Princesses

Princesses

The Six Daughters of George III

FLORA FRASER

JOHN MURRAY

© Flora Fraser 2004

First published in 2004 by John Murray (Publishers)
A division of Hodder Headline

The right of Flora Fraser to be identified as the Author of the Work has been asserted by her in
accordance with the Copyright, Designs and Patents Act 1988.

3 5 7 9 10 8 6 4

A CIP catalogue record for this title is available from the British Library

Hardback ISBN 0 7195 61086

Typeset in Monotype Bembo by Servis Filmsetting Ltd, Manchester

Printed and bound by
Clays Ltd, St Ives plc

Hodder Headline policy is to use papers that are natural, renewable and recyclable products and
made from wood grown in sustainable forests. The logging and manufacturing processes are
expected to conform to the environmental regulations of the country of origin.

John Murray (Publishers)
338 Euston Road
London NW1 3BH

For Peter Ross, Stella Elizabeth, Simon Tivadar and
Thomas Hugh

Contents

List of Illustrations   ix
Family Tree   xii
Preface   xv

Book One: Youth   1766–1783

1. Early Days   3
2. Growing Up   22
3. The Younger Ones   43
4. Adolescence   61

Book Two: Experience   1783–1797

5. Brothers and Sisters   79
6. Fear   101
7. Hope   121
8. Despond   142

Book Three: Scandal   1798–1810

9. In Spirits   167
10. Agitation   189
11. Outcry   214
12. Passion   231

Book Four: Maturity   1810–1822

13. Breaking Up   249
14. Emancipation   272
15. Daughters in Distress   294
16. Princesses at Large   313

CONTENTS

Book Five: Piano Piano   1822–1857

17. Royal – Queenly Dowager   333
18. Elizabeth – The Largesse of a Landgravine   351
19. Augusta – A Princess for All Seasons   370
20. Sophia – The Little Gypsy   380
21. Mary – Last of the Line   389

Notes   400
Select Bibliography   449
Index   456

Illustrations

Section One

1. Francis Cotes, *Queen Charlotte and the Princess Royal*. Royal Collection.
2. John Fisher, *The White House, Kew*. Orleans House Gallery.
3. Johann Zoffany, *Queen Charlotte with Members of Family*. Royal Collection.
4. Benjamin West, *Sketch of Royal Children Playing*. Victoria and Albert Museum.
5. William Westall, *Buckingham Palace – East Front*. Royal Collection.
6. Henry Edridge, *George III*. Royal Collection.
7. James Fittler, *George III and Queen Charlotte with Children on Terrace at Windsor*. British Museum.
8. Thomas Gainsborough, *Princess Elizabeth*. Royal Collection.

Section Two

9. Sir Thomas Lawrence, *Princess Amelia*. Royal Collection.
10. Richard Livesay, *The Duchess of York presented to George III*. National Trust.
11. Richard Cosway, *George IV*. National Portrait Gallery.
12. Richard Cosway, *Princess Mary, after Duchess of Gloucester*. Royal Collection.
13. James Fittler, after George Robertson, *South East View of Windsor Castle with Royal Family on Terrace*. Royal Collection.
14. Henry Edridge, *Ernest, Duke of Cumberland, after King of Hanover*. Royal Collection.
15. Andrew Robertson, *Princess Sophia*. Royal Collection.
16. Charles Wild, *Frogmore House*. Royal Collection.
17. Sir William Beechey, *Charlotte, Princess Royal, after Queen of Württemberg*. Royal Collection.
18. *Frederick, King of Württemberg*. Wedgwood Museum.

19. Unknown artist, *General Sir Brent Spencer*. From Smythies' *History of the 40th Regiment* (1894). Owner photograph.
20. Sir William Beechey, *Princess Augusta*. Royal Collection.
21. Thomas Lawrence, *Sir Henry Halford*. Royal College of Physicians.
22. After unknown artist, *The Hon. Charles Fitzroy*. From Childe-Pemberton's *The Romance of Princess Amelia* (1910).
23. Andrew Robertson, *Princess Amelia*. Royal Collection.
24. Robert Hicks, after William Marshall Craig, *Apotheosis of Princes Octavius and Alfred and Princess Amelia*. National Portrait Gallery.

Section Three

25. William Thomas Fry, after George Dawe, *Princess Charlotte Augusta of Wales and Leopold I*. National Portrait Gallery.
26. After Abraham Wivell, *William Frederick, 2nd Duke of Gloucester*. National Portrait Gallery.
27. Henry Edridge, *Princess Elizabeth*. Royal Collection.
28. Richard Dighton, *An Illustrious Visiter from Hombourg, Frederick VI, Landgrave of Hesse-Homburg*. National Portrait Gallery.
29. Johann Frederick Voigt, *Princess Elizabeth, Landgravine of Hesse-Homburg*. Gothic House Museum, Bad Homburg.
30. Johann Paul Fischer, *Charlotte, Princess Royal, Queen of Württemberg*. Royal Collection.
31. Henry Bone, after Sir William Charles Ross, *Princess Augusta*. Royal Collection.
32. John Simpson, *Sir Herbert Taylor*. National Portrait Gallery.
33. W. & H. Barraud, *Captain Thomas Garth*. Private Collection.
34. P. H. Heath, *A Change of Performance at Astley's*. British Museum.
35. Sir Thomas Lawrence, *George IV*. Royal Collection.
36. After unknown artist, *King William IV and Queen Adelaide*. National Portrait Gallery.
37. Queen Victoria, *Queen Victoria*. Royal Archives.
38. Sir William Charles Ross, *Princess Sophia*. Royal Collection.
39. Augustus Liddell, *Princess Mary, Duchess of Gloucester*. Royal Photograph Collection.
40. Antoine Claudet, *Queen Victoria, Mary, Duchess of Gloucester, Prince of Wales and Princess Alice*. Royal Photograph Collection.

PHOTOGRAPHIC CREDITS: 1, 3, 5, 6, 8, 9, 12-17, 20, 23, 27, 30, 31, 35, 38, The Royal Collection © 2004, Her Majesty Queen Elizabeth II; 2, LBRUT Art Collection, Orleans House Gallery; 4, Victoria and Albert Museum © V&A Museum; 7, 34, the Trustees of The British Museum; 10, Upton House (Bearsted Collection), The National Trust, NTPL / Angelo Hornak; 11, 24-26, 28, 32, 36, The National Portrait Gallery, London; 18, Image by courtesy of the Wedgwood Museum Trust, Staffordshire; 19, 22, British Library; 21, The Royal College of Physicians of London; 29, Gothic House Museum, Bad Homburg; 33, Private Collection; 37, 39, 40, The Royal Archives © 2004, Her Majesty Queen Elizabeth II

THE PRINCESSES' FAMILY

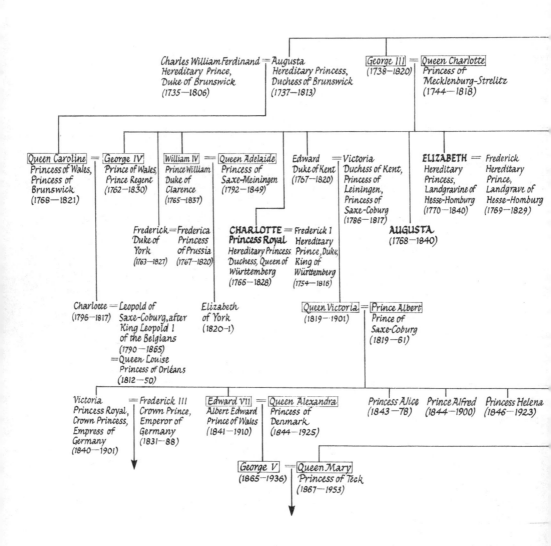

Charles William Ferdinand = Augusta
Hereditary Prince,   Hereditary Princess,
Duke of Brunswick   Duchess of Brunswick
(1735—1806)   (1737—1813)

George III = Queen Charlotte
(1738—1820)   Princess of
Mecklenburg-Strelitz
(1744—1818)

Queen Caroline = George IV
Princess of Wales,   Prince of Wales,
Princess of   Prince Regent
Brunswick   (1762—1830)
(1768—1821)

William IV = Queen Adelaide
Prince William   Princess of
Duke of   Saxe-Meiningen
Clarence   (1792—1849)
(1765—1837)

Edward = Victoria
Duke of Kent   Duchess of Kent,
(1767—1820)   Princess of
Leiningen,
Princess of
Saxe-Coburg
(1786—1817)

ELIZABETH = Frederick
Hereditary   Hereditary
Princess,   Prince,
Landgravine of   Landgrave of
Hesse-Homburg   Hesse-Homburg
(1770—1840)   (1769—1829)

Frederick = Frederica
Duke of   Princess
York   of Prussia
(1763—1827)   (1767—1820)

CHARLOTTE = Frederick I
Princess Royal   Hereditary
Hereditary Princess   Prince, Duke,
Duchess, Queen of   King of
Württemberg   Württemberg
(1766—1828)   (1754—1816)

AUGUSTA
(1768—1840)

Charlotte = Leopold of
(1796—1817)   Saxe-Coburg, after
King Leopold I
of the Belgians
(1790—1865)
= Queen Louise
Princess of Orléans
(1812—50)

Elizabeth
of York
(1820—1)

Queen Victoria = Prince Albert
(1819—1901)   Prince of
Saxe-Coburg
(1819—61)

Victoria = Frederick III
Princess Royal,   Crown Prince,
Crown Princess,   Emperor of
Empress of   Germany
Germany   (1831—88)
(1840—1901)

Edward VII = Queen Alexandra
Albert Edward   Princess of
Prince of Wales   Denmark
(1841—1910)   (1844—1925)

Princess Alice
(1843—78)

Prince Alfred
(1844—1900)

Princess Helena
(1846—1923)

George V = Queen Mary
(1865—1936)   Princess of Teck
(1867—1953)

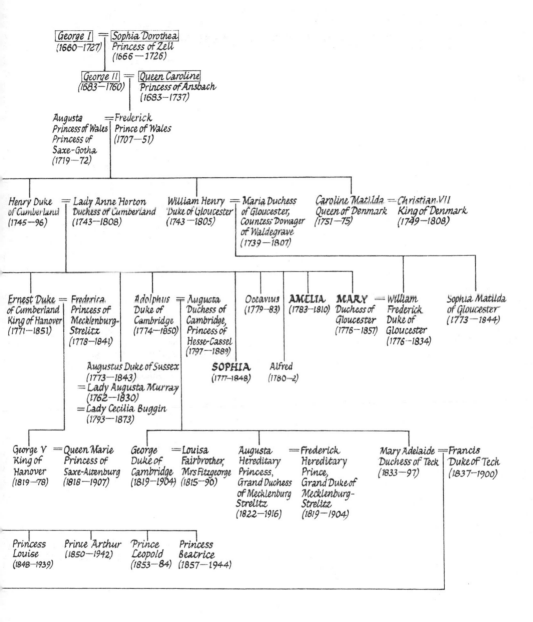

George I (1660–1727) = Sophia Dorothea Princess of Zell (1666–1726)

George II (1683–1760) = Queen Caroline Princess of Ansbach (1683–1737)

Augusta Princess of Wales Princess of Saxe-Gotha (1719–72) = Frederick Prince of Wales (1707–51)

Henry Duke of Cumberland (1745–96) = Lady Anne Horton Duchess of Cumberland (1743–1808)

William Henry Duke of Gloucester (1743–1805) = Maria Duchess of Gloucester, Countess Dowager of Waldegrave (1739–1807)

Caroline Matilda Queen of Denmark (1751–75) = Christian VII King of Denmark (1749–1808)

Ernest Duke of Cumberland King of Hanover (1771–1851) = Frederica Princess of Mecklenburg-Strelitz (1778–1841)

Adolphus Duke of Cambridge (1774–1850) = Augusta Duchess of Cambridge, Princess of Hesse-Cassel (1797–1889)

Octavius (1779–83)

AMELIA (1783–1810)

MARY Duchess of Gloucester (1776–1857) = William Frederick Duke of Gloucester (1776–1834)

Sophia Matilda of Gloucester (1773–1844)

Augustus Duke of Sussex (1773–1843) = Lady Augusta Murray (1762–1830) = Lady Cecilia Buggin (1793–1873)

SOPHIA (1777–1848)

Alfred (1780–2)

George V King of Hanover (1819–78) = Queen Marie Princess of Saxe-Altenburg (1818–1907)

George Duke of Cambridge (1819–1904) = Louisa Fairbrother, Mrs Fitzgeorge (1815–90)

Augusta Hereditary Princess, Grand Duchess of Mecklenburg Strelitz (1822–1916) = Frederick Hereditary Prince, Grand Duke of Mecklenburg-Strelitz (1819–1904)

Mary Adelaide Duchess of Teck (1833–97) = Francis Duke of Teck (1837–1900)

Princess Louise (1848–1939)

Prince Arthur (1850–1942)

Prince Leopold (1853–84)

Princess Beatrice (1857–1944)

Preface

I first became curious about the six daughters of George III when I was researching *The Unruly Queen*, my biography of their sister-in-law Queen Caroline, in the Royal Archives. The princesses' close involvement in their brother George IV's quarrels with his wife led me to wonder why they were not all themselves married to foreign princes and busy with child-bearing, or at least with their own marital difficulties. Rumours of affairs, secret marriages and pregnancies in their contemporaries' journals fuelled my interest. Above all, the princesses' letters – confidential, conspiratorial, allusive – in the Archives intrigued me. And so I started *Princesses*.

At first I was unsure of my subject. The princesses' letters were often difficult to read, sometimes illegible. And others were less inquisitive than I about these shadowy sisters from a Regency past. The conversation with those whom I told of my project tended to be short: 'George III's daughters? Who did they marry?' *No one in particular.* 'How many were there?' *Six.* 'Any brothers?' *Nine.* End of conversation, or a coda: 'Fifteen children! All by one woman?'

But I was not put off. As the princesses' story and the extraordinary circumstances of their existence took on form and substance, I grew ever more absorbed. No one could have guessed, when these princesses of England were born, that any particular struggle would be theirs – except to secure a foreign prince for a husband and successfully to bear him heirs. But each of them was forced, by successive strokes of fate that *Princesses* describes, into subversive behaviour and even acts of desperation. Their letters reveal the transformation of these attractive, conventional princesses into resilient, independent-minded women. The sadness is that this transformation occurred only as a result of spectacular illness that their father George III suffered, and that destroyed their mother Queen Charlotte's domestic happiness. Earlier admirable, the Queen did not behave well to her daughters in later years. But she had been greatly tried.

Given other circumstances, the letters of these six royal sisters might have been filled only with Court gossip, pomp and fashion. Instead their correspondence makes harrowing reading, revealing the humility with which they met pain and horror, the tenacity with which they pursued their individual dreams, and the stratagems they devised to endure years of submission and indignity. For some but not for all of the princesses, there were happy endings, their letters dwelling more on family news and less on family suffering. For all of them, I developed the greatest respect and admiration, and I hope that readers of *Princesses* will share those feelings.

I thank Her Majesty The Queen for kind permission to consult and publish the papers of the daughters of King George III. I am also most grateful to Pamela Clark, Registrar of the Royal Archives, her predecessor in that post, Sheila de Bellaigue, and Jill Kelsey, Deputy Registrar. I owe thanks besides to all in the Royal Archives, especially Allison Derrett, Maud Eburne, and Angeline Barker, for generous help and advice during the preparation of this biography. I would also like to thank Oliver Everett, formerly Librarian to The Queen, for his constant encouragement of my project, and Stuart Shilson, Assistant Keeper of The Queen's Archives, for his friendly professional advice.

The daughters of George III, as inhabitants of many royal residences, as sitters to many artists, and as decorative artists themselves, have left their mark on the Royal Collection. In that context I urge readers of *Princesses* in this year of publication to visit the magnificent exhibition at The Queen's Gallery, London, *George III and Queen Charlotte: Patronage, Collecting and Court Taste*, or to study the accompanying catalogue edited by Jane Roberts. I would like myself to thank Jane Roberts, Librarian to The Queen, Christopher Lloyd, Surveyor of The Queen's Pictures, Hugh Roberts, Director of the Royal Collection and Frances Dimond, Curator of the Royal Photograph Collection, for much generous help. I am in addition grateful to many other curators and members of staff at the Royal Collection, including Siân Cooksey, Martin Clayton, Gay Hamilton, Shruti Patel, Prue Sutcliffe, Bridget Wright and Margaret Westwood. I also record my thanks here to Susanne Groom, Joanna Marschner and their colleagues at Historic Royal Palaces for much helpful advice.

The six daughters of George III corresponded mightily all their lives. So *Princesses* is a book in which I have drawn heavily on private British family papers, and I would like to thank all their owners for allowing me to make use of them, and many of them for memorable hospitality. Among those I especially thank are: Sir Peter and Dame Elizabeth Anson, the Marquess of Bute, the Earl of Home, Richard Jenkins, the Earl of Pembroke, David

Scott and David Smythe. I am in addition indebted to, among others, Robin Harcourt Williams, Andrew Maclean, Charles Noble and Michael Shepherd for their professional advice.

I am also most grateful to the archivists and staffs of all the County Record Offices where papers relating to the princesses are deposited, and whom I visited or corresponded with. Carl Harrison at Leicestershire Record Office, Sally Mason of Buckinghamshire County Archives, and David Rimmer at Gwent Record Office are among others who have given me great assistance.

I owe thanks to Michael Borrie, of the British Library Department of Manuscripts, to Christopher Kitching, of the Historical Manuscripts Commission, and to Ian G. Brown, at the National Library of Scotland, for advice about the whereabouts and extent of various collections of papers. I would also like to thank the staffs of the British Library, of the London Library and of the Public Record Office for their help, and John Saumarez Smith of Heywood Hill for much generous advice.

I would like to thank Prince Ernst August of Hanover for permission to consult family papers, and for an illuminating discussion about the House of Hanover in Germany and in England. Two of the princesses married into other German royal families, and I would like to thank Dr Iris Reepen for her great assistance to me on two memorable research trips. We saw castles, collections, archives and curatorial departments from Bad Homburg and Frankfurt to Stuttgart and Ludwigsburg and, on the other side of Germany, to Greiz in Thuringia.

Thanks are also due, for help with manuscripts in Germany, to Eberhard Fritz at the House of Württemberg Archives in Altshausen, to Johann Krizsanitz of the House of Hanover Archives in Hanover, to Anja Moschke of the Thuringian State Archives in Greiz, and to Gerta Walsh and Ursula Stiehler of the House of Hesse-Homburg Archives in Bad Homburg. In addition I would like to thank the staffs of the State Archives in Stuttgart and in Hanover for their help and advice. Thanks also go, again in Europe, to Monique Droin-Bridel in Geneva and to Silke Redolfi at the Fundaziun de Planta, Samedan.

In the earlier part of the twentieth century British royal documents were purchased with enthusiasm by American collectors and bibliophiles, and innumerable letters of the princesses and their circle then found their way across the Atlantic, some of which I have consulted. I am most grateful to Roger Horchow for arranging introductions for me at various American libraries; to Stephen Parks and his colleagues at the Beinecke and Lewis Walpole Libraries, Yale; and to Robert Parks, Inge Du Pont and others at the Pierpont Morgan Library, New York, for help and advice. I am also grateful to Stephen Crook and others at the Alfred A. Berg Collection in the New York Public Library.

I would also like to thank, among others who have shed light on the princesses' artistic output and on their sittings to artists: Henry Adams, Norman Blackburn, Elizabeth Fairman, Charlotte Gere, Bryony Kelly, Martin Royalton Kisch, Stephen Lloyd, Amy Meyers, Lucy Peltz, Marcia Pointon, Aileen Ribeiro, Nancy Richards, Jacob Simon, Kim Sloan, Kay Staniland, Arthur Tilley and Lord Ullswater. In addition I thank Matthew Bailey and Tom Morgan of the National Portrait Gallery Picture Library for their help in providing images.

For sharing with me their knowledge of places important in the princesses' story here and in Europe I thank among others: Gotthard Brandler, Kathleen A. Burgess, Dr Fritz Fischer, Kurt Hoffmann, Dr Heinz Krämer, Julian Litten, Sister Manda, Dr Klaus Merten and Christopher Woodward.

Others I owe thanks to are: Maureen Attwooll, Clarissa Campbell Orr, Kate Chisholm, Leo Cooper, Amanda Foreman, Michael Holroyd, Giles Hunt, Rana Kabbani, Linda Kelly, Mark Le Fanu, Lowell Libson, Sacha Llewellyn, Giles MacDonogh, Philip Mansel, David Michaelis, Sir Oliver Millar, Mimi Pakenham, Diane Nash, Michael Nash, Andrew Roberts, John Rogister, Francis Russell, Stephen Simpson, Paul and Daisy Soros, Gina Thomas, John Wardroper and Edmund White.

For professional aid during the researching and writing of *Princesses* I am, as ever, grateful to Leonora Clarke for typing my work. I owe thanks also for research or help at different times to: Georgie Castle, Georgina Gooding, Linda Peskin, Carole Taylor and Otto Wilkinson. I thank Katarina Ardagh for translation from the German, and Barbara Peters for checking printed sources at the British Library. And I am most grateful to Lesley Robertson Allen, to Rowan Yapp of John Murray and to Diana Tejerina of Knopf for their professional help with the production of the manuscript and illustrations. I thank Reginald Piggott for providing the family tree, and it gives me great pleasure to thank Douglas Matthews for compiling the index.

I am fortunate beyond words in my agent, editors and publishers here and in America, and they are all too distinguished to need my praise. Nevertheless I wish to thank Jonathan Lloyd, my literary agent, for his rock-solid encouragement of this project. I thank Peter James for his steely editorial work. I am grateful to Bob Gottlieb for, among much else, crucial advice during narrative crises. I thank Sonny Mehta of Knopf in the

US for his steady support. And I am delighted to be publishing once more with Roland Philipps and with John Murray (Publishers) in England.

I am grateful for good conversation and stimulating professional advice from my mother Antonia Fraser and, until recently, from my grandmother, the late Elizabeth Longford. I thank Sheila de Bellaigue, Christopher Hibbert and Jane Roberts for reading the manuscript at different stages and for their valuable comments. I thank also Jane Birkett for reading the proofs with such care. Finally, I have, throughout the writing of this book, had the unflinching support of my husband Peter Soros, to whom, with my children, I dedicate it.

June 2004

BOOK ONE
YOUTH
1766–1783

I

Early Days

~

TOWARDS THE END of September 1766 the Prince of Wales, who was only four, told a lady at Court that 'about next week' he reckoned they should have 'a little princess'. George Augustus Frederick, the eldest son of King George III and Queen Charlotte, was known to be precocious. His mother's Mistress of the Robes called him 'the forwardest child in understanding' that she ever saw. And so, far from doubting the child's prediction, his confidante, Lady Mary Coke, added in her journal, 'I find the King and Queen are very desirous it should be one [a girl] and hope they shall have no more sons.'

The additional information probably issued from Lady Mary's friend Lady Charlotte Finch, who had been appointed royal governess the day after the Prince of Wales's birth on 12 August 1762. Lady Charlotte and her deputy, or sub-governess, Mrs Cotesworth had since received into the nursery establishment two further princes, Frederick and William, in 1763 and 1765. To these ladies, who looked after their boisterous charges in the summer at Richmond and Kew, and in the winter at the Queen's House in London, as much as to the royal parents, a baby girl represented a hope of dulcet peace and feminine charms.

In the event, George, Prince of Wales was confirmed as a prophet in the land when his mother Queen Charlotte, at the age of twenty-two, gave birth in London to a baby princess the following Monday – Michaelmas Day, 29 September. The celebrated anatomist and royal obstetrician Dr William Hunter hovered with the King and the King's mother, the Dowager Princess of Wales, in an adjoining room at the Queen's House, the royal family's private residence overlooking the Mall and St James's Park.★ But nothing untoward took place in the crimson damask bedchamber next door to require their presence. Lady Charlotte Finch, who had moved up to nearby apartments at St James's Palace the evening before to

★ The Queen's House is today part of Buckingham Palace, as the royal residence was rechristened when enlarged in the 1820s.

oversee the practical arrangements for the new baby, wrote in her journal that night: 'At a quarter past eight this morning the Queen was safely delivered of a Princess Royal. Passed all morning at the Queen's House ...' That date, 29 September – the quarter-day when, in the greater world, rents became due and, in the royal household, salaries were paid – was to be long dear to the Queen, who was not sentimental by nature, as the day she gave birth to her 'Michaelmas goose'.

Names were awaiting the baby Princess: Charlotte, for her mother; Augusta, for her father's mother; and Matilda, for the King's sister Caroline Matilda, who, aged fifteen, was leaving England within a few days to marry the King of Denmark. (The English Houses of Parliament gave economical thanks on the same occasion for the birth of the Princess and the marriage of her aunt.) But, as her new governess's journal entry indicates, by none of her Christian names was King George III's and Queen Charlotte's eldest daughter to be known. At birth, her proud father and sovereign of England had bestowed on her for life the style of Princess Royal, and this (shortened to Royal by her family) is how she was always known in England – although, curiously, the style was only officially granted her years later on 22 June 1789.

The Stuart King Charles I's eldest daughter Mary had been, in 1642, the first English princess to have been styled Princess Royal. She was eleven and leaving England to be the bride of William of Orange, the future Stadholder in Holland. No other princess was so honoured until 1727, when the Hanoverian King George II of England styled his daughter Anne – who also became a princess of Orange and lived until 1759 – Princess Royal, when she was nineteen years old. King George III's decision in 1766 to make his daughter while still a baby a princess royal in part reflected England's recent surge in prestige since his accession in 1760, notably with the successful outcome of the Seven Years War in 1763. But it also reflected the unreserved and almost awestruck delight that he exhibited as a young father – some felt, to the detriment of royal dignity – in his infant daughter.

The day after the Princess Royal's birth, her three brothers, George, Prince of Wales, Prince Frederick and thirteen-month-old William, came up to London to inspect their new sister. Prince William, till now the baby of the family, was a general favourite at Richmond Lodge, the King's house in woods adjacent to Kew Gardens, where the royal children generally lived during the summer months. As it was not a large house, the children's attendants – their governess Lady Charlotte Finch among them – were mostly lodged in houses grouped around the King's mother's house, the White House in Kew Gardens, and the children spent much of their time there.

A few weeks before the Princess Royal was born in September 1766, Miss Henrietta Finch, one of Lady Charlotte's daughters, wrote to an absent sister:

> We saw the King and Queen last night, they was in Mama's parlour. We stayed in the room the whole time, they was vastly good humoured and enquired vastly after you. Little Prince William was undressed quite naked and laid upon a cushion, the King made him stand up upon it. I thought I should have died with laughing at his little ridiculous white figure.

The King adored Prince William's sturdy elder brother Prince Frederick, who was aged three when his sister was born. A year earlier Lady Charlotte Finch recorded the royal father's close involvement in all his second son's doings in the autumn of 1765:

> Mr Glenton the tailor is the happiest man in the kingdom. He has been sent for to make a coat for Prince Frederick, and when he came, was ordered to go and take measure of him in the room where the King was. At which he was so astonished and so terrified that his knees knocked together so, they could hardly persuade him to go in. And when he was there, he did not know what he did. And when he came upstairs, he begged he might stay till the prince came up, for he owned he did not know anything of his measures. However, he has made the clothes so excessively neat and fit, that when he brought them home, the King spoke to him himself and commended them. And he is now so happy you cannot conceive anything like his spirits. He is now making another suit for Prince Frederick. However, it is only by way of dressing him in them sometimes, as the King is fond of seeing him in breeches ... The Queen likes to keep him a little longer in petticoats.

It was evident that the King did not dote on his heir, a less manly child than Frederick. In this sultry summer of 1766, Miss Henrietta Finch noted encouragingly, 'I think the King grows very fond of the Prince of Wales, though he does certainly snap [at] him sometimes.' The King's coolness towards his heir was not lamented as it might have been. It was understood by all that, in the Hanoverian succession, there was an unfortunate tendency for the monarch and his heir to have differences. And the Prince of Wales's sophistication and insouciant charm continued to attract many admirers, not least his mother and governess. Queen Charlotte was always to love her firstborn best of all her children, and Lady Charlotte recounted her eldest royal charge's *bons mots* with pride.

Asked earlier that year if he found tedious the hours spent in a darkened room that custom prescribed following inoculation against smallpox, the

Prince replied, 'Not at all, I lie awake and make reflections.' Lady Mary Coke, visiting Lady Charlotte Finch and her charges at Kew shortly before the Princess Royal's birth, found the Prince, as she graciously put it, 'comical'. When she left off playing with him, explaining that she was expected at his great-aunt Princess Amelia's, the Prince looked her up and down before asking, 'Pray, are you well enough dressed to visit her?'

The princes were among the few privileged visitors to view the Princess Royal at the Queen's House at this point. From the fashionable sandy Mall, and indeed from Green Park and from St James's Park north and south of it, the courtyard and modest redbrick façade of this royal residence were open to view. But while all Society made formal enquiries after the health of mother and child, they made them at St James's Palace, that warren of great antiquity with suites of apartments for royal servants jostling state rooms and throne rooms which sprawled north of the Mall. At this palace, as well, officials of the Court of St James's received royal and imperial felicitations from other Courts of Europe on the Princess's birth – and took in coachloads of mayoral addresses on the subject besides.

Here at St James's, in the dilapidated state apartments, the King held his levees and gave audience to ministers. Here ambassadors presented their credentials. Here the Queen received Society twice a week at formal drawing rooms. And here, on the King's and Queen's birthdays, Court balls followed the drawing rooms. Other high days and holidays of the reign – Accession Day, Coronation Day and the King and Queen's wedding day – were all marked too. Here, in due course, the Princess Royal would make her debut, signalling that she was of an age to take a husband. But for the moment the only ceremony beckoning her there was her baptism, which would take place in October in the Chapel Royal, St James's.

At the Queen's House – which the King had bought two years after he ascended the throne as a London home to which he and the Queen could retreat from the fatigue of public life at St James's Palace – mother and daughter recovered. The Queen rested in rooms decorated in a style reflecting her Continental upbringing and showing a great deal of taste, as a visitor to the Queen's House recorded the following spring when the royal mistress was not in residence: 'The Queen's apartments are ornamented, as one expects a Queen's should be, with curiosities from every nation that can deserve her notice. The most capital pictures, the finest Dresden and other china, cabinets of more minute curiosities … On her toilet, besides the gilt plate, innumerable knick-knacks … By the Queen's bed … an elegant case with twenty-five watches, all highly adorned with jewels.'

Evidence of children on that occasion was lacking, and now too, in September 1766, the focus of celebration, the Princess Royal, was nowhere in sight downstairs at the Queen's House. Queen Charlotte, observing the prevalent custom among Royalty and society at this time, did not breast-feed her children. Shortly after birth the Princess Royal had been whisked upstairs to somewhat different surroundings – the attic storey, far from fres-coed staircases and damask chambers – to forge an intimate relationship with a mother of two named Mrs Muttlebury, who had been selected as her wet-nurse.

Mrs Muttlebury had been carefully vetted as a milk-cow in August 1766 – not only by Lady Charlotte Finch, a mother of four herself, but also by Dr Hunter and even by Mr Caesar Hawkins, the King's Serjeant-Surgeon, and by his brother Mr Pennell Hawkins, Surgeon to the Queen – in pre-paration for her important task. First she had had to bring for her critics' inspection the child she was then suckling, then she was asked to show her elder child too, to see if it thrived. Only then, in return for a formidable salary of 200 pounds, and a hundred, after her employment ceased, for life with the interest of the royal family permanently engaged for her own children – was Mrs Muttlebury retained to devote herself for six months unconditionally to breastfeeding the royal baby. (A limner's or painter's wife was put on warning as a substitute wet-nurse should Mrs Muttlebury's milk fail before the royal infant appeared.)

But Mrs Muttlebury remained somewhat bewildered by the honour done her. 'She told Mama she had not the least notion of anything she was to do,' recorded Lady Charlotte's daughter Sophia, 'and begged her to tell her ...' She was surprised to hear she must provide a maid – 'I suppose from a notion of having people to do everything for her,' commented Miss Sophia. 'Mama told her of several other expenses, viz providing her own washing, always wearing silk gowns morning and evening ...' The royal baby should come into contact only with superior materials – tussore and brocade and Mechlin lace for ruffles, as supplied by Lady Charlotte.

It was a world unto itself, that of the Princess Royal and Mrs Muttlebury. The wet-nurse was allowed no visitors, not even her own children, to divert her from her duty. Up on the attic floor of the Queen's House, among plain mahogany furniture and striped ticking mattresses, and at Richmond Lodge, the country retreat which the King and Queen inhabited from May to November, the Princess Royal grew. Lady Charlotte Finch, the royal governess, supervised the arrangements for this new addition to the royal nursery. But, mostly, she was engaged with the three princes, who spent their days with her at her house in adjoining Kew Gardens.

The attention of the Princess Royal's parents downstairs was meanwhile diverted elsewhere. Two days after her birth, as we have seen, on 1 October 1766, her aunt Princess Caroline Matilda married King Christian VII of Denmark by proxy in London in the Great Drawing Room at St James's. For want of a husband her brother Edward, Duke of York stood groom. And for want of a father – the fifteen-year-old Princess had been born posthumously, months after a cricket ball fatally injured her father, Frederick, Prince of Wales in 1751 – her brother William Henry, Duke of Gloucester gave her away. 'Before she set out in the procession,' a wedding guest noted, 'she cried so much that she was near falling into fits. Her brother the Duke of Gloucester who led her was so shocked at seeing her in such a situation that he looked as pale as death and as if he was ready to faint away.'

When the Archbishop of Canterbury christened the Princess Royal on 27 October 1766, the new Queen of Denmark was among her godparents, but that in its turn was a proxy appearance. Caroline Matilda had embarked for Copenhagen and for a fateful dynastic marriage overseas that her brother, King George III, was bitterly to regret having arranged.

Another of the Princess Royal's aunts, Princess Augusta, had not fared well in a foreign land either. Her sophisticated soldier husband, the Hereditary Prince of Brunswick, taunted her with a succession of mistresses, and she took disconsolately to religion, and to trumpeting the superiority of her native land. In England two years after her 1764 marriage, and with an infant son, Prince Charles of Brunswick, in tow, she told anyone who would listen that she hoped he would in due course marry his new cousin, the Princess Royal.

There was another royal marriage in the air at the time of the Princess Royal's birth. Her fainthearted uncle William, Duke of Gloucester married beautiful Maria, Dowager Countess of Waldegrave on 6 September – but was too afraid to admit the fact to his mother or brother. For Maria, although the widow of the King's former governor and the mother of three beauties, all of whom were to marry well, was herself illegitimate. She was the daughter of Sir Edward Walpole, Horace's brother, and of a Miss Dorothy Clements who some said had been a washerwoman and, others, worse.

The Duke of Gloucester and the Dowager Countess of Waldegrave prosecuted their romance at Windsor, a castle conveniently neglected by the Court since the days of Queen Anne. Maria and her daughters had apartments in the deserted royal stronghold, and her father, Sir Edward, inhabited a country house at Frogmore, close by. When the Duke took a house at St Leonard's Hill in the Great Park, the town gossip became unstoppable. 'As soon as the castle clock at Windsor had struck twelve', ran one account, 'and of consequence all was quiet', Lady Waldegrave 'ordered a rocket to be let off in the great walk in Windsor Park, which it seems was the signal, for soon after it a Royal chaise came down, and out of it a certain Duke, who usually passed the remaining part of the night in her lodgings.' The irregular arrangement, the truth of which neither party owned to anyone, became a talking point – had they or had they not married? And if they had, when would they own it?

The baby Princess Royal knew nothing of her aunt Caroline's and uncle Gloucester's marriages in the year of her birth. But the time was not far off when, while she was still an infant, her future as well as that of her siblings would be dramatically determined by the King's unmeasured response to the consequences of these and other marriages of his own siblings.

Towards the end of November Lady Charlotte Finch wrote in her diary, 'To the Queen's House at eleven o'clock, the hour I have fixed every day for giving the Princes their lesson.' At this time of year the royal family and attendants settled in town for the winter – Lady Charlotte and others in apartments at St James's Palace – and the damp Kew and Richmond houses were abandoned until summer weather the following May made them habitable again.

In Mrs Muttlebury's quarters, women known as 'rockers' soothed the Princess Royal when she cried by pulling her cradle, a thing of gleaming wood, soft mattresses and silk coverlets, to and fro on strings. Household accounts show that Mrs Muttlebury had the use of a nursing chair in her bedroom, while Mrs Chapman, the 'dry-nurse' who looked after the baby's other needs, was in a more modest room with harateen or coarse linen covers. Lady Charlotte, however, had superior red and white check covers to her chairs, and the Princess Royal, gifted with a good memory, recalled the colour and check of these chairs years later when recounting how, as a child, she jumped off one of them, pretending to descend from a bathing machine into the sea.

The Queen's German dressers, the formidable Mme Schwellenberg and her deputy, Mrs Hagedorn, shared the attic quarters with the royal children and their attendants. Mme Juliana Schwellenberg, who had come with the Queen from Germany, was of immense value to her mistress. In guttural English she kept all comers away from her beloved Queen with an unholy enthusiasm for her task which irked others. Swollen with self-importance, she was heard to say that what was good enough for the Queen was not good enough for her, and a page, Robère, would always crouch outside her door, ready to speed to her assistance at the peal of a silver bell. Fortunately for the King and Queen below – in view of the racket that all these various inhabitants could make – the original owner of the house, the Duke of Buckingham, had soundproofed the upper storey, with 'floors so contrived as to prevent all noise' over his wife's head.

The week after the princes joined their sister in town, they 'as usual' visited their grandmother Augusta, Dowager Princess of Wales, on her birthday at her home, Carlton House, a short distance down Pall Mall from St James's Palace. This year they were joined by their two-month-old sister on one of the first airings she took outside the walled brick garden behind the Queen's House. Their grandmother was widely reviled in England – partly for the simple fact of being German, partly for the influence, following the early death of her husband Frederick, Prince of Wales, that the politician Lord Bute had exerted on her. Some accused the Princess of having taken the Scots peer as her lover. Other xenophobes held – more accurately and with more import for the lives of the grandchildren who visited her on 1 December 1766 – that she had brought scrofula with her into the Hanoverian royal family of England from the Saxe-Gotha line.

Scrofula, a horrifying disease giving rise to scars and chronic swelling of the lymphatic glands – in the neck especially – led at best to intractable inflammation of skin, bones, joints and other parts and to a weakened resistance to other disease. At worst the tubercular disease spread to the lungs and proved fatal. Scrofula – also known as the king's evil – was already believed to have been responsible for the death of one of Augusta's children, would be adduced as the cause of the death of another within a year, and those with imagination believed it would weaken the succession. With some satisfaction every ailment and death in the royal family over the next century would be claimed when possible for what became known as the 'family disease'. But, ignoring the fatal inheritance she supposedly brought him, the Dowager Princess's son the King paid his mother every respect and made sure his children did too.

On 18 January 1767 the Princess Royal was on display with her brothers at a drawing room at St James's marking her mother's official birthday – she had now graduated to wearing a 'pink and silver watered tabby [or taffeta] coat'. But Lady Charlotte Finch, who had ordered the outfit, could not be present. Having suffered the death of one daughter in the year Prince William was born, she was now in mourning for her estranged husband, the Hon. William Finch.

Finch had died on Christmas Day 1766 after a period of hideous mental instability which had begun after his wife's appointment as royal governess, and which had led her to take her children and leave the marital home in London for apartments in St James's and for a house in Kew. The wonder is that Lady Charlotte, who presided over all nursery matters with competence and grace, was not undone by her double duty – to her royal charges and to her own three teenage daughters and her son at Eton. She continued to rule the royal roost and to order her children's lives with a zest stoked by reference to devotional works, her energy flagging only when her royal employers insisted on keeping her with them in the evenings after the children were in bed. For not only were their young children a central focus of the King and Queen's day, between public business, but, eschewing the formal dining that had been the rule at Hampton Court and St James's Palace during the reign of the King's grandfather George II, this royal couple liked to dine every day at home with the same small selection of their household in attendance.

Horace Walpole was apoplectic about the King and Queen's decision to live a retired life. He wrote in the summer of 1764 from Strawberry Hill, his spectacular Gothic villa near Twickenham, 'The Court, independent of politics, makes a strange figure. The recluse life led here at Richmond, which is carried to such an excess of privacy and economy, that the Queen's friseur waits on them at dinner, and that four pounds only of beef are allowed for their soup, disgusts all sorts of people. The drawing rooms are abandoned ...' Walpole had earlier praised the new Queen's unshowy appearance and behaviour on her arrival from Mecklenburg-Strelitz in London in 1761, which had disappointed some hoping for great beauty and hauteur. 'She looks very sensible, cheerful, and is remarkably genteel ...' he wrote. 'She talks a great deal – is easy, civil, and not disconcerted.' And he had perspicaciously noticed the taste she showed for the decorative arts, and her enthusiasm for the burletta – comic opera – and for the theatre.

'The Queen is so gay,' Walpole added, shortly after her arrival, 'we shall not want sights; she has been at the opera, *The Beggar's Opera* and *The Rehearsal*, and two nights ago carried the King to Ranelagh ...' Fortunately he was not privy to the opinion of English opera that Queen Charlotte later shared with her brother Charles in Germany. 'They sing but like parrots.' He, and others, praised the Queen's passion for music, as well as her playing on the harpsichord and singing at weekly concerts with her brothers- and sisters-in-law. (The King, a less sure performer, sometimes in private accompanied her on the German flute.) Walpole's disappointment when the couple lost that initial enthusiasm for gaiety was all the greater.

The King and Queen did not buckle. Complaints on every side – not least from the select few who were chosen to be their intimates every evening at cards and to have as entertainment the company of the royal children – continued to dog their life of retirement. But the King was well satisfied, and the Queen was determined to love and obey her husband, and to defer to his wishes – in particular, the lust for a plain life which he visited on her and their children. 'If there is a shade in her character,' one of her intimates was to aver, 'it was due to a natural timidity.' This timidity, to which her children later testified, was later in many instances to test the whole family, when the Queen insisted on bowing to the King's desires in matters where she felt very differently from him.

It was hardly surprising that the King wanted some kind of domestic respite. Much had occurred in the course of the six years since Prince George was told, while riding across Kew Green with his mother's mentor, Lord Bute, that his grandfather King George II – a man he hardly knew and whose closest companions at Richmond were his spinster daughters Caroline and Amelia – had died, and that he had become, at the age of twenty-two, King George III. Lady Charlotte Finch's then loving and sane husband William had been present at the palace on 25 October 1760, and wrote to his wife, 'My dearest dear', that the King had died of an apoplexy at seven or eight in the morning. He had been particularly cheerful, 'dressed, drunk his chocolate, and then retired as usual [to the water closet]; soon after a noise was heard of something having fallen, upon which one of the pages opened the door and found him upon the floor stone dead.'

The following year, the new King, anxious to secure both a companionable consort and the succession – of his four brothers and two sisters then living, none as yet was married – seized on Princess Charlotte of Mecklenburg-Strelitz to be his queen. She was a seventeen-year-old princess of 'very mediocre education', according to the reports, from an unimportant north German Duchy, and spoke no English. Hence, ran his thinking, unlike grander brides, 'being isolated, she could never involve England in affairs of the Continent'. The Queen was only too happy to adhere strictly to the line that the King had instructed her to follow in politics on her arrival in London – not to meddle. 'Having been brought up without pomp and in the simplicity of a small court,' as a diplomat informed the French Foreign Minister, Choiseul, 'she has no knowledge of politics, and no idea of intrigues, or of the interests of Princes.'

The English found her 'plain', criticized her complexion as sallow, and noticed her spreading nostrils and mouth, but the marriage was an immediate success; an astute courtier observed that they had an immediate air of pleasure in each other. To his delight the King and his new, submissive Queen appeared to agree on all things, especially the need to live a good Christian life.

Within a year of his marriage, in 1761, the King had an heir, George, Prince of Wales. Within two years he had shown himself a patron of the arts, embellishing the new Queen's House with libraries and with collections of paintings from Italy. And when, by September 1766, Queen Charlotte, speaking accented but fluent English, was a mother of three sons at the age of twenty-one and heavily pregnant with her next child, they could not fault her fecundity.

But the weekly drawing rooms and levees over which the King and Queen presided at the ancient palace of St James's, emphasizing England's power, where all was splendour and formality, were exhausting. And party politics were a further minefield for the inexperienced new sovereign and his consort to circumnavigate while they built their marriage – of vested landed interests and patronage centring around the powerful Whig and Tory families. In the six years since his accession, the King had had five different administrations – led, in turn, by the Duke of Newcastle, the Earl of Bute, George Grenville, the Marquess of Rockingham and, since July, William Pitt, newly Earl of Chatham. These changes brought, in turn, five Oppositions to contend with. And the King could hardly be blamed for wishing for a little domestic comfort in such trying circumstances.

The Queen was a great favourite with her ladies, and, even if she might have wished for more gaiety, she still sparkled in the small domestic setting her husband imposed on her. 'She is timid at first,' according to a report on her character, 'but she talks a lot, when she is among people she knows … She is capable of friendship and attachment to those who attach themselves to her.' The beneficiaries of the Queen's entertaining commentary on Court life or of her remarks on the books she consumed were her ladies at Court who had travelled abroad and imbibed Enlightenment ideas, like Lady Charlotte Finch, or who were foreign themselves, like Lady Holderness, the Dutch wife of the eldest princes' new governor. With these intimates the Queen carried on a rattling, vivacious correspondence which might well have surprised her husband or even her children accustomed to their dependable but somewhat austere mother. 'The Queen did not see this,' she wrote in a postscript to a particularly lively letter to one of her ladies in which she had commented on some absurdity of Court life.

In the year 1767, the Duchess of Northumberland wrote with admiration of the royal nursery arrangements: 'The Queen sees everything, but says nothing.' This was by marked contrast with the King, who was prone to go up and check on his sleeping children at six in the morning, to the discomfiture of their half-dressed attendants. No detail of their life was too small to interest him. But just as he knew every facing of every military uniform and did not know why the American colonies were rumbling with dissatisfaction, so he had no particularly good grasp of his children's different personalities.

A remarkable portrait that the artist Francis Cotes created in early 1767 of the Princess Royal asleep in her mother's lap shows how the child must have appeared in her first year of life. 'The Queen, fine,' wrote Horace Walpole in the margin of his catalogue on viewing the painting exhibited at the Society of Artists show later that year, 'the child, incomparable ... The sleeping child is equal to Guido.' In November 1767 a new son, Prince Edward, displaced Royal as the baby of the family when she was just thirteen months old.

Unfortunately for the Princess Royal, even before Prince Edward's arrival the Queen's careful childcare arrangements were a distinct failure in the first year of her eldest daughter's life. For Lady Charlotte, that incomparable governess who apart from anything else spoke 'the purest Tuscan' following youthful years in Florence, was suddenly consumed by her own concerns and those of her children. Not only was she dealing in her few hours of private life with the trauma of her husband's death, and with the management of her four children, but the health of her beloved eldest daughter Charlotte was failing, and her case increasingly resembled that of Frances, the daughter who had died two years earlier from tuberculosis.

When the Princess Royal was weaned from Mrs Muttlebury's ample bosom in April 1767 on to a diet of pap, she found no Lady Charlotte Finch in command of a highly organized nursery. The royal governess had embarked on a desperate and ultimately unsuccessful tour of watering holes with her eldest daughter. Mrs Cotesworth, the sub-governess, was left in charge of a bevy of nurses who dealt as well as they could with the demands of the royal children. The Prince of Wales told Lady Mary Coke that the Princess Royal 'lived at the Lodge [in Richmond] with the Queen and ... was extremely pretty'. But until Lady Charlotte returned in November, having buried Miss Finch, the royal nursery – with three children under three, and the Prince of Wales and Prince Frederick five and four respectively – was in a degree of confusion.

Order, restored with the grieving Lady Charlotte's return and further improved when a French mademoiselle was taken on to assist with the Princess Royal, came under threat again soon enough. For six days after

Prince Edward's first birthday – he was born on 2 November 1767 and named after his lately deceased paternal uncle Edward, Duke of York – the Queen gave birth to a second daughter. As a sense of injury was to be one of Edward's most developed characteristics, it is perhaps appropriate that he had an opportunity to experience it so early.

Princess Augusta Sophia, second of the daughters of George III and named after her paternal grandmother and after her mother who was christened Sophie Charlotte, was born on 8 November 1768. Anatomist Dr Hunter again hovered in the adjoining room, while Queen Charlotte went through her travail at the Queen's House with a female midwife. It was an extremely swift labour, lasting an hour and a half. But then Princess Augusta was the King and Queen's sixth child – and besides, in a long life, she never gave anyone any trouble if she could help it. The labour was not without another kind of incident. The waiting father was extraordinarily eager that the child about to enter the world should be a girl – so much so that Dr Hunter, anxious that, if it occurred, the repugnant alternative should not be regarded as his fault, protested. 'I think, sir, whoever sees those lovely Princes above stairs', the doctor ventured, 'must be glad to have another.' 'Doctor Hunter,' the King replied, 'I did not think I could have been angry with you, but I am; and I say, whoever sees that lovely child the Princess Royal above stairs must wish to have the fellow to her.' The agitated King then interrupted his wife's labour to repeat the dialogue to her. The Queen was no doubt relieved to give birth to a small and pretty girl, a foil to the Princess Royal, who was destined to be among the most loved and loving of the royal children, and to win the grudging respect of one with no liking for the House of Hanover as 'certainly the best of the whole family'.

Princess Augusta was in later life to display an eye for the absurd that marked her out. An incident that occurred during a public reception at St James's Palace shortly after her birth is worth recalling in that context. Traditionally, a few days after members of Society had paid their respects, members of the public came to enquire after the health of the royal mother and child, and were rewarded with 'cake and caudle'. The latter was a mixture of thin gruel and wine served to women in childbirth and to their visitors. Traditionally also, the throngs – mayors and corporations included – who passed through the chambers of the Palace were ludicrously greedy. At the 'enquiries' for Princess Augusta, two young ladies, having drunk deep of the caudle, made a bid to carry off 'a large quantity of cake, and some of the cups in which the caudle had been served up'. Detected, the inebriated misses were allowed to go free after a severe reprimand, and after begging a pardon on their wavering knees.

Princess Augusta was swiftly absorbed into the ebb and flow of royal family life, and was so accommodating as to spend her first Christmas – with her wet-nurse and brother Edward – at Lady Charlotte Finch's apartments in St James's Palace, while the Princess Royal and Prince William were inoculated against smallpox, a disease that was often fatal if caught, at the Queen's House. Lady Charlotte, never having had smallpox, customarily remained with those royal children who had not yet been inoculated. Lady Mary Coke visited the Queen's House on Boxing Day 1768 and found Prince William 'excessively full' of spots, while the Princess Royal had 'not twenty all over her'. She told her correspondent that she was surprised to find the Princess Royal a healthy child, 'for instead of colour in her cheeks there is a yellow mark, which I should never think denoted health.'

In defiance of Lady Mary's pronouncement, Princess Royal was back at her lessons with her French teacher, Mlle Anne Dorothée Krohme, without delay. Her education, destined to be a great source of pleasure and interest to her, had begun when she was a mere eighteen months, in the spring of 1768. The King and Queen, however, had shown a bewildering lack of manners in 'poaching' Mlle Krohme from their intimate friends the Holdernesses, who lived across the river from Richmond at Sion Hill where she was their daughter Lady Amelia d'Arcy's beloved governess.

'The whole was transacted', wrote Lady Mary Coke, 'before any notice was taken to Lord and Lady Holderness; that is to say, the proposals were first made to Mlle Krohme, which seems, I think, a little strange, and does not, I think, please them.' It was indisputably in the English royal family's interest that the Princess Royal should speak and write French fluently. Later she herself was to ask repeatedly of a niece's governess: 'Do not you soon intend getting in somebody in playing to accustom her to hear French spoke? If she does not learn early, she will never acquire the accent ...' For the Princess Royal was destined for marriage on the Continent, and to a great Protestant prince, where French would be the language of the Court, regardless of whether German or another tongue was the language of the country. Presumably anxiety on this point led the royal parents to treat their friends the Holdernesses with such unusual discourtesy.

Within a few months, as it turned out, the hijacked Frenchwoman returned to her own country. 'She says herself for only a short time,' reported the vigilant Lady Mary Coke, 'but others think that a melancholy in her temper, which has been observed by their Majesties, made them think her improper to educate the Princess Royal, and that she is not likely to return.' A substitute was found in the form of Mlle Krohme's cousin Julie, who proved thoroughly popular, as she acted as the Queen's unofficial secretary as well as her daughters' French teacher.

The Princess Royal's memory – and in due course that of Princess Augusta – was trained before reading and writing were even thought of. Thirty years later she had not forgotten the pleasure she took in her early lessons, and endorsed the method employed with her to a niece's governess, when that Princess was just two: 'Pray begin to employ her, as early as possible, with some reasonable little things, for everything in which memory alone is required can be learnt early. Let her have little prints of the history of the Bible – tell her the stories and they will already get in her head and she will never forget them …' The Princess Royal was an apt pupil. She and her siblings were to have, after this early training, an uncanny recall of names, faces and incidents, even from childhood, as well as a remarkable grasp of historical facts.

Remembering other less pleasant scenes from childhood, Princess Royal spoke of the importance of 'breaking' children of any 'sad passions' to which they might be subject, although she advocated 'gentleness' to subdue 'temper'. But above all else, and here she followed her mother, she believed, in the education of princesses, that 'making her a good Christian' rather than concentrating on making a 'wonderful' child full of accomplishments was, with the duty of guarding her from 'folly', the chief labour for a princess's superintendents.

A little folly, however, was sometimes permissible in the royal nursery. In late September 1769 Princess Augusta, at nearly eleven months, and Royal – a couple of days before her third birthday – were dressed up with their brothers for 'an entertainment given at Kew in the house assigned to the young Princes by Lady Charlotte Finch …'. Princess Royal represented Columbine in a dress of crimson and black, ornamented with gold. ('Her royal highness appeared rather too plump for the character,' was one onlooker's comment.) She and Princess Augusta sat in a shared pavilion in Lady Charlotte's apartment, 'a sort of illuminated temple, very picturesque'. Princess Augusta wore a 'well-fancied dress of silver gauze, with painted gauze wings at her shoulders, and a chaplet of flowers on her head'.

The eldest princes, meanwhile, in Hussar dresses of white satin trimmed with fur, awaited their parents in a military tent. They were joined there by a charity boy, Master Blomberg, whom, on a misguided impulse, the Queen had taken in some years before to be a companion to her eldest sons, and who now wore a 'Mercury' dress. The Prince of Wales by no means liked this addition to the nursery, Lady Charlotte Finch's daughter Henrietta sighed, adding that he took no pleasure in sharing his possessions with Master Blomberg or anyone else. He was happy, nevertheless, to make all around him cry while he took theirs. Later the Princess Royal was to write with feeling that taking a 'humble companion' for children in an 'exalted situation' was a 'sad thing'.

When the King and Queen arrived, the two eldest princes emerged from their pavilion to perform a 'warlike dance, to martial music'. Then Prince William, in harlequin dress, stepped out of another pavilion that he shared with Edward, a Bacchus with trailing ivy leaves, and made two or three trips around the room 'with the true harlequin step (which he had learned very perfectly)'. And finally Princess Royal, his Columbine, came out and accompanied him in the dance as well as a child of not quite three could, while Princess Augusta was carried round the room 'fluttering her little silken pinions, like a real sylph'.

The Princess Royal was later implicitly to criticize these tableaux, and declare that she did not like 'wonderful children'. Displays of their accomplishments stoked vanity, she asserted, perhaps remembering not being a 'wonderful child' herself. She found music 'horrid' later, while some of her brothers and sisters were both very musical and fairly 'wonderful' as children. Moreover, when Princess Augusta was a month old, Lady Mary Coke found her 'the most beautiful infant I ever saw'. But she was not so kind about the child's elder sister. 'I forgot to ask you', she wrote to a correspondent, 'if you did not think the Princess Royal very plain.' Lady Mary's criticism was to be, if not accurate, prophetic. The Princess, though never 'very plain', was never to be beautiful, as her sister Augusta would be, or elegant, as her mother was. And although her figure and height would be in her favour, her reputation was established early.

The royal parents at any rate heartily applauded this exhibition of their children's prowess, although the atmosphere was tinged with sadness. This performance was a farewell gift from Lady Charlotte, whose Etonian son Lord Winchilsea was now ill. No longer trusting the spas of England after her experiences at Bristol and Scarborough with her poor daughters, she took her son abroad to Nice.

The princesses' parents continued to cultivate their rural idyll at Richmond and Kew. Prince Frederick had told Lady Mary Coke in the month before Princess Augusta's birth that the King had been 'working in the garden, cutting down trees, and that he had carried away the boughs'. Before she left for Nice, Lady Charlotte Finch told Lady Mary that the

Queen at Richmond, not pregnant for once, 'wears an English nightgown and white apron … 'tis a dress his Majesty likes; formerly nobody could appear before the Royal family with a white apron …' And Lady Charlotte added that the King had ordered her to wear this homely dress too. Lady Mary Coke's outrage knew no bounds when she heard, in July 1769, that the King and Queen with the Queen's brother Prince Ernest – on a visit from Mecklenburg – and Lady Effingham had walked through the town of Richmond without a single servant. 'I am not satisfied in my own mind', she wrote stiffly, 'about the propriety of a Queen walking in a town unattended.' There was really no limit to the King's liking for living 'in a retired manner, but easy of access'.

But in fact outside the rural bliss constructed at the royal residences on the Thames – at Richmond Lodge with its shabby Indian paper on the walls and its rolled lawns and orange trees outside, and at Kew in Lady Charlotte's house with views of passing traffic on the Thames – there were strained relations between Crown and country in this year following Princess Augusta's birth. At home, and to the King's fury, the radical Mr John Wilkes had been returned as Member of Parliament for Brentford, just across the Thames from Richmond. News from the recalcitrant British colony of Boston in America was hardly more encouraging. Horace Walpole wrote, days before Princess Augusta's birth, of the new Parliament: 'A busy session it must be. The turbulent temper of Boston, of which you will see the full accounts in all the papers, is a disagreeable prospect.'

When the silk weavers of Spitalfields in London, who supplied their costly fabric for Court levees and drawing rooms and royal birthdays, protested – and rioted – against foreign imports of silk in 1769, the King and Queen naively attempted to turn public opinion in their favour and seduce the Spitalfields weavers with an additional opportunity for them to display their wares at a 'junior drawing room' at St James's presided over by the seven-year-old Prince of Wales in a crimson silk suit and his three-year-old sister, the Princess Royal, reposing on a sofa in a Roman toga, also of silk.

The Queen was excessively proud of the silken tableau that her children created at St James's, and declared it fit to be painted. But the vain effort to woo public opinion broke up when the London mob, yelling defiance, drove a hearse into the Palace courtyard. The Prince of Wales said afterwards that he 'thanked God it was over', and told Lady Mary Coke two days later, when she hoped it had not fatigued him, 'Indeed, Madam, but it did, and the Princess Royal was terribly tired.' There was no attempt to repeat this public display of the royal children.

Tempers could fray in the royal nursery itself, as when, exasperated by Prince William, his nurse Mrs Abbott 'had not only the presumption to strike him, but knocked his head against the wall'. The affair attracted some publicity – Lady Mary Coke heard of it in Vienna – and Mrs Abbott was dismissed. This was an offence, lèse-majesté, that could not be overlooked by the Queen and Lady Charlotte. The offender's pension, however, was paid to her for the remainder of her life – an indication, perhaps, that it was felt that she had had much to try her.

Lady Mary Coke recorded on one occasion that the Princess Royal's 'temper was a good deal tried by her brothers, who pulled her about most unreasonably'. She now regarded the Princess as 'much improved', and, perhaps necessarily, 'the best humoured child that ever was'. The Queen was to write to Lady Charlotte in 1771 with some relief after the royal governess returned from a journey, 'They never can be in better hands than yours.' Three years later, with her family still growing, she wrote that she was 'thankful to providence for having worthy people' about her children.

Inevitably, when Lady Charlotte had returned unexpectedly to London in the spring of 1770, leaving her son in Nice, there was speculation that the Queen was 'a-breeding' again. Lady Charlotte could not comment, as there was – despite the frequency of the occurrence – a coyness at Court observed about the Queen's very visibly increasing person. The tattlers were proved right. A wet-nurse, Mrs Spinluffe, was in place at the Queen's House by mid-May, and Princess Elizabeth – named after her maternal grandmother, with a nod to the great Tudor Queen – was born there on 22 May 1770.

With the birth of a third daughter and seventh child, Princess Elizabeth, King George III and Queen Charlotte, had they been otherwise, might have seen fit to draw their childbearing to a close. But it would never have entered the King's head. On hearing that a lady of his acquaintance, already blessed with nineteen children, was lying in with her twentieth, he wished sincerely that she might have twins. And it would not have entered Queen Charlotte's head at this point to have ideas of her own on the subject.

The elements of a formula for the education and management of princes and princesses continued to evolve. The Princesses Royal and Augusta acquired an attendant they doted on, Miss Mary Dacres, in the year of Princess Elizabeth's birth. The sister of a rear admiral and a Cumberland connection of an intimate of the Queen's, Lady Effingham, Miss Dacres appears in the nursery accounts as the princesses' 'dresser'. On Miss Dacres the Princess Royal and Princess Augusta showered affection, and while Lady Charlotte and Mrs Cotesworth taught them to read,

Miss Dacres managed their 'passions' and was patient with Royal's stammer – 'hesitation in speech', that princess later recorded, was 'unfortunately very common on all sides of the Brunswick family' – and Princess Augusta's shyness.

These princesses were unusual and fortunate among European princesses – and, still more so, among girls in England – in having such high-minded and bookish parents who treated their education seriously and took great care over their attendants. They were also unusual and fortunate as young royal children in having parents who preferred their children's company and that of a small domestic circle to the glamour and turbulence and power-broking that characterized most other great Courts in full flow. But they were to be unfortunate in having parents who could not – given their public duties, given the number of children they continued to produce, and given the domestic and foreign calamities that were soon to strike the royal family – adequately oversee the implementation of the utopian child-rearing policies they earnestly advocated.

2

Growing Up

~

LADY MARY COKE went to breakfast with Lady Charlotte Finch at Kew on 19 August 1771, specifically 'to see the young Princesses, who are with her early in the morning: the Princess Royal I think the most sensible agreeable child I ever saw, but in my opinion far from pretty: the Princess Augusta rather pretty, but not so well as she was last year'. She did not see Princess Elizabeth, now nearly fifteen months, but conceded that Prince Ernest, who had been born ten weeks earlier, on 5 June at the Queen's House in London, was a 'pretty infant'.

Lady Charlotte had become director of the princesses' education, and the princesses had begun their daily drive over to her house at Kew from Richmond Lodge, earlier this year, when the Prince of Wales and Prince Frederick acquired their own establishment at Kew, complete with governor, sub-governor and tutors. A merchant's house opposite the Dowager Princess of Wales's residence, Kew House, and known as the Dutch House, with a garden gate on to the riverbank, was duly redecorated for the princes, and became known as the Prince of Wales's House. The previous August, Queen Charlotte had signalled the coming move in a birthday letter to the Prince of Wales that she requested his governess to read to him: 'Time draws near when you will be put into the hands of governors, under whose care you will study more manly learning than what you have done hitherto.' At the age of seven, in England, boys' education became the province of their fathers and they went 'into men's hands'. The Prince of Wales and his brother had remained beyond the usual age in the care of Lady Charlotte. The courses of the tight-knit junior royal family were dividing, and the princesses would now receive most of their education at Lady Charlotte's own new house on the river at Kew and see little of their elder brothers.

Lady Charlotte in her turn would see little of her former charges. Her son George, who had recently succeeded his uncle as Earl of Winchilsea, wrote from Christ Church, Oxford, where he was now an undergraduate, hoping his mother liked her new abode and its 'charming situation'. 'It must be quite new to you to have a garden gate to yourself,' he added encouragingly. Lady Charlotte's sister, Lady Juliana Penn, however, was sympathetic about her inevitable demotion, and wrote after seeing the Prince of Wales and Prince Frederick installed as Knights of the Garter this summer of 1771: 'I felt a great part of the beauty of the sight was your work, and what must give you pleasure, in seeing your two sweet little princes brought up by yourself to be fit for anything that can be expected from them. The world indeed does you justice and they were admired by every creature that looked on them.'

From now on, the princes' governor, Lord Holderness, and his deputies would receive compliments on their prowess. And the following spring, in 1772, a house facing St Anne's Church on Kew Green was assigned to Prince William and Prince Edward, and a 'tall and showy' Hanoverian army officer in his thirties, General Budé, was appointed their instructor. As a royal nursery attendant later related, Prince William 'exulted beyond measure going into men's hands. His very housemaids, he said, should be men.' The appointment of an officer rather than a university man as his instructor was no doubt an additional pleasure, as Prince William was of 'a strongly marked military turn'. Third and fourth in line to the throne, the younger princes – and Prince Ernest and any other princes who should be born – were destined for the army and navy, not for government, and their education need not include the subtler points of constitutional law.

The admirable Lady Charlotte's path lay now with the females of the species, and for a while she and the sub-governess, Mrs Cotesworth, undertook the whole of the princesses' education at Kew, bar the rudiments of the French language, which Mlle Julie Krohme supplied. 'Till we were seven or eight children,' the Princess Royal later wrote, 'we had no English teacher, Lady Charlotte Finch and Mrs Cotesworth having taught us all to read. But the Sub Governess's [Mrs Cotesworth's] ill health preventing her giving us the proper attention, Lady Charlotte could not teach us all and begged Mama to take some clergyman's daughter to assist her. Notwithstanding which Lady Charlotte continued to read with Augusta and me everyday sometimes two but always one hour.'

In 1774, Lady Mary Coke wrote a more forthright account of Mrs Cotesworth's health problems: 'It has been said a long time that she had taken to drinking, which must make her very improper for that employment.' Perhaps also Lady Charlotte Finch had a little less relish for her task as royal governess, now that the excitement of moulding the heir to the throne was no longer hers. Be that as it may, in July 1771 she undoubtedly did governess and clergyman's daughter Miss Frederica Planta honour in calling her to be 'about the little Royal family'. She was 'to teach them to read first English, and the other languages after that', wrote Miss Planta's sister Elizabeth. A governess herself, Miss Elizabeth Planta followed the affair with interest, although she disparaged the terms and conditions of the employment, including the salary of £100 a year: 'Her appointments are quite mediocre.' Still, her sister was at Kew as she wrote, ready to attend the princesses when they came from Richmond Lodge, and her accommodation was paid for, as were her chairmen – porters who carried her sedan chair – when the royal family was in town. 'The future promises des avancements,' Elizabeth concluded dispassionately.

Unfortunately, Frederica was still bound to an employer, Lady Hoskyns, who liked having her children's governess filched by the royal family no better than had the Holdernesses. And she was a good deal more vocal about the inconvenience. She accused Miss Planta of 'having made underhand applications' to the royal household, and wrote in terms, Miss Elizabeth considered, that 'showed very vividly that she regarded her own interests much more than those of my sister'.

At last Lady Hoskyns was made to cede the invaluable Miss Frederica Planta, but not before the Queen herself had expressed her displeasure at Lady Hoskyns's obstructiveness. The appointment was one much to the Queen's taste. Key to her interest in attendants employed about her daughters was that they should be not only Christian but the right kind of Christian. Following Lady Charlotte Finch – mentor in much – she subdued her temperament and exorcised the frustrations of her position by a passionate meditation on sermons and exegeses on the Bible, but she was utterly intolerant of agnostic brands of Christianity.

The Misses Planta followed, in their Christian faith, their father Andreas, a respected pastor in London and founding librarian at the fledgling British Museum. One of those Deist Christians who found themselves able to reconcile recent geological findings with the Story of Creation, he had emigrated from his native Switzerland, when that 'republic of letters' became dominated by philosophers who decried his brand of faith. In London he and his wife settled happily, their son Joseph succeeding him as librarian at the British Museum and four of their five daughters becoming governesses. (The fifth married and fled the world of education for Philadelphia in America.)

And so the princesses had their English teacher, and Miss Planta, 'mistress of seven languages' – including Latin and Greek – 'and a most pious Christian', settled into the community of royal preceptors and tutors and governesses at Kew. The Queen had written to Lady Charlotte: 'I am sorry that I myself have not more time to spend with them [the royal children] and therefore am thankful to Providence for having worthy people about them.' She and the King were certainly prepared to fight fair and foul to secure those 'worthy people'.

State portraits by Allan Ramsay and by Zoffany of the King – auburn haired and pink cheeked – and of the Queen – dark, slight and grey-eyed – were copied in these years and sent abroad to confirm the young couple's status. They were sovereigns of a mighty kingdom following the triumphant end of the Seven Years War in 1763, and of a growing commercial empire, and the Queen's diamonds in her portrait were commensurately dazzling. Chief among them were those that sparkled on a stomacher the King had commissioned on their marriage for £60,000. 'The fond [or background] is a network as fine as catgut of small diamonds,' the Duchess of Northumberland had recorded in 1761, 'and the rest is a large pattern of natural flowers, composed of very large diamonds, one of which is 18, another 16, and a third 10 thousands pounds price.' Lord Clive, better known today as Clive of India, added, among other riches, to the Queen's store of jewels presents from the deposed Great Mogul of India, Shah Alam: 'two diamond drops worth twelve thousand pounds'.

But in the midst of their public life the royal couple continued to attempt a domestic life, whether in town at the Queen's House or at the Lodge in Richmond parkland, once the property of the King's grandfather George II. The princesses were still brought down to visit their parents after breakfast and, now of an age to do so, visited after their parents' four o'clock dinner. The King continued as devoted and eager a parent as ever, carrying Prince Ernest as a baby around in his arms and sitting on the floor to play with him, just as he had when the older children were infants.

But now, while the King and Queen attended to public business, after breakfast the princesses were driven off to Kew and to the schoolroom at Lady Charlotte's or, when in town, climbed to their brothers' old schoolroom at the Queen's House. All the princes and the princesses, at their father's behest, pursued a programme of *mens sana in corpore sano*, which excluded meat from their diet except on certain days, and included daily airings in the garden of the Queen's House in town or walks in Kew Gardens come rain, come sun. It featured as well a discussion of improving subjects selected from a ponderous commonplace book that the King had kept since boyhood.

The princesses' schooling in London in the winter months with Lady Charlotte and her subalterns was instructive, and their hours with their parents at Richmond Lodge or at the Queen's House were precious, but their days at Kew, given the environs where they took their airings, were inspiring. They were old enough to have their imaginations fired on their walks by the strange fancies that the architect Sir William Chambers had placed in the gardens to entertain their grandmother. There was a Chinese pagoda modelled on one he had seen on his travels to Shanghai, a model Alhambra and even a Gothic cathedral, besides innumerable temples. And in the years since their grandmother had established a botanical garden and a menagerie at Kew in 1760, there had come exotic visitors bringing booty from foreign lands to enchant the children.

This very October, following his voyage with Captain Cook to the South Seas, the young naturalist Sir Joseph Banks presented the King and Queen at Richmond Lodge with an Australasian crown and feathers. He also brought to the botanical gardens that occupied part of the Kew property an extraordinary plant with orange and blue shoots from the Cape of Good Hope, and named it the Strelitzia, in graceful compliment to the Queen's native land of Mecklenburg-Strelitz. In the menagerie in a different part of the gardens, another first fruit of Captain Cook's voyage to the South Seas – a kangaroo from Botany Bay – was proudly placed, a mate brought over, and a successful breeding programme instituted. Not surprisingly, Kew was to have a powerful hold on all these princesses' memories and imaginations in later life.

The princesses now saw little of their elder brothers and of tag-along Prince Edward, except when their paths crossed while out on airings. The boys, so recently part of a boisterous family group and meeting their parents twice daily, were now forbidden to stray from the sphere of their houses at Kew – except for those improving walks in the grounds of Kew and, in the case of the eldest two, Sunday dinner, which they took with their governor Lord Holderness and his wife at Sion Hill on the other side of the Thames. Otherwise, spartan conditions reigned in the boys' establishments. Meat was rationed, and even when fruit tart was on the menu it was 'without crust'.

The Prince of Wales and his brother were, to begin with, obliging pupils and anxious to please all their instructors, although Prince Frederick later condemned one attendant as having been 'used to have a silver pencil-case in his hand while we were at our lessons … and he has frequently given us such knocks with it on our foreheads that the blood followed them'. But the King instructed the princes' governors and preceptors to administer beatings when appropriate. One of the princesses later claimed to have seen her eldest brothers 'held by their tutors to be flogged like dogs with a long whip'. The boys, trusting or fearing their father, did not complain. Other boys of their age endured worse at schools, and their regime, with a certain want of imagination, was the same as their father's had once been.

These indignities the princesses were spared, and the Princess Royal, condemning harshness as counter-productive, later declared, 'I love a steady, quiet way with children.' She also wrote, echoing her mother, 'On the whole I believe that example does more than precept … I think the more they [children] are led to everything, and fancy it is by their own instigation, the better.' But the princesses probably suffered other ordeals by way of punishment for poor behaviour. Royal thought severe measures – tying girls' hands was a practice of the time – should be the response to 'a lie, or the proof of a bad heart … alone'. But for 'ill humour' she endorsed 'great firmness and coldness', and her prescription 'for bad lessons' was interesting: 'the making learning a favour and the not allowing her to learn the next day if she is idle'.

'My pen is not capable of tracing a quarter of what I feel at the moment of your departure,' Queen Charlotte had written in July 1771 to her brother Prince Charles, who had just left England for his duties as military governor of Hanover after a long summer stay. Her newborn baby, Prince Ernest, was no consolation – nor was the offer her other brother in England, another Ernest, made to delay his return to Zell in the Hanoverian electorate where he was governor. 'My pleasures are finished for the year by our separation,' she wrote.

The Queen did not know how truly she wrote. Over the coming months she and the King were to be plagued by family and political crises in the world that lay outside the well-managed promenades of Kew. In the American colonies there was growing discontent with the King's decision that they should be taxed and the revenue raised put to their defence. Thirty years before, the then Prime Minister Sir Robert Walpole had been wary of such a measure when it was proposed to him in 1739. 'I have old England set against me, and do you think I will have new England likewise?' The King had lit a 'long fuse' when he insisted on Prime Minister Lord North exacting duty on newspapers and other printed material in the colonies with the Stamp Act. In March 1770 a mob, incensed by the continuing tax on tea, had attacked the Customs House in Boston. Five of the assailants had been shot, but the protests grew bolder. Within two years, another mob was to board a revenue cutter, the *Gasparee*, and burn it. Within six, the American colonies were to declare their independence from the Crown, and a bloody war would be launched.

The King was to be similarly obstinate in a situation at home which he regarded as a challenge to his authority, and which he could not control – the behaviour of his younger brother the Duke of Cumberland.

The King's relations with his brothers and sisters had never been easy. His parents had always favoured lively Prince Edward, Duke of York, over him and had greeted his own more faltering essays into social intercourse, 'Do hold your tongue, George: don't talk like a fool.' Given that the Duke of York liked nothing better than to roam expensively in Italy, the King was perhaps less sorry than he might have been when his brother died in 1767. (Lady Mary Coke, who, without much justification, had considered herself practically affianced to the Duke, was devastated.) But now it was the King's brother Henry, Duke of Cumberland who posed a problem. He had shown his character at his brother the King's wedding in 1761. When someone had questioned his early departure from the family group on the wedding night, he had replied, 'What should I stay for?... if she cries out, I cannot help her.'

The Duke, having succeeded his uncle 'Butcher' William, Duke of Cumberland, as ranger of Windsor Great Park, caroused at the Ranger's residence there, Cumberland Lodge, and on the Continent with his mistress Lady Anne Horton. Lady Anne was the daughter of an Irish peer who sat on the Whig benches, and her constant companion was her sister Lady Elizabeth Luttrell – known in all the capitals of Europe as a hardened gambler.

The King was furious and confounded when the Duke of Cumberland handed him a letter to read on 1 September 1771, while the brothers were out walking in the woods at Richmond. It informed him that the Duke had married Lady Anne, and was now looking for greater Parliamentary provision as a married man. The King described his reaction to this news to his brother the Duke of Gloucester: 'After walking some minutes in silence to smother my feelings, I without passion spoke to him to the following effect. That I could not believe he had taken the step in the paper, to which he answered that he would never tell me an untruth.'

The scandal this mismatch brought on the royal family, and the harm it did to the King's endeavours to create a more moral atmosphere at Court, made him and others think longingly of the system that obtained at many Continental Courts to deter this sort of thing. The Duke's conduct, the King wrote to his mother, was 'his inevitable ruin and ... a disgrace to the whole family', and he encouraged him to go abroad. 'In any country,' the King told his brother, 'a prince marrying a subject is looked up[on] as dishonourable, nay in Germany the children of such a marriage' – a morganatic match, as it was termed there – 'cannot succeed to any territories but here where the Crown is but too little respected, it must be big with the greatest mischief. Civil wars would by such measures again be common in this country; those of the Yorks and Lancasters were greatly giving to inter-marriages with the nobility.' He went on, 'I must therefore on the first occasion show my resentment, I have children who must know what they have to expect if they could follow so infamous an example.'

This letter made very uncomfortable reading for the Duke of Gloucester, who – although five years his junior – the King regarded as 'the only friend to whom I can unbosom every thought'. Gloucester, weak and flaccid except in the pursuit of women, made a perfect recipient for the King's laborious thought processes. On this occasion, the message of the letter was clear. Gloucester must settle the question that perplexed Society. had he married Lady Waldegrave or not? For the King to have one brother married to a commoner and with family among the Whig Opposition in the House of Commons – five of the new Duchess of Cumberland's brothers and her father had seats there – was unfortunate. Were Gloucester married, too, and, should he wish to go into opposition, he could count on the political support of those strong Whigs the Walpoles and Waldegraves, as Maria belonged to the first family by birth and to the second by her first marriage.

The Duke of Gloucester answered approvingly, soothingly, condemned his brother Cumberland's behaviour and added for good measure that he himself would never marry. Honour was apparently satisfied, and Gloucester, pointedly leaving Lady Waldegrave in England, went abroad to Tuscany where he almost immediately fell ill with a 'bloody flux'. For companion-able nurses, fortunately, he had the attentions of not one 'Madame Grovestein' from Holland but two. In January 1772, however, Lady Mary Coke in Vienna heard from Lady Charlotte Finch in England, 'the Royal family does not flatter themselves with the Duke of Gloucester's recovery ... the accounts are so bad as to leave little room for hopes.' He was then at Naples. And as late as March, having flitted to Rome, the devoted Grovesteins hot on his heels, the itinerant Duke was still 'at death's door'.

In England, meanwhile, the King's 'resentment' was immediately manifested in the announcement that those who visited the Duke of Cumberland and his new Duchess would not be welcome at Court. But he went further, despite the pleas of his mother, the Dowager Princess of Wales. She, more concerned for the dying Duke of Gloucester in Italy, preached family harmony in the case of Cumberland. 'All I beg of you is,' she wrote to her son the King in November, after expressing her chagrin that Henry had behaved so badly, 'do not have vengeance against him in your heart and if he has the good fortune to be quit of his wife, pardon him.' She knew her eldest son's capacity for resentment. Instead of listening to her, the King meditated a Royal Marriages Act, making it illegal for members of the royal family to marry without the previous consent of the sovereign. With his brother Gloucester's assurance that he was a bachelor, this and other provisions in the bill that the King personally drafted should deter him from ever making an honest duchess of his bastard Walpole mistress. And looking ahead, the King would be sure of controlling his own children's marriages.

The brooding lawmaker had other family matters to attend to. His mother, who had been suffering from agonizing throat pains, had been much affected by the initial reports of her son Gloucester's imminent death abroad and by the family strife over her other son Cumberland's marriage. By the end of November 1771, her situation had deteriorated – 'her speech grows less intelligible, she hourly emaciates, and her dreadful faintings towards night must soon put an end to a situation that it is almost too cruel to wish to see', the King reported. No one thought she would last a fortnight. Her malady was now described as 'a cancer in her mouth and risings of the viscera'.

But the redoubtable Dowager Princess lived on and on beyond the prescribed fortnight. 'Nothing ever equalled her resolution,' wrote Horace Walpole. 'She took the air till within four or five days of her death, and never indicated having the least idea of her danger, even to the Princess of Brunswick [her daughter], though she had sent for her.' Ghastly with illness, the old Saxe-Gotha Princess dressed and received her son the King and the Queen in a travesty of their usual evening ritual on the last night of her life, Friday, 7 February 1772. She 'kept them four hours in indifferent conversation, though almost inarticulate herself, said nothing on her situation, took no leave of them – and expired at six in the morning without a groan'. The Princess was unpopular to the last: her coffin was hissed and booed on its way to its resting-place in the royal chapel of Henry VII in Westminster Abbey. Meanwhile, Prince William, who was tender hearted, asked Miss Planta to read him the funeral service, and 'wept bitterly'.

There was more to come. On the day before the Dowager Princess died, Horace Walpole had written to his friend Horace Mann, 'No more news yet from Denmark, which is extraordinary, but one should think therefore that nothing tragic has happened, or Mr Keith [the English Minister in Copenhagen] would have dispatched messengers faster. You may imagine the impatience of everyone to hear more of this strange revolution...'

Whether the Dowager Princess was apprised or unapprised of her daughter Caroline's misadventures, the story that arrived in London at the end of January 1772 gripped Society and horrified the King. Queen Caroline of Denmark, the royal princesses' aunt who had married the King of that country two days after the Princess Royal's birth, had been lying in bed in the early morning on 17 January, after a masked ball that she and the King had given. Hearing a commotion below, she believed that it was the servants clearing up, and called for quiet.

It was, in fact, the King's stepmother, the Dowager Queen Juliana, and her son Prince Frederick, confronting the King with evidence of the Queen's adultery with Count Struensee, the Prime Minister. The King, whose mind was weak but affectionate, resisted for a time their demand that he sign a death warrant for his favourite Minister and an order for his wife's imprisonment. But they persisted. Struensee had been seized earlier as he left the ball. And now into the Queen of Denmark's bedchamber sprang armed guards, who bore her off to the fortress of Kronborg.

The English Minister at Copenhagen, Sir Robert Murray Keith, was the hero of the hour in England when it became known there that he had threatened that gunboats would be trained on the offending capital if the Queen was not released. But for the King – and in due course for his daughters – when Keith's despatch reached him, this was a defining hour. For two months his sister the Hereditary Princess of Brunswick had poured into his ear complaints of her husband's adultery and contemptuous treatment of her. Now his sister Caroline had been, as he saw it, 'perverted by a cruel and contemptible court'. When she was released from Kronborg, he sent her to live in the city of Zell in his Electorate of Hanover, where his brother-in-law Ernest was governor, and where their sister Brunswick became a constant visitor. There he hoped that 'by mildness' Caroline would be 'brought back to the amiable character' she had previously possessed.

King George III never forgot his sisters' fates in foreign Courts beyond his control, and it weighed heavily with him that he had promoted the matches. This would prey on his mind with fatal consequences when his own daughters came of an age to marry. His brother the Duke of Gloucester was to hold that the King believed his daughters did not wish to settle out of England. Meanwhile his sisters, who had never been close, forged an agreeable friendship on a foundation of religion and tears. And Lady Mary Coke summed it up – the Queen of Denmark had exposed herself, so too had the Duke of Cumberland with his disgraceful marriage, the Princess of Wales had an 'incurable distemper', and the Duke of

Gloucester was, 'with one foot in the grave, lavishing his poor remains of life in pursuit of his intrigues with Madame de Grovestein. This is a picture full of shades.' It was an evil hour for the English royal family, and was felt to be so by no one more than the King.

The reputation of the monarchy, however, was even more severely tarnished when the King drove through his ill-considered Royal Marriages Act at the end of March 1772 with the reluctant assistance of his Prime Minister, Lord North. The temper in the House of Commons was inflamed. The MPs did not hesitate to speak ill of every member of the royal family, and the recently deceased Princess of Wales came in for a great deal of abuse.

Furthermore, on 16 September, just over a year after the Duke of Cumberland had broken the unwelcome news of his marriage to the King at Richmond, another storm broke. The Duke of Gloucester told the King that he too was married – had been married, in fact, since 1766, secretly but perfectly legally. The ceremony had taken place days before his niece the Princess Royal's birth.

All through the brouhaha about their brother Cumberland's marriage, it transpired, Gloucester had played a false part. Lady Charlotte Finch told Lady Mary Coke at Kew that she thought the Duke of Gloucester very ungrateful to the King. (Coke, with more important things on her mind, decided at the drawing room on 22 September 1772 that Princess Elizabeth was now 'much the prettiest', when the three princesses saw company in the old drawing room.) And the reason for divulging this information now? The Duchess of Gloucester, as Lady Waldegrave was revealed to be, was expecting their child in May of the following year.

The King turned on his once favourite brother and not only barred him from Court, declaring that, as with the Cumberlands, anyone who visited the Gloucesters would not be welcome at Court, but instigated a humiliating and vindictive investigation by the Privy Council into the validity of his brother's marriage. His supposed object was that there should be no doubts about the child's legitimacy. In the meantime, his own wife, Queen Charlotte, appeared in satin and ermine at the January drawing rooms in 1773 until a week before she gave birth on the 27th of that month to their sixth son and ninth child, Augustus. The Queen, naturally stoic, rarely had sympathy for the woes of pregnant women, but even she might have felt a pang for the Duchess of Gloucester concerning the ordeal that now awaited her.

The Privy Council hearing took place days before the Duchess was to give birth, and she was forced to appear to defend the marriage, despite her condition. A flurry of depositions later, the King conceded on 27 May that the marriage had been valid after the Privy Council registered it as such, and the child born two days later – Sophia Matilda of Gloucester – at the Duke's house in Upper Grosvenor Street was duly given the title of princess. Any sympathy the Queen might have felt for her sister-in-law was no doubt extinguished when the Gloucesters summoned members of the Opposition to attend the birth.

The unchivalrous Privy Council enquiry had been most unfortunate, not least for its author. It earned the King the hatred of Horace Walpole, fond uncle of the Duchess of Gloucester, who had earlier been well disposed towards him. Walpole took revenge on the King in his later writings on the Court of King George III. As for Princess Sophia Matilda of Gloucester, her mother wrote that she seemed to smile at all the world to make up for being unwanted. But Horace Walpole was less enthusiastic about what he called the 'royalty of my niece and nieceling'. Asked by a lady at Court if he had seen the infant and was she not very pretty, he replied curtly 'that he had no idea'. All he knew was that she was very red.

Following the example of the Cumberlands, the Gloucesters left England with their baby daughter and, as Lady Mary Coke observed in December 1773, 'I wonder after having made such disgraceful marriages that they cannot stay at home, as they certainly do nothing but expose themselves when they come abroad.' Both couples spent their time running from Continental Court to Court to establish whether, if their own King would not receive them, anyone else's would. Meanwhile, the King and Queen and family were isolated not only from the London Society that he shunned, but from the other members of the royal family. As a result, and because the King and Queen did not encourage their daughters to make friends with other children, dreading 'party', the princesses' youth was spent almost exclusively with each other, their younger brothers and their attendants.

The Queen had written to her brother Charles in March 1772, 'We have changed our home this summer. We exchange Richmond for Kew, our chez nous will be better and the solitude greater than ever.' With the Princess Dowager's death, her summer residence at Kew – the White House, or Kew House – became available to the King and Queen. While the building in Kew Gardens could accommodate only the royal parents, their daughters and a skeleton household, the princesses could at least wave to their elder brothers in the Prince of Wales's House opposite, whose northern windows gave on to the Thames. Should they so choose, the princesses could walk from the gardens of Kew House into the back of Prince William's House, which fronted Kew Green. Following Prince Ernest's birth in 1771, Prince Augustus and then Prince Adolphus were born in 1773 and 1774. These 'younger princes', as they were known, acquired in due course their own house – known, imaginatively, as Prince Ernest's House, at the top of the Green, close to Lady Charlotte Finch's house.

In other houses on Kew Green, in Kew Village, by Kew Bridge and by the ferry over to Brentford the rest of the royal household was disposed. They might not be perfectly housed, but the royal family had left Richmond Lodge, which it had long outgrown, for good, and in due course it was demolished. Kew became a full-blown royal campus, which the royal children rarely left during the summer months, where servants intrigued against each other, and where tradesmen in the village that had grown up around the church on the Green vied for preferment.

The two younger princesses – Augusta and Elizabeth – and their brother Ernest enjoyed a rare outing from Kew at the end of June 1773, when they were four, three and two. They were despatched 'in great state' to visit their great-aunt Amelia, daughter of King George II, at her villa at Gunnersbury outside London – one of the few relations whom they were allowed to meet. 'They were all dressed in the clothes they had for the King's birthday and the two princesses had a great many diamonds. They came in a coach of the Queen's,' reported Lady Mary Coke,

> with six long-tailed horses, four footmen, and a great many guards. The Princess had the whole apartment above stairs open for them to play in, and a long table in the great room covered with all sorts of fruit, biscuits, etc of which they ate very heartily. There was also music for Prince Ernest who, though only two years of age, has a fondness for it very extraordinary in one of that age. The moment he heard it he danced about the room so ridiculously as made everybody laugh: then laughed so excessively himself as very much diverted the Princesses! They stayed two hours without tiring HRH or themselves, and said they were sorry to go.

Their days were rarely so exciting.

In the autumn of 1774 a domestic fracas threatened the peaceful campus, and the relationship between the Queen and Lady Charlotte soured. The health of the princesses' sub-governess, Mrs Cotesworth, finally failed, and she left royal employ. While searching for a replacement, Lady Charlotte Finch requested that she should herself devote fewer hours to the royal children. The Queen, believing the trouble with Mrs Cotesworth had been exacerbated by Lady Charlotte's increasingly skimpy attendance on the royal children, wanted her instead to devote more hours to her charges. 'I am fully convinced', wrote the Queen, 'that besides the dependence you can have upon those that are there for a constant confinement' – the sub-governors and sub-governesses 'lived in' – 'your presence as the first not only will encourage them in theirs, but will make them look upon it as a less confinement. This I swear by experience for though with my sons Mr Smelt [the princes' sub-governor] is to be depended upon, yet Lord Holderness's presence in the house [the Prince of Wales's House] for so many hours is the only and essential thing that prevents those under him from repining.'

Lady Charlotte's reply – or at least her draft on 31 October 1774 – was magnificent; not for nothing had she grown up at the Court of King George II. 'The attendance I have hitherto given has been regularly a double daily attendance of two and oftener three hours in the morning and from before seven in the evening till dismissed by your Majesty, besides numberless occasional and additional attendances.' She, besides, ever made her own concerns 'except when of a particular or melancholy nature, in which I shall ever acknowledge the indulgence I have met with from both your Majesties' give way to the duties of her place, 'as everything belonging to me has experienced'.

And now as she advanced more in years and very much declined in spirits, Lady Charlotte wrote:

> How can I without deviating from my own principles undertake an additional duty of a kind for which I am conscious I am growing every day more unfit, as your Majesty must know what an uncommon stock of spirits and cheerfulness is necessary to go through the growing attendance of so many and such very young people in their amusements, as well as behaviour and instruction, besides ordering all the affairs of a nursery.

A letter that Miss Planta wrote in 1774, giving an account of the royal children to her sister in America, describes the 'so many and such very young children' to some purpose. The royal children, she recounted, had 'all fine skins and blue eyes, some of them have brown hair, particularly Princess Augusta' – Prince Edward was also a very dark child – 'and they are all straight and healthy, and from what we can judge at present, are sensible and good tempered ... In short, they would attract attention, though they were clothed in rags. Their dress is as unadorned as their rank will permit ... their diet is extremely plain and light.' Referring to the children's attire on their parents' birthdays and on feast days, she wrote, 'the little sword the boys wear, makes one laugh. Imagine to yourself little Prince Augustus at eighteen months old, in his nurse's arms with a sword by his side, and a "chapeau bras" under his arm; such was his figure.'

Asking the Queen to 'signal' to her the additional attendance required, Lady Charlotte wrote, 'I shall either endeavour faithfully to discharge it, or humbly and fairly own my incapacity for it ...' The old warhorse had one further feint to make. Speaking of her own wish for 'the real good of the children', she was ready, should the Queen wish it, to resign her office 'into the hands of any person younger and more fitted for it'. No further request was made for any 'additional attendance' from Lady Charlotte. Moreover, she had written of having 'really nobody I wish particularly to recommend' as sub-governess, but she had in fact selected a candidate – Miss Martha Gouldsworthy – whose good health and lack of family or friends seeking her company were of prime importance.

Lady Charlotte's daughter Miss Henrietta Finch describes the consternation that their family at St James's was thrown into by a message from the King and Queen after dinner one stormy night in September 1774 to say they would come and drink tea – and the good use the Finch family made of the occasion to promote Lady Charlotte's candidate. 'I was fortunately in a sack and hoop,' Henrietta wrote to her sister Sophia, 'which looked a little dressy, but my hair catted up without any curl, in a new way, and not so well consequently as it might be done.' The royal party was 'so good humoured – particularly the King – who I am more in love with than ever ... He gave me an opportunity ... (by speaking of Miss Gouldsworthy) to make mention of her good temper and cheerful spirits ... things I knew would recommend her to him, more than anything.'

'Gouly', as Miss Martha Gouldsworthy became known, was the successful candidate, and was soon an established fixture in the princesses' lives, chaperoning them from Kew to the Queen's House or St James's, sitting at their lessons with masters, and supervising their preparation for lessons with Miss Planta. She walked with them at Kew between their morning and afternoon lessons, sat with them while they 'worked' – sewed – and generally clucked after them (snatching an hour for dinner) from before breakfast until she escorted them to bed.

The princesses were not only fortunate in their sub-governess Gouly, but, aged eight, nearly six and four, were cheerful students in the schoolroom. For the benign Miss Planta, their 'English teacher', used a variety of educational aids to develop – from an early age – their memories and knowledge. 'I believe they all love me,' she wrote, 'and I have gained their affection by making their learning as much play as possible ... I have put together a set of cards which contains the history of England, or more properly an idea of it, and have reduced the chronology of England to a game, by means of which the Princesses are better chronologists than I was three years ago.'

Miss Planta was nothing if not optimistic. She put Princess Elizabeth, at the age of four, to learning by this method 'the succession of Kings according to their several lines'. But she had help from the princesses themselves. 'One thing more, common to them all,' she noted of the royal children, 'is a very retentive memory.' The Princess Royal, who later advocated teaching her niece from Bible pictures, also recommended – perhaps from personal experience – having the child begin a 'short history of England' once she had learnt to read. 'And have her accustomed,' she wrote, 'as soon as she is finished reading, to give a little account of her lesson and then lead her to make some slight reflections on what she has learnt.'

There was no escaping an element of classroom grind – namely, the need to acquire good handwriting. This affair was taken very seriously, as all the princes, especially when serving abroad, and the princesses, on marrying abroad, would be required in later life to maintain a large correspondence with members of their own and other royal families. The Prince of Wales, whose father the King employed no secretary but undertook all his own official correspondence himself, had begun the process when he was five with Mr Bulley, a writing master.

Now it was the turn of the Princess Royal and her sister Augusta with their writing master Mr Roberts to cover sheets of paper, shakily ruled, with such maxims as might do, faithfully inscribed in copperplate writing. (Perhaps Mrs Hannah More, the Sunday-school pioneer, who was a near relation of Mr Roberts, furnished some of the maxims.) The process took time, and would not be complete until they were well into their teens. It was among the most wearisome elements of their education. However, a geography teacher was also employed for the princesses from when they were young to display to them the extent of their father's dominions, and the lands of others, and it is said that jigsaw maps of Europe were employed in the nursery. There were also in the King's libraries in the Queen's House full-scale models of the forts which guarded English property in America and India and further afield, to excite the children's imaginations.

In many ways, the education which the Queen and Lady Charlotte ordained for the princesses would be as rigorous as that that the King ordained for his sons, for the Queen wrote that she thought women with a good education would be capable of as much as men. Princesses' deportment, proficiency in music and dancing, and skills with needle, paintbrush and pencil were traditionally important, but in Lady Charlotte and Miss Planta the Queen had provided her daughters with accomplished women as teachers who themselves read English, Continental and classical literature for pleasure. And now the princesses began to learn German from the Reverend Heinrich Schrader, of the Savoy Chapel, to add to their French.

The Princess Royal was, in 1774 and at the age of nearly eight, 'a noble girl', in Miss Planta's opinion. 'She looks the daughter of a King,' she wrote:

> She is remarkably sensible, the propriety of her behaviour is very great, and she has shining parts. She speaks French very well, is well versed in ancient history, and to my knowledge, there is not an event of importance in the history of England, she is not pretty well acquainted with. She writes well, makes pertinent observations on what she reads, and has a competent knowledge of geography.

Miss Planta was writing a private letter to her sister Mrs Minicks in America, who had begged a description of her royal charges. Aware that the letter would be shown around her sister's circle, Miss Planta might not have been above exaggerating the princesses' achievements under her tutelage, but there was little need. The Princess Royal was always a quick, calm and competent student, whatever the subject of study. It was outside the schoolroom that this 'noble girl' would experience difficulties, and Miss Planta's reference to her 'shining parts' obscures these.

The Princess Royal savoured her position as eldest daughter of the King – sometimes to the point of arrogance – but she also stammered, especially in the presence of her mother. Furthermore, for all the learning she would acquire and despite the attentions of the royal dancing master, M. Denoyer, she was a clumsy dancer, possibly because she had no ear – and certainly no liking – for music. So although she looked every inch the daughter of a king, she was a self-conscious and awkward one, who was aware of her failings. And the Queen, a naturally elegant woman with a fine appreciation of music, could not understand it.

A painting two years later by Benjamin West, an American artist the King favoured, shows the Queen and Princess Royal at congenial 'women's work'. They are embroidering a length of silk. But the Princess looks strained and uncomfortable, and appears to be seeking her mother's approval for her work. The Queen seems distant and oblivious of her daughter. It is a far cry from Cotes's intimate rendition of their relationship at the Princess Royal's birth.

Miss Planta's report card for the Princess Royal, though full of admiration, betrays little affection. Her portrait of five-year-old Princess Augusta, on the other hand, is full of love. 'Princess Augusta is the handsomest of all the Princesses,' she announced. 'She is five years old, of a small make and very lively, and when compared to Princess Royal, very childish. She wants, however, neither feelings nor parts and will, I dare say, unfold to advantage.' She went on, 'It is amazing how much the little creature knows of the history of England, down as far as James I,' and she revealed her method of imparting it. 'I chose some striking facts in every chapter and dressed them in words adapted to her capacity and then told them as diverting stories. This method has taken, and she tells them again in words of her own, with as much pleasure as she would a fairy tale.'

The Princess had also learnt to repeat such maxims as 'To be good is to be happy, angels are happier than men, because they are better.' 'Any things of this kind she often repeats to herself, and is generally extremely influenced by them,' wrote Miss Planta. But when not influenced by them Princess Augusta threw quite violent tantrums. Miss Planta had her revenge: 'I displeased her today, by saying, I would go to Otaheite' – or Tahiti – 'to be English teacher to the Otaheite children.' This remarkable declaration needed, at the time of writing, no explanation. That summer, following Captain Cook's voyages to the South Pacific, an Otaheitan 'prince' called Omai had appeared in London, and made his bow – as Sir Joseph Banks's guest – at Kew in July. Miss Planta's remark, or rebuke, to Princess Augusta reflected the boundless curiosity about the natives of Tahiti that resulted from this exotic visitor's appearance. But Princess Augusta would not succumb to it. 'She says, indeed she cannot part with me,' Miss Planta reported to her sister.

And what of Princess Elizabeth? From the attentions of her wet-nurse Mrs Spinluffe, she had passed into the care of her sisters' dresser Miss Mary Dacres, and from there into Miss Planta's hands. As a third princess, she had not rated the attention that the Princess Royal had commanded as firstborn of the species. No artist detailed her infant wardrobe or depicted her doll as had Humphry and Cotes and Zoffany for the Princess Royal.

Nor was Princess Elizabeth the subject, as Princess Augusta had been from birth, of anxious and minute comparisons with an elder sister, where she was judged prettier or less pretty, more 'sensible' or less 'sensible' than the other. As foil to her elder sister, Princess Augusta features in a celebrated Zoffany group portrait of the royal family in Van Dyck dress when it numbered two parents, four sons and two daughters. Princess Elizabeth – seventh child – appears once in a Zoffany conversation piece as a baby, then not again till depicted by Benjamin West.

Her primary distinction, and an unfortunate one for a princess, had been that she was a fat baby. At the age of three she was still fat, but Miss Planta discovered great potential in her. She traces a determined personality that was to be key for this artistic Princess's survival in a world where her sisters' looks and figures would be widely admired. 'Princess Elizabeth is a lovely little fat sensible thing and so tidy', she exclaimed, 'that she never leaves her needles, or scrap of work without putting them all in a tiny bag, for the purpose.'

As we have already heard, Miss Planta dwelt on Princess Elizabeth's achievements in learning the lines of succession, and then revealed that the three-year-old was not always a paragon. 'Her reward to being good, is giving me a flower or some such trifle, and I make it a point not to accept anything from a naughty child.' Elizabeth and her sister Princess Augusta later separately recalled that Lady Charlotte Finch had taught them – as soon as they could speak, Elizabeth said – to memorize for recital the maxim, 'Content is wealth, the riches of the mind, / And happy he who can that treasure find.' Unfortunately, frustration rather than contentment was long to be the tenor of this gifted girl's life.

Even that harsh critic Lady Mary Coke thought when she saw the three girls on 25 October 1774, with two of the young princes in 'what is called the queen's apartment', that 'the Princesses are much improved'. She wrote, 'The two youngest are really pretty, especially the Princess Augusta.' But Lady Mary had private information to impart about Augusta: 'I'm told she is not so agreeable as the Princess Royal. She tells long stories which is not a good habit.' However, she recorded with more pleasure that on the child's sixth birthday, 8 November 1774, an entertainment and supper were projected, which the Duchess of Argyll and Lady Betty Stanley were to attend. But in this sort of situation Princess Augusta was not at her best. Her elder sister may have stammered, but Augusta was painfully shy, and in this sense was much more 'childish' than her sister.

Princess Augusta's comfort and enjoyment lay within the family circle, and in this setting she showed early on the large-minded and rational character that was always to distinguish her, as her brother the Prince of Wales reported to his governor Lord Holderness, who had gone abroad to recover his health in the autumn of 1774. The Prince wrote, 'Last Sunday, William, Edward and Augusta were talking together about pistols, and Edward complained that his brothers had pistols but he had none. Upon which Augusta turned to William and said, "Give one pistol to Edward and then you will be equal". "O Madame", said William, "if I have not a pair of pistols I am worth nothing".' Seven-year-old Prince Edward's response is not recorded, but, just as the elder brother guarded his privileges, so did the younger one resent them. On one occasion, Prince Edward was told that Prince William was going to Court. 'Then,' said the younger brother, 'I shall button myself up and go to bed.' Upon being asked why, he replied that, if he were not accompanying his elder brother to Court, it must surely be because he was ill and needed his bed.

The princesses' youngest brother, Prince Adolphus, born on 24 February 1774, was weaned the following spring, and the Queen wrote with relief on that occasion, 'Adolphus seems to relish the taste of potatoes and apple pudding extremely well, nor did it disagree with him, of which I was very fearful.'

And there were other things to be fearful of. In America, the colonies were in ferment. Despite conciliatory proposals from the House of Commons, as Prince Adolphus supped his apple purée at Kew in April 1775, the first shots had rung out in a skirmish between British troops and American patriots in Lexington, near Boston. As the situation darkened, the English government was forced to despatch more troops to General Howe, commander-in-chief across the Atlantic – and hire still more from German warlords as General Washington proved Howe's superior.

In the meantime, what with America and the princes in need of subjection, exhortations for the daughters of King George III to 'be good' came more than ever thick and fast. Their mother's love had always been conditional. In the spring of 1775 she had written from Kew to Lady Charlotte Finch: 'If everybody is well behaved at the Queen's House of the female party I should be glad to see my daughters on Wednesday morning between 10 and 11 o clock.'

The princesses learnt that, as the King's rule was benevolent, so any infringement of it – their uncle Gloucester's defiance, the American colonies' violent assertion of independence, let alone their own brothers' dissidence – was to be abhorred and punished. Thus the royal children grew up to detest alike highwaymen, Opposition politicians and General Washington. And in later – if not more mature – years, they were to deplore the measures of Catholic emancipation and Parliamentary reform, which ran contrary to their deceased father's will. Nourished on the legend of the blood of Englishmen shed on American battlefields and on the sin of lèse-majesté, few of the princesses would venture to stray over the lip of conservatism – except those who determined to launch their own rebellion against their father. For the others, and most of all for Princess Augusta, whose brothers and sisters teased her when they were older about her 'rage militaire', their politics were to be an expression of loyalty to their father.

Just before their mother was due to give birth to her eleventh child in late April 1776, the elder princesses went with her to observe a thousand guardsmen march off to take ship for America. Queen Charlotte wrote to her brother in Hanover, 'the affair is so interesting that it possesses me entirely'. In particular, the reluctance of the Quakers of Pennsylvania to take up arms appealed to her. Her husband's reaction was more violent, for he could never understand why the colonies should wish to revolt against a benevolent Crown. But the Queen did not voice her sentiments openly, and the princesses at Kew learnt a specific form of patriotism during a childhood in which remote conflict in America anguished their father and returning generals brought not eagles to lay before him, but increasingly sombre budgets.

The Declaration of Independence which Washington and other principals signed on 4 July 1776 was to enlarge the American patriots' ambitions and further to incense the King. The conflict was not to end until 1783, after France, Spain and Holland had joined arms and nearly all Europe had formed an armed neutrality in 1780 to resist the British seizing American goods from their ships. These seven fruitless years of war were to change the reputation and character of England as firmly as the end of the Seven Years War had assured her a new prestige and power. The eventual loss of the colonies was – unlike the outcome of the royal Dukes' rebellions and that of their nephew the Prince of Wales – not to be punishment and removal of privileges but liberation and a scot-free, not to say tax-free, existence.

Princess Augusta, however, when recalling her childhood, spoke not of the generals who came to report on the progress of the war, but of games of cricket and football and hockey: 'When she was a little girl, she played at all these games with her brothers, and played cricket particularly well.' Her elder sister Royal, by contrast, advocated learning through play with dolls. The play at Kew could certainly get quite rough. On one occasion, Princess Augusta recalled, the Queen's brother Prince Ernest of Mecklenburg-Strelitz was visiting and nearly had his eye knocked out when his nephews swarmed all about him and one got on his back and clawed at his face. For all the segregation of princes and princesses, in Princess Augusta's memory, at least, they were much together. And her younger brother Ernest later fondly remembered days at Kew: 'How gay did the Green appear ... from the middle of May till the beginning of November, and how cheerful did the Green look on a fine Sunday evening when all the servants in their red liveries were strolling about and sitting under the old trees by the church, and every house was inhabited.'

3

The Younger Ones

~

A NEW CHARACTER WAS now added to the group of princesses, a sister
born nearly ten full years after Princess Royal, a child born in war-
time as her elder sisters had not been, a child with three elder sisters and
seven elder brothers whose needs would come before hers, and a child who
would have, of all the royal siblings, by far the most commonplace mind.
Nevertheless of all the princesses, Princess Mary – as the girl born on 25
April 1776 was to be christened – would have the most self-confidence and
exhibit the most tenacity in achieving her desires, for she was to be the
beauty of the family. Princess Mary reigned serene, and for eighteen
months enjoyed the attentions – at £200 a year, with a pension of a hundred for life to follow – of wet-nurse Mrs Anna Maria Adams, sister to the
elder princesses' beloved dresser or nurse, Miss Mary Dacres.

The even keel of the royal children's life at Kew over which Lady
Charlotte Finch and the princes' governors presided was rocked violently
in the spring of 1776. But Princess Mary's birth was not responsible, nor
was that of her cousin Prince William of Gloucester on 15 January 1776,
at the Palazzo Teodoli in Rome, although his mother, the Duchess of
Gloucester, exclaimed on 5 October of that year in a letter to her friend
Elizabeth, Lady Nuneham that her son was 'the surprise of all Rome'.
Although only nine months old, his prodigious intelligence, she wrote
fondly, caused a furore among her friends, as did his unswaddled limbs.
'Several ladies have followed his fashion in dress,' the Duchess informed her
friend, 'and some new born babies are now stretching and enjoying their
limbs at liberty, who but for him would be bound up like mummies.'
Unfortunately, evidencing their royal uncle's disapproval of their existence,
this Italianate prodigy and his elder sister, Princess Sophia Matilda of
Gloucester, were undignified by the title of royal highness and were unpro-
vided for by Parliament.

The convulsion occurred at Kew in April 1776 and took the form of a
'junior rebellion' when Princess Mary was a few days old and the
Declaration of Independence in America two months off. Lord Holderness,

the Prince of Wales's and Prince Frederick's absentee governor, returned from the Continent to find the boys laughing in his face, and the Dutch House, or Prince of Wales's House, at Kew alive with disobedience. With many apologies for the need to distract the King even for a moment from affairs of importance across the Atlantic, Lord Holderness and the sub-governor, Mr Leonard Smelt, resigned. The whole household was swept away, and new and grimmer preceptors installed. But the shockwaves that the princes' rebellion had caused in the community of Kew were not to be so easily brushed aside.

The Prince of Wales might still learn to box and fence and construe in Greek, and the new governor, the Duke of Montagu, might put on paper details of a Spartan regime, but the Prince had felt his power, and the struggle between royal father and son, which was to strain the princesses' loyalty to both, had begun. 'He is rather too fond of wine and women,' the seventeen-year-old Prince was to write of himself in the autumn of 1779. If this was fantasy – he was still in the hands of governors, to whom his father had earlier deplored the Prince's 'bad habit … of not telling the truth', as well as now his poor German – the wish would soon be father to the act. Suddenly with war in America, and the princes out of control, life at Kew was not so safe. 'You shall always hear that I have been good,' Princess Augusta wrote to her dresser. The princesses must be good for everyone.

'Unhappily for me we have begun to hunt deer at Windsor,' the Queen wrote to her brother Charles, 'and since that moment all rational occupation cannot take place.' A few months after the junior rebellion at Kew, as the rebel American colonists congregated in Philadelphia, fancy led the King of England to take up the sport of hunting at the ancient seat of Windsor, following the example of numerous monarchs from William the Conqueror, who built the castle, to the last of the Stuarts, dropsical Queen Anne, who pursued her quarry in a curricle. For a lodging King George III chose a house facing the south terrace of Windsor Castle that he had until recently rented out to Lord Talbot, and here he and the Queen stayed for the first time in early July 1776. It would be charming once the brown woodwork had taken on 'une autre face', the loyal wife told Charles.

But the Queen's decorative schemes had to be put on hold, and her enthusiasm for Windsor flagged, after the King, with his architect Sir William Chambers, decreed that the house as it stood was far too small and that a new one, the Queen's Lodge – a veritable barracks, with seventy rooms – should rise in its place. 'The King is building it,' the Queen wrote, informing Charles that the house was to be a gift to her, 'but

I am buying the furniture and I settle my accounts the moment they are delivered. Besides, I am in treaty for a garden and house next door to it, for which I am paying £4000.' In the meantime, the King and Queen occupied apartments in Windsor Castle itself. As they had found six years earlier when they stayed there for the installation of their eldest sons as Knights of the Garter, it was cold, uncomfortable and inconvenient.

From this point on, when not occupied with public business, the King indulged himself to an unusual degree, in hunting and supervising the building of the Queen's Lodge – with battlements on top to match those of King William the Conqueror on the Norman castle opposite. The royal couple spent a commensurate period of time, sometimes two days a week, at Windsor. 'Ma vie sera tout à fait campagnarde,' the Queen prophesied on 18 June 1776. With the demands of Court levées and drawing rooms occupying another three days, she increasingly fretted that she was with her children only on Fridays and Saturdays. After a few years she wrote to her brother with exasperated good humour, 'It is true we are pilgrims on earth, for we are very often at three different places in a week.'

The Queen valued the months at Kew from May to October as prime time for inculcating in her daughters the principles of orthography, religion, royal genealogy (Hanoverian and other), history ancient and modern, geography and languages. At Kew neither she nor her daughters nor any of the ladies who supervised or taught her daughters 'dressed' until shortly before dinner – and when they did, they employed their wardrobe women rather than hairdressers to attend to their coiffure. In 1777 the royal mother could not necessarily count on more than five years in which to conclude her plan of education for her eldest daughters at Kew and elsewhere before they took up the burdens associated with marriage which had deflected her from her own studies. Even now, when in London the two eldest princesses began to attend their parents in public – to breakfasts, to the play, to the opera. Their curled and powdered heads, their polonaises and 'gew-gawed' or bejewelled necks and arms entranced the public when they issued forth, and were described in flattering detail in the newspapers. But their mother, equally bedecked and bedizened, regretted the hours lost to what she called 'rational occupation', while accepting the need to encounter Society.

The princesses had a first exposure to Windsor – a place that would be as much a part of their lives as Kew – in the summer of 1777, when they were of an age to appreciate the grandeur and history of the place, as well as the hugeness of both Castle and park. A new attendant, Miss Mary Hamilton, formed, with the princesses, part of an enormous royal caravan that travelled to Windsor in the earlier part of August, and stayed in apartments in the Castle. They were there to inspect the rising Queen's Lodge, and to celebrate the beginnings of a late-come but earnest Hanoverian royal residence at William the Conqueror's stronghold. The principal celebrations were fixed not for 1 August, the sixty-third anniversary of the accession in 1714 of the first Hanoverian King of England, George I – but for 12 August, his great-great-grandson George, Prince of Wales's fifteenth birthday.

The princesses and their brothers and immediate 'family' were housed temporarily in towers and eyrie apartments on the east and south fronts of the Upper Ward, or in the state apartments occupying the entire north front with a view of Eton College chapel across the Thames. As for other members of the household, some had to climb the many steps to apartments at the top of the historic and moated Round Tower in Middle Ward which divided Upper Ward from Lower Ward. Others needed to be of a religious or humble cast of mind, as they were appointed apartments in the Deanery adjoining St George's Chapel that Edward IV had built long before in the centre of the Castle buildings, or were lodged in the almshouses reserved generally for the quaintly named Poor Knights of Windsor. To make way for this royal assault, indignant tenants had been ejected from grace-and-favour lodgings everywhere within the Castle which time and monarchs had so long forgotten.

Some of the alterations to the Lodge that the Queen had made were finished, seven or eight rooms or so, and on the eve of the Prince of Wales's birthday she and the King took the princesses over to view them. A day or so earlier, Miss Hamilton had seen them and wrote that the rooms were 'furnished in a style of elegant simplicity ... beautiful paper hangings, light carved gilt frames for looking glasses, worked chairs and painted frames, every room different. Curtains of fine white dimity with white cotton fringe – one set of chairs are knotted floss silk of different shades, sewn on to imitate natural flowers ...'

What made more of an impression on eleven-year-old Princess Royal and her sisters than some rooms furnished with the Queen's familiar elegance, or even the state rooms inside the castle – which had a tendency to admit rain – furnished by their Stuart kinsman King Charles II, were the festivities arranged for their brother's birthday. And what no doubt made most impression of all was that their lessons on that day were deferred in honour of the event.

Cannons fired and bells rang to mark the day, and the royal family activities included a carriage procession through the Home Park and a tour of a newly built country house in the locality, before they dressed in their best in the evening to walk on the terrace beneath the south wall of the Castle that was the place of popular promenade. Even sixteen-month-old Princess Mary, who Miss Hamilton described as 'a lovely elegant made child', wore a lace frock over a blue silk coat, and was carried out of the Castle gate to take part in the procession. Both she and her elder sisters – 'with their hair dressed upon high cushions, with stiff large curls powdered and pomatumed, small dress cap and diamond ornaments set in a formal manner such as stars etc.' – were admired greatly. Their satisfied attendant, Miss Hamilton, thought that they looked uncommonly well and that the sophisticated costumes 'suited them despite their tender years'.

The King was delighted by the enthusiasm and respect the townspeople of Windsor showed for the royal crocodile on the terrace, flattening themselves against the curtain wall of the Castle so as not to touch their exalted visitors and periodically shouting their regard. Miss Hamilton, who was shepherding the princesses' younger brothers behind them, recorded the scene: 'There was a great crowd, each saying aloud what they thought, without restraint ... a host of nobility, fashionable persons, pretty women, smart girls, coxcombs, and abundance of clergy'.

Slowly the royal family processed to the end of the terrace, the King constantly halting to accost someone in the crowd, and bringing the rest of the family behind him up sharp in a flurry of silks and polonaises, powdered curls, dress-swords and governesses. At last he decreed the 'terracing' at an end, and the royal family finished the evening, listening from their apartments within the Castle to Sir George Lennox's regimental band play in the quadrangle before their windows.

The princesses returned to Kew and to their studies the following day, but their brother's birthday celebrations were the beginning for them of a long and not always happy association with Windsor, bringing with it dissipation of the children's paradise that was Kew. The King their father would fire several of his daughters with the new enthusiasm he felt for all things rural, equestrian and agricultural. Long walks in the mud and riding and hunting in the rain would make of them true English countrywomen, as their Hanoverian aunts and great-aunts had not been. But the softer and more civilizing influence of their mother, who regarded long walks as barbaric and pined and suffered from crippling headaches within the thick walls of the Castle while the rest of the family braved the elements, would diminish – and her temper would fray.

There was dissipation of a happier kind, however, at Kew this summer when pretty young Miss Hamilton, who enjoyed giving the children treats, provided for the elder princesses and for Lady Charlotte's granddaughter, Miss Augusta Feilding, in her apartment there a 'little entertainment of fruit, flowers, cakes, tea etc.'. First the children played in the garden. Then Lady Charlotte, Gouly and Mrs Feilding joined them, and they played at Dumb Crambo, with forfeits 'which gave rise to much amusement in framing punishments'. The princesses were 'quite rakes', recorded the successful hostess, 'as Lady Charlotte allowed them to stay up till 10 o'clock'. When the party was at last at an end, wrote Miss Hamilton, 'the flowers were tied up in nosegays and Princess Royal had the distribution of them, the cakes, etc.'.

The younger princes, Ernest, Augustus and Adolphus, also enjoyed Miss Hamilton's ministrations. She lodged – and held her party – in the house that had recently been appropriated to their use on Kew Green, and that was now known as Prince Ernest's House. On one occasion, when she formed part of the princes' escort back to Kew from Windsor, they would not leave her, although they now had, with their new establishment, their own attendants. They even came into her room at Prince Ernest's, she wrote: 'the dear children had so completely found out my weak side'.

For the Queen, the King's enthusiasm for Windsor engendered many logistical problems. Four days after the excitement of the Prince's birthday at Windsor, Prince Frederick's fourteenth birthday was spent in the comparative calm of Kew, but later that month of August 1777 it was decided that all his brothers and sisters should be present to celebrate Prince William's twelfth birthday at Windsor. Under Miss Gouldsworthy's and Miss Hamilton's supervision, coaches shipped the three elder princesses, their three younger brothers and Princess Mary, in her wet-nurse Mrs Adams's care, from Kew to Windsor and back again, with an escort of Light Horse to protect them en route. Mrs Adams was a useful member of the nursery for such expeditions, but when her charge was eighteen months old in October 1777 an event that was not unfamiliar in this royal family occurred. The approaching birth of a new baby dislodged the old wetnurse from rooms that would be needed for the new one.

From the Queen's House, Princess Augusta wrote to Miss Hamilton's mother, shortly before the new baby was due, introducing herself and saying she hoped to encounter Miss Hamilton, who was at Kew, 'when she comes to see the cradle of the new child Mama is to have ...' And she wrote again to her new correspondent, saying, 'I hope you are as well as I expect. My dear friend your daughter, tell her when you see her that she is very good to me.' Princess Augusta, aged just nine in the winter of 1777, was from an early age consumed with the problem of 'being good' and troubled by her lapses from that holy state.

Princess Sophia was born at the Queen's House on 3 November 1777. 'I was taken ill and delivered in the space of fifteen minutes,' the Queen informed her brother Charles the following month. On this occasion, the King was very likely not hovering, as he had done so anxiously for the births of his elder daughters. While Queen Charlotte and the midwife, Mrs Johnson, were taken unawares by the speed at which the child shot into the world, the King was working against the clock, as the French moved closer to declaring war on Britain in sympathy with the Americans and in indignation against the English embargo of French ports.

Princess Sophia's sisters, too, were preoccupied, as their beloved dresser Miss Dacres had suddenly abandoned her employment to become wife to their brothers' page, Mr Henry Compton. Their letters to Miss Dacres on her departure and on her October marriage show how dependent they had been on this companion of their early childhood.

Princess Augusta's response to the terrible loss of Miss Dacres was markedly mature, although her handwriting was huge and unformed. 'I am very sorry that you do go away from me,' she wrote on 20 October, 'though at the same time I am glad that you will be happy. I hope sometimes you will come and see me and I hope that you will lead a happy life. I hope your sister [Mrs Adams, who had just quitted her post as wet-nurse to Princess Mary] is well. Dear heart, you can't conceive what I felt when Mama told me you was to be married to Mr Compton. It caused me many tears when I heard it.' The Princess rationalized her feelings in a letter to Gouly the same day: 'Dear Miss Dacres is a great loss to me, for I love her with all my heart. I would [not] have lost her for all the world, but you know one can't have always what one wants. She is the first loss I have had, for Mlle Krohme was a loss to me but not such a great one as Miss Dacres.' When Mlle Krohme had died in April 1777, it was the Princess Royal who had been greatly affected.

The birth of Princess Sophia did not long distract Princess Augusta from writing affectionate letters. 'My sisters and me have got in the lottery [a prize of] twenty pounds and what I have got is for you,' she told 'Cuppy' – this was the name Prince Adolphus had manufactured for Mr Compton's new bride – on 4 November. 'I desire that you will always remember your poor child,' she entreated her former dresser in another – undated – letter. 'I assure you that she was very sorry when the Queen told her that you was to go away from her.'

'I shall always remember how my dear Mrs Compton loved me,' wrote Princess Augusta again, manfully to the new Mrs Compton. 'And now I begin to repent that I did not behave well to you ... I promise you that you shall always hear that I have been good.' Pursuing this theme, she was to write to her mother from the Queen's House on Boxing Day 1777,

> Dear Mama, I am very glad to tell you that I am very good; this morning I behaved pretty well and this afternoon quite well. All my brothers and sisters send their duty to you and Augustus in particular for he told it to me about six times, give my love and duty to Mama, little dear Sophia is quite well and little Mary is pretty good. Dear Mama I am your most affectionate dauter December 26 1777 Augusta Sophia Queens House London.

The Princess Royal's response to Miss Dacres's happy change of circumstances was distinctly less affectionate than that of her younger sister. 'How could you be so sly as not let anybody know of when you was to be married?' the Princess Royal upbraided her former attendant the day after Princess Sophia's birth, and wished her joy of a marriage 'done, done, never to be undone'. She tried blackmail: 'I beg you will not go till after the christening.' She was only sorry it was so soon. 'I do not think you love me though I do you ...' wrote the unhappy Princess. Her angry refrain did not quickly diminish. 'I am very much hurt at your loss,' she wrote three days later, '... too soon of a week, of a year, at least I think so.' For a month or more the Princess Royal bombarded her with requests and directions. 'Princess Royal presents her compliments to Mrs Compton and begs she will do her the favour to come to breakfast next Sunday at nine o clock,' ran one note. 'Pray do tell me where your house is that I may kiss my hand to you every day, when I walk by your window,' ran another. But it was swiftly followed by a rebuke. 'Mr Compton told me it was his fault that I did not see you at the window ... It was a baulk ... I hope to see you there tomorrow.'

The Princess Royal's amour-propre and sense of grievance were assuaged when Mrs Compton visited and showed contrition. And in addition the Queen and Lady Charlotte were taking steps to introduce the Princess Royal to an adult world. Earlier in the year she had been present at a private performance at the Queen's House when the actor David Garrick had read from his tragedy Lethe. 'Today,' Royal wrote grandly to Mrs Compton on 5 December 1777, 'I went on an airing with mama.' But the Princess Royal was not out of the nursery yet. Thanking Mrs Compton two days later for another visit, she announced, 'I now write by the light of the fire; laying on the ground.' And on the day after Boxing Day she wrote to her mother, 'Tomorrow I give a breakfast to my brothers and sisters and some other people. Last night we saw a magic lantern of Mrs Cheveley's which made me laugh very much.' She ended politely that she hoped the Queen had been able to go to Windsor.

Seven-year-old Princess Elizabeth was direct in her affection to her former dresser. She drew an accomplished picture of Cuppy's new home on Kew Green and sent it, inscribed 'this is your house', to her with the message, 'My dear Mrs Mary I love you with all my heart ... I and my sisters wish that you will come to see us ... Mary says your name very often.'

Mrs Henry Compton was not to enjoy the princesses' regard long, for she died the following autumn at Kew, after giving birth in September 1778 to a daughter named Augusta. The princesses, however, had already transferred their affection to Mary Hamilton, the well-born young woman whom the Queen had appointed in April 1777 to join Lady Charlotte and Miss Gouldsworthy as 'a third lady to be at the head of the establishment'. Although Miss Hamilton later wrote that she 'never in [her] life had the least desire to belong to a Court', this clever, lively – and young – companion was to play a major part in the princesses' lives for five and a half years. The papers Miss Hamilton preserved after she had left royal employ include such examples of indentured schoolroom labour as the following improving text, copied out by Princess Augusta, aged nine, in her best – but not very good – handwriting on 17 July 1778: 'Recreation, moderately used, is profitable to the body for health, and to the mind for refreshment: but it is a note of a vain mind, to be running after every garish pomp or show.'

Rather more revealing is the following scrawl by the same author written from Kew House:

> My dear Miss Hamilton, I am very sorry for the blow I gave to you the night before last. I am very sorry indeed, and promise you I won't do so any more. I have written to Gouly and she has forgiven me, because I have been very good with every body and her too, and I learnt very well with Monsieur Guiffardière. I read very well, and I said my verses well also. I beg you will forgive me, for indeed I will be very good to you, and I will mind every thing you bid me. I am very sorry that I hurt Miss Gouldsworthy. I promise you I won't do so any more. But I hope I have not hurt you, and I was very sorry to find you put brown paper and arquebade upon your breast. I hope it will be of no consequence to you for I assure you that if it is, it will make me very unhappy. I am your ever affectionate Augusta Sophia.

And early in their acquaintance, discovering a taste for writing and for finding new correspondents, Princess Augusta wrote, while sitting with Miss Hamilton, a letter to her companion's mother in Derbyshire: 'My dear Madam, I hope that you are well Miss Ham sends her love to you but pray don't forget to write to Miss Ham. Madam I am your most obedient servant AS.' But then, apparently dissatisfied with these formal pleasantries, she added on the front: '28 November 1777, London, at night. Madam, Miss Ham. has a very bad headache, but for all that, she sat down and has writ you a very long letter and I shall be very angry with you if you don't thank her.' And finally, on the back fold, she added:

> Dialogue between Clare and Eloise at Lambeth in Cornwall.
> E: My dear friend, I had the pleasure to see your little brother last night. Pray, has not he got a wig, for he had something like one?
> C: He had, my dear, for he did tear his hair off his head. He is very sorry now that he has tore his hair off his head.
> E: He was very handsome before he had that trick.
> C: So he was.

And there the dialogue ends, with a note from the dramatist, 'And good night, I am very sleepy.'

The Princess Royal's letters to Miss Hamilton, on the other hand, like those she wrote to Mrs Compton, are full of threats and scolds and teases. 'Princess Royal presents her compliments to Miss Hamilton,' she wrote shortly before Christmas 1777, 'and begs to know why she would not kiss her last night.' And in the early part of the next year the Princess Royal, aged eleven, was in commanding form:

> Madam, I am very sorry that you did not sleep well last night. I beg you will lay down and then not think of any thing but of a flock of sheep, and if you do not do that I shall not love you in the least, and I know that you will be very sorry for that, and if you do what I desire I will love you very much. Madam, your friend, Charlotte Augusta Matilda.

Miss Hamilton was quite up to such tricks, and called the eleven-year-old autocrat's bluff next morning. The Princess Royal had to concede: 'Madam, Though you did not think last night of a flock of sheep, yet as you did sleep more than the night before, I will love you a little bit. Pray give my love to your mama.'

Brought to heel, the Princess Royal wrote three days later on 17 January, 'My dear, I thank you for your note, and I hope you think I minded what you told me, and that it will encourage you to continue your correspondence with me.' And then she put a note in Miss Hamilton's workbag: 'Day and night I always think of you, for I love and esteem you.' And she wrote again: 'My dearest Hammy, I that love and adore you, think it very hard, that you will not kiss me today. I will tell you why I love you,' she added, attempting to subdue her feelings. 'This is the reason, for it is that I think you have a good character.'

The awkward, hungry notes continued, sometimes twice a day. The Princess wrote late in January: 'Ma chère, Je vous assure que je vous aime de tout mon Coeur et je vous prie d'avoir la bonté de m'accorder votre amitié et si vous avez cette bonté vous me rendrez fort heureuse.' But she had not finished there. On returning to the Queen's House that night from drinking tea at Gouly's apartment in St James's, the Princess Royal's first thought was of Miss Hamilton, who had had the evening off. And she sat down to write: 'When we came home, only think, we went all three in Lady Charlotte's [sedan] chair, and she walked on the side. I hope you was much pleased with the play and the farce. I assure you of my love and promise you always to continue it.'

Romantically, the lovesick Princess signed another note a couple of days later, 'your most affectionate unknown friend'. She sent her love to Miss Hamilton's mother in Derbyshire: 'tell her that though I have not the happiness of knowing her, yet I love her because she belongs to you'. And she added, 'Pray give me your love, for I wish for your love so much that I think you must give it to me, My dearest love, your little affectionate friend, Charlotte Augusta Matilda'. She returned to the theme two days later, afraid that she had made Miss Hamilton ill on some account. 'Pray love me for I love you so much, and so it is fair. The publicans and sinners even loved those that loved them,' she wrote with muddled logic but clear-eyed determination.

Despite the Princess's declarations of affection, she made her attendant's life difficult in time-honoured fashion, as the following letter of 6 February shows: 'My dearest Hammy, I am very sorry to have tormented and hurt you, in not learning my lesson for Monsieur de Guiffardière, but I promise you to do my utmost for to know it perfectly tomorrow.' M. de Guiffardière, a French émigré doctor of letters, had been chosen as the princesses' principal master this year, and he was to suffer much at their inky hands. Later this year Princess Augusta begged Miss Hamilton to ask M. de Guiffardière 'to not tell that foolish thing I did this morning, for I promise that I won't do so any more'. (It had been a bad morning. Augusta was also seeking forgiveness from Gouly for 'being so foolish this morning about my rhubarb'.) There would be more good intentions and inattention to follow from the princesses' younger sisters over the next decade. Inclined to lose his temper with poorly prepared pupils, in this opening year M. de Guiffardière was full of hope. Eventually beloved, he was to dedicate to his royal pupils his *Cours élémentaire d'histoire ancienne, à l'usage des LL. AA. Royales, Mesdames les Princesses de l'Angleterre*, published at Windsor in 1798.

The princesses had lost another long-standing teacher this year. Although a Miss Planta continued to be the elder princesses' English teacher, and to teach them other subjects including their own royal history, this was not Frederica Planta but her sister Margaret or Peggy. So discreet, so efficient and so self-effacing was the Planta family that when on 2 February 1778 Miss Frederica Planta died suddenly, she was immediately replaced by her younger sister. And her brother Joseph was only sorry to disturb the royal household with arrangements for removing his sister Frederica's body from the room it occupied at St James's Palace. As a Miss Planta continued to be the princesses' companion, sit, walk and sup with them, and draw the same salary, many people never noticed the substitution. Besides, there were so many attendants now for the royal children that it was difficult for anyone to keep up with them – except for the children themselves.

Miss Hamilton appears to have directed the energies of her emotional pupil the Princess Royal effectively back into her studies. Besides M. de Guiffardière and the new Miss Planta and Mlle Suzanne Moula, the French teacher who replaced Miss Krohme, the princesses had other tutors for specific subjects ranging from their writing master Mr Peter Roberts to their geography master Mr George Bolton, and to dancing and music masters. In addition, the Princess Royal and Princess Augusta continued to learn German with Mr Schrader. By the time the royal family took up residence at Kew for the summer months, the Princess Royal was writing on a more respectful note: 'My dearest, I beg you will forgive me intruding upon your morning leisure, but must beg that tomorrow you will breakfast with me. I am very sorry to find that you have so bad a headache, and beg that if tomorrow you have such another you will not think of coming to my breakfast.'

Her mother the Queen believed the Princess Royal to be a steady, conscientious pupil, and indeed she was when interested. When she was twelve, in 1778, for the first time an artist, John Alexander Gresse – known in London as Jack Grease – was employed as drawing master to the princesses, and the Princess Royal found something of a métier. With Gresse and other art masters Royal began 'drawing heads' every week, or copying Old Master profile drawings by Leonardo da Vinci and other heads by Italian and English eighteenth-century artists in her father's library. The results were creditable, and marked the beginning of a passion for drawing and painting copies of superior originals in the pursuit of artistic excellence – as Sir Joshua Reynolds in his fashionable *Discourses on Art* advised.

In March 1778, the French broke off diplomatic relations with England and the King was at work from six in the morning until midnight without respite. 'I speak, read and think of nothing but the war,' wrote Queen Charlotte with energy, having recovered quickly from the birth of Princess Sophia. 'Je deviendrai politique malgré moi.' But busy King George III marked the birth of his fifth daughter – a round-headed, fair-haired baby with blue eyes – and sought Parliamentary provision in the spring of 1778 for the princesses and for his younger sons, which he had neglected to do until this point, and even for those of his brother Gloucester as princes and princesses of the blood. Although other woes would accrue to her lot, as she lay in her cradle round-faced Princess Sophia was assured of £6,000 a year for life, to be paid to her on marriage or on her father's death. Her brothers were to receive £8,000 on the same terms, and her cousins Prince William of Gloucester and Princess Sophia Matilda of Gloucester won respectively £6,000 and £4,000 on their own father's death.

The Queen wrote to the King in April 1778, 'Dear little Minny [Mary] remains quite uneasy about not finding you anywhere in the house, every coach she sees is Papa coming and nothing satisfies her hardly but sitting at the window to look for you.' For the King spent much of the summer months of that year reviewing troops at camps in locations varying from the West Country to Warley Common in Essex and Cox Heath in Kent, visiting the fleet at Portsmouth and elsewhere, and making preparations. These covered the vexed subject of arrangements for the care of the royal family against a French invasion that became a real threat the following year.

But the family still found time for a fleeting visit to Windsor to inspect the Queen's Lodge. 'It is astonishing to see the progress ... since last year,' Miss Hamilton wrote; 'it is a spacious elegant structure, though standing on a confined space of ground.' And the celebrated botanist Mrs Delany was lost in admiration at the effect of the Queen's interior decor: 'The entrance into the first room [in the Queen's Lodge] was éblouissante after coming out of the sombre apartment in Windsor, all furnished with beautiful Indian paper, chairs covered with different embroideries of the liveliest colours, glasses, tables, sconces, in the best taste, the whole calculated to give the greatest cheerfulness to the place ...' The Queen and the princesses – Mary and the baby Sophia included – all lodged with the King and necessary attendants at the unfinished house for the few days they were at Windsor this summer. The Queen was later to refer to a neighbour's unfinished country house as 'unfurnished, unfinished, dirty and uncomfortable to the greatest degree', and to complain of it as not appearing 'the least cheerful'. She expanded on her theme: 'A thing the most essential in a country place, is its being cheerful; for else it is not worth living at it.'

But the King was content, and surveyed energetically all the 'improve-ments' in a smart new 'Windsor uniform' – a blue coat with red collar and gold buttons – which he had devised, and which, it was decreed, not only he but all his sons and the equerries and male members of the 'family' were always to wear while resident at that place. When a royal cavalcade of 'fifty-six personages', counting the thirty-three servants in attendance, descended on the elderly Duchess of Portland and her companion Mrs Delany at Bulstrode, the King and all his 'attendants' besides wore this smart new uniform 'of blue and gold'. Bidden to Windsor the following day with the Duchess to meet the remaining royal children – seven only having accompanied their parents to Bulstrode – Mrs Delany does not record whether the King, appearing at the head of all his seven sons, again sported the 'Windsor uniform'. But she described young Princess Mary as 'a delightful little creature, curtseying and prattling to everybody'. And the child engaged Mrs Delany herself in conversation while they looked down from a bow window in the Castle at the crowds on the terrace below.

Mrs Cheveley – or Che Che, as she was known to the younger princes and princesses, who adored her – was the younger girls' nurse, and had been their elder brother Ernest's wet-nurse. Once described unforgettably as 'rather handsome and of a showy appearance and a woman of exceeding good sense', she was very much the younger children's champion and took enormous pride in all their doings. She wrote after one visit to Windsor: 'sweet Pss Mary has conquered and captivated every human being that has seen her. There never was a child so consummate in the art of pleasing, nor that could display herself to such advantage.' Prince Ernest was her other favourite; she called him 'my boy', and described him approvingly as 'rude', 'big' and 'noisy'. 'I do not know that I have a right to hold the scales when Prince Ernest is to be weighed …' she wrote, admitting her partiality.

Mrs Delany shared Mrs Cheveley's admiration for her charge when the royal children partnered each other, over at the Queen's Lodge, in minuets and country dances. The little 'ball' ended with the 'delightful little Princess Mary', a spectator all this time, dancing with her brother Adolphus 'a dance of their own composing'. Lady Charlotte Finch had not lost her touch in twenty years of organizing displays of the children's skills for their parents and guests to admire. Mrs Delany was less taken by the performance of the Princess Royal, observing with some surprise, when the girl danced with her eldest brother – a beautiful dancer – that she had 'a very graceful, agreeable *air*, but not a good *ear*'.

One of the Duchess of Gloucester's nieces who had apartments in the Deanery had written early on, echoing Lady Mary Coke's earlier remarks on the lack of formality at Kew: 'The King and Queen live at Windsor rather in too easy a style.' And the Duchess's niece Miss Laura Keppel – no friend to a family who did not recognize her aunt – further remarked of the King and Queen: 'They make themselves, I think, too cheap. They walk about the park as other people do … They know all the tittle-tattle of the place and the Queen sits in the room Lord Talbot's servants used to sit in to see everything that passes. I wish they had not thought of coming to Windsor …' she concluded.

But the royal family had come to stay, and in the summer of 1779 they were finally installed for good in the Queen's Lodge – 'our new habitation, just the thing for us', Queen Charlotte wrote approvingly. 'The new building of offices advances very well and the Duke of St Albans's house' – to be known as Lower Lodge – 'will be finished by the beginning of autumn.' Usefully the garden of Lower Lodge connected with the southern stretches of the Queen's Lodge garden. And so the children housed in either place – including a new Prince, Octavius, born that February – might come and go with ease. At Kew, at the top of the Green, Prince Ernest's house had meanwhile been acquired to accommodate that Prince, his two younger brothers, Augustus and Adolphus, and a swarm of attendants.

Prince William had left home – and a vexed relationship with his younger brother Edward – at the age of fourteen in June 1779, to board the *Prince George*, Rear Admiral Robert Digby's flagship, at Portsmouth, and enter the Royal Navy as an able seaman. The impetuous Prince was cock-a-hoop. Less so was one of his tutors from Kew, Dr Majendie, whose unpleasant task it was to share the boy's stateroom, monitor his behaviour on deck and on shore, and attempt to din some Latin and Greek into the royal recruit's head. General Budé and the other tutors remained at Kew with dark, clever Prince Edward, who continued, in his solitary splendour, to be unpleasant to his elder brothers and haughty to his attendants. The princesses wrote to William in letters that spoke in every sentence of their affection for him, but Miss Hamilton noted that the Princess Royal was the only one of the royal children who seemed at all affected when their brother departed.

Mrs Delany, visiting Windsor this summer, found the sight of the King carrying around in his arms by turns Princess Sophia, not yet two, and the latest arrival, Octavius, delightful. Princess Mary – in a 'cherry-coloured tabby' or frock and 'with silver leading strings' – could not quite put a name to her interlocutor of a year earlier, but made her a 'very low curtsey' and greeted her: 'How do you do, Duchess of Portland's friend?' Less benign members of the small Court sighed at their seclusion, and reserved a special dislike for the now established practice of terracing, or walking on the terrace – whatever the weather. 'Bring heavy shoes,' ran one dismal note from Miss Gouldsworthy during an especially rainy spell at Windsor to Miss Hamilton at Kew, 'the gravel on the terrace is so wet, thick shoes will not suffice.'

The royal females themselves were not above joining in the complaints. This summer, on 26 September, nine-year-old Princess Elizabeth wrote to Miss Hamilton at Kew from Windsor: 'I ought to have told you that Lady Holderness and Lady Weymouth [two of the Queen's ladies] [are here]. You know how I do dislike her, and like Lady Holderness, but I do promise you that I will take a great deal of care not to sit by her at dinner.' The Queen herself wrote to Miss Hamilton the following year on 20 August: 'Mrs Vesey ... is in this neighbourhood and come twice to Lady Courtown in order to see the Royal Family upon the terrace. I made her two curtseys from the window and was told my politeness had almost thrown her down. I was sorry to find that I had been doing mischief.' The princes' and princesses' liking for the company of their social inferiors – the nurses and pages and housekeepers and grooms at Kew and Windsor – and their tendency to make confidants of their attendants was of their parents' making, and born of the seclusion in which they were kept.

The Queen was worried above all about the effect of this seclusion on her beloved eldest son. His liking for 'low company' and his influence on his younger brothers were not lost on her, and in private she and the King began to think of sending their second son Frederick to Germany to embark on a course of military studies there – away from the elder brother who was fast becoming, in their gloomy view, unfit to be useful to the world.

Meanwhile, Miss Hamilton was in the unhappy situation of having excited the Prince of Wales's first amorous attentions. It being Princess Mary's turn to be inoculated against smallpox by Surgeon Pennell Hawkins with her brother Dolly in the spring of 1779, Miss Gouldsworthy had remained with them some weeks at Kew, while they lay in darkened rooms. During a previous inoculation the Queen trusted that 'some Providence which has hitherto given me uncommon success in all my undertakings will not withhold it from me this time, as I can say it is not without praying for his assistance as the greatest and best of medicines I can put my confidence in'. Providence was kind again, and Mary and Dolly came through their ordeal, although not without the three-year-old Princess, who was full of spots, being very fretful, especially when stopped from itching those on her scalp.

Miss Hamilton was obliged to take Gouly's 'post at the marble table', against a wall of the drawing room in the Queen's House, where the sub-governess was accustomed to spend her evenings standing while the elder princesses, seated within a family circle, 'worked' and read and played cards. Their companion, the sixteen-year-old Prince of Wales, was inspired to expostulations of excitement by his nightly viewing of sentinel Miss Hamilton, and he poured out his admiration for his sisters' attendant in a series of impulsive letters that he smuggled to her over the course of the summer and autumn. Between − rejected − requests that he and his corre-spondent exchange lockets with romantic mottoes, the Prince revealed that he hoped he and his brother Frederick were to move to his grandmother's former home, Carlton House on Pall Mall, within the year, abandoning governors: 'towards midsummer we are both of us to dash in to the wide world'. In preparation for this worldlier role, the Prince stole into Miss Hamilton's apartment at Kew and seized a bouquet she had worn in her bosom to place it in his.

Like many who would come after her, and like his mother before her, Miss Hamilton appealed to the intelligence, feeling and sense she believed the Prince to possess: 'I want to raise your virtues, for you have virtues. You have a heart too good ever totally to eradicate the love and admiration of what is virtuous.' But she shuddered at the Prince's impetuosity, and her side of the correspondence consisted more and more of remonstrances − about his liking for the company of his servants and grooms, about his habit of cursing like them. She had had her last reprimand delivered on New Year's Eve 1779, after the Prince informed her − to her horror − that he had shifted his affection to a new object of admiration, an actress, Mrs Mary Robinson, whom he had contrived to meet. 'A female in that line', Miss Hamilton prophesied earlier in the month, 'has too much trick and art not to be a very dangerous object.'

And now this boy so long secluded from the world did indeed plunge into vice, climbing out of his bedroom at Kew to keep midnight appoint-ments with the actress − and, consequently, entering into an opposition to his father that would sorely try his sisters' loyalties. Within months, Mrs Robinson was suing for breach of the many, many promises that her besot-ted young lover had made her, and the King had to pay her £5,000 in set-tlement of her claim.

To add insult to injury, the Prince took up with his reprobate uncle the Duke of Cumberland, who favoured the Whig cause. Long forbidden to appear at Court, the Duke was welcomed back into the fold with his brother Gloucester by the King after they supported him in restoring order in June 1780, when London was convulsed by serious riots. Under a banner of 'No Popery', with a willing London mob at their heels, Lord George Gordon and others, who objected to Parliamentary proposals to free Catholics from restrictions passed a century before, captured the streets, let loose prisoners and burned the Lord Chancellor Lord Mansfield's house and library at Kenwood.

The King decreed that his brothers – but not their wives – should meet his children. So one week the Duke of Gloucester came. The next the Princesses Royal and Augusta, with their elder brothers, and the three little princes duly received the reprobate Duke of Cumberland, according to the Queen's commands, in the Gallery at Kew House. The Duke stayed half an hour during which 'the elder Princes, à l'ordinaire, made the little ones as noisy as possible', wrote Gouly. But the main point had been established, in the King's view – the princesses had not enquired after the health of their uncles' duchesses. He failed to foresee that his brother would seem an object of glamour to his sons, and that, when the princes took their uncle back to their own house, where he remained till ten o'clock, it would be the beginning of an unwelcome friendship, and of a penchant for the Whig party.

4

Adolescence

~

THE QUEEN HAD written wistfully once of Bath, the watering place, which she said was 'as full as an egg' with fashionable summer visitors – English and foreign nobility among them – dancing and sniffing out scandal. Now she wrote, 'I fear for my daughters one day or another, because one has to know the world to judge it, and to know how to behave there.' Being alone, she went on, the tendency was to create a wicked world which had no basis; and on entering that world, it vanished into the air. The Queen also expressed doubts to her brother Charles about the wisdom of a policy which she intimated to be now not hers but the King's – of keeping their elder children, and particularly their daughters, in the country and out of the way of a world which she did not believe to be any more wicked than it had ever been. 'As we all do the same as each other, our conversation cannot be animated, and our life is too uniform and retired for us to gain knowledge of the world.' It was not stimulating, she declared.

Horace Walpole, who had rejoiced in the Queen's appetite for gaiety on her arrival in England and regretted her subsequent seclusion, would have agreed with her. Indeed had the Princess Royal been allowed to go about in the world a little, or permitted some friends of her own age, a fracas that developed in the summer of 1780 and came to a head shortly before her brother Prince Alfred was born in September might never have occurred.

The Princess Royal and Princess Augusta were left under the care of Miss Gouldsworthy this June, while Lady Charlotte and Miss Hamilton led a party of invalids in search of sea breezes and bathing machines at Eastbourne on the Sussex coast. Princess Elizabeth had been suffering from disfiguring boils that spring, and Prince Edward was sickly; Princess Sophia and Prince Octavius would profit from the change of air. Princess Mary remained with Gouly and her two elder sisters at Kew, while nurse Mrs Cheveley accompanied the younger children to Eastbourne.

Prince Edward with his retinue was lodged separately, but the two parties met each morning in the relaxed atmosphere of Compton House, a delightful villa in the neighbourhood with a library and garden pavilion. Here Prince Edward worked with his tutor, the Reverend John Fisher; here Princess Elizabeth read the Psalms and the chapter of the day with Lady Charlotte Finch and attended to 'various lessons from Lady Charlotte and myself in the absence of her teachers', as Miss Hamilton recorded.

Among the early writings of the royal children that Miss Hamilton preserved is a ruled sheet on which Princess Elizabeth wrote out six times in some previous year, with varying degrees of success, 'Forgetting of a wrong is a mild revenge.' Three times she failed to fit the last word on the line. But she was by now an accomplished penwoman, having at the age of nine and a half on New Year's Eve 1779 copied out: 'Superiority in virtue is the most unpardonable provocation that can be given to a base mind, innocence is too amiable to be beheld without hatred and it is a secret acknowledgement of merit which the wicked are betrayed into when they pursue good men with violence.'

'Sometimes Mr Fisher stays and obligingly instructs the pss in drawing, or she is again employed by lessons,' Miss Hamilton told her colleagues at Kew. Princess Elizabeth was fortunate in her instructor. Her brother Edward's preceptor or tutor, the Reverend John Fisher, was a gifted amateur artist, and the trouble he took with her at Compton House suggests that he recognized the flair that she was to bring to a remarkable career as a decorative artist.

'Princess Elizabeth and my sweet engaging child Pss Sophia are playing about like butterflies in the sun and culling wild flowers on the grass,' wrote Miss Hamilton, turning to less weighty matters, 'whilst I am watching them and scribbling to you.' The Queen at Windsor wished she was with them, and was to write, in the last month of her pregnancy, to her brother Charles in Germany, 'I don't believe a prisoner wishes more ardently for his liberty than I wish to be rid of my burden ... If I knew it was for the last time I would be happy.'

Now she wrote to Lady Charlotte: 'How happy should I be to make dear Sophia a visit in her bathing machine and how surprised would you be to find me in it, hélas! I must only think of it; in thoughts I am very very often with them all.' The Queen admired from afar Elizabeth's 'steadiness' in undergoing what the mother termed 'that dreadful operation of bathing'. 'You will allow her I am sure great merit', she had told Lady Charlotte, 'in feeling so much, saying nothing and yet doing what was right.' Lady Charlotte herself stayed well clear of the bathing machine.

The Queen teased Miss Hamilton:

Pray can you tell me what punishment is to be made use of when the physician recommends bathing in the sea and it is not complied with? I am very impatient to have that point determined as I intend practising it upon a certain Miss M H who promised Dr Turton to wash herself quite clean, and who since her arrival at Eastbourne pretends to be a little fearful, for I dare not make use of the word which begins with a C for fear of shocking your delicacy …

Queen Charlotte wrote to Lady Charlotte Finch in July 1780, 'Tell Miss Hamilton I hope soon to answer her letter. She makes me guilty of breaking a commandment, for I envy her writing so well.'

Princess Royal wrote to Miss Hamilton this summer from the Queen's Lodge: 'Dear Hammy, I have behaved well in every occasion except last Wednesday, that I danced ill. I am very sorry to be obliged to add that, but alas it is too true. However, I hope that you will not give me quite up, since I have done everything else well, and that [sic] I dance better last Friday.' But the Princess Royal had greater sins to report, and wrote again at greater length: 'My dearest Hammy, I return you ten thousand thanks for your letter, which is filled with the most undeniable truths. I have not now much time and therefore must defer for the present to give you an ingenuous account of myself, which I am afraid will not be very pleasant, but I hope with the next post to send you one which will please you better and give you more satisfaction.' Turning to domestic news with relief, she added:

We have been at Windsor, Miss Planta and M Guiffardière accompany us there. I have one hour every morning with the latter. Mama has worn the trimming you saw me work her last summer. She has ordered me for the present to put by my waistcoat, not because it was too great a piece of work for me but because she was afraid as I have not much time to work, it would dirty. I have bought myself a little Spa toilet for two guineas, which contains everything that can possibly be wanted. Pray give my love to all those it is due. Pray tell Elizabeth that next week I shall write to her.

This letter was very likely in reply to a remonstrance from Miss Hamilton. The Princess Royal had been behaving less than well to her attendant Miss Gouldsworthy, who wrote from Kew, worn out from having escorted the elder princesses three times in a week to the Queen's House: 'I return to this dungeon … heated to death and wishing … for the hour of going to bed.' A month later she complained of 'being dragged for two hot hours upon the terrace at Windsor'. Meanwhile, Miss Planta, the princesses' English teacher, decried the damp at Kew, and ascribed her rheumatism of the last two years to the insalubrious surroundings.

In July Miss Planta wrote that the Queen would be most unhappy when she heard of the Princess Royal's conduct to Gouly: 'Miss G is much dissatisfied with the Pss R's conduct and I am sorry to say it is far from amiable.' Miss Planta had warned her pupil of the consequences to come: 'Unless she corrects herself in time, the Queen will grow indifferent to her.' But Gouly, that much tried sub-governess – who had now been with the family for nearly five years – tendered her resignation, which the Princess Royal had plainly hoped would be the result of her behaviour. She said to all and sundry that she wished Miss Hamilton – for whom she still had a passion – would replace Miss Gouldsworthy. The angry young Princess – fourteen on 29 September, six days after Prince Alfred's birth – did not get her wish. Miss Gouldsworthy remained at the Queen's request, and the Princess Royal's rage subsided once the Eastbourne party – and dear Hammy – returned in October.

The Princess Royal's sister Princess Augusta had a more equable temperament, and was much happier within the family circle, as a letter she wrote to Miss Hamilton the year before shows. It was the morning of her eleventh birthday:

> My dear Hamy, This morning I waked at four and I found all my presents. But I would not look at them for fear that I should disturb Gouly and Princess Royal. At half after six the maid came in to make the fire. Then I waked a second time and I looked at them and I assure you that I liked them very much and when I came to the beautiful little purse you was so good as to give me I was as happy as a Queen, for if your present had not been what it was I should have had no play purse for tonight. As soon as I come to Kew you shall see all my presents ...

Now she wrote from the Queen's Lodge in July 1780: 'Dear Hamy, I am now (as you see) performing my promise. You must promise to answer all my letters or else I will not write to you. We are now come to Windsor and for our sins are forced of Sunday evenings to walk on the terrace. I hope you mind and never show the scrawls that I write to you. We now always dine at the castle, for the King is fitting up a library here as well as at Kew.' After adding the information that 'We now do our hair in a new sort of fashion, we wear hats all day and no caps,' she ended, 'My dear Hamy, the letters having to go in half an hour, I can write now no more. My dear Madam, I am with the most profound respect your most humble and obedient servant as I know you like those titles.'

Augusta was cheerful, but other tempers were riding high in Windsor, including the King's in the course of a tempestuous general election this August. Irritated by the Whig party's plan of economy for the Court, he went into one of the silk mercers' in the town and said, as one anecdotalist had it, 'in his usual quick manner, "The queen wants a gown – wants a gown – No Keppel – No Keppel".' The mercer was convinced that he should vote for the Tory candidate in lieu of Admiral Lord Keppel, the Whig MP who had recently seen off the French fleet, and 'all the royal brewers and butchers and bakers' in the town followed suit. Further, the princes' page Billy Ramus and some of the Queen's band who lived at Kew Green were ordered by the King to appear at the Castle on the eve of the election, and 'were put to bed at Windsor so as to vote as inhabitants'.

But Admiral Lord Keppel had his admirers within the royal family. Prince Augustus, aged seven, was locked up 'in the nursery at Windsor for wearing Keppel colours'. Presumably he had been dressed up by his elder brothers, for, in a first display of the sympathy with the Opposition that enraged their father, the Prince of Wales and Prince Frederick became ardent Keppelites during this bitter local contest. Indeed, the Prince of Wales would not speak to an equerry who cast his vote for the Tory candidate, Mr Peniston Portlock Powney – widely known as 'The King's Pony' – who gained the seat.

Princess Augusta, for her part, found the political hullabaloo at Windsor tiresome, and wrote to Miss Hamilton: 'I wish that the election was at an end for the noise is inexpressible. I believe that if you had all the children of Sussex all together in one room could not if possible be greater [sic].' She was herself busy with a new pastime, making a coin collection:

> Col Lumsden showed me some shillings, half crowns and one guinea of Q Eliz that one of the drummers dug up from under Herne's Oak. They are to be sure very curious … My collection goes on very well, for General Freytag [the Hanoverian Minister] has given me some German coins of the late King [her great-grandfather King George II] and of the present King [her father].

At Eastbourne a month later, Princess Elizabeth received a letter from her father with less controversial news. 'I was made glad to hear that my dear mama was so well and that I had got another brother,' she wrote in reply. 'Sophia says she has got a little grandson; Octavius she calls her son. Last night Lord and Lady Dartrey drank tea with Edward and me.' Alone of the princesses and princes, Princess Elizabeth was to preserve a fondness for her brother Edward in later years, which was perhaps promoted by these months they spent together.

> The cannons fired from the ships, and from the beach both yesterday and today. I was so overjoyed when I had your letter this morning, my dear Papa, that I could not settle myself to write. I beg my best duty to my dearest Mama. I have the pleasure of telling you that my brothers and sisters are well. I remain my dear papa your most dutiful and most affectionate daughter Elizabeth

Four months after the birth of Prince Alfred, her fourteenth child and ninth son, the Queen rejoiced in January 1781 to find that 'the new year is begun without the want of a nurse'. And indeed as the next two years wore on without that need arising, there may have been agreement between husband and wife at this point that their family could be said to be complete. Nevertheless, the Queen and all the family were sincerely sorry to lose another of their number. While Prince William pursued his midshipman career in the Atlantic, the King despatched Prince Frederick in December 1780 to Hanover to pursue the military studies for which the boy had already showed some aptitude.

Over the course of the new year, the royal schoolroom and nursery were in some confusion. Not only had Miss Hamilton leave of absence for some weeks to nurse her mother in Derbyshire but Lady Charlotte Finch sailed for Lisbon to nurse her son, Lord Winchilsea. Stalwart Miss Gouldsworthy's health declined so badly that she had not the breath to stoop to a writing table, Miss Hamilton told Lady Charlotte in early September. And to cap it all, one of Mrs Cheveley's own three children had a bad eye, requiring her to take the whole brood to Margate for a month.

When she returned from Derbyshire, Miss Hamilton kept the absent Lady Charlotte informed about the progress of the princesses back home, writing on one occasion:

> I must tell you a little anecdote of Pss Mary's. When Lady J P [Juliana Penn, Lady Charlotte's sister] came last night Pss M said, I am glad Lady Joully is come. One of her sisters told her she ought to call her Lady Juliana. 'Oh,' says she, 'I don't care how I call her, God bless her – I love her – she is so like dear Ly Char.' And Pss Sophia, who is my great great favourite, says 'Ly Cha is very ill natured to stay so long.' She is continually enquiring after you.

Lady Charlotte Finch was still in Portugal, embroiled in family crises of her own, when the Princess Royal made her debut, not yet fifteen, at the King's Birthday on 4 June 1781. Not only the Princess, but her mother, the masters and attendants who had coached her for the important event, and the whole household had to steel their nerves. But all went well. From Caldas on the coast north of Lisbon, Lady Charlotte wrote to Princess Elizabeth of the 'satisfaction' the King and Queen must have had 'in seeing dear Princess Royal's first appearance at the ball on the birthday'. She thought of it 'continually', she wrote, 'tho, as my dear Princess Elizabeth will conceive, with almost as great regret, that I should have been absent at such a time; I can think of nothing that can make me amends for such a disappointment, till the time comes for my dear Princess Augusta and Princess Elizabeth to be called forth upon the like occasion, when I have no doubt they will do themselves as much honour as Princess Royal has done.'

Princess Elizabeth wrote to Miss Hamilton, 'Last Wednesday William returned home from Portsmouth.' The princesses' beloved brother, now nearly sixteen, had stories to tell of being present at two sieges of Gibraltar, but his naval superiors in general were tried by his liking for drinking and brawling. 'I hope you are better and will continue so,' Princess Elizabeth wrote. 'Augusta and me have got a delightful house [at Windsor] which is called the Lower Lodge, the rooms are delightful and very pleasant. I hope to see you in them soon, my dear. I hope you have not had so much thunder as we have had here. Mama has read a very fine sermon and two very pretty Spectators.'

The princesses took their cue in relationships with their attendants from their mother, who continued to endear herself to all her daughters' attendants by the attention and great civility she showed them. 'My dear Miss Hamilton,' she wrote on one occasion, 'What can I have to say? Not much indeed! But to wish you a good morning in the pretty blue and white room where I had the pleasure to sit and read with you *The Hermit*, a poem which is such a favourite with me that I have read it twice this summer. Oh what a blessing to keep good company. Very likely I should never have been acquainted with either poet or poem was it not for you.' And again the Queen wrote to the same correspondent:

> My dear Miss Hamilton, I find it with regret, that notwithstanding all my envy I cannot obtain that agreeable style of writing both you and Lady Charlotte Finch are possessed of. I grieve and fret for days about it, but it avails me nothing else but making me dissatisfied with myself, which is the true way of preventing my poor head to make any real progress in such a desirable talent. I shall therefore renounce all claim to elegance of style and desire you to be contented with a very simple natural way of writing, well meant at all times but making no pretensions whatever. Having prepared you for this I may without the least fear of offending your feelings upon

that subject say anything that occurs to me without being criticized. I mean by that, severely, for a little will do me good, as I love to improve. Pray do not think me too old for that. It would be mortifying indeed.

But in June, when Miss Hamilton tried to resign in a letter stressing her delicate constitution, the Queen was as iron: 'The contents of your letter I am inclined to take as the effect of low spirits and therefore won't indulge you with an entire belief of what you have said ...' If her attendant persisted in her opinion, she must inform no one but the Queen, until the latter had gone through the 'disagreeable' business of finding a 'proper person' to replace her.

At the Prince of Wales's nineteenth-birthday ball at Windsor in August, which lasted till six in the morning, Miss Hamilton wrote, 'the Queen, Pss R and her sisters wore different coloured clothes, trimmed with silver and were all very fine', while their brothers and father and others danced in the full Windsor dress uniform. 'I wish I could convey a proper idea of the very brilliant and magnificent appearance of St George's Hall which was the supper room,' she wrote earlier in the letter. 'It put me in mind of descriptions in the Tales of the Genii.' Without incident the Princess Royal opened the ball with her brother, over 2,000 candles illuminating their progress down St George's Hall, and there were even rumours of an approaching marriage – to none less than the Emperor of Austria – to confirm her adult status after a bold-faced English duchess in Vienna suggested her as a bride to that elderly and widowed sovereign. On His Imperial Majesty's replying with courtesy that he thought the Princess might prefer a younger husband the determined peeress replied, 'That is nothing, I married to my first husband an old man, and it did very well.'

At chapel on the birthday morning, Miss Hamilton wrote, the gentlemen wore 'the undress uniform, the ladies, hats – smart polonaises – the hair well dressed, white cloaks, etc – each dressed agreeable to their own taste, except the princesses, who all wore rose colour trimmed with gauze'. Apropos of the Prince of Wales and churchgoing, Miss Hamilton noted demurely that he had taken up shooting and was very fond of it. 'This morning he was going to set out [for a shooting party] as we went to chapel, he has quite left off attending divine service. On Sunday mornings,' she added pointedly 'their Majesties and the psses attend both the chapel and cathedral [the name by which St George's Chapel was known].' The Prince of Wales did not as yet enjoy independence in Carlton House in fashionable Pall Mall, but he had achieved a level of autonomy, having his own apartments in town at the Queen's House as well as in the Castle at Windsor.

Meanwhile, Princess Augusta sent to Lady Charlotte Finch at Caldas what her governess described as 'not only the most gracious, but the most entertaining' two letters she ever received. 'I have read them over and over again with the greatest pleasure.' She went on to mention 'a dear little girl here, that is excessively like my sweet Princess Augusta who dances delightfully, she is the cleverest little creature here and I am quite fond of her, I believe you can guess why'. Lady Charlotte encouraged Princess Augusta's new hobby. She was acquiring 'the different coin of this country to add to your Royal Highness's collection', although she had found no medals. She spoke of the formal dress for little girls in Portugal, and appeared to think of Princess Augusta, whom the first Miss Planta had earlier thought 'childish' for her age. And indeed, although in duty bound to follow her sister into the world, now that the Princess Royal had made her debut, twelve-year-old Princess Augusta was still fully occupied with her lessons.

In February 1781 she had copied out: 'No character is more glorious, none more attractive of universal admiration and respect than that of helping those who are in no condition of helping themselves.' And a month later she had written to Miss Hamilton, who was ill, from a schoolroom at St James's Palace, 'My dear Hamy, I am very sorry that it was not in my power to write to you this morning but I was a-doing my French lesson and I could not leave it off for to write ... I looked when we came into the court to see if I could see you at the window but I don't believe there was so much as a fly to be seen. We were very anxious to hear how you was, but nobody could tell. I am sorry that as I am under the same roof as you ... I cannot see you.'

But she could also be upon occasion an unruly schoolgirl. 'Madam,' she wrote to Miss Hamilton, 'I beg your pardon for what I did to you this morning. I promise you I won't do so any more. I beg you will forgive me and indeed I won't do so again. Indeed I shall be very sorry if you go away from us, for indeed I love you very much. Indeed I won't behave ill to you again. I am very much ashamed of what I did and said this morning, upon my word, and won't do so again.' And she wrote again: 'Madam, I beg that you will have the goodness to forgive me for all the impertinences I did you. I promise you that I won't do so any more and promise you that I will do everything that you bid me.' A small piece of paper bearing the faded inscription 'Augusta Sophia, Queen's Lodge, Windsor, August 14th 1781' was docketed by Miss Hamilton with the words 'As a mark of affection,

Princess Augusta Sophia pricked herself with a pin and wrote this in her blood to give Miss Hamilton.'

The King was increasingly caught up in business about the war in America, especially after the news in November 1781 that the British commander-in-chief, Lord Cornwallis, had had to surrender in humiliating circumstances at Yorktown on 19 October to the American forces. The princesses grew up in an atmosphere rarely free of increasingly gloomy discussion about the great struggle overseas. Princess Augusta was nevertheless, under the influence of her father, to become particularly patriotic and fervently attached to the idea of the British soldier as the apogee of all that was valorous.

Prince Frederick in Hanover had been adventuring: 'I was about one week ago in the mines of the Hartz where we were obliged to go down ladders for above thirteen hundred feet and up again, as for me I did not feel it in the least, but Grenville complained that his wrists ached the next day so terribly he could hardly stir.' But nothing could compare with the glamour of Prince William joining the English forces deployed against the American rebels in New York. His sister Royal wrote to him in March 1782: 'I hope that you do not really think that there is even a possibility of your being forgot at home, for indeed if you have the smallest suspicion of it, you do us all very great injustice, for you are generally spoken of several times in the course of the day.' She wished that she could have seen him skate: 'I am sure that before the end of the winter you will be able to do it very well.' (As William was not yet adept, the other officers would skate along pulling him on a sledge over the frozen Hudson river, shouting, 'Hooray for the Prince, hooray for the Prince.') 'All my brothers and sisters send their love to you. Octavius is very much improved since you have seen him by his change of dress,' she ended.

At home Princess Augusta's behaviour was still erratic, and she was often repentant. 'I assure you my dear Hamy', she wrote in the summer of 1782, 'that it is my most earnest desire to please the King and Queen and you, and that I will be obedient to everything you say and that I will put off childish things from this day forward and for ever more, and that I will always take it for granted that I should never be told anything if it was not for my good.'

But when the Queen broke the news in 1782 to this younger daughter that she was to appear at the King's Birthday that year, the thirteen-year-old 'was perfectly silent for some time' from surprise. So the Queen told Lady Charlotte Finch, who was at the seaside at Deal this year – with

Prince Alfred, who had recently been inoculated, and Mrs Cheveley. She added that, from not wishing her daughter to dwell upon her coming debut, she had told her of it only two days before it was to occur.

The Queen recorded that, even so, her daughter – who had not by any means grown out of her childhood shyness – 'grew more timorous' as the moment of her appearance approached. Public life of any kind and crowds in particular held terrors for this Princess. 'We are ... for our sins ... forced of Sunday evenings to walk on the terrace,' she had written two summers before at Windsor. But she 'went through it very properly', the Queen reported to the royal governess with relief after the Birthday that June; and 'her behaviour was approved of'. The newspapers, she went on, had been very kind to the juvenile debutante, saying that 'the world admired the elegance of Princess Royal, and not less the modesty of the Royal Augusta'. Princess Augusta may have been formally 'out', but she was still a child. 'I am very much obliged to you my dear Hamy,' she wrote in September, 'for having let me have a fire and assure you that you shall not be mortified by my proving that you did wrong, but I will not only be obedient to you and not meddle with it and not only be obedient about that but about all things which can give you any pleasure.'

Into this picture of domestic tranquillity – barring the Prince of Wales's dissipations in the equerries' room after dinner with his parents, and some debauchery in town – came, unannounced, death. Shortly after Princess Augusta made her debut in London in June 1782, Prince Alfred endeared himself at Deal to – among others – an old bluestocking lady by waving at her when asked to do so. He was at the seaside resort to recover his strength after being inoculated against smallpox. But he did not profit from his bathing. His face and especially his eyelids were still troublesome, with eruptions from his inoculation, and his chest continued weak. Nor did a session of horse riding – what his mother termed the 'four-footed doctor' – answer, an activity which Mr Pennell Hawkins the Queen's Surgeon had recommended, disapproving of the child being carried around in Mrs Cheveley's arms. Prince Alfred's chest continued to be a problem on his return from Deal, and the doctors convened at Windsor in August to discuss his case. But it came as a complete shock to the family when they concurred in the opinion that the child could not survive more than a few weeks.

None of the fourteen royal children had ever been in more than passing poor health, or less than an advertisement for the skills of the Hawkins brothers, Mr Pennell and Sir Caesar (a baronet since 1778), who inoculated them and attended them in illness, and of Augustus Brande, the Mecklenburg apothecary who had set up shop at Kew. At one point when the

Queen sent to her brother Charles a medical book that contained, she wrote, 'the manner in which they care for children here from the moment of their birth', she boasted, 'Follow our method a little, and you will find that your children will become strong as anything.'

After prolonged bouts of fever, Prince Alfred – not yet two – died at Lower Lodge, Windsor in late August, despite the dedicated nursing of Lady Charlotte and Mrs Cheveley. They, first among others, received mourning lockets of pearl and amethyst containing curls of the dead boy's light gold hair. The household did not, however, go into mourning, as it was not prescribed in the case of deaths of children under the age of seven. Alfred's small body was buried with full honours at Westminster Abbey beside those of larger men of greater note, and his death affected the whole household. The Queen 'cried vastly at first', Lady Charlotte reported, 'and … though very reasonable' – she dwelt on her good fortune in having thirteen healthy children – was 'very much hurt by her loss and the King also'. The King, who was a blunt man, found his own comfort. He said that if it had been three-year-old Octavius who had died, he would have died too.

Princess Augusta had another cross to bear later this year. In November she wrote on a piece of paper for Miss Hamilton:

> 'Question: Do you think I have behaved well this summer? Ans: (Pretty well upon the whole.)' By your saying pretty well, I perceive you mean not quite yet what you could wish for. Therefore I hope that at the end of next winter when I ask you the same question, you will be able to answer 'Yes,' that I may have the pleasure of seeing that I have made you happy and improved myself, which I always mean to do.

But there was to be no such appraisal the following November, for six days after Augusta penned her memorandum Miss Hamilton departed, to live with her friends in London. Leave had at last been granted by the Queen for her resignation, and Miss Hamilton, like Miss Dacres before her, passed quietly out of the secluded circle within which the princesses existed.

Six months later, however, deeply agitated, Miss Hamilton made her way to the Queen's House, seeking confirmation of a hideous rumour. Miss Planta wrote from Kew on 5 May 1783 to confirm the truth of what she had heard. 'My heart bleeds for the King and Queen for indeed you see in them the resigned Christian in the afflicted parent,' wrote the English teacher. 'I need not say more to you, who were witness to the melancholy event which happened not many months ago [Prince Alfred's death]. I believe we shall remain here till the last duty is paid to the dear departed angel.'

Out of the blue at Windsor a few days earlier, from being his usual ebul-
lient self, Prince Octavius had sickened over a period of less than forty-
eight hours, and, despite the frantic attentions of all the royal doctors, had
died at Kew at 8.40 in the evening of 3 May. Although he had been inoculated with Sophia weeks earlier, smallpox had had nothing to do with his
death. Mrs Cheveley, who had nursed him as she had nursed Alfred, was
unfortunately firm on the point. So rumours that he was a victim of his
Gotha blood, and that both he and Alfred had succumbed to the 'family
disease' – sometimes named as scrofula, and sometimes as 'a weakness in
the lungs', or tuberculosis – circulated. Whatever the cause of the child's
death, the King was quite undone by it. As Princess Augusta was later to
recall, the next day her father passed through a room at Windsor, where
the artist Gainsborough was putting the finishing touches to portraits of
the royal family. The King sent a message to beg the artist to desist, but, on
hearing that the work on which he was engaged was the portrait of Prince
Octavius, allowed him to continue.

At the Royal Academy summer exhibition a week after Octavius's
shocking death, the royal family inspected Gainsborough's 'numerical'
work – oval heads of the King and Queen, and of all their children, exclud-
ing the absent Prince Frederick. There in the bottom right-hand corner
were Octavius, bright eyed and golden haired – just as he had been in life
– and diminutive Alfred, still in baby clothes, 'painted by remembrance'.
The princesses, trained not to show emotion in public, were overcome and
cried, regardless of their company. These portraits of their dead brothers,
when hung in the Queen's House and when later engraved, became life-
long talismans for the princesses of what had been.

Over the Birthday in June 1783 hung the cloud not only of the coming
peace negotiations with a victorious America, but of Octavius's death. The
King was at least as cast down by his four-year-old son's death in May as
he was by the negotiations that in Paris that September would accord the
American rebels full independence and establish an American republic.

But, for the Queen and for her daughters, there were immediate con-
cerns to divert them from their grief. In July, Princess Royal and Princess
Augusta acquired their first ever lady-in-waiting – Lady Elizabeth
Waldegrave. It was a practical acknowledgement that, at rising seventeen,
Princess Royal now took drawing, painting and even the dread music lessons to avoid idleness rather than because her education was incomplete.
The Queen warned her old friend Lady Holderness, who had recommended Lady Elizabeth, to put the new recruit on guard: 'See her and tell
her my way of things, particularly how I hate intrigues and that I must insist

that in case she ever sees anything improper in the princesses' behaviour I must be told of it, and that I am the person she must talk to.'

At the age of thirty-nine, the Queen herself was expecting a fifteenth child, conceived after Prince Alfred's death and due early this August. A cradle with satin curtains and a matching coverlet was made ready. Mrs Johnson, who had been first employed as royal midwife seventeen years before at the Princess Royal's birth, was in attendance. And on 7 August 1783 Queen Charlotte gave birth to a sixth princess, named Amelia in compliment to her wealthy great-aunt in London.

The birth of Princess Amelia at Windsor – the only child of the King and Queen to be born there – acted as a tonic on her father's spirits. While grieving for Octavius, he was as proud and possessive a parent as though Princess Amelia had been his first child. Amelia was to be the most turbulent and tempestuous of all the princesses. She would show a strength of will that would surprise and divide her doting relations, but as yet, beneath the ivory satin curtains of her cradle and under the coverlet embroidered with garden flowers, she was merely the latest royal baby in a long line.

The birth of Amelia did not obliterate for her sisters the memory of their brothers Alfred and Octavius, but they did not dwell on the death of the latter, as their father did. Three months after Amelia was born, the King wrote to Lord Dartmouth that every day 'increases the chasm I do feel for that beloved object [Octavius]'. The artist Benjamin West probably best soothed the King's 'woe', if he astonished others, with a huge painting entitled *The Apotheosis of Prince Octavius* exhibited at the Royal Academy the year after that Prince's death, and featuring Prince Alfred perched on a cloud and stretching out baby arms in welcome to his elder brother. Way below, an earthly landscape features Windsor Castle, from which Prince Octavius has presumably been launched.

The King's feelings of political frustration about the humiliating final stages of the American war had led him to consider abdicating the throne of England and retiring to Hanover. Amelia's birth, following so swiftly on Octavius's death and followed itself a month later by the firing of the Tower guns signalling peace between England and the new United States of America, was felt, and was always to be remembered within the family, as a time of hope and redemption.

For many years Amelia was to repay this investment in her by being quite as beautiful and winning a child as her brother Octavius had ever been. With hindsight, it is possible to say that she was a child of whom too much was expected. 'Our little sister is without exception one of the prettiest children that I have ever seen,' the Princess Royal, in September, wrote with satisfaction to her brother William, who had been despatched the previous month to Hanover. (His parents had been horrified at his rough sailor's manners and hoped that a course in his father's Electorate would prepare him better to be an officer.) She regretted that, being absent, he would miss Amelia's christening, and, with the material rather than spiritual comforts the day would bring in mind, wrote, 'I wish that I could send you some of the plum cake in my letter ... but that being impossible you must be satisfied with my wishes.'

So great was the gap in age between the Princess Royal and Princess Augusta and their baby sister, that the elder sisters, at nearly seventeen and nearly fifteen, stood godparents – with their brother the Prince of Wales – when the Archbishop of Canterbury baptized the child on 17 September 1783 at the Chapel Royal, St James's. Princess Elizabeth, whose debut had not yet been decided upon, looked on with her younger brothers and sisters. Princess Amelia was the fifteenth child of King George III and Queen Charlotte to be christened there – and, although no one knew it, she was to be the last. Before the chapel would again host a royal baptism, one or other of the children gathered around Amelia's font must first take a bride or groom.

BOOK TWO
EXPERIENCE
1783–1797

5

Brothers and Sisters

~

ONE THING WAS certain. Over the Queen of England's dead body would her sister-in-law the Duchess of Brunswick succeed in the campaign she had recently resumed to secure the Princess Royal as a bride for her ill-favoured son, the Hereditary Prince of that duchy. 'I would much rather keep all my daughters with me for ever than see them marry there,' the Queen wrote to her brother Duke Charles in July 1783. The King's sister Augusta – Duchess of Brunswick since 1780 – had recently married off her own eldest daughter Augusta, at the age of fifteen, to the Hereditary Prince of Württemberg. The King rejected his sister's advances in November 1782, saying that he intended none of his daughters to leave home before they were seventeen. He later ignored the Duchess's riposte, 'Your princesses must be very different from all other girls, if they did not feel themselves unfortunate not to be established.' The Princess Royal turned seventeen in September 1783, but her father made no plans to interrupt her round of education 'reasonable occupation' and entertainment with her sisters in England.

Details of that round follow from the correspondence that Princess Augusta struck up with her brother William in Hanover: 'We walk for two hours of a morning and our instructions last from eleven till two. Then I have an hour's English reading from three to four and sometimes go out with Mama,' wrote Princess Augusta on 6 November 1783. One imagines her sucking her pen and thinking what next to say. Inspiration came: 'We went the other day to Baron Alvensleben [the Hanoverian Minister at the Court of St James's] at Ham Common who gave us a very handsome breakfast. From thence we went to Hampton Court Palace, which I think very fine. Last Thursday we went to Kew, and we drove around Richmond Garden, where there are great alterations for the better. We always go to town with Papa and Mama, and then go to the drawing room and the play. Sometimes we play at cards in the evening, sometimes work, and draw.' But Princess Augusta's letter was not finished. William had sent her a 'pin' or brooch bearing a 'shade' or silhouette of his profile, Augusta had sent him some of her hair. 'I cannot help once more thanking you for your dear little shade which

I love being your gift and being yourself. You cannot have more love for my hair as you are so good to say you have than me for this pin.'

Given time and practice, Princess Augusta would become an excellent and reliable source of family news. But the Queen did not now encourage her daughters to write to their brother. 'Their mornings are so taken up with their different masters,' she wrote to William in February 1784, 'that unless they make use of every moment, they hardly can find time for writing letters.' And the Queen wrote to William of a promised gift: 'I shall be glad to have your picture, but give me leave to advise you that your income is not that of your elder brothers.'

William, for all his sisters' good wishes, was failing to reap the advantage of the courses in Hanover which his father had hoped would teach him to become a useful officer. His governor, General Budé, commented on the Prince's 'great hauteur … extremely good opinion of himself' and 'lightness of character. All he hears in praise of his brother [Frederick] excites his jealousy, not his emulation.' And a passion William developed for the daughter of his uncle Charles of Mecklenburg, 'Lolo' or Charlotte, ended with that Princess, on Queen Charlotte's advice, being despatched to her maternal grandmother in Darmstadt to evade the importunate Prince.

The elder princesses at home revelled in William's attention, the Princess Royal writing on 30 March 1784: 'I wish that the air balloon earrings that you sent me could transport me through the air, that I might see you and Frederick, and that after having spent a few hours with you, I might return in the same way.' Princess Augusta hoped, too, and for the same reason, that 'the air balloons were brought to perfection'. But she added, not knowing how famous one Vincenzo Lunardi would become within a few months, 'I don't think that will be very soon.'

But, like her father, the Princess Royal was incapable of writing without casting a damper on things, and her letter had begun, 'My dear William, I am very happy to hear from the Queen that you pass your time pleasantly at Hanover. Perhaps you may wonder that, knowing this, I should be selfish enough to wish you to be here, where you would certainly not enjoy as many amusements. But, however, there are some pleasures which I do not doubt would afford you much satisfaction.' And she wrote of Mary and Sophia attending the opera for the first time the night before, 'they were very much entertained with the dancing'.

While the schoolroom – with its lessons in history, geography and needlework – was still the usual province of the younger princesses Mary and Sophia, the three eldest were much with their parents. Their 'instructions' came more and more often from art masters and music masters, and from those among them who had some speciality or 'fancy work' to offer – painting on velvet, etching, sculpting in wax or in clay, and even 'blotting', the art of creating landscapes out of ink blots. And of course the princesses continued to draw – daily, nightly. Mrs Delany attests to them sitting with their mother round a large table after dinner with 'books, work, pencils and paper' spread out. The Queen, always on the alert for dispelling 'oisiveté' or leisure time with 'reasonable occupation' for her daughters, made sure that they pursued these studies as seriously as though their lives depended on it.

The Princess Royal etched her image of Prince Octavius in 1785, copying a copy by her drawing master, John Gresse, of the Gainsborough original. In addition, she made five etchings of languorous ladies, entitled *The Five Senses*, which she copied from drawings by Benjamin West, apparently made for her specific use. (West was everywhere at Windsor – even called in, when the Queen and her daughters were with their hairdresser at the Lodge, to give his opinion of the arrangement of jewels in their hair.) In the King's libraries in London, Kew and Windsor were remarkable sets of drawings by artists ranging from Leonardo da Vinci to Piazzetta, and even prints by John Hamilton Mortimer, who specialized in theatrical portrait heads. With this splendid resource to hand, and with the guidance of John Gresse, the princesses copied the heads of philosophers, of peasant children and of turbaned Saracens. Princess Elizabeth even produced much later a portrait of Lady Charlotte Finch, copying the image from an earlier miniature.

Just as at Kew, like their mother and the other ladies of the household, the princesses did not 'dress' till dinner at Windsor, but wore morning gowns. Thus on a visit to Bulstrode in 1783 all five princesses, and the other ladies of the party, wore 'white muslin polonaises, white chip hats, with white feathers'. The Queen alone was distinguished by a black hat and cloak. Cloaks and greatcoats were useful when the need came to broach the great outdoors, or even just the wind in the passages at Windsor. Even after the princesses had 'dressed', they did not always appear in splendour. On an evening visit in 1779 to Bulstrode they wore, like their mother and her ladies, 'blue tabby, with white satin puckered petticoats, with a blue border, and their heads quite low'. Mrs Delany noted on a visit to the Queen's Lodge in the autumn of 1783: 'All the royal family were dressed in a uniform for the demi-saison, of a violet blue armozine, with gauze aprons, etc.' The Queen was distinguished by 'the addition of a great many fine pearls'.

For high days and holidays, and for appearances in public – at Court, at the theatre, at the Ancient Music concerts of which the King and Queen were so fond – the princesses were dressed distinctively, either exactly alike or in the same dress in different colours. As early as the Princess Royal's thirteenth birthday, for instance, she was in 'deep orange or scarlet' – by candlelight, Mrs Delany could not distinguish which – with Princess Augusta in pink and Elizabeth in blue. In addition their dress generally referred to or replicated that of their mother's grander production.

Augusta wrote of attending five oratorios in Lent 1784 with her mother 'and once to see Mrs Abington the famous comic actress'. Dresses were needed for all such public occasions, as well as for Court appearances, and the Queen and her milliners in consultation at the Queen's House generally chose the cloth for the princesses. The princesses had their own part to play, choosing trimmings, painting fans and buying, with their pin money, cheap ornamental jewellery. But the Queen experienced financial woes, which she described to her brother Charles: 'My expenses with five daughters, of whom the oldest appear at Court and are always with us in public, require all the economy imaginable. A sum immense. Their masters, servants and wardrobes above all consume a considerable sum' – the last item, she estimated, between £1,500 and £2,000 pounds a quarter.

Although the King was to add £8,000 annually to the Queen's income of £50,000 beginning in August 1786, the following month she presented her Lord Chamberlain with a paper her Treasurer, Lord Guilford, had given her at the end of July, showing a shortfall of £11,000 to be paid. When the King enquired about these debts, the Lord Chamberlain 'told him it was likely to be worse rather than better as the Princesses grew up'. On Princess Mary and Sophia at that date the Queen reckoned to spend a thousand pounds each a year, and even on Princess Amelia, who was then just three, £500. Later Princess Mary was to confirm that she and Sophia had a thousand a year, but she added that her three elder sisters received double that sum. Where possible, the Queen kept the younger children in clothes made by country dressmakers, and their food was plain. But otherwise she appears to have made no economies. Her instinct was to give her children – and especially her elder daughters – the very best, particularly where their education was concerned.

The Queen found educational opportunities even where others saw only pleasure. At the theatre in 1783 the royal family thrilled – like the rest of the theatre-going public – to Mrs Sarah Siddons's displays of disdain and indignation in her great role as *The Mourning Bride*. 'It was worth the trouble of a day's journey to see her but walk down the stage,' wrote one admirer. But then the Queen summoned the tragedienne, as she had once summoned David Garrick, to give readings at the Queen's House. Mrs Siddons was too stately to feel much awe as she waited to perform in her sacque, hoop, double ruffles and lappets. She reasoned that she was in her natural element, as she had frequently 'personated' queens on the stage. But the appearance of the King on one occasion, pushing Amelia in her cane baby chair, and the child, released, showing an interest in the flowers at her bosom did help the situation. 'What a beautiful child. How I long to kiss her,' Mrs Siddons said aloud. But young Amelia had her own ideas, and 'instantly held her little hand out to be kissed, so early had she learnt the lessons of Royalty'.

Garrick too had been disconcerted by the royal family's lack of expression – and lack of applause – when he read to them, but Mrs Siddons was more confident. With queenly grace she wrote later, 'Their Majesties were the most gratifying of audiences, because the most marvellously attentive.' Her reward was to be appointed 'reading preceptress' to the princesses – she was, according to Mrs Papendiek, the diarist wife of a royal page, appointed to 'teach the two youngest princesses to read and enunciate' – although the post was 'without emolument'. At any rate, she read plays to the royal family on a regular basis at the Queen's House, and performances from Mrs Siddons at Windsor became an established treat for the princesses on their birthdays. The King and Queen generally commissioned the great actress, with scant regard for her art, to enact 'sentimental comedy'.

The three eldest princesses were becoming a familiar sight in public, in attendance on their parents – all 'uncommonly handsome, each in their different way', according to one observer: 'The Princess Royal for figure, the Princess Augusta for countenance, and the Princess Elizabeth for face.' The Prince of Wales had the royal favourite, Gainsborough, paint them as a group this summer – for the salon at his new palace, Carlton House. When exhibited by the painter, the princesses' polite faces – masks of impersonal beauty – fascinated the public. Only their different accessories hinted at different personalities and tastes. The public could choose to see the images again when Gainsborough showed the painting two years later. The Carlton House salon, for which the painting was destined, was not yet ready to receive either real-life or painted princesses.

The Prince of Wales was proving, like his brother William, a less than tractable son. At the general election in March 1784, when the Duchess of Devonshire famously kissed a butcher to secure his vote for the Whig candidate Charles James Fox, the young Prince gave a party to celebrate the victory that followed. An introduction to a Catholic widow, Maria Fitzherbert – an intimate of the Duchess of Devonshire – sealed the callow Prince's fate. He became obsessed, the plaything of his emotions – in which frustration predominated, when Mrs Fitzherbert refused to become his mistress. He had taken no notice of expense in rebuilding Carlton House. In pursuing a Catholic with extravagant offers of marriage, as he now did, he took no notice of two distinct acts of Parliament which forbade any such activity.

Mrs Fitzherbert, with great good sense, paid little attention to the Prince's offers of marriage, until startled into consent after the frustrated Prince stabbed himself. The play-actor Prince so frightened his lady-love with groans and cosmetic pallor that she agreed to have a ring placed on her finger – the Duchess of Devonshire provided it. Next day Mrs Fitzherbert fled – and did not stop till she reached the comparative safety of Aix-la-Chapelle.

Mrs Fitzherbert was wise to depart. The ring-giving, though scarcely a contract of marriage, had come too close to an act – namely, the heir apparent's marriage to a Catholic and without his father's permission – which would have been illegal on two counts. Had the couple married, by the Act of Succession of 1689, which forbade the Prince's marriage to a Catholic, and by the 1772 Royal Marriages Act, which invalidated his marriage without his father's permission, the Prince would have forfeited his place in the succession. As matters stood, no harm had come to the throne from the Prince's theatricals. But when, as he had to, he revealed his growing debts to his father, the King, who had heard all about his bedroom theatricals and was already furious with him, was disinclined to help. As a result of all this, the princesses saw little of their eldest brother at this time.

The King was barely more pleased with William, writing in August 1784 that, with thirteen children, he could not afford to pay any of the Prince's further debts. He despatched Prince Edward, a son of whom he had higher hopes, to join that paragon Prince Frederick in Hanover. With great economy the ship that took Edward across the North Sea to Hamburg in May 1785 found both Frederick – newly created Duke of York and Albany – and William waiting there. The Duke of York was to lead Edward into good ways at Hanover, reprobate William was to board the ship and set sail for the West Indies.

In their letters to their brothers abroad, the princesses did not mention a very cautious offer of marriage that was aired in the summer of 1785. Some at the Court of Denmark were eager to secure 'a Princess of England' as a bride for their cousin the Prince Royal of that important state, but they had heard at St Petersburg 'that the King of England would not consent to send any of the English princesses to Denmark'. Hugh Elliot, the British Minister at Copenhagen, joined in the intrigue with zest and journeyed to London in June expressly to discover the truth of this.

The Prince Royal was willing to break off 'other engagements' that were being considered in favour of an English bride, he announced. But the King was dismissive of the proposal: 'After the treatment my late sister received, no one in my house can be desirous of the alliance.' (The Crown Prince was, of course, the product of that unhappy marriage between King George III's sister Caroline and King Christian VII which had seen that Queen exiled and living out the last few years of a short life under her brother's protection in Germany.) The King firmly discouraged 'all negotiation ... till time may show to both Courts that it would be right to think of it', which would not be before the Prince Royal succeeded his father. But the proposal, and especially the Danish Court's apparent preference for Princess Augusta over her elder sister, caused a stir in the family circle. Even a year later, M. Guiffardière, who took liberties others did not dare to, made Princess Augusta blush with some teasing references to her imaginary fondness for the plays of a particular country, which, it emerged, was Denmark. 'How can you be such a fool!' was her response.

Princess Augusta was still happy at home with her sisters – and 'doted on' the company of her younger brothers Ernest, Augustus and Adolphus. Adolphus, benevolent if not blessed with brains, was a general favourite. Augustus, intelligent and bookish, had romantic aspirations to join the navy, although he suffered attacks of asthma. And handsome, boisterous Ernest was quite as entertaining and unmanageable as he had been as a child. The King arranged, rather than promoted, the education of these younger princes, just as the Queen did not lavish on the education and upbringing of the younger princesses the thought and care that she had given, and that she continued to give, despite their advancing ages, to that of their elders.

Prince Ernest was to claim of their life at Kew, 'we used to sup alone and be as lonely as monks'. But their preceptors were on the whole young and cheerful, and he exaggerated. Everyone in the royal household enjoyed the company of the younger princes, certain in the knowledge that they would soon be following their elder brothers abroad. Princess Augusta gives a flavour of the princesses' relationships with these younger brothers in an account she wrote of a visit in 1785 to Nuneham Courtenay, a magnificent country villa near Oxford and home of the Harcourts, one of the few 'fashionable' couples to hold key positions at Court.

The royal party, including the King and Queen, the three eldest princesses and Princes Ernest, Augustus and Adolphus with a tutor, set out in three chaises and a coach from Windsor at seven in the morning so as to be at Nuneham for breakfast. 'A very good one indeed!' commented

Augusta, 'and I think I was one of them who relished it the most, though I had eaten a sandwich before with the greatest appetite ...' That misdemeanour was 'my sisters' fault', Augusta wrote in exculpation, 'for they ordered that some might be put in the carriage'.

Only a day's visit was planned, but in the interval before dinner in the octagon room Lord Harcourt mentioned to the King that 'he had a private key of Christ Church Walk, and that he could see Oxford without the least trouble ... and that if his Majesty would like to make Nuneham his inn, it would make the owners of it very happy.' Princess Augusta reported her father's reply, 'Why, Lord Harcourt, it's very tempting,' and went on:

> Mamma, my brother, sister, and myself (not by far the least delighted of the family) kept our wishful eyes upon the King, who fixed his upon Mamma; and upon her saying, 'I will do as you please,' he said, 'Well, with all my heart let us stay'. During all this conversation, I think our countenances were so curiously ridiculous, and I don't doubt that our soliloquies were as much so, that anybody must have laughed if they had looked on us, without knowing why we looked 'so strange, so wondrous strange'. For my part, I know I could not refrain from saying, 'And O ye Ministers of Heaven protect me! For I shall be in despair if we do not stay.' However I was so completely happy when I found we did not go back till the next day, that my spirits rose mountains high in half a second. 'Thank you, my dear Lady Harcourt,' 'God bless you, Lord Harcourt, heaven preserve you both', 'You are the very best people in the Kingdom after Papa and Mamma'. These were the sayings for the rest of the day.

Princess Augusta's account of the royal children's conversation on the subject of the bedrooms in the fashionable mansion they were to inhabit is compelling.

> 'Dear Augustus' (said Ernest), 'think how amazing good of Lord Harcourt; he has promised me that I shall sleep alone. I have seen my room, it has a yellow damask bed. I have got a toilette too, with fine japan boxes on it. Beautiful Lady Jersey has that room when she is here. I suppose it is a great favour to let me have it; I fancy strangers in general are not allowed to sleep in it...'
>
> 'Say what you please' (says Augustus), 'Lord Harcourt has given me a much better room. I have got a fine view out of the window; and what signifies a damask bed when one has not a fine view. Besides, I am next room to Co Co [Lady Caroline Waldegrave]; and I shall knock against the wall and keep her awake all night.'
>
> (Adolphus), 'I suppose you none of you have seen my room, I have got a tent bed in it; I should have you dare speak against a tent bed. It puts me

in mind already that when I am an officer, and that I am encamped against an enemy, I shall have one then.'

'Well,' cries Princess Royal, 'mine is a charming room; the dear Duchess of Ancaster sleeps in it when she is here; I shall tell her of it when I see her. I am to take care of Augusta tonight, she sleeps in my dressing room.'

'Your dressing room, madam! Your nonsense,' said I, 'I think it the best room; for I can see into dear Lady Harcourt's passage, and maybe I shall see her in it tomorrow morning. Lord, how happy I am to get a little look of her whenever I can.'

'So we went on all day long,' concluded Princess Augusta, 'and I am sure we shall never hear the last of it, it was the most perfect thing that was ever known.'

The younger princesses had remained at Windsor during this foray under the eye of Mlle Charlotte Salomé de Montmollin, their new French governess, who had previously been briefly with the princesses' cousins, the Württemberg children. She was, according to a contemporary, 'one of the best and finest work-women to be met with', and taught Princess Mary and Princess Sophia, and in due course their sister Amelia, 'a thousand ingenious uses of the needle'. Among the accomplishments they accrued were fancy needlework, beadwork and the netting of silk purses. Miss Jane Gomm, a governess last employed in Prussia, who had been educated in St Petersburg, joined them in 1786 as English teacher, and supervised the rest of their education.

Princesses Mary and Sophia wrote letters in beginner's French to their father recounting their daily doings at Windsor, Sophia writing: 'I hope my cold gets better soon, because I do not dare to read with Mlle Montmollin, and that grieves me, because we read such nice things together.' Mary, too, reports on her sister Sophia's 'rhume' while giving an account of an evening at Mrs Delany's house in Windsor: 'We played dominoes and we were very well amused.'

Mrs Delany had been installed by the King and Queen this autumn in a house at Windsor cheek by jowl with the Queen's Lodge, and lived in a permanent daze at the condescension of the royal family who made a habit of stopping in unannounced to see her. The King, in particular, treated Mrs Delany's house as an extension of his own. But her house also served as a useful retreat in the evening for his youngest daughters. Mrs Delany records in her diary Princess Mary's good voice, and Sophia's softer tones, as they played and sang Handel's 'Hallelujah' chorus for her on one of these evenings. 'My dear papa,' Princess Sophia wrote again to the King in French,

... You will hear with pleasure that my dear Mary has had the best lesson she ever had in her life with Mademoiselle Montmollin and I am doing the same, because I do not want to fall behind. On the contrary I shall always try harder and harder, and what I like above all is the history of the Greeks. My dear Mary wants to write to Mama this evening for the first time. I wrote yesterday so today she has her turn. Believe me, my dear Papa, I shall always be your respectful daughter, Sophie.

The appetite for books that Mlle de Montmollin fostered in her charge was not to diminish. All her life, Princess Sophia was to be a voracious and adventurous reader in French and in English. Appropriately then she was the dedicatee of the best-selling children's book, *The Story of the Robins*, which Mrs Sarah Trimmer, a prime mover in the Sunday-school movement and daughter of George III's clerk of the works at Kew, published in 1786. But the younger princesses were not always studious. 'We had great pleasure yesterday in seeing our brothers,' Princess Sophia informed her father in a letter, 'we played at "poule" [a French card game] and greatly enjoyed ourselves.'

The younger princesses' letters to their parents show how much they lived apart from them, sometimes with the younger princes at Kew, often at the Lower Lodge at Windsor – usually with Princess Amelia and Che Che, or Mrs Cheveley, too. When the Queen arranged for Mrs Siddons to read at the Queen's Lodge in April 1785, it was for the benefit of her elder daughters. After John Adams, the first American Ambassador to Britain, had delivered his compliments and a bow on presentation to the Queen, and she had returned a curtsey, the Princess Royal and Princess Augusta, as well as the King and Queen, all spoke to him 'very obligingly'. A meeting in July of that year between the Queen and Mme de Genlis, whose books had so crucially guided the education of the elder princesses, did not lead the Queen to make any new experiments with her younger daughters' upbringing. There was much that was done on the model of their elder sisters' plan of education, and still more that was makeshift about the younger princesses' education.

These princesses were less disciplined than their elder sisters, as the history painter John Singleton Copley discovered when he embarked on an ambitious group portrait of the three children, complete with family pets. Years before, Johann Zoffany had painted a successful, if stiff, group of King, Queen and the elder princesses and princes in Van Dyck costume. Copley's experience was quite different. 'During the operation the children, the dogs, and the parrots became equally wearied,' wrote an observer. 'The persons who were appointed to attend them while sitting complained to the queen; the queen complained to the king and the king complained to Mr West, who had obtained the commission for Copley.' The artist contrived to finish the work and, charming and pouting in a baby carriage with a fringed parasol, Princess Amelia steals the show. But Copley had had enough. He returned to history painting, and never took on another portrait commission.

During an outbreak of whooping cough at Windsor in December 1785 which laid low all six princesses, and had attendants, physicians and parents running from one house to the other, Princess Mary, who was later to be very careful of her health, reported to her father, 'I cough much more than my sisters, but I hope things will go better.' In general, the princesses were in good health. Certainly Princess Elizabeth appeared so when, in front of Mrs Delany, the Queen made her daughter try on a pair of stays and rejected them as too small. The teenage Princess, mortified, insisted that they did fit, but her mother overruled her and sent for a larger pair.

Princess Elizabeth had seemed, if annoyed, in perfect health on this occasion. But a few days later Mrs Delany was concerned, as all at Windsor were. Elizabeth was suddenly extremely ill – she was diagnosed first 'with an inflammation on her lungs', and then with severe 'spasms'. Mrs Papendiek, the page's wife, wrote that it was a 'scrofulous abscess on her left side'. Her parents feared for her life, the images of Alfred and, in particular, of Octavius's sudden sickening in their minds, as well as the Dowager Princess of Wales's Gotha blood. The Princess was bled twice in forty-eight hours. At an early January conference, the London doctors did not know what else to suggest. The New Year's drawing room was abruptly cancelled, and it was thought that Elizabeth had only days to live. And then she recovered, to the bewilderment of her doctors, if to their relief.

Had the royal family but known it, there was calamitous news of a different kind in another quarter. The Prince had married Mrs Fitzherbert in December 1785, having prevailed on her to return from France and listen to his serious proposal that they marry secretly but legally, at least in the eyes of her Church. The deed was done in extreme secrecy at Mrs Fitzherbert's house in Park Street, Mayfair, on the 15th of that month, under cover of an evening party. Nevertheless, the news crept out, and within months a set of well-informed cartoons with titles such as *All for Love* and *Wife or No Wife*, informed an avid public of the ceremony.

After this clandestine marriage, Mrs Fitzherbert played the part of hostess at Carlton House, a house where, in Horace Walpole's opinion, every ornament was 'at a proper distance, not one too large, but all delicate and new' – and all in the French taste. 'How sick one shall be, after this chaste palace, of Mr Adam's gingerbread and sippets of embroidery,' wrote Walpole. The task of renovating and decorating the Prince's grandmother's house had been agreed by Parliament in 1784 at a figure of £30,000. Unfortunately, work on this palace of 'august simplicity' had to stop shortly after Mrs Fitzherbert became its mistress with costs running £220,000 over budget. The Prince had no funds, and his father refused to contribute.

Abandoning London life – and debt – for the moment, the Prince retired to the seaside at Brighton in 1786, where he lived quietly with Mrs Fitzherbert, and occupied himself making essential repairs to a small 'marine villa' – destined, many years and many, many thousands of pounds later, to become Brighton Pavilion, that fabulous tortured product of Eastern opulence and princely extravagance.

Meanwhile, although the sharp anxiety about Princess Elizabeth's health had decreased, she was so weak that she spent much of this same year – 1786 – at Kew. In January, Queen Charlotte wrote of her being struck by a 'new series of attacks'. And then again in August the Princess was at Kew, with Gouly attending her, and with Sir George Baker ministering to her. Her 'long illness' was never specifically diagnosed, but, involving spasms and supposedly a scrofulous abscess, it was probably tubercular in origin. The rumours that had circulated in the old Dowager Princess of Wales's life, that she had brought from her native Saxe-Gotha a 'king's evil' prevalent in that family – tuberculosis of the lungs – had been given weight not only by the deaths of her own children and by a mysterious illness the King suffered in 1765, but by the deaths of Prince Alfred and Prince Octavius. The royal family was by now widely held to have an 'hereditary weakness in the lungs' and several of the children had besides a well-developed tendency to violent spasms.

Elizabeth was not to be free from suffering entirely for another two years, and she was to write long afterwards in a Book of Common Prayer, 'This prayer book was given me by General Gouldsworthy in 1786, during my great illness, and has ever proved my truest and most comforting friend in all my distresses.' She also spoke feelingly of care administered by the General's sister Miss Gouldsworthy: 'She never was away from me any part of the day and she was so very good as to have a chaise longue brought into the room that she might sleep by me. I always loved her extremely, but my illnesses have made me love her and esteem her ten times more.'

Rumours later spread that during this time – and in a later year – Elizabeth gave birth to not one but two children, and that the father was a royal page called George Ramus, whom she married. William or 'Billy' Ramus, the most likely candidate, was page in several households at Kew

over a number of years, and there were others of his family in royal employment too, but no George. There seems no substance to the story which
includes the King being present at the wedding. It probably arose after one
of Billy's family was dismissed, and can itself be dismissed.

The year at Kew away from her family was in many ways formative for
this third Princess, this seventh child. Not only was Elizabeth away from her
elder sisters, but even her three noisy younger brothers, and the governors
and tutors who tried to control them, were no longer there. In July 1786
the three younger princes were ordered abroad by their father to the
University of Göttingen near Hanover, where they were to learn German
and pursue a military education. As a result Kew was a haven of peace, an
ideal place for steady study, and Princess Elizabeth always spoke with gratitude of the Smelts, with whom she spent a great deal of time there. Leonard
Smelt, the elder princes' former sub-governor, had settled at Kew, with his
wife following his resignation, and remained a royal favourite. He and his
wife encouraged Elizabeth in a 'course of reading' that occupied her for
much of the year. Moreover, she had Mr Smelt, a noted amateur artist, to
encourage her in her drawing. And the festoons of painted roses that decorate Queen Charlotte's teahouse in the grounds of Kew Gardens, by repute
the work of Princess Elizabeth, and the Hogarth prints varnished on its walls
may have been produced in this year away from ordinary occupations.

At the beginning of July 1786, with the departure of their brothers for
Göttingen, the princesses had a new correspondence to begin. Princess
Augusta wrote to Prince Augustus soon after he had set off, hoping that
the seasickness he had suffered would not make him give up his thoughts
of being a sailor. 'I beg if you are so good as to answer this letter that you
will let me have some account of Frederick and of Edward, for I shall be
more inclined to believe what you and your brothers say about him than
anybody else ...' She wanted to hear 'if you are pleased and happy at
Göttingen, in short every particular concerning you. You will think me
certainly mad to be so inquisitive but every little thing that happens to you
is most interesting to me. I forgot to tell you that Mrs Oaks has dressed us
some excellent spinach and I could not help mentioning it as I know she
is a great favourite of yours.'

The Princess Royal gave advice on how her brother could prevent the
tinnitus of which he complained:

> I wish that you could find some means to stop your ears for to prevent your
> hearing the variety of false sounds of which you complain. Perhaps custom
> may use you to them, but, if it has not that effect, I should advise your keep-
> ing a canary bird which will out-scream all the other noises. Pray in your

next letter let me know how you like German. I hope that when you have studied this language long enough for to understand what you read you will read Gellert. His works will do you and every body that reads them good. He is a favourite author of mine.

While their brothers began on an extensive curriculum, the Princess Royal turned to what really interested her this year, her expanding circle of female friends. She told Augustus: 'the Miss Howes are gone into the country, therefore I cannot give them their message that you send them. A fortnight ago I spent a charming evening with them. They left London the next day and I am afraid that we shall not meet for two months.' Besides Miss Mary and Miss Louisa, Lord Howe's daughters, there were other new female friends named by the Princess Royal in these letters. 'Lady Harriot Elliot [Lord Chatham's daughter, recently married and now expecting a baby] in her present situation cannot venture to come to Kew which prevents my having the pleasure to see her, but I hope that we shall meet in November, for she will then come to London and, I hope, be able to come frequently to the Queen's House.'

In the meantime, on 5 August 1786 the King appeared in his wife's dressing room at the Queen's House with an announcement that dumbfounded her and their two eldest daughters who were with her: 'Here I am safe and well as you see, but I have very narrowly escaped being stabbed.' Lady Harcourt received an account of what had prompted this declaration from her sister-in-law, Mrs Harcourt, who had the tale 'exactly and with a candour that does him honour' from the King. The King had alighted earlier that day at St James's, and made to take from a woman standing there a petition she held out to him. Upon which she drew a knife and tried to drive it through his side.

> He said that if he had not happened to have seen the woman preparing her petition, and from her eagerness kept his eyes fixed on her he could not have escaped, for she was close to him, and on her drawing the knife from the paper he stepped back. That she aimed a second blow, but was caught by the Guard, and a servant wrested the knife from her hand. It was a large servant's eating-knife with a horn handle, made sharp on both sides ... he is not sure whether it struck against him or not, but he thinks it did not. He said he called to them directly to take the knife from her but not to hurt the woman, for he was not hurt.

The would-be assassin, Margaret Nicolson, 'lived servant with Mrs Rice', Mrs Harcourt heard, and had 'left her ... from being wrong in her mind. She is so certainly on this subject, and Monro [Dr John

Monro, superintendent of the lunatic asylum known as Bedlam] declares her so.'

The thanks given for the King's escape included an address from the senate of Oxford University: 'upon the miraculous escape that he had of being murdered by that wicked mad woman', as the Princess Royal put it, 'who, if she had succeeded in her horrid attempt would have made us the most wretched family in the world. But providence who watches over all things was pleased most mercifully to preserve the life of the best of kings and of fathers.' Princess Augusta described to her brother Augustus the royal family's stay at Nuneham this year, which preceded the solemn ceremony at Oxford: 'I was particularly pleased with the sermon, which was preached by Lord Harcourt's chaplain Mr Hagget ... Good God! My dear Augustus how miserable how abject and how low should we have been thrown if ... we had had such an unheard of misfortune.'

Princess Elizabeth, upon recovery from her 'great illness', was filled with energy, and wrote in November 1786 to Augustus: 'Having been some length of time separated from all the family, as well as masters, I now must make up for the time I have been without them.' She had begun to learn the harpsichord, and wished to sing the praises of London now as well as Kew: 'never has a winter begun more delightfully for me than this one has. I trust in God it will continue so. The constant kindness and affection I receive from Papa and Mamma adds very greatly to it and all the amusements they can think of for us, we are always sure of having.' Still occupied with her studies, she wrote to Augustus, five months later, 'It has not been in my power to write for some time as the day passes very quickly with all my different employments. So that trying to perfect myself in everything, I hope, will plead my excuse which, if I did set about to do, must be very long.'

The Princess Royal was less contented. 'My dearest Augustus,' she wrote in the new year of 1787,

I have been very much mortified by a provoking rash, which prevented my being at the birthday. I had the last month worked very hard for to complete four fans and two muffs which were intended for that day. On the Monday I finished everything expecting with the rest of the family to go to London on the Tuesday but hélas, when I was a going to get up, I was so red that it would have been dangerous to have moved me. I therefore remained at Windsor, which I shall leave next Monday if no fresh misfortune prevents my going to London.

She took some comfort in the fact of 'several other young ladies who have been prevented going to the birthday, Lady Charlotte Bertie by a fever,

Lady Frances Bruce by a cold, Miss Howes by being at Bath. The eldest of them having a complaint in her stomach has been ordered to spend six weeks at those wells. I am very sorry for it, as it prevents my enjoying their company, particularly that of little Mary, who you know is a great friend of mine, and was that of poor Lady Harriot.' (Lady Harriot Elliot had, to the horror of the Princess Royal and friends – and as a warning that there were perils as well as pleasures consequent on marriage – recently, and very soon after her marriage, died in childbirth.)

She continued, in her old admonitory style: 'Pray, do you understand German enough yet to read plays? For if you do, that is the most likely way to make you learn to speak it tant bien que mal but however you must walk before one runs ... Pray give my love to my brothers and believe me your ever affectionate sister, Charlotte Augusta Matilda...'

'Since I wrote last, I have had the pleasure to spend many evenings with dear Miss Mary Howe,' the Princess Royal recorded soon after, 'who I think more charming than ever.' But Miss Howe was cast down. 'She is very low at the thoughts of parting from her sister, Miss Louisa, who is going to be married to Lord Altamont, an Irish peer of great fortune.' Princess Elizabeth, two months later, added to this picture of sisters parted by the demands of matrimony, not a future apparently in prospect for the princesses themselves: 'Louisa Howe is not as yet concluded with Lord Altamont, but will be soon. She is prettier than ever. Her sisters are miserable at the thought of parting with her, particularly Mary, who has always lived with her ever since she was born and constantly slept in the same room. But they have the pleasure of thinking that she will be perfectly happy, as everybody gives him the best of characters.'

Princess Augusta was the brothers' most faithful correspondent, giving them news of each other now that they were separated. She wrote to Prince Augustus at Göttingen in April 1787: 'I thank you for your pretty letter and in return send you a shade of your humble servant, which I fancy you will find like from the forehead to the upper lip. I kiss that, and then the chin is like, for I must say that I don't think that pouting lip like mine, though mine is nearly as thick as Edward's.' She added, having good information from Hanover, 'By the by I understand that Edward is grown quite a giant. If so, I hope he will never be a grenadier or else he will be quite a frightful sight. Pray send me your shade and I shall love it as much as your sketch, which I would not part with for the whole world. I hope you are still determined to go to sea. It is the finest profession in the world and you are made for it.' But for all her encouragement, Prince Augustus's severe asthma was to put an end to those dreams.

'I had a letter from dear William last week,' the newsletter went on.

He is at the island of Nevis in the West Indies. He says he is happy as the day is long and that the *Pegasus* is his whole and sole delight and pleasure. He has a little band of music that serves to make his ship's company dance, and he says, 'I doat to see my men happy.' Everybody speaks well of him and I believe him, as I always did, a very hearty good honest English tar, liking better a hammock than a bed and plain salt beef than all the fine dishes and luxury that townspeople fare upon. He always wears his uniform and curls, and yet looks as well dressed, and more of a man, than any of the fashion- able powder monkeys, and talks of affectation in a man as the one thing in the world that takes the same effect upon him as an emetic. God bless you my dear boy, believe me your affectionate sister and friend, Augusta Sophia. I have got so bad a headache, I can hardly see, so can write no more.

Augusta continued a fluent correspondent, sending off descriptions of scenes at home that would appeal to or interest her brothers, including an account of a royal doctor's lingering death after he attended her and her sisters for measles:

Poor Sir Richard Jebb lived just long enough to see us all in a recovering state, but was so ill when he attended us and so very weak, that he was very near dying at Windsor and was in that state when he left us, that he was obliged to lay on mattresses in his coach and to go through the park, as he could not bear the shaking of the stones. We did not see him for some days before he went away, he was so thoroughly adying. But as we were on the same floor, we heard constantly how he was. And nothing gave him any pleasure but when us sick ones either sent to enquire after him – or that the last people he attended were the King's children. For he loved nothing so much as Papa. He quitted Windsor on the Thursday and died the Tuesday after, much regretted by everybody who knew him.

The princesses' return to health coincided with the excitement of their brother Frederick's arrival at Windsor on 2 August 1787, after six years away in Germany. 'Joy to great Caesar!' wrote Princess Augusta. 'Our dear dear Frederick just arrived this afternoon when we were at dinner. I am overjoyed to see him! Quite quite drunk with joy and spirits but not spir- itual liquors.' While the reprobate Prince of Wales's birthday on 12 August went unmarked for the first time by cannon fire at Windsor, four days later the King and Queen gave a great ball there for his younger brother, the Duke of York. Princess Elizabeth for one enjoyed it so much that she wished to stay on, but 'as everyone went away I could not possibly stay to dance capers alone so I also returned to bed'. But all the King's pleasure in his second son's arrival in England and in his military successes abroad was to be swiftly spoilt by the alacrity with which he joined the Prince of Wales's parties of pleasure at Newmarket and elsewhere.

Augusta had another source of satisfaction. Her father this year permitted her to have a door broken through from her bedroom at Windsor to the little dressing room on the stair, so that she had two rooms. 'I have two nice bookcases on each side of the chimney and my harpsichord so that altogether I am more comfortably lodged than I can express.' She was learning the harpsichord, like her sister Elizabeth, with Charles Horn, a new music master. She enjoyed it so much that she had begun composing, and a minuet and a march were already to her credit. 'You see what an enemy to mankind luxury is. I have been seven years at Windsor with only one room, and now that I have two, I find the total impossibility of ever submitting to live in one again ... ' she wrote. There was a very 'neat' wallpaper in her new apartments and her friends had done many pretty drawings. But as she told her brother Augustus in August, the shade or silhouette he had just sent her had pride of place. It was 'hung up just over against where I now sit', she informed him, and she thought it 'very like ... I look at it as often as I come in and go out of my room and constantly when I am in it.'

News later that month that Prince Augustus was suffering from 'another attack' of his 'terrible complaint' – asthma – led his sister to write again: by way of cheering the invalid, she described a recent family outing to Hampton Court. 'We did not go into the old straight walks that are seen from the windows for they are like the oldest part of Kensington Garden, but we went to the maze or labyrinth ... It is certainly the most tantalizing thing I ever saw for I thought myself near out of it often. And then the shortest turn brought us far from the end of it. Old Toothacker the foreman is still there. I assure you he makes a very venerable appearance in the old gardens for now he has left off his wig and wears his own hair which is quite grey. It improves his looks very much.'

Royal joined in the chorus of pleasure at the Duke of York's return, but wrote less happily to Augustus of her lot, which included going to the Ancient Music concerts which specialized in Handel's music: 'I think that my dislike for music rather increases.' However, she continued to draw a great deal and looked on it as one of the most entertaining ways of employing herself. 'This summer my drawing has not gone on as well as usual, on account of my having been forbid during three months after the measles to apply my eyes to anything.' But she had now begun again and hoped to make up for lost time. 'Mama has been so good to me,' she wrote, 'that she has now taken Miss Meen, a flower painter, to instruct me till we leave the country in colouring flowers. I continue every Monday heads with Gresse. Indeed if I do not come on I must be wanting in capacity, for I have every advantage and therefore no excuse but my own stupidity if I do not improve.'

At least reports of the younger princes were better. 'The other young fry at Göttingen are the happiest of beings: they constantly write to me of the different entertainments they have both at Göttingen and Rotenburg,' Augusta told William. Prince Edward had been despatched, after two years in Germany, to university in Geneva with his governor, General Wangenheim. She heard that 'as he is exceedingly attached to his profession, he preferred Hanover', a centre of military excellence. 'But he soon made up his mind to quit it as it was by the King's desire.'

The princesses' daily round continued. Errands for their mother brought the elder princesses into the backstairs sphere, to be commented on by the author Fanny Burney, who for five years had a position as second keeper of the robes to their mother. The Princess Royal brought Miss Burney the Queen's snuffbox to be filled and 'took her leave with as elegant civility of manner as if parting with another Queen's daughter'. If the Princess Royal's regal manner disconcerted Miss Burney, she praised Princess Augusta, as did others, for the easy friendship she showed all the attendants in the house. When Miss Burney gave a workbox to Augusta's wardrobe woman to put on the Princess's table on her birthday, the courtier received her reward. She was led by none other than the Queen into Augusta's room, where the Princess was seated at her desk writing letters and was thanked for 'the little cadeau' in 'a manner the most pleasing'. Princess Elizabeth came asking Fanny's superior, Mrs Schwellenberg, to send a basin of tea into the music room for Mrs Delany, and all the attendants in the tearoom 'rose and retreated a few paces backward with looks of high respect'. But Miss Burney rather noticed Princess Elizabeth's bluntness – which she prided herself on: 'Miss Burney, I hope you hate snuff? I hope you do, for I hate it of all things in the world.'

Nor were the younger princesses exempt from Miss Burney's scrutiny. Princess Sophia, 'curtseying and colouring', came looking for her mother's dog Badine, which the Queen was accustomed to leave in Miss Burney's care while she was at early prayers. The author begged permission to carry the basket to the Queen's room, but Princess Sophia insisted on taking it herself, 'with a mingled modesty and good breeding extremely striking in one so young'. Princess Mary Miss Burney encountered earlier the same morning in the Queen's Lodge when the Princess was 'capering upstairs to her elder sisters'. She 'instantly stopped and then, coming up … enquired how her mother's attendant did, with all the elegant composure of a woman of maturest age'. Miss Burney had already seen how three-year-old Princess Amelia could be 'decorous and dignified when called upon to act *en princesse* to any strangers, as if conscious of her high rank, and the importance of condescendingly sustaining it'. Now she reflected: 'Amazingly well are all these children brought up. The readiness and the grace of their civilities, even in the midst of their happiest wildnesses and freedom, are at once a surprise and a charm to all who see them.' But the princesses were also trained to be civil when in the midst of their wildest misery.

Miss Burney saw how the Princess Royal performed many secretarial tasks for her mother, including, on one occasion, efficiently labelling a 'new collection of German books, just sent over', while keeping up a conversation. In the spring of 1788, the Queen wrote to her botanical mentor, Lord Bute, offering him 'a sight of the beginning of an herbal from impressions on black paper'. The Princess Royal and she together, she explained, meant to attempt this work of pressing plants – 'not only the leaves, but the flowers and stalks, which I believe had not been done before with any success'. With the summer before them, the Queen declared blithely, and with the assistance of Mr Aiton, the royal gardener, she hoped to take her specimens 'quite in the botanical way'.

With the encouragement of Sir Joseph Banks, director of the royal gardens at Kew, and of the head gardener there, the Princess Royal had already begun to copy, with growing skill, nature in the form of botanical specimens. She began with a wavering painting of a lily. Soon she was drawing parts of the flower as well, and writing Latin inscriptions beneath flower paintings, copied from the engravings illustrating John Miller's *An Illustration of the Sexual System of Linnaeus*. 'There is not a plant in the Gardens of Kew ... but has either been drawn by her gracious Majesty, or some of the Princesses, with a grace and skill which reflect on these personages the highest honour,' wrote the author of *The New Illustration of the Sexual System of Linnaeus* a decade later. Mrs Delany's astonishing flower mosaics cut from paper were a shining example. And no doubt Lady Charlotte Finch, who took up botany, and Miss Hamilton, who was an enthusiast, encouraged their work. Confirming royal interest in this new branch of the natural sciences, the Queen, in 1784, had accepted the dedication of Lord Bute's *Botanical Tables*: 'I am much flattered to be thought capable of so rational, beautiful and enticing amusement, and shall make it my endeavour not to forfeit his good opinion by pursuing this study steadily, as I am persuaded this botanical book will more than encourage me in doing it.'

She appointed the Princess Royal her assistant in the spring of 1788, as the Princess's 'natural steadiness never makes her shun labour or difficulty'. She added, 'I do not mean any reflection upon my other daughters, for all are equally amiable in their different ways.' But she and Royal had left the initial execution to M. Deluc: 'The specimens of plants being rather large, it requires more strength than my arms will afford, but in the smaller kind I constantly assist.'

How long would the Princess Royal be content to act as her mother's secretary and 'scholar'? She was never at her best in her mother's company. Furthermore one observer described her as 'born to preside', which she could certainly never do at her mother's Court. 'Timidity, with a want of affectionate confidence in the Queen's commands and wishes, always brought her Royal Highness forward as ill at ease,' wrote another courtier, 'while out of the Queen's presence she was a different being.' Mrs William Harcourt, Lady Harcourt's sister-in-law, added: 'Princess Royal has excessive sensibility, a great sense of injury, a great sense of her own situation, much timidity: without wanting resolution, she wants presence of mind, from the extreme quickness of her feelings, which show themselves in her perpetual blushes. She has excellent judgment, wonderful memory, and great application ... She is unjustly considered proud, and a peculiarity in her temper is mistaken for less sweetness.'

The King and Queen had both been against the matches proposed so far, but they could not hope to fend off for much longer the matter of the Princess Royal's marriage – not now that she was rising twenty-two. Her letters to her brothers make it clear that marriage was on her mind. Did her 'timidity' make it impossible for her to speak of it? Or was it an unmentionable subject?

All agree that, whatever the Princess Royal's relationship with her mother, she dearly loved her father, 'whom she resembled in many points of character, and she was his comfort and [his] darling'. On 3 July 1788 she therefore wrote from Windsor to her brother Augustus in a less collected state than usual to give a hurried family bulletin: they had stayed unusually long – a fortnight – at Kew, owing to an unexpected bilious attack that had seized the King.

> My dear Augustus by this time knows how ill our dear papa has been. His complaint was very disagreeable and indeed alarming for the time that it lasted – the spasm beginning at three in the morning, and continuing till eight o'clock in the evening. He is, thank God, perfectly recovered, but is advised by Sir George Baker to drink the Cheltenham waters, which are particularly good for all bilious complaints. We are to go to Cheltenham on

the twelfth. Lord Fauconberg has lent papa his house. Lady Weymouth, Mr Digby and Colonel Gwynne are to be of the party, also Miss Planta and Miss Burney. Mary, Sophia and Amelia are to remain at Kew during our absence with all those that belong to them.

The Queen wrote a supplementary letter to Prince Augustus the next day, ascribing her husband's 'violent attacks' to 'the dryness and heat of the season … everybody has been troubled by this complaint …'. More on her mind was the farmers' and country gentlemen's anxieties about the harvest in these arid conditions – and for once with reason, as she suggested. 'Providentially' an abundance of rain had come in good time, and 'everything bears a prosperous and plentiful aspect'.

She could not have been more wrong. The kingdom was about to be plunged into chaos and confusion. But in an excellent frame of mind the small royal party, as described by the Princess Royal, set off for Cheltenham and in good hope that the King would soon be fully recovered. The patient himself, unperturbed by his ailment, had no doubt, he wrote to Prince Augustus, 'that the efficacy of the waters which are not unlike those of Pyrmont, the salubrity of the air, the change of scene, privation of long conversations at St James's and, above all, the exercise of riding and good mutton will do what may be at present wanting'. And the King too was to be proved wrong.

6

Fear

⁓

'NEVER DID SCHOOLBOYS enjoy their holidays equal to what we have done,' wrote the Queen after the July 1788 visit to Cheltenham. 'The King went there without any guards,' which pleased the local people. 'At various times have they thrown out that he was better guarded without troops walking among his subjects whose hearts were ready to defend him ...'

Lord Fauconberg's house, with a charming view of the Malvern Hills, had so few rooms that, even with only a skeleton staff accompanying the King and Queen and their elder daughters, Miss Planta had to take her tea with Miss Burney on a landing. All arrangements were rustic. When Miss Burney, plagued by illness, consulted an apothecary brought in to dose the Princess Royal for influenza, he thought mightily before suggesting a saline draught. On a visit days later to Worcester the Princess Royal divided the orgeat she had been given for her own influenza, and put half by Miss Burney's bed.

The royal family strolled 'on the walks', and bought fairings and novelties which they distributed among their ladies and sent home to the younger princesses. At first, such was the curiosity of the local inhabitants about their royal visitors, the crowd around Lord Fauconberg's house was 'one head', as, on the way, every town had 'seemed all face'. But the extravagances of the initial welcome died down, and there was little to do in the little spa once the invalids of the party had walked at six in the morning across a couple of fields and an orchard to the wells to take their daily dose.

The King informed Sir George Baker in London that his bilious complaint was lessening, and enquired what that daily dose should be. Baker wrote, 'no one except the drinker can possibly determine it. It is in general experienced to be a weak purgative.' Baker conceived that a pint drunk every morning would act on the bowels sufficiently, but if the King wished to drink more, he would not object unless sleepiness or headache followed. He did beg, however, that the King should not take strong exercise.

Fatigue, when taking the waters, was counter-productive, as it heated the constitution.

The King heeded Sir George to the extent of not riding his usual thirty miles a day. Instead, he embarked with his wife and daughters on a series of exhausting days out. Having written ahead to the Prince of Wales's former tutor Dr Hurd, now Bishop of Worcester, with warning of his intention to attend the Three Choirs Festival and visit the china manufactory there, the King with his womenfolk meanwhile surveyed the model jail and hospital at Gloucester, where an enormous crowd surrounded them. They travelled to Stroud, where they inspected every stage of the process for making jackets at a clothing manufactory. And they visited, in addition, various seats of the nobility. At Lord Coventry's house, Croome Court, the princesses sat stiff on stools with no backs, provided for them at the specific request of Lord Harcourt. But the formality of the visit abated when some young farmers, having found their way into Lord Coventry's cellar, clambered into the King's coach and sat there, despite remonstrances from coachman and postilions. The King, it was known, had a great fondness for the 'harmless sportings' of country people, and no disciplinary action ensued.

One of the King's preoccupations at Cheltenham was a promised visit from his second son Prince Frederick, Duke of York. The Duke was loath to leave Oatlands, the house near Weybridge on which he had just taken a lease. But the King was determined, and at last the Duke relented. Elated, the King was next concerned to have his son near at hand, but there was literally not a room to spare in the Fauconberg house. The King solved that difficulty by buying a sturdy timber house that stood on the outskirts of the town, and having it dismantled and re-erected on Lord Fauconberg's land. (He also caused a well to be dug in his host's garden, averring the quality of the water there to be infinitely superior to that in the celebrated wells a few miles off.) Unfortunately, for all the King's energy, the Duke stayed only one night, pressure of business forcing him to fly off again – in the direction of Newmarket races. For male companionship, the King instead took to raising his equerries from their beds at six in the morning with a holler.

The stay at Cheltenham was punctuated by the arrival of letters from Princess Mary and Princess Sophia at Kew, and even from Princess Amelia, who turned five there on 7 August. While the King and his daughters were taking the waters under Sir George Baker's direction, the doctor had another patient at Kew. Princess Mary had developed a 'tumour' in her arm, and Mr Charles Hawkins – Caesar's son and Pennell's nephew, who had become the King's Serjeant-Surgeon on his father's death two years before – had to operate. Princess Sophia wrote to her father in French, to thank him for a 'charmante' present, and to add, 'Amélie est enchantée de son joli cadeau ... Le bras de ma chère Marie continue d'être toujours le même et grâce à dieu elle ne souffre pas beaucoup.'

Princess Mary wrote, too, describing her sufferings from her arm, or rather from the 'part swelled up to my shoulder'. 'How happy I was when I awoke to receive your kind letter and the beautiful present you were so good to send me. Amelia was so delighted to hear there was something for her,' she continued, 'that she came upon my bed to receive it, and means to wear it today.'

Princess Amelia made a sprawling attempt at a signature to a letter to her father this same day, which an attendant – probably Miss Gouldsworthy – acting as scribe and coach for the flood of information she had to give, wrote for her. 'My dear Papa,' the letter ran, 'I am very much obliged to you for the very pretty belt, and I am to wear it today when I dress. Pray give my duty to Mama, I hope you are quite well after the waters. Pray give my love to my sisters, and I hope when they come back that they will be very well. Minny [Princess Mary] feels pain when she puts on [the] poultice, I always do hold her hand ... Pray tell Augusta and Elizabeth, I intend to write to them very soon, so I do to Princess Royal. Lady Ely and Mrs Bonfoy come today. My dear Papa I am your affectionate daughter Amelia.'

Sophia wrote again, in English this time. 'My dear Papa, I am very much obliged to you for the charming letter you was so good as to write me, and for the charming descriptions it contains.' (The royal party was now at Worcester staying with Bishop Hurd for the choral festival.) She was very happy to hear that one Lady Reid had made acquaintance with General Gouldsworthy – Gouly's brother and the King's equerry – and she expected 'to hear in a short time that he is gone to make her a visit'. Gouly desired her to send her duty to him 'and is very much flattered at your remembrance of her'. But the burden of Sophia's letter was excitement. Princess Mary still being *hors de combat* following her operation, the younger sister had received permission to attend one of the children's balls that were held in private houses, at which boys and girls practised their dance steps in forgiving company. 'I am very much obliged to you, my dear Papa, for letting me go to the ball and my dear Mary is so good as to say that she is very glad I am. Mr Hawkins has given her leave to come down stairs which you may suppose makes me very happy.'

Unfortunately, this promising letter alone survives from the Princess's progress into adolescence. Princess Sophia, favourite charge of many of her governesses and attendants, a girl who stirred an elderly Lord Melbourne to speak of her charms in youth – 'he always thought Princess Sophia, when young, though very pretty, very like a gypsy', he said – can only be glimpsed through the eyes of others until November 1790, when, at the age of thirteen, she writes a small and somewhat secretive hand.

Princess Mary wrote two days later from Kew to thank her father for another letter. 'Indeed I do not see anything extraordinary in my behaviour in being glad that Sophia should go to the ball,' the elder sister wrote priggishly, 'for I think it is only what I ought to have done.' It was Princess Amelia's fifth birthday that day and, although she missed her parents, Mary told them, the little girl was 'vastly pleased' with the presents they sent, and 'laughed exceedingly' at the nutmeg grater in the shape of a wooden shoe the King sent – surely a souvenir of the Cheltenham 'walks'.

The royal sisters and parents were reunited at Kew in mid-August, and the yearly round began again with a ball at Windsor on the 29th for the Duke of York, and a drawing room in London two days later, new clothes for the King and Queen's wedding anniversary on 8 September, and new clothes again on the 22nd, for Coronation Day. Princess Augusta promised, in a letter she wrote to her brother Augustus, a long account of 'that most blessed of spots, Cheltenham' in her next. But this letter was dedicated to her regret on hearing he had been so ill, and her relief at knowing that he was recovered.

> I hope, my dearest, that you will take proper care of yourself ... And that you will not be displeased with me when I ask you if you take exercise enough. For you know how much you used to be out in the air when you was in dear old England. I thought that phrase of 'old England' would make you laugh and that is, added to air and exercise, what I shall next recommend by way of a restorative. A little mirth, even in an illness, makes one feel better, and I am very sure that, if I was with you two or three days talking over old stories and telling you several new ones that have passed since you are gone, that you would soon pick up your good looks and spirits.

Princess Royal's letter to poor asthmatic Augustus was, if sincere, decidedly more sombre:

> perhaps this very illness ... is a great blessing, since it has confirmed all the good principles that have been instilled into you, and made you see the comfort that religion fills the soul with, when we have reason to believe that all other comfort will soon be withdrawn from us. Indeed, my dear brother, every day convinces me more and more of the truth and comforts of religion. For never does anything vex or really afflict me that, if I have recourse to prayer, I do not instantly feel relieved, being convinced that my father, which is in heaven, knows what is best for me and only afflicts me for wise purposes.

Recommending her dear Augustus, with his 'serious turn of mind', to read 'a German book, that I am very fond of, which is Haller's letters to his daughter', the Princess turned to news of a concert, which was to be held at the Castle on her birthday. 'We were to have had a great entertainment, as Mrs Siddons was to have read a comedy, but alas she has leave of absence from the managers, and is some hundred miles from London for a month. Therefore it would have been quite cruel to have sent for her.' The Princess Royal would 'at least try to keep awake during that evening, which will indeed be something new for me to do at harmony. I am afraid that you will not have a very great opinion of me from this confession, as in general a love of music to distraction runs through our family, of which I alone am deprived. Pray, my dear Augustus, do not love me less for my want of ear, and consider that music is almost the only thing that we differ about. In drawing we are both artists and I hope by the next messenger to send you a proof that I have not lost my time since my return from Cheltenham.'

Princess Elizabeth joined in the correspondence, rather rushed: 'You have not heard as yet, I suppose, that Lord Carmarthen is going to be married to Miss Anguish – everybody gives her the best of characters. Mrs Fox [Lady Charlotte Finch's niece and the princesses' friend] was brought to bed last Saturday of a daughter. Lady Louisa Clayton [Lady Charlotte's sister] was with her at Plymouth. Now my dear, Adieu, believe me affectionately yrs Eliza. My best love to Ernest and Adolphus I will write soon to both of them.'

Although the Queen was in playful mood on her eldest daughter's birthday, instructing Miss Burney to 'bring down the two "Michaelmas geese"' – Miss Gouldsworthy's birthday falling on the 29th as well as the Princess Royal's – the evening concert was a lugubrious affair, lasting from eight until midnight with an interval for tea. Fischer the oboist played once; the rest of the performance, according to Lord Ailesbury the Queen's Chamberlain, was 'very indifferent, particularly the Windsor singers'. But the King was cheerful, 'and continued to talk with satisfaction of his Worcestershire tour, and to think that Cheltenham had been of use to him'.

The Princess Royal was happy with her birthday presents, which she described to her brother Augustus: 'Mama gave me a beautiful watch and chain of green enamel set with pearls. Prince of Wales a diamond hoop ring, and Frederick a blue enamel ring with a large diamond in the middle and set round with smaller ones.' But she was less satisfied on another topic. One by one, her friends, and even the ladies who had attended her and her sisters, were marrying and having children. Mary Hamilton had married

Mr Dickenson. Lady Caroline Waldegrave was now affianced to Lord Cardigan, while she, the Princess Royal, had only dancing partners – and those chosen for her by Lord Ailesbury. When the ball was over she accompanied her parents back to the Upper Lodge, at the age of twenty-two nowhere nearer her objective of 'settling'.

The next princess due to celebrate a birthday was Sophia, who would be eleven on 3 November. But between the Princess Royal's birthday concert and that day, the dull regularity of the royal family's routine was to be overturned. Sophia's birthday – and still more her sister Augusta's birthday on the 8th – would be days for anxiety and fear rather than celebration, and the close harmony which ruled the King and Queen's lives together shattered. Nor would the princesses' relationships with their parents ever be the same again.

It began in the week of 16 October 1788. The King, aged fifty, complained of a rash on his arm, and showed it to his daughter Elizabeth, who told Lady Harcourt that 'it looked very red and in great weals, as if it had been scourged with cords'. The Princess advised her father to take care, but he proceeded with his normal punishing routine. On the Wednesday, he took only a cup of coffee and dry biscuit for breakfast, as it was a levee day, and, after having no dinner, ate only pears at supper at the Hanoverian Minister's. The following morning, Thursday, he walked around Kew and Richmond gardens in the morning dew, then failed to change his stockings, only pulling off his wet boots before driving into town with the Queen and princesses. He was afraid he would make them late, for dressing for the drawing room.

That night at Kew he became very ill. At 1 a.m. the Queen ran out of her apartments, 'in great alarm, in her shift, or with very little clothes'. As the pages attempted to 'retire', she ordered them to go for Mr David Dundas, apothecary at Richmond. He came forty minutes later and revived the King, who in turn sent for Sir George Baker. His note, inscribed '7.25 a.m.', informed Baker that he had had a 'spasmodic bilious attack'. The King was suffering acute pain in the pit of his stomach, which was shooting from side to side and into his back, making breathing difficult. He told his doctor that 'of late he had been much tormented in the night by a cramp in the muscles of his legs, and that he had suffered much from the rheumatism, which … made him lame'.

The King did not get better quickly. In fact, his legs swelled after he took the senna that Sir George prescribed. The royal family's return to Windsor was delayed, as he was still feverish. And indeed it was not till the morning of 21 October that the King, although he had had a bad night's rest, wrote that he felt able to see Mr Pitt, his Prime Minister. With amazement, Pitt received a private note from Sir George Baker, saying that the King was in a state 'nearly bordering on delirium'. William Grenville, a member of Pitt's Cabinet, wrote equally confidentially to his brother the Marquis of Buckingham on 23 October 1788: 'a part of the K's disorder is an agitation and flurry of spirits which hardly gives him any rest'. And at Kew itself Princess Augusta was employed by the Queen on the 23rd, in extreme secrecy, to beg Sir George not to permit the King to leave Kew and attend his normal round in London until he was fully recovered: 'Mama desires you would express it not as hers but as a wish of your own.'

The King meanwhile wrote to his son Augustus on the 24th, informing him that the spasm in his stomach that he had suffered on the 16th, 'with the consequences of removing it', had left him too ill to write earlier, but he was going to St James's that day, to show he was not as ill as some had believed – though he added that he would 'certainly have for the rest of my life a flannel clothing next to my skin'. He was more concerned about Augustus's poor health at Göttingen than his own, and with preparations to send his son south to the milder climate of Nice for the winter.

At the levee that day at St James's, which the King did indeed attend, his swollen legs, wrapped in flannel, appalled more people than his presence reassured. Prime Minister Pitt noted what the King himself named his 'bodily stiffness'. Two days later, William Grenville thought the King's appearance at the levee 'an effort beyond his strength, but made with a view to putting an end to the stories that were circulated with much industry. He has, however, considerably weakened himself by it ...' And Grenville hinted that 'The present situation is sufficiently embarrassing; but if it turns out ill, all sense of personal inconvenience, mortification, or disappointment, will, I fear, be lost in considerations of infinitely greater moment.' But a veil of silence had fallen over the King's health. Following the levee he had travelled to Windsor where he spent the anniversary of his accession, 25 October, generally a joyful occasion, with his family. Unfortunately, the King was not at all well. When his coach drew up at the door of the Queen's Lodge and the King saw his four younger daughters waiting there, he had a hysteric fit. Later, Miss Burney saw him by chance, and he spoke with 'a rapidity, a hoarseness of voice, a volubility, an earnestness – a vehemence ...' She wrote: 'it startled me inexpressibly'.

The King seemed to have lost all power over himself. At Sunday Matins in St George's Chapel, he started up, as the sermon was to begin, 'embraced the Queen and Princesses, and then burst into tears'. He said to Princess

Elizabeth, '"You know what it is to be nervous but was you ever so bad as this?" With great presence of mind, she answered, "Yes",' and he became calmer. The scene took place in the royal pew close to the altar, so no one else witnessed it. But the King was undoubtedly very ill, of which he was aware. Once back at Windsor he had said to his equerry General Gouldsworthy, 'I return to you a poor old man, weak in body and in mind.' And during these days, sitting in a chaise with the Queen, he listened to her stating her belief that God did not try his servants beyond their capacity. 'Then you are prepared for the worst,' he said, with a hand encircling her waist.

Sir George Baker reassured the Queen that the King was not as ill as he seemed. Bringing in the King's favourite Windsor physician, Dr William Heberden, as his partner, Baker counselled putting a blister on the King's head with his wig to be worn over it. But the princesses watched with horror as their father's hold on his world crumbled. The meals at which he had been so punctual lay waiting for him now. The Queen was distracted. Yet no one dared to call a halt to the King's activities. With mottled skin and swollen legs, rapid and hoarse in his speech, he became a frightening figure. He took his daughter Augusta and then the Princess Royal out in his carriage for airings, and told them quite unexpectedly of plans he was formulating for their more or less immediate marriages in Germany. He would take them to Hanover in the summer, he said, and make his Court there as gay as possible, attracting all the young princes of Germany. He regretted that he had not made matches for them as yet: he had been held back only by the 'pain the idea of parting from them' had caused him. He would be happy with such choices as they themselves should make, if they did not make mésalliances. The extent of their husbands' territories was as nothing besides his wish for their happiness. And there was much more ...

It was what the Princess Royal had wished for, but stated under these circumstances – and told rapidly, hoarsely, excitedly – these plans could only upset her and her sister. 'Though there was nothing improper in what he said,' wrote Lady Harcourt, 'yet he spoke with a degree of eagerness and rapidity that was distressing to the Princesses.' The Princess Royal came in from the airing on which she had heard of these plans for her future and gave the Queen what Fanny Burney took to be a good account of the episode. But the Princess spoke in German, which she was well aware Miss Burney did not know.

Officially the King's illness was a rheumatic complaint and, in the doctors' words, 'it appears now as if everything has thrown itself upon his nerves, which has given him a very violent degree of agitation which noth-

The Princess Royal, as a sleeping baby, with her mother, Queen Charlotte.
The Queen, although elegant, was sallow, and the child inherited her glorious
complexion from her father, George III

The White House at Kew. The central building in the royal estate on the Thames, where the daughters of George III spent much of their childhood

Royal family al fresco. Baby Elizabeth reaches for her mother from the arms of royal governess, Lady Charlotte Finch, while the Queen, with the Princess Royal at her knee, restrains the princesses' elder brother William

Augusta and Elizabeth, wearing caps, at play with their younger brothers in 'frocks'. Up till the age of seven the daughters and sons of George III shared nursery and education

The princesses' London home, the Queen's House in the Mall, and birthplace of all but
one of George III and Queen Charlotte's fifteen children

George III wearing the 'Windsor' uniform and standing before an 'improved' Windsor Castle. The King and his family were the first of the Hanoverians to live in the ancient royal stronghold

Royal crocodile at Windsor, with the youngest children, in the arms of governesses, at its head, and their elders behind, in pairs. The princesses' attendants complained bitterly of the heat and fatigue of these public processions

Princess Elizabeth, aged twelve. One of a set of gold-framed ovals of the royal family that George III commissioned from Gainsborough

ing but rest and quiet will remove'. But neither the royal family nor the household at Kew was convinced, and London was full of strange reports. Miss Burney at Windsor wrote on 3 November: 'we are all here in a most uneasy state. The King is better and worse so frequently, and changes so daily, backwards and forwards, that everything is to be apprehended if his nerves are not quieted.' The Queen burst into tears when Miss Burney was with her, but more often closeted herself with Gouly, to ask how her brother found the King. 'Sometimes she walks up and down the room without uttering a word, but shaking her head frequently and in evident distress and irresolution ...'

'The Queen is almost overpowered with some secret terror,' Miss Burney wrote. The drawing room on the 4th was put off, 'all the house uneasy and alarmed'. The following day the King went out with the Princess Royal for another airing, 'all smiling benignity', but he badgered the postilions with contradictory orders and got in and out of the carriage twice. In conversation with Sir George Baker the King's speech was 'very unconnected and desultory'. A man of rigorous punctuality, the King kept dinner waiting, deferred coffee and the evening concert till well past their appointed times, and did not go to bed before two in the morning. He spoke of going to Hanover when he got well. But would he ever get well?

The mounting anxiety at Windsor came to a head on the evening of the 5th. At dinner that night at the Queen's Lodge, where the King and Queen and princesses were joined by the Prince of Wales and the Duke of York, the King was in a terrible way. He had no longer the least command over either his body or his tongue. 'His eyes', the Queen later told Lady Harcourt, 'she could compare to nothing but black-currant jelly. The veins in his face were swelled, the sound of his voice was dreadful. He often spoke till he was exhausted and the moment he could recover his breath, he began again, while the foam ran out of his mouth.'

Somehow the awful meal was got through, while the King, speaking without stopping, praised the Duke of York and forgave the Prince of Wales. The company, according to Lady Harcourt, was 'drowned in tears'. The King at one point – the conversation turning to murder – seized the Prince of Wales by the collar out of his chair and threw the corpulent young man across the room. The Queen, as soon as she could, left the table and made for her room where she fell into strong hysterics, Lady Elizabeth Waldegrave comforting her. While the King followed her there, the Prince of Wales in the eating room burst into tears and was only prevented – he believed – from fainting when Princess Elizabeth rubbed his temples 'with Hungary water'. The King's physical symptoms were now subsidiary to his symptoms of mental disturbance. Members of the royal family and of the royal household who gave accounts of this dreadful dinner spoke of the King's 'delirium'. Sir George Baker went further. The King was 'under an entire alienation of mind', he wrote in his diary.

While the household were still ignorant of the exact events in the eating room, the atmosphere throughout the Queen's Lodge was highly charged. 'A stillness the most uncommon reigned,' wrote Fanny Burney. '... Nobody stirred; not a voice was heard; not a step, not a motion ... there seemed a strangeness in the house most extraordinary.' In the apartment where ladies of the household customarily dined and dispensed tea to those equerries not in waiting, all was mystery. No equerries came, and Miss Burney and Miss Planta sat without talking. The former was 'shocked' at she scarcely knew what; the latter 'seemed to know too much for speech'. Confirmation that something was afoot came with news that the evening concert had been cancelled and the musicians ordered away, But when the Queen's reader Mme de la Fite came from Princess Elizabeth they were no better informed. She had found the Princess 'very miserable' but unconfiding.

The royal family's private drama had shifted to the King and Queen's apartments. The King, on being told that the Queen was unwell, said he would take care of her himself, then insisted on removing her to the drawing room. Here he made a sort of bed out of one of the sofas for her to lie on, and then placed Princess Royal, Princess Augusta and Princess Elizabeth round it. With all the candles except two put out, the unhappy woman and her daughters were forced to remain in this funerary arrangement while the King talked fondly and deliriously on.

When the time came to retire for the night, the King eventually agreed to move into the dressing room next door to the bedroom he shared with the Queen, on being told that she was really ill. And ill indeed she was. From this evening on, the princesses saw their mother crushed, despairing and unwilling to take any sort of lead. For thirty years she had played the queen consort with all her might, bearing child after child, organizing childcare and education, managing household and Court life, dispensing charity and encouraging the arts. Now, with her husband 'under an entire alienation of mind', the Queen wilted.

While the princesses went to their rooms upstairs, the Queen sat upright in her bed, with Miss Gouldsworthy on a chair at her side, and listened to the King next door as he talked without stopping. Once he came into the room and pulled back the curtains to check, with a candle held to her face, that she was really there. 'Gouly,' he said, addressing his daughters' governess of fifteen years, '... they said the King was ill, he was not ill; but now the Queen is ill, he is ill too.' He stayed half an hour. In the morning the Queen was still trembling from the anticipation of another such visit, but still desperate to hear, through the door, what the King was saying and to judge his mental state. 'I am nervous,' the 'poor exhausted voice' cried out. 'I am not ill, but I am nervous: if you would know what is the matter with me, I am nervous.'

What was the matter with the King? The question plagued the doctors – for now there were three. In the night, Sir George Baker, feeling unwell – or unable to attempt alone a diagnosis of such a portentous illness – sent for fashionable Sir Richard Warren, a favourite in the Whig households of London. He had no more special knowledge or experience of cases of mental illness than Sir George, but he was the Prince of Wales's own physician. The King refused to see Warren when he arrived, and Warren had to base his diagnosis of the case on what he could glean by listening through the door. He pronounced the King's life to be in the utmost danger, and declared that 'the seizure upon the brain was so violent, that if he did live, there was little reason to hope that his intellects would be restored'.

This statement overwhelmed the Prince of Wales as much as his mother and sisters. If his father was unfit to rule, as seemed the case, then the Prince or the Queen were the obvious candidates for regent. If the King died – and he seemed, leaving aside his mental impairment, all at once mortally weak and debilitated – then the Prince automatically became king. Leaving aside his filial feeling for the King – and the Prince was decidedly tender-hearted – he had reason to exult privately at the opportunities presented to him. Not the least of his concerns for the last few years had been the pressing need to clear his debts, or at least to receive a larger annual grant. Chief among the opponents to this project had been William Pitt. As regent – or as king – the Prince could at a stroke dismiss Pitt, call Charles James Fox and the Whigs into office, and name his sum. Although he was genuinely moved by his father's plight, the Prince waited with growing excitement to see whether he would maintain his state of delirium, sink further, or recover. The doctors, deeply uncomfortable at the idea of diagnosing insanity or something resembling it in a monarch who might then recover, called in a third consultant, Dr Henry Revell Reynolds, to help them in their deliberations.

The Queen – the other obvious candidate for regent – wanted none of it. She had settled into a modest suite of rooms far removed from the anteroom where the King continued to babble. There she cried aloud, 'What will become of me! What will become of me!' (As Miss Burney, who said she could never forget 'their desponding sound', averred, the words 'implied such complicated apprehensions'.) The Queen recommended leaving all arrangements to the Lord Chancellor. The question of a regency she appeared to regard as none of her business, and likewise she seemed to have no faith in the doctors' ability to cure her husband, apparently regarding his death as inevitable – and insupportable. The princesses were almost more alarmed by their mother's staying in bed all day – an unheard-of occurrence – than they were by their father's plight. She received them, dressed in a dimity chemise that served her as dressing-gown and a close gauze cap, and the princesses, confronted with her in this unfamiliar condition, struggled, 'from a habit that is become a second nature', to repress all outward grief.

In Lower Lodge, Mlle de Montmollin, Miss Gouldsworthy and Miss Gomm – with Lady Charlotte Finch as overseer – kept the younger princesses busy. Five-year-old Amelia was impervious to adult fears. Mary and Sophia ate their dinners like good little girls, but the future looked very black.

On 6 November, the Prince of Wales and Duke of York spent the night with a selection of gentlemen and attendants on an arrangement of chairs and sofas placed in the antechamber next door to where the King paced and talked. At one point he entered the room before the pages could stop him, apparently with the intention of going to the Queen. Distinguishing his sons in the darkness by the stars on their coats, he asked what they did there, and could only be persuaded by the use of some force to return to his room.

At Windsor on the 7th, Mr Pitt learned details from the Prince of the King's conversation and behaviour over the past few days, showing the 'derangement' of his mind. To substantiate the Prince's opinion, the three doctors, Baker, Warren and Reynolds, were then called in to give their opinion. 'His Majesty's understanding is at present so affected', they said, that there did not appear to them 'any interval, in which any act that he could do, could properly be considered as done with a consciousness and understanding of what it was about'.

They spoke of the 'disorder' either being 'locally fixed on the brain', in which case they anticipated it being permanent and life-threatening, or then again not life-threatening. Or it might be a case of 'a translation of a disorder from one part to another'. They might be able to remove it, but then it might 'attack some part where it might be dangerous to life'. They concluded their desperate ramblings with the more intelligible statement 'That on the whole there was more ground to fear than to hope, and more reason to apprehend durable insanity than death.' Later that day, the Prince wrote more coherently still that the King was now 'in infinitely a more dangerous state than he has hitherto been, having no recollection whatever'. The Duke of York came out from the King's room to look over the shoulder of one Court reporter, the Prince's 'creature' Jack Willett Payne, and bid him say that the King's situation was every moment becoming worse. His pulse was weaker and weaker and the doctors believed it was impossible for him to survive long. 'All articulation even seems to be at an end with the poor King,' Payne wrote, two hours later. The monarch was in a 'most determined frenzy'; poultices, or 'cataplasms', had been applied to his feet, and 'strong fomentations' had been used without effect. The general agreement was that, if the King did not recover within twenty-four hours, all was over.

It was Princess Augusta's twentieth birthday on 8 November, a day when it had been intended that Mrs Siddons should read a play before a large company. The birthday passed instead largely unremarked. With tears her birthday present from her mother was offered. The Queen had wondered whether it was right to give it in the circumstances. With tears, Princess Augusta received it, and made a silent curtsey.

But the King recovered his physical health, at least, within twelve hours, passing a bowel movement and perspiring heavily, after which he fell into a profound sleep at midnight on the 9th. He woke within hours, with no fever, but his case was hardly better, for, according to Payne, he awoke 'with all the gestures and ravings of the most confirmed maniac, and a new noise, in imitation of the howling of a dog'. He did not have a lucid interval through the night, according to the Duke of York, who sat up with him. He raved all next day on the theme of religion, and of his being inspired, and also of Dr Heberden and of the Trinity and of the Queen. A new horror dawned, that the King would be permanently insane, yet healthy.

During these anxious days, the Prince remained at Windsor in his apartments in the Castle. He sent an urgent message to Charles James Fox in France, begging him to return, but he was not otherwise politically active. He confided his own plans for the future to no one, unless to his brother York. His creature Jack Willett Payne was not so reticent, and he had appeared at the Whig bastion, Brooks's Club, and gave vivid imitations of the King in his distress, mimicking his spasmodic gestures and revealing that he 'howled like a monkey'. As late as the end of October it had been given out that the King was unable to attend the weekly levees and drawing rooms because he was 'dropsical'. Few believed that, odd rumours having circulated about his behaviour in Cheltenham. It was whispered that his attack at Kew had been delirium, or even 'alienation'. But Payne's account, from inside the Castle itself, was of a mania on a different scale.★

Several courtiers, in a desperate attempt to reduce the damage, and to the derision of Whig Society, announced that they had suffered a period of insanity themselves with no lasting effects. 'You see how I am now,' a very sane Lord Fauconberg offered, after revealing that he had had a strait waist-coat on for a week once upon a time. But the floodgates of gossip were opened with Payne's contribution. One Whig, 'Fish' Crawfurd, writing to the Duchess of Devonshire, was sure of the King's case: 'the humour to which his whole family is subject has fallen on his brain, and ... nothing will save him except an eruption upon his skin'. In some parts of the country, the King's near-death calcified into confident reports of his actual death, mourning was prescribed in the newspapers, and tributes paid to him.

Far from dying, the King had found a new lease of life. He was still alive, and gaining strength physically. But on the night of Tuesday, 11 November 'the ramblings continued', equerry Robert Fulke Greville recorded, 'and were more wild than before, amounting alas to an almost total suspension of reason'. 'No sleep this night,' he added wearily. 'The talking incessant throughout.'

The Prince of Wales now 'took the government of the house into his own hands'. All was done and only done by his orders. His sisters passed all their time with their mother, who 'lived entirely in her two new rooms, and spent the whole day in patient sorrow and retirement'. The princesses did not go for walks, they did not ride, they did not even go to church. They lived in an atmosphere of whispers and silence and dread. News came from the King's room that he was talking much, and with great hurry and agitation, of 'Eton College, of the boys rowing, etc'. He complained of burning, perspired violently, and called to have the windows opened. By the evening he was turbulent and rambling, and at three in the morning he had 'a violent struggle, jerking very strongly with his arms and legs'. He had not slept for twenty-nine hours. The only edict to emerge from the Queen's rooms was that the Archbishop of Canterbury should 'issue out public prayers for the poor King, for all the churches'. John Moore, the Archbishop, accordingly produced a moving prayer, and Fanny Burney went to St George's Chapel that Sunday to hear it read.

★The King's agonizing abdominal pain and his mania were almost certainly both symptoms of an acute attack of porphyria, a hereditary metabolic disorder which was then unknown to medical science.

The elder princesses were anguished by their father's state. One morning he attempted to jump out of the window, and in his loquacity did not hesitate to reveal various state secrets to anyone in the vicinity. But he was quieter, too, and arranged his watches and conversed rationally and ate bread and butter and drank tea with relish. His daughters accepted it all and hoped that the care of his poor jumbled mind and weakened frame would result in his recovery. However, as the days went by a new source of tension at Windsor developed. As he waited for Fox to return and direct affairs, the Prince began to be less amenable to the wishes of his mother and less moved by the plight of his father.

Members of the Whig leadership – Lord Minto, the Duke of Portland and especially Richard Brinsley Sheridan – made contact with the Prince and argued for action. The Whig doctor Sir Richard Warren pronounced the King's recovery in doubt, and, prophesying a period of years during which the King would be incapable of conducting public business, or indeed of attending Parliament, urged a regency. The King himself was aware in his clouded mind of this possibility and had informed his doctors that he lived under 'an absolute government, no, a republic, for there are three of you'. He begged them, when they had resolved something, to tell him of it, and he would give his order. 'But let not these pages', said the humiliated monarch, 'say to the King, "You must and must not".' The other doctors differed with Warren and predicted the King would recover, thus pleasing the administration and putting in doubt the need for a regency. The King believed that he had recovered already, and asked General Gouldsworthy to go to Eton and obtain a holiday for the boys to celebrate his return to life. Gouldsworthy was also to prepare the Queen for the firing of the guns at noon, and to order Handel's Dettingen Te Deum in church.

Attempts were made to check the King's ceaseless flow of words – he spoke on the 17th for nineteen hours, and not surprisingly developed a catch in his throat – and even to shave him, which he had resisted. But, after being shaved on one side, he rose and would not allow the operation to continue. As he had not been shaved for a fortnight the effect was bizarre. 'Cabal flourishes,' Lord Sheffield wrote. Yet the cause of the caballing was not melancholy but rather gay. The King talked for sixteen hours on 21 November, until the doctors set him to writing to divert him, when he made notes on *Don Quixote*. 'He fancies London is drowned, and orders his yacht to go there,' Sheffield continued. 'He took Sir George Baker's wig, flung it in his face, threw him on his back, and told him he might stargaze. Sir George is rather afraid of him. In one of his soliloquies he said, "I hate nobody. Why should anyone hate me?" Recollecting a little, he added, "I beg pardon, I do hate the Marquis of Buckingham."'

As Fox returned from France and the Houses of Parliament adjourned for a fortnight, to resume business in December with a debate over the regency, the Prince was elated, his sisters desperately unhappy.

During the afternoon of 24 November there was a flurry of movement within the walled garden that lay behind the Queen's Lodge at Windsor. And now into the garden, emerging into the walled space and moving down the sloping ground in the direction of the trees and shade at the other end, came a hesitant band of princesses. Their father's doctors, at their wits' end to know how to deal with an unprecedented royal malady, had that morning in conference had an idea: 'they thought they would try what effect the letting him see his children in the garden would have'. The forlorn hope was that the deranged King, looking on from a window, would gather strength from the mere sight of the daughters for whom he pined in his confinement.

Despite the doctors' determination to try 'the effect', the King had become agitated at the prospect earlier in the day, and had endeavoured to forbid the scheme. 'No, I cannot bear it; no, let it be put off till evening, I shall be more able to see them then,' he begged. But the doctors were adamant, and outside the girls now trooped to take part in the experiment. For a moment all was still on the lawn. The younger princesses were unaware of the watcher at the window. And then, startled, they looked up. There was their father struggling at the windows, making efforts to open them, gesticulating at his daughters and banging in frustration on the pane. But how could this be their father, this pale and haggard man wearing a nightgown and nightcap in the middle of the day? And now others appeared at the window, and the King was removed from sight.

While the elder girls were still shaken and the younger ones stared uncomprehendingly, a gentleman appeared with a request from their father that they would come nearer. They approached, and their father called to them through the window. But by now the Princess Royal was quite overcome, as was Princess Mary, on whom the horror of the scene had not been lost. The matter was decided when it appeared that Princess Elizabeth was about to faint. 'And, in truth,' Mrs William Harcourt wrote to Lady Harcourt, 'they all seemed more dead than alive when they got into the house.'

The princesses, love their brothers though they did, could not but feel uncomfortable about the growing hostility towards their father. As the Prince plunged deeper into politicking, he became more callous towards his father's suffering, and even took to mimicking him and his mania in public. The Duke of York, not to be outdone, mimicked his father to some friends in a coffeehouse. Their sisters did not know of these excesses, but of one turbulent act of the Prince's they had personal knowledge. At the end of November, the headstrong Prince drove his three elder sisters and Lady Charlotte Finch around Windsor one evening. Apparently he drove with such ferocity that countless lampposts were left shattered in his wake.

The King's close confinement at Windsor was coming to an end. 'There is not only no impropriety in removing him to Kew,' wrote the doctors on 27 November, 'but it is advisable.' They declared that a 'change of place and objects' would facilitate recovery, while 'air and exercise' was 'necessary for His Majesty's cure'. The princesses left for Kew with their mother and an assortment of ladies on the morning of 1 December 1788. They found the house – not usually used in winter – freezing and with their names daubed in chalk by the Prince of Wales on the various apartment doors. Fanny Burney was grateful for a rug which the Queen gave her, though it was a very small one. The news was then broken to the King that they had gone before, and he was invited to join them at Kew House. He had been anxious for the Princess Royal to accompany him in his carriage, which could not be allowed. He had lascivious thoughts in this state, although they generally focused on an elderly lady-in-waiting, Elizabeth, Lady Pembroke.

At first, George III refused to leave Windsor, his favourite residence, and became so frantic that 'they were obliged for the first time to threaten him with a strait waistcoat'. Finally, he hobbled past a mournful gauntlet of members of the household who lined the passage of the Queen's Lodge and, braving crowds who clung to the railings outside the house to see him go, departed back to the house at Kew where he had first been taken ill.

At Kew the King occupied a suite of three rooms, with two equerries or pages always in attendance. The Queen, as at Windsor, took a separate suite of rooms – in this case, a bedroom, the drawing room and the gallery on the first floor – and the princesses had their apartments beyond hers. The house, never designed for winter habitation, was so cold and draughty that the Vice Chamberlain, Colonel Digby, of his own accord and shuddering at the 'naked, cold boards', sent out to purchase not only carpets but sandbags for doors and windows to stop the wind whistling through the rooms. 'The wind which blew in upon these lovely Princesses', he declared, 'was enough to destroy them.' But they were made of sterner stuff. The dullness of those hours when the crocodiles of royal children snaked around the shrubberies and lawns seemed, to the princesses in retrospect, an idyll. Now at night, in company with the other inhabitants, they feared that they heard the King, though his apartments faced towards the garden and only the animals in the menagerie could hear his cries.

The day after Parliament met following the November adjournment to consider the King's case, seventy-year-old Dr Francis Willis joined the medical team at Kew. Willis was a 'mad-doctor', a physician who devoted himself to the care of the insane at an asylum at Gresford near Lincoln where, with his two sons John and Thomas, he supervised 800 lunatics. Queen Charlotte found Willis's arrival hard to bear. It announced to the world, as much as if the King had been placed in the care of Dr Monro of Bedlam, that he was now regarded as a madman. Moreover, with the Lincolnshire doctor – a rough man with none of the sophisticated manners of Baker or Warren – came the odious instrument then commonly employed in the management of the mentally ill, the strait waistcoat or straitjacket.

On 8 December, Willis, examined by a House of Commons committee keen to establish the prognosis of the King's case, declared that he had treated no fewer than thirty patients a year with mental disorder for twenty-eight years, and he believed, like Baker, that the King would recover. Three months was, in his estimation, the normal time of recovery for nine out of ten people who had been placed in his care. But he submitted that the King's cure might take a little longer. 'When His Majesty reflects upon an illness of this kind, it may depress his spirits, and retard his cure more than a common person.' At any rate, he saw no 'present signs of convalescence'.

Lady Charlotte Finch led the Queen and princesses in prayer on the Sunday. The prayers that they said so fervently seemed answered when the King appeared to be recovering day by day, and he even went for a walk in the Gardens. In another 'experiment', Mary and five-year-old Amelia were held up to a window so that he could see them. But 'when he had fixed his eyes upon them, he pulled off his hat, which in his agitation he flung one way, his gloves and cane another, and ran into the house' – where he burst into tears. Next day, 13 December, despite this scene, the King's incessant pleas to be allowed to see his 'Emily', Princess Amelia, were answered, and she was brought to him. (At night he rolled to and fro, reciting her name and asking her wraith how she could let him be subjected to these humiliations.) He 'pressed the Princess Emily in his arms who cried very much and was frightened'. In just a few weeks the King had become very thin, and he had grown a beard. Furthermore, his speech was rambling, though he tried to check it in front of his daughter, and even his movements were wild and abrupt. Princess Amelia was hurried away, and that night Dr

Willis took the decision to 'confine' the King for the first time in the strait waistcoat, and he remained in it till morning.

Four days later, the waistcoat was employed again. Dr Warren reported from Kew that the King had become 'very unquiet ... had no sleep during the whole night, and was confined by Dr Willis early this morning'. Dr Warren released the King from this confinement at ten in the morning, and left him eating breakfast but talking at the same time in 'a very disturbed manner – the whole resembling our worst Windsor days'. The following day the King was even more 'agitated and confused', Sir Lucas Pepys informed the Prince of Wales, 'perhaps from having been permitted to read *King Lear*, which he is now reading and talking about'. The King's mind, although turning on a few subjects only, was not deprived of guile or logic. When a doctor forbade him the play, he asked instead for Colman's *Works*, which he knew contained the original 'altered by Colman for the stage'.

Such was the King's fear of the straitjacket, so docile did he become when threatened with it, that the punitive measure came slowly to be regarded as having magical curative powers. Both family and politicians began to afford Dr Willis a certain respect, although the King remained wary of him. On one occasion when the monarch was castigating him for having left the Church to join the medical profession, Dr Willis objected: 'May it please your Majesty, Our Saviour went about healing the sick.' 'Yes,' replied the King, 'but I never heard that he had £700 a year for doing so.'

The case appeared hopeless. The King was 'good humoured, but as incoherent as ever', wrote Baker and Reynolds on Christmas Eve. He slept one hour or maybe two a night, and Christmas Day 1788 was a sad day at Kew. The bells of St Anne's Church on the Green clamoured, but none of the inhabitants of Kew House joined the congregation. A regency appeared inevitable.

And then, without warning, the King began to improve. He was 'in a much more composed and collected state yesterday than he has been hith-erto', the report of 28 December read. On New Year's Day, Dr Willis reported that the King had played several games of backgammon with him, and 'conversed in a collected, sensible manner yesterday evening for seven hours'. The King, he believed, was 'more himself than I have ever seen him since I have had the honour to attend His Majesty'. So the question now arose, and was to grow more urgent: was the King to be judged incapable of conducting public business and even of going down to Parliament because for an hour or two a day he was 'raging'? The Whigs deemed him incapable; Pitt and the Tories now believed, or affected to believe, that he was on the verge of a full recovery. Before the point could be resolved, the King worsened again.

The princesses themselves were spared the sight of their father after the failure of the November and December 'experiments' at Windsor and at Kew until he again seemed on his way to recovery. Visiting him on 17 January 1789, and seeing him play a game of piquet, the Queen judged – and Dr Willis agreed – that he had behaved with propriety. The following day the King's request to see his daughters was granted, although he had awoken 'never more disturbed in his life'. (After the princesses had gone, the King told one of his pages that the Queen had consented that 'Esther' – Lady Pembroke, the elderly lady of the Court for whom he had conceived a passion – should come to him.)

On another occasion the King called to Miss Burney whom he had spied in the garden, and when she desperately tried to get away he lumbered after her to try her nerves a little further. But while the King was still for hours at a time 'very deranged, his looks wild', he was also now rational for long periods. The manner of his greeting Royal and Princess Augusta and Princess Elizabeth on one occasion was affecting. He told them he had been reading *King Lear*, to which they could think of no response. But, the King continued good-humouredly, 'in some respects he was not like him, he had no Goneril, nor Regan, but only three Cordelias'.

In the course of February 1789 the Queen took twelve-year-old Princess Mary to visit her father. 'Twice,' she believed, 'he was going to say something wrong, but he put his hand upon his mouth, and said "hush" and then in a moment spoke properly'. Princess Sophia read to him from a *Life of Handel* later in the month. Although there were worse days, on 26 February the doctors announced: 'There appears this morning to be an entire cessation of His Majesty's illness'. And the following day the glorious news was posted on the railings of the Queen's House: 'A perfect recovery.' The prayer for that recovery, which the Queen had instigated, and which was read in all parish churches on Sunday mornings, had at last been answered. It was discontinued, and a prayer of thanksgiving substituted.

7

Hope

~

ESPERATION AND HUMILIATION were alike over, and in euphoric
mood the Queen and her daughters – all but Amelia – drove to
London with the Willises on 10 March 1789 to enjoy the illuminations
there that marked an end to the progress of the Regency Bill. Sir Joseph
Banks had illuminated his house with a transparency of Hygeia, and Sir
Nathaniel Wraxall described the city splendour: 'London displayed a blaze
of light from one extremity to the other; the illuminations extending ...
from Hampstead and Highgate to Clapham, and even as far as Tooting;
while the vast distance between Greenwich and Kensington presented the
same dazzling appearance.' The royal ladies stayed out till one in the morning, revelling in this public display of affection and support for the recovered King.

Meanwhile, at Kew Princess Amelia led her now benign father to a
window to observe the transparency – shining with representations of the
King, providence and health – and illuminations that the Queen had had
the painter Biagio Rebecca create in the Palace courtyard. She first knelt
to him to speak lines written, at the Queen's request, by Miss Burney and
ended, with appropriate action: 'The little bearer begs a kiss from dear Papa
for bringing this.'

Four days later, the King and Queen and the elder princesses travelled
to Windsor from Kew: 'All illness over, all fears removed, all sorrows light-
ened,' as Miss Burney put it. 'The King was so well as to go on horseback.'
And Mr Leonard Smelt, the Prince of Wales's former tutor and now
Deputy Ranger of Richmond Park, wrote some days later with satisfaction from Windsor to Miss Hamilton: 'Their majesties and the three eldest
princesses came here last Saturday, and the improvement in all their appearance is as rapid as the most attached and sanguine of their subjects could
wish it – The youngest princesses, I understand, come here in a few days
as, excepting the attendance on the drawing room (which the papers will
inform you is only for the Queen and the princesses), the residence will be
solely here for some time.'

Public anxiety and medical speculation about the 'family disease' that was held to have afflicted the King surfaced now in newspaper and magazine articles. And the King's own reactions to his illness, and sentiments about his imprisonment at Kew, emerged. He did not forget the impertinences served upon him and indeed the humiliations to which he had been subjected. Some months later, he 'talked of the coercion and asked, how could a man sleep with his arms pinioned in a strait waistcoat and his leg tied to the bedposts'. When the Archbishop of Canterbury and others counselled against the service of thanksgiving for his recovery in St Paul's Cathedral that the King demanded, he replied, 'My Lords, I have twice read over the evidence of my physicians on my case, and if I can stand that, I can stand anything.'

Were the princesses disturbed by the widespread understanding that their father's illness was hereditary, and alarmed that their prospects as brides in Europe might be affected? Time might tell soon enough, as the King's promise of November the year before to make his Court at Hanover 'gay' for aspirants to his daughters' hands had survived his illness. Or at least he threw out a 'hint' in March 1789 to Prince Augustus, back in Göttingen after wintering in the south, that he might receive a 'call to Hanover', as he contemplated a visit. And his equerry Robert Fulke Greville noted that the subject of a visit to Hanover was much on the King's mind.

His daughters, meanwhile, were celebrating the end of their own confinement. For the four months of her father's illness, the Princess Royal told her brother Augustus later in the year, she had written nothing. Princess Elizabeth told a friend she had seen nobody during those months. Now they more than made up for it, and on 15 April the Queen, Princess Augusta and Princess Elizabeth admired at the play an ingenious transparency featuring the King's recovery, while Mr Bannister, the leading actor, led the audience in six rousing choruses of 'God Save the King'. 'I always did and ever shall glory in being born an Englishwoman,' Elizabeth wrote to Augustus, as they prepared for the great Thanksgiving planned for the 23rd in St Paul's Cathedral.

On that day, the King and Queen drove down to the cathedral in splendour, in the gold coronation coach drawn by the famous Hanoverian Royal Creams. And the Queen, stalwart in her demonstrations of loyalty to the King here and at the drawing room, armoured herself with all the jewels the King had given her on marriage. Even Augusta, usually 'so careless as to what she was dressed in, provided only that she was dressed', and Elizabeth, 'usually anxious to forget that she was burdened by being great', dressed sumptuously for the service – in a prescribed uniform of imperial purple silk and patterned gold muslin over white satin. Only the Prince of Wales and Duke of York resisted the festive mood – they pointed at their parents in church, ate biscuits and burst into fits of laughter.

The King withstood the rigours at the Thanksgiving of the 'good old Te Deum and Jubilate' he had wanted. But many commented on his extreme loss of weight and altered appearance. His face, wrote one, was 'as sharp as a knife, and … his eyes appeared therefore more prominent than before … He appears extremely weak in his manner of walking.'

The princesses launched themselves into further celebrations – including rival fêtes given by the French and Spanish ambassadors – for their father's recovery. For a gala celebration on May Day at Windsor of which the Princess Royal was hostess, they painted dozens of fans with the motto 'Health to one and happiness to millions'. The Whigs boycotted a ball at White's, the government club in St James's, but the princesses and other ladies sparkled in a 'uniform' of white and gold with purple bandeaux inscribed with the now familiar acronym GSTK in diamonds. The Queen thought highly of this ball, 'as all the world was in accord and of the same opinion'. But her Whiggish eldest daughter was of a different view, and preferred Brooks's ball the other side of the street which *all* Society attended the following week.

The King, still frail, did not attend these festivities, and he found that his head for business was somewhat impaired. He wrote in May that 'lassitude and dejection' made it difficult for him to take quick or satisfactory decisions, and complained of fatigue: 'I am not yet able to copy my own papers.' Telling Pitt that he would attempt for the meanwhile only to 'supervise' his ministers' work, and relying on time to complete his cure, he continued to take bark, with tartar mixed in, as directed by Dr Willis, now back at his Gresford asylum. And he continued to make plans for Hanover.

The King missed a piquant encounter at the ball following his Birthday drawing room on 4 June between his daughter Princess Augusta and the Duke of Richmond's heir, Captain Charles Lennox, whom the Queen had pointedly invited – to her son the Prince of Wales's fury. A week earlier, Lennox had fought a duel with the Duke of York, his commanding officer in the Coldstreams, after publicly insulting his brother the Prince. 'The Duke of York had one of his curls shot off, and when the King and Queen heard it, the first showed very little and the second no emotion at all, and both said coldly that they believed it was more Fred's fault than Lennox's,' wrote an indignant Whig. The royal parents had not yet forgiven their eldest sons their behaviour during the King's illness.

When the dancing began, Lennox joined with his partner in the royal family's set. The Prince of Wales left that set with the Princess Royal, before the Captain could 'turn' her. But the Duke of York with Princess Augusta remained. And so Augusta danced with the dashing Captain, creating in the circumstances a sensation. Indeed, the manuscript of *The Claustral Palace*, a projected book detailing the romances of the princesses and for that reason suppressed, features handsome Captain Lennox as Augusta's earliest lover.

A rash of lovers and suitors and even a bridegroom might have followed for Augusta in Germany had the King stuck to his plan of setting up shop at Hanover. Unfortunately, Dr Willis counselled against the proposed trip as too strenuous, and advised the King to take 'a few dips in the sea' instead as a final guarantee of his health. This suggestion took root with the King, and led him – anxious that he might not 'entirely recover the vigour of mind and the inclination of taking the same active part' that he had done 'for above 28 years' without 'thorough relaxation' – to plump for Weymouth. This was a rather staid sea-bathing resort in Dorset, thirteen hours by coach from Windsor, where his brother Gloucester had a house.

And so early in the morning of 25 June 1789 the three elder princesses departed Windsor for Weymouth, part of a caravan of eight coaches loaded with luggage and supplies – Lyndhurst in the New Forest their first stop. The Queen, the princesses and all the ladies, noted Miss Burney, wore 'riding coats of the Windsor uniform, which is a new dress taken up this year', for their journey. The younger princesses – Mary, Sophia and Amelia – stayed behind at Lower Lodge at Windsor with Gouly and Lady Charlotte Finch.

En route to Weymouth the party stopped for a few days in the ancient New Forest in Hampshire. It was the King's first visit to this royal hunting ground, and at its entrance a local baronet, Sir Charles Mills, waited to present him with a brace of white greyhounds with silver collars. Hereditary Keepers of the Forest then escorted the royal party to the 'King's house' at Lyndhurst, where the Duke of Gloucester received them. Princess Augusta, at least, was greatly taken with the New Forest, and some years later fantasized to an admirer of living in a cottage there.

Miss Burney, another of the party, remembered instead the experience of passing through Salisbury further down the route to Weymouth: 'a city which with their Majesties, I could not see for people! It seemed to have neither houses nor walls, but to be composed solely of faces.' The roads, according to one observer, were 'lined with every human creature of every rank and every age, in chariots, coaches, carts, on horseback, upon asses ...

all come to see, and holler, and scream their true loyalty and joy … every field and every hedge was robbed of every flower to wreathe garlands and crowns'.

The princesses had their first sight of Weymouth Bay on 30 June, and of the harbour and the rolling hills of Portland Isle beyond, as they descended the steep hill leading to the town that curved round the bay. The Duke of Gloucester's house, Gloucester Lodge, lay at the end of that great sweep, the southernmost part of an elegant terrace of houses. Next door was the Royal Hotel, and immediately in front of the Lodge door was the public esplanade, leading to the shops, circulating library, theatre, assembly rooms and other appurtenances of a popular seaside resort. Across the esplanade lay the sands, the public bathing machines and the sea itself. Their lodgings, in short, commanded no privacy whatsoever.

For the princesses it was an entirely new sensation (except for Elizabeth, who as a ten-year-old had stayed at Eastbourne) to see and hear the sea, to walk on sand and, of course, to bathe – and all in public. Their father's first attempt at sea-bathing on 7 July was not without incident. The 'dipper' or bathing attendant who rolled the bathing machine containing the sovereign forward into the waves made the most of her moment. The windows of the machine were inscribed in gold 'God Save the King'. The dipper wore a plain flannel dress tucked up, and no shoes, but her girdle and a bandeau in her hair were both inscribed again 'God Save the King'. And there were others waiting to proclaim their loyalty. When the King descended from the back end of the machine to duck under the waves, a band of musicians, concealed in a machine alongside, appeared and struck up 'God save great George our King'.

The Queen wrote diplomatically a few days later, 'Elizabeth and Princess Royal go in the sea every other [day],' and her husband had been in twice – but had been stopped by a pain in his ear. The royal party also sailed, and the princesses were 'frequently' rowed about in 'ten oar cutters' manned by the oarsmen – 'very smart fine dressed men', wrote his mother the Queen – of their brother Prince William (who in May had been created Duke of Clarence and St Andrews). But the sailor Duke's ungrateful sister Princess Royal told her brother Augustus that she no more liked sailing than she liked music. On one occasion it took six hours to get back to Weymouth from Lulworth Castle, the winds were so strong.

The royal family did not slump on reaching home. Mrs Siddons, summering in Weymouth with her small son, was playing Mrs Towneley that night for their benefit. And so they went, 'such figures to the play as were never seen before', wrote Princess Royal, 'for we only stopped by Lady

Pembroke's to put a little powder in our hair and went in our cloth great-coats!' Mrs Siddons, for her part, rejoiced to see the King so well, she had never seen him so handsome in her life, 'and the Queen is absolutely fat', she wrote to Lady Harcourt at Nuneham Courtenay.

Royal's patriotic younger sister Augusta enjoyed the opportunities which sailing on the frigate *Southampton* afforded to learn about her father's navy. 'I went all over the ship ...' she wrote. 'The first ship I ever saw both inside and outside, the most enviable of things, and the most elegant and clean.' 'I am a famous sailor,' she boasted in late July. She had barely sat down, 'and stood while they hove the anchor, and while she tossed about in a capital manner. Lady Elizabeth Waldegrave was the only one of the ladies who was sick.' Entertained by everything to do with her new-found passion for the sea and the navy, Augusta told with gusto of the method by which she had ascended the side of the ship. It was a 'very mild and safe ceremony which bears a very false and ridiculous name ... whipping. It consists of being drawn up her [the ship's] body in a chair by two cables. It seems tremendous to the ear, but as I would trust my life in the hands of a British sailor, I thought myself as safe and secure as in my own room.'

Others across the Channel were less safe. In late July, the Queen at Weymouth heard that, following the storming of the Bastille on the 14th of that month, the French Minister of Finance, M. de Foulon, had escaped, but was then discovered. 'They intended to hang him, but the cord break-ing, they beheaded him.' She also heard that the Queen of France was to be forced to go with her son the Dauphin to give thanks for the Revolution at the Cathedral of Notre Dame. 'The poor unfortunate Princess, what a bitter potion is hers,' wrote Queen Charlotte with feeling. 'I pity both the King and her, and wish anxiously that they may meet with some well dis-posed people to extricate them hourly out of their great horrible distress.' The Queen was waiting for the morning post to know how the French Queen had gone through 'this mortifying scene'.

The *Magnificent*, a seventy-four-gun ship of the line, sailed round the coast to stand off Weymouth Harbour, and Mr Pitt drove down from London to discuss developments. But events in France did not deter the royal family from their programme of sailing and sightseeing, and in mid-August they embarked on an ambitious journey to Exeter, Saltram and Plymouth. Their appearance so far west caused many demonstrations of loyalty – not least from a housekeeper who gave a child a morsel of the King's dinner when he had done, and said 'she might talk on it when she was an old woman'. At Plymouth, the royal party was saluted by 'every ship, every fort, and every battery', and next day the King went to Saltram

Victualling Office and inspected supplies. More to the royal ladies' taste was a visit to Mount Edgcumbe, where the Queen cut a sprig of myrtle from a bush and said, 'I will carry this home, and plant it myself in a pot; I will send it home, and always have it, and always keep it.' When they departed downriver, their hostess, Lady Mount Edgcumbe, said the 200 boats on the river looked 'like a wood' with their oars lifted in acclamation of the monarch restored to health. And she was quite sure her husband George would not be satisfied till he had raised a triumphal arch to commemorate the visit.

The King was well, they could rejoice, but the Queen was much changed. Her hair till the previous year had been a light brown. During the King's illness it turned white. She was also so bowed and stooped with suffering that, according to several diaries, she had shrunk in height. And shortly after New Year 1789 was rung in so dolefully at frozen Kew, Fanny Burney recorded that the Queen had lost so much weight that her stays went twice round her. Mrs Siddons's testimony at Weymouth eight months later makes it appear that that phase of intense grief was over.

These were the physical effects. But the Queen's personality had undergone a sea change. The horror of those four months had struck deep. She had been drawn, for the first time ever, into politics. There she floundered, attempting desperately to follow the King's firm orders never to meddle with party. And she was attacked by the Whigs – her beloved Prince's party – whatever she did. Now she dreaded drawing rooms and balls and even her favourite concerts for fear of obloquy. On her return to Windsor and London from Weymouth in mid-September, she was most happy at home, when one of her daughters, or her readers, M. Deluc or Mme de la Fite, or even Miss Burney or M. de Guiffardière, read aloud to her, distracting her from the daily round.

Unfortunately, the King's lewd remarks during his illness about his preference for Lady Pembroke, his repeated expressions of dislike for the Queen and his assertions that she frightened all her children had also had their effect. The Queen was never again to be that gay centre of her intimate circle, that nimble correspondent of her brother and sons, the firm administrator of the several households. The humiliations and insults heaped upon her by the King, the hatred he had conceived for her, had confounded her. Even after he was declared officially well, for some time he harked after Lady Pembroke. The Queen developed a terrible temper that did indeed frighten her children, and she became capricious in her treatment of them and of her attendants.

Years before, Gainsborough had painted the Queen as he might a lively actress moving across the stage. Benjamin West had painted her again, the composed mother of thirteen children. When the young painter Thomas Lawrence painted her, on her return from Weymouth, she was inattentive and edgy. One of the princesses sat reading to her but did not pacify her mood. The artist proposed she wear jewels, perhaps to inject some much needed sparkle into the picture, and she refused. In the end she allowed her pearl bracelets with the King's portrait to be introduced into the sombre painting, but she would not model them herself, and her hairdresser's daughter was given that employment.

Princess Amelia, Lawrence's other sitter at Windsor in September 1789, was a good deal easier – until the painter gave two drawings to her elder sister and only one to her, 'The child ran to her father telling him in grief that she was sure that Mr Lawrence did not like her as much as her sisters ... The child's sorrow prevented the progress of the portrait for that day, and until the presents were equalized.'

Typical of the Queen's sombre mood were her continued reflections in July on the French Revolution, occasioned, she believed, by 'the want of principle and the neglect of all duty to God and man'. Again she wrote: 'I often think that this cannot be the 18th C in which we live at present, for ancient history can hardly produce anything more barbarous and cruel than our neighbours in France.' The Queen's reflections on the revolution in France were leaden, but at least it made her more cheerful about the future of England. It was a country with 'much to bless itself for', she declared, 'a king is returned to us, the illness has made him even more dear to his people ...'. And, telling her son Augustus that the King had resumed his levees, she ended: 'I have hopes that we shall soon come to go on in our old way.'

Princess Augusta's opinion of events across the Channel was more robust, if not more sophisticated, than her mother's. 'Poor France,' she wrote to Augustus, 'she's penny wise and pound foolish, I pity the King – I hate the nation – Indeed they aren't worth hating – I only hold them cheap.' She settled down, having greatly enjoyed her summer, to lessons on the harpsichord with her music master, Charles Horn, who had come to England as a valet seven years before. Now, as music master to the royal ladies he occupied a place last held by John Christian Bach, who had died in 1782.

The Princess Royal had been anxious to get back to her drawing lessons with Richard Livesay, Benjamin West's apprentice, when they were at Weymouth. Princess Elizabeth was drawn both to music and to art. The princesses were all busy when the New Year bells of 1790 tolled, as their new lady-in-waiting and friend Lady Mary Howe attests: 'You heard before of my having painted the Queen's parrot,' she wrote to her married sister Louisa in Ireland, 'it's beautifully framed and to be hung up in town. I have also given my handsomest nonpareil [or pink parakeet] to Princess Elizabeth. She is so very fond of birds that I was happy to give it up to her. She is painting Miss Moser's great flower piece most astonishingly well, and Princess Royal finishing a beautiful fan for the Queen, with feathers, flowers, insects, shells ... figures and landscapes, I think it one of the prettiest I ever saw.'

Miss Mary Moser, whose work Princess Elizabeth was copying, was the leading flower painter in England, and one of only two female artists who had been elected founder members of the Royal Academy. The Queen, busy both purchasing art and creating it, wrote to her brother Charles on 2 February asking for colours to paint botanical specimens in gouache – some prepared, some in powder form. 'I wish much for those from Nuremberg,' she wrote, 'as the place best known for this sort of painting.'

Princess Augusta wrote from Windsor to her brother Augustus at the end of February, 'Trifles and enormities both serve the world with a great deal of talk for a little time ... Emperors' deaths and a fashionable new carriage, a new dance at the Opera, the birth of an heir apparent to a Crown, the forwardness of the season and new gowns or caps or such like nonsense give topics of conversation, all in their turns, and one talks of each of them with the same avidity as were they all of the same consequence.' But she, like her other sisters, envied Augustus the travels he now undertook in search of better health.

Rome was 'of all places abroad the one I wish most to see', she told him when he reached the Holy City. When he was in Florence, Princess Augusta wrote that she longed to visit the Uffizi Gallery, and Princess Elizabeth chimed in: 'Of all places in the world Italy and Switzerland are the countries out of England I most wish to see.' By contrast, their own amusements recently had consisted in music at home and once a week music in Tottenham Court Road. And the Princess Royal wrote, 'I suppose that you now both read and speak Italian with ease, having had such a favourable opportunity of learning it and that language not being very difficult ... If you recollect the picture that Zoffany painted of the Tribune, I beg that you will let me know whether you think it like.' She knew that he had introduced paintings and objects from other rooms, but she wanted to know 'if in other particulars he has followed the original close'.

The King's recovery continued, and on 1 March Princess Augusta observed: 'He continues his old pursuits just as he formerly used to do, only that he has left off coursing. Therefore he has parted with his greyhounds to hunt hares with a very pretty pack of harriers he has just got.' But the King's thoughts of taking his daughters to his Electorate had faded with his return to the routine of government and recreation. Two months later the princesses' brother Edward didn't think their father at all likely to go to Hanover.

The King attended his Birthday this year, and his third daughter, Princess Elizabeth, yawned. 'A great many minuets were danced – indeed (entre nous) so many that when the country dances began, I was more inclined to sleep than to begin dancing again.' Another princess there, on the other hand, was alive with mortification. Unfortunately neither illness nor recuperation at their father's house had made the King – or Queen – soften towards the Gloucester children, as became clear when Princess Sophia Matilda of Gloucester made her debut on this occasion. The Princess was an odd sight to begin with. She was 'not dressed well in a very old fashioned style – her gown was very magnificent but the hair was dressed quite out of the fashion ... after her own direction', wrote an uncharitable relation. 'She herself has not the least idea of dress and she will not be guided by anyone else.' But then 'she was placed in a corner with Miss Dee [her governess] and Their Majesties just spoke to her as they would to any common person'.

Worse followed. The Gloucesters *père et fille* had to wait three-quarters of an hour in the ballroom, while the royal family ate dinner before the ball, a meal to which they had expected to be invited. When the ball opened, Sophia Matilda 'danced very well but nobody paid her the least respect, and after the King and Queen were gone she was treated quite as a common person and pushed about'. At last the Prince of Wales took pity on his cousin, and advised her to go home. Little though they knew it, the King and Queen's callous treatment of the Gloucester children was to rebound much later on one of their own.

Princess Augusta complained to her brother Augustus of the race days on Ascot Heath rather than of any ball: 'we were there for 5 hours which – added to another, half of which was spent in going and the other in coming home – we were cooped up six hours in a coach in hot and dusty weather ... you may suppose I was very agreeable company when I came home – for I was almost asleep, and amazingly cross that those horses lost, for whom I wished, so that I found it was charity not to wish for any one in particular'.

Prince Augustus, now aged seventeen, was pursuing his campaign, begun long before, of persuading his father to send him to sea as a midshipman: 'The fine and noble description of the British fleet, which are preparing [for war with Spain] have roused in me a double desire, which haunts me day and night … The blood of a British subject boils within me and I wish to be witness to what is going forward.' But it was not to be, as the Queen told the disappointed romantic. His health made it impractical.

Prince William, on the other hand, had rejoined the navy on promise of war against the Spanish, and was at anchor at Torbay, full of 'zeal for the sea service', as Princess Augusta told their brother Ernest. And she wrote to Augustus: 'Dear little Amelia has got through her inoculation remarkably well and quick – She has had no spots in her face and not altogether thirty about her body. I think her grown and looking better than she has done of a great while.' Her elder sister agreed: 'She [Amelia] is the most charming little girl that I ever saw, her understanding and quickness are astonishing for her age. If she grows up as she is at present, I shall be very much disappointed if both her and Sophia are not superior to most women.' The superior Sophia, who was reading Campe's *Kinder Bibliotheque*, had an artistic project in mind, fostered by the gift from her sister Mary of her 'picture'. 'My intention is to have a locket made of all my brothers and sisters' hair,' she wrote. And she was writing to all her five brothers abroad, to the Prince and Duke of York and to her sisters, for that purpose.

The previous summer Princess Royal had fretted at having got 'behind', during the visit to Weymouth, with her drawing: 'The time that I have lost which is dreadful this year … I did little or nothing.' Now she explained to her brother Augustus: 'I should have answered sooner, had I not been totally prevented doing anything by the Queen's furnishing two rooms at the house she has bought at Frogmore, and my painting with stencils the chairs for one of the rooms, and cutting out in paper several ornaments, which things could not be completed without time. On Amelia's birthday we breakfasted there.'

Queen Charlotte's purchase from a Mr Floyer of his rambling farmhouse with eleven rooms to a floor at Frogmore in the Home Park at Windsor was something of a surprise to all. But Lady Harcourt wrote an account of their first festivity there to her husband:

> We were all dressed beyond our usual morning dress before eight. We then went over to the chapel, returned to fetch the little princesses, and then proceeded to Frogmore. Pss Elizabeth (who had been there from 7 o'clock) met the Queen in the hall and presented her with a basket of flowers. Three of the rooms are made very pretty. The Princesses have painted the borders, not only for the papers, but for the curtains and chairs, upon white glazed linen. The servants' bell ropes, flower tubs, flower pots, and flower baskets are also of this manufactory, and filled with a profusion of oranges, limes, various plants, and ornamented with large swags of ribbons – vastly well.

Among all the babble of family news, there was one item in December 1790 of especial interest to King George III and Queen Charlotte's second daughter. 'We have just now a Prince of Württemberg here,' wrote Augusta's mother, 'who has served every campaign against the Turks. He seems a very amiable young man, religious, modest and agreeable. He is but 27 years old.' The Duchy of Württemberg was, like Hanover, part of the Holy Roman Empire, which had existed in Europe since the tenth century – since the fourteenth as a limited elective monarchy – and which featured circles of electors, princes, dukes and counts.

This catalogue of virtues commended him to the Queen, but she did not mention something that must tell against him. Prince Ferdinand was the younger brother of another soldier, the Hereditary Prince of Württemberg, whom the King's niece Princess Augusta of Brunswick had married and accompanied to St Petersburg ten years earlier when she was fifteen. When the Hereditary Prince and their three children – two sons and a baby daughter – left Russia, Augusta did not leave with them. And shortly after she was imprisoned by the Empress, Catherine the Great, in the castle of Lohde for unspecified immorality. Despite loud protests from the Brunswick family – and remonstrances from King George III – to St Petersburg, Augusta was still there in 1788 when she died.

The tale was murky, and the Hereditary Prince of Württemberg cast as its villain by his mother-in-law, the Duchess of Brunswick, and by others. There were widespread rumours that he had an ungovernable temper, and, again, that his wife had only turned 'coquette' after he had himself indulged in open amours at the Russian Court. But it would appear that the English Princess Augusta did not dislike his younger brother. Returning from church on Christmas Day, she wrote to Augustus: 'I hope you don't think it vulgar to wish you a happy Christmas, but I was used to do it when we were children and that time I never think of but with an undisturbed pleasure. A time when we were sensible to no greater care than a tumble or a scratch which a kiss and a beg pardon would make up for in a moment.' And she repeated her mother's news: 'I forgot in my last letter to tell you that we have made acquaintance with Prince Ferdinand of Württemberg, a Lieutenant General in the Austrian service. He has served against the Turks, and is now come to England for a few months.'

On 3 January 1791 Prince Ferdinand wrote to Lady Harcourt, one of those among the Queen's ladies who keenly wished to see the princesses married: 'The Prince Ferdinand Duke de Württemberg has the honour to present his most respectful homage to Lady H, and will have the honour of paying his court tomorrow at midday. He thinks himself very happy to promise himself the advantage, so long desired of …' And meanwhile cheerful, stout Elizabeth was going up to town from Windsor to get her birthday clothes, and the King and Queen had promised them a ball – 'it will be but a little ball which (entre nous)', she wrote, 'I like much better than a great one, we shall have but 14 or 15 couples which is just the pleasant number.'

A week later, the Princess Royal described at length this Twelfth Night Ball at which Prince Ferdinand was present, and which took place in the Salle d'Armes at Windsor Castle. The princesses dined at the King's table with the Prince, two other tables were some way off. They danced from 8 p.m. till 4.30 a.m. in the King's Salon, and in other rooms some of the chaperones played cards. Augusta says little, except that she danced with her brother William, her cousin William and the Duke of Dorset, and with Ferdinand. But the Württemberg Prince was her acknowledged suitor and members of the household, hearing of his beauty and elegant manner, rejoiced at the idea of her – 'certainly the most beautiful creature one could wish to behold' – securing such a bridegroom. Augusta could look forward to a travelling life as the wife of a distinguished Continental soldier, and, for a settled home, an elegant palace in Stuttgart with opportunities for walking and riding and gardening.

Alas, by the time the next Court ball came round – the Queen's birthday ball on 18 January – Mrs Papendick records that 'the King had refused his suit, and he sat in the background and would not come forward'. The King himself was magnificent on this occasion in a dark brown coat 'embroidered with gold and stones', and the Prince of Wales wore a 'dark purple spangled all over and quite superb'. But Augusta condemned the dresses she and her sisters had worn for the occasion – 'very handsome gowns but very heavy – at least mine was so'. It had been a 'horrid dull ball', with 'a good deal of fussing and dressing' and 'a good deal of fatigue from morning to night'. It would seem that she as well as the Prince was suffering from her father's refusal to let them marry. The only mystery is that the Prince appears not to have asked for the Princess's hand in marriage until the day after this ball.

'Your kindness to me inspires in me gratitude and confidence', he told Lady Harcourt on the 19th. 'As proof of this, Madame, I ask you to permit me to ask you the favour of remitting the enclosed to their Majesties.' ('The letters I was desired to give to the King and Queen contained a proposal of marriage for the Princess Augusta,' noted Lady Harcourt.) The following day Prince Ferdinand wrote to her again: 'I have just yielded to the Prince of Wales who has invited me for the third time to go to his terre [estate] in Hampshire, tomorrow morning. As it could be that their majesties might have orders for me during the few days I will be absent, I beg you to make clear my earnest wish to return as soon as possible to London, if that was the pleasure of their majesties.' But no message came for the Prince to interrupt his Hampshire stay, and on Saturday the 22nd he was out hunting there with the Prince.

The King presumably found reason to object to this unexceptional match on the ground of the suitor's consanguinity with the Hereditary Prince. Or, and this was the explanation the household endorsed, because Prince Ferdinand was 'two removes from the dukedom, besides which the King would not let the younger Princesses marry before the elder'. It was, at any rate, a very public refusal, when all had been expecting a favourable answer to the dashing officer's suit.

On the 29th Augusta reminded herself, in a letter to her brother Augustus, of her unhappiness during the darkest days of her father's illness when all seemed bleak: 'If such a great light could come forth from such utter darkness though I always had hopes – I mean our dearest father's recovery – after his shocking illness – I am sure we ought never to despair and submit patiently to everything.' And she found consolation in the religion that had supported her during that time. Of taking communion, she wrote three months later: 'When I reflect on what an occasion the ceremony was instituted and by whom ... I try as much as lays in my power to make myself worthy of receiving it, and ... go to the table with all the calmness I am mistress of, and always return with an inward satisfaction and a fervent desire to remain in the good resolutions I have taken.'

Putting away thoughts of love and marriage, Augusta incarcerated herself in literature. M. de Guiffardière, who had teased her about an earlier suitor, the Crown Prince of Denmark, recommended the Abbé d'Olivet's French translation of *The Thoughts of Cicero*, knowing her taste for 'serious reading', and she kept a copy in London and at Windsor. She went through a course of reading with 'Grif': Thomson's *Seasons, Les Saisons* by the Chevalier de St Lambert, *Les Jardins* by M. de Lille and this same de Lille's translations of Virgil's *Georgics*: 'Having the advantage of Grif's remarks and explanation of what I did not quite understand,' Augusta wrote, 'I never passed any time more pleasantly in my life.' She thanked God that she could be by herself without ever feeling alone, thanks to books and music, dancing and a little work. Indeed, she was somebody who needed hours to herself. 'I don't think I have spent the day to my liking', she wrote on a later occasion, 'if I have not been an hour alone – I require that little quiet and then I am equal to do anything. But unless I have my reading and thinking quietly and by myself I am totally done up for.'

The King had now rebutted proposals from the royal houses of Denmark and of Württemberg. Later this year, the widower King of Sardinia asked for the hand in marriage of a princess of England, the condition being that she become a Catholic. George III turned down the heretical proposal instantly, the easier because the bridegroom was older than he was. As her husband turned down suitor after suitor for her daughters, the Queen became despondent. When her younger daughters' French teacher, Mlle Charlotte Salomé de Montmollin, married this summer, one of her colleagues remarked that the Queen took as much trouble with the trousseau as though it had been her own daughter marrying. And how she wished that were the case! Meanwhile Charlotte Salomé's cousin Julie took her place.

The Princess Royal, meanwhile, grew discontented and solitary, and railed against her mother for inviting to Windsor the daughters of government families who, she said, 'could not amuse the King, but only ran idly about the house, interrupting everybody'. Rudely, she instructed her lady-in-waiting to 'tell all these visitors that she never received anyone in the morning'. Princess Elizabeth meanwhile dedicated herself to a bevy of artistic projects; Princess Augusta took refuge in friendships, and her family. The arrival of letters from brothers continued to be for all the princesses red-letter days. 'My great joy at finding it on my dressing table', Elizabeth wrote to Augustus of one letter of his, 'caused a general laugh for I quite screamed.'

Unfortunately this year Augusta lost Lady Elizabeth Waldegrave, whom she called her best and dearest friend, to the altar. Admittedly, she would still see her former lady-in-waiting, as she had married Lord Cardigan, Governor of Windsor Castle. But Augusta wanted acknowledgement of her generosity in blessing the match. 'Don't you think I behave very handsomely upon this affair?' she asked Augustus, before adding, 'you must allow me to feel a great deal upon this occasion, as in our situation a true friend is the most valuable of possessions'.

The careful catalogue of her friends which the Princess now made for her brother was not large. First came her family, then there were those that 'have been with me from my childhood' – Lady Howe, Lady Harcourt and Lady Cremorne; these were her 'particular friends'. Of the 'younger people' she favoured Lady Caroline Waldegrave, Lady Frances Howard and Lady Mary Howe. She said firmly, 'And I feel that quite sufficient. I have of course many pleasant acquaintances, but there is a wide difference between such and friends.' As for Lady Char and Gouly, she declared, 'I never can mention them with any body else … owing everything to them.' This was a princess who loved to confide, but felt the difficulty of forming new friendships, she noted, 'too suddenly as they may prove fatal to us'. She wrote without emotion, 'The highest disadvantage in our elevation is the being subject to flatterers and false friends – both of which are shocking calamities to which we are liable.' To her delight, in April the King and Queen appointed two of her 'particular friends', Lady Elizabeth's sister Lady Caroline Waldegrave and Lady Mary Howe, 'to be our ladies'.

The elder princesses' unmarried state was acutely on show this June when their younger sister Mary made her debut, aged fifteen, at the Birthday ball. The Duke of York had written to Augustus on 29 March 1791, 'You would hardly know your younger sisters, they are so much grown and so much improved, particularly Mary.' Her dark hair and pale skin had always made her stand out among her sisters. Now came the moment when she would for the first time dance at Court and further-more lead off the first minuet. For her sisters standing beneath her in the set, it was also a moment that would nudge them – six, eight and nine years older than her – into the shadows of spinsterhood.

Princess Mary like her mother was ardently interested in clothes, and savoured her dress for the Queen's birthday: 'the colour of the gown is green with gold spots and stripes, the trimming is to be crepe, with a little running pattern of gold spangles. I think it will be very pretty.' Her younger sister Sophia – a foot shorter and looking much younger than she was – declined to describe the dresses for the birthday – 'They are always the same sort of thing.' In 'a great shew of royalty', later that year Prince William of Gloucester – only a few months older than Princess Mary – and his elder sister were made welcome at the King's Birthday. But Mary's appointed partner was her brother Prince William.

Unfortunately, at twenty-five the veteran of more than nine years' active service at sea, Prince William relied on strong drink to cheer all social occasions, and his sister's debut in society was no exception. He arrived incapable from alcohol, and Mary had to sit disconsolate in her gown and spangles while another couple led off the dance. Prince William did not mend his ways. Later that year he plied drink on his mother's learned reader, M. Deluc, at a dinner given by Mrs Schwellenberg, and the poor man became tipsy just before he was to go to the Queen. But Princess Mary's beauty had at least struck many beholders – her cousin Prince William of Gloucester for one, and her two eldest brothers for others, who thought they saw a way of turning it to their advantage.

While the French King and Queen's plight disturbed other crowned heads of Europe – news of their flight from Paris in June 1791 was swiftly followed by that of their capture at Varennes, and of the abolition of the monarchy on 16 July – the Prince of Wales in London and the Duke of York in Berlin were writing of the twenty-one-year-old Crown Prince of Prussia as a suitor for one of their sisters.

The Duke of York had left England that month for the Court of Berlin, hoping to enlist as a volunteer in the Prussian army in a war against the Austrians that did not in the event transpire. But he remained there, rekindling romantic feelings that he had harboured ten years earlier in Berlin for the King of Prussia's daughter by his first marriage, Princess Frederica. And there he received a letter from his brother the Prince of Wales, written from Brighton and outlining his remarkable suggestion that their sister Royal should marry Frederica's half-brother, the Crown Prince of Prussia.

Not only was this youth of twenty-one unknown to Royal; he was also four years younger than her. And it was at this point that the Duke of York remarked in a letter to his brother that the Prussian heir would make a better bridegroom for Mary, and indeed he believed the Crown Prince already had her in mind. The Prince of Wales's plan was, to the Duke of York's mind, unfeasible and, anyway, he was far too preoccupied negotiating his own match with Princess Frederica at the Prussian Court and in correspondence with their father to be an envoy in this matter.

But the Prince's account of his conversations and his correspondence in May with their sister the Princess Royal shows just how desperate and nervous she was, shortly before Mary's debut. 'I had occasion to go to the Queen's House,' the Prince began, 'and sit with my mother, where our eldest sister also was, with whom I joked much in a good-humoured way about herself ...' Afterwards the Princess begged him never to tease her again in that way before her mother. He did not know 'how she suffered for it afterwards'. A few days later the Princess Royal poured out her heart in a private interview with her brother. All her sisters were favoured over her. In addition, she spoke of 'the violence and the caprice of her mother's temper which hourly grows worse'. And her parents made no attempt to supply any sort of establishment for her – at home or abroad. She was kept under 'constant restraint ... just like an infant'.

Failing marriage abroad, she would be happy, she said, astonishing her brother, to marry the Duke of Bedford, his friend. Indeed, he said, she seemed eager for it. 'She says she is grown to a time of life that will not admit of any scheme of this sort being long postponed.'

The Princess Royal's plans, radical though they were, were most interesting to her brother, in that they might be of assistance in his attempts to secure loans on the Continent. He was at present negotiating through an agent, Zastrow, a large loan from the Landgrave of Hesse-Cassel, and Zastrow had said he had heard the King of Prussia would be 'ready to assist' with more money, if his son the Crown Prince married a princess of England. When the Prince rashly mentioned this to his sister, she seized upon it, only to have her dreams shattered by the Duke of York's response.

The Duke of York thought no more highly of her other scheme, to marry his friend the Duke of Bedford. It was perhaps with the Duke in mind – a leading Whig and agriculturalist – that she had fulminated against those idle daughters of government. But in her rage against the world the Princess Royal now said, according to Mrs Papendiek, that 'she had never liked the Queen, from her excessive severity'. She added 'that she had doubted her judgement on many points, and went so far as to say that she was a silly woman'.

The Bedford plan was, like the Prussian plan, dismissed by her brothers as one their father would never agree to. The project of an establishment and independence, which the Princess Royal had introduced with such fire, crumbled into cinders. And Royal, baulked of her attempt to escape, retreated from the family circle, while her younger sister Elizabeth whiled away the wet hot summer with long drawing lessons from Mr Gresse. At the Lodge at Frogmore, where she and Augusta and the Queen went almost every day, Elizabeth sat in a room with her sister and read, wrote and 'botanized', while their mother sat in another room – very small and green – across the passage where she did likewise. On Saturdays, the younger princesses, having no lessons, came too. But Royal was rarely there.

In February this year, the Queen had written to her son Augustus – about to embark, for his health, for the south – a letter describing the mild winter in England: 'No frost nor snow, and everything in blossom. The hazels, lilacs, primroses, wallflowers, polyanthus, are all out this present time, in Kew, Richmond and Windsor gardens.' Four days earlier she had begun to plant, with the help of a Yorkshire clergyman, 'who undertakes to render this unpretty thing pretty', the neglected garden at Frogmore. From that day accordingly she dated 'the beginning of my little paradise' where Mr William Aiton, the gardener at Kew, had finished making her a greenhouse. She was also taking up the botanical studies that the King's illness had interrupted, again with a vengeance. 'Curtis's books of botany, Lees, Sowerby, and Miller's English garden calendar and dictionary are to be my chief studies when there, and the drying of plants – both foreign and natives – an endless resource. Of the former I make a collection and have hitherto gone on with great success.'

The Queen's immersion from that time on in her houses and gardens at Frogmore was to please some of her daughters more than others. Elizabeth was an enthusiast from the beginning, and wrote this year: 'Our few days in the country every week suit me extremely and Mama's little cottage at Frogmore fills my thoughts at present very much.' She had just been there with Augusta and 'It looked in beauty, at least we wish to think it did ...' Elizabeth described to Augustus the 'shades' or silhouettes that she was now making from black paper with amazing dexterity – not only portraits but whole scenes of figures, often mothers with children and, very, very often, babies. 'I shall enclose two or three of my cuttings out, and if you like them, I will send you more. But you must remember that I do not draw figures, and cut out these without drawing them first.' She declared herself content with her secluded life: 'It is a very lucky thing for me that I do not live more in the world, for I am sure it would not do for me.' But Elizabeth often declared an airy lack of interest in the world while being a keen participant in it. Of a regiment stationed at Windsor and said to be 'the finest regiment ... quite perfection,' she wrote, 'I do not understand anything about it!'

The younger princesses were despatched to Nuneham and the Harcourts in the late summer of 1791, for their elders were once again off to Weymouth, where the King, who had been looking 'full and bloated', could bathe. 'I shall take *Don Quixote* as my companion, which is very rude of me when I add that I go in the carriage with Pss Royal and our 2 ladies,' wrote Elizabeth a week before they set out in early September, 'but I cannot keep up conversation for a whole day.'

The King bathed with energy at Weymouth, and rode desperately hard also – thirty-two miles to Lulworth in the heat one day, and perspiring violently. But he was judged to be well. His wife was not. 'The Queen looks, I think, very ill,' wrote Mrs Harcourt, 'and, by all accounts, has been so low and languid, that nothing but real illness can account for it.' She had, in addition, been troubled by a bad foot for six months. But above all, Mrs Harcourt was interested in news about the Duke of York and his bride. They married in Berlin – on his sister Princess Royal's twenty-fifth birthday, 29 September 1791 – in a double ceremony in which the bride's sister Wilhelmina married the Prince of Orange.

'We have nothing to do with any former attachments she may have had,' Mrs Harcourt wrote, and did not elaborate. All the reports were that the couple were deeply in love and talked of nothing but retiring to England, 'and living with and for each other'. Upon hearing that Princess Frederica's brother the Crown Prince of Prussia was to accompany his sister to

England, Mrs Harcourt wrote with excitement, not knowing of the Princess Royal's disappointed hopes: 'We shall see which of our three goddesses will have the apple.'

But the Crown Prince did not come. And to Queen Charlotte's discomfiture her brother Charles's motherless daughters, on whose education she had advised, scooped the pool. His daughter Louise became the bride of the Crown Prince of Prussia on Christmas Eve 1793 and in due course queen of that country. Her younger sister Frederica married two days later the Crown Prince's younger brother, Prince Louis of Prussia.

Augusta bathed for the first time this year at Weymouth. 'I like it very well, and think it will do me good, I feel very hungry, all very good signs, first hunger, and then faith', was her tepid response to the sensation. She preferred joining a party that sat in one of the bathing machines, working, while Lady Mary Howe read aloud. And she walked along the strand almost in the sea – 'the spray is charming and the sands so soft to walk upon that I am quite delighted. It is quite an indulgence to me who am tortured with the bad gravel on Windsor Terrace.' At Weymouth, the princesses and even the Queen walked about with only a lady, and went into the few shops as they pleased. But there was little enough to do. When they went to the play twice a week, ladies of their circle secured the boxes to either side 'to keep off improper company'. Alas, they could not improve the quality of some of the actors' performances. For entertainment, Princess Augusta was reduced to making an attendant's young son – with 'little legs like two sticks ... feet like little bits of sealing wax' – dance round the room while she played her harpsichord.

The arrival of the clever, sophisticated Duchess of York in November altered the Princess Royal's mood for the better – although the Prussian Duchess had a love of music which the English Princess could not share. The Duchess brought a £30,000 dowry, and the English cartoonists, for the first time, featured Princess Amelia. She was held up by the Queen to greet the Duchess of York – indicating greed on the royal family's part to get the Princess's large dowry. In fact, the Duke of York, a man in love, spent £20,000 on jewels for his bride. The Princess Royal described her new sister-in-law as a 'charming' little woman, and praised her as very industrious. With the Duke Frederica settled down at Oatlands, the luxurious house complete with games room and pool and grotto that he had furnished three years earlier.

But Royal was distressed that her brother Augustus complained of her silence. She could not, she said, 'write such long letters as Eliza ... our life is so much the same ... the history of one day, that of every day ...'. She couldn't think what her sister filled her pages with. 'Besides,' she continued, 'ever since we parted, our society is so much altered, and the people we live with so unknown to you.' She asked him, rather, to tell her about the pictures he had seen, and the snowy Alps. (All the princesses thrilled to the idea of travel. Princess Elizabeth was reading Pennant's *Tours of Wales*, and meant to try next his *Tours through Scotland*.) How, she wrote, she envied Augustus his sight of Rome; were she there, she would not leave a single spot unseen of that great city. With M. de Guiffardière's ancient history lessons to the fore, she added, 'The statues are amazingly fine by all accounts, but I am afraid very few of them are not a little broke.' Meanwhile, the Queen asked Augustus for some Italian fan leather 'quite white for to paint on, and if besides you will send us some Naples fan mounts I shall be much obliged to you'. Fan painting was a favourite hobby of hers and of the Princess Royal and Elizabeth, she explained. The princes might travel or marry and settle. The princesses had their 'work' to do.

8

Despond

~

PRINCESS AUGUSTA WROTE on 3 February 1792: 'Elizabeth and me (who were always each other's best friend) are sitting opposite each other at the same table and talking between whiles.' They had been quiet that New Year, while they discovered what entertainments their new sister-in-law the Duchess of York, who was visiting, might like. But the Duchess was not unnaturally distracted. Following their joint declaration at Pilnitz, in September 1791, her father the King of Prussia and the Emperor of Austria signed a defensive alliance against France this month, based on the repugnance they felt for illegitimate republican regimes.

'What joy it must be to Papa and Mama and all of us to see how fond they are of each other,' wrote Sophia, nevertheless, of her brother Frederick, on whom she doted, and of his Duchess. Sophia was now included with her sister Mary in more of the family doings, and found the farce, *The Town Hunchback*, 'very laughable', though Mary did not. 'The little idol Amelia' still ate in the nursery, as Miss Burney on a visit in January noted, and the six-year difference in age between Sophia and her younger sister was also apparent in the elder sister's note: 'Amelia played about the room with Lady Douglas's two daughters and with Lady Harrington's little girl, Lady Anna Maria Stanhope. Mary and me played at cards.'

While the Duchess of York's father and brothers prepared to go to war over France's demand in March 1792 that Prussia's ally Austria withdraw from territories in Flanders, her new family in England felt no such call to arms. They were living in more or less domestic contentment, or at least idleness. The Prince of Wales was at Brighton with Mrs Fitzherbert, who was incidentally angry that the Duchess of York would not treat her as belle-soeur or sister-in-law. Prince William, Duke of Clarence had set up house with the celebrated comic actress Mrs Jordan at Bushey, and even Edward had found happiness, at Quebec, with a Mme de St Laurent. Only the princesses' younger brothers were without known romantic attachments – Ernest and Adolphus in the Hanoverian cavalry and infantry, and, at Portici near Naples, Augustus. From there this last Prince, disappointed in his hopes of a naval career, was considering academe as an alternative. He wrote to his former tutor Dr Hughes on 10 January 1792: 'very probably next October in a year I shall be going or gone to Cambridge or Oxford; but ... this is a great secret'.

The princesses continued to spend much of their time at Frogmore Farm, Mr Floyer's house which the Queen had rechristened Amelia Lodge. When Miss Burney visited the royal ladies at the Queen's House in May 1792, the Queen opened her 'work repository ... a very curious table and work bag in one', and showed her a sample of the chair covers she was making for 'her cottage at Frogmore'. It was Princess Elizabeth's twenty-second birthday that month, but, no suitor beckoning, she wrote instead for Lady Harcourt's amusement an answer to a hypothetical advertisement: 'Rug Lane 1792, To the person intended for getting all proper people for the Queen's small establishment at the Cottage Royal at Frogmore.' She sought 'the place of housekeeper', and went on, 'Now my love, I am a pretty good hand at conserves, pickling, and so forth ... When I lived with the late Lord Orford [Horace Walpole] I gave great satisfaction to him and Miss Polly. I was a great favourite of the latter's, I used to read to her. In case of that's being wanted, I could read to her Majesty, as I am told she is fond of that amusement.'

The Queen was indeed 'fond' of reading, but had a way of dealing with books given or even dedicated to her that were not to her taste. She deftly put *Dinarbas*, for instance – a turgid sequel to Dr Johnson's *Rasselas* by a lady author – into Fanny Burney's hands, for 'some account', as the Queen put it, 'of its merits' before she read it. Miss Burney praised it, and even recommended it to the princesses' attention: 'I am sure their Royal Highnesses could read nothing more chastely fitted for them.' For reward, she received later in the year the author Miss Ellis Cornelia Knight's new publication *Marcus Flaminius*. Like many others, Miss Burney believed the princesses isolated from the world, allowed to read neither novels nor newspapers without their mother's permission. And the princesses traded on this supposed isolation to appear blank-faced and innocent, while a constant diet of letters and newspapers and Court gossip – as well as the books that circulated among the household – kept them immensely well informed of what was 'moving' in the world.

For Elizabeth and for the Queen, the purchase of first Frogmore Farm, or Amelia Lodge, and then the neighbouring Great Frogmore estate in 1792 featuring Frogmore House offered distinct possibilities. The Queen was to avoid both the cares of her position and her husband. Elizabeth seized on the opportunity the acres of neglected garden at Frogmore House afforded for designing architectural 'surprises' in the Gothic or Olde

English style as well as small buildings on the more established classical model, both being then fashionable. Moss huts, Gothic ruins and octagonal temples appeared in the grounds under her direction. And while the French Queen's creation, Le Petit Trianon, lay neglected at Versailles, the Queen of England and her daughters established what she called a 'terrestrial paradise' in the Home Park at Windsor.

Fanny Burney, hovering around the passages and corridors of the Queen's House on the King's Birthday, was invited by Princess Elizabeth to join them in the state dressing room where the Queen was sitting with her head attired superbly for the drawing room, her Court dress awaiting her at St James's. All the princesses (bar Princess Amelia) and the Duchess of York were with her. In the background stood M. de Luc, Schwelly, Mme de la Fite and Miss Gouldsworthy. For this day was to be fourteen-year-old Princess Sophia's debut at Court.

With five princesses now 'out', established routines of thirty years were ending. This summer, Lady Charlotte conducted Princess Amelia daily to her mother in the White Closet at the Queen's House, as she had escorted so many royal children since she was first appointed as governess to the infant Prince of Wales in 1762. But Lady Charlotte was now old, deaf and unwell, Princess Sophia writing this autumn, 'I am grieved to death about her, she is if possible more kind to us than ever. Indeed, both Gouly and her are so good to us that we should not be deserving of having such treasures about us, if we did not feel their kindness in the highest degree.'

Lady Charlotte resigned from her post in November 1792, and with the New Year the Queen must look for other governesses and companions for her younger daughters. Even the Queen's dresser, Mrs Schwellenberg, who had ruled backstairs longer than Lady Charlotte had the schoolroom, was now a very sick dragon. Too ill to preside in the eating room where she had persecuted Miss Burney and others, Schwelly rose from her sickbed only to attend the Queen at her dressing and at her going to bed. The Old Guard was passing.

Unfortunately, the princesses' remaining attendants did not pull well together as Mary and Sophia completed their teenage years, and as Amelia approached them. Miss Gouldsworthy, though unremittingly kind to all her charges, even to those who abused her, was often ill. And Miss Burney's opinion of the two 'English teachers', Miss Planta and Miss Gomm, was that they 'humiliate, dislike and distrust each other ...'.

Princess Mary of all the sisters adored children, and she enjoyed hearing from Fanny Burney about a nephew's fantasy island called Protocol. 'Had we been alone', wrote Fanny, she was sure Mary 'would have insisted upon hearing every particular'. Mary, intensely interested in the world around her, was no great student, but Sophia and Amelia were naturally quick and avid readers. It was a pity that the Queen had no educational aspirations for them, as she had had for their elder sisters. Instead, with Mlle Julie de Montmollin their instructor, they became beautiful needlewomen, adept at lacemaking, crochet work and all kinds of fine embroidery. But their handwriting, in contrast to their elder sisters', was shocking, the very texts of their letters less assured, their knowledge of history, geography and botany skimpy, and their artistic and musical education sketchy.

This year, for the first time, the younger princesses were allowed to join their sisters at Weymouth, where the royal party proceeded in mid-August, and Mary vividly remembered her first sea bathe there half a century later. Her bathing dress was a 'regular one' made for the occasion, which 'no floating about deranged. If all the world', she recalled, 'had been looking on, they would of [sic] seen me as well-dressed as if in a drawing room.' She remembered the fatigue of bathing. 'I began with jumping into the sea from the first step of the machine, but I would not go on so doing, and then the two bathing women dipped me into the sea which saved much fatigue and I liked it much better.' However, the experience did not agree with her. At last 'I was obliged to lay down and could not walk at all, so that it was given up.'

They were at Weymouth for the Princess Royal's twenty-sixth birthday, but she did not raise the subject of her future. No one wanted to dispute with the King now, for fear his old and shocking illness might re-emerge. On being informed this year that the great Dr Burney's remedy for depression was to compose canons to solemn words, the King told the musicologist's daughter that he, too, found that grave or difficult employment composed him when ill or disturbed.

The prospects of the princesses marrying abroad had anyway diminished as the prospect of full-scale European war loomed. Shocking news arrived from Paris – of the mob entering the Tuileries Palace on 10 August, of their killing the Swiss Guards, and other Swiss in the English Minister's house – and of the French royal family taking refuge with the National Assembly.

Still worse news came. The Prussians, who with Austria had declared war on France in July, assembled an allied army at Coblenz. Hoping to take advantage of the social and military chaos in France, the army marched on Paris under the command of the famed but elderly Duke of Brunswick – and was routed by French cannonade at Valmy on 21 September. Next day, the French republic was declared, and – further news came – the French had defeated an Austrian army at Jemappes and taken Flanders.

Weymouth, by contrast, remained the most peaceful town imaginable, where the King and Queen of England went weekly to the public assembly rooms, and took tea in friendly fashion with people 'with a claim to their notice' in an inner room. On her return to Windsor, Princess Elizabeth wrote to Lady Harcourt on 3 October 1792: 'Of all parties to Weymouth this has been infinitely the most agreeable to me ...' Only breakfast at an inn on the way back had been a disappointment: 'anything so disgusting I thank God I never saw before and never wish to see again, bad butter ... plum cake as stowage for the stomach'. She hoped Lady Harcourt would pardon 'the badness of my handwriting, but I have so horrid a pen that it is scarcely possible to write, and another thing is that I am scrawling, while my hair is dressing'.

Sophia wrote on 14 November of having been to see 'Mama's new house [at Great Frogmore], in time it will be charming. Pray tell Lord Harcourt (for I assume it will amuse him) that we went all over the house not excepting the kitchens and cellars which are very good.' In January the Queen had written of her plans for a Gothic cottage at Frogmore Farm which the architect James Wyatt was to design. (The King had also given her the long elm walk which used to lead to Shaw Farm and she had planted 4,000 trees there, on the advice of her new consultant Major William Price.) But, as we have seen, the Queen had persuaded the King to buy her the much larger neighbouring estate of Great Frogmore, and so all ideas of a cottage were at an end. Amelia Lodge was demolished and its grounds united with those of Frogmore House, the Queen's new residence.

Meanwhile, the princesses' brothers Ernest and Adolphus, to their delight, were under arms. Following the trial and execution of Louis XVI in early January 1793, an emboldened France declared war on Britain and the United Netherlands (which comprised the Austrian and Dutch territories in northern Europe). Austria, Prussia and Holland dispatched their finest generals to lead their armies in the coalition that responded to this aggressive move. Hanover was supplying nearly 4,000 men out of a force of 20,000 that the states of the Holy Roman Empire were drumming up against the French. And King George III yielded to his sons' pleas to serve. Accordingly Adolphus was ordered in November to join the Hanoverian Foot Guards, and Ernest the Hanoverian Light Dragoons.

Adolphus, aged nineteen, was thrilled to be off to join the coalition: 'I always have wished to make a campaign.' And the King of England had insisted that his second son the Duke of York, aged twenty-nine, be appointed commander-in-chief of the British forces, who set off with the declared intention of knocking France out of Flanders and restoring order – and with the undeclared intention of thereby acquiring some part of the French West Indies. Lady Harcourt was moved to compose 'A song written on the occasion of the Guards being sent to the Continent under the command of HRH the Duke of York, 16 Feb 1793'. But Miss Lucy Kennedy, a lady diarist with apartments in Windsor Castle, tells us that Princess Sophia fell extremely ill at that leave-taking. 'She went with the family to Greenwich to see her brother, the Duke of York with the British Guards, embark for Germany ... It affected P.S. so much, that she fell into fits, which have increased, and continued ever since ...'

In the early summer of 1793, following the Duke of York's departure and a bad bout of chickenpox, Princess Sophia was three weeks in bed, the Queen told her brother, with a bad 'swallow'. She remained alarmingly ill for many months, and Miss Kennedy called her illness in October 'a violent nervous disorder'. She elaborated: 'She takes from 50 to 80 [fits] in the 24 hours, falls back in her chair, more or less convulsed, recovers soon, does not complain of pain, and goes on with her work, or book as if nothing had happened, until she sinks again. Sir Lucas Pepys attends her.'

To try and cure this puzzling complaint, Princess Sophia was first sent for six weeks to Kew, with her sister Mary and Lady Charlotte Bruce, Mrs Gouldsworthy and Mrs Cheveley for companions. (Che Che slept in Princess Sophia's room as she had slept in those of other royal invalids whose lives were judged in danger.) But on 8 July her sister Elizabeth wrote to Lady Harcourt: 'I make no scruple of telling you that Sophia is just the same – patience itself, but making us all very uneasy, though we are assured she is not in the least shadow of danger, which we must thank God for. You know well enough how many unhappy hours that makes me pass in every sense of the word. But at Court, one learns deceit ...' Elizabeth gave way to 'low spirits' only in her own room.

'My swallow has improved within these last few days,' wrote Sophia to the King from Kew House on 19 August, and spoke of her gratitude to her father during her 'long and tedious illness'. But in the autumn and back at Lower Lodge she was nervous and paranoid: 'Many more unpleasant things have passed since we met; Princess Royal and Lady Cathcart [their new lady-in-waiting] ... I strongly suspect are at the bottom of everything ... my reasons I will give you when we meet ... I have very good ones and I heard many a story that Princess Royal has repeated to the Queen.' She ended by begging: 'You will not mention to any of my sisters what I said to you.'

At the beginning of October, Sophia was despatched by her alarmed parents to Tunbridge Wells with Lady Cathcart, Lady Charlotte Finch's replacement, and Mrs Cheveley as attendants, to drink the waters there. Mrs Kennedy wrote:

she was not told of it, until the coach drove to the door, in hopes the flurry of spirits, and agitation would make her weep, which it did violently, which relief made her perform her journey better than they could have expected … The queen only told Lady Cathcart and Mrs Cheveley the day before, took no leave of her [Sophia], and took all the Royal family to Frogmore immediately after breakfast … when they returned at 12 o clock, she was gone. They all wept much, especially Princess Mary, who had never been separated [from her] one day in her life.

But the 'cure' answered, and Sophia could write of her mysterious illness on 15 October to the King, 'My faintings are less, though not as much diminished as I could wish, as to my swallow with your leave I will not mention that.'

The royal family had anxieties this autumn other than Sophia's health. In August, after the Hanoverian troops had successfully taken Valenciennes from the French, the Queen had written, 'Thank God my sons behaved well.' But on 6 September the French attacked Hanoverian forces – among them Adolphus – retreating after dark from Dunkirk. In the hand-to-hand fighting that ensued, Prince Adolphus was 'wounded in the shoulder, and had a deep cut with a sabre so near the eye that it is a wonder it escaped'. So General William Harcourt wrote from the British lines to his wife, and off flew Mrs Harcourt to the Queen's Lodge with her letter. The Queen was much affected by the news of her son's wounds, 'and the Princesses all cried very much'.

The King heard simultaneously from the Duke of York of a desperate and unsuccessful sortie the British forces had made to try and take Dunkirk from the French on the 6th. (When the Duchess of York received word at Oatlands of these events, she finished her game before opening the despatch, as befitted the granddaughter of Frederick the Great.) The Duke was safe, if humiliated, and the British forces had to lift their siege anyway soon enough and go to the support of the Hanoverian army, which had been forced to retreat still further. Here at least Adolphus could rest from his wounds, and here he received orders from his brother to make for England and a full recovery.

Adolphus's sisters had last seen him seven years before, when he went off, a skinny twelve-year-old, to study at the University of Göttingen. Elizabeth wrote from Weymouth on 17 September 1793, '… I am at this moment the happiest creature with my brother [Adolphus] who is quite an angel …' But Adolphus was puzzled by changes that he observed, and he wrote later, 'I am very sorry to hear that the ill humour of a certain person (you know who I mean) [the Queen] continues so bad: particularly her behaviour towards dear Mary and Sophia is so very singular, as they certainly by no means deserve it. What can possess her to be so odd and why make her life so wretched when she could have it just the reverse?' Mary, Adolphus said, was 'a charming creature, and one of the sweetest tempered girls I ever saw'. But the Queen could not shake off the misery and feelings of doom that the King's illness and the fate of the French royal family had engendered in her. Steely of purpose, she worked on an 'entertainment' she and Princess Elizabeth had planned for Coronation Day – 25 October – and ordered 'a certain quantity of green paper' stained the colours of laurel and oak leaves. She wanted thin rose-coloured paper too, and some 'for fashioning yellow and dark red roses'. But the celebration had to be postponed after Queen Marie Antoinette was executed in Paris on 16 October.

'Augustus is hourly expected. I do not understand why he is so long a coming,' Elizabeth wrote in September. But, as the political situation in Europe declined, Augustus lingered abroad, although the King had called him north from Rome in May. The King and Queen had heard then that he was romantically inclined towards the Earl of Dunmore's daughter, Lady Augusta Murray, who was travelling with her family on the Continent. But they had no inkling that he had married her – secretly and in defiance of the Royal Marriages Act – in the Hotel Sarmiento in Rome. And, before he answered his father's call to head north, Lady Augusta became pregnant.

When Augustus did arrive, his mother showed herself well aware of the passion he had formed in Italy, saying to Elizabeth when Lady Augusta arrived in England in October: 'I see it is not over, by the agitation Augustus is in.' Elizabeth could say little. Fear of discovery did not prevent Augustus and Augusta, back in England, from going through another marriage ceremony at St George's, Hanover Square, on 5 December 1793. They also had clandestine meetings before the birth of the coming baby – not only in London, but at an inn in Windsor. Prince Augustus crept away there between engagements at the Castle – including his confirmation at St George's Chapel two days before Christmas.

The King and Queen continued to follow anxiously the progress of the British forces under the command of their second son in Flanders. 'There is a subscription set on foot in most of the towns in England for procuring flannel waistcoats for the British troops, now serving under the Duke of York. The conductor of the newspaper called *The Sun* has offered to receive all the donations ...' Miss Kennedy wrote. 'Everybody is interested about this charity. Her Majesty has ordered 2000 flannel waistcoats to be made immediately.' But the British campaign was going badly.

Adolphus, recovered, was sent back to the theatre of war early in the New Year, and Ernest, still out there, was moved, to his disgust, into the heavy dragoons. The Harcourts' sister-in-law Mrs William Harcourt, who was at Tournai with her husband the General, became reacquainted with the boy she had known at Windsor over seven years before. 'He is excessively liked here,' she wrote, 'but would not do in England; he talks too much, and I am sure he would not bear the life of Windsor three days. He is a true Hussar; but open, lively, and very good-natured.' On further acquaintance with Ernest, Mrs Harcourt noted, 'I have some difficulty in endeavouring to make him behave well.' When they paid a visit to a convent where he had been quartered the previous summer, she added despairingly: 'He would kiss the Abbess and talk nonsense to all the poor nuns. I know a thousand traits of the goodness of his heart, but I fear he is too wild for England.'

But the princesses now were occupied most of all by their brother Augustus's coming departure for Leghorn, since Elizabeth and Sophia at least knew that he was about to become a father. Mrs Kennedy recorded, 'On Monday the 13th [January 1794] the Royal Family all went to the play, the Princesses wept the whole time, and both K and Q looked grave. The two young Princes were to set out early next morning, Prince Augustus to Rome, and Adolphus to join the army and [the] Duke of York ... The King thought it was better to go to the play, that it would keep them all more composed, but it was [a] pity as they could not compose themselves ...'

That very day at Lower Berkeley Street, Lady Augusta gave birth to a son, whom she imaginatively named Augustus. But the Prince had barely time to see his son before he was off on *L'Aquilon* and ordered back to Italy. Princess Elizabeth, fearing their father's wrath, had prevented her brother from handing the King a confession that he had written on 9 January. She even produced the exact terms of the Marriage Act to warn him against revealing his secret to their father. But she may not have guessed just how implacable the King was to be when the news leaked out.

'Today the King told me', runs Queen Charlotte's diary for 25 January, 'that the Lord Chancellor had acquainted him yesterday after the levee with the disagreeable news of Augustus's marriage with Lady Augusta Murray ... That the register was found. And that he had given orders to the Chancellor, the Archbishop of Canterbury, and the other Ministers to proceed in this unpleasant business as the law directs, Augustus having married under age being against the Marriage Act.' She added: 'Also orders were given to stop Lady Dunmore and her daughter joining him or leaving England.' After this account of the measures the King had taken, she wrote further on the 29th: 'we went into my room to read, then acquainted the Princesses of their brother's imprudent match with Ly Augusta Murray. Then read and wrote till one ... '

The King spared Lady Augusta and her family no humiliation, hauling them before the Privy Council to make affidavits, until, on 14 July 1794, the Arches Court of Canterbury declared both Prince Augustus's marriages to have been a 'show or effigy of a marriage' and therefore null and void. Hence the Prince, the Court declared, 'was and is free from all bond of marriage with the said Right Honourable Lady Augusta Murray'. And the Prince's son, the King's firstborn grandson, was declared illegitimate.

The King had made his position clear when his brother Cumberland married Lady Anne twenty years before: 'I must ... on the first occasion show my resentment, I have children who must know what they have to expect if they could follow so infamous an example.'

Prince Augustus, weeping with frustration, remained on the Continent. Lady Augusta, barred from joining him, lived – on a pension from the King admittedly – in retirement at Teignmouth with their baby son, who, owing to the shenanigans surrounding his birth, was not even baptized until he was two years old – and then as 'Augustus Frederick, son of Augustus Frederick and Augusta Augustus Frederick'.

Barely two weeks after Prince Augustus's marriage was discovered, the King suffered another humiliation at the hands of his sons. The Prime Minister came to him and made it clear that the Duke of York had to be withdrawn from his command. His inexperience was having disastrous effects; he should never have been placed in command. The King tried to save face and appoint the Duke of Brunswick, his brother-in-law, in his son's place, but Brunswick, still smarting from defeat at Valmy, refused. And on 14 February 1794, diverting attention from his recall, the Duke of York brought with much pomp to England the standard once carried by Louis XVI which the British forces had seized from the French.

The recall proved disastrous for the Duke of York's marriage. The Duchess, still caught up in Prussian affairs, showed little respect for the husband who had so publicly been proved an inadequate commander, and he turned in his discomfiture to his brother the Prince of Wales for the comfort of revelry. The Duchess stayed at Oatlands, pursuing musical and charitable projects and amassing a menagerie of animals in place of a husband. No child was ever born of this union which had begun so well, and which had been intended to secure the Hanoverian line, given the Prince of Wales's disinclination to make a dynastic marriage. And so, although it was an amicable separation, and the Duke visited Oatlands at regular intervals, the succession to the throne was endangered once again.

Meanwhile, on 10 May 1794, Ernest, who was nothing if not brave, had been leading a charge at Tournai, when he was badly wounded in the eye, and had to return to England to recover. He did not lose the eye, but a film settled over it, and, as he had been shortsighted before, his chagrin was considerable. The great sword-cut in his cheek he regarded with some satisfaction, following his education in Germany, where duelling scars were a source of pride. But this tall, handsome and energetic Prince's career as a cavalry officer seemed in doubt, as he rested in England and reviewed the family he had not seen for eight years.

For a time there was only Adolphus, of all George III's sons, serving on the Continent, and he was mostly confined to barracks in a defensive position near the Prussian border. (Edward was stationed with a garrison in Canada, from where word of his excessive love of discipline only slowly reached critics in England.) In March, however, Prince William of Gloucester, aged eighteen, was sent to join his cousin Adolphus in Flanders, and the Duke of York returned there later in the year.

Fortunately, Lord Howe, father of the princesses' friends, scored a tremendous naval victory, known afterwards as the Glorious First of June, to divert the nation's attention from the calamitous campaign that Britain had waged in Flanders. The Queen and princesses, accompanied by Prince Ernest, drove down to Portsmouth to congratulate the victor when he arrived on his flagship, the *Queen Charlotte*, and Princess Elizabeth afterwards wrote to Lady Charlotte Finch: 'Of all days of my life, this is the one that I may indeed call the proudest.' Augusta told Fanny Burney two years later that 'when she was at Portsmouth at church, she saw so many officers' wives and sisters and mothers helping their maimed husbands, or brothers, or sons, that she could not forbear whispering to the Queen "Mama – how lucky it is Ernest is just come so seasonably with that wound in his face! – I should have been quite shocked else, not to have had one little bit of glory!"'

But all was not well. And on 25 July Elizabeth wrote to Lady Harcourt that they were bound the following month for Weymouth, in search of rest for the King. 'I think it absolutely necessary,' she said bleakly, citing 'much hurry of mind, owing to unpleasant business, sleepless nights but much better this last week'. The King was ill again, although not so ill that it had been publicly announced. The Queen was about to call in Dr Willis's son Thomas for an opinion. 'That is the true reason why I did not write, but never write to me on the subject, nor own to the family that I have mentioned it but the truth will out to you ...' She wrote, 'We never talk on the subject and continue doing the same things as we have always done, going to chapel, breakfast, reading, work and drawing. Sometimes squabbling takes us till dinner, after that we sit together unsociably till card time when we have a little conversation.'

From Weymouth Sophia reported to Lady Harcourt on 24 August, 'Going to sea is as usual our greatest amusement – that is to say the greatest to those that love it but for my part I prefer land.' And of her father, she wrote, 'I cannot say some people are bright by any means – however, better than when we left Windsor.' She confessed, 'I find that at present very much my spirits are very weak. I am easily overset. However I struggle as much as possible.'

Down to the anxious household at Gloucester Lodge at Weymouth the Prince of Wales drove at the end of August, and announced to his parents his earnest desire to marry – and marry soon – his aunt the Duchess of Brunswick's daughter, Caroline. Very typically, he had ended his relationship with Mrs Fitzherbert in cowardly fashion by having his brother Ernest call on her with the information that the Prince would be visiting her no more. But he could not end their secret marriage of 1785 without openly acknowledging it. Now the Prince disregarded the danger his bride Caroline would encounter crossing Europe to reach him, and he disregarded the fact that he had never met her. He owed so much money that to get his debts paid by Parliament he would have to indicate his wish to settle down, so that he could demand the income of a married man. And he had fixed on his unknown cousin as the bride most likely to win his father's approval most swiftly, as being his sister's child.

The King, still far from well, approved the scheme, but the Queen, who knew much more Continental gossip than her husband, and who was decidedly less fond of the Brunswick family than he, was dismayed. Not only had the chastity of Caroline's deceased sister, the Hereditary Princess of Württemberg, been in doubt, but the Queen had counselled her widower brother Charles only months before against considering Princess Caroline as a second wife. She had heard that the Princess was so flirtatious that a governess was deputed to follow her round the ballroom to prevent impropriety.

Neither husband nor son listened, and by December the matter was set in stone. The Princess in Brunswick had eagerly accepted the flattering offer, the King had announced the Prince's intended marriage to Parliament, and the Queen and princesses in England were busily preparing for the bride's arrival. As the New Year came in, Lady Charlotte Bruce remarked that the Queen and princesses and some of the ladies had been 'as closely employed for three weeks in embroidering dresses for the birthday and the forthcoming marriage of the Prince of Wales, "as if they had been working for their daily bread"'.

When Mrs Harcourt had joined her husband General William Harcourt – the new commander-in-chief – at the British lines in Flanders in December 1794, she had found the army 'weak and sick'. Every foggy night they expected another attack. But this did not stop her speculating about one of the Allied officers she found there – Prince Frederick of Orange – as a husband for one of the princesses. His father the Stadholder was rich, and the wife of his elder brother the Hereditary Prince – the Duchess of York's sister Wilhelmina – was too amiable to let any younger brother's spouse feel inferior.

Mrs Harcourt was easily seduced. Prince Frederick of Hesse, another officer present, spoke of a nephew's hope for an alliance with one of the princesses, and after spending an agreeable day in December with the scion of the Hesse house in question, Mrs Harcourt felt no hesitation in declaring for Hesse over Orange: 'He is the only man worthy of our Princesses; he even deserves Princess Augusta, angel as she is.'

When the French took Holland in January 1795, putting an end to British military operations on the Continent until 1807, and the Orange family fled their Court at The Hague for exile in England at Hampton Court, Prince Frederick of Orange, at least, ceased to be mentioned as an eligible groom for the princesses. And matchmaker Mrs Harcourt had to abandon other speculation when she was deputed to leave her husband and escort the Princess of Brunswick to her destined husband in England.

In London the princesses cheered on their brother as his marriage approached, and with it the Parliamentary debates on the size of his income. Augusta wrote to him in February 1795, thanking God that 'all things wear a good face'. Elizabeth told him in the same month, 'If you are ever in want of a friend ... remember the corner room at the Queen's House.' The groom himself was in a state of steaming disappointment, however, by the time his bride arrived in London in April. The money paid by Parliament had covered his debts, but had left him – in his view – with a tiny income, on which he could barely afford to maintain Carlton House and his Marine Villa at Brighton. His bride, he argued, far from being the golden goose he had hoped for, would instead merely bring him nothing but expenses.

The meeting of the Prince and of his cousin Princess Caroline was perhaps doomed, given the groom's resentful feelings towards their coming union. At that ceremony – in the Chapel Royal, St James's – the Prince was drunk. On their wedding night he was drunker. But the person who should have been most concerned at the Prince's deficiencies, Princess Caroline, did not show any outward perturbation. Fair-haired, sharp-nosed and sloe-eyed, she smiled and nodded at all those who were presented to her in this new strange land whose language she had only just begun to learn.

But it was not all bad at the beginning. On 13 May, the Princess Royal wrote to Lord Harcourt of the preparations at Frogmore for a proposed nuptial fête she and her sisters and mother were giving for the Prince and his bride. 'I am a little like Mary in *The Fête Champêtre*,' she exclaimed, 'running every way and doing little to the purpose.' And she instructed him to tell Lady Harcourt of the dress for the occasion: 'all the fair that are assembled at the cottage are to endorse the uniform of shepherdesses, and strut across the lawn in muslin gowns and elegant fancy hats. However we do not complete the fair vision by bearing a crook, as we fear mischief might move among so many belles, were they trusted with offensive weapons.'

The Princess Royal could be, as her mother's former Assistant Keeper of the Robes wrote, 'very gay, and very charming; full of lively discourse, and amiable condescension'. Like all the other princesses – and the Duchess of York – she subscribed to Heideloff's *Gallery of Fashion*, an expensive magazine showing the latest modes. Like Princess Augusta, the Princess Royal apparently managed well on £2,000 a year, loved jewels, and bought from Duval. When her art master, John Gresse, died in 1794, she did not repine, but tried out new teachers.

Despite this evidence of loving the material world, it is noticeable in her mother's diary of the previous year that Royal often now did not form part of the crocodile of princesses that the Queen led – to Frogmore, to St George's Chapel, to the Ancient Music concerts at Tottenham Court Road, to Kew. Even when she accompanied her family, she was not always a willing companion. On 24 August 1794, the Princess Royal left the church at Weymouth 'on account of the heat', according to Queen Charlotte's diary. Her continuing resentment towards her mother, her wish for escape from the state of subjection in which she considered she was kept, and her belief that such escape was impossible, had resulted, in short, in withdrawal from the world.

Suddenly there was a bridegroom in view, and in August 1795, walking on the sands at Weymouth, Princess Augusta teased her elder sister, calling her 'Duchess of Oldenburg', while Princess Elizabeth wrote of her sister's 'maiden-blush cheek' being 'turned into a damask rose' whenever that

Duke's name was mentioned. For in a match fostered apparently by Mrs Harcourt and by the Prince of Wales, the Princess Royal was now seriously considering as a husband Prince Peter of Oldenburg, a widower with children, and cousin and heir of the reigning Duke of that name. She wrote to her brother: 'I am perfectly convinced that the Duke of Oldenburg's character is such that could this be brought about, it would be the properest situation, and knowing your kindness, shall leave it totally to you.'

News came while the princesses were at Weymouth that their sister-in-law the Princess of Wales was pregnant, and the Queen diligently sent pigs to Brighton to provide bacon and ham for the Princess. But the Prince was never there. Indeed, his sisters were grateful for his presence in London in November 1795 when a mob surrounded their father's carriage and abused him and his government. Afterwards a hole was found in one of the windows, indicating that someone had fired at him. And Elizabeth, who had been drawn to the window of the Queen's House by the hubbub far off, recorded, 'When the coach turned round the corner of the end of the Mall near this house the hooting, screams, and horrid sayings which reached my ear, being at the open window, it scared me in a manner which no words can ever express.' Princess Augusta told Lady Harcourt that at the play next night 'my poor agitated mind was more fit for a fireside than for pomp and noise'. When they came out, they faced a mob once more, and the Prince of Wales and Duke of York – the chief objects of hatred that evening – dispersed it, to her relief, by riding off in separate directions and so leaving them a clear passage home.

At the end of the year, while his own marriage was complicated by a passion he had discovered for Lady Jersey, a grandmother, the Prince of Wales encouraged his maternal uncle Ernest of Mecklenburg-Strelitz to endorse the Oldenburg alliance. But meanwhile, whether by coincidence or stimulated by rumours of the approaching Oldenburg match, the Princess Royal had received a proposal of marriage from quite another quarter – and it was not one that, at first, pleased her father.

On 13 November 1795, de Wimpfen, the Württemberger Minister in London, sought an audience with Lord Grenville, the British Foreign Secretary, and suggested the Hereditary Prince of his country as a bridegroom for the Princess Royal. The Hereditary Prince was the elder brother of Prince Ferdinand of Württemberg, who had proposed four years earlier for Princess Augusta. But he was also a widower with three children. And his deceased wife was the King's niece, Princess Augusta of Brunswick – and the Princess of Wales's sister. The Hereditary Prince had, at the least, abandoned his wife in Russia, when he took their three children back home to Stuttgart. The King replied to Grenville: 'In the course of the summer I was astonished at the Duchess of Brunswick mentioning in a letter to me a desire of such an alliance, but knowing the brutal and other unpleasant qualities of this Prince, I could not give any encouragement to such a proposal.' He therefore ordered Grenville to refuse the request, and he continued, 'if he will not take a gentle hint, I have no objection to his adding that, after the very unhappy life my unfortunate niece led with him I cannot as a father bequeath any daughter of mine to him'.

But the Hereditary Prince was not daunted. A month later, he himself wrote to the King: 'The eminent qualities of Mme Princesse Royale, no less her virtues universally acknowledged, have given birth in me to the most lively desire to see my fate united with hers.' And the King of England, under pressure from the Imperial Court of Russia – the Hereditary Prince's sister had married Catherine the Great's son, the Emperor Paul – began to shift from his earlier position.

Slowly another story began to emerge in which the Empress Catherine, with whom Augusta of Brunswick had been a favourite, had persuaded the Princess to stay in Russia when her husband left with their children, against his wishes. Catherine had tired of her protégée, in this story, and banished her to the castle of Lohde, where Augusta duly died. It was a shocking story, to be sure, but one in which the Hereditary Prince seemed to show no worse than anyone else involved. This story emanated from the Russian Court, where the Hereditary Prince's sister, wife of Catherine's son Paul, was now empress, and keen to promote her brother's cause.

The Prince of Wales's own marital situation did not improve, not even when his wife gave birth to a healthy girl on 7 January 1796, who was named Charlotte Augusta – good Hanoverian names. Princess Mary wrote from Windsor on the 9th, 'I am almost distracted with joy at the birth of my little niece. I am sorry for my brother and sister [-in-law]'s sake that it was not a boy as I believe they both wished it, but I am sure in a very short time my brother will be as much pleased that it is a girl.' She went on: 'Papa is so delighted it is a daughter. As you know, he loves little girls best. He was, I am sure, more kind than I can ever express to us in a speech he made to Lord Jersey, which was: "If the Prince of Wales is blessed with such a daughter as mine are to me, he will be a happy man indeed." ... I may say in return that, if my brother is as good a father to my niece as the King has always been to us, she will be a very happy little girl.'

But the Prince was truly het up. He wrote a will the night that Charlotte Augusta was born, condemning her mother on every count and leaving the few groats he believed he possessed to 'my Maria [Fitzherbert], my wife, the wife of my heart and soul'. This testamentary bequest occupied twenty-six pages.

The Queen, so practised in the business of childbirth, had sent cradles to Carlton House and had appointed rockers and nurses, dry and wet. Lady Elgin became governess to the baby destined for a majestic calling. From the first, it was pretty much established that Princess Charlotte of Wales was to be the one and only child of the Prince's marriage to Princess Caroline – and hence heir to the throne following her father.

The Prince had no justice on his side. He had taken a dislike to his cousin which largely hung on his continued love for Mrs Fitzherbert, although, a fastidious man, he found Caroline's slatternly approach to dressing and even washing off-putting. The Queen took his side, at least partly from a dislike of the Princess's mother. The princesses, for too long accustomed to defend the Prince against all comers, were beguiled by their brother's stories of his wife's insubordination. They sympathized with him and made few attempts to see their cousin and sister-in-law. And so the Princess of Wales found no support in the unknown country of England – except, indeed, from her uncle the King. But, powerful though he was, the King could not command his son to reconcile with his niece. Besides, he believed that wives should obey their husbands. And the princesses, when they tried to be even handed, failed too. Princess Elizabeth wrote to her brother on 6 June 1796 of the King 'constantly saying that you should never yield to the Princess, and she must submit which every woman ought'. She added, 'He has said and re-said that you must be supported by the whole family, for, if you was to fall, the rest of the family would soon follow.' The reference was unmistakably to the Duke and Duchess of York, whose amicable separation had already caused England's ally the King of Prussia some grief.

Meanwhile, the negotiations for the Princess Royal to marry the Hereditary Prince of Württemberg began – and proceeded at a snail's pace. The Württemberg commissioner who had been despatched to London that month was Count Zeppelin, the intimate friend of the Hereditary Prince since they had been brothers-in-arms in the Russian military service. Indeed, he was said to be such an intimate friend that the previous Hereditary Princess had objected, and the King's reference to the Hereditary Prince's 'brutal ways' may have been occasioned by such rumours. At any rate, on 4 May Count Zeppelin had 'a long conversation with M. le Comte de Woronzow' – the Russian Ambassador to London – 'who informed him of the zealous interest taken by the Empress [of Russia, the Hereditary Prince's sister] in respect to the object of M. de Zeppelin – and he [Woronzow] had the most positive orders of Her Imperial Majesty to use any means in his power to her name to facilitate its accomplishment'. Two days later, Zeppelin made the formal proposal in his master's name for the Princess Royal's hand in marriage, and on 4 June the Hereditary Prince wrote to an English baronet, Sir John Coxe Hippisley, who had interested himself in the affair, of his joy at the successful outcome of 'my dear Zeppelin's negotiations'.

The King's response was cautious, and he wrote of his daughter to the Hereditary Prince from Kew on the 15th, 'In an affair so essential to her happiness it would have been contrary to my duty not to leave her per- fectly free in taking time to fully reflect' before declaring her sentiments. He gave his consent to the match, but he could not think of sending his daughter to Germany until it was in a more tranquil state. Likewise, he stated: 'You must defer coming to this country until circumstances are such that it [the marriage] can take place.'

The Prince in Stuttgart was impervious to snubs, and the Princess Royal wrote on 7 September to the Prince of Wales to say that she had received 'a very handsome letter' from him. Everything that had been anathema to her was enchanting now. 'We were out to see the line,' she reported, describing the spectacle of part of the British fleet sailing in formation past Weymouth Bay. Generally the Princess hated her family's daily pursuits – music, cards and the sea – but on this occasion, she added, 'I own I was much amused.' Baron de Rieger, the Württemberg Envoy Extraordinary, left Stuttgart for London with the marriage contract in his luggage on 3 October, charged by the Hereditary Prince to tell the King 'of the happy change in our affairs ... the tranquillity of this country'. And the King, resigning himself, told Lord Grenville on 6 November: 'Baron Rieger is to arrive in the course of this month to conclude the treaty of marriage.' Promptly next day the Baron duly arrived, and presented his credentials from the Duke and Hereditary Prince to the Duke of Portland.

Unfortunately, towards the end of that month the Princess Royal caught jaundice, and was 'as yellow as a guinea'. But, her sister Augusta wrote, she bore 'the inconvenience of the complaint with uncommon patience and Sir Lucas Pepys foretells the greatest good from it'. Early in the New Year she wrote again to Lady Harcourt: 'All the spare time I have is devoted to poor Pss R who, after a week's amendment, is worse than ever ... It is a detestable complaint and I fear, will not leave her as soon as she thinks. She is as yellow as gold and as weighty as lead – suffers more than she ever ought to do and is as patient as a lamb.'

Jaundice, wicked weather, reverses on the Continent in the war against France, and many other obstacles notwithstanding, the determined bride was dressed and ready when the Prince, having disembarked on her native coast from the *Prince of Orange* packet on 10 April 1797, appeared at the Queen's House on the evening of the 15th for their first interview. Princess Elizabeth wrote to Lady Charlotte Finch immediately afterwards, 'We are just come upstairs and I can say with great truth and pleasure that nothing could go off better than the interview of this evening with the Prince of Württemberg. My sister is very well pleased with him, and I really think that he appears delighted with her. He has a very handsome countenance, is certainly very large – but very light with it and a most excellent manner. In short, we are all pleased with him.'

'Very large' indeed: Frederick, Hereditary Prince of Württemberg had a huge stomach, so large and round that Napoleon said of him: 'God put him on earth to see how tight you could stretch, without bursting.' 'Sensible and well informed' he might be, '... though not exactly the picture of a young lover', as Lord Grenville wrote. But his appearance was a gift to the London cartoonists, who seized on this German prey and dubbed him the great 'Bellygerent'.

The Princess Royal did not flinch from her purpose, although a private letter of 13 May from Windsor told Fanny Burney she was 'almost dead with terror and agitation and affright at the first meeting – she could not utter a word – the Queen was obliged to speak her answers'. The Prince said courteously that he hoped this would be the last disturbance he would cause her, and paid court successfully to her sisters until she was recovered.

A note written by the Princess Royal exists from the days that followed: 'My dearest Lady Harcourt, I have received the Queen's commands to acquaint you that if you wish to see my trousseau, she desires that you will be so good as to be at the Queen's House tomorrow morning at eleven o'clock. Pray mention this to nobody, as the Queen does not wish it to be spoken of.' And among the gowns and dresses laid out at the Queen's House were two complete sets of baby clothes, one for a girl, one for a boy, till the age of three. Most of the dresses, however, were unmade. Queen Charlotte, who had taken on the task of equipping her daughter, had merely selected material to be made up in Germany according to fashions there.

As for the wedding ceremony itself, the Queen declared that she and no other would dress Royal for the occasion, as Augusta told Miss Burney when the latter said she had heard 'the bride had never looked so lovely'. Proclaimed the younger sister, ''Twas the Queen dressed her! – You know

what a figure she used to make of herself, with her odd manner of dressing herself; but Mama said, "Now really, Princess Royal, this one time is
the last; and I cannot suffer you to make such a quiz of yourself; so I will
really have you dressed properly." And indeed', added Augusta, 'the Queen
was quite in the right, for everybody said she had never looked so well in
her life.'

Augusta's light-hearted recital does not disguise the tension that existed
between Royal and the mother she was about to leave. But the Queen
spoke admiringly of Royal insisting on embroidering her 'wedding gar-
ment, and entirely ... well knowing that three stitches done by any other
would make it immediately said it was none of it by herself'. With her
mother's sanction, the silks she used were white and silver, her right as
eldest daughter of the King, although, marrying a widower, she should,
according to etiquette, have been in white and gold. James Bland Burges,
as knight marshal of the King's household, walked ahead of the tremulous
Princess and her husband 'immediately after the drums and trumpets, and
in front of the pursuivants and heralds'. And in the accomplished cartoon
by James Gillray entitled *The Bridal Night* that depicts this scene, not only
does the coronet, 'set with brilliants', that the bride wore, shine, but a bag
marked £80,000 floats above the procession.

The new Hereditary Princess of Württemberg brought to the marriage
a dowry of £80,000, which would become her widow's jointure if she survived her husband. The King, citing the uncertainties of Continental war
and hence the uncertainties of currency valuation, insisted on keeping the
sum lodged in Britain. The Hereditary Prince did not argue, but he protested on another point, 'extended a finger and said, "not a ring to show"'.
In Germany it was the custom for the bride to give the groom a present of
value. Even the Princess's hair in a ring surrounded by brilliants would
answer for his marriage. The Harcourts returned a dusty answer: 'I hope
... that upon reflection the Pce will consider that every country has its own
customs, and that it is as reasonable that he should at present be satisfied
with those established here, as it will soon be for the Princess to adopt those
of the place she is going to. It would be very painful for her to find that
there was dissatisfaction, after all the pains that have been taken to show
every attention.'

The Princess Royal was up early on 2 June 1797 to make her departure
with her bridegroom on this great adventure, having said her goodbyes to
her sisters and parents the evening before. 'The parting was very severe,'
noted her niece Charlotte's sub-governess, Miss Anne Hayman. 'There was
to be no leave taking by mutual agreement, and the sisters dropped away

one by one the evening before. But when the King went to wish the Princess of Württemberg good night, she fainted in his arms, and he was obliged to leave her in that state, not daring to encounter the scene that might follow.'

Her brother the Prince of Wales walked about Carlton House till midnight, meaning every instant to go and bid his sister farewell, but, feeling too much, he put it off till morning. When morning came, he was too affected to depart the house, and then it was too late. The new Princess of Württemberg, however, the night before forgotten, 'sailed in good spirits'. Her family was less sure than she was of a successful outcome to this step into matrimony, less sure of her husband and of his character. Five years later, on 11 October 1802, Queen Charlotte wrote of the Hereditary Prince to her brother, 'I agree with you, he is agreeable in society.' Among the Hereditary Prince's friends in England were Sir Joseph Banks, with whom he stayed, and who advised him on an agricultural and manufacturing tour he made of the country while he waited for his bride to complete her arrangements for departure. 'But he has a vanity which made him detested in England,' continued the Queen. 'He did not know how to govern his bad humour in the presence of the women of my daughter's suite, and for a man who prides himself in knowing the world, that was to forget himself entirely. In a few words, he displeased us totally and his departure was not regretted.'

But the new Hereditary Princess was at last in a situation, as Miss Burney wrote, to make her happy. 'She is born to preside,' wrote the novelist, 'and that with equal softness and dignity; but she was here in utter subjection, for which she had neither spirits nor inclination ... her style of life was not adapted to the royalty of her nature, any more than of her birth; and though she only wished for power to do good, and to confer favours, she thought herself out of her place in not possessing it.' If that power came at a price, the Princess Royal was never to regret her marriage. Exhilarating was the moment after a night at Harwich when the Hereditary Princess stepped aboard the *San Fiorenzo*, and that when she stepped ashore at Cuxhaven, to be greeted by her brother Adolphus. 'He is grown much larger since he left England and having let his hair grow as long as Ernest's was, it has altered his appearance very much,' she wrote to the Prince of Wales.

The couple proceeded to Hanover, in her father's Electorate, for balls and drawing rooms, all etiquette and formality at Herrenhausen, and then on through the countryside, where 'the peasants enquired which was the King's daughter', and asked the King to come and visit them. The Princess had her first encounter with Mme de Spiegel, who was to be her lady-in-waiting at Stuttgart. Onward she drove to Brunswick, to Nordheim, to Münden, and to the gates of Cassel, while her mother in England wrote to her brother Charles, 'I have just separated from my daughter Royal. It cost us much, God hopes she will be happy. The Pce has esprit, worldliness, and knows how to get what he wants. They are both at an age when they must know how to discern what true contentment consists of, and, first youth being past, they must endeavour to make themselves mutually happy.'

The Prince, who had gone ahead, greeted the new Hereditary Princess – with full honours and with his two sons – at Heilbron, frontier to the Duchy of Württemberg, on 23 June. Prince Wilhelm and Prince Paul were, their new stepmother wrote, 'so like my brothers that I was both pleased and overcome'. And the next day, arriving at Stuttgart, she met both her parents-in-law. That evening, at Ludwigsburg, the massive castle in the country where the Württemberg family liked to live as much as possible, she met her nine-year-old stepdaughter Catherine. All three of her stepchildren were to be encouraged by their father to call his new wife 'Maman'. And for the first time ever this new bride and stepmother, who had been known as 'Royal' by her intimates, was known by her husband as 'Charlotte'.

Timid the Princess Royal might appear in company, nervous and sometimes reduced, for fear of stammering, to speaking little, but she had achieved her heart's desire – to marry. On her arrival at Ludwigsburg she found her husband Fritz had sent ahead a copy of Gainsborough's portrait of her dear father to hang in her closet. Whatever his faults as a husband to her cousin Augusta, this Prince of the Holy Roman Empire seemed determined to please her.

BOOK THREE

SCANDAL

1798–1810

9

In Spirits

~

THE KING HAD found parting with his eldest daughter very painful, and was hardly better disposed towards his new son-in-law than was the Queen. He resented the Hereditary Prince's attempts to secure his interest for the Duchy with letters and even via petitions from the Princess. The Hereditary Princess had to reassure her father that, on her instructions, the Prince would write no more, as the King disliked answering letters. Accordingly, when they heard at Windsor that the Prince had had an accident out shooting in Germany, no great sympathy was felt for him.

But at Scharnhausen, the Hereditary Prince's country retreat near Stuttgart, it was a major drama. The Hereditary Princess told her father she had been 'seized with ... an unaccountable uneasiness' after she had seen her husband mount and ride off. She could not go on with her book, but went up 'to sit with Madame de Spiegel in her room'. Fifteen minutes later that lady was called out to go to Prince Wilhelm, the Prince's son, and when she returned she begged Royal to join her in the garden. 'The moment that I had reached the bench I burst into tears,' wrote that Princess, 'entreating that she would acquaint me with what had happened to my husband. She then by degrees told me that he had fallen from his horse.'

After a short time her stepson Wilhelm came out to bring Royal into the house. She found the Prince in bed, 'and he then told me himself that his arm was broke. It is a great mercy that he was not killed, as in the first fall he broke the right arm in the joint ... and afterwards, as it was on the side of a mountain, rolled four times. His eyes was much bruised but providentially not hurt essentially.' With great presence of mind, as the Hereditary Princess lovingly wrote, 'before they could lift him off the ground, [he] ordered his son to go to Madame de Spiegel, to desire that she would break it to me in the gentlest manner and gave directions that I should be taken into the garden, that I might be spared the pain of seeing him lifted out of the coach.' Royal was entranced by this proof of her husband's consideration for her. Their being in so remote a part of the country, the surgeon could not arrive for hours to set the arm, but when Royal went to her husband, 'he kept laughing and talking with me for above three hours, when he insisted on my going to supper, and the moment I left him he fainted away'.

The princesses in London were, as Miss Hayman, in attendance on their niece Charlotte, observed at the Queen's House a few days after Royal's departure, 'very pleasing and affable, but still lamenting, I believe, the loss of their sister'. But by early August Princess Elizabeth had become callous, telling Lord Cathcart that her brother-in-law in Württemberg was none the worse for his mishap. 'No more has happened than a broken arm … notwithstanding he never quits his room.'

Princess Elizabeth, however, had grown in confidence since she had published a book in 1795 entitled *The Birth and Triumph of Cupid*, containing some twenty-four designs she had made on that theme, engraved by the Queen's 'Historical Engraver' Mr Peltro Tomkins. The following year, the plates were republished as *The Birth and Triumph of Love*, accompanied by a set of 109 Spenserian verses on the same amatory theme by that enterprising young man of letters – and subsequently member of the King's household – James Bland Burges. A connection of Martha, Lady Elgin, when she was one of the Queen's ladies, and a sometime Foreign Office employee, Burges enjoyed versifying in assorted magazines of the day. He had his reward when he learnt in November 1794 that all the princesses copied and kept his verses, considering him 'an astonishing genius', and that Princess Elizabeth was in addition the author of some anonymous poetry he had received. At a drawing room shortly thereafter, his 'Muse' – Princess Elizabeth – asked him the names of some French émigré officers awaiting presentation, and their introduction was effected.

'I will satisfy your curiosity about my epic poem', wrote Burges to a friend when busy at work the following year on his Spenserian verses, 'on condition that you will confine what I say to yourself for the present … I have already finished the first book of it in the metre of Spenser's *Fairy Queen*, but not in his antiquated language. How the idea may have been executed is not for me to say; but the idea in itself is so entirely original, that I am confident nothing like it is to be found in any language. I caught it from some drawings of Pss Elizabeth, and I am writing this poem for HRH.'

On Twelfth Night 1796 the poem was complete, and Lady Elgin wrote from the Queen's Lodge to Burges that she had given it to the Princess, whom she saw briefly. 'I was … most completely gratified by her manner of reading,' wrote Burges's champion, 'and the delighted expressions that burst out, I may say, as she went through the lovely poem.' The Princess, not wishing to have her Cupid 'mortified' by being set aside, did not show it to the Queen, as the Oranges were on the point of arriving to dine. But while she was showing it to Mr Smelt, the Queen came in and, as Princess Elizabeth herself wrote, 'I had the pleasure of putting into Mama's hands Sir James B B's most beautiful and elegant poem … my poor little foolish silent Cupid owes all its worth to the poetry, for I never saw him before in the favourable light you all did, till he was privileged with verse.'

Burges had considered that, if the publication he envisaged of the manuscript he was working on were a success, 'it will place me not very low among the English poets'. Princess Elizabeth was more modest, and sent a copy of her original Cupid engravings to Lord Harcourt, with the note: 'As you was so very good as to wish to have a copy of *The History of Cupid*, I do beg your acceptance of it. It is in so terrible an undress, that I am really afraid to send it.' Nevertheless, she wrote, 'I send it the moment I received it, in hope that it might give you a moment's amusement, which if it does, will gratify me very much.' All the princesses in different ways relied on Lord and Lady Harcourt as sounding boards for the great world, from which they were aware they lived secluded. Ever since her 'great illness' at Kew, Princess Elizabeth had felt sustained in her artistic endeavours by Mr Smelt. In this new adventure of publication, Lord Harcourt, who was not only a distinguished amateur artist himself but also a noted patron of poets and artists, supported her.

Once encouraged by publication, there was no stopping the Princess. (She may, in 1794, have been author of the illustrations Tomkins provided for an edition of the royal ladies' favourite volume of poetry, Thomson's *The Seasons*.) And Tomkins executed soon after a further set of engravings from her drawings, entitled *The Birthday Gift or The New Doll*. In March 1796, Princess Elizabeth wrote to Lady Harcourt:

> As I make it a rule never to push, I was not so lucky as to get near you [at Court]; which you will now have occasion to be sorry for, being troubled with one of my very stupid notes; which will be made double so, by being forced to name the insignificant present of the 'Delights of a new Doll,' which I shall be very much flattered if you will accept. I send you two copies, one for yourself, one for Mrs Damer, if you don't think it impertinent. I forget whether I ever sent you the engraving of the dancing dog.

Lady Harcourt, whose work Horace Walpole had wished to publish, provided in return by way of compliment *Philip, A Tale*, dedicated to Princess Elizabeth.

When Miss Burney visited the royal family in July at Windsor to present to the Queen her new novel *Camilla*, Princess Elizabeth was still full of her own publishing venture. She related 'the whole of her own trans-action, its rise and cause and progress, in the Birth of Love', wrote Miss Burney in her journal. But Miss Burney failed to record these details, judg-ing that she must abridge her account of her visit to Windsor there, else she would never finish. She had energy enough however to note, of her own book, that Princess Elizabeth had exclaimed, 'I've got leave – and Mama says she won't wait to read it first.' With permission so graciously given, 'I wrote immediately to order six sets, bound in white and gold,' recounted a delighted Miss Burney, one for each of the Queen's daugh-ters.

While her sister Royal was glorying in the sumptuous palaces of Stuttgart and Ludwigsburg, set in a land of plenty famed for its Rhenish wine and romantic forests, Princess Elizabeth had a very different view of how best to live in a changing world. She wrote from Kew to Lord Harcourt, thanking him for arranging a trip to inspect Strawberry Hill, where Horace Walpole worshipped the Gothic and classical past: 'My life has certainly been spent at Court, but my actions and affections have ever been guided by sincerity and truth, and have no tint whatever of a cour-tier. At this place my great hoop is dropped, and my plumes lowered so that the Pss is left in town and the humble miss steps forward.'

Princess Elizabeth did not, for all that, abjure luxury. The Queen gave Miss Burney in July 1796 an account of her new house at Frogmore, of 'its fitting up, and the share of each Princess in its redecoration'. Miss Burney had already heard from a Windsor correspondent of Princess Elizabeth's work there painting ceilings and designing buildings in the gardens. And when she visited the princesses' different apartments at Windsor this summer, she spoke of Elizabeth's as the 'most elegantly and fancifully orna-mented of any in the lodge, as she has most delight and taste in producing good effects'. In consequence, the artistic Princess knew what it was to be in debt and, James Bland Burges claimed, she had said she would soon go to jail.

But Elizabeth had a liking for comfort of a more substantial kind too, which her friends the Harcourts enjoyed supplying. She thanked them in December 1796 for 'the best Bath buns that ever were eat which saved me from a lethargy of cold which I suffer with more than ever. Now picture me sitting in the fire with all my different comforts round me in my own room, in the act of copying, when a knock at the door made me turn and your kind present entered the room. I will own to you the moment the box was open I looked with an anxious eye to see whether you had sent me a few lines.'

The Princess Royal withdrew, and then departed for another life. Princess Elizabeth resorted to Bath buns for comfort. Their younger sister Sophia found a confidante, as the troubles worsened between the Prince and Princess of Wales, in the shape of Miss Frances Garth, who had been appointed sub-governess to the couple's daughter, Princess Charlotte, on her birth in January 1796. Miss Garth, niece of the King's equerry Colonel Thomas Garth, had been companion to Lady Harewood, and was a plain, modest young woman with a talent for embroidery and fancywork. Princess Elizabeth on one occasion wrote to thank her for a cloak she had made for the Queen: 'so perfect a piece of work, which Mama says is done more like a fairy than anything else'. The Queen added that it was the only cloak that had ever fitted in her life. Sophia, alone of the princesses, felt that the Princess of Wales was unfairly treated, and Miss Garth struck her fancy. But Miss Garth may also have acted as an emissary, with the Princess of Wales's encouragement, for a romantic correspondence – or something more – between Princess Sophia and Miss Garth's uncle the Colonel.

Fanny Burney visited the Queen's House on Sophia's twentieth birthday in early November 1797, and was interested both by her appearance and by her self-consciousness:

> She had a pair of spectacles on, which, with her uncommonly young face – its shape being as round as a baby's, and its colour as rosy – had a most comic and grotesque appearance ... She is so near-sighted, that she is almost blind; and the Queen now permits her always to wear spectacles. 'And I want her', said Princess Augusta, 'to wear them at the play, where we are going tonight; but she is afraid, she says, of some paragraph in the newspapers; but what, I ask her, can they say? That the Princess Sophia wears spectacles! Well, and what harm can that do her? Would it not be better they should say it, than she should lose all sight of the performers?'

Augusta herself, although shy, was not vain. She 'let the hairdresser proceed upon her head, without comment', wrote Miss Burney, 'and without examination, just as if it was solely his affair, and she only supported a block to be dressed for his service ... And when he begged she would say whether she would have any ribbons, or other things, mixed with the feathers and jewels, she said, "You understand all that best, Mr Robinson, I'm sure – there are the things – so take what you please."'

Sophia supported her sister-in-law the Princess of Wales with difficulty, her mother and sisters being partisans of the Prince. On one occasion the Princess said, 'I perceived you withdrew from me, but I saw your motive, and approved greatly.' In June 1796, when Carlton House was ablaze with emotion after the Princess of Wales had forced the resignation of her husband's lover, Lady Jersey, as her lady-in-waiting, Sophia wrote in flattering terms again to Miss Garth, hoping she would wear the hair she sent around her neck: 'Your uncle also told me you had desired him to give me your duty. Indeed, be assured you will, in time if not already done, turn my head.'

The uncle of whom she spoke was Colonel Thomas Garth – major-general from January 1798 – with whom Frances Garth lived after her father's death. He was one of the King's favourite equerries, and was much with the royal family.

On another occasion, Sophia, thanking Miss Garth for helping her with a troublesome piece of needlework she had sent her, wrote, 'O! Were I my own mistress how often I would fly to you.' She was glad the accounts were good of the Colonel. 'May I beg you to thank him for his remembrance of me, and to mention how sensible I am of his not having forgot me, and that I am very sorry I have not seen him for so long.'

Thomas Garth was a small man, 'a hideous old devil' according to one account, and marked by a claret-coloured birthmark that extended down over one eye. In compensation, contemporaries speak highly of his wit and, indeed, of his stories of his own soldiering adventures in the West Indies. At any rate, Sophia had entangled herself romantically with him by the autumn of 1798. Her sister Mary wrote in September to the Prince of Wales: 'As for General Garth, the purple light of love toujours le même'. While this may or may not have been a cruel allusion to the General's birthmark, or just a quotation from the poet Cowper, a daughter of one of the Queen's ladies later recalled, 'the princess was so violently in love with him that everyone saw it. She could not contain herself in his presence …'

A year earlier, in the summer of 1797, with Miss Garth now a woman of the bedchamber to the Princess of Wales and part of that estranged Princess's establishment at Blackheath, Princess Sophia wrote that she had found an emissary to be trusted with correspondence for Miss Garth when she accompanied the Princess of Wales to Carlton House to see Princess Charlotte: 'His name is Robinson, he has lived with us many years and may be depended upon – He will therefore walk to Carlton House with his son, who will I trust be allowed to give you my letter without further enquiries …'

Far away from the intrigue that sometimes characterized royal family life in England, the Hereditary Princess of Württemberg was absorbing the new country over which she would preside with her husband when the Duke his father died. 'She has won the hearts of all who have seen her from her great affability and desire to please,' wrote an English resident there, Sir

John Stuart. Sir John considered the Princess 'particularly fortunate' in her choice of Grande Maîtresse, or Mistress of the Robes – Mme de Spiegel. She was 'a woman of great merit, nearly her own age, of much information, of irreproachable moral character, and who has conducted herself with great propriety in her own family through difficult circumstances'. Charlotte also had acquired Mme de Spiegel's young niece and daughter-in-law as ancillary ladies – 'Her RH treats them as if she was educating them herself with all the good humour possible.' Stuart considered the Prince and Princess had made a wise choice in appointing ladies from outside the Stuttgart 'Circle'. 'Another generation must pass before the ravages made by the Duke Charles' – Fritz's uncle and a former reigning Duke – 'in the morals of every rank can be repaired,' wrote Stuart ominously.

It was of another generation that the Princess wrote to her father on 30 August 1797 in some excitement: 'The Prince has desired me to present his humble duty to your Majesty and to express his great regret at not being able to write. But not having it in his power to do more than sign his name with his left hand he does not think it respectful to acquaint your Majesty in that manner he has reason to hope that I am with child '

They were off to the Prince's house at Ludwigsburg to escape the heat of Stuttgart as she wrote. Court functions, balls, assemblies and levees took place in that city at the Neupalais or new palace – a huge Baroque edifice accommodating within its gilded marble corridors, as well as state rooms, a multitude of doors and staircases leading to apartments for all the branches of the ducal family. In the small town of Ludwigsburg, halfway up the hill, a former duke had built an enormous palace rivalling Versailles in size, featuring wall-to-wall classical paintings and Pompeian rooms, and commensurate acres of garden. But, just as at Windsor the royal family lived in the shadow of the Castle in the Queen's Lodge, so at Ludwigsburg the Hereditary Prince and the rest of the family inhabited more informal residences abutting the Palace.

That October, congratulating her father on the British naval victory of Camperdown, Charlotte resumed a plea for his aid, as Elector of Hanover, for her new home, Württemberg, at the forthcoming Congress following the conclusion of peace between Austria and France. The Ducal House of Württemberg had lost so much – in both territory and revenue – by this 'cruel war', she wrote. Looking with confidence to the future, she added that, in supporting the Prince, her father would be 'taking in hand the interest of a son sincerely attached to your family, of your daughter and of your grandchildren'. While the Duke had sent Count Zeppelin to Vienna and then on to St Petersburg to seek the backing of those imperial Courts, the Princess believed her father's support would be most effective. The friendship between her husband and Count Zeppelin may have been more than platonic, but it does not seem to have disturbed Royal: Zeppelin was welcome at Court, with his wife and daughter. (His friendship with one Count Karl Dillen was anyway judged now to be closer than that with the Hereditary Prince.)

From Scharnhausen, four months pregnant, Royal wrote in late November 1797 to England – now standing alone though firm against France – of the 'dreadful' times, of the new King of Prussia's difficult inheritance, and of Austrian regiments marching daily through Stuttgart. To her husband, who was away shooting, she wrote on the 22nd an account of how she passed the hours. It had snowed all morning the day before, and when darkness fell, she and Mme de Spiegel had worked and drawn for five hours till nine. Falling back on patterns familiar from Frogmore days, she was embroidering a chair cover with eagles and, she wrote to Fritz on the 23rd, she hoped to finish it that day.

This peaceful way of life came to an end at midnight on 22 December 1797 when Fritz's father dropped down dead. And as his mother's health weakened, Royal increasingly had the care of her stepdaughter, who had been living with her grandmother. Also, with the theatre of war now moved to an area north of Switzerland, the Duchy, positioned between France's eastern frontier and Austrian territories, had become a favourite route for both French and Austrians on their way to attack each other's territories. The damage the troops did as they passed through, to say nothing of the foraging and plundering that went with such mass movements, was fast impoverishing the normally wealthy Duchy. Earlier in December Royal had written to her father in England that the Austrian artillery were now marching through the country – and in heavy rain – for the fourth time that year, and that Austrian troops passed frequently through Stuttgart on their way to their new Turkish territories.

Frederick wanted Royal to rest, to abjure long drives. Royal, following the example which she had seen her mother set so often, intended to continue a normal life until the last month of her pregnancy. Her husband did not wish her to attend a card party of English émigrés from Switzerland that she had arranged. Royal dismissed his worries: the Court doctor, M. de Weimar, was on hand, and her health seemed good.

Another of George III's children was hoping this winter to marry and provide further grandchildren. Prince Adolphus had been invited in August by the Prussian King to join a family party at Pyrmont with the Crown Prince and Princess – a Mecklenburg cousin, Louise – and with another, widowed cousin, Princess Louis of Prussia and her two children. (Prince Louis had been killed in action the previous year.) Years before, Prince William had been smitten in Hanover by their cousin Charlotte or Lolo of Mecklenburg. Now his brother Dolly fell passionately in love with her younger sister Frederica, the widowed Princess Louis, and in December won her agreement to their engagement. The King in England sanctioned the match, made his son a colonel and even bought Dolly a house on the Leinestrasse in Hanover for a married home. But the marriage contract would have to wait, he warned, until Parliament – sore from war expenses – was in a mood to grant his son the income of a married man.

The very public if unofficial separation that had taken place between the Prince and Princess of Wales did not commend to Parliament the idea of financing another royal marriage. The King ordered a great Thanksgiving at St Paul's for the naval victories of that year – Camperdown in October against the Dutch, and Cape St Vincent in February against the Spanish – and, for good measure, Lord Howe's victory on the Glorious First of June in 1794. But neither the Prince nor the Princess was present. After a good deal of wrangling over carriages and appeals to the King he decreed that their finances allowed neither of them to appear. Unfortunately, the couple's wrangles, as much as the prospect of the Thanksgiving, gave the Queen a wracking headache which prevented her appearance at the drawing room – 'crowded with heroes' – on 12 November preceding it. By December that year the Prince was petitioning the King for a full separation from his wife, but the King refused it.

Meanwhile in Württemberg the new Duchess, although six months pregnant, had to throw off her previous 'retirement' when her husband inherited. Sir John Stuart had written, 'I imagine she will not think her situation so agreeable, when Duchess. If she indulges herself in retirement then, she must become unpopular at a German Court.' But although the new Duchess informed her father that, from economy, she was to take no more ladies to reflect her new station, and her husband meant to keep his father's establishment, she happily moved into the new palace at Stuttgart. 'This evening I am to have an English card party,' she wrote to her father. 'We are in hopes that many who have left Switzerland will settle here, at least till they see what turn affairs are likely to take.' The previous year the French had made of Switzerland a Cisalpine Republic. 'Every moment the people come in to move some of the furniture. My new apartment is both fine and convenient, as on one side I have my private rooms and on the other those to receive company.' The portrait of her father, she wrote, was to be hung in her 'favourite closet'.

They moved, too, into central apartments in Ludwigsburg, a palace where 'everything had been allowed to go to ruin' and no doors shut, and lived with workmen all around them while Royal neared her time. They were planning to make Stuttgart and Ludwigsburg comfortable and 'to attempt nothing more', she said, citing that reprobate Duke Charles's 'folly of constantly launching into the expense of building new palaces and neglecting the old ones'. She would send her father a plan of the alterations at Ludwigsburg when all was complete, but wondered, as they were to have a menagerie there, 'will your Majesty forgive my entreating you to send us a pair of congaroos [kangaroos] which would be a great pleasure to us?'

The death of her mother-in-law in March 1798 gave Royal yet another 'undertaking': 'I am now very much taken up with Trinette' – Catherine her stepdaughter – 'who, unless she has lessons, never leaves me for a moment. One thing gives me great pleasure ... that from the beginning she took to me very much, and her age being the same as my dearest Amelia's makes her doubly interesting to me.' She was grateful to her father for the advice he gave her 'to try by my example to imprint those principles [of religion] on the mind of Trinette ... I trust I shall succeed in my endeavours to make her, as far as I can, go through the same course of religion that Mama made us read with Schrader [the German Reform Church pastor in London].'

The move to Stuttgart came at last, and from there Royal wrote to England, a week before the baby was due, that she had taken the Sacrament with her husband: 'I own I felt a great deal of joy at being enabled to go to the altar, as I think that when one has fulfilled that duty, one's mind is better enabled to go through any undertaking in life.' And then the baby did not come. For three weeks the Duchess lay in a state of suspended animation, while the Duke fussed about her. And Princess Amelia, in England, wrote lightly that there was no word of the sprouting branch of the Württemberg family. The 'heat and the confinement' of Stuttgart made both Duke and Duchess long for the country and Ludwigsburg where they would go after her confinement. Admittedly it was the 'fashion' in Germany not to stir for six weeks after childbirth. 'However, I plead mama's example and then they must submit,' she wrote on 13 April, set on leaving within the month. Looking still further ahead, she pressed Mr Charles Arbuthnot, the British envoy who had come to congratulate the Prince on his accession, to stay on till the christening, there to act as the King's representative. Her conception of all that was to come was at last realized. All was in place, when the pains began. The Princess prepared herself and the accoucheuse and ladies gathered.

But then all Royal's hopes and dreams foundered. Her labour produced a stillborn daughter. The Duchess 'having been delivered of a dead child and having suffered very greatly in her lying-in', Mr Arbuthnot began a difficult letter to the Prince of Wales, 'so much fever ensued that for a short time the physicians were apprehensive for her safety'. The Duke of Württemberg's Chamberlain, Baron de Wimpfen, wrote more openly on 30 April 1798 to Sir John Coxe Hippisley: 'Her Royal Highness continues to manage as well as is possible in her situation, but she does not yet know of the death of her child, for which they are preparing her ...' But then, when the body of Fritz's father lay in the palace of Stuttgart, where his widow was, Fritz had a newspaper printed and given to his mother, falsely declaring the body, which she had wished to see, to be instead at Ludwigsburg. Medieval indeed.

When the Duchess was told the evil news of her baby daughter's death, her husband told her also of their subjects' concern for her health. Even the country people came into town to get news of her, and the bourgeoisie were planning a fête for her recovery, an event unheard of in the annals of the Duchy. 'We consider the death of the child as a true sadness,' wrote Wimpfen. 'It was a beautiful big girl who, in becoming a new bond of union and tenderness for father and mother would have contributed strongly to her Highness's happiness. We must hope for the future, today all the wishes are united for her recovery.'

The Duchess wrote to her father from Stuttgart on 4 May: 'Do not think me ungrateful to Providence for the many blessings with which I am surrounded when I say that the loss of my dear child has deeply afflicted me. I trust that I feel this as a Christian and submit with resignation to the will of the Almighty, but nature must ever make me regret the loss of the little thing I had built such happiness on: when I do this I frequently blame myself as God has made her happier than my warmest wishes could have done.' She thanked God for her husband's affection and attention in her distress – 'I am doubly sensible of this happiness as it falls to the lot of so few people in our situation of life ...' And she even thanked Mr Arbuthnot for his courtesy in giving up the ball he had planned to give to the Duke in honour of the birth of her child. The preparations having been made, he had proposed to give it instead in honour of her recovery. He 'had the goodness to give it up when he heard how deeply I was afflicted at the knowledge of the death of my child'.

Four days later the Duchess was stronger. 'Though I shall long silently mourn my child ... were it in my power to recall her to life I would not do it. These times are not those to make one pity children it pleases God to save from the miseries of this life.' The doctors had advised the Duke to take his invalid wife to Deinach, a 'famous water drinking place ... where I am also to take the baths of Liebenzell which they assure will perfectly cure me'. In the meantime they moved to Ludwigsburg and she was carried into the garden there, hoping soon to be able to walk to the large English garden the Duke was laying out at a distance from the house. Her husband, still tender, made a flower garden outside her dressing room for her more immediate enjoyment, and a year later she was to take pleasure in 'drawing the flowers that blow there'.

In the months following the stillbirth, Royal was 'very busy' with her drawing, and by August could tell her father that she walked a great deal – 'generally two hours a day and near five or six English miles in the woods and often in the fields. I am afraid that my pace is sometimes a little irksome to the other ladies but having now obtained that they divide themselves, and that some walk in the morning and the others in the evening I go on in my old way, as I find it agrees very much with me, as notwithstanding all this exercise I continue very fat, without it I should be a perfect sight.'

A portrait commissioned by her husband of Duchess Charlotte about this time shows her golden haired and smiling, but grown sensibly more matronly, in a muslin dress. Schweppe, the artist, may have been exercising some restraint with his paintbrush. The Princess Royal had, of all the three eldest princesses, always been noted for her good figure, but following her pregnancy and the stillbirth of her child, she grew larger with every year until it was eventually reported that she had no shape – like snow. A year after the stillbirth, she was to write uneasily to her father that she was now nearly as large as her husband. The mind boggles. The Duke had by 1802 a piece cut out of the whist table at home to accommodate his stomach, although when he was in London an accurate observer, Sir Gilbert Elliot, told his wife that the bridegroom's belly was not as large as had been advertised. But, although the Duchess ceased to mind about her size, she did not forget the hopes she had had of her dead daughter.

No more children came, although she hoped for them and kept till her death the baby clothes she had brought from England. 'If ever the Almighty blesses me with girls, it shall ever be my object to have them constantly with me, and to try gently to correct little faults,' she wrote, in one of many long letters of advice she composed for Lady Elgin, governess in England to her two-year-old niece Charlotte. They contained the wisdom that she would have wished to have lavished on her own child's education. But, as she wrote to Lady Elgin a few days after the anniversary of her daughter's stillbirth, she did not think she would wholeheartedly enjoy seeing her niece: 'The sight of all children is a pleasure mixed with pain.'

Princess Charlotte enchanted others, including her grandfather the King. He played with her on the carpet at the Queen's House as he had done thirty years earlier with his own children. She sang 'Hearts of Oak' for him, and in return he bought her a large rocking horse. 'She is the merriest little thing I ever saw,' wrote her sub-governess when she was one and a half. 'Pepper hot too, if contradicted she kicks her little feet about in great rage but the cry ends in a laugh before you well know which it is.' Her aunt Royal hoped that she would one day be a bond of union – even a magnet – between her parents, but she was to be more a bone of contention.

Princess Mary reported that Weymouth this September 1798 was 'very dull and indeed stupid' after the fun of Windsor, for within two weeks Princess Sophia was ill with 'cramp in her stomach', and it was 'a perfect standstill of everything'. She wrote to the Prince about his 'amiable left hand', Mrs Fitzherbert, to whom he thought of returning – and to whom the following year he did return. The Prince's estranged wife and their daughter were now both settled out of London, the former at Montagu House on Blackheath and her daughter and attendants in the village of Charlton near by.

Princess Sophia was continuing her correspondence with Miss Garth, and was pleased that she had looked 'fitter than for some time past' when she walked on the terrace. At Weymouth, when she had recovered from her illness, she rode out with her father every morning, which 'does not make me a little vain', and in the evenings they went to the theatre where Kemble and Mrs Mattocks were in residence. Sophia finished by giving Miss Garth an account of her uncle, General Thomas Garth: 'he is very well but not over and above pleased with Weymouth; notwithstanding he is all good humour and as cheery as ever; you know he is no small favourite of the dear King's'.

The General's principal period of attendance each year on the King was during the three winter months, but as Major-General of the district he had a house near Weymouth, and so was a constant visitor there.

Meanwhile, Princess Amelia, youngest of the six princesses, was having an adventure of her own at the staid sea-bathing resort of Worthing. At her sister Royal's wedding the year before, Amelia, an excited fourteen-year-old debutante, was the tallest of all the sisters with big bones, a fine bosom and mid-brown hair. Further, according to Miss Burney, she had 'ruby lips' and 'an expression of such ingenuous sweetness and innocence as was truly captivating'. The King adored her, while Amelia herself worshipped her eldest brother the Prince, and of all her sisters loved the motherly Mary most. Her life, unlike those of her elder sisters and as befits that of the youngest child of such an enormous family, had been till now free of care. When the King recovered from his 1788–9 illness, the doctors said that the Queen should from now on address herself entirely to his needs. 'Then I pity my three younger daughters, whose education I can no longer attend to,' she said. Amelia was then five. The King later inscribed a book that he gave to his eldest daughter, 'For the Princess Royal, governess to her five sisters' – and there was some truth in his words. According to Mrs Papendiek, the Princess Royal took a great interest in her youngest sister's education at least, and gave her lessons. But there seemed nothing to pity Amelia for in having such a serious scholar and affectionate sister for a tutor.

And then her health became alarming. On 8 October 1798 Amelia should have been celebrating, with the rest of her family, Nelson's annihilation of the French fleet at the Battle of the Nile, of which word had just reached England. But in the summer of this year, as Nelson was chasing the French fleet, she had developed terrible inflammation and pain in the joint of her knee. With Gouly, and Gouly's brother General Gouldsworthy and other attendants, she was sent in August to Worthing, where, it was thought, she would be more quiet than at Weymouth, and where Dr Thomas Keate, an excellent surgeon, especially in the matter of wounds and injuries of the arteries, and Sir Lucas Pepys attended her. Amelia confirmed in a letter to her father at Weymouth that she could never have reached that resort. Even the short journey to the Sussex coast from London had been agony.

Every morning in August, in pursuit of a 'perfect cure', she sat out in 'a little garden near the sea', and all afternoon she sat out on the sands. A sofa that the Prince of Wales sent her was pulled up on board a barge attached to a sloop named the *Fly*, for her to lie on and better enjoy the sea air, but the motion disturbed her. 'I find my leg at present much the same,' she wrote to her father on 9 August, 'but certainly the vapour and warm sea bath are of use and therefore I hope that I shall soon be able to assure you I am better.' Her brother the Prince was assiduous, and in early August visited her from Brighton further along the coast with more presents. 'The hats are very pretty and fit me exactly,' she wrote in thanks. Later in the month she was out on the barge again, this time in 'a cot which is a very clever invention as it will prevent my feeling a great deal of the motion'. But there was still no 'material amendment' in her knee.

Princess Amelia, aged fifteen, was determined not to complain to her parents. 'Oh dear, *that* I cannot help saying, but complain I will not,' she wrote to her English teacher, Miss Gomm, adding, 'I have given over dining with the ladies, as having no appetite, the smell of meat was very disagreeable to me.' But she underwent treatments that appalled her. 'Only think of my being electrified,' she exclaimed, 'you well know my horror and fright for it, but I put that aside as well as I could the moment Mr Keate told me he wished me to try it. I must ever think it horrid. It hurts very much when it is upon the knee, although it is done in the slightest manner possible.' On her arm it was nothing in comparison, 'though it was done stronger'. To her 'feels [feelings]' the knee seemed the same but Dr Keate said it was better, and she had an appetite. 'Laudanum to a great degree is left off,' she told the Prince on 28 October. 'I have attempted to stand up – It gave me very severe pain though I did only do it for half a minute.' The Prince visited her again, and the Duke and Duchess of York called on her.

When Miss Burney saw Amelia one morning this summer at Sir Lucas Pepys's house, the Princess, 'seated on a sofa, in a French grey riding dress with pink lapels', seemed as lively as ever. But her condition became clear when, on leaving the room, she had to be 'painfully lifted from her seat between Sir Lucas and Mr Keate'. Grateful for all, Amelia did wish, in her pain and discomfort, that she could have just one sight of her sister Mary's shining face. 'Oh dear, never can there be such another angel in this world.' Amelia's only fear was that the angel was too perfect to be long for the world. She swore she should die if Mary did. On her parents' Coronation Day, the *Fly* sloop, commander Captain William Cumberland, fired a 'feu de joie' out at sea, and as she wrote the band was playing a last song out of *Blue Beard*. Mary and she had sung that 'almost the minute before my lameness seized me', she recalled sadly.

When the doctors Sir Lucas Pepys and Mr Keate attended on 13 November and solemnly ordered her to keep her leg down, Princess Amelia obeyed and no longer laid it on the sofa. Sir Lucas, physician in ordinary to the King since 1792, was inclined to be dictatorial and very firm in his manner. 'It is four months since I have let it hang, and therefore of course it hurts,' she wrote bravely. She complied also with their directive that she ride, and General Gouldsworthy lent her one of his horses, Frolic, for an attempt out on the downs where no one could see her. Eventually came success. Sir Lucas's prescription and the electrifying answered – or the knee healed naturally. By Christmas Amelia was back in London. 'I go on riding every day, and now canter,' she wrote, and was on her way to join the family for Christmas at Windsor.

A curious story exists about this sojourn at Worthing relating to Amelia and Robert Keate, nephew of surgeon Thomas Keate, who assisted his uncle with the royal patient there. In her August letters she told the King that he seemed to be 'a very modest, civil young man and anxious to do what is right'. But she also told the King 'how attentive and anxious to do right' was Captain Cumberland. He took her out, lying on a sofa imported for the purpose, to recruit her health on his barge. Nevertheless in early September, when the older Keate had to leave Worthing periodically to attend another patient, young Keate became responsible for her case – 'his nephew, who is very gentle, attends me, you know', Amelia told her father. Given the curious circumstances of her isolation, with only Gouly and Mrs Cheveley and General Gouldsworthy for companions – even Lady Charlotte Belasyse, Amelia's lady, was called away to Yorkshire – it seems perfectly possible that the young nephew and Princess enjoyed during this summer at the least a tender relationship. But there the matter did not end. Lord Glenbervie learnt from the Princess of Wales twelve years later details that she had heard from the Duke of York about this Worthing sojourn – that 'being engaged one day' there, Keate had sent his nephew to Amelia, 'who communicated an infection to her from whence all her subsequent illness originated'. We shall see that this gossip chimes with fears about her fertility – and with detailed descriptions of symptoms that tally with those of venereal infection – that Amelia herself expressed later in extremely confidential letters.

For the moment, Amelia was restored to health and the following summer could join the rest of the family at Weymouth – where the princesses had their niece Charlotte to dote on. Amelia gloated over the baby one afternoon when, all by herself, she collected her from her nap and gave her her tea. Amelia, when not in pain, continued to be lively and enthusiastic. She was also religious. On 24 December 1799 she was confirmed by the Archbishop of Canterbury in St George's Chapel, Windsor. She believed that 'the consequence these two days have been to me' would long endure, for her happiness depended on it.

Others in the family were not so blessed. After a period of some months in which she had not answered his letters, Prince Adolphus had heard in Hanover on 27 March 1799 that his beloved fiancée Frederica, widow of Prince Louis of Prussia, had married the Prince of Solms the day before. Admittedly there had been obstacles in the way to their own match, as the King was still waiting for peace to ask Parliament for a grant for the marriage. But poor Adolphus was beside himself with grief and mortifi-cation in the house on the Leinestrasse in Hanover that he had so lovingly prepared for his bride.

Among the comings and goings of officers and battalions and regiments at Windsor, one arrival was of significance for Princess Augusta herself – that of General Sir Brent Spencer, an Irishman who commanded the 40th Somersetshire Regiment. Since becoming an ensign at the age of eight-een, he had been almost constantly in the West Indies. But now, aged thirty-nine and a bachelor, he returned from an ill-fated expedition with the 40th to the Helder under the command of the Duke of York. When he brought despatches from the Helder to the King at Windsor, Sir Brent made such a favourable impression on the monarch that he was appointed one of his aides-de-camp, and took up residence at Court.

But Spencer did not long remain with the King – perhaps fortunately, since he was 'anxious and fidgety when there was nothing to do', as a con-temporary put it, 'but once under fire like a philosopher solving a prob-lem'. Soon he was away again, off to command the 40th in the Mediterranean – Menorca, Malta and then to Egypt with Abercromby's expedition to force the French out of Alexandria and Cairo. But he had made an impression on Princess Augusta, whose siblings had always teased her about her 'rage militaire', and she had equally affected him. She had written in 1793, 'I intend for the rest of my life to be very despotic until I have a Lord and Master, and then (unless I break the great oaths and prom-ises I shall make when I marry) I shall give myself up to his whims.'

Now Princess Augusta dreamt of having Sir Brent Spencer not only for a lover but for a husband, as she later recounted. But she did not yet reveal her feelings, strong though they were, to Spencer himself. He, for his part, caused much ill feeling when he unaccountably broke his engagement to his cousin Miss Canning this year, but whether this was on account of unspoken feelings he had himself for Princess Augusta cannot be known. It was dangerous for any private gentleman to have feelings for these prin-cesses, when the King their patron would not allow even princes to come near them – unless the princess herself gave encouragement. In due course Princess Augusta would give that encouragement, in pursuit of private happiness within the confines of the Royal Marriages Act, an ambition that she had long pondered. The intensity with which she pursued that goal would startle those she entangled in her scheme – Sir Brent, perhaps, as much as anyone.

The Prince of Wales meanwhile had returned to Mrs Fitzherbert, and Princess Augusta wrote to him on 25 August 1799, without apparent irony, 'how very much it stands to your mutual credit, that old friends sincerely and unalterably attached, should come together again'. A year earlier she had written that all the sisterhood felt concern at 'the dejected appearance you made. I am not such a child as for you or anyone else in the world to suppose me ignorant of the cause ... After such real affection, not to say adoration on your side, and I am confident from all I have heard pretty near the same on hers, I am certain it is nothing less serious than a reconciliation, which would surely make both of you happy.'

Other unorthodox arrangements proved too fragile to withstand the displeasure of the author of the Act. In Berlin out of the blue Prince Augustus's wife Lady Augusta Murray had appeared at his side, alarmed to hear he was ill. After an interval of six years apart the Prince and his lady lived contentedly for a time, and even provided for their son Augustus a sister, Augusta. But the Prince was recalled to England by his father, and not long after his arrival there in May 1800, his Berlin sojourn with his wife and son and their daughter's birth appeared like a dream – as did his promises to Lady Augusta of eternal fidelity. Shrugging off all encumbrances, Augustus took up his father's offer of apartments at Kensington Palace and became an avid bibliophile. He welcomed visits from his brothers and sisters at Kensington, but bad health, he claimed, kept him away from Windsor.

Meanwhile in the spring of 1799 in Württemberg Augusta's elder sister Royal had believed herself in real, not romantic, danger as the French drew near. But she had resisted her husband's attempts to send her to safety. Her sister-in-law Princess Ferdinand, a target as the wife of an Austrian general, had left for Hanover on hearing the report that the French intended marching through the Duchy. As the daughter of the King of England, the Duke argued, Royal would have also a special value to the enemy. But with the stepchildren, and her ladies, she remained in Stuttgart and Ludwigsburg – keeping up lessons in engraving with Friedrich Müller. She preferred not to be parted from her husband, she told her father: 'some days ago I was low with the thoughts of what might happen but now that the decisive moment approaches I am perfectly calm'.

Notwithstanding her calm, Royal lamented to her father the ruin of the country. The French armies under the command of General Moreau were in and out of the city, eating all they could find, stealing cattle as they pleased, and the Austrian generals imposed equal demands. The Duke dissolved the Stande or Parliament when it advocated making peace with the French, and offered stout promises that he would never leave his people – only to renege on that when the Helder disaster appeared to render flight essential. The Duchess reluctantly agreed to go to Wengen in September

1799, but after a few days she was celebrating her release from captivity. The menace had passed for the time being.

The next spring, however, there was no way out. To Erlangen in the Prussian King's Franconian lands the Württemberg women and children retreated in 1800. Here in a flat landscape of conifers and sand, far from the fruitfulness of Württemberg and in a small house, Charlotte, Trinette and Paul sat down to endure the war. By a touch of fate, the pair of kangaroos she had requested from England were their companions – an intelligent chamberlain at Stuttgart had divined they would be of interest to the royals in their exile. This was not what Charlotte had expected when she adopted that diamond headdress and had her hair pulled into ringlets for her wedding day. She had hoped above all to be a mother, but she had certainly also looked forward to exercising the power of her position as the matriarch of a major Continental power.

Stoic by nature, self-abnegatory by upbringing, Princess Charlotte Augusta Matilda, Duchess of Württemberg looked out over the desert sand and identical pines in the shifting light and fretted that the French would destroy the improvements she and Fritz had so recently made at Ludwigsburg. Meanwhile, her husband the Duke of Württemberg, with his son Wilhelm, was energetically attempting at Vienna to redress his altered fortunes, and those of his Duchy. He expressed himself as bitter against Britain, which had done so little to aid his country considering their new family connection. And the Mintos heard that he was among those eager to separate themselves from the fading Holy Roman Empire and seek their fortune with Napoleonic France. Colleagues remonstrated with Minto for listening to the Duke, but the diplomat stood firm:

> Besides the natural claim he seemed to have as an ally and relation of our own Court to support from an English minister in his relations with this Government, it seemed impossible to refuse a ... kind and friendly ear to the lamentations and claims of a prince whose ruin seems so much a consequence of this relation and engagements to us ... It is not his merits, but his misfortunes, or rather ruin in a common cause that my indulgence is directed [to]. I admit also that he is no apostle of our cause, and I can easily believe all you say of the mischief done by his indiscreet and perhaps ill affected language. Yet I have not nerves to resist altogether, or rather feel some indulgence for the cries and clamour of a real *agonie*. For he is at present struggling in the very convulsions of political death.

In England Charlotte's sisters had recently recovered in May 1800 from convulsions of a different nature. Huddled outside the royal box at Drury

Lane Theatre behind their mother, who was waiting to join her husband once he had taken his bow, they heard a shot. At first they thought it was a 'squib' backstage. Then the King waved the Queen back, saying, 'Don't go forward, a man in the parterre has fired a pistol.' The Queen, worried that her younger daughters would faint, said nothing, for fear of uttering a 'bêtise'. For two minutes the theatre was silent. 'You could have heard a pin drop,' the Queen told her brother. Then, with the marksman apprehended, the King advanced, showing himself safe and unharmed, and a hubbub, with 'cries of joy', erupted. But the actors were too frightened to start the comedy, and the audience wanted to know what had happened. 'Finally,' reported the Queen, 'an actress was pushed onto the stage.' The actress announced, 'I have the pleasure to tell you the man is in custody,' and the comedy, very badly performed, began. There was no political intention, at least, in the attempt on the King's life, as Sheridan, the theatre manager, discovered on questioning the marksman. James Hadfield, a hospital orderly who had tried to murder his child two days before, joined Margaret Nicolson, the King's earlier assailant, in Dr Monro's asylum, Bedlam.

Sophia wrote to Miss Garth on 25 May of 'the miraculous escape of my most perfect and angelic Papa', at the same time complaining of having been very far from well 'with a complaint in my stomach'. The year before she had been afflicted by this complaint, as in earlier summers, including that first occasion in 1793 when she had stayed for so long at Tunbridge Wells and again in the summer of 1798. She had been forbidden 'any kind of fatigue or hot rooms' this time, and therefore would not be at the Birthday, although she told Miss Garth that she would accompany her parents in the following month – July – to Weymouth.

In the event, Sophia and Amelia set off a day before the rest of the royal party, and stopped for the night en route at General Gouldsworthy's house outside Salisbury. It was said that Princess Sophia was still so weak she had to be carried up the stairs there. The rest of the royal party pursued their usual headlong course by coach from Windsor to Weymouth, there joining on 31 July the younger princesses and Prince Ernest, newly Duke of Cumberland, who was taking a course of sea bathing. (The King had provided royal dukedoms for both Ernest and – at last – for Prince Edward in Canada, who became Duke of Kent, in April 1799.)

After taking an airing on the sands in a 'sociable' (an open carriage) with her sisters Augusta and Elizabeth on the 2nd, Sophia was ill off and on at Weymouth in the early days of August until the 8th, when the Prince her brother – with whom she was still on cool terms, due to her support for his hated wife – heard from Amelia: 'at last we have the prospect of seeing our dear Sophia restored to health very shortly'.

Dr Francis Millman attended the Princess, and by 15 August she was judged well enough to take another airing on the sands. Progress continued slowly, and she benefited from the 'warm bath', or bathing in heated seawater, while the rest of the royal family made 'aquatic excursions'. The King rode about Dorset with his son Ernest and with General Garth for companions, while the Queen and the other princesses 'worked' or took airings on the sands. Finally, in early October Sophia was declared fully recovered, and the extended royal visit came to a stop. And shortly before she left with the royal party for Windsor on the 8th, Dr Millman received the King's congratulations and a baronetcy, although it was later said that the King put his daughter's recovery down to eating good roast beef.

At any rate, the party returned to Windsor, after the extended stay at Weymouth, in high good humour to prepare for celebrations to mark the new century. These were to commence on New Year's Day 1801, but there were to be other celebrations soon – for, after seven years of war, peace was at hand.

In December 1800 the Duchess of Württemberg and her children – as she called Paul and Trinette – were threatened directly in the 'paper house' in which they lived at Erlangen. Moreau, having defeated Archduke John, was headed for Vienna, but other French forces had taken Nuremberg and their troops were now constantly marching through Erlangen itself. They were 'quartered in all of the villages around about, which makes me an absolute prisoner', wrote the Duchess. Only the day before she tried to walk round the town, then saw a patrol which stopped them in their tracks. Later that month, during exchanges between the Austrian and French positions, 'one could hear every shot as distinctly as if we were at a Review', but there was no decisive outcome. 'The whole day there is nothing but firing to be heard. God grant the Austrians success,' she wrote with remarkable calm.

The Austrian outlook was hopeless and the Emperor sued for peace on Christmas Day. The Treaty of Lunéville, signed on 9 February 1801 and confirming Campo Formio, put an end to the Holy Roman Empire, concluded the War of the Second Coalition, and closed the eighteenth century with complete victory for France on the Continent – though not as yet in the newly United Kingdom of the British Isles. Over the New Year, congratulating her father on the union of Great Britain and Ireland and wishing him well for the new century, the Princess Royal wrote in disgust that the Austrian troops had simply thrown down their arms on hearing of the armistice.

A few days later she had more delicate information to offer from her husband, who was still in Vienna. The Duke had had to send a representative to Paris. His instructions were to keep in the background and 'come forward' – only when there was no thought of continuing the war, of course – to make a separate treaty with France. The Duke could not, Royal pleaded, maintain war against the might of France with only 7,000 men if Austria had made peace. The English, who had been suspicious of Royal's husband at Vienna, were confirmed in their opinion of him, as he took the first steps towards alliance with Napoleon, and pulled with him Napoleon's foe, the King of England's eldest daughter.

10

Agitation

~

E VEN AS THE Peace of Amiens was being celebrated, Princess Elizabeth
mentioned to Dr Thomas Willis in March 1801 'a very delicate subject – the cruelty of a fabricated and most scandalous and base report concerning P.S. [Princess Sophia]'. The rumour was that she had given birth
to a child at Weymouth the previous summer. 'Such a report', wrote Willis
indignantly, 'must in its nature be false as those who are acquainted with
the interior of the King's houses must testify.' But the rumour or 'report'
was almost certainly true.

Princess Sophia was in no doubt about the origin and fount of the
rumours – her brother, the Prince of Wales, who so disliked her championing of his estranged wife. 'He has trifled with my character, and a
young woman's character once gone is not so easily regained,' she
averred. For even before Lord Glenbervie and Princess Elizabeth gos-
siped and protested, Princess Sophia had confided in her oblique way –
to Lady Harcourt on 30 December 1800 – her distress at the stories that
were circulating about her. Referring to a 'private conversation' they had
had, and to her happiness that she had 'had courage to begin it', she
wrote:

> the excessive kindness of your manner has, I assure you, greatly soothed my
> distressed and unhappy days and hours ...
>
> I have no doubt that I was originally to blame, therefore I must bear
> patiently the reports, however unjust they are, as I have partially myself to
> thank for them; but, dearest Ly H, when I reflect of the difference of your
> behaviour and that of others, it shows me how insincere the generality of
> this world are, and how one ought to value and revere a true friend, which
> is most justly styled the most precious jewel in life. It is grievous to think
> what a little trifle will slur a young woman's character for ever. I do not com-
> plain, I submit patiently, and promise to strive to regain mine, which, how-
> ever imprudent I have been, has, I assure you, been injured unjustly.

For all her fighting words, Sophia almost certainly gave birth at
Weymouth – in circumstances which remain mysterious – to a baby who

was baptized in the parish church there on 11 August 1800. The infant was described in the parish register as 'Thomas Ward, stranger' or foundling, 'adopted by Samuel and Charlotte Sharland', and as having been born on the 5th of that month. Samuel Sharland, a colonel of the Weymouth Volunteers, had a prosperous tailoring business on the Weymouth esplanade, and the birth of his own child was noted earlier in the month in the same register.

There is no doubt about Thomas Ward's existence or about his presence during the first few years of his life at the Sharlands' house on the esplanade at Weymouth. But great doubt surrounds the whole business of his birth, including his birthplace and his birthdate – notwithstanding the date given in his baptismal entry. The child may have been born when Sophia stopped en route at General Gouldsworthy's on 30 July, or somehow, somewhere when she reached Weymouth – not necessarily at Gloucester Lodge, the royal residence on the esplanade, where there was little privacy. Sophia later said that it was her 'old nurse' who was with her at that dreadful time, and stopped the story from coming out then, but gives no further details. Apparently she did not realize for a very long time into her pregnancy that she was having a child.

Still more doubt obscures the identity of the child's father. General Thomas Garth is, of course, the natural candidate, given Sophia's 'passion' for him. A teasing letter without a date and addressed to 'My very dear, dear General' – almost certainly General Garth – refers to their exchange of rings and in other ways convinces the reader that their relationship was intimate. And less than four years after Sophia had given birth, Glenbervie was writing, 'The foundling which was left at the tailor's [Samuel Sharland] at Weymouth about two years ago, is now in a manner admitted by the people about the Court to be the Princess Sophia's and, as the story generally goes, by General Garth ... It is now said the Queen knows the child to be the Princess Sophia's, but that the King does not, but that the Queen thinks Garth the father.'

As if to confirm part of the opinion that Glenbervie ascribes to the Queen – that General Garth was Thomas Ward's real father – the equerry went on to adopt and educate the child at Harrow, renaming him Tommy or Thomas Garth in the process, making him his heir, and fostering his career in his old regiment. The letter Sophia wrote in 1805 referring to her 'old nurse' shows plainly that she was the child's mother. Nothing would appear to be clearer than that, by some lapse in morals or contraception, Sophia and the General had together conceived Tommy Garth in the autumn of 1799. For evermore the Princess was to bear the shame of this ill chance, forfeiting all hope of marriage or domestic happiness. And the General behaved honourably by the boy in giving him his name, if his adoption of young Tommy unhappily confirmed the rumours that he was the illegitimate offspring of the equerry and the Princess.

But Glenbervie inserted an astonishing caveat into his story about Tommy Garth's parentage. After his remarks about the General openly maintaining the child, he added, 'But the Princess of Wales told Lady Sheffield the other day, that there is great reason to suspect the father to be the Duke of Cumberland. How strange and how disgusting. But it is a very strange family, at least the children – sons and daughters.'

This claim by the Princess of Wales, which probably issued from one of Cumberland's brothers or even from the Duke himself, who was 'underhand the great friend of the Princess of Wales' this year – that he was the real father of his sister's child – was to dog Sophia for a long time. As the child grew up, sly references to the story multiplied, and the matter ended by exploding into the public arena when Tommy Garth was nearly thirty years old. Old letters from Sophia to General Garth complaining of Ernest making 'attempts on her person' were supposedly among other documents bandied about at that time to prove that her brother was responsible for her pregnancy.

That Ernest made 'attempts' on Sophia or, in plain language, tried to rape his sister is certainly possible or even likely. The Prince – that boisterous, rude darling of his nurse Mrs Cheveley – knew no boundaries where appetite or decency were concerned, and all his life not only used the grossest language about women, but made the grossest of physical assaults on them – all women, married, unmarried, young, old, innocent and knowing. As a young soldier on the Continent he had to be restrained from trying his luck at a nunnery. In later life one of his victims' husbands committed suicide.

However, let us not forget to whom Sophia wrote these letters complaining of her brother's 'attempts' – to her lover, General Garth. And while Ernest had the opportunity to be the father of Tommy Garth – he was at Windsor during the late autumn of 1799 – Sophia's letter to 'My very dear, dear General' makes it perfectly plain that her relationship with the equerry was long-standing, consensual and intimate. In other words, if an 'attempt' by the Duke of Cumberland was responsible for the child to which his sister Princess Sophia gave birth at Weymouth, rather than the more regular attentions of her lover Garth, she was particularly unlucky. That Garth was the father of Princess Sophia's child is the commonsense and probable, if unromantic and not so scandalous, answer.

Before we leave Tommy Garth in 1801 still at the Sharlands', not due to take up residence for another three years at the home his 'adoptive' father General Garth provided for him at Ilsington Manor at Puddletown near by, it will be as well to quote the undated letter from Sophia already mentioned: 'Though I never can be really angry with you, my very dear, dear General, yet at this moment I almost am so, for you have indeed been excessively naughty. How can you, my dearest General, go on so long, when you do not feel well, without seeing Dr Turton?' This physician to the royal household, who died in 1806, was no doubt required to alleviate General Garth's chronic gout from which he unromantically suffered agonies. Sophia continued:

> Your dear ring has given me some tremendous pinches, but I have bore them like a heroine. If you looked at your little finger when you were so naughty, I believe a certain little ring would have been impertinent enough to have given you a pinch. I think you deserve it – And now, my dearest General, do not forget that, when you are neglecting your own health, you are the cause of giving many unhappy moments to those who love you. And that was the case yesterday, for, as we were going to dinner, I heard you were not well and till the evening, when I saw Miss Gomm, did not know you was better. Therefore, you may easily imagine, dinner went down but so so, but, upon looking at the ring, I was frightened to death and ate like an Alderman.

The letter concludes:

> I assure you I do all in my power (which God knows is but little) to please my sisters, but alas! I fear I do not succeed – I can say no more at present. My heart is too full, but, though I own I am not happy, yet I shall never forget you, my dear General, to whom I owe so much. Your kind remembrance of me is a cordial. Your calling me your S makes me as proud as Lucifer ... I love you more and more every day. God bless you, my dearest dear General. Think of me tomorrow at 2 o clock. I shall then be happy for two minutes as I shall be speaking to dear Gooly once more.

The King was ill. How ill was unclear, but in mid-February 1801, he told General Garth out riding that he was 'very bilious and unwell' and had not slept. It seemed that he had stayed too long in church on the Friday, which had been a fast day. 'The weather was so snowy and cold that His Majesty became excessively chilled.' Shortly thereafter the symptoms of thirteen years before that had so alarmed the royal family and disrupted public business came flooding back – colic, sweating and hoarseness – and led to acute delirium and coma.

Thomas Willis had visited the King on Monday, 16 February at the Queen's House, and was satisfied, after spending an hour with him, that the patient had a severe cold and was hoarse but nothing more. Yet within days, although the King attended a Council – convened, out of respect for his ailment, at the Queen's House – he was 'hurried' and dwelt on his illness of 1788. He told Henry Addington, the incoming Prime Minister – Pitt had resigned over the question of Catholic Emancipation on the 5th – that in 1788 his father Dr Anthony Addington had counselled quiet.

Quiet was what he needed now, and a week after he had first felt symptoms he confided in Thomas Willis, 'I do feel myself very ill.' Sunday, 22 February 1801 saw the arrival of the Reverend's 'medical' brother Dr John Willis and of four burly 'keepers' from Dr Thomas Warburton's asylum, both sanctioned by the Duke of York and Addington. Following the pattern of years before, the Opposition began their 'speculating, anticipating and arranging' of Cabinet posts in the new regency government they felt would soon ensue. For on 27 February Dr Willis, according to the Prince of Wales, 'not only thought that the King could not understand what he read, were he disposed to read but that he could not, to the best of his judgement, know a single letter'. How then could he sign his royal assent to public acts? Pitt's resignation and Addington's substitution as prime minister still needed his confirmation. Russia was establishing an Armed Neutrality league in the Baltic to menace British shipping as she attempted to violate French commerce there. And at a time when Austria and France had made peace, and the Continent was at last quiet – albeit in the stranglehold of France – there was a growing appetite in England for peace. If the King were incapacitated, who would commission the preliminary discussions with France on that delicate subject?

The King's very existence rather than just his sanity seemed in doubt on 2 March. The princesses gathered with the rest of the family at the Queen's House, expecting his fever to end in death. But a stray suggestion from Addington, of putting a pillow of warm hops under the invalid's head, had a miraculous effect. The King slept, he grew stronger. He 'cries at almost anything', the doctors wrote, and he still 'became so puzzled' – when reading state papers – 'that he grew hurried and angry'. But they wrote their final bulletin, predicting complete recovery, on 11 March, and the King accepted Pitt's resignation on the 14th. He even accepted, through the unorthodox medium of the Reverend Thomas, the need for proposals of peace, and signed them. Princess Augusta wrote with relief to Lady Harcourt on 16 March: 'We are as well as can be expected, considering what we have gone through – and though all the great distress and horror is now over, we now feel much oppressed from fatigue of mind and hurry of spirits.' Her mother hoped to see Lady Harcourt the following day, she went on. 'But of course it depends upon the hours we spend with the King or when we are in expectation of being sent for.'

The Queen held a drawing room on 26 March at the Prime Minister's insistence and much to the King's displeasure, when he found that Dr Willis had so blistered his legs that morning that he could not appear. Princess Augusta later recalled her own anguish at this time: 'When I was very miserable and unhappy at St James's last winter I told Lord Harcourt that I never would be happy again. And he was so very good as to say, "O fie, le bon temps viendra." And I was so obliged to him and so incredulous and so low that I could only say, "God knows!" To which he again replied, "He does know best and does best for us all." I always tried to think so, but my mind was too oppressed then to say more.'

In the meantime, while the King's mind was wandering, King Frederick William III of Prussia had issued a proclamation declaring that he was compelled to take 'efficacious measures' against Hanover, and Prussian troops duly occupied the King of England's beloved, if obscure German Electorate. Adolphus, leaving his house on the Leinestrasse in Hanover, was back in England by mid-April 1801, where he found his father recovering – but once more in confinement and in rooms that had originally been prepared at Kew House for his own arrival. The King was there alone with the Willises and their keepers. The Queen and the princesses, in deep distress, lived across the way at the Dutch House, or Prince of Wales's House.

The King had seen his eldest son on 15 April for the first time in a month, and received him with 'every mark of love and fondness', speaking of his happiness in embracing him on the day he dismissed Dr Willis's keepers. He knew of Nelson's victory in the struggle for domination of the Baltic, when that Admiral destroyed the Danish fleet in their own harbour of Copenhagen. But 'of the condition of Hanover none had ventured to talk to him', and he repeatedly declared he was a dying man, and determined to go abroad to Hanover and make over the government to the Prince. The Queen and Prime Minister between them became so agitated by his behaviour that, only days after he had embraced his son and celebrated his freedom, the Willises cornered him on 20 April at Kew, where he had gone to convalesce at the Prince of Wales's House. While the church bells rang on the Green summoning the inhabitants to hear the prayers of thanks for the King's recovery, the eager doctors imposed on the object of those prayers their will and the straitjacket. 'I will never forgive you as long as I live,' said the King. From April to late May he recovered slowly at Kew House, seeing nobody but the Willises – not even his son Adolphus, who inhabited the same house. The Willises were his constant companions as he walked round the gardens or signed official documents. Even after he was better, they stayed until the end of June on Kew Green to supervise him.

During this time the King took the interests of the Princess of Wales and her rights over her daughter almost painfully to heart. Elizabeth wrote to Dr Willis after a visit to her father in June 1801, when the princesses and the Queen, who camped at the Prince of Wales's House, were at last allowed to see their father, now he was recovered: 'The subject of the Princess is still in the King's mind to a degree that is distressing from the unfortunate situation of the family.' He meant to build the Princess another wing to her house at Blackheath, and take care of Princess Charlotte himself. But the Princess of Wales had spoken to Elizabeth in some alarm about all the schemes the King had for her. He was 'heated and fatigued', Elizabeth said ominously. Dr Robert Willis, a third Willis brother called in, said that there was an increase in 'hurry', and his brother Thomas concurred in this opinion: 'His body, mind and tongue are all upon the stretch every minute ...' But the King was set in his mind, not only to spend a period of convalescence at the Lodge at Weymouth which he had finally bought from his brother the Duke of Gloucester now that his confinement was ended, but to lend his support to his niece the Princess of Wales in her battles with her husband the Prince. Days after he had reconciled with his son on his first recovery, Glenbervie reported, the King rode down to Storey's Gate and over Westminster Bridge to visit the Princess at Blackheath with only the Duke of Cumberland and two equerries in attendance. 'She had just breakfasted and was still in bed, and was very much surprised when they brought her word the King was at the door ...' She arose immediately and went down to hear from the King 'his entire approbation of her conduct and his affection for her'.

One cannot exclude the possibility that the King's hostess left a bedfellow when she went to greet her father-in-law. Princess Sophia wrote to Miss Garth from Weymouth in the summer of 1801, expressing a new caution about her sister-in-law, whose independent ways at Blackheath were leading to rumours of love affairs. 'I think it a blessing you are not mixed in her [the Princess of Wales's] confidence, as you can never be blamed; once and once only, and that was at Kew, Elizabeth said she thought the Pss confided in you; I ventured at random to say I thought not ... as to the Pss I never name her to my sisters ...'

Meanwhile the King's virtuous eldest daughter, the Duchess of Württemberg, had returned to her husband's Duchy after a year in exile, and she recorded, 'I shall never forget the way in which they received me; the whole road from Lourch [Lorch] to Ludwigsburg was crowded with people. The Duke and his sons came three miles to meet me. Words can but feebly express the gratitude we feel to the Almighty for having restored us to our home.' The kangaroos came safely home, too, and very shortly, none the worse for their journey, provided two young joeys for the admiration of the citizens of Ludwigsburg.

Royal thought fondly of her niece in England and wrote, 'Pray tell little Charlotte that I send her a fan and when I go to Stuttgart shall not fail to bespeak some silver toys if she continues a good girl.' But on hearing from General Melius, her husband's envoy to England, of her niece's 'musical genius, speaking and repeating French well, and of her pretty manner', she was a little hurt that 'she displayed all these accomplishments without showing any timidity'. In Württemberg the Duchess continued to supervise the education of 'the children', as she called her teenage stepchildren – Catherine, 'who certainly puts me much in mind of dear Elizabeth and has a very amiable good heart', and Paul, who was 'a very comical boy and, in my partial eyes, his manners are like Adolphus's'.

But her delight now was in the gardens and grounds of Ludwigsburg: 'After having been so many months deprived of flowers I feel double pleasure in attending to them and to a very pretty aviary the Duke has been so good as to build for me and to fill with common birds, as I object much to fine foreign ones which would not give me more pleasure and would cost much more trouble.' But all the delights to be savoured on her return from exile paled beside the arrival of a letter her father wrote her from Weymouth, three days after the Willises and keepers had been dismissed for good. 'It diffused on my whole countenance such a look of happiness that the first question my children asked me was what had given me so much pleasure, that they might share in it.'

Information that the King had 'taken to botany' led the Duchess to rejoice: 'You will find it a constant source of amusement.' She had herself bought a garden at Ludwigsburg of seven acres, with a house – 'though in good repair, like old Frogmore and I have made it very comfortable by papering some of the rooms'. And she now tried to 'acquire some fresh knowledge every day', having a good gardener who understood both kitchen and flower garden, and a greenhouse and hothouse, 'for flowers all winter long'.

Furthermore, the Duke increasing her land with the gift of an adjacent three-acre field, the Duchess was able to make hay three times that
year, and feed the two Swiss cows she established there – and a calf born
that September. But she worried, as a good Duchess should, about the
field mice which threatened the potato harvest. Some farmers let their
hogs into the fields to devour the mice, but then they ran the risk of
swine fever. In graceful compliment to her father, she observed, 'Your
Majesty having taken so much to farming is very much admired abroad
and looked on as one of the great causes of the improvements in
England.'

At Stuttgart in the late autumn, the Duchess occupied herself with
copying some dogs from Ridinger engravings, after a spell of damp weather
had prevented her drawing or working – 'it gives me violent headaches'.
She showed her work to the Stuttgart engraver Müller, and 'he appears
satisfied with those I have finished of late, which encourages me very much
to apply [myself]'. At her new house, the Matildenhof, Royal began also
to paint the celebrated Ludwigsburg porcelain with images derived from
the engravings of Ridinger and others. The palaces of Stuttgart and
Ludwigsburg filled with her painted and gilded products – cups, vases,
plates and even plaques set into furniture.

The Duke had given her two very fine flower paintings, which, she
believed, were by Breughel. 'I intend to attempt to copy them but whether
it will be in colours or in black and white I am not yet determined.' She was
delighted with a visit that she had had in November from Lord Minto, the
British Minister at Vienna. 'Indeed,' she declared then, 'it is impossible for
those who have not been parted from their family to imagine the joy one
feels at meeting with anybody who can give some account of all those one
loves. I am like an infant on those occasions …' She pressed the diplomat to
take home to her father an account of her house at Ludwigsburg, her 'favourite spot'. If possible, she contrived to spend one day there every week 'and
watch a little my workmen, who grow very idle if they are not followed'.

But she had other business in December 1801 which she hoped another
British diplomat – Lord Cornwallis, envoy to the Peace of Amiens deliberations – could bring forward: 'Though I understand Great Britain does
not intend to interfere publicly in the interest of the Continent … one
word from your Majesty would have great effect and be highly flattering
to the Duke, who is much attached to you and has been one of the greatest sufferers by the war.' The Duke was still waiting for the restitution of
territory and financial recompense he had been promised at the Lunéville
peace earlier that year.

At Weymouth meanwhile Royal's sisters endured long weeks of ennui, going to the playhouse nearly every night, and sailing on the days the King bathed, so as not to fatigue him, although they would rather have walked or ridden. But, as Sophia wrote on 25 July to Lady Harcourt, they did not complain. 'How trifling are our amusements when compared with the blessing of his returning health; all that should be put aside; no self in the case, and his health be our only object ... there never existed so good a man, a husband and a father.' By the end of the summer the King had recovered, but he looked an old man, stooped and less firm on his legs when, on 1 October 1801, he signed the preliminary articles of peace between England and France.

Princess Augusta in London wrote to Lady Harcourt with relief and regret mixed:

On Sunday I read a letter from my sister [Royal] in good spirits, and all happiness at the Peace – I, who am prudence itself, answered her yesterday that I was glad she was so happy, and that the telegraph had brought her such good news – but did not tell her what I will tell you, that she feels like an inhabitant of the Continent and I, like a proud Islander. Talk of the Continent now! It's all chatter and as good as mouldy cheese.

I heard a long account the other day about the wonderful work the French would set about as soon as their lads returned from their different armies, and amongst other things that they would build a formidable navy. 'So much the better,' said I, 'let them build, and we will take their ships' ... It's no disgrace that we cannot build ships like them and we ought to own that we cannot. Why, Eliza don't grind her colours, grind her scissors, and yet nobody draws and cuts out like her. It's all stuff to suppose that one can do everything ...

Now what a prose I have been led onto, but you are so good you will excuse your spoiled child. And you must recollect for my excuse that I have been so very long thinking only on one subject [the King's health] that now thank God as I have no uneasiness on that head, I may let my head run upon various subjects – that, it is always ready to do it is like a wild colt, running and galloping de çà, de là, partout.

On New Year's Day 1802 that 'inhabitant of the Continent' the Duchess of Württemberg reported to her father the King from Stuttgart that it had snowed above eighteen inches in town and three feet in the country. 'A man was froze to death last night who had lost his road.' She was hoping that 'the road will be sufficiently beat' in a week's time to go in a sledge, 'a favourite amusement of mine and particularly so of all the young people here as these parties end in a ball'. The Duchess's amusements were innocent enough, although conscientiously in May she hoped her father could do something for the Duke with the First Consul in Paris. She did not know that in March her husband Frederick had signed a private treaty with Napoleon, surrendering his possessions on the left bank of the Rhine in return for nine towns formerly Austrian. He was preparing the way to be created elector.

The Duchess kept her father informed of her employment: 'I have bespoke a room to be painted and furnished in humble imitation of the seat at Frogmore but ... I believe it will only turn out a bungling piece of work.' Later in the year English visitors including her brother Adolphus, on his way back to Hanover, described her father's building plans – to restore Windsor Castle to 'its ancient Gothic beauty' and to complete a new castellated palace on the river at Kew, 'Lulworth Castle improved'. 'I hope that your Majesty will allow me to draw you some chairs with a pen on velvet to be placed in this new palace, and that you will be so gracious as to decide whether they shall be flowers or landscapes,' she wrote.

Despite all, the Queen was perturbed by what she heard from Ludwigsburg. Royal had written to her of her cousin the Princess of Thurn and Taxis – 'spirited and agreeable society, very pretty and with a charming figure'. Sadly, wrote the Queen on 11 October 1802, 'I don't think the Princess can say the same of my daughter. I hear from all the English she is enormous. In other respects she does as much good as she can, and studies to make herself respectable by her conduct. That's the essential, but still I don't think one should neglect the exterior wholly.'

Brother Adolphus was searching the Continent for a bride, and he concentrated entirely on the exterior of his sister's stepdaughter Catherine when he rejected her as a bride. For a year now Adolphus and Augustus had, like their brothers, been royal dukes. The King had created Augustus Duke of Sussex and Inverness, while Dolly became Duke of Cambridge, in November 1801. And this Royal Duke was fastidious. Princess Catherine was, following her father's and now her stepmother's example, as fat as could be – as fat, indeed, as his sister Elizabeth and not as tall, nor as pretty, he noted. Besides, he added, 'knowing the violence of her father and mother, I own I am afraid'. He continued his pilgrimage.

At Weymouth this year Amelia at nineteen delighted in the doings of her six-year-old niece Princess Charlotte. 'I have dressed our dear little love from tip to toes for tomorrow [the Prince of Wales's birthday] and dear Mary has dressed me for the day,' she wrote. Fashion-plate Princess Mary had given her younger sister a dress that the elder described as 'in my own style – to make her look less like an old woman than usual'. But Amelia's odd style of dressing did not prevent her from conducting a very open romance with one of the King's favourite equerries, General the Hon. Charles Fitzroy. He had apparently stayed behind as part of her escort the previous summer when she remained with Miss Gomm, her English teacher, at Weymouth for her health a few days after the rest of the party left for London. Her refusal to hide her relationship with Fitzroy, Lord Southampton's second son, her hanging back and riding with him, her insistence at playing at his table at cards, brought down on her the twittering disapproval of Miss Jane Gomm. But Amelia was impervious to such criticisms, as her elder sisters might not have been.

Princess Elizabeth for her part wrote to Lady Harcourt, 'Now, if you wish to hear of Weymouth, shut your door and your window, and I will … say in a whisper it is detestable, and I continue my prayer, "Oh, how I long to be married, be married, before that my beauty decays etc".' (She had no particular candidate in mind, but a review at which the French princes, including Louis XVI's cousin Louis Philippe, paraded before her father would soon concentrate her thoughts.) The days were odious, and the evenings, after 'an hour's German', dressing and dinner, were as follows:

> Read to the Queen the whole evening till cards, when I play at whist till my eyes know not hearts from diamonds and spades from clubs. And when that is over, turn over cards to amuse the King, till I literally get the rheumatism in every joint of my hand … News there is none, but who bathes and who can't, and who won't and who will, whether warm bathing is better than cold, who likes wind and who don't, and all these very silly questions and answers which bore one to death and provoke one's understanding.

There was festivity at the New Year at Frogmore with a children's ball given in honour of the princesses' niece, Charlotte. She 'never was not in any one of the figures and danced with great dignity and looked, if I may say so, what she really is born to be', wrote her aunt Mary, 'but perfectly the life and spirit a child ought to have with it which makes it the more surprising …'. The children supped upstairs afterwards, 'in those two rooms' at Frogmore 'that open into each other with large folding doors, the plateau was filled with children's toys and you cannot think what a new and pretty effect it had'.

As Charlotte grew, and the divide between her parents widened, her aunts in England and in Württemberg thought not only of her wellbeing as a child, but of the character she would bring to the role of sovereign one day. The presence of a docker's child at her mother the Princess of Wales's house at Blackheath alarmed them. Not only was this hardly proper company for the future Queen of England, but the Princess said 'everybody must love something in this world', and lavished attention on this infant, Willy Austin, to the detriment of her relationship with her visiting daughter. These children's balls at Windsor were an opportunity for her to make 'proper' friends. And the Prince her father put in an appearance: 'all good humour, and as you know he can be when he likes and intends to please and be pleased, his manner to the King was just what it always ought to be and the pleasure he expressed concerning his child and his admiration of her was really quite charming'.

By the autumn of 1803 Napoleon was concentrating his considerable forces on the project of an invasion of England, and 100,000 men stood ready at Boulogne to cross. 'We are expecting the French but many say that they will not come, but it is as well they should be expected,' Elizabeth declared stoutly.

The Queen meanwhile told her brother that she and her daughters were amusing themselves at Frogmore 'with a good read, working there on a long table under the shade of fine trees'. But while Augusta listened to the Queen read *The Lay of the Last Minstrel*, far away in a white medieval tower near Frankfurt the Landgrave of Hesse-Homburg wrote on 12 January 1804 to King George III. 'My eldest son [the Hereditary Prince of Hesse-Homburg] has had only one wish for some time,' ran his letter, 'on which his happiness depends; to obtain the hand in marriage of your second daughter, Princess Augusta, and he presses me so strongly to place his wishes at your Majesty's feet that I cannot refuse his prayer. He has no titles to speak in his favour, except his moral character, and the campaigns which he has made with honour in the Imperial service.' But Augusta never got to hear of this proposal. As was his custom, the King refused the honour. But he could not refuse a letter from his son-in-law of Württemberg, who had a new title, if no moral character, to inform the King of. The Diet reconstructing western Germany on a Napoleonic model had decreed that he was to be one of the electors of the Holy Roman Empire.*

This came as a bitter blow, especially as the King of England's own Electorate of Hanover had been lost to the French almost immediately the war began again in May 1803. 'We have had little contact with the continent since the French entered Hanover,' the Queen informed her brother

*On New Year's Day 1806 the Elector of Württemberg was proclaimed King, and later that year the Holy Roman Empire was abolished, being replaced by Napoleon's Confederation of the Rhine. The Holy Roman Emperor renounced his ancient title and became known as emperor of Austria.

two months later. 'The affair of Hanover is a coup de foudre for the King, but he is well.' And Elizabeth wrote to Lady Harcourt, 'The accounts of Hanover almost killed me, as in every sense it was a most melancholy event for the family and all the little hopes we had been building since the treaty of Amiens – like the treaty of Amiens – vanished into air.' However, she continued with gusto, 'as long as England shall be England, I still do hope we shall do. I think everybody may be of use, women as well as men, and we should be getting all our old linen together, making lint bandages and everything useful in that way ...'

In September Augusta had apologized for the penmanship of a letter she sent to Lady Harcourt, but she was writing in Amelia's room: 'Dear Amelia is famously untidy with her inkstand and her pens are six inches deep in black mire.' That autumn, untidy Amelia composed one of several last testaments that she would execute when illness overcame her. All were dedicated to her lover General Charles Fitzroy, 'who nothing but my unfortunate situation parts me from, as I feel assuredly I am the chosen of your heart as you are of mine – I leave you everything I have ...'.

Illness was to turn Amelia's mind hard and suspicious, but now her family still hoped for her perfect recovery from her different ailments. 'Through God's assistance we may see her what she was,' wrote Princess Elizabeth in December 1803. And Amelia herself told Lady Harcourt: 'God knows my heart is gratefully devoted to my family, I possess the greatest of blessings, kind parents and sisters ... Our dear King who is our sheet anchor, and whom we look up to next to Heaven is well. If he is preserved to us I think we must do well.' She loved the Prince almost as much, and complained to him, 'It is ages since eleven of us have been together.'

But the royal family was soon to need their ministering energies for another invalid. As Napoleon was crowned emperor of the French in January 1804, across the Channel the King caught a cold, and a 'rheumatic attack' with malaise and 'hurry' followed. Princess Mary, whose cardinal virtue was calm, wrote in distress: 'The King never left us till half past seven o'clock. Such a day I never went through.' And the Marquess of Buckingham told his brother of 'the certainty of the King's insanity having returned, which is now universally known, and makes a strong sensation'. Once again the King was for a few days in danger of his life, then he recovered.

This time the King agreed that he was ill. He gave the keys to the private drawers of his desks to the Queen, dismissed his pages for the meantime and awaited medical help – and restraint. A new character, Dr Simmons from St Luke's Hospital for Lunatics, was called in, the presence of the Willises being judged likely to bring on dangerous convulsions in their former patient. Although this new doctor – and his keepers – used the same methods the Willises had employed, Prime Minister Addington reported, 'He submits cheerfully to the restraints which he believes to be necessary,' and the King was in a straitjacket night and day. As he was on the road to recovery by 26 February, Simmons was able to declare his methods effective. Princess Elizabeth wrote, after it was over, 'I have never quitted my mother's room morning noon or night ... I am told I am very much altered, look 20 years older. So adieu to looks of any kind, mes beaux jours sont passés.'

By the end of April the Queen could tell her brother that the King was getting better. 'But one does not recover so easily at 66 as at 50.' And indeed for the rest of a harrowing year the King was to veer from cool and collected to wild and sometimes lascivious behaviour, and back again. One event at least pleased him, the reappearance of Pitt as prime minister, He was 'better than I have seen him yet, delighted with Mr Pitt whose presence and conduct have worked a miracle', wrote Elizabeth in May.

'The King (with Dr Simmons at his side) used to ride out at the same time with a great cortege of Princesses and their ladies, equerries, attendants, and frequently some of the Royal Dukes,' an equerry's wife, Mrs George Villiers, later recorded. Her husband, a favourite of the King's, was called to Kew in June 1804 to 'be always at hand to attend upon the King' while the monarch was recovering, and the Duke of Cumberland's house on the Green was offered to his wife and children, so that 'he might have no reason for going away'. Mrs Villiers tells us that she dined every day with the Queen and princesses at the Dutch House: 'I never saw any daughters ... show such assiduous and affectionate devotion to their father ... perhaps none so much as Princess Sophia and Amelia.' In the sad, enclosed world of Kew that summer, these two princesses became intimate with Theresa Villiers, whom they called 'Tant Mieux', and her husband George, whom they dubbed 'Savage'.

Mrs Villiers's friendship with Sophia was to fade but with Amelia it increased daily. However, she wrote, the Princess never spoke of 'the attachment that existed between her and General Charles Fitzroy, second son of Lord Southampton ... From 1804 ... till the year 1808 she never once alluded to it ...' (Amelia was equally discreet with her sister Mary, with whom she was to be on the closest of terms, but to whom she never once spoke of her 'attachment'.) Mrs Villiers added how strange it was that the King, 'though perfectly unconscious of the attachment', never missed an opportunity – when he recovered – of 'placing Princess Amelia under the care of General Fitzroy, whether in dancing, riding or on any other occasion'.

Although the King rode out and gave other appearances of functioning normally, the Prince of Wales felt justified in accusing ministers of conspiring to hide his real condition from Parliament and the country. He begged the Lord Chancellor to regulate the matter – preferably by the Regency Bill of 1789. In July he bewailed the 'extraordinary' circumstance of any king exercising his royal powers while being kept under personal restraint, and begged the Queen to join him in declaring the King incapable.

Princess Augusta wrote to Lady Harcourt on 3 July of 'the constant state of anxiety we live in … it makes me very low, but that I am so used to now, that I can bear it better than I did six months ago … I think it a great mercy we have so little company,' she concluded, 'as a made up face with a heavy heart is a sad martyrdom.' Kangaroos proving a leitmotif in times of affliction for the royal family, she recounted how there was a tame one in the menagerie at Kew that fed from her hand. To her relief, if not that of the Prince, on the 20th of that month the King was declared restored to health. He left Kew for Windsor, and a few days later prorogued Parliament.

The Prince, abandoning plans for a regency, was now exercised by the very odd ideas the King had about Princess Charlotte, but, as Amelia told him, 'All I can make out about you is that until the doctor leaves us he will take no steps to see you or the Princess.' Simmons, having lingered a further month to observe the King, finally departed towards the end of August. The King wrote immediately to Princess Caroline and to his granddaughter's governess Lady Elgin, requesting that they meet him at Kew, the late scene of his confinement. There he told the Princess of Wales that he meant to take her daughter under his care and that of tutors at Windsor, where Caroline might visit her freely. Indeed, he would provide a house there for her convenience.

Three days later, a furious Prince failed to appear at a meeting to which the King had called him at Kew, where he meant to impart this information. Princess Amelia, sending a snuffbox to her brother a few days earlier, had stressed that all their comfort depended on that meeting: 'I am more wretched than I can express … could an extinguisher fall on the whole family as things are it would be a mercy.' Nevertheless, the Prince did not appear at Kew. Instead a note from him was handed by Edward to the King, waiting with his other sons – including Augustus, who had just returned to England – and the Queen and princesses. 'The Prince is ill,' the King announced, and set out forthwith for Weymouth.

'The Queen was much frightened,' wrote Augustus of the awful day at Kew, 'as were all my sisters.' A month later, when Princess Amelia fell from her horse out riding with her father, the King insisted, with unwonted severity and when she was plainly suffering, that she remount and continue. With the Prince's failure to attend the meeting still in his mind, he said that he had one child already who lacked courage. He would not have more.

When the King reached Weymouth, at six in the morning, he was 'less hurried than could have been expected', wrote his daughter Sophia. 'He went to bed for an hour, and since that has not been off his legs, but I trust in God after a few days he will be more quiet as we must make allowances for his joy at this moment finding himself quite at liberty.' But, she added, 'I am sorry to say, he means to wear the uniforms of the different corps ... which is vexatious.' All that summer, according to unkind witnesses, the King dressed in heavy Hanoverian boots and wore great gauntlet gloves, an odd choice of dress for a bathing resort. Buckingham wrote to Grenville, 'My accounts from Weymouth are the same. Mens non sana in corpore sano.'

But there was worse. Lord Grenville had heard from his brother Buckingham in May that, when the King drove out, his sons accompanied him. The Queen and princesses, meanwhile, followed in another conveyance, as he had shown himself to be 'lost to all propriety of conduct in their coach'. The Queen did not now allow the King into her bedchamber, placing two German ladies there and then retaining two or three of the princesses who stayed until he had left the apartment. The fear or disgust the Queen had felt for the King was strong enough to resist the entreaties of ministers, doctors, nature and 'duty', according to a memorandum from Weymouth the Prince of Wales received in September. Lord Auckland wrote to Lord Henley that month, 'Within the family there are strange schisms and cabals and divisions among the sons and daughters. One of the two youngest of the latter dines alternately with the Patron [the King] and nobody else.' Lord Hobart wrote to Lord Auckland the same month, 'It is a melancholy circumstance to see a family that had lived so well together for such a number of years completely broken up.' Dr John Willis had told him confidentially, he added, that 'things would never be quite right'.

The royal parents, dissatisfied and irritable with each other, effectively separated on their return from Weymouth, when they both took up residence in Windsor Castle, in accordance with the King's new project of inhabiting the Castle itself and pulling down the Queen's Lodge. But they lived in separate apartments in different parts of the Castle. The Queen bemoaned the loss of her comfortable warm rooms at the Queen's Lodge, occupying now with her daughters the south and east towers that looked over the Long Walk and the Home Park. The King moved into the northern wing once lived in by Queen Elizabeth, and there his conversation which had been at times 'very childish' at Weymouth became sober and composed.

Other family rifts healed. In November 1804 the King and Prince met at last, 'a day that has created feelings in me never to be forgotten', wrote Princess Amelia. 'The dear king I think wonderfully well. To me he appears more placid and calm than I ever saw him since his illness.' But the King wrote next day to his niece at Blackheath, saying that he now 'wished to communicate a plan for the child's happiness'. And so began a series of conferences at the Princess of Wales's house which alarmed the royal family. Two weeks later Sophia wrote to Mrs Villiers:

> Well my dear, I am completely miserable. The dear angel [the King] gone to Blackheath and probably will not be home till dark. How late it was last night, he could not have been home till one. All this worries us to death. I thought him most hurried when he came in to our dinner, very good humoured, but in a sad fidget, after dinner he talked of nothing but this sad story, but not one word of anger escaped him ... the old Lady [the Queen] is in high glee, I suppose at the dear man's absence – How unnatural, how odious!

Sophia did not relish her growing role as her father's confidante, and, a few days later, remarked that she wished she had a new dictionary 'to do justice to all my heart feels'. The Princess of Wales at Blackheath told of having to leap over sofas to escape the King's passionate lunges, and a housemaid was apparently caught by the King and locked in a stable with him. 'He is all affection and kindness to me,' wrote Princess Sophia, 'but sometimes an over kindness, if you can understand that, which greatly alarms me.' She hoped the Princess was prudent: 'I believe he tells her everything.' Her father's 'flow of spirits' disturbed her.

At Weymouth that summer two physicians speculated that Sophia herself suffered already in some part, and was likely to suffer more, from what people persisted in calling the 'family malady' – that scrofulous tendency which, in her father's case, was held to have 'fallen upon' his brain. As someone who lived on her nerves, Sophia felt keenly her father's changes of mood – and sexual attentions. As she said sorrowfully to Mrs Villiers, 'I wish I did not feel as I do, for these feelings have ever been my misfortune. I wish sometimes I had all the bonhomie of a princess, it would be better for me, but though born a RH, I must feel like the rest of you, and this your kind heart will forgive.' Sophia had been prone to 'spasms' for nearly ten years now, but these 'feelings' and the 'nervous' condition from which she had suffered this summer were apparently new. They were to recur.

Yet Sophia was no supporter of her eldest brother: 'Does he really fancy, because he is the rising sun, anything he says, it is to be swallowed whole?' she asked. But her venom was reserved now for her troubled mother, whom she saw as the chief agent of her father's unhappiness. She recorded that the Queen 'was not pleased at the dear angel's desiring her to go over the castle with him. She said she was "not an enthusiast". How true that is. God knows, her enthusiasm consists in nothing but eating black puddings and German dishes at Frogmore.'

Sophia's spirits were so broke, she declared, that she hoped, 'when my duty to the best of fathers is at an end', that she could then 'retire from this worldly scene and end my days in quiet'. Buckingham, always in the know, declared shortly before Christmas that 'appearances at Windsor are most unfavourable'. Even in her relations with Princess Elizabeth – who, with Princess Augusta, was sympathetic to the Queen – there was no peace for Sophia. The elder sister told the younger, who was writing to Mrs Villiers, to say the Queen was in a delightful humour. 'At this I hesitated,' reported Sophia. 'Eliza then left in a huff saying, "Well say what you like, nobody wants you to say what you do not feel, but it is very unfortunate that people see with such different eyes".' For her part, Elizabeth wrote on Boxing Day that she had been 'more unhappy this year than any one year of my life'.

The King kept to his cold northern apartments at Windsor, where General Sir Herbert Taylor, his new private secretary, now joined him every day. Remarkably he had managed till now his vast correspondence himself. But an unexpected blow, the loss of sight in his left eye the previous summer, had left him persevering with the aid of a green eyeshade. Now the oculist Phipps declared that there was no way to save the right one, short of couching the cataracts, and Taylor proved an able amanuensis. It was said that Princess Mary developed romantic feelings for him, and that they were reciprocated. But gossips were always eager to ascribe to the blameless, beautiful Mary some romantic attachment.

The father the princesses had known when they grew up was now hardly recognizable. The energetic and authoritarian King of their childhood was now a stooped and blind old man on whose behalf Sir Herbert conducted public business, and to whom he related the progress of the war. The King's love of farming and of the countryside and hunting could no longer be realized with much vigour, in his poor state of health. He went out for stilted walks with his equerries and pages, and in the evenings music was his one solace. And yet he remained stubborn on the same points which had tried him years before. He would still not yield on the question of allowing Catholics into Parliament – and he would still not yield on the question of his daughters getting married.

'The kinder the angel King is to me, the more desirous I am of keeping in my own humble sphere ... not asking to court popularity and make my little self of consequence,' Sophia wrote in January 1805. She told Mrs Villiers of an unpleasant ride with her father when he had alarmed her with his hurried expostulations, 'What! What!', and said 'much against the Queen'. He said to Sophia, 'I look upon you as my friend and I will tell you that I cannot go on as I do, she has turned me out of her room, and a friend I must and will have ... I shall find somebody else.' When the King said he saw she did not approve of this, Sophia simply said, 'I lament it.'

With her elder sisters, who were more forgiving towards their mother, Princess Sophia reported, she was highly out of favour, and Sir James Bland Burges heard that the princesses now spent hours in their own rooms and were rarely together. Sophia wrote of their situation: 'to have the whole talked over and canvassed now makes me wretched. It is not that I am invisible to his [the King's] faults, but I know what he was. And can I love him less, when I reflect that this sad change arises from the will of God? And indeed this house is made so truly uncomfortable that I cannot wonder at his flying from it.' A day later she avowed, 'The Queen's manner to the Angel is, in a word, shameful. Indeed I believe she has lost her head and her heart for I am sure it is as hard as a stone.'

In the meantime a new governess, Lady de Clifford, was chosen for Princess Charlotte, 'the quantum of access ... to be allowed to the mother' was decided, and in February Charlotte was established at Windsor. The King wrote on the occasion of Caroline's first visit to her: 'It is quite charming to see the princess and her child together, of which I have been since yesterday a witness.' Now that she had the 'advantage of excellent air and a retired garden' at Windsor, which would be the young Princess's residence for the greater part of the year, he believed his granddaughter would make satisfactory progress in her studies, 'which have certainly been little attended to'. And, his mind at peace, the King was well at last. 'All the hurry of his manners is gone – he never said "hey!" once or "what" twice together,' wrote the Princess of Wales's Privy Purse Miss Hayman, 'and indeed was as quiet and collected as possible.'

The Queen brought up with her more pliant husband in April 1805 the subject of a proposal from her brother Charles in Mecklenburg. He wished his son, the Hereditary Prince, to marry one of their younger daughters. She had not 'named the subject to any of the Princesses', the Queen told the King, 'for I have made it a rule to avoid a subject in which I know their opinions differ with your Majesty's. For every one of them have at different times assured me that, happy as they are, they should like to settle if they could, and I feel I cannot blame them.' The King was remarkably gracious in return – 'My dearest Queen, After having had the good fortune to possess such a treasure come from Strelitz, it is impossible for me to hesitate a moment, if my daughters wish to marry, to declare I would like to see them allied with this house above all others in Germany.' Four days later the Queen wrote to her brother in encouraging terms. The King had agreed that the Hereditary Prince of Mecklenburg-Strelitz should come – in July – but he should be aware, he stressed, that the princesses' dowries were fixed in England. He went on, 'I cannot deny that I have never wished to see any of them marry: I am happy in their company, and do not in the least want a separation.' Still, he would not oppose what they felt would add to their happiness.

The Queen advised her nephew, in fact, to visit only after the royal family had made their summer visit to Dorset. 'The stay at Weymouth is sad. We have very mediocre lodgings and the place really only exists as lodgings for invalids.' She suggested coming after the summer because, in any event, nothing in the way of settlements could be arranged till Parliament met in the autumn.

By chance, Mrs Delany's niece, now a Welsh matron Mrs Waddington, saw all the bridal candidates for the Mecklenburg Prince, as well as their elder sisters, in Lady Charlotte Finch's apartments at St James's this summer. About to join their mother and embark on a drawing room, the princesses with their hoops took up almost all the space in the very small room. Elizabeth was conspicuous by her size in a blue gown, not to mention 'eleven immense yellow ostrich feathers on her head', which Miss Waddington said 'had not a very good effect'. But Princess Mary shone for her 'beauty' and taste combined. Her headdress was 'a large plume of white ostrich feathers, and a very small plume of black feathers placed before the white ones: her hair was drawn up quite smooth to the top of her head, with one large curl hanging from thence almost down to her throat. Her petticoat was white and silver, and the drapery and body … were of purple silk, covered with spangles, and a border and fringe of silver.' Then the call came for the princesses to attend the Queen, and Mrs Waddington observed, 'if they had been anyone else, I must have laughed at seeing them sidle out of the room, holding their hoops with both hands'.

Was Princess Mary – the calm, bland beauty, the fashion plate, the nurse – the bride for the Mecklenburg Prince? Or would he choose troubled, attractive Sophia, or passionate Amelia? Mary was undoubtedly the one without complicated ties to England. Romantically she had only ever been known to favour distantly her cousin Prince William of Gloucester and, before that, more faintly, a man whose proposals of marriage, it was said, she had refused, still another cousin, Prince Frederick of Orange, who had died – and, of course, General Taylor.

The trip to Weymouth this summer was remarkable only for the suffering of both King and Queen. The Queen endured crippling headaches 'in the back part of my head', an inheritance, she declared, from her mother. Only drops from her Kew apothecary, Augustus Brande, relieved the 'tormenting evil'. The King's eyes were so bad meanwhile that he could not recognize people coming into the room – not even, some said, his own children. He had taken an aversion to his green eyeshade and would not even wear it under his hat.

Under these circumstances the princesses, so subject to their parents' moods, were out of sorts. 'Nothing can be more dull than this place not a creature we know,' Sophia wrote. 'General Fitzroy I have only seen for a moment; thank God somebody else is not here,' she added, thinking presumably of General Garth, who had made her dread going out the previous year when he walked about the town with young Tommy Garth.

Princess Sophia was herself not well, being dosed regularly with laudanum. She was mortified to be taken ill on board the yacht, in the middle of dinner with the King in his cabin, and 'carried upon deck more dead than alive'. In that state, 'spasmed all over', she remained till they came to anchor. She continued, well or ill, in her passionate hatred of their mother – 'She makes my blood boil in some things' – and in her compassion for their father's sufferings. There was nothing absolutely wrong or incoherent about him, she said, 'but a triviality about him that greatly alarms me, for it is so unlike himself'.

The Queen's misdeeds consumed her, especially her refusal to share her bed with the King, extending now to fitting locks on the bedchamber door. 'Will you believe it possible that she keeps us there [in her bedchamber] and at last says, "Now, sir, you must go, for it is time to go to bed" – My God ... how can she refuse him anything?' Sophia wished she were the King's little dog: 'what a little Fidel I would be and lay all day at his feet'. And, expressing her wish to escape these scenes, Sophia claimed that, 'could astronomical observation be made', their Windsor neighbour the astronomer William Herschel would see that 'there was a just mistake in my birth, for surely I never was intended for an R H'. Of 'those dull [assembly] rooms', the Princess exclaimed, 'Oh ye Gods, how deadly dull it is, and only think of our going to the Master of Ceremonies' ball and sitting in a circle there – I wished myself a kangaroo.'

Back in London the royal family received in early November news of the victory at Trafalgar that put an end to fears of invasion and of enemy sea power for the duration of the war. The King and Queen were overcome. 'But you know of old,' wrote Princess Elizabeth to Lady Charlotte Finch, her former governess who was now in retirement, 'they place the victory with gratitude at the foot of the throne of grace and though they feel happy, far from exalted.'

Trafalgar put an end to French hopes of naval supremacy, but meanwhile the Napoleonic armies had beaten the Austrian forces into submission when they rose up against their conquerors that summer. As the wife of a Napoleonic elector, the Princess Royal was obliged to abandon her horticultural schemes at Ludwigsburg, and the ouvrages, the ormolu and the porcelain with which she was embellishing all the palaces of the Duchy. In October she fled the advances of the Austrians, once her husband's overlords, for the safety of Heidelberg. There she received the welcome news – from her point of view – that the French had defeated the Austrians at Ulm on the 19th. 'Most providentially the [river] Neckar rose in the night which stopped their [the Austrians'] march,' she informed Lady Charlotte.

With the French defeat of the Russians, the Austrians' allies, at Austerlitz in December 1805, the Continent was truly under French dominion – to the Queen of England's fury. Writing earlier in the year to suggest that her nephew the Prince of Mecklenburg-Strelitz come from Strelitz, she had been so confident that a match would occur that she was led to 'picture one of her daughters in the home where she had been so happy'. But when she had hoped the Prince would visit, in the autumn, the King had called for delay, given the uncertain state of the Continent. At the end of the year, the Queen told her brother that the King had said to tell him that nothing had changed. 'As soon as I see the moment this alliance can take place, I will tell him,' the King told her. 'If only', the Queen wrote crossly, 'on the Continent they had encouraged the soldiers with Nelson's order, "England expects every man to do his duty", and that was all the orders given that day. If Mack and Prince Aursberg [Auersperg] had thought like that, Vienna would not be in the hands of the tyrant.'

The Princess Royal had further details of the French campaign that had so destroyed the chances of one of her sisters joining her on the Continent. And they could not fail to disturb and fascinate her family in England. Just before the Ulm campaign began, the Emperor Napoleon himself visited her and her husband at Ludwigsburg on 2 October. The previous day his marshal, Ney, had taken up residence in the palace of Stuttgart, after the Elector had made a spirited defence of his state against the 'violent Austrians'.

'You will easily believe, my dear brother,' she wrote to the Prince,

> that this was not a pleasant moment for me, but I should despise myself, could I, out of weakness, at such a moment have left my husband ...
>
> Certainly, the Emperor Napoleon's enemies have done him great injustice. I can say with truth that he went out of his way to be attentive to all the Electoral family, but most particularly so to me. Soon after his arrival he made me a visit and sought to say something polite to all present. I am convinced that he wishes to have peace with Great Britain, for he not only spoke with regard of the King, but of you, dear brother, on different occasions with esteem ...

The Electress's belief that her conduct would do the Electorate no harm had been confirmed days later, before she wrote to her brother. As she wrote to Lady Charlotte Finch, 'by an article of the treaty [of Pressburg, signed on Boxing Day 1805] the Elector has been acknowledged by these two sovereigns [the Austrian and French emperors] as King of Württemberg'. The new King ordered a general thanksgiving upon hearing the news, 'and I was obliged to dress in the greatest hurry', wrote the new Queen, 'to attend him to church ... the whole day was filled up by drawing rooms dinners plays and redoutes'. Royal had determined that Lady Charlotte should be 'the first of my friends acquainted with this alteration in my situation'. Writing to her brother the Prince now, she asked for 'that same place in your affection as Queen that I have enjoyed under so many different names'. (The new Queen did not succeed in this wish with her mother. 'Ma très chère Mère et Soeur', she tried writing to Queen Charlotte. 'You may guess how it was received,' wrote Lady Bessborough. The new King of Württemberg meanwhile put an enormous gold crown on top of his palace in Stuttgart to announce his new dignities to all the birds of the air.)

Royal mentioned to her brother, besides Napoleon's visit to Stuttgart on his way to victory at Ulm, that of his Empress, Josephine, 'on her road to Munich'. Both visitors had been charming, the Empress 'a very well-bred pleasant woman [who] does a great deal of good'. Josephine's son,

Royal wrote meditatively, was about to marry Princess Augusta of the ancient house of Bavaria – 'the settlements are very great'.

Years later Napoleon himself recalled his meeting with Royal: 'She soon lost whatever prejudices she might have originally entertained against me. I had the pleasure of interfering to her advantage, when her husband, who was a brute, though a man of talent, had ill-treated her, for which she was afterwards very grateful.' Two years later Royal 'contributed very materially towards effecting the marriage' of Napoleon's brother Jérôme, King of Westphalia, with her stepdaughter Princess Catherine of Württemberg.

II

Outcry

~

ON HEARING THE news of the death of Prime Minister William Pitt in January 1806, Princess Amelia wrote with some acumen, 'I do not fear the present moment so much as the future, for you know with him [her father], distress blazes out long after the blow.' A blow was coming which would distress the King as much, in its way, as the death of his long-serving Prime Minister. For a few months later the Prince of Wales's lawyers placed before the new Prime Minister, Lord Grenville, papers containing such allegations against the Princess of Wales that the King felt he had no option but to appoint – on 29 May – a Secret Commission of four Cabinet ministers to look into the charges.

The papers not only alleged outrageous behaviour with various men on the part of the Princess of Wales, but also claimed that she had given birth to a son whom she was raising in her own house in the guise of an adopted child. It was further alleged that the Princess had announced her intention at a future date of declaring the boy, called Willy Austin, hers – and naming the Prince as his father. The King's instructions to the committee were that they should 'enquire into the truth of the written declarations touching the conduct of her RH the Princess of Wales'. To her daughter-in-law the Queen sent a message by Princess Elizabeth on 31 May that Caroline would not be expected at the Queen's House on the King's Birthday the following week – 'nor in the evening, nor in the morning'. And three days after the Birthday, on 7 June, the Duke of Kent appeared at Blackheath to warn his sister-in-law that within hours many of her servants would be sent for to Downing Street, to be questioned on the evidence they had given – earlier in the year and without her knowledge – to the Prince of Wales's lawyers.

The Princess of Wales spoke of returning home to Brunswick. But on the first day at Downing Street the child whom the Princess had indeed looked after in her house since shortly after his birth four years before was proved beyond any doubt to be William Austin, son of an unemployed docker and his wife. Nevertheless there were other parts of her conduct that the Commissioners viewed with grave concern, and so they reported to the King in July 1806. The King passed the document without comment to his son, beyond saying, as the Prince told his sister Amelia, that the Commissioners' conclusion was 'they could not, as a result, recommend to the King not to receive the Princess, nor to receive her'.

The Prince, furious, still vowing divorce and vengeance on his estranged wife, sought his sisters' company. Princess Amelia wrote to Charles Fitzroy: 'Do you know the Prince's visit made me very nervous, for I love him and yet how all my brothers concern me in their characters.' The Prince told Amelia that 'The King was very kind to him and he thought him remarkably well ... he was sorry the King wd talk so little to him on the subject [of the Princess], that he had tried to bring the subject forward but could not.' Amelia continued, 'The Prince does not mean to let the thing rest here and he swears, if she is received, he will not put his foot into this house or at Court. But he persists that he is sure whatever the K does is not meant unkind to him, and that he is forced into it, and not does it unkindly.'

The Prince, she declared, said the Princess was 'a perfect streetwalker'. And he said to her in front of their sister Mary, 'I tell you what, my dear Amelia, the Princess says, if things don't quite end to her satisfaction, she will bring forward many things she has seen and heard here of your sisters, and will say the K allows things here which he finds fault with in her. Don't be uneasy, it cannot injure your plans and perhaps it might prove a blessing and make you all much happier.' Amelia went on:

> I felt myself colour. Minny laughed. And had she not been present, I really think I could have ventured to speak.
>
> He then asked about the ride, 'Who rode?' I said, 'General Spencer and Taylor.' 'And who did Augusta ride with?' I said, 'With us.' 'No no,' says he. 'I know all.' 'She did not,' I said. 'Ranger [Spencer's mount] was near her, but she rode amongst us.' He then said, 'I know you all. If things turn out well, I shall often come here and ride with you, and we shall, I hope, have many a comfortable pleasant chat and ride, and I will tell you all I see and think.' He appeared good humoured.

There was much that the Princess of Wales could have 'brought forward' about the behaviour of her sisters-in-law had she wished. And she continued to tell Lord Glenbervie privately ever more scandalous snippets about the birth of Tommy Garth, now five years old and living for the last three years at General Garth's house near Weymouth. But Sophia's affair with General Garth was over, its demise hastened by his habit of parading the boy about Weymouth when the royal family was in residence. In

January 1805 the Princess wrote to Mrs Villiers: 'I agree with you that it is very, very desirable that some check should be put to the odd conduct of a certain person [General Thomas Garth] ... At the same time I will candidly avow to you that that person is very difficult to manage, and thus I have more than once endeavoured to point out to him how ill-judged it was allowing ... the younger object [Tommy Garth] to be with him.

'All my entreaties proved very useless', she continued, 'and I merely received a cold answer, that it was selfish and that I could not pretend affection as I never had expressed a desire of even seeing what God knows was out of my power [her illegitimate child]. This wounded me beyond measure, for my conduct had shown but too plainly that I am not selfish, and I own to you that what hurt me the more was the indelicacy this year of knowing it so near me and that I never could go through the town [Weymouth] without the dread of meeting what would have half killed me, had I met it [the child].'

After further remarks on Garth's conduct, Sophia vowed 'to try in my poor way to serve what I ever must feel an instinct and affection for [Tommy Garth]'. At the same time she recognized that she could never go 'abroad', that is marry a foreign prince. She declared, '... I never could answer it to myself to marry without candidly avowing all that has passed ...' Sophia continued,

> ... there is one love to whom I am not indifferent, I will not name him till we meet, and it is this, my beloved friend, that I think of with fear and trembling; could it some time or other be allowed, I think it would make me happy, but though I know the difficulties and above all, I feel that, did he know the full content of this story, he might think me very unworthy of him. And how could I blame him? For I know but too well how I have lost myself in the world by my conduct, and alas, have felt it *humbly*, for many, many have changed towards me ... The person in question bears the most honourable character and was very kind about me at the time of this sad story ...

Would settling with this unknown man with a respectable name in England be wrong, given her shameful situation? This was the quandary Sophia now expressed to her confidante. As the years passed, so did these references and allusions by the princesses to a future – after their father's death, or possibly after his symptoms made a regency necessary – multiply, when much would be possible that was not now.

Shortly after she wrote this letter, Sophia declared that she had been in pain since the Queen's birthday drawing room: 'From my head to my heels I know not a spot free from pain; the weight of the clothes [at the birthday] almost destroyed my poor stomach, and just now I feel a perfect rag.' But within days she was elated by a speech from the object of her affection: 'That evening he did find me out and came up of himself, said he was delighted to see me and lamented his misfortune in coming to Windsor on the very day I was taken ill, to which I answered I was very much obliged to him; we then spoke upon indifferent subjects and [he] at last said, "Pray take care of yourself and do not be ill again for you are of too much consequence to give this fright to your friends too often".'

This speech was enough for Sophia to savour, to build upon, to treasure and repeat – although she was never to 'settle' with this unknown man of 'honourable' character, or any other. 'I have lost myself in the world by my conduct,' Sophia wrote in 1805, and it was unfortunately true. There was little she could do to change that, especially when General Garth thrust her illegitimate child in the way of Society.

In July the following year the General wrote to his niece, Miss Garth, that he had 'some idea of remaining in town a month, and this I cannot do without my family, in short, I cannot live longer without the child'. He added, referring to the Princess of Wales, of whose household his niece was still a member, 'I am not sure I expressed myself to HRH sufficiently respectful or grateful for the superb present made the child, nor indeed did I know how to act, yet I hoped I have not been wanting in respect – if I have, make me so, I beg. The present was too great for the child – Mine on my life and honour, if there is truth in woman, and no ways under the influence of the abominable and idle stories set about the world.' So it would appear that, although they had now quarrelled, Sophia had earlier assured the General that Tommy Garth was his and not her brother's child.

'It is so delicate a thing to attack the honour of a woman,' wrote the Duchess of Brunswick the following month – in August 1806 – to her brother the King, when he delayed responding to the Commissioners' Report, beyond asking the Cabinet to discuss it, and requesting that a copy of it be sent to his daughter-in-law, which was done on 11 August. She and the Duke of Brunswick begged him to publish the particulars of the Delicate Investigation and to receive their daughter. Indeed, she asked for her daughter's innocence to be proclaimed, else the King's and Queen's characters would suffer 'in the eyes of all Europe'. She ended: 'I close this letter with tears.' But the eyes of Europe were elsewhere. That August pusillanimous King Frederick William III of Prussia at last went to war against Napoleon and his Grande Armée – and was soundly beaten for his pains at the battles of Jena and Auerstädt in November.

The commander he employed to head the disastrous force was the Princess of Wales's father, whose attachment to Prussia was so great that he came out of retirement at the age of seventy. Badly wounded at Auerstädt in October, and carried to safety on a litter, near blind in one eye, he begged Napoleon, moving northward, to show clemency to his Duchy of Brunswick. The Emperor agreed, on condition that the Duke abandon the service of the Prussian enemy. But the old Duke replied that as long as he could use his limbs and vital air was in him, he would defend his King and country. He died from his wounds on 10 November at Altona, his wife and the rest of the Brunswick family having scattered in advance. Princess Elizabeth from Windsor wrote in December of Napoleon's victories and his establishment of the Confederation of the Rhine, which included Brunswick and other conquered territory: 'whole countries ruined, burnt, pillaged ... in short, the Duke of Brunswick's death is a most happy release'. But the Princess of Wales in England, on hearing the news of her father's death, fell ill, believing, according to the politician Mr Spencer Perceval, '... it is intended that she shall never be permitted to see the King again, at least not to see him alone.' In October she had sent a spirited defence of her conduct to the King, drawn up by her lawyers, but she had heard nothing in response.

The King wrote at last in January 1807 to say that he would indeed receive her, and that no further steps were to be taken against her. But he noted that there had 'appeared circumstances of conduct on the part of the Princess which his Majesty never could but regard with serious concern'. The evidence of flirting and the allegations of lovers had startled the King, who had fortunately no memory of his own unrestrained and inappropriate behaviour with his daughter-in-law in earlier years. The Princess, furthermore, stood accused of abusing members of the royal family – calling her cousin William, now Duke of Gloucester since his father's death in 1805, the 'grandson of a washerwoman', and Prince Ernest 'a foolish boy'. The rest of her brothers-in-law she thought 'very ill made and [they] had plum pudding faces, which she could not bear'. Adolphus, besides, looked like a sergeant, 'so vulgar with his ears full of powder'. 'Honourably acquitted; but a reprimand' was Caroline's summary of the letter from her father-in-law.

But then the Prince decided that, before his wife should once more be received, his lawyers should respond to the report – 'that I may not have to charge myself with any possible hazard affecting the interests of my daughter and of the succession'. And so, uncomfortably, while the King awaited the arrival of his widowed, stateless sister, the Duchess of

Brunswick, who had begged a home, he waited too for his son's lawyers to permit him to receive her child once more.

A change of ministry brought an end to the affair, and in April the King at last received the Princess. But, as Princess Elizabeth noted, the public had taken very badly the royal family's treatment of the Princess of Wales, both over the Delicate Investigation, as the enquiries at Downing Street became known, and over her father's death. It was believed, the princesses lamented, that none of the royal family had paid her any visit even of condolence during her bereavement. And although it was not true, it soured the public mood against the Queen as well as against her son, the chief offender. At the Birthday in June 1807, which both Prince and Princess of Wales attended, husband and wife did not speak but came out 'close together, both looked contrary ways, like the print of the spread Eagle'.

The matter of the Princess Royal's happiness with her husband had for some time concerned her parents. One matter on which they were united at least was the infamy of the turncoat Napoleonic King, her husband. Despite all the difficulties of gaining private access to the Queen of Württemberg – a title the royal family in England did not accord her an English lady secured from Royal the following: 'when peace was settled, she would put her favourite plan into execution, that of seeing her family. But as long as certain matters were not settled [the acknowledgement of the Kingdom of Württemberg's existence by her father's government] she could not go.'

Royal's concluding words were:

> I should be afraid of contributing to the ruin of the House of Württemberg, for Bonaparte has eyes and ears everywhere, and you know best what we have to fear from the great preponderance of power. Tell this, Madam, to your obliging correspondent [a Mr Horne] and thank him for the interest he takes in my behalf. Request him to inform my dearest father not that I am happy, for this would be telling an untruth, but that his Majesty's love and the care he is graciously pleased to take on my behalf amply compensates for all my sufferings.

That very summer she had the pleasure mixed with pain of seeing her stepdaughter Trinette depart for Paris, where, in the presence of an avuncular Emperor Napoleon and of her own father, the Württemberg Princess married none other than the Emperor's young brother Jérôme, King of Westphalia. A year later Royal wrote to her brother the Prince. Napoleon and Tsar Alexander had meanwhile met at Erfurt in September 1808 to concert plans for partitioning Turkey and to renew their alliance formed in mid-river at Tilsit the previous year. She told him, 'I am indebted to the French for the pleasure of conversing with you, dear brother ... little did I hope to have it in my power to recall myself to my friends when the King my husband set out for Erfurt to visit Emperor Napoleon, who at his first interview with him enquired most particularly after me and hearing how much I was affected with not being able to correspond with my family, was so good as to desire the King to acquaint me that he would undertake to have my letters sent to England.'

That July of 1807, Royal's aunt, the Duchess of Brunswick, who knew what it was to suffer from 'the great preponderance of power' vested in Napoleon's small person, arrived in London. She was 'very deaf and look- ing much older than she ought at her time of life. Her memory fails her very much, and her whole system is very much shook.' But she took a house at Blackheath next door to her daughter the Princess, and invited her brother the King to dine on 'all the German dishes that you like – send me your bill of fare that it's to your taste'. Her daughter Caroline invited 'par- ticularly old fogrums and old cats' when the Duchess came to dine. Princess Charlotte was allowed by her father to dine on Sundays at her grand- mother's. 'It is settled that my mother don't go to the royal family without me,' wrote Caroline that July. 'By that means it will come all again upon the footing as it was two years ago.' In this she was very much deceived.

Eleven-year-old Princess Charlotte was now much with her aunts the princesses at Windsor, according to the King's desire that she be educated there. But her mother was no longer granted the easy access that the King had envisaged and accorded her before the Delicate Investigation, and the offer of a house at Windsor was not made good. When in London, Charlotte, her governess Lady de Clifford and a gossiping female house- hold filled Warwick House, a tall, narrow seventeenth-century building at the end of a dark alley behind Carlton House, where the Prince forbade his wife to go.

In the absence of mother and father, the princesses cooed over Charlotte and dressed her up in clothes like a doll or the daughters they did not have and lavished inexpensive jewellery on her. Her resemblance to her father – and her looks were very boyish – delighted them. But her wilfulness – and she could be imperious with the ladies of her household – and her tan- trums, which had now become rages, dismayed them, as did her dislike for books in particular and education in general. The elder princesses and Queen Charlotte were especially distressed by Charlotte's disdain for liter- ature, and not even the enthusiasm of her tutor Bishop Fisher, who had as a young man taught Charlotte's uncles and given her aunt Princess

Elizabeth art lessons, succeeded. Her passion for horses and riding, however, Augusta and Sophia and Amelia could all sympathize with, even if
the Queen complained that her granddaughter whistled like an ostler and
walked like a groom.

Among other entertainments for Charlotte at Windsor was the cottage
with a thatched roof and rustic porch that her aunt Elizabeth took on a
lease from a farmer at Old Windsor and rebuilt. Inside, Elizabeth kept her
collection of teapots in all kinds of shapes and designs and other ceramics
which she had been acquiring for nearly ten years. Several times a year she
invited the rest of the family to join her, usually in celebration of a family
birthday, and then the cottage was en fête with garlands of artificial roses.
It was a perfect answer to Elizabeth's earlier wish to be a plain farmer's wife.
She should be a farmer herself instead, with fields of corn whose harvest
she could compare with those of her father's Flemish and Norfolk farms.
The public, who had previously admired Elizabeth's artistic productions,
learnt of her new avocation from an article in the *Lady* magazine which
featured her cottage, with a field of bristling corn in front.

Princess Augusta, meanwhile, wrote from Windsor to thank Lady
Harcourt for a 'very happy day' at Nuneham in the autumn of 1807. She
confessed that she had 'not for a long time been so free from care, though
at times (even in that delightful spot) I could not help thinking of my soldiers and sailors, my anxiety on their account having oppressed my mind
beyond measure. Judge then what my happiness must have been when we
were stopped in going up Henley hill with the intelligence that
Copenhagen had really surrendered and that we had met with very little
loss.'* General Spencer had been appointed in July to the command of a
brigade in the British expedition against the Danish capital, and when the
British navy captured the Danish fleet in September, the General distinguished himself in the successful attack on the Danish land forces.

'Still my heart was very ill at ease,' Augusta wrote,

> until I came home and heard that all my friends were safe – Since the troops
> sailed which is seven weeks today, I have never had an instant's comfort pass-
> ing what might be the consequence. But thank God all is well – all is as it
> should be. We have acted like truly brave men – sensible men, steady and
> not vengeful. I only wish you could have seen my face, it was perfectly broad

---

* The precarious peace established between Britain and France by the treaties of Lunéville
and Amiens in 1801–2 soon broke down, and Napoleon – after failing to invade Britain –
tried to wage economic war by means of his Continental System, which was designed to
squeeze British trade. France's attempt to enforce that policy in the Baltic led to British military activity in Denmark.

with delight, for my pride is as much gratified as my heart. Today the *Gazette* has not lessened these delightful sensations, but it has added to my gratitude to heaven to think what dangers they escaped.

The *Gazette* paid due tribute to General Spencer's part in the hostilities, and to Augusta's relief he returned home in October. She could confide in few – Lady Harcourt was a chief comforter – about her anxiety for the General's safety. She too thought ahead to a day when her father's objections to members of the royal family marrying commoners might no longer stand in her way.

The following spring Spencer left for Gibraltar with 5,000 men to co-operate with Sir John Moore against the Russian fleet at the mouth of the Tagus river. When he joined Arthur Wellesley at Cadiz, and supported him in the battles of the Peninsular War that followed at Roliça and Vimeiro,★ Spencer's exploits gained him the Order of the Bath, and his grateful superior, Wellesley, wrote: 'There never was a braver officer or one who deserved it better.' But the experience of waiting at home in England without news tried Augusta's nerves. She wrote in June to Lady Harcourt of reading the Thirty-fourth Psalm, and 'my sweet comfort the 94th …'. Both had often, 'in the multitude of sorrows which have encompassed my heart … refreshed my soul. We have had good reports from Spain by the *Alcmene* frigate,' she added. 'I trust they are true, and I trust your fellow servant General Spencer may again show us what bravery and discretion can do, for he joins all these great qualities in one. I am very anxious for him, for he is one of my Elite friends in the bunch with you. It is very small but choice.'

Two months later she wrote in relief: 'The Gazette will have informed you of the dangers and valour of the army, and that of Sir Arthur Wellesley and General Spencer … every army officer and man did their duty to the utmost.' One of her brother Frederick's aides-de-camp had stood by Spencer under fire, she reported. 'He says he never in his life saw anything like his coolness, good temper, intrepidity and steadiness – that he was, if possible, greater on the 21st [at Vimeiro] than on the 17th [at Roliça] and that his conduct on the first day was enough to establish his military character, if it had not been often seen before, and each time with credit to his head and heart.' Her father's happiness at the news of these 'great Peninsular victories', she declared with joy, was 'not elated and noisy, but

★France's declaration of war on Portugal in 1807 in support of her Continental System and her invasion of Spain the following year started the Peninsular War, with the British backing nationalist risings against the French invaders, who were in turn backed by Russia.

only calm, smiling, and content and gratitude to heaven for having helped his endeavour.'

Princess Elizabeth was taking steps to secure her happiness. In February 1808 she passed some happy hours with their old nurse Miss Dacres's daughter Augusta Compton, in whom the princesses had long taken an interest. Elizabeth sent her 'a little box for your work which I have long prized, I mean the top for it was your mother's work for me when I was five years old. The netting I did myself.' Elizabeth stayed at her cottage in March when Amelia was infectious with the measles and thought of going to live there permanently. She even sounded out Miss Compton as an agreeable companion, who shared her skills in drawing and was otherwise accomplished. 'The cottage scheme was a delightful one and like yourself' – the Prince would have financed it – 'but between friends a mate not being there (who I hope makes its appearance one day though time flies) it would have been lonely.'

Bidding the Prince happy birthday in August – the sisterhood sent him some china – Elizabeth told him that she had opened the doors of her dear little cottage to her neighbours to celebrate. 'I am new from top to toe.' The King was relatively well this summer, but the family seems on this occasion and others to have shielded him from anything unfamiliar on the ground that it might strain his nerves – even an event as innocuous as a visit to his daughter's cottage. 'We had all the natives [inhabitants of Windsor and environs] on Thursday,' Elizabeth wrote to the Prince of their parents' wedding anniversary, 8 September 1808, usually a red-letter day in the Court calendar, 'but my mother very wisely proposed nothing gay as it is cruel by my father …' The doctors had prescribed absolute regularity – to the point of monotony for all around him – in his diet, his exercise and, in so far as was possible, his duties.

Spencer Perceval, Prime Minister since 1807, could not however shelter George III from the worries that Wellesley's and Sir John Moore's expeditions to Portugal and Spain brought, following the French invasion of the latter country and Joseph Bonaparte's installation there as king. The King received full details of Wellesley's triumphs at Vimeiro and Roliça in 1808. As Princess Mary wrote in July, he was cheered by 'the spirited conduct of the Spaniards which appears to continue through that country'.

Meanwhile Miss Gomm had handed in her resignation in March 1808. 'Gouly will miss her sadly,' wrote Princess Mary, but later that month Miss Gouldsworthy, 'in consequence of declining health and increasing deafness', thought it advisable to retire from her situation. So Princess Mary informed her old nurse, Mrs Adams. Miss Gomm and Miss Gouldsworthy set up home together in a small house in Hill Street in London, but Princess Mary said gloomily of Gouly, 'Thirty-four years constant habits and never having been used to the trouble of housekeeping etc will go deeper and deeper with her.' A boiling tale underlay her calm news of two governesses hanging up their slates and anticipating a retirement together. It was a story that would have a tragic resolution within only a very few years, and that had reached one of many crisis points when Princess Amelia caught the measles in March and was blooded and blistered for it.

Miss Gomm, suffering from an attack of guilt that she had allowed Princess Amelia so long to prosecute her affair with General Fitzroy, tried simultaneously to confess all and to 'save' Amelia from 'being ruined'. Seeking an interview with Princess Elizabeth, the governess had no more joy than when she had brought up the matter with the Queen four years earlier. The Queen, on hearing that Miss Gomm in her distress described *her* as contributing to Amelia's ruin by sanctioning the romance and indeed planning to sanction the Princess's marriage to her lover once the King was dead, was 'outrageous', or outraged. Elizabeth tried, not altogether with success, to prevent Miss Gomm from uttering further on the subject. But matters had gone too far, and while Amelia and Fitzroy continued to meet, to ride and to play always together at cards – headlong to ruin, as Miss Gomm saw it – resignation for the governess herself was the only route forward.

'We have had great and sad changes this year,' wrote Mary, and she did not find they were any the better for them. But by her twenty-fifth birthday on 7 August 1808 Princess Amelia was calm. Lady Charlotte Finch, to celebrate the day, sent her a snuffbox, having counselled her never to use one before that day. Other presents she received ranged from a lace vest and sleeves to a necklace of gold chains and monkey heads from her brother the Prince, and a gold turban from Princess Elizabeth. But she was no longer extravagant, she wrote. Though there were 'squibs' in the papers about her 'economy in dress' when it became known that she had set her maid Mary Gaskoin to make her 'birthday petticoat', the Princess declared that she was proud to scrimp, 'which I shall continue to do till I am clear [of debts] and therefore think it much more honourable than buying things I cannot pay for'.

Her debts were not small. To David Bolton, a tutor – and father of the earlier royal tutor Sir George – who had acted as investor and more often lender to the princesses and their brothers for some years now, Princess Amelia owed £9,000 – but it was a tangled web which the royal siblings could not divulge to their parents, who were still their financial masters. When Princess Sophia asked for the return of the £5,000 that she had invested with Mr Bolton, she was told he had lent it to her brother

Frederick. Among other services Charles Fitzroy performed for Amelia was the writing of letters to that 'rogue' Bolton to attempt to set her financial affairs in order.

Princess Elizabeth of all the sisterhood was the most agitated this year. The acquisition of her cottage at Old Windsor had delighted her the year before, and she had written to Lady Harcourt of a visit to Nuneham: 'The blues of the flower garden I shall never forget, but I must be troublesome and beg you to ask Flora how she manages your beautiful hydrangeas for in my life I never saw anything to equal them – I have spent my whole morning at the cottage walking about and determining what shall be done – for I must plan a great deal, and the flower garden shall be as pretty as I can make it. You cannot think how well it all looked today and having settled my plans I am quite enchanted.' She would have loved to remain at Nuneham, and longed to ask: 'Will you receive me without my canister at my tail and feel as if you had any of your friends with you?' Princess Elizabeth dubbed 'the HRH' a garrison round her and her sisters. 'I wish I could cut through that fence, maybe a rabbit hole would let me through though my size comes in my way, Modern dress might let me squeeze out, we live in strange times, I will not give up,' she wrote.

But this year all seemed only to fuel her discontent. 'We go on vegetating as we have done for the last twenty years of our lives,' she wrote on 11 September 1808. 'I am just going to walk so cannot write as much as I intended, besides which the wind is so high that it stupefies me.' For the first time, at thirty-eight she was at odds – severely – with her mother. She and her sisters vegetated alongside the Queen, she wrote. 'My madre goes out very little, though she thinks she does, and takes so little exercise that I believe it unwholesome.' The Queen was, as a result, growing very large.

Elizabeth had begun a regimen of walks at eight in the morning, 'for the sake of not losing the use of my legs'. Nothing was going to shift the weight which she had carried all her life, and which she did not have the height to carry off. Her pretty face and full bosom nevertheless show to advantage in engravings of the Beechey portrait, originally commissioned for the Prince, and now often ornamented with an easel and paints to mark her fame as an amateur artist. As she said, 'All my amusements keep me at my desk'. At Windsor Castle she wrote cosy scribbles to her brother the Prince. She cut out silhouettes, painted borders to books and decorated china. She japanned panels and boxes. And in 1804 she had published a book of plates entitled *Cupid Turned Volunteer*, dedicated to her sister Augusta. Two years later came *The Power and Progress of Genius*. If sedentary, she was nothing if not energetic.

She told the Prince that she kept equanimous even in the rain of the last four or five days by drinking sugar and water at night. As he knew, 'It requires not only a great flow of spirits to follow up a day's duty,' she wrote, 'but a degree of submission which seldom falls to the lot of any but a RH which to make you smile I tell you *en secret* is the canister to my tail.' She added, 'When scribbling to you I blow all my stiffness away and write *comme une bourgeoise*, or why may I not say the cottager, whose comforts have been so much owing to your unparalleled kindness.'

Days later Elizabeth wrote again in a panic, 'having heard a letter of confidence has been written to you on my subject by a person who shall be nameless'. She referred to a letter that Louis Philippe, the impoverished Duke of Orleans who was living in Twickenham with a number of other French princes in reduced circumstances, had written to her brother. In it he referred to his wish to marry Princess Elizabeth – and possibly to her acquiescence in the scheme, which had been promoted by Edward, Duke of Kent. Edward had spent some years in North America with Louis Philippe, when the French Prince was in exile there, and had continued the friendship in England.

Unfortunately the Queen heard of this letter and asked Elizabeth what she knew about it. 'I thought it more honourable,' wrote Elizabeth, 'by her and just towards myself, to let her know I was not ignorant of what had passed with my sentiments and feelings upon it.' To her brother she wrote: 'If there is no possibility of the thing now, I only entreat you ... that you will not dash the cup of happiness from my lips, yet. Believe me, whatever I may feel at present – and flattered at having been thought of ... if I did not hope and flatter myself I might make them [Louis Philippe] happy, I would not think of it ...' Louis Philippe, son of Philippe Egalité and grandson of Louis XIV, was Roman Catholic, but she was unruffled. There being no soul 'near them that might worry or plague on the score of religion I do not fear it for you know I hate meddling, having no turn for gossiping, and being firm to my own faith I shall not plague them upon theirs'.

There were many advantages to the scheme. Three years her junior, Louis Philippe was a handsome man. At thirty-eight, Elizabeth could hope at least for a child, and they would, for want of a home in France, remain in England, where she would become not a cottager but a householder, and independent. But there was of course an impediment.

The Queen, when she received her own letter from Louis Philippe, said firmly, 'It can never be.' Elizabeth told the Prince, 'She will never hear of it again.' The Prince of Wales wrote back in support, encouraging her to hold fast – 'be prudent and silent and I trust happiness may yet be your lot'.

Brother and sister of course both referred to what might take place after their father's death, or during a regency. 'All I wished', wrote Elizabeth of her interview with her mother,

> is that she had named it, that I might have acted by her with the degree of honesty ... I thought she would have deserved, which was, 'Let me accept it, but never mention it while that life is preserved to us.' Do you think, my dear brother, I would have wished it brought forward after all I have seen? Good God no, and I think by the whole manner of the conduct they would have agreed to what may be unfortunate to us, but which will make everything *couleur de rose* afterwards, by considering my father before ourselves – I said that day on which my mother spoke with me, 'You shall never see a wry face.'

And Elizabeth swore she never would. 'Without being a perfect good daughter,' she wrote, 'I never can make a good wife.'

Nevertheless, during her discussion with her mother when she was 'almost wild', Elizabeth determined to 'Never Give It Up'. The reason was, she said, that 'it was hinted many, many things had been brought forward and rejected without a word from us, and therefore we felt the sun of our days was set'. One proposal at least in recent years had not been made known to the Princess in question. Prince William of Hesse Philippsthal Barchfeld – 'a good looking young man yet poor in every way' – proposed for lovely Mary, to no effect. Without her mother's knowledge, Elizabeth was sorrowfully determined to proceed with the Orleans match under the protection of her brother the Prince, as a future project. And Augusta, she said, 'has really stood forward nobly for me'.

Elizabeth reported to her brother in November 1808 that the Duke of Orleans was anxious that the Prince should 'insure the legitimacy of children, should there be any ... if the least doubt should arise as to their legal situation she should feel he was scandalizing the world', as well as ruining Elizabeth, 'and entailing misery on his children'. Elizabeth begged the Prince to send for Orleans, who was about to depart for Spain, so that her suitor could 'hear what you have said to me from your own mouth'. She had herself been 'examining the business more closely', since she and the Prince had spoken: 'I find no marriage whatever can be looked upon as valid without the Sovereign's consent which alone makes the law.'

Princess Elizabeth was looking ahead to a time when her brother would be 'sovereign', and was anxious to assure the Duke of Orleans that the Prince would without fail consent to – and so legalize – their marriage and children. But she was wrong in her facts, and would appear to have misunderstood the Royal Marriages Act, if she had secured a copy of it. After the age of twenty-five the King's children could, on giving twelve months' notice to the Privy Council, marry a suitor to whom their father – or those who succeeded him as sovereign – had previously objected, or even one to whom they continued to object. There was, however, one proviso of which Elizabeth may or may not have been aware – that the Houses of Parliament should not, during the term of notice, declare their 'disapprobation' of the match. And in the case of a penniless French Catholic and émigré prince, that 'disapprobation' might possibly be forthcoming.

In the event the project foundered. Louis Philippe decided that the opposition was too strong, and the wait too open-ended. Princess Sophia added a sad note on 5 October: 'Eliza's conduct towards my mother is perfect, and I lament her total want of confidence in her children.'

These were difficult years for the Queen. She had slid into a depression, in which her nerves were irritable and her temper short. 'The Queen's temper is become intolerable, and … the Princesses are rendered quite miserable by it,' Lord Glenbervie had commented four years earlier. The pleasure she had taken in her reading, her flower garden, her clothes and her children was vanished. Her little jokes with her ladies and fanciful letters to her brother dried up. She never spoke on the subject but she dreaded the extreme symptoms of this nameless illness to which her husband periodically succumbed. Her sons ranged from unfilial, like the Duke of Cumberland, to wastrel, like Clarence and Kent. Her beloved Prince of Wales alone, on whom she saw she might soon become dependent, she pursued with blandishments. The last thing she wanted to do was lose any of her daughters – or to inflame her husband's symptoms by proposing that one of them marry a Frenchman, a Catholic and the son of Philippe Egalité, who had early favoured revolution in France!

The discussion of putative children and their legitimacy acted to inflame Princess Elizabeth's maternal instincts. Writing at the end of November of a Mrs Fulford's pregnancy she confessed that she herself was 'always wishing (don't tell) to be in that way myself (I mean properly)'. Her correspondent was Augusta Compton, who could be trusted not to divulge these longings. Miss Compton heard, less controversially, of the painful blisters Mary had had applied to her feet for her gout. 'The caustics tortured her and inflamed the foot sadly.' The result was that she was back lying on her couch in her room. Elizabeth was enjoying mornings at the cottage *en fermière*. She was altering the garden and planting it for spring.

Over the winter Elizabeth's hopes of matrimony, high in November, were whittled away. But a sentence in a letter to her brother – 'If you have anything more to say you can write me a line, for I should like privately to know how the message is taken' – ends the affair. By September 1809 Louis Philippe was writing gracefully to the Prince of Wales to announce his engagement to King Ferdinand IV of Naples and Sicily's daughter, Princess Maria Amalia, and to say how sorry he was not to be joining the Prince's own family. (He was made commander-in-chief of his father-in-law Ferdinand's Sicilian forces.)

During March 1809 there appear to have been a succession of messages and even a 'principal adviser'. Elizabeth walked with her sister Mary, who was not in on her secret, and fobbed her off when she said she knew the identity of the 'person supposed to be the principal adviser'. But these may have referred to a scandal that now engulfed the royal family. On 27 January 1809, the Radical MP Gwyllym Wardle, formerly a lieutenant-colonel in the army, moved to appoint a committee to investigate the Duke of York's conduct as commander-in-chief of the armed forces. Frederick was accused of having abused his position to profit from the sale of army commissions that his mistress Mary Anne Clarke had arranged. Elizabeth wrote, 'It is most cruel to see people wretched enough to try and ruin all the Royal Family which I am persuaded is their great wish.'

Although the Duke appeared, by the end of a long and publicly aired hearing, to have taken part in none of the commerce himself, as Mrs Clarke's lodger in town he had undoubtedly shared in the proceeds at her ever more luxuriously appointed house. And culpable of leniency, laziness and negligence – as well as of adultery – he was removed from his position as commander-in-chief.

In December Elizabeth, her thoughts of matrimony extinguished, turned back to old friendships and to dependable friends. She asked Lady Banks to tell her husband Sir Joseph that they had feasted on the mushrooms she had sent over. 'Now I have two ridiculous questions to add to your collection of conundrums,' she added. 'When is the Queen like a farmer? Answer, when she cuts her corn, and Why is the soul like a thing of no consequence? Because it's immaterial.'

And she confided in that repository of private royal thoughts, Lady Harcourt. She hoped to see her old confidant Lord St Helens – 'my dear and invaluable Saint' – at Christmas. Seventeen years older than Elizabeth, the retired diplomat and lord of the bedchamber was a great connoisseur of the arts.

It is always holiday with me when he is here, for I love him to my heart and may say it. There can be no harm as I do not see why one may not speak

the truth. There is no man of m y acquaintance I love so well, and his kindness to me is never varied, and that is a thing I never forget. His advice is
my rudder, his approbation my delight, and I have that respect and regard in
that quarter that even a disagreeable truth I could bear from him which from
others I could not take, and I am quite sure he would not say it if I did not
deserve it, and I should be monstrously hurt if I did not flatter myself he
liked me.

You see I am honest, maybe too much so, but that is the nature of the
beast. You know, young men I never could bear, and though there may be
exceptions to every rule … any young man I like, I must think older than
his years. But that you seldom find, and then I am sure I never was from my
earliest days a person to please men in general, and though not at all shy, I
always dreaded showing off. And if ever I was such a fool and tried to be
agreeable, I have often gone to my bed thoroughly dissatisfied and displeased
with myself.

And now, I am neither young enough nor fool enough to run into that
error. I take things as they come and people as they are and leave the matter
to chance, whether I turn out pleasant or not. Half the world I associate
with, I don't care if I ever see again. So they become indifferent and also
stop gaps, I mean men. Women, better to see them nothing other than very
agreeable in society, but not for one's room or intimates. Others such as my
Saint at all times, minutes, days, nights … but God knows, they are not
found often, they are diamonds without flaws.

The Princess was right, these 'diamonds without flaws' were not easy to
find. But the unfortunate outcome of her nuptial negotiations with the
French Prince was not to deter her from seeking other means of escape.

12

Passion

~

Pₚᵣᵢₙ... **RINCESS AMELIA'S PASSION** for General Fitzroy continued to rage, her open assertions of it causing difficulties in a household where feelings might run deep but were customarily confided *sub rosa*, or carried unspoken to the grave. And she thought and dreamt and acted always with her eventual marriage to Charles in mind. Some time before her twenty-fifth birthday, she wrote to him:

> How dearly and gratefully I do love you, my own CFR. I am miserable without you. Yes, judge of my feels [feelings] by your own. I do want you much more than you have an idea of. I am sure we must be hours together before we knew each other. The joy would be so great, I mean to keep you in bed for a week at least when we marry. We must somehow settle to meet. I think at Ernest's we might, if you would come in plain clothes and if I could get Hely the man out of the way.

When Amelia turned twenty-five in August 1808, her obsession with Fitzroy twisted in her side still more. For, as we have seen, under the terms of the Royal Marriages Act, she had reached the age when she no longer needed her father's consent to marry. But in the event she never gave the required notice to the Privy Council on her twenty-fifth birthday or thereafter, for fear of inflaming her father's condition. She did, however, write numerous letters to her beloved Charles and even, as we have seen, a number of wills in his favour, in which she, like her sisters Elizabeth and Augusta, looked ahead to a day when their brother, as sovereign, would allow her to marry. Younger, more impetuous than her sisters, Amelia also now dreamt of a clandestine marriage.

'Dear Lord E, how I love him,' Amelia wrote of Lord Euston, Charles Fitzroy's uncle, who had been let into their secret plans:

> Do you think he could settle how to be called in church, or get a licence, and when I am next in town, I could manage it. With a licence I might, for I might go to Dumergue [the royal dentist] with Mrs Tant Mieux [Mrs Villiers] and then meet you and go to Chapel St, where, with a clergyman

and licence we might be married. That would be the best of any plan, I think – and if witnesses were necessary, and Tant Mieux did not like to be one, Lord E, I am sure, would, or any of your mother's old servants.

Although Fitzroy seems from Amelia's side of the correspondence to have played a supine part in the relationship, he dared much in openly accepting the affections of one of the King's daughters. And he sometimes showed himself as rash as his lover. When one of Princess Amelia's ladies, Lady Georgiana Buckley, tried to alert the King to his daughter's romance, which was clear to all with eyes to see it, Fitzroy said he would resign if 'those devils', the Buckleys, stayed. But the Queen did not dismiss the offender for many months, until Lady Georgiana's 'flippant' talk about the royal family provided an excuse. The misfortune, Princess Sophia said, was that, when 'all does not swim for them', Princess Amelia and Fitzroy lost their heads and acted on the impulse of the moment. But they never did put into effect their scheme of marriage by special licence or otherwise.

In part, the matter of witnesses was a difficulty. Unless Amelia gave notice of her intention to marry to the Privy Council, any witnesses to any marriage she contracted, the clergyman who officiated and possibly Fitzroy as well would be subject to the strange penalties of 'praemunire' with which the Royal Marriages Act threatened those participating in an unlawful marriage. Supposedly they would be stripped of all their possessions. In practice, as had happened in relation to the marriage of Amelia's brother Augustus to Lady Augusta Murray fifteen years before, all involved would be disgraced, and the marriage declared null and void.

The Princess nevertheless wrote eagerly of her future as Fitzroy's wife. Where she could, Amelia made purchases towards the married life she envisaged, commissioning silver to be engraved with their initials intertwined, buying furniture inappropriate to her present circumstances but to be installed one day at Sholebrook Lodge, Fitzroy's house in Northamptonshire. 'Promise our bedrooom and your dressing room may be quite close for I shall be in and out all the time we are dressing.'

Passionate and single-minded, Amelia created in her mind and in her letters a world of 'ifs' and 'one days'. Attempting intimacy everywhere while true intimacy was denied them, she sought by her letters to create a union of 'hearts' where marriage there was none. 'For years have I considered myself his lawful wife,' she wrote of Fitzroy, 'without ever enjoying my rights.' And she declared: 'No two ever loved or were so tried as we, and instead of separating us ... it has bound us tighter and more sacredly together ... I can never help praying and hoping a time yet may come when the Almighty may bless and join us in persons, as we are in hearts, ever inseparable.'

In other uninhibited letters to Fitzroy Amelia went into Chaucerian detail, recalling the pleasure of the hours of intimacy they snatched together. And she revelled in their every encounter: 'Oh God I am almost mad for you, my blessed and most beloved Charles. You are more dear to me and mine than ever today ... Oh God, that dear soft face, that blessed sweet breath ... ' More often, prevented from enjoying such 'ecstasy', she wrote of what she longed for: 'I should like to cuddle to you ... and then talk over everything unpleasant ...'

And again, and poignantly, she wrote without shame and in detail about her womb and other sexual organs which she feared were diseased, and would leave her unable to bear Charles's children: 'Don't be angry or shocked, but do you think my spot being out is likely to prevent my having children if I was married to you? And what is its being out owing to? I ask you anything. I say anything to you, so don't be angry. But if you are, pray tell me. I should hate to disgust you, you dear, dear soul ... Don't be angry, but from all I have suffered in those parts, I have often thought and dreaded having a cancer in my womb.' She asked, 'Could you not, my darling, consult any good surgeon and say it was a relation in the country who had been ill?' He could tell the surgeon this fictitious relation's husband was 'uneasy', or suspicious, so that Fitzroy could not 'betray the name'.

And all the time she was busy, thinking up how they could next meet. 'You cannot be more anxious, my blessed darling,' she insisted, writing of their mutual wish to meet, 'than I am for it. I own I think it will be safer when you leave the dear [the King]. However, you had perhaps go home first ... then I shall be sure of Mama's being in her room with the dear ...' She had another idea later in the letter. Could Fitzroy somehow get 'the key [hanging] by St George's Hall', she asked. 'Is it practicable?' Then he could explore 'those little rooms one day, when we are perhaps at breakfast. Try the back staircase and where it leads to.' They rode next to each other when they could in the royal cavalcade, and they touched feet or knees or reached for each other's hands under the card table in the royal drawing room. The rest of the time, Fitzroy was more often than not out riding with the King, or playing backgammon with him in his northern apartments in the Castle. Amelia wrote in one hurried note, '... I am just returned from walking on the Terrace ... I walked three times under the window where you were playing at backgammon, and I think you may guess what I felt and longed for.'

233

Alone in her room, with her pen ever ready to confide her thoughts, Amelia reflected deeply on her relationship with Charles. She reasoned that it would have been that of husband and wife, but for their father's ban, and so in the eyes of God it was such. 'I wish you had known no other woman but me and yet so far being preferred to all by you after, that, I think, insures its lasting more than anything.' She declared on another occasion, 'I hate your speaking to a soul but me. It robs me of my right, my only right. How could you say I had not wore your watch lately? How little you must observe me, as you must know I never go without it, and so particular am I that, unless forced to be gewgawed, I never wear but what you give me.'

Between her bouts of letter writing Amelia was being treated for an acute pain in her side which caused her to suffer this spring of 1809. 'By God, if ever I lost an atom of your kindness, affection and good opinion,' she said, hoping to bind Fitzroy to her, 'may some charitable being destroy me, for what a wretch I should be.' But, under the weight of her suffering, her charitable feelings towards some of her family declined – noticeably towards her mother and her sister Elizabeth, whom she called 'Fatima', no doubt in allusion to her size. But for her father Amelia retained an affection and sympathy which nothing eroded, although he was the cause of her unhappiness over not marrying Fitzroy. And this double vexation, that his life stood in the way of her marriage, for which she longed, that his death which she dreaded would allow her wish, preyed on her mind.

'Why is he so tried?' Sophia asked, after the eye surgeon Phipps had put leeches on the King's blind inflamed eyes without result. 'Dark and unknown indeed are the ways of providence.' With the help of his secretary, General Taylor, the King dealt reliably enough with his official correspondence, although it was a laborious process. In his private affairs he became easily agitated. 'He cannot find his things without assistance,' Princess Sophia explained to her father's master of music Sir William Parsons, and he trusted only one servant to arrange his property. Princess Sophia, that partisan of her father, in April 1809 thought it was anxiety preying upon her sister Amelia's mind that caused her to appear so ill. 'She looks wretched,' she noted, 'and just a skeleton.' And she wondered that her mother and elder sisters Elizabeth and Augusta should 'think so lightly of dear Amelia's illness'.

The Villierses persuaded Amelia to seek advice for the troublesome pain in her side from a Quaker doctor they favoured at Staines, Dr Robert Pope. A cough plagued her. 'I go out in the garden,' she wrote in May, 'but I am tired of self and believe I never shall recover.' She told her brother the Prince of Wales, 'None but your dear self know what human feelings are, none of my family do but you, I like to think we resemble each other.' He and she, twenty-one years apart, equally felt 'to their full extent the blessings of love and friendship,' she wrote, referring to his relationship with Mrs Fitzherbert. He could therefore judge what she must feel, 'deprived as I am of the enjoyment of either'. For now in this illness her relationship with Fitzroy had been nearly extinguished. She was not well enough to go to chapel, or downstairs, or out riding. Those meeting places on which she had so depended were one by one excluded. A favourite poem of Amelia's had been:

> Unthinking, idle, wild and young,
> I laughed and danced and talked and sung;
> And, proud of health, of freedom vain,
> Dreamed not of sorrow, care or pain …

The Princess of Wales had once supposedly detected one of Amelia's ladies leaving a note in a hedge when out for a walk during a fête at Frogmore. On plucking it from the hedge, before General Fitzroy could come upon it, the Princess – and her companion the Duchess of York – found marked on it the Roman numeral XII. According to the tale, the Princess put the note back where she found it, then kept Amelia in conversation till past midnight that evening, so that she could not keep the meeting.

The days of unthinking idleness and assignations were over. Sorrow, care and pain were from now on the Princess's lot, as she submitted to different doctors' prescriptions for what was then known as consumption, now as tuberculosis. But she managed her illness with courage. First she summoned Mrs Williams, who had years before been her wet-nurse, to be her companion at Windsor when the others went to town for the Birthday. Mrs Williams was her nurse when Dr Pope ordered a seton, or silk cord supposedly efficacious as a drainage device, to be drawn through a fold of skin on Amelia's chest. Then, in mid-July, again on the orders of Dr Pope – 'No medicine having in any way removed the pain in her side' another seton was introduced into that troublesome area. Four days later Princess Elizabeth, though regretting her sister Amelia's delicate health, was writing of her 'perfect cure' as being sure, albeit a considerable way off. But she was overly optimistic.

Amelia was too weak – following the insertion of this seton into her side – to attend a housewarming at her sister Elizabeth's cottage to celebrate the Prince's birthday in August. But a few days later, still determinedly following Pope's advice, she wrote to ask her father to allow her, with Princess Mary as her companion, to go to Weymouth for a 'change of air'

– a formidable journey for someone in her state of health. She told the King that the royal doctor Sir Francis Millman concurred with Pope's view that 'there was great tenderness remaining' in her lungs, which accordingly needed strengthening with warm baths and the mild air of Weymouth – and even with sailing.

The King consented, and expressed himself as desperately sorry that he could not, on account of his eyes and public affairs, go with her. Amelia departed, not neglecting to write a spirited new will before she went, leaving all, as usual, to her Charles: 'Nothing but the cruel situation I am placed in of being daughter to the King, and the laws made by the King respecting the marriages of the Royal Family, prevents my being married to him, which I consider I am in my heart and which vow and sole object has been my comfort and guide these last ten years and can end but with my life.'

Of her sister's fateful journey to Weymouth, Princess Mary wrote, 'Her suffering was such that it was impossible for her hardly to speak.' Nevertheless, she did all she could to keep up the spirits of Princess Mary and their lady, Lady George Murray, 'assuring us whenever she could, she felt better'. Princess Augusta wrote of her sister on another occasion: 'I never saw so good a disposition, so thoughtful and considerate to those about her, so afraid to fatigue them by their sitting up with her, I never saw anybody more careful to disguise her sufferings, for fear of vexing others; and truly it is most vexing to see her so long in such a sad state of health.'

Amelia's health was becoming more than vexing. She wrote to her wet-nurse Mrs Williams, some days before setting out for Weymouth, that she had given up calomel. (She called only for 'salts or lavender water' when the shooting pain in her side was at its worst, Mary told the King from the bathing resort.) And the silk setons, at Pope's direction, were to be changed for india rubber the following day. 'I feel very nervous as the hour [of departure] approaches and yet I must hide it.'

Amelia felt secure in her confidences to Mrs Williams, as did Mary when she wrote to her own wet-nurse Mrs Adams, or Elizabeth to Miss Compton. The princesses' correspondence with Lady Charlotte Finch dried up, as the royal governess was ill and old for some years before dying in 1813. But the favourite confidante of all the sisters – Lady Harcourt – remained a faithful correspondent, even after she left Nuneham on her husband's death in 1809. Others to whom the princesses wrote, known for a shorter time, were to prove less trustworthy.

Dr Pope was waiting for his patient at Weymouth, and, after applying leeches to Amelia's side, declared himself 'much better satisfied'. He then

Princess Amelia, aged eight,
right, by Lawrence. *Below*,
always the youngest in a family
group, Amelia was petted by all, and
was her father the King's favourite

Above left, George, Prince of Wales, the princesses' eldest brother, and *above right*, Princess Mary, the 'beauty' of the family. *Below*, beyond the terrace, Queen's Lodge and Lower Lodge, Royal residences at Windsor

Prince Ernest, Duke of Cumberland, *left*, was energetic but unbridled in his appetites. His relationship with his sister Princess Sophia, *below*, became the focus for hideous rumour

Frogmore House, the retreat near Windsor Castle owned by the Queen where the princesses read, drew, painted and gardened

Above, the Princess Royal, on the point of departure as a bride to Germany, with her husband Frederick of Württemberg, *below left*. And, *below right*, Princess Augusta's admirer, General Spencer

Although Princess Augusta is represented here as wearing thin slippers, on long tramps about Windsor and elsewhere the daughters of George III wore thick shoes and even heavy boots

Sir Henry Halford, *above*, an enterprising society physician who won the confidence of the princesses. But when Princess Amelia begged him to persuade her father to allow her marriage to Charles Fitzroy, *right*, Halford refused

Left, Princess Amelia in a blue riding costume. After her early death the deluded King often summoned her, with other children who had died young, back to life

returned to Staines, but the invalid he left behind showed no signs of progress, being afflicted by shooting pains and liable to moan in her sleep. She was carried out into a bathing machine opposite the house, fitted out with a couch, but the exertion was too much for her. After being winched up on board a yacht and placed on a couch on deck so as to benefit from the sea breezes, Amelia ended by fainting on leaving the ship. The motion of the sea had proved more than she could stand 'on account of the pain in her side'. Princess Mary, Amelia's companion, prayed that her sister 'would find some benefit from all the tortures she has submitted to go through'. Her father wrote, offering advice from Windsor that to obtain the benefit of maritime air they should try placing her on a bed in a tent in a field with the flaps open. The answer came: recent heavy rain made that idea impractical.

Amelia had been hope itself when she first arrived at Weymouth. She declared to her father, 'Everything recalls former times, and I like your knowing everything about us, and that we are under your roof.' The King's footmen carried her very well upstairs, she added bravely, and her rooms were very comfortable. Dr Pope, after applying the leeches to her side, on his departure had left full instructions for her treatment with Mr Beavor, a local apothecary. An airing on the sands had not relieved the pain, she admitted, but she worked, read and wrote in the King's room looking to the sea where she sat 'entirely', she told him on 14 September. But Mary reported to the King that, although her sister was indeed 'constantly employed', she could not sit up as well as she had before leaving Windsor. 'A degree of languor prevails at times that is painful to witness.'

The King's response was to lament to Amelia on 19 September 'the absolute necessity of resorting to remedies which in their momentary effect are so distressing'. In early October Pope went down to the resort to make still larger 'issues' or openings in Amelia's side. She survived them, although her flesh was now tender to the touch as well as being inwardly painful. He spoke of bleeding her, to see the state of the blood. As for the dressing of the 'issues', Mary had never seen her more in pain. (Mary Gaskoin, Amelia's maid, had been trained by her mistress to apply 'caustic' to the skin that was now permanently inflamed around the setons.) But still Amelia went down to the bathhouse to immerse herself in the warm water there, until the cold wind began, and then made do at the house with a slipper bath. Her bravery was dauntless.

At last in November the hapless invalid was allowed to return home – 'this obstinate pain in the side yields to nothing', Princess Sophia heard the month before at Windsor. And the day before she set out on that journey home Amelia wrote wearily to her father, 'this journey had not answered and yet everything has been tried that was recommended'. But Amelia did not go back to the tower in the Castle which she shared with Mary and Sophia. Pope said the Castle 'would not do', from being 'too elevated and my rooms to the eastward'.

Instead the King made ready for his daughter's return to Augusta Lodge, a house on St Alban's Street close to where Lower Lodge still stood, which Princess Charlotte had earlier occupied. And Amelia from Weymouth was pliant, merely begging the Prince: 'Don't tell the Queen I can feel any pleasure in seeing her, for I can't, and Eliza some day or other shall hear my mind.' She begged her brother not to think her ill natured, but 'neither affliction or pleasure ever led me near the Queen or Elizabeth, after all I have experienced in that quarter'.

At Augusta Lodge, Amelia settled in early November in rooms on the ground floor giving onto a pretty garden 'and very quiet', with Princess Mary and Mrs Williams. The King visited her every day. 'Alas, his blindness prevents his seeing how she is reduced as thin as death,' wrote Mrs Kennedy, the Windsor Castle diarist, and he flattered himself with hopes of her recovery. The Queen also called every day but never asked after Amelia's health, her invalid daughter declared. 'I hear General F.R. is returned, and the Queen was particularly cross to him. She always tells me how very agreeable Sir Brent Spencer is and Col Desbrowe [Disbrowe], but regularly names no one else except Münster [the Hanoverian Minister] ...' complained Amelia. But others heard that Fitzroy himself had for some time — before her illness removed her from the world — been treating Amelia with 'great harshness' and cross words. It is possible to sympathize with his predicament, in having his bold seduction of one of the King's daughters go so horribly wrong. Not only had he, from the beginning, acted as Amelia's factotum and dealt as best he could with her money worries, but he had been her confidant for her agitations and suspicions about her family, and also for her worries about her gynaecological disorders. And now the lover who was obsessed with marrying him, who ordered accoutrements engraved with their entwined initials for the home she envisaged them sharing, was apparently dying.

Painful examinations followed, with the Queen's favourite Dr Millman and Amelia's preferred medic Dr Pope 'the best part of the day ... in and out of her room'. When the former declared that 'the calomel had been pushed too far at Weymouth' by the latter, a liver specialist, Dr Saunders, was called in to examine Amelia with the King's friend Dr Heberden. The principal cause of Princess Amelia's disease was then declared to be 'an inflammation which has taken place in the back part of the right side', and that had caused 'a considerable swelling' there. 'From its origin being in the neighbourhood of the liver', Amelia told the Prince, the doctors thought it probable that that organ was 'disordered in its functions'. (In modern terms, Amelia's tuberculosis had spread from her lungs to her liver and other organs.) They believed that 'a discharge of matter externally' might occur naturally, which would not be 'unfavourable'. Amelia pathetically told the Prince that the King was pleased with Pope's honesty when, responding to these criticisms, he said he had not observed the swelling. 'They say it will be a long case,' she added.

A month later further and greater opinions were sought, when Millman and Saunders suggested closing the seton in her side, as arduous a business as opening it. Sir Henry Halford and Dr Matthew Baillie came down from London to give their opinions of the case. Amelia was ecstatically grateful to her father, who willingly paid for the expensive consultation. 'The desire to consult others, at a moment when additional torture is suggested, appears to me both natural and reasonable,' he wrote. The doctors spoke against closing the seton and effectively joined with Pope to form her medical team, but the New Year of 1810 brought no relief. An outbreak of St Anthony's fire or erysipelas around her face and eyes – a bright red and spreading skin infection – oppressed Amelia's spirits further, and she had to suffer a blister applied to her head to drain it off, on Pope's orders.

No better, Amelia now found it difficult to digest meat, and after an effort to eat cold chicken, had a severe spasm. Her diet became one of laudanum, beef tea, brandy and a few strawberries and grapes. Leeches were placed around her head, which she bore bravely. Mrs Adams replaced Mrs Williams as head nurse in May, but Princess Mary and Mary Gaskoin, Amelia's maid, stayed. The compass of Amelia's love had grown very small, as her brother York later avowed.

Though she kept up remarkably high spirits through months of 'constant torture', Sir Henry Halford spoke of her 'constant retching and exhaustion'. Visitors were rationed further, and one of them, her sister Augusta, said she 'never saw such suffering'. Amelia read and wrote of *Clarissa* – she was on the fourth volume – that 'there was much to like and much to abhor' in its pages. Against hope she imagined a future with Charles, and commissioned from London firms more silver, with the initials CFR and AFR intertwined and surmounted with coronets, for the home she longed to have with him. And from I. and L. Tuck, her brothers' jeweller, she ordered a hair bracelet initialled A and C, with hearts and hands locked.

After her brother the Prince had delicately insisted she make a will, she wrote to Charles on 28 July 1810: 'Should my cruel situation continue to separate our persons, be assured my heart is and long has been joined and united with yours. I live but for you. I love you with the purest affection, the greatest gratitude.' Nevertheless this document she wrote for him to open when she was 'no longer an inhabitant of this world', and to tell him of the existence of her will, and of her choice of executors – the Prince, and her brother Adolphus, who had visited her at Weymouth.

Even in extremis the Princess made one last effort to win her heart's wish – from her doctor Sir Henry Halford in early September. She begged him to seek on her behalf permission from her father for her marriage to Fitzroy. He copied his answer to her – refusing her request – to her companion Princess Mary. In his opinion, he told Amelia, such a 'communication' would:

> entail great wretchedness upon yourself and misery upon all the Royal Family for ages to come … the end hoped to be obtained would not be secured thereby and … the attempt would be followed only by bitter reflection … this blow to the King's peace of mind must be so heavy as to endanger the loss not only of his Majesty's happiness but of his health. As a physician I cannot help putting this result in a most prominent point of view … what must be our reflections [those of the royal doctors] in knowing that we had consented to be the immediate instruments of such a calamity … A case has occurred undoubtedly in inferior life to almost every physician in which he has thought it his duty to interfere between the anger of parents and the certain death of his patient but no resemblance can be found between your RH's unhappy case and one in inferior life. The circumstances here are peculiar and unparalleled.

A weakened Princess Amelia read Halford's letter with 'astonishment and regret', as she informed him. Already earlier that year she had described the doctor to her brother the Prince as 'so good a courtier that he does not venture to oppose anything the King and Queen like'. Now she reminded the egregious Halford that he had 'solicited and obtained' her confidence, 'at an early period of our acquaintance by making the most friendly offer of assistance and consolation'. But now that he was convinced her disease was 'more that of the mind than the body' and that 'affliction' was shortening her days, he had nothing to offer but:

> an exhortation to filial duty and respect to my parents. I trust I know my duty on that subject, as well as what I owe to my dearest brother the Prince

... and I am only sorry that a gentleman like yourself, whose skill and abilities no one can doubt, should think so meanly of me as to believe me deficient in either, or that my conduct is likely to be such as to become the object of impertinent remark at the corner of every street in every town in this island ... I have asked nothing of you but secrecy. From that I do not release you, though I cannot but apprehend that the sentiments contained in your letter are the suggestion of some part of my family.

She ended imperiously, 'this subject is never again to be named between us on any account'.

By the end of September Princess Amelia had been confined to her bed for a fortnight, having suffered a further outbreak of St Anthony's fire – this one 'literally from her head to her heels ... The torture she undergoes from the violence of the fever is so great that she can only be moved in a sheet. She says her bones feel as if they were breaking, and the soreness from the agony of the eruptions is indescribable.' Nevertheless she was all piety and resignation, and, when alone with Augusta, thanked her for all the comforts that were daily thought of for her. 'It would break your heart to see her,' wrote Augusta to Lady Harcourt on 26 September, 'but even now she looks so beautiful, so holy, so clean, so nice in her bed – You won't mind my naming all these details because you love her as I do.'

When she was still well enough to write, Amelia had sent a note to Lady Harcourt: 'Don't mention having heard from me, for people are very kind, but I feel unequal to writing to many and therefore if it is known, I may offend some even of my own family ... though I see no one now but my own family every day, yet during your stay here, I do hope I may just get sight of you if possible for a minute.'

Princess Augusta secured at least one meeting between Amelia and her General, recorded in a letter to him from Mary Gaskoin, who had opened the gates of the house to let him in. The Princess wished Fitzroy, while out riding with Princess Augusta, to 'express in the strongest terms' how much they both felt 'the very great kindness' she had shown concerning this visit.

But the Princess was dying. Princess Elizabeth wrote on 19 October: 'There is no hope of our dear Amelia who is gradually sinking to an early grave by illnesses which have never been able to be got the better of.' Her sister had taken the Sacrament, she said, and ever since had 'appeared to have said adieu to the world'. She was now 'waiting her awful summons ... with a degree of firmness ... which is truly heroic if not angelic and heartily prays to be released'. Miss Ellis Cornelia Knight, the author and one of the Queen's readers at this time, records seeing her in late October.

'Taking off her glove, she showed me her hand, it was perfectly transparent.' The Princess, who had loved music, could not bear the sound of a pianoforte, even in another room. Princess Augusta gave her instead a bird, 'which sang very sweetly, and with a very soft note, and she took pleasure in listening to it'.

Augusta wrote to Lady Harcourt on 26 October: 'Our beloved Amelia is absolutely going out like a candle ... Her physicians assure us she cannot recover, but the poor dear King flatters himself [that she might], however, because they cannot say they see the signs of approaching dissolution in her face ... I dread when the fatal close takes place, it will be a very great blow to him ... her state is deplorable, that is, the pains of the body, for she is the greatest possible example of the immortality of the soul ... affections as tender and delicate as they were ever at any period of her life.'

On Sunday, 28 October, Sir Henry Halford wrote to the Prince of Wales: 'I am grieved to inform you that the King has passed a night entirely without sleep.' Over the previous two days, as his patient's situation had deteriorated, Halford had called in Dr Matthew Baillie and then Dr William Heberden junior and David Dundas, Serjeant-Surgeon since 1792, as the King began to exhibit the symptoms that his family dreaded – he was nervous, prone to tears, his nights became disturbed, and his pulse quickened. His appearance at the fiftieth anniversary of his accession on Thursday, 25 October had frightened everyone. 'As he went round the circle as usual,' wrote Miss Knight, 'it was easy to perceive the dreadful excitement in his countenance.'

Meanwhile Amelia had softened towards her mother. She 'cut off a lock of her hair' after one frightful seizure, 'gave it to Her Majesty, thanked her for all her kindness, hoped her own sufferings and her anxiety would now soon be over, but hoped also she would remember her and sometimes think of her.' Mrs Kennedy heard from another of the Windsor ladies that the Queen was 'the picture of grief, cannot shed a tear and endeavours to keep up to support the King, who weeps all day long, but rides out every day as usual, and the Queen goes to Frogmore for an hour most mornings'.

The King usually visited his daughter at three in the afternoon. One day he was standing weeping by the fire when Princess Mary said, 'Sir, Amelia desires you will come to the bedside.' Amelia said, 'My dearest father, this ring shall tell you my wishes,' and handed him a ring she had had made specially. She had had some of her hair put under a crystal tablet set round with diamonds, and in the crystal was engraved the motto, 'Remember me.' Reading the motto, the King embraced his daughter and said he 'should think of her, and lament her every day he lived, for she was in his heart's core. That it should be on his finger as long as he lived, and go into his coffin with him.' Princess Mary had gone on her knees to prevent her sister from giving him the ring. But Amelia was resolved on it, and resolved in all she did, even asking that the bird that Augusta had lent should be restored to her two days after her death, so as not to awaken too many cruel reflections.

In her 'last hours' the twenty-seven-year-old Princess Amelia spoke to her attendants at Augusta Lodge:

> 'I am dying, send for the chaplain, to pray with me.' All thought her so weak that she would not be able to join with him, but she did do it and in all the fervour of devotion repeated the prayers after him, and, upon his stopping, 'Sir,' said she, 'you have left out one prayer – the absolution, which I desire you to repeat.' 'Your Royal Highness must then allow me to ask you some previous questions.' She acceded and after that thanked him, and said, 'Now I must ask you a question – do you think that my great sufferings have been laid upon me because I am a sinner above all others?' 'By no means,' he replied. 'Do you think', she said, 'that when my soul departs, I shall go into the bosom of my saviour through his merits and mediation?' He answered in the affirmative. 'Now then,' said she, 'I have nothing to ask.'

On Thursday, 1 November Augusta went to her sister, and Amelia's words, 'Dear Augusta I love you, I always did love you,' were within days to be 'like heavenly sounds' in her sister's ears. For early the following morning Amelia was seized with convulsions, then 'fell into a stupor between 11 and 12'. At noon Princess Mary, sitting by her bedside, put aside the curtain to look at her, then said, 'Sir Henry, I do not hear her breath, pray come and look.' The doctor felt Amelia's pulse, then lit a candle and, having examined the Princess, closed the curtain. 'Your Royal Highness must suffer me to lead you to the Queen, who is in the house,' he said. Mary remonstrated, saying, 'Oh, she is dying and I will not leave her.' 'Madam, she is dead,' came the grim response, 'and you must leave the room, for I must go and acquaint the Queen.' While Sir Henry wrote to inform the King of his daughter's death, Princess Mary wrote to Charles Fitzroy, before quitting Augusta Lodge: 'My dear Fitzroy, Our beloved Amelia is no more but her last words to me were, "Tell Charles I die blessing him." Before I leave the house I obey her last wishes.'

Princess Augusta described her own reaction to her sister's death in a letter to Lady Harcourt on 6 November:

> God knows I had never looked forward to dear Amelia's life being spared – and her sufferings were so great and her frame of mind so angelic, that

except for my own deprivation of a sister I doted upon, I could not wish the tortures prolonged. At the same time the suddenness of her death has been a severe shock to us all, especially to myself – for seeing the Queen's coach when I returned from my ride I said, 'I am glad it is here for it shall carry me directly to my beloved Amelia.' And little did I think that angel now gone to another and a better world, and that poor Mary had just got out of the coach at the castle. I saw Mary as soon as I could collect my ideas at all, and then I went to the Queen, both of which were duties I wished to fulfil as soon as possible, and since that time I have scarcely shed a tear.

The King was too ill for several days before and after Amelia's death to understand anything, let alone that she was dead. The Foreign Secretary, Lord Wellesley, had heard the King sobbing before he went in to see him on 29 October – 'most dreadful – a sort of wailing, most horrible and heartrending to hear'. Still Halford had hoped 'the [King's] malady would last a short time'; Baillie thought of months. But now his mind was gone. 'His excess of feeling has been too much to bear,' Elizabeth wrote to Augusta Compton, 'and the long suspense between hope and fear has been the fatal cause of his illness.'

'The violence of the [King's] disorder was at a horrible height,' wrote Mr Speaker Abbott of 2 and 3 November. While Amelia lay dying at Augusta Lodge, it had already been resolved by the physicians supervising her father's treatment that they would 'control and govern' his case, but would do well to 'have some of the mad people under them'. At their request Dr Simmons came down to Windsor, but on finding he was to be 'under' the physicians, went away again. On the day Amelia died, a mad-house keeper from Kensington with two assistants was introduced into the King's apartments at Windsor, with instructions that they were 'not to be afraid of employing the necessary means of restraint, but were at the same time never to lose sight of the King's rank'. Dr Henry Revell Reynolds, who had attended in all the previous illnesses, was called in as additional physician the following day, the 3rd.

When he first suspected he was becoming ill the King charted his own descent into alienation. He remarked that at its inception he had dreamt the same dream which heralded each of his other illnesses, and he named the causes of his former illnesses, ending 'and now it is poor Amelia'. He told Sir Henry Halford that, if his case required medical supervision, he and any other physicians attending him should admit to their consultations no 'medical man specially engaged in the department of insanity'. But, three days after Amelia's death, the King's ministers were resolute that – despite Simmons's refusal to act – the attendance was required of a medical man 'whose practice and experience have powerfully been directed to that species of disorder with which it has pleased God again to afflict his Majesty ...'. The Prime Minister Spencer Perceval wrote to the Prince of Wales on 5 November: 'Doctor Robert Willis is proceeding down to Windsor this morning for that purpose.'

The King still could not take in the fact of Amelia's death, though Sir Henry Halford attempted to impress it on him. The King had written to Amelia on his seventy-second birthday that June, as they applied the cupping glasses to her head once again at Windsor: 'There is no object nearer my heart, no blessing for which I pray more fervently than that you may be restored to me.' Now, when told that his prayers had failed, he resorted to believing that she had died but had risen from the dead. Lord Auckland commented on 5 November that it was 'not easy to conceive a more terrible visitation of mental misery than that of feverish insanity added to total blindness', and very hard to imagine a king ruling in such circumstances.

Amelia's sisters were torn between bracing themselves for their sister's funeral and fearing for their father's sanity. Augusta said of Amelia in her letter to Lady Harcourt of 6 November: 'You who loved her dearly will understand the delight it is to me to talk of her and how happy I am she is to be buried where I live. The same good and merciful God who gave her to me, had a right to take her to himself whenever he thought fit. I am thankful for the time I had the blessing of possessing her.' She received back the bird that she had lent Amelia, and she asked Amelia's nurse, Mrs Adams, to secure for her from her sister Mary 'any one little box belonging to poor dear Amelia – either the writing box or the red leather box and any one book which she has read in much during her illness. I cannot help asking this for I had rather have a book than anything. Don't name it till you think it quite right.' The 'circumstances of horror' in which they had been for some days concerning the King 'added greatly to our afflictions', Augusta confessed, 'and we may indeed say we are borne down with grief.'

Elizabeth wrote to Lady Harcourt on the 9th, four days before Amelia's funeral was due to take place in St George's Chapel: 'I now shudder when I think of what the angel King will feel when he knows the worst for as yet, though it has been named, he cannot believe it. Three days later, however, 'restraint was taken off', after the King at last comprehended his daughter's death.

Amelia's funeral took place the next day, 13 November, at eight o'clock in the evening. 'There was no parade, only the hearse drawn by eight of His Majesty's fine black horses, escorted by a troop of the Royal Household Blues and Royals with drawn swords.' The Prince of Wales and the Duke of Cambridge, Amelia's executors, followed in a coach and six, while the Castle bell tolled the short distance that the coffin travelled from Augusta Lodge to St George's Chapel. Amelia's other brothers, cloaked and booted, met the body at the west door of the church, which was itself illuminated by two rows of guardsmen bearing flambeaux. Lady George Murray and three others of Princess Amelia's ladies – wearing long white crêpe veils and long white gloves – supported the pall, while eight of the King's Beefeaters carried the coffin into the chapel. All Amelia's brothers were 'in floods of tears the whole ceremony, particularly the Prince'. But her sisters and mother, according to etiquette, were not present for the service, nor for the moment when the Beefeaters lowered Amelia's coffin into the royal vault below the chapel. Remaining in their apartments in Upper Ward, they had heard only the tolling of the bell, to announce the passage of the hearse into the Castle.

The King in his northern apartments knew now that his darling Amelia was dead. With his mind gone, it seemed that a period of regency must ensue. Princess Elizabeth wrote some weeks later, 'Distress and misery has so long been my lot that I have no longer the power of tears.'

BOOK FOUR

MATURITY

1810–1822

13

Breaking Up

~

THERE WAS, BESIDES the sadness of Amelia's death and of her father's reaction to it, the matter of her will. Amelia's maid Mary Gaskoin, herself to die of tuberculosis within months, received, according to her mistress's directions, all the clothing that had been found in the Princess's apartment at the Queen's House: 'a variety of court dresses, fans and other ornaments of dress'. Everything else Amelia had left to Charles Fitzroy, but the Prince of Wales and the Duke of Cambridge, as executors, moved swiftly to overturn the will. A bereaved Fitzroy received the brothers – at their most charming. He agreed that it would only do Amelia's reputation harm if it were known she had left nearly all her possessions to him. The brothers assured him they would pass on much of what she had left to him – a 'large number of packing cases … removed from HRH's different apartments' and now lodged at Mrs Villiers's house. There were books and furniture, plate – Amelia had had half of it engraved AFR and CFR – and china. Fitzroy was later to contest this arrangement, but for the moment the princes' graciousness won the day.

Knowing nothing of the urgent bargaining taking place between the Prince of Wales and General Fitzroy to reassign the dispositions of Amelia's will, in the days following her funeral on 13 November 1810 the King took his own measures, assuming his daughter to have died intestate. According to Mrs Kennedy, he 'called for his strong box, took out some gold and bank notes, parcelled them and had them put up in different papers, sealed, and then called for pen and ink and directed them himself to the Queen, saying, "I must perform my promise to my dear departed child." They were little legacies to her attendants and to the poor.'

But that night the King was feverish and sleepless, and they 'restrained' him at three in the morning. For a good month the delirium and sleeplessness persisted, with acute pain at times from a bowel complaint. Towards the end of November the Privy Council examined the physicians – Halford, Heberden and Dundas one day, and Baillie the next – and Dr Robert Willis, all of whom spoke 'with confidence' of the King's ultimate recovery. The politician George Canning had indeed believed, before Amelia died, that 'the one shock' of her death would probably accelerate the King's recovery. But it was not to prove so, and by mid-December, when they were examined by Select Committees in the Commons and Lords, the physicians' answers about the King's recovery were less firm.

Princess Elizabeth wrote with feeling of the proceedings at Westminster, calling them 'the vile examinations what kills us, yet I am determined not to despair'. Princess Mary, meanwhile, having nursed her sister for over eighteen months without pause, was recovering from a collapse brought on by 'worry and anxiety of mind', her elder sister wrote. The King, Mary told Mrs Adams, was not worse, but 'at a standstill, says nothing quite wrong but nothing quite right and talks a great deal more than he might or than the physicians like'. Courteous Sir Henry Halford had to divide his time at Windsor between 'upstairs' – the south apartments, where Princess Mary lay heavy headed – and 'downstairs' – the north apartments, where the King walked and talked and forgot to sleep. Sir Henry steadied the nervousness in Mary's usually placid head by a blister 'on the back part of the head where the great trembling of the nerves is'.

The atmosphere in the chambers of Westminster in December was muted and without any of the frenzy that had characterized the Machiavellian extravaganzas of 1788–9. The machinery for a regency had been in place since 1789 when the King's recovery had stopped the third reading of Pitt's bill, and the doctors' reports now convinced the Parliamentary Committees that a regency, or 'substitution for the deficiency in the executive power', was now called for. On 20 December Perceval introduced in the House of Commmons a Regency Bill with restrictions.

The Whigs, who expected to be called on to form a government, worried that the Prince as regent, with the restricted powers that were proposed, as they had been in 1788, would be unable to carry on public business at all. Others, the Tory Prime Minister Perceval among them, expected to be turned out if the Prince was appointed regent. They worried more about what would occur, should the frail seventy-two-year-old King be declared well once more and no regency ensue.

In January 1811 – despite a period of paroxysms in late December – the King's health seemed better. He walked on the terrace outside his rooms for an hour in mid-month and asked to go 'upon a particular part' of the south terrace next day, 'that it might be seen that he was alive'. Eight days later on the 26th he talked 'in the most collected manner' for over an hour with Perceval and the Lord Chancellor, Lord Eldon. The physicians had asked the politicians to give the monarch an account of what was passing in Parliament, as 'His Majesty's understanding and comprehension were perfect to every purpose of such a communication.' But he would not discuss public affairs, and, as often as they tried to bring him to talk of them, 'turned the conversation with much dexterity …'.

With the Regency Bill nearing enactment at the end of January, Perceval returned to tell the King of its provisions on the 29th, and stressed that it allowed for him to take up the reins of government immediately he recovered. George III countered that at his age he should be thinking of retirement, but evaded overtures from Perceval regarding a voluntary resignation of his powers. And the next half-hour was 'not so good', wrote Perceval after he came away.

The King's vacillating sanity placed his Cabinet in a predicament for the last time a few days later when the Lord Chancellor came down to Windsor on 5 February to see if he were fit to give his royal assent to the Regency Bill. Although that day the King was calm and collected, Eldon thought it politic not to obtain his signature, and the bill was passed with the assistance of the unequivocally rational Great Seal, enabling the Prince to be sworn in on 6 February at Carlton House as prince regent of the United Kingdom – with restricted powers to be reviewed after a year.

The Prince's decision on becoming regent to keep his father's Tory ministers caused some consternation among the Whigs, but they chose to believe his assurances that he would never forgive himself if his father recovered and found his ministers gone. Sir Henry had indeed told the Prince that news of a change of ministry would 'produce such an exacerbation … as might put an end to his life'. The Whigs waited impatiently for February 1812. If the King were not better by then, the Prince's regency would be confirmed and unrestricted, and then, the Prince intimated sorrowfully, he would no longer feel compunction about introducing his own advisers. Meanwhile, a Queen's Council of seven privy councillors – including Lady Harcourt's brother, the Archbishop of York and Lady Charlotte Finch's son Lord Winchilsea – was established to advise the Queen on the King's care at Windsor, and to visit the monarch weekly to remark on his condition. The princesses, who had not seen their father since those dark days surrounding their sister's death, now began again to pay him visits with their mother – visits which were sometimes painful to endure, and which sometimes raised their hopes. The King, Mary told Mrs Adams after her first visit in early February 1811, had greeted the announcement that the bill was passed 'with much composure and calmness'.

'His Majesty is recovering,' Mrs Kennedy wrote optimistically that month. 'He walks every day upon the terrace, attended by Drs Willis and Heberden. The terrace is shut up from the public, but the people walk in the park and see him with pleasure daily recovering.' His attendants were replaced with pages. There was a brief flurry of activity in late spring when the other physicians concurred briefly with Heberden's advice that the King could not recover without stimulus. 'This day,' wrote Mrs Kennedy on 20 May, '... His Majesty rode out on horseback for the first time with the Princesses and only attended by his equerry and gentleman as usual – no physician. He rode up the Long Walk in the park, appeared in great spirits, was out for about an hour. When he got back to the Castle, Dr Willis stood at the door to receive him. He stumbled getting off horseback and laughing said, "Don't report me ill, Doctor, it is only the old man not so alert as formerly."'

The next day the King unexpectedly spoke to Elizabeth of Princess Amelia, and declared he would not have her live again, her mind was so perfect when she was taken. His daughter was comforted to think he accepted what had happened. Mary's hopes for a full recovery weakened, however, when, from her room, she saw her father return from another ride with her sisters. She 'really was quite overcome at seeing him so much altered on horseback'. He appeared to her to sit his horse 'with great difficulty and as if he was very weak'. Earlier he had had to struggle even to get his boots on to his swollen legs. He did not succeed, 'despite much pulling from the jackboots', and finally, in cloth shoes, struggled on to his mount at 'Sophy's door'. He did not enjoy the ride, despite his anxiety to go, and when Princess Sophia said it was his dinner hour, he turned back immediately.

The King tried to check and contain himself in his daughters' presence, especially towards the end of each week. The Council members paid their weekly visit of inspection on a Saturday, and he was determined to master himself and be declared well. He occasionally displayed the wit that had distinguished his illness in 1788–9. When he heard that the Prince was giving a fête or ball at Carlton House on 5 June, and asked if it was true, the Queen replied that it was designed to mark his own Birthday, and 'at the same time assist trade'. The King replied trenchantly that he saw no reason to 'put oneself out of the way to help trade'. But after the Queen had gone, Bott, the King's page who served as his eyes, said the orders his master gave that day to imaginary subordinates were more than usually extravagant.

The King, in hopes of being allowed to attend the Regent's fête at Carlton House – a fête, sumptuous at the time, that grew in its extravagance in people's minds as time and the war went on, till it ranked with banquets of antiquity – and feeling fever coming on, even submitted to restraint. But there was no suggestion that the princesses should themselves attend the merriment. Their part was to kneel as vestal virgins at the tomb of their father's sovereignty, mourning its passing. 'Is there no balm in Gilead?' the Book of Jeremiah demanded in the cold church that they attended every morning. They might well have cried in response, that indeed there was none, as the tortuous days slipped by.

During his daughters' visits, the King occasionally meditated on Princess Amelia's attachment to Fitzroy. But he had already accepted Sir Henry Halford's bland account of Amelia leaving what she had to Fitzroy, in return for his attendance on her out riding and on journeys. And his mind did not rest long on any subject.

The King's recovery did not last. At the end of May the princesses wrote with sadness of a 'new system' that was about to operate 'across the quadrangle' in their father's apartments – a system sanctioned by the Council and Cabinet in which the physicians' and mad doctors' positions were to be reversed. Dr Robert Willis, on 1 June, assumed the 'whole responsibility of the sick room', and, recommending extreme quiet for the King, forbade for the moment communication with his family. Furthermore, the blind King's pages were removed from their responsibilities at his side, and instead burly keepers were supplied by Willis from his asylum in Lincolnshire. As for Halford, Baillie, Heberden and Dundas, though they might see the King every day, they were to observe only his physical wellbeing, and no longer occupy themselves with his mind. They could do nothing without the consent or presence of Dr Robert Willis, not converse with the King, nor – as Dr Heberden had wished – provide any stimulus for him.

General Herbert Taylor resigned as the King's secretary shortly before the 'new system' came in. One of his last tasks was to lock away in presses throughout the King's apartments and library state, historical and private papers that he had dealt with since 1805. At different times, the King had handed him papers 'in great number from various presses, table drawers, bureaus, boxes etc', and he had found others in bureaux and presses in the State Apartments at Windsor, in the Great Lodge in the Park, in the Queen's House and at Kew. Taylor's work completed, he gave to the Queen the King's 'private key' to all the presses. With this locking away of the King's vast correspondence, with the paperwork that had been his chief tool as monarch sealed up and by recourse to which, even after his blindness, with Taylor's help, the sovereign had so often confronted the Cabinet, the apartments 'across the Quadrangle' grew quiet.

But there was one last eerie communication from those apartments. At an Ancient Music concert in London just before the 'new system' came into effect at Windsor, the Duke of Cambridge announced that his father had made the selection of all the music that followed – passages from Handel, the King's favourite composer, all of them 'descriptive of madness or blindness, particularly of those in the opera, *Samson*; there was one also upon madness from love and the lamentation from *Jephtha* on the loss of his daughter'. The resonance of the music was felt throughout the assembly, and the monarch's absence was underlined when the concert ended with 'God Save the King' – a king 'who was sometimes', as his daughter Princess Mary put it, 'so sensible of his own situation'.

But the King was not always so alert to his circumstances. As the British army – General Spencer with it – forced its way forward in Portugal and won great victories at Almeida and at Fuentes de Oñoro, at home the Treasury computed the frightening cost of these Peninsular expeditions. The new expense of maintaining in state a Regent's Court – even on lines not considered by the Regent himself sufficient to his position – as well as an establishment at Windsor for the ailing King and another for his wife and daughters, was also painfully felt.

The country would have to economize somewhere, now that the Prince could to some degree claim that he had to be magnificent. Commissioners were therefore appointed, and carried out their brief – to make plans to reduce the King's and Queen's establishments, and transfer the appurtenances of state to their son's new Court – with mathematical rigour. The King, 'employed with the bedclothes', sorting them by night and spending his day in his apartments 'singing, laughing and talking a great deal to the queen' of very trifling subjects, cared nothing for the changes around him that were meditated. But the princesses were humiliated and mortified by the 'reductions' that they began to understand would be required of them.

The Queen rarely displayed her feelings, even in private. Her daughters spoke occasionally of her temper, and Princess Mary lamented that she seldom showed herself warm or affectionate. 'Her unfortunate manner makes things much worse,' Mary wrote. Only when she spoke of the Prince did a glow suffuse the Queen's sunken features, and she was neither support nor companion to her daughters in their distress. In these sad times a visit in early June from Princess Charlotte, now aged fifteen, was very welcome. 'Her spirits do us all good and keep the house alive,' remarked her aunt Mary; '... she says everything that comes into her head and is very clever at the same time.' Charlotte's hoydenish ways, however, did not earn her aunt's approval. She 'requires much softening down, more than any young female I ever saw', said Mary, 'both as to manner and voice'. Charlotte's own response to life at Windsor was 'Heavens, how dull.'

For seventeen days in July 1811 the King suffered 'paroxysms' and was completely 'lost, not knowing one soul or giving any marks of reason'. A month later his daughter Mary commented, 'Nobody who loves the poor King can wish his life to be prolonged an hour.' And in August Princess Augusta told Amelia's old nurse Mrs Williams that she had all along had a bad opinion of this illness of the King's, 'because his affections could never be worked upon'. In all his other illnesses he had rejoiced to see his daughters, she added, and had even been vexed, sometimes 'beyond measure', when they left – inconsolable in the 'forenoon', though they were to return in the evening. Now he told his daughters his schemes or complained to them as to anyone else, and wished them goodbye without concern. On 15 August, Augusta declared not dispassionately but with finality: 'Since the 28th of May I have never seen him, but at a distance – and now probably I shall never see him again, For', she explained sadly, 'under his melancholy state I would not see him for worlds, as I cannot serve him. I could do him no good, and he would not know me.' Since July the King's memory had become very impaired.

Windsor, in a diarist's words, took on 'an Asiatic stillness', with the Queen and princesses living far across the quadrangle and under considerable financial restraint, and the King often under physical restraint in his northern apartments. There was, the doctors agreed, 'perfect alienation of mind'. His daughter Mary remarked that his changeable days were like 'the shield in Homer which represents a city in war during the day as well as in peace in the evening'. Sometimes he was dosed with laudanum to counter his paroxysms, sometimes he was put in the strait waistcoat to curb violence. And he indulged for hours in fantastic thoughts and dreams – among them that Princess Amelia was alive and living at Weymouth, that King George I was a huge expense to him at the Great Lodge, that Prince Octavius was alive and his other sons dead. He refused to be shaved, on the ground that he was too young to have a beard, he planned for Princess Sophia to marry Prince Octavius, and he announced that the Duke of Clarence was to marry the Princess of Wales, and emigrate with her and the Queen to Botany Bay in Australia.

The doctors were nonplussed. The large imaginary company that the King summoned up in his mind's eye was sometimes so turbulent that he put his hands to his ears to block the noise out. He also liked to have lavender water applied to his head. This suggested to them that something

was going on 'within the head with which the mental disorder is associated'. However, the nature of the 'wrong' was not clear enough for them
to 'found any practice upon it'.

Every medicine or management they tried 'disagreed' with the King.
They even prevailed on the Queen to allow Drs Simmons and Monro and
Dr John Willis to observe the King in October and November. For in the
closing months of 1811, with the restricted regency coming up for renewal
or closure in February of the following year, members of the Council –
the Chancellor Lord Eldon among them – visited the Castle and 'expressed
great disappointment ... that not one of the physicians in constant attendance could give any comfort'. There was no sign of the King recovering.
Mary wrote in October to Lady Harcourt, 'Sir Henry Halford, Baillie,
Heberden, Willis and Dundas call the last month the very worst they ever
witnessed ... the King was all day Friday under confinement and the whole
of the night from the Friday to the Saturday.' Within weeks, unless the
King surprised his doctors, his son the Prince would become regent without restrictions.

Princess Augusta, meanwhile, had an opportunity during her ride on
the morning of 10 October to have 'a very long and serious conversation'
with General Taylor. 'We spoke of what might take place when the year
expired ...' and of the 'great and important changes' that would almost certainly take place then in the royal household. The physicians and Council
might possibly want the King to be nearer at hand at Kew, and it had much
to recommend it. 'The Queen's House in point of lodging would be
better, but it would be most cutting to our feelings', she wrote, 'that the
King should be within a stone's throw of the Regent's House where all the
royal horses must reasonably be fixed – and that he could not stir out in the
garden for a little air without being overlooked by all the houses in
Grosvenor Place ...' At Kew, though necessarily in different houses, she
went on, she and her sisters 'would not be so far off from him, as we are
here across the Quadrangle'.

The Princess went to her mother, to forewarn her of these plans, and
found her obdurate. She would never leave Windsor, Queen Charlotte
said, even when Augusta told her that it would be impossible for a large
establishment to be kept up there for the King. Probably, Augusta said,
the King's attendants, 'which were only those of State', would be dispersed, while those who were his 'private friends' – his equerries and
Taylor and a few others – might be continued. 'For everything would be
done with respect and kindness, but ... his family must be very much
reduced.'

Princess Charlotte, visiting her grandmother and aunts in late October, not unnaturally was unhappy herself. Her aunt Elizabeth wrote: 'She in her heart hates being here and confessed it yesterday. She said three days was enough, more was horrid ...' Elizabeth declared herself 'never in favour' with her niece, 'for you know I will not toady. Therefore I come out with the truth, and truth is often too rightly told to please a lady's ears.'

Amelia, when alive, had complained of Elizabeth's plain speaking and lack of sympathy during her unhappiness. And Mary, as she had been Amelia's favourite, was now Charlotte's. 'She has been all kindness to me but otherwise you know that I am always happy to quit the castle,' noted Charlotte. Meanwhile Elizabeth said of her niece, 'I do not think her at all improved, self-opinionated to a great degree, and holding every soul as cheap as dirt.' Her governess, Lady de Clifford, had no control over her whatever, 'and I believe she is so clever that she does not mind her in the least. I hope these visits will not harm her head but everyone here shows her so much adulation, that how can it be otherwise?'

Towards the end of November the Council proposed to the Queen that they should bring in Dr John Willis and Dr Simmons to help Dr Robert Willis manage the King's case. The Queen fended off Simmons successfully, but failed to keep John Willis at a distance, even when she cited the promise she had given her husband years before never to let that doctor have his management again. Overruled by the Council, she wrote to her brother with colossal understatement, 'It is not a situation designed to lift the heart.' When Dr John was introduced to the King on 23 November as a new doctor who would assist Dr Robert in the management of his case, George III did fall into a violent rage. But he appeared to have no memory of that time at Kew in April 1801 when Dr John had cornered him and kept him captive. The royal patient returned to arranging imaginary concerts, playing his harpsichord and 'exerting his power of sending various individuals to the lower world'.

Princess Mary herself was dejected, writing in January 1812, 'No one that really loves the King ought to pray for his life being prolonged a moment in so deplorable a state.' And a few days later on 4 February her father was declared, in a question-and-answer session between Council and doctors, unlikely to recover. 'Is it insanity?' the Council questioned. 'Yes,' the doctors replied firmly, and a full regency was inaugurated that month.

With the passing of the unrestricted Regency Bill, an uncontroversial and necessary measure, if a lamented one, the Prince Regent acquired all the powers that his father had held. The Prince's decision to retain Perceval and his father's Tory ministers, however, on the same plea as before, that he could never forgive himself if the King one day cast off his delirium and suffered a relapse on finding the enemy Whig party in power, was spectacular.

At Windsor the Queen and the princesses, while regretting the need for a full regency, were happy, as stout defenders of the King, that his ministers should remain in power, although the King himself, under the care from now on of both Willises and their keepers in his northern apartments at Windsor, knew nothing of the matter. But the Dukes of Portland and Devonshire, Lord Grey and the other leaders of the Opposition were from now on the Prince's implacable enemies; Princess Charlotte, a fervent Whig, rushed from her father's table when he proposed a toast to Mr Perceval. And, as in a game of cards, the Whigs picked up Charlotte's mother, Caroline, Princess of Wales, when the Tories dropped her as a Court card of lesser value now that they had the Prince in their deck.

The previous autumn the Prince had outlined to his sisters at Oatlands the measures he intended to include, for their happiness, in the Regency Bill, then being drafted. Sophia, giving her address as 'The Nunnery, No. 3 Castle Court', wrote to him afterwards: 'My heart overflows with gratitude for all your noble and generous intentions towards us …' And she hoped that 'your kindness to four old cats' would not cause the Regent any trouble with his ministers. 'How good you are to us … Poor old wretches as we are, a dead weight upon you, old lumber to the country, like old clothes, I wonder you do not vote for putting us in a sack and drowning us in the Thames. Two of us [Augusta and Elizabeth] would be fine food for the fishes, and as to Minny and me, we will take our chance together.'

If the ministerial arrangements pleased the Queen, the financial arrangements that the Prince was making for his sisters occasioned in her some bitterness, or 'jealousy of your kindness', as Princess Mary told her brother. The Queen said that no one appeared to feel for her, but that she thought it best not to discuss anything with her daughters. Nevertheless, Princess Augusta was worried to death by their mother's revelations, her sister Mary believed. 'Poor soul … she has, I believe, spoke more to her than to any of us.'

In Parliament there were eyebrows raised at the additional sums of £9,000 that the Prince wished settled on each of his four sisters in England. But they had their supporters, notably in the person of William Fremantle MP, who spoke movingly of the princesses and of 'the filial affection and amiable and captivating submission with which they have borne the calamities which have lately fallen upon them. Throughout the Empire,' he

declaimed, 'there can be but one sentiment on their conduct and sufferings. Every father of a family may truly say to his children, imitate but the
virtues and the example of your Princesses the King's daughters, and my
wishes will be gratified.' The Regent's and Mr Fremantle's wishes were
granted, and Sophia thanked her brother for 'the energy you have shown'
and 'the steadiness with which you have persevered on our account'.

With the additional £9,000 a year came a new carriage for each of the
princesses, plus a page and a footman. The livery was to be the same as that
of their brothers – crimson, lined and trimmed with green, very handsome. Furthermore, the princesses could now appoint a new lady each on
half-duty at £300 a year. But when General Taylor brought the princesses
letters to sign regarding their proposed allowances, the Queen became
enraged that Mr Perceval had not written to her. Augusta replied boldly
that in this delicate matter it had been right for the Regent instead to speak
to her. The Queen looked 'very steadfastly at me', wrote Augusta to her
brother, 'and said with a kind of suppressed anger, "That may be, but still
I think I ought to have been addressed straight to myself".' It was all very
wearing.

Princess Elizabeth was no less affected. 'The changes are great here,
which has nearly broke my heart,' she reported to Miss Compton on 29
February. In January, before the passage of the Act, she had written of the
disagreeable duty of parting with old friends among the household: 'I wish
to do everything handsomely, properly and soberly.' Miss Planta had
resigned, and Elizabeth told Lady Harcourt, 'The Queen has behaved like
an angel, she gave her a present of £100 a year. Augusta and me intend to
make it [up to] three, for she then will be comfortable. She thinks of going
to Bath ... You may suppose she was violently affected and how much
pleased at our mother's kind and gracious conduct.'

When the day came in February to make the final farewells, Elizabeth
recorded:

> It was Miss Planta's last day and she was the picture of misery and breaks her
> heart. Which of course affected us much, and leaving after so many years
> and having done her duty thoroughly, made me ... recollect nothing but the
> good. Then came a servant, he was a porter on the King's side [of the quad-
> rangle] who had belonged to us, to tell us he was going. There was another
> scene. And so it went on all day – grief and vexation of spirit. Every hour
> something springs up to rend our hearts – letters from other servants, occa-
> sioned by the present melancholy change. It will be soon over, but these days
> are misery to us. This morning my sisters have persuaded our dear old Cox
> ... the old servant in the Queen's ladies' room, to retire ... she has behaved

extremely well and really like a sensible woman, thoroughly a gentlewoman. She came into my room and I said, 'I hope you will be happy.' 'I cannot be otherwise,' she responded. 'You have all done everything to make me so.'

Elizabeth noted sorrowfully, 'I appear like a brute to everybody ... I can scarcely bring myself to see them. It so totally unhinges me, and this a.m. it has seized my bowels and made me bilious.'

Other servants and members of the royal households left, too, if they felt their dignity forbade them remaining under the new arrangements, where only five tables instead of twenty were to be 'kept', so that equerries would dine with doctors, and ladies of the bedchamber with keepers of the robes. 'I look forward with a degree of dread to all we have to bear still,' Elizabeth wrote. Displaying a certain guilt, she added, 'If anyone thinks we are much pleased with the idea of an establishment, they must think we are born without hearts and feelings. God knows it is a most bitter pill to swallow for the cause' – the King's illness – 'is death to us.'

The King's merino sheep in the Home Park at Windsor, procured for him from Spain and Portugal by Sir Joseph Banks, were sold off. The Staffordshire Regiment and the Blues and Royals were no longer to guard the Castle. The Queen's German band was dismissed. Castle Street in Windsor no longer echoed to the hooves of the King's glossy saddle horses, and Highflyer, Perfection and Othello were sold off, and Spanker, Frolic, Traveller and Boldfeather too. But there was for Princess Sophia, when she felt well enough to resume her riding – she had been plagued by 'cramps' for some months – room for comfort. She and Augusta, the only equestrians among the princesses now that Amelia was dead, took ownership of Skyscraper and of five further mounts.

They might have splendid new establishments, a carriage and a lady each, but, Elizabeth wrote, 'You may depend that we do not intend doing anything extravagant or silly, we only wish to have that degree of liberty which is right ... The trials of these years have made me more sedate and more willing to yield on many points than I ever was. In short, a home sans ma mère I hate the thought of.' But of course with an income of £13,000 any of the princesses could now set up their own households, were they not subject to their mother's wishes.

Princess Augusta no longer felt subject to those wishes, and wrote a letter to her brother on 5 March on a very confidential matter. She reminded him that, when her heart was 'full of care' one evening after dinner four years before, she had told him, as she had earlier told the Duke of York, the secret of her heart – her love for General Sir Brent Spencer.

The Prince of Wales had responded then that he had often marked 'a gloom' upon her countenance which, he was certain, 'proceeded from some secret cause of anxiety'. No action was possible then, but now, writing her letter, Augusta looked to the Prince's sanction for a 'private marriage' with the object of her affection. Though Sir Brent was not her match in birth or station, it had been twelve years since they were first acquainted, and nine since their attachment had been 'mutually acknowledged'. She was now forty-three.

'Long and great has been my trial, and correct has been my conduct,' Augusta proclaimed with feeling. In the circumstances, she begged the Prince to stand witness at the secret marriage she craved. If he thought it not proper to attend himself, she asked him to send Frederick in his place to give royal sanction to the match. Almost as ardently, she desired her mother's blessing, but she wished the Regent to broach the matter to the Queen. Though her consent was not necessary, Augusta wanted her mother to acknowledge that her daughter had never shrunk from any of her duties, 'though suffering martyrdom from anxiety of mind and deprivation of happiness'. In the event, Princess Augusta did not send her letter to her brother until June, while her mother continued to be cold and difficult with her daughters.

Anxiety about an approaching drawing room – the first in eighteen months, and one marking the return of the Queen and princesses to public life – brought forth a tirade from the Queen on 2 April directed at her daughters. The occasion was another letter written to her by Augusta. It began by thanking the Queen for 'the many years she had so liberally provided everything for us', and mentioned the resolve the princesses had taken to go about in Society despite their father's condition. When Augusta came in from her ride after breakfast, she had her answer. 'I was fully aware', the Queen wrote, 'that the happiness of an independent establishment must carry the idea of liberty with it, and ... this may perhaps be the last time that any one of you may be inclined to take a mother's advice.' But, she warned them, 'your situation is very different to that of your brothers'. They were duty bound to appear in public. 'Your sex and ... the present melancholy situation of your father' must be counted in. And, the Queen declared, 'the going to public amusements excepting where duty calls you would be the highest mark of indecency possible.'

Finally she addressed the visits the princesses had begun to make to their brothers in their new coaches and carriages. 'You never can be in the house with those that are unmarried without a Lady – even that pleasure, innocent as it is, should be considered before it is done.' Bidding Augusta keep in mind that 'no age whatever is exempted from being criticized', the Queen closed her letter by saying that she had seen that Augusta had fixed her course so she would not say more.

Her mother's reply was 'written in anger', Augusta told her brother the Prince, 'and I put a person in a passion and a person that is drunk upon the same footing'. Hence she would not copy it to him, and, when she saw the Queen in the evening with her sisters – their mother had dined alone and cried a great deal – the Queen smiled and said nothing. Augusta said nothing in her turn.

The quarrels between the Queen and Mary and Augusta did not occlude the joy brought by the Regent's visit to Windsor on his father's Birthday in June 1812. Elizabeth was suffering from a bout of St Anthony's fire on her face, and Sophia was still invalid. But Mary and Augusta and the Queen were a harmonious trio for the occasion. The Prince Regent crossed to the northern apartments his father occupied, and stood silent spectator of the King's activity for some time. 'He was struck', Mary reported, 'with the King's good looks.' The Regent, however, thought their father had 'grown very fat and large'.

When, on the 12th of this month, Princess Augusta sent her March letter to the Regent and begged him to show it to her mother, saying of it, 'there is not one syllable not strictly true', she enclosed a covering note: 'I feel that the longer I delay the making my sentiments known to you, the more completely miserable I grow, particularly as I do not nor cannot name the subject on which I have written to any one but yourself ...'

Augusta's March letter would have moved a stone: she had originally been led to speak to the Prince when the General was abroad, and her 'anxiety for his safety and welfare' had been 'put to the trial for a second time'. She told the Prince that the General had offered to give up his 'situation about the King', to spare her unhappiness, which she forbade. 'A third time he was ordered abroad, and painful as the thoughts were of our being separated again, it was a mutual consolation to us both', she wrote, 'that you and dear Frederick ... were apprised of our attachment.' Had the General fallen, she knew they would have shared her sorrow. Now that the General was returned, 'I am sensible', she said, 'that should you agree to our union, it can only proceed from your affection for me, and your desire of promoting my happiness, and that of a worthy man ... of course it will be necessary to keep it a secret and ... it must be quite a private marriage ... Nothing is more repugnant to my principles ... than the not acting with candour to every individual, and more particularly towards my own family, but ... there is no duplicity in silence.' As for the Queen, 'if she merely thinks of my birth and station', she could not approve, 'but that is the only reason she can object to it and I shall never blame her for it'. Augusta ended, 'I am proud of possessing the affection and good opinion of an honest man and of a highly distinguished character.'

She continued, it seems, to possess that 'affection and good opinion', even though no answer from her brother, not even a letter from her mother exists, and it seems unlikely that any marriage took place. The only material evidence of Augusta's relationship with her General is a locket bearing her miniature and taken from his neck after death, with an accompanying card claiming that they had married. It is a claim impossible to substantiate.

Before she had sent her letter, Princess Augusta with Princess Mary had been the Regent's sisters with the appetite for town. Shortly after the King's Birthday of 1812 they dined one day at York House, the next at Carlton House. But, Princess Mary told Mrs Adams, 'all this has been done with great difficulty and given us much pain and sorrow'. She could not enter into particulars in a letter, but, she wrote, with obvious reference to the Queen's opposition, 'if you knew everything you would think we are quite right'. Miss Kennedy wrote compassionately at Windsor of the Queen and princesses, 'They have been shut up so long, that they have lived a most melancholy life.'

Sophia's health yielded under the strain twice within eighteen months. Only weeks after she had nursed Amelia for the last time, Mary found herself looking after her other younger sister, Sophia, when she was 'much subdued' and had a 'bilious fever' for five weeks. Halford and Baillie both feared that her case resembled Amelia's. 'And in many things she puts me so dreadfully in mind of poor Amelia, it makes me quite sick,' wrote Mary, who had known her dead sister's case better than any doctor. These morbid feelings did not, in fact, herald any deterioration in Sophia. She grew thinner, her niece Charlotte noticed, over the year, and was quickly fatigued, but she continued to ride out, getting into a post-chaise that followed behind when her energy dimmed.

But on the King's Birthday in 1812 Sophia remained with Elizabeth at Windsor, the younger sister very ill once more with spasms and other symptoms that so reminded her sisters of Amelia's case. Halford and Baillie rather now feared she was 'nervous'. It was a nebulous condition, but it was one that was now to persist for years, not months. It effectively immured Sophia in her rooms at Windsor, and – by association with the invalid King in the northern apartments of the Castle – this incarceration easily gave rise to rumours about her health to join those others that circled about her. Six years later Dr Baillie's sisters answered enquiries from a guest, the novelist Maria Edgeworth. Princess Sophia was 'not insane', they told her, 'only nervous and weak'. Miss Edgeworth recorded, 'this is the truth, and nervous is not here used as a soft equivocal word'. The Misses Baillie also quelled the rumour that Amelia had died 'a martyr to the King's evil and all scars and sores – absolutely false'. Their brother had seen the Princess 'after death', and 'her neck and every part of her was free from all scar or sore or swelling or any symptom of that disease'. But one of the Misses Baillie started new hares – 'all about her children true', noted Miss Edgeworth, 'Fitzroy her husband I think she said but am not sure – was not always kind to her'. And she added: 'The princess [Sophia] is married, it is believed, to General Garth. Miss Baillie says you would be surprised if you saw him.'

Leaving aside the accuracy of the information Miss Edgeworth acquired about the two princesses, Sophia's letters to Sir Henry Halford show her very 'nervous' indeed. Usually clear-headed and lively in her correspondence, she now betrayed extreme anxiety and morbid sensitivity in matters of no moment to a person in normal health. Halford was her lifeline, her dependence was all on him. He heard from her daily in letters that listed in equally minute detail the dishes she had tried to eat and the range of emotions through which she passed while she lay in her bed at Windsor.

For Princess Mary, the purchase of 'finery' to set off her good looks had always been a pleasure. Now, with a new lady, Lady Isabella Thynne, as chaperone, and with her more capacious purse, she made frequent visits to West End haberdashers and mantua makers. Sophia, too, had looked forward to emancipation. She and Mary had made a pact to share the costs of a coach, a chaise and two footmen out of their handsome new incomes. Mary, visiting her brothers and her friends in London in defiance of her mother, had sole use of the stable, as Sophia lay in her room, guarding her 'cramps'.

Her nerves frayed, Sophia was 'quite overcome' when news of a terrible incident in Parliament reached her in May 1812. An assassin, John Bellingham, shot dead Prime Minister Spencer Perceval. 'To think that we live in a country that could produce so great a monster,' exclaimed Princess Mary. Princess Elizabeth, like Sophia, was 'truly overpowered' and 'completely overset'. The whole House of Commons felt horrified, she recounted, and 'all party animosity' put to one side when 'poor Mrs Perceval and her twelve children' were recommended for a pension.

Perceval, apart from his earlier championing of the Princess of Wales, had been a politician greatly to the princesses' liking. He had protected the interests of the King. In addition, he had been largely instrumental in the successful passage of the Regency Bill and of the provision for the princesses. They were right to mourn his passing and regret the advent of his successor, the tremulous Lord Liverpool.

Princess Elizabeth, declaring herself a 'bad courtier', went less and less to London in her search for independence. She wrote of her rooms in the Castle that they were 'altered, old friends with a new face', with the help of her new income. Her old bedchamber too was changed into 'an elegant sitting room and all as pretty as possible, my old china perfect and altogether it is quite the thing. It has been an amusement, and the only one I have had.' Ever industrious, Elizabeth claimed to have 'of late been idle to an excess', but she shared with Miss Augusta Compton her latest artistic achievements. She had done 'some few drawings in a slight state ... on blue paper'. Had she had more to copy she would have been happy, but her supplier had gone into Wales. She wished she had Augusta's 'hand and pen' to make all her studies and books perfect, and, searching perhaps for a companion in her artistic projects, she offered to her friend another cottage close to her own at Windsor.

Augusta Compton's father, the Queen's page Henry Compton, had died recently. 'Do you think to live in town or in the country?' Elizabeth opened, moving on swiftly to enquire, 'how was you to like being near here?' She could, she explained, 'manage' – that wonderful new income – a 'very pretty little cottage which I think I can get', where Augusta could live rent free, and with a friend if she liked. 'Be honest and tell me', Elizabeth concluded, 'if you do or do not like the idea.' Elizabeth continued eagerly with her plan for Augusta Compton to be her companion in the country. 'The room below is lovely,' she wrote on 13 June of the cottage she had acquired; 'you may make as pretty a room above if you will sleep in one of the back bedrooms.' Within the week, Miss Compton was at Windsor, which offered Princess Mary the opportunity for some sharp words about her letting down her maternal relations by spending time with Elizabeth's maids. Mary concluded, 'without she keeps herself up properly ... I cannot ask Miss Townshend and many of the respectable people at Windsor to visit her'.

Elizabeth did not see this, Mary added – and there perhaps lay the real burden of complaint. It was, after all, Elizabeth who did not 'keep herself up properly' but dined in her 'cottage' with pages' wives and maids and – in Augusta Compton's case – the daughter of a nurse and page. Elizabeth was, in short, becoming eccentric, and prizing low rank and humble origins in her companions above other qualities. And as she inhabited her old countrywoman's role at Old Windsor, her figure grew still larger, and her cheeks rounder.

Elizabeth had new criticisms to make *en princesse* of her niece Charlotte, who in June 1812 had been sent, for the sake of her 'studies', to live at Lower Lodge in Windsor. The sixteen-year-old, going up to town every two weeks to visit her mother, dined at the Castle every other evening, after the hours spent with music teachers and art masters and riding out with her aunts were over. The Princess of Wales made attempts to see her daughter more than once a fortnight, and was met with rejection when she drove down unexpectedly to Windsor. The Queen – and Lady de Clifford – inflexibly applied the Prince's orders, that the Princess should never see her daughter in any of his houses, and as such Lower Lodge was now counted. Pausing to order in pigeon pie from the Castle Inn as she awaited a kinder response that did not come, the Princess of Wales drove back to London to bruit about the story of her husband's cruelty and left her daughter at Windsor to a 'more than usual sleepless night' after what Charlotte described as a day of 'events, doubts and uncertainties'.

Such was the tension between her parents, that Charlotte's mind, when not occupied by 'study', ruminated 'upon everything that is uncomfortable, and happiness fled', and in these painful circumstances she even came, from disliking it, to value 'study' – learning from the Griesbachs (musicians in the King's band) and drawing 'landscapes and figures' on alternate days. Her thoughts had earlier more naturally flown to waltzing and billiards and 'gymnastic games'. Twenty years or more after those aunts whose company she scorned had sought independence, as they were finding a measure of it, she now sought it too, declaring, 'This cannot go on very long … Emancipation cannot be far away, I trust …' She longed for a time when it would be 'in my own power, my own act and deed, independent of everybody', to take her own course of action. Meanwhile her mother's actions 'put us all into a great fury', Mary told Mrs Adams on 12 July. And, she concluded mournfully, Charlotte had been 'neglected to a degree that is quite dreadful and I own I begin to fear she has very little heart'.

Charlotte had turned against her aunt Mary, who, she wrote, was 'the carrier of everything back again to the Prince, whose great favourite she is, as well as Princess Elizabeth. There is but one difference, that the former [Mary] being a fool, cannot contrive things so well as the other [Elizabeth] who has cleverness and deepness, both; had she the scope to exercise them, she would be a second Duke of Cumberland, having all his dark propensities of dark deceit, and also Princess Mary is a very good handle, that is all, for she is too great a repeater.' Princess Sophia was now Charlotte's favourite: 'When I see her with the rest of her family, I can hardly believe she belongs to them — so wholly different is she in thoughts, opinions, manners ... Her nobleness and rectitude of mind renders her no favourite here. The constant scenes of intrigue, of tracasseries she can but ill support.' And the King's situation made Sophia further miserable in her niece's opinion: 'Her health is impaired by her acute feelings, not for herself but those she loves.' As Sophia had once fought Caroline's battles, Charlotte noted, her aunt now fought hers at the Castle.

Princess Mary recited the 'heartbreaking' facts about the King's condition. 'I fear now not the smallest prospect of his mind ever coming round,' she wrote. In addition to his old delusions he had a new idea — 'that he is surrounded by most of his old friends that have been dead at least fifty years'. He was almost wholly occupied by this phantom assembly, and was quite happy, except when asked to turn his attention to something else. 'He puts himself into violent rages,' Mary told Mrs Adams on 24 August, 'which, entre nous, require restraint.' Most sobering of all, he did not appear to mind the restraint. 'He is grown very thin, looks many many years older,' she concluded, but he was still very strong.

The King remained all this time in his own world, speaking tenderly of Princess Amelia, his hold on reality sometimes loose, sometimes only a fraction less than perfect. His sons Augustus, Edward and Adolphus took him out walking on the terrace, and he talked of making alterations at the Weymouth house he was never to visit again. Faced with this blind, unknowing husband, the Queen — whose duty it was, under the Regency Act, to visit him once a week and stand silently observing him — was a broken vessel. 'Poor woman, her dreadful alarm and fears get so the better of her, she appears so dreadfully cold,' wrote her daughter Mary. Only Charlotte, 'open hearted and artless', who 'cuts all her jokes with the Queen' as she did with her aunts, beguiled the old lady into good humour. The Queen was 'surprised but certainly full as much amused' as her daughters by Charlotte, 'and very good-natured to her, and inclined to join in the fun'. That fun, Princess Mary commented tartly, was 'without end'. Still, she believed now, 'a great deal of good may be done with her'. Charlotte's outspokenness, careless manners and ungainly deportment would yield, in her opinion, to 'care and constant attention and good example and talking to her as a friend (not as a governess) ... we have still very good ground to work upon'. Mary sounded only one note of alarm. When she went into Charlotte's room at Lower Lodge — the room that used to be Amelia's — her niece was standing at her dressing table, just as that earlier occupant had had the habit of doing. It could have been Amelia standing there, wrote Mary in sudden distress.

Nothing disturbed the King in the sad calm of Windsor. Elizabeth, establishing a new tradition, organized at Frogmore, on the Prince's suggestion, the fêtes to mark her brothers' birthdays and other high days and holidays, that had once been held in the Castle. Princess Charlotte dreamt of Parliament granting her an establishment of her own, while her preceptor, and previously her uncle Edward's tutor John Fisher, now Bishop of Salisbury, read to her from Mrs Hannah More's *Hints for Forming the Character of a Princess*. ('This I believe is what makes me find the hours so long. I am not quite good enough for that yet,' she complained.) Augusta, Sophia and Mary made an expedition to Lord Liverpool's country home with their mother and ladies, and came away with a higher opinion of the new Prime Minister.

And then Princess Charlotte wrote in mid-November from Windsor to her clandestine correspondent Miss Mercer Elphinstone – a Whig! – that the Regent had come down to Windsor with a most welcome message. Charlotte was to be three days in the week at Warwick House, her London home, in the winter, 'to have such masters as I had not here, and such amusements as the time will allow, the opera, play, dinners at company at Carlton House and those of his brothers who can give them ... Two princesses are to go up to the Queen's House, to break the ice for them of new liberty.' She added dramatically, 'Here is the hitch. The Queen is outrageous, and will not hear or allow either of them to go without her. There has been a terrible fracas about it all, nor is it over yet, for nothing more can be done or said till the Regent returns.' The princesses thought that he would be very angry 'at her opposing his orders'. Charlotte herself was not particularly thrilled at the idea of being 'seen out under the charge of a parcel of old maids'. The society she would see would be 'ministerial', or Tory, while she was still a committed Whig. Nevertheless, she admitted, it would be 'at least something to get away for a day or two from this odious place'. Therefore, she sent her thanks to the Regent.

The Regent, by way of avoiding further disputes, wrote on 29 November to say that he wanted Charlotte to be present at the State Opening of Parliament, when he went down in person to the House of Lords. Furthermore, he wanted his sisters to attend her, else she could not go. 'It made it quite impossible we could refuse going,' wrote Mary to Mrs Adams, 'as we never ought to stop any amusement for Charlotte. It therefore is decided.' Mary and Elizabeth were to go. Mary lamented the 'great deal of disagreeables' it caused them, and it placed them in a 'sad and most awkward situation'. The 'disagreeables' of course came from the Queen. 'We can only do for the best,' Mary finished. But it came to a head in a 'dreadful scene' on a December Sunday, Augusta informed the Regent.

The Queen wrote her own account of the scene. 'Elizabeth, by defending her own conduct, struck in a most violent manner upon a Holy Book, saying that she would have an oath that she had done all in her power to please.' The Queen believed that her daughter wished to hit her. Augusta wrote that her mother used 'hard expressions'. It was particularly painful, she observed, for Elizabeth, who was the most attached of all the princesses to her mother. 'Sad and cruel is the return she has met with.'

Elizabeth and Mary resolutely took their places in the House of Lords with Charlotte beside them at the State Opening of the new Parliament. But their return to Windsor brought a further outburst from their mother. 'She told them that she would never forgive them,' Augusta reported to the Regent on 2 December. 'Eliza said, "May God forgive you for saying so".' The Queen saw their public endorsement of the Regency Parliament as a betrayal of the King. 'She won't allow that any of us feel for the King's unhappy state of mind.' Mary wrote: 'Today the Queen still appears to very great disadvantage and when we are with her *cuts* at us very deep, but we do all we can not to mind it.'

The Queen ended by commanding her daughters to name the subject no more, but Augusta, for one, felt 'most deeply' the injustice with which she treated them. The Regent attempted to assuage matters with conciliatory letters, but the Queen remained 'silent and very distant with us and out of humour', Mary told him. The princesses were careful to do nothing to offend, and were anxious that the Queen should master herself before her granddaughter, and that Charlotte should not notice how 'uncomfortable' the Queen's manner was with her. With the once protective King, though yards away, insensible of his daughters' predicament, the Queen, swollen with dropsy, hounded her daughters with rages and angry predictions of disaster.

The princesses could not keep the Queen's unhappiness from her granddaughter. 'The Queen exposed herself ... before Charlotte', wrote Mary on 9 December, 'at breakfast this morning in her manner towards us.' Mary found it difficult to know what to say to her niece, who had plainly taken in her grandmother's bad humour. 'You have been long enough at Windsor now', Mary offered, 'to know the Queen has not a good temper, and the kindest thing you can do by us is never to provoke the Queen.' The Queen's black mood lasted all day. She dismissed them all hurriedly from breakfast, as if she 'could not contain herself at all'. When they saw her again at dinner, she dispensed the coffee in summary fashion and sat in her own room without speaking a word, while Elizabeth read to her.

The atmosphere of tension and hostility persisted. But in the middle of December the princesses launched a protest. The Regent – the Queen's favourite child and the supreme power in the land – would have to try to make her see reason, they declared to him: 'We have neither health or spirits to support for any length of time the life which we have led for the last two years.' Unless the Regent could 'secure' them from this 'treatment' from their mother arising from 'compliance' with his wishes that they attend his daughter to town or fulfil other entirely reasonable engagements in London, they believed the intention must be 'to force us to quit the paternal roof'.

Their mother having forbidden them to mention this subject to her, they begged their brother to ask her to explain to him 'her present and future intentions with respect to the line which she means to adopt towards us'. If they were forced to quit their mother – and father – at Windsor, they wrote determinedly, they would ask his protection in establishing new residences. They were very serious about this, especially Augusta and Mary.

When George, Prince of Wales, Duke of Cornwall and Prince Regent exerted himself, there was no being more charming, sympathetic or adept at oiling troubled waters. And there was no being in the world more susceptible to his gracious manners than his mother. After a visit to Carlton House and an interview with the Regent, the Queen, charmed and soothed by her eldest son, relinquished her belief that the princesses' duty was to remain at Windsor without relief. The princesses accepted, in their turn, their mother's assertion that she had misunderstood them. Within days mother and daughters were back in daily domestic contact. Mary, recently so enraged with the Queen, asked Mrs Adams in Dorset to send some 'baked apples' for her, 'which she is told Devon is famous for'. And she wrote that she was as 'busy as a bee making things for the poor to give on Christmas day', and had just finished an immense drawing for the Queen, which was to be put up at Frogmore.

Princess Charlotte, soon to be seventeen years old and still ensconced at Lower Lodge with masters and governesses and nursemaids, might show her legs indecorously when she sat down, alternately mistrust and adore her warring mother and father, gossip with her old nurses and conduct clandestine correspondence with Whig misses. But she, and her desire for amusement, also represented her aunts' lifeline to an independent and adult life in London. Even Sophia, 'very nervous, very low', hoped to dine at Carlton House and attend the next drawing room. The passage of the war and the politics of the Houses of Commons and Lords became quite suddenly the province of these mature princesses. Casting off the remnants of the wretched cocoon in which they had slumbered for so long at Windsor, Augusta, Mary, Elizabeth – and Sophia when well enough – prepared to take London by storm.

14

Emancipation

~

IN THE MIDST of the princesses' new independence, with their mother resigned to their new life in London, and with her strong feelings that this showed disrespect to the King softened by the Regent's blandishments, there was extra need for them to attend town. Their niece Charlotte had lost her governess and chaperone. 'We have lived in the high road to town for the last fortnight,' wrote Princess Mary cheerfully to Mrs Adams in January 1813, 'in consequence, entre nous, of Lady de Clifford having resigned, and the difficulties were great in trying to make the new arrangements.'

She was being economical with the truth, even when she added, 'The Prince has therefore begged the Queen to assist him, and that has caused much anxiety and as yet nothing is settled.' Lady de Clifford had been asked to 'quit directly' after it was discovered she had condoned her charge's flirtations the previous year. Not one by-blow of an uncle – George Fitzclarence, the Duke of Clarence's son – but two, the other being Captain Charles Hesse, an illegitimate son of the Duke of York, had ridden alongside Charlotte's carriage in the Great Park at Windsor without protest from her governess. But Charlotte, indifferent to Lady de Clifford's removal, wanted her fidgety replacement, the Duchess of Leeds, to be named her lady-in-waiting. She also wanted to purloin her grandmother's reader, Miss Knight, and have her named 'lady companion'. Other girls of seventeen, she said, were not subject to governesses.

The Regent huffed and puffed, his mother cried at Miss Knight's perfidy when she accepted the position, and her daughter Mary wrote, 'It really is very selfish of the Queen not to consider the consequence it is to find proper people for Charlotte.' It was true, nevertheless, that Charlotte went under the aegis of her grandmother and aunts to a series of London events including the Queen's birthday drawing room – and to a ball at the beginning of February which the Regent gave in his daughter's honour.

Princess Mary was cheerful about these outings, unaware of the bilious tone of her niece's letters. A few days after the Carlton House ball, which went on till past six in the morning, Princess Charlotte wrote, 'I really enjoyed it and though very far from well, exerted [myself] to the utmost, and danced down every dance. Princess M[ary] opened the Ball, though it was given for me, and was always the couple above me, as jealous and ill natured the whole night as she could be. I did not care, as I am not quite so mean as to care about trifles.' In Charlotte's opinion: 'There is a cabal and a wheel within wheel about everything,' and she held Princess Elizabeth and Princess Mary, in particular, to have great influence over her father: 'It is infamous to make such a use of a brother ... as Princess Mary does of the Prince Regent towards her ... Their low jealousy was let out yesterday at dinner, and in the evening at the fête it was obliged to be concealed. They could not endure [me] being heard and seen, the Prince Regent being pleased with me, and his having gone for the partners for me, and having left me to make choice of them.' She wrote of her father with delight, 'He was just opposite to what he had been before.'

William, Duke of Gloucester, though absent from London on military duties, heard tell of 'grand doings' at 'the Court of Carlton House'. He moved, with his sister Princess Sophia Matilda of Gloucester, uneasily between his cousin the Regent's new Court and his aunt Brunswick's and cousin Caroline's houses. Princess Mary reported to her brother, who was always morbidly interested in the doings of his estranged wife, that the party had been only family at Kensington Palace when Charlotte visited her mother on her birthday: just Princess Sophia Matilda of Gloucester and her lady, and Charlotte's maternal uncle, the Duke of Brunswick – a widower – and his two young boys.

Despite a rapprochement that had existed for many years now between William, Duke of Gloucester and his sister Sophia Matilda and their cousins the King's offspring, he and Sophia Matilda had never been given the titles 'royal highness'. And the omission rankled. It was suggested – perhaps to account for the romantic vacuum of Princess Mary's existence – that the Duke had proposed not once but many times to his beautiful cousin, who had been born Her Royal Highness at the Queen's House months after plain Prince William's own birth in Rome; and that her refusals rankled too. But there were other rumours, that the Duke of Gloucester was 'always in love with somebody ... very amorous'. It was also said that he was 'a good man, but amazingly stupid, tiresome and foolish' – which would explain why anyone might reject him.

Princess Mary was cast down when Mr George Villiers – husband of Mrs Villiers and once the King's favourite equerry until his dismissal for peculation – turned blackmailer. In his possession, he wrote to Sir Henry

Halford, were letters from Princess Amelia and from Princess Mary to his wife regarding 'the subject which', he declared, he knew to be the cause of the younger Princess's death. 'In the number of years Mrs Villiers was intimate in our house, I cannot pretend to say', Mary wrote, 'that I may not have written many things I should be very sorry appeared before the public.' And that Amelia died of a broken heart, she believed, she had quite possibly asserted, although she did not recall that she had explicitly mentioned General Fitzroy's name. But she was defiant. 'I don't care what he says or does to the living, however disagreeable, but to disturb her poor ashes is more than I can stand.'

The matter was resolved, quietly, discreetly, General Taylor and Sir Henry Halford with Sir Benjamin Bloomfield, the Prince's secretary, employing what was to become over the years, in defence of several of the princesses' reputations, an effective mixture of emolument and emollience – with belligerence as a last resort. The princesses' sister-in-law the Princess of Wales, however, had no such supporters in positions of power when the Regent refused to read a letter she wrote protesting that she had lately had no access to her daughter. But she had as supporters the Whigs, she had the public, and she had her brothers-in-law, the Dukes of Kent and Sussex, and her cousin the Duke of Gloucester, who for their own reasons wished to spar with the Regent.

Caroline's letter, published in *The Times* as the 'Regent's Valentine' on 14 February 1813, rehearsed old arguments. But her mother, the old Duchess of Brunswick, died in the midst of a new Parliamentary committee being appointed to examine the conduct of her daughter, and the evidence collected in the Delicate Investigation being revisited. New waves of sympathy and applause met Caroline's every appearance in public, even as she was being driven by debt – and a wish for greater privacy in which to indulge a new friendship with a handsome Italian music master – to move out of Kensington and into a rented house in Bayswater. But, while the Princess of Wales gained public sympathy, she lost much of the confidence her daughter had till now placed in her. The Regent forced Charlotte to read the Parliamentary Report, which was mostly a commentary on the charges brought against her mother seven years before and going back to a time when Charlotte was a small child.

Many bitter recollections came back to the young woman who read the evidence for the first time. She wrote six months later, 'after the publication of things I was wholly ignorant of before, it really came upon me with such a blow and it staggered me so terribly, that I never have and shall not ever recover [from] it, because it sinks her so very low in my opinion …'.

She continued: 'it has taken away any feeling of respect or duty ... I will add that I think she had her aggravations, that she was ill-used, and is still now more than before, after this double clamour ...' But, she said, 'the horror of the knowledge of the whole can never make those feelings ever return again that might have allowed influence'.

The burial of the Duchess of Brunswick disturbed her nieces the princesses at Windsor, recalling, with its night-time ceremony, the laying to rest with similar honours of their sister Amelia. They heard the bell toll. As before, soldiers of the Blues and Royals, holding flambeaux, surrounded St George's Chapel, while the Duke of Brunswick, cloaked and booted as his cousins had been before him, honoured his mother as they had their sister.

Royal, the Duchess's eldest niece, had recently renewed correspondence with her family in England, after her husband realigned himself with the Austrian and Russian emperors following years as a Napoleonic satellite. She explained to Lady Harcourt, 'Having been so many years deprived of letters from my friends and of all English newspapers, I am a little like a person who has been in India, and returns home quite ignorant of most transactions which have taken place in England.' Many of her first letters were, in fact, concerned with the depreciation of her income since 1805, thanks to a fluctuating foreign exchange. And she wrote now, begging on her stepsons' behalf, for a share – as Augusta of Brunswick's children – of their grandmother the Duchess's estate. With unusual tact, she did not ask for any sum for the Duchess's granddaughter Trinette, now Jérôme Bonaparte's wife and Queen of Westphalia, perhaps judging a Brunswick inheritance unlikely to be forthcoming for Napoleon's sister-in-law.

Another disruption occurred in the stillness of the Castle to alarm especially the Queen. Princess Augusta wrote to Sir Henry Halford from Windsor on 2 May 1813: 'The chambermaid Davenport (who has been very strange for a long time past) went raving mad in the night and at five this morning she flew down to the Queen's door.' Davenport knocked and called out to Mrs Beckedorff who went out to her. Davenport declared she would see the Queen, and Princess Augusta too. Upon Mrs Beckedorff telling her 'in her mild way' that she would not wake the Queen but that she should see her in the morning, the chambermaid 'threw herself on the floor and swore and screamed in the most violent manner'.

The matter passed out of the royal ladies' hands when Dr Willis's men, hastily summoned from across the quadrangle, placed the girl under restraint. 'In that state', wrote Augusta with horror, she was now – 'thank

God' – gone to London. And, Dr Millman, for whom her mother had an 'adoration', not being available, Dr Baillie came to quiet the Queen. The Queen would be seventy the following year, and not only were her nerves fraying, but she suffered increasingly from headaches and from bowel complaints – a debilitating duo. Sir Francis Millman, her doctor of many years, who her dresser believed 'understands the Queen better than all the world put together', spoke of a cure or rest at Bath or at another watering-hole, but the Queen refused to leave the King. Her temper and her nerves were now accepted by her daughters and those who inhabited their reduced circle.

At Frogmore, where Queen Charlotte continued to botanize and garden, they had, she said, 'a very small society'. 'With walks, reading, work and a collection of engravings,' she wrote flatly, 'our time passes, if not joyously, at least reasonably, and that is all *qu'il nous faut.*' Entertainments now were always subject to the Queen's calculation – were they seemly, given the King's condition? When one of the princesses wished to sit for her portrait to Henry Edridge, the Queen said 'she would allow no painters to come to the Castle as she did not think it proper, ill as the King was'. Princess Mary circumvented this neatly six months later by saying she would sit to Mr Thomas Lawrence the next time she went to town. When Hanover was restored that year to England, and Adolphus went out to head the new civil government, his mother's first thought was of the King, who knew nothing of the matter. She lamented that her husband was denied the pleasure of hearing of the return of this possession whose loss had caused him such suffering.

In some ways the Queen was still energetic. She joined with her daughters in advising Augusta Compton to accept in marriage Captain Thomas Baynes, a retired naval captain with a post at the Royal Naval Asylum at Greenwich, whom she had refused earlier in the year. The Queen hoped Augusta Compton's 'natural shyness' would not get the better of her good sense, and Princess Mary, too, was swift to urge haste. 'Pray don't let her go on with a long courtship,' she wrote to Augusta's aunt, Mrs Adams, 'it is such nonsense – in particular, with so old a man as her intended.'

It was 'downright folly', wrote Princess Elizabeth, to resist, and she did not stint on her wedding presents to her protégée, giving 'some dimity for petticoats, two silk gowns, a small lace veil of Brussels, one of patent, not too long, and a skirt of Honiton [lace], a wedding work box'. She continued, 'I shall send more things by and by.' When the wedding day neared, Elizabeth was beside herself. She rejoiced that Augusta had 'determined to quit that vile class, you know what I mean [spinsters]. Don't let anyone know my sentiments, for else I shall bring a hornet's nest about me but my language is that of truth seldom spoke anywhere, particularly near the dwelling of HRHs.' Augusta had set her a good example, she added, and she would follow it whenever she could.

In August, when Mrs Baynes was on honeymoon at Hastings, Elizabeth wrote again: 'A married woman is a much more respectable and estimable one than a tabby, the thing of all others I hate, though alas! It is my own case. But maybe your wedding may bring me luck ...' She had eaten Augusta's wedding cake 'by the pound', and trusted it would have a proper effect. (According to the old wives' tale, a good helping of wedding cake made spinsters radiate eligibility.) If not, she said, 'men must be blind, and Phipps [the royal oculist] must couch them [remove their cataracts], that's all.'

But it was not Elizabeth who had eaten that wedding cake to effect. Princess Charlotte, nearly thirty years her aunt's junior – barely come out, at seventeen – was suddenly mooted as a bride. For in August 1813 the Hereditary Prince of Orange brought despatches to the Regent from his patron, Arthur Wellington, that announced a great victory over Marshal Soult's forces in the Pyrenees. And the Regent seized his appearance in London to impress upon his daughter the dynastic opportunities of marriage to this unprepossessing boy, Prince William of Orange. Lord Yarmouth was sent as his emissary, to tell Charlotte that all must wish her to be 'well together' with her father. The Regent's sisters Elizabeth and Mary – whom Yarmouth called 'intriguantes in every way except being women of gallantry which might be the case too, but there he did not meddle' – governed her father now, he said. How much more easily might she do so, Yarmouth wheedled, with so superior an understanding? But until Charlotte was married, with her own establishment, how could it be, he sighed?

At first Princess Charlotte resisted. She might say she was free of her mother's influence, but Caroline had stigmatized the Oranges, when they lived in exile at Hampton Court before proceeding to Berlin, as 'intriguing and violent'. Furthermore, a friend in London who met the Prince said Charlotte would think him 'frightful ... as thin as a needle. His hair excessively fair, to match a complexion that is burnt brown by the sun; eyes that have no expression at all, but fine teeth that stick excessively out in front.' And so Charlotte declared herself at Frogmore one August afternoon, to another of the Regent's emissaries, 'very much in favour and in preference for everyone to the Duke of Gloucester'. She wrote to her confidante Miss Mercer Elphinstone, 'I added that I had considered it long and in no hurry, and was convinced of the propriety.' 'Good God, I can hardly believe you are serious,' came the reply of her father's deputy. The Duke of Gloucester's attachment to her aunt Mary was common rumour. And Charlotte, well pleased with her effect, 'laughed heartily after they were gone'. Even the reminder that she could not marry the Duke of Gloucester if the Prince forbade it did not disconcert her. 'I assured them nothing was so easy as to make a public declaration that I would never marry anyone else.'

Two months later, the Regent held forth to his daughter so strongly and in such indecent language against the Duke of Gloucester, her supposed object of affection, that she hardly knew which way to look – 'especially as he repeated it twice over'. He accused her of being in love with the Duke of Devonshire – whom, as it happened, the Duke of Clarence favoured that winter as a groom for his illegitimate daughter, Sophia Fitzclarence. But eventually, on the advice of Lord Grey, the Whig leader, who counselled that opposition to her father must not commence her public life – 'which God grant may be long and glorious' – Charlotte accepted her fate. Her aunt Mary advised her to marry – although she did not promote 'Slice', as Gloucester was known, but rather 'the Orange'. And Charlotte had an interview in December with William, whom she described as 'shy, very plain, but he was so lively and animated that it quite went off'. When it was done, the Regent took her into the other room, and, on his asking what she said to it, she hesitated. He was 'so alarmed that he cried out: "Then it will not do".' When Charlotte indicated, rather, that she approved what she had seen, he exclaimed in still greater agitation, 'You make me the happiest person in the world.' And without a second's pause he called in the young Prince, 'took us both into another room and fianced us, to my surprise'. He took their hands and joined them and gave them his blessing. 'And when it was over, and I was walking with him [William of Orange], we were both so excessively astonished that we could hardly believe it was true,' Charlotte ended her tale.

'Whether it was summer or in spring', his daughter was 'equally to be married', the Regent told his mother days later on Christmas Eve at Windsor after she had expressed her surprise at the heady course of events. And when the Queen attempted to give her granddaughter some 'good advice', the Prince was no less impatient. The royal family was gathered to attend Charlotte's confirmation, which had been planned rather more carefully than her engagement. Not surprisingly, at the end of her confirmation, 'so awful a ceremony that I felt during it and afterwards exceedingly agitated', Princess Charlotte saw 'traces of agitation visible upon all their faces' when she met her family afterwards.

But the match, so suddenly come forward, so urgently forwarded, was not destined to stick. Charlotte worried about a black box containing her letters to her admirer Captain Hesse which Mercer seemed unable to extract from him. She worried about her mother, 'a very unhappy and a very unfortunate woman who has had great errors but is really oppressed and cruelly used'. She worried about her aunt Sophia, especially when Dr Baillie, her mother's doctor, said that 'he saw … no end to her illness … that hers and Amelia's sickness were precisely the same, though not origi-nating from the same causes … having no digestion at all it is greatly to be feared she will sink under it, having so little strength'. It seemed that no medicines would remain in Sophia's stomach.

Charlotte also worried that Mr Augustus d'Este, her uncle the Duke of Sussex's son by Lady Augusta Murray, was quite her 'shade'. All the previ-ous summer he had pursued her on her daily drives in the Park in her til-bury; now he was again in evidence, for instance, at the Chapel Royal – 'opposite to me the whole time of service, never taking his eyes off me and imitating every motion of mine'. When she went to Kensington Palace to see her mother, where the Duke of Sussex also had apartments, d'Este was 'planted behind one of the pillars of the colonnade watching me'. An extravagant letter from the boy – Charlotte took exception to her bastard cousin's use of his father's royal crest – finished the matter, for she sent it to her uncle Sussex with a request to be no further disturbed.

In June 1814, the Prince of Orange reappeared to play a part in the fêtes in London that marked the Allied victories culminating in the imprison-ment of Napoleon on Elba, and the successful restoration of the Bourbons to France. All the French princes paraded, and the King of Prussia came with his general, Blücher, who was loudly cheered. The Russian Emperor, Alexander, and his sister, Grand Duchess Catherine (widow of Prince Peter of Oldenburg, son of the Prince of the same name who had once wooed the Princess Royal), came, and put up at Pulteney's Hotel. The Prince Regent did not dare visit them there for fear of being hissed, of which the Grand Duchess declared herself very glad. She had come to London with a thought of marrying the Regent, but took a strong dislike to him. The Hereditary Prince of Württemberg, though a married man with children, attracted her instead.

The Prince of Orange, whose father had been restored to the throne of Holland the previous winter, and the Hereditary Prince of Württemberg – and his brother Paul – were among countless young princes who made their way to London this June, to begin the jockeying for position in the new Europe that would be continued at the Peace Congress to be held in

Vienna shortly thereafter. A handsome prince in the Russian service, Prince Leopold of Saxe-Coburg, made Princess Charlotte's acquaintance when she visited the Grand Duchess, and asked if he might wait on her. His brother was much in favour with the King of Prussia, and his sister was married to the Prince of Leiningen, but his – successful – effrontery was noticed, given that Charlotte was engaged to the Hereditary Prince of Orange. No one knew that, among the mêlée of princes, and while engaged to William, Charlotte had also met and given her heart to Augustus Frederick, a nefarious cousin of the Prussian King.

Meanwhile, Charlotte's aunts were not without visitors during these days of fêtes and celebrations. And their sister Royal had written to Lady Harcourt from Ludwigsburg that she hoped 'the various visits which will take place in England will ... have some influence on my sisters' future situation. This is a subject I have much at heart, and trust the Almighty will bless them and reward them already in this world for all they have gone through ...' She herself had had to decline her brother's invitation to join the imperial and royal visitors in London, as she was 'so very apt to be sick in a shut carriage and off and on constantly spit blood with a violent spasmodic cough'. Sir Thomas Tyrwhitt, the Regent's envoy, believed that the cough was a pretext and that Royal's husband was furious not to have been addressed on the matter himself. But Royal begged him not to pursue the matter – she said she would be the loser for it. And still she prayed daily that her sisters might yet have a chance to marry.

In 1788, as we have seen, only days before the King of England became ill for the first time, he had said he would take his daughters to Hanover, there hold a court, and invite all the German princes to attend. His daughters might choose whom they wished, within moderation. Now the German and other princes had come instead to England – and, with Princess Charlotte affianced, they looked afresh at her older aunts. The King of Prussia was seeking a bride to act as mother to the seven children his adored wife Louise had left him. The Russian royalties were scouting for brides for their brothers, the grand dukes. Dynastic alliance with England, above all, rather than heirs and maidenly charms was what was desired at this time of acute anxiety on the part of all the imperial and royal houses of Europe.

Princess Elizabeth had remained at Windsor while her brother led a great party of emperors and kings and generals to the Ascot races: 'I went into my room to sit in my great chair with my books, my papers and writing things, intending to employ myself all day.' About three o'clock she was startled to receive a note from Mary, written at the race ground. The

Emperor Alexander of Russia and his sister, the Grand Duchess of Oldenburg, were on their way to visit her.

Elizabeth dressed and summoned her wits to entertain her distinguished visitors, no doubt making something of the connection between them – her brother-in-law the King of Württemberg being their maternal uncle. 'When they were gone I sat down to recover myself,' the invalid wrote. The next moment, the door opened and from without 'they said, the King of Prussia'. This time there was a double connection to explore. Louise, the adored wife of Frederick William III, had been Queen Charlotte's niece, and he himself was half-brother to the dear Duchess of York. 'I almost dropt,' she wrote the following day, 'for I did not expect him. He is very shy, very modest, looks manly, good and melancholy ... you will allow it was awkward for me, as we had never met and there was no soul to introduce either him to me or me to him.' It gave her the 'headache ferociously'.

Although Elizabeth did not know it, her sister's stepson, Prince Paul of Württemberg – first cousin of the Emperor and Grand Duchess, and the Princess of Wales's nephew for good measure – had behaved shockingly that day at Ascot. He got the Hereditary Prince of Orange blind drunk, for the second time. The first time, at Carlton House, Princess Charlotte had been present to observe it. The Prince's stepmother, Royal, disclaimed all responsibility from Ludwigsburg, telling the Regent that she had warned him in April that they could not be answerable for Prince Paul's conduct. 'For thirteen years he has done nothing but offend his father by the improprieties of his conduct.' But Princess Charlotte seized on the displays to refuse outright to marry the Hereditary Prince of Orange. She was as summary with him in this great matter of state as she had been with young d'Este. She wrote to her aunt Mary of 'an explanation which took place between me and the Prince of Orange and which terminated in a manner which will, I fear, give you pain; but in my situation it was unavoidable. Our engagement is at an end ...'

The real truth was that Charlotte feared she would be forced to live in The Hague, and she felt very strongly that her presence in England was her mother's protection against further designs – divorce, persecution – that she was aware her father would meditate with her gone. If she also felt that her father's remarriage and the birth of a son – an heir apparent – might follow divorce, it was hardly surprising.

There were so many advisers pressing in with information and hypotheses on this unfortunate young Princess – ranging from her father and his government to her uncles Sussex and Kent, to Lord Grey and Mercer

Elphinstone for the Whigs, to her mother's lawyer Henry Brougham. And then there were the visiting dignitaries who put a finger in the pie, such as the Duchess of Oldenburg, the Tsar's sister, who saw Holland as a useful Russian satellite and wanted the Prince of Orange as a bridegroom for her own sister. In the midst of it all was Charlotte, with her jutting bosom and hips and her fresh face and chestnut ringlets – outfacing her father's wrath, and, as it happened, utterly in love with Augustus Frederick of Prussia, whom Miss Knight had allowed into Warwick House after Princess Charlotte had asked him to come and visit her.

The hothouse atmosphere of royal London exploded when the Regent appeared at Warwick House, demanding to see his daughter. Miss Knight said, on the Princess's instructions, that she was too ill with a swollen knee to descend, but then offended the Prince by saying she must contradict a report that Prince Leopold of Saxe-Coburg, an officer in the Russian service, had been secretly visiting Warwick House. The Regent said grimly that he knew that rumour to be false, and that equally he knew of a certain Prussian prince who had been the visitor in question. The upshot was that Charlotte learnt she was to be incarcerated with some old ladies of the Queen's in a lodge in Windsor Great Park for her criminality in receiving Augustus and rejecting William of Orange. For sanctuary she fled by hackney carriage, bad knee or no bad knee, to her mother at Connaught House, the Princess of Wales's house in Bayswater.

It was a chastened Charlotte who left, as her father had originally directed, a few days later for Cranbourne Lodge in Windsor Great Park. At Connaught House her mother had rejected her daughter's impassioned plea to save her from the prison her father meant to condemn her to. (The failure of her many relations among the visiting dignitaries to call on her, for fear of losing the Regent's favour, had left Caroline wretched and humiliated and she was now set on going abroad.) Charlotte's uncle Sussex had, with the other advisers who drove up to the house in Connaught Street, counselled obeying her father.

Indeed, the lawyer Henry Brougham had led the quivering Princess to a window that overlooked Hyde Park and had spoken of the potential scene should he show her to the populace that would gather there next morning with the advent of a Parliamentary election. Blood there would be, and marches and riots in her defence, but the English public would never forget that she was the cause of that bloodshed. Just as surely as Charlotte's aunts had had to obey their father thirty years before, so this wilder, more headstrong Princess – seeking emancipation as they had before her – agreed to be driven to Carlton House and to do her father's bidding.

At Cranbourne Lodge, to compound her hurt, Charlotte learnt from her father that her mother was preparing, in the wake of Napoleon's expulsion from France and the restoration of his satellite kingdoms to their former sovereigns, to travel to her brother William's restored Duchy of Brunswick. It was a trip that the Princess of Wales had often meditated during her years of distress in England before her father's death and the incorporation of her homeland into Napoleon's Empire. The Regent had 'no objection', and had no wish to 'interfere' in his estranged wife's plan. Her daughter wrote, 'I really am so hurt about it that I am very low ...' But Princess Mary told the Regent, 'I congratulate you on the prospect of a good riddance. Should a storm blow up and the ship go to the bottom I will send you a small fashionable pocket handkerchief to dry your tears – it will be the only black gown I shall ever put on with pleasure.'

Charlotte slowly recovered from a year and more of exceptional agita-tion and distress at Cranbourne Lodge which, after all, turned out to be a 'very cheerful and very good' house, 'the view lovely'. She visited Weymouth in company with her chaperone, Lady Ilchester, and General Garth, her grandfather's former equerry, and bathed in hope of a cure for her knee, which swelled unaccountably. And she forgave her aunts and grandmother for their previous behaviour. Indeed, she found her aunt Sophia a strong ally when she expressed fears that the Regent had not entirely lost sight of reviving the Orange match. 'The thing was impos-sible,' said Sophia firmly. Charlotte came away, more relieved than she had felt for some time, 'though I still see mountains and hills before me are to be passed over, if not quite inaccessible'.

All the princesses were utterly convinced that Charlotte, despite her youth, should marry. 'The country and your family wish you to marry, and I am sure all who really love you must too,' said Sophia, 'for you never can be happy or enjoy anything like liberty or comfort going on as you do now, so subject and subjected.' Royal wrote to Lady Harcourt: 'Il n'y a nulle rose sans espine [there is no rose without a thorn], but I believe that it is ever better for Princesses in particular to be settled.'

The Princess of Wales's failings were a subject on which the Queen and the princesses had 'naturally agreed' with the Regent – all bar Sophia. But Caroline had departed now for the Continent. And the Queen began, as Charlotte observed, 'to have her eyes opened and see now ... that the Regent only used her as a cat's paw'. The Queen meanwhile told the Regent, 'You do not see Charlotte at all to advantage. She is quite differ-ent with us, I assure you.' But he answered, 'You always say so, I know. It is very unfortunate, but she appears to me half in the sulks.' And Charlotte never lost her fear in her father's company.

The only princess whom Charlotte was wary of was Mary. She suspected her of still being likely to take the Regent's part if he tried to revive the Orange match. And she regarded her also as something of a rival. Mary, after all, though she was thirty-eight next birthday, was the beauty of the family, and Princess Charlotte, heir presumptive though she might be – and sought by many – had little confidence in herself. When Charlotte mentioned Prince Leopold of Saxe-Coburg, she said she believed Princess Mary 'coloured not a little' and then was made 'quite satisfied and cheerful again' when Charlotte said he did not suit her taste.

Charlotte concluded darkly, nevertheless, 'I suspect there was something or other.' But when she questioned her aunt Sophia about Mary's feelings, Sophia said irritatingly she knew nothing of it. 'If there is any tendresse, it is all her side certainly,' concluded Charlotte. However, when she departed for Weymouth that winter, she gave Mary credit for 'feeling it exceedingly, as she had the example of poor Amelia before her eyes too fresh, easily to forget and not to feel uneasy about my knee'. Indeed, Mary also expressed her astonishment that the Regent was not more unquiet. 'If the country takes an interest in me and about me,' wrote Charlotte gloomily, 'that shall stand to me in lieu of family and everything else.'

At Weymouth Charlotte was discomposed by her attendant, General Garth, pressing his 'adoptive son' Tommy Garth on her – 'a more lovely boy I never beheld', she admitted. But she 'was taken aback' when the General paraded the boy on the esplanade, and when Charlotte stopped overnight at his house at Ilsington he said, 'Pray see and speak to him, as he would be dreadfully mortified if you took no notice of him, but don't let him be seen or let your ladies see you take any notice of him.' Furthermore, the old General said roughly that Princess Charlotte should not believe any of the abominable stories she had heard of his birth. Charlotte nearly fainted.

'It looks like this,' she explained, 'that not being able to torment her [Sophia] now any longer with the sight, he will continue it upon the relative she loves best besides the Duke of York, a sort of diabolical revenge that one cannot understand.' However, her ladies, Lady Ilchester and Mrs Campbell, she wrote, believed that 'it cannot be and is not Garth's child, that he has the care of it, and is proud and vain that it should be thought his, and knowing he has it in his power probably to disclose whose it is, if offended, makes him so very bold and impudent about the whole thing.' The feeling in the county, on the other hand, she said, was 'that there is something to come out yet and that if it ever does, it will turn out to be some secret marriage or something of that kind'.

Charlotte was no stranger to stray children with question marks over their parentage, following her childhood with a mother who adopted first a French orphan, Edwardine Kent, and then a docker's son, Willy Austin. She was also happy to guess at those children's parentage, believing them both to be her mother's, and the elder child – whom her mother had just married off to an aide-de-camp of her brother's in Brunswick – the daughter of a military hero, Sir Sidney Smith. She had the same black hair as his, she said. As for Billy Austin, removed from Dr Burney's school at Greenwich and tagging after the Princess of Wales as she toured the Continent, the Delicate Investigation and childhood memories had convinced her he was the child of the naval officer Captain Manby. 'As for my mother taking a flight to Turkey,' Charlotte opined, reporting rumours that became fact some months later, 'I should not wonder at it, as it is quite possible for her to do anything strange and out of the way.'

Charlotte herself had decided to do something very reasonable by the time she left Weymouth – and marry Prince Leopold of Saxe-Coburg, the young man who had asked to visit her that June. 'That I should be as wholly occupied and devoted as I am to one [Prince Augustus of Prussia], and yet think and talk and even provide for another would appear unnatural in the highest degree were it written in a novel, yet it is true. It is not overstrained.' On Charlotte's return to Windsor, Mary's became the room at the Castle where she most often found herself, and in January 1815 she seized an opportunity to confide to Mary her marriage plans, when her aunt asked if there were any one prince she had seen in England that she did not dislike the appearance of. She said that she was 'not in the least in love' with Prince Leopold, but that she 'had a very good opinion of him' and would rather marry him, for that reason, than any other prince.

But then her hopes were dashed. 'Only think of Elizabeth and Augusta saying to me just before we parted for the night', Charlotte wrote on 26 February, 'how much they hoped I should be tormented and worried no more on the P[rince of] O[range] business, how they longed for an answer from me which might set my mind at rest.' And Princess Royal had written from Stuttgart, 'saying the reports were that Lord Castlereagh was going to Brussels' – the new Orange capital – 'on his way to England. That, if it was true, she only hoped to God it was not to renew any more torment or worries for me.' Charlotte went on, 'the letter came to wash down again all my air-built hopes of quiet'.

Princess Mary told the Prince that she and her sisters were trying to encourage the Orange match, as they knew his feelings on the matter. Charlotte had a more committed supporter in Princess Sophia. 'As for the O[range] business,' she wrote to her niece, 'I have my doubts whether all hopes are yet given up at headquarters [Carlton House]. They still flatter themselves that the event may take place. At least, so I hear. But I live so very much to myself, and so very retired, that I do not learn much. My health ... does not allow me to trudge about sufficiently to get much information.' And she was 'in complete quarantine' with her family, as their ideas did not agree.

The Queen, however, was strong in support of her granddaughter. She was 'deeply overcome, and she wept which is very uncommon for her', wrote Charlotte. 'She was very affectionate to me, implored me on her knees not to marry ever a man I did not like, that it would be endless misery ...' She did not wish to encourage Charlotte to disobey her father's wishes, the Queen told her granddaughter. But, Charlotte recorded, she insisted that, 'in what so wholly concerned my earthly happiness and well-doing, I had a right to have my own opinion, and by it to be firm.'

As the country flamed in riots over the Corn Bill, and it was written on the wall, 'Prince Regent, dissolve this Parliament directly or your head shall pay for it,' the Queen was firm herself with her son, saying sternly: 'Prince of Wales, you must, if you persist, talk to your daughter yourself. For both myself and mine choose to keep quite out of it, as we will never press what will, we know, make Charlotte miserable.' Charlotte's own unhappy conclusion was 'The Prince must be gone mad if he goes on persecuting me with his abominable Dutch man.'

On the Continent, Royal was at last diverted from her niece Charlotte's peccadilloes by news of Napoleon's escape from Elba. 'His landing in France at the head of so small a body of men would have appeared romantic', she warned the Regent on 16 March 1815, 'to all who were not acquainted with the talents and good fortune he displayed till last year.' The Queen of England, suffering from erysipelas and a swollen face, was as anxious as her daughter in Württemberg – and was to become more so, when another marriage scheme divided the royal family, making the Regent's and Charlotte's tussles over her choice of bridegroom look feeble by comparison.

The final conflict of the Napoleonic Wars was played out on the fields and farmland around Brussels in June 1815, and Royal's supporter Napoleon, vanquished for ever, was despatched to the remote Atlantic island of St Helena. Ernest, Duke of Cumberland, with many others, headed for a Continent no longer, as the older royal houses of Europe saw it, in chains to an upstart. And while others prepared to gather once more at Vienna to fight for territory, Ernest – saturnine and scarred – found, at his mother's old home of Strelitz, a bride. Unfortunately, the woman he wished to take as his wife was his cousin Frederica. A woman of fascinating and natural manners, she had also, when a widow with two children by Prince Louis of Prussia, jilted Ernest's brother Adolphus for the Prince of Solms. Solms then divorced her, citing her 'loose behaviour'.

The Prince Regent gave his assent to the marriage in Strelitz – and opened Carlton House to the couple when they wished to say their vows again in England in 1815. But the Queen, who loved her brother Charles more than anyone in the world, could not bring herself to receive her niece, his daughter and now her daughter in law. She feared that 'her [Frederica's] character is so well known in this country that it may cause you many difficulties', Mary wrote of her mother to the Regent, 'which don't strike you at this moment ... Should the Princess of Wales ever come to England again (and find the Pss of Solms well received) it may place us all under great difficulties.'

The Queen's nephew the Hereditary Prince of Mecklenburg-Strelitz came begging her to reconsider, and still she could not. When he retaliated by sending a 'very improper letter', his aunt declared to all her children 'that she never will see her nephew again', and she commanded them 'to have no further communication with him'. Given the Queen's 'adoration for her own family', Mary wrote to the Regent, 'the feeling herself under the necessity of acting against them is one of the greatest trials she could have in the world,' and the Queen's health deteriorated from this summer of 1815. Elizabeth asserted to her brother Sussex, 'as she acts from principle and a thorough knowledge of the King's opinion, she cannot err'. The princesses meanwhile were persuaded by their mother to write an uncomfortable letter to the Regent, the day before their brother Ernest married in England, avowing their intention to follow the Queen's 'line ... in the propriety of which we entirely concur'. The next day the miscreant couple were married at the Regent's home. And Charlotte believed that her uncle Ernest must have had her father in his power in some way to cause him to upset his mother and sisters so.

The Prince Regent ignored his mother's advice not to recognize his immoral sister-in-law. But he was eager to know details of his daughter's past passages with that immoral woman his estranged wife. And Princess Mary had acted as confessor to Charlotte, when, on Christmas Day 1814, she told a rambling tale of her visits to her mother over the past years.

Charlotte was at the time distraught on account of lawyer Henry Brougham's reports about Caroline's behaviour on the Continent. 'There is no hazard or risk to serve my poor mother that I would not run if it would be of any avail,' she told Miss Elphinstone. But she could not conceive that breaking her promise to her father not to write to her mother would do anything but mischief. 'When he talks of her being completely in a man's power I do not exactly know to what extent of evil I am to prepare myself,' she wrote fearfully of Brougham's reports.

Charlotte's recital to Mary included an account of how the Princess of Wales had taken her and Captain Hesse by the hand and shut them in a bedchamber with the words, 'I leave you to enjoy yourselves.' Much else followed, to the grim satisfaction of the Prince Regent, to whom Princess Mary wrote immediately a full account of her conversation with her niece. 'I never knew whether Captain Hesse was her lover or mine,' said Charlotte forlornly.

After she made her confession, Charlotte passed the night 'in the horrors ... I fear so terribly that I may have tended ... to incriminate her ... She is still my mother and as her child I have no right to cavil in her conduct.' Charlotte begged Mary – 'you are perhaps a more impartial judge than the Prince' – to tell her if she had acted justly. 'Except it be absolutely necessary,' she wrote, 'I hope all that passed in your room yesterday will be kept sacred within your bosom.' But of course Mary had passed it all on.

Once the rupture of Charlotte's engagement had become known, other princes did not hesitate to visit the Regent's Court, some latecomers being two Austrian archdukes in the autumn of 1815. 'I have such a dread of foreign princes, the sight as well as the name of them alarm me from the idea of some intrigue or other going on for my marrying some one of them, that I am on the *qui vive*,' Charlotte confessed, longing for Leopold to appear and declare himself. Of another prince who appeared, the Hereditary Prince of Hesse-Homburg, she wrote: 'a husband *in petto* for me too, I suppose ... the best thing I can do to make all easy and equally pleased is to marry them all at once in the lump. He is not a man at all calculated for me or that could make me happy.'

Indeed, beside smooth young Leopold, the mature and soldierly charms of the Prince from Homburg stood no chance. They were not always on show, anyway, as he was often obscured by pungent plumes of smoke rising from his beloved meerschaum pipe. There was too the reek of tobacco that clung about his hairy person – he boasted, besides a full head of hair, bushy sideburns and luxuriant whiskers – to discourage Charlotte.

Meanwhile, the Prince whom the Princess had once declared herself willing to marry, the Duke of Gloucester, had at the ripe age of forty, proposed to a wealthy widow, Lady Monson – and been rejected. Under this blow, wrote Charlotte, 'my cousin seems strangely to have kept his dignity and love of pride etc. She has done more than anybody else ever effected, I believe' – she meant, jokingly, in getting the Duke to propose. But Charlotte was soon cast down by new reports about her mother who, it was said, had taken as her lover an Italian who acted as her travelling courier. 'I am in despair at what you tell me about a courier. I had not the slightest or smallest suspicion of the kind … Surely, surely, my dear Marguerite,' she wrote to Mercer Elphinstone, 'there can be nothing there, a low common servant, a servant too. And yet you seem to insinuate it from the influence he has in disgracing the boy Austin.'

Charlotte was distracted from these meditations when she won her object, and the Prince Regent finally agreed to Prince Leopold as a suitable choice of husband for her. On a cold damp morning in February 1816, she came flying over to the Castle from Cranbourne Lodge with a 'face of delight' to show her aunts her father's 'perfect' letter on the subject. Later that month her suitor arrived from the Continent and was interviewed by his prospective father-in-law at the Pavilion at Brighton, where the Regent was increasingly spending his time. (His latest inamorata, Lady Hertford, could not abide London, all her comfort was 'destroyed' there, and so anyone, government ministers included, wishing to hold the Regent's wavering attention had to go down to the Sussex coast.) Princess Augusta, who had visited her brother in January, was delighted with her brother's taste: 'The house is quite beautiful, the ground floor entirely Chinoise of the very best taste – and magnificent, the bedchamber storey all plain handsome, good, substantial furniture.' Prince Leopold found the corps diplomatique who assembled there less entertaining than the Princess. 'Who would have thought that I could have put a morsel in my mouth sitting with an ambassador?' she wrote. 'But I did or I must have starved.' He complained of the oppressive heat of the rooms, which was doing immense damage to his chest, and Charlotte was all solicitude.

The marriage went forward, despite the Regent's ill humour. As host at Brighton to the young fiancés and suffering from the gout, he wheeled himself about in a 'merlin chair', not being able to put his feet to the ground, 'and in that sits the whole evening with his legs down', wrote Charlotte. The Queen, who told her son that this was a match she most highly approved of, gratified her granddaughter by consulting with her about 'fine lace' and other items for her trousseau before ordering it. Charlotte had delightful evenings with Leopold, 'full of long conversation on different subjects interesting to our future plans of life ... A Princess never, I believe, set out in life (or married) with such prospects of happiness, real domestic ones like other people.'

And although the wedding was being planned according to 'some old documents' Lord Liverpool had found relating to her aunt the Princess Royal's marriage, Charlotte considered herself luckier than that Princess. When they were in town, she and Leopold met daily, 'and she did not', she wrote of her aunt, 'after the first day till they were married'. But then the Princess Royal did not have so many sexual escapades or such bizarre parents to discuss. Leopold hoped very much that the Prince Regent would not pursue his prospective mother-in-law for a divorce. He dreaded the 'éclat'. 'We did not say much about my mother,' wrote Charlotte, 'as he told me honestly her conduct was so notorious and so much talked of abroad that he was as well informed as everyone else about her.'

By mid-March 1816 Parliament had voted a generous sum to the bridal pair, and had agreed to the purchase of Lord Clive's house, Claremont in Surrey, as their residence. The nation was caught up in the love affair that blossomed between Charlotte and her fiancé, and their marriage, which took place on 2 May before an imported altar in the drawing room at Carlton House, was widely celebrated. 'Everyone complimented me upon the composure and dignity of my manner, and the audible manner in which I answered the responses,' Princess Charlotte wrote from Oatlands, which the Duchess of York had lent the bridal couple for their honeymoon. 'It all seems to me like a dream, and I ask if it is not so sometimes to myself, and I forget it all for a time, and then it comes back in full force. I cannot say I feel much at my ease or quite comfortable in his society, but it will wear away, I dare say, this sort of awkwardness.' Also Charlotte and Leopold both found the 'air of the house' at Oatlands 'quite unwholesome, it is so infected and impregnated with the smell and breath of dogs, birds, and all sorts of animals' – the Duchess of York's close companions for many years since she and the Duke had amicably parted.

Charlotte declared that the foundation of her own marriage was 'very reasonable and therefore there is less chance of its ever being otherwise than with most others; indeed, on the contrary, I am more inclined to think that it will improve. I do not see how it can fail to go on well, tho sometimes I believe it is best not to analyse one's feelings too much or probe them too deeply or nearly.' She had not completely forgotten Prince Augustus Frederick of Prussia.

While Charlotte became a wife and the mistress of her own house at Claremont, with firm hopes of becoming a mother as well, lightning struck out of a clear blue sky. Princess Mary, aged forty, followed her niece to the altar and married her first cousin William, Duke of Gloucester on 22 July 1816. Lady Albinia Cumberland described the scene to her daughter:

> Well, the wedding is over! Dear Princess Mary looked most lovely and angelic – really. Her dress a rich silver tissue of dead silver … no trimming upon it – lace round the neck only. Diamond necklace. The hair dressed rather high. The diamonds put round the head, something in the form of a diadem. When everybody was assembled in the saloon, the Dukes of Cambridge and Clarence handed her in. She looked very modest and overcome. The Prince Regent stood at the other end to the Duke of Gloucester. She stood alone to the former, quite leaning against him. Indeed she needed support. I pitied the Duke of Gloucester for he stood a long time at the altar waiting till she came into the room, giving cakes, carrying wine etc … She then went to the Queen and her sisters, and was quite overcome, was obliged to sit down, and nearly fainted …

Lord Eldon, the Lord Chancellor, said afterwards of the new Duchess of Gloucester that 'her behaviour was so interesting and affecting at the ceremony. Even the tears trickled down *my* cheeks.' Impossible for the Princess not to miss the presence of her father at this sacred ceremony. But the King inhabited a world of his own at Windsor, full of its own ceremonies. On one occasion, alone in the room with Willis, he 'took leave of all his company before he went to bed as if the room had been full of people'. When Dr Willis attempted to hurry him, the sovereign bowed acceptance: 'But I beg Lord Hardwick may first tell his story to Mr Smelt.'

Princess Mary wrote when the Duke's offer had just become public, in late June, to a friend who was a recent bride herself, 'it is difficult to describe what my mind is suffering at the prospect of leaving my first and most beloved of homes'. She declared, however, that, as the Duke's seat, Bagshot Park, was so close to Windsor, she would hardly spend a week without seeing her mother and sisters. And she wrote warmly, 'The Duke of Gloucester made so good a son himself' – his warring parents were both now dead – 'that he enters into all my feelings in regard to my family and my wish to take my share of duty in the attendance at Windsor in illness or in any distress.'

What had precipitated this marriage? The Duke of Gloucester had lately, as we have seen, proposed to another lady, and so was presumably in the mood to marry. Perhaps his thoughts had turned to marriage when his cousin Charlotte 'declared' for him. With marriage he won the coveted HRH, and even became a field marshal, as Leopold had done weeks earlier. But if it was true that he had earlier proposed to his cousin Mary twenty or thirty times and she had rejected him, why did she now accept him? Not much had changed in his circumstances to make him more or less attractive than at any time since he had become duke in 1805. Married life would centre on a town house, Gloucester House, which faced Hyde Park to the west, and, in the country, Bagshot Park, where the Duke was accustomed annually to shoot his way through the autumn and winter months. Nevertheless Princess Augusta believed Mary had 'every prospect of happiness'.

Mary herself guarded that prospect of happiness, and refused to allow her brother Ernest to visit her at the Queen's House before her marriage. 'I am quite certain', she wrote, 'the Queen would be greatly offended if he came into her house, and secondly, was he to say anything against the Duke of Gloucester, it would place me in a most awkward situation.' Mary was marrying a cousin from a 'weaker branch of the family', whom most if not all of her brothers had long regarded as a tiresome fool, and she, quite reasonably, did not wish to hear it said.

One of the chief reasons, it emerges, that Mary accepted Gloucester, or even possibly promoted the match herself, was that she hoped, as a married woman, to see more of her adored Prince Regent. 'I hope', she told him, 'I may be permitted to find my way into your room occasionally of a morning when in town. I shall be very careful never to get out of the carriage until I know you can receive me.' In return she directed him, 'Come when and as often as you please to my house, it will be the joy of my life to see you.' She had told the Duke 'how completely and entirely my happiness depends on my remaining on this blessed footing with you and all my family.' She ended this document that spoke only of her ties to her own family and of none to the Duke, 'I trust and hope my intended marriage will rather add and increase ... my devotion to my family, and that as a married woman I can come forward and be of more use to you all than I can now.'

Charlotte wrote a few weeks after Mary's marriage: 'I have seen the Gloucesters twice. They seem very comfortable and happy. He is much in love, and tells me he is the happiest creature on earth. I won't say she does as much, but being her own mistress, having her own house, and being able to walk in the streets all delights her in their several ways. He is not at all in favour with the regent, who quizzes him and shrugs up his shoulders at him upon all occasions ...' Charlotte herself found the Duke of Gloucester 'tiresome', but, after he and the Duchess had stayed at Claremont in August, wrote, 'though they are not the most agreeable people in the world, still they are exceedingly good humoured, good natured, kind and easily pleased ... the Duke seems very fond of Mary and to be very happy; he is certainly all attention to her, but I cannot say she looks the picture of happiness or as if she was much delighted with him.'

15

Daughters in Distress

~

Princess charlotte had not been entirely enthusiastic about her aunt's marriage. The new Duchess of Gloucester gave tit for tat. 'Our visit to Claremont went off very well,' Mary wrote on 29 September 1816, 'considering that we went to see two people completely engrossed with each other ... I doubt that the sort of life they are now leading can last, but I wish it may with all my heart.' Mary had very little conversation with Charlotte, who had once confided in her. 'She really appears ... to have no eyes or thoughts but for the Prince of Coburg and he is much in the same state.' Charlotte herself admitted with delight, a month after marriage, that her 'reasonable marriage' had flowered into a love match.

Her own husband, averred the Duchess, was 'all affection and kindness and has no object but my happiness'. She wrote of 'a marriage which promises every comfort' and of the Duke's 'honourable character and excellent heart'. And they both thoroughly enjoyed the marriage feast that her sister Princess Elizabeth contrived in their honour at her cottage at Old Windsor – a splendid fête, with rustic emblems and trophies of plenty and fruitfulness, jostling 'pan pipes twisted with tassels', trumpets, fifes and drums, painted on a blue background. The guests danced in a tent, and were offered a 'sandwich supper', and Elizabeth told Mrs Baynes that, if she had let her imagination have fair play, there would have been turtle-doves in pairs and cupids in every corner.

The new Duchess endorsed the work of the Duke's steward, Mr Edmund Currey, who had done much recently to make the estate into a first-class shoot. For Princess Mary was grateful, as she learnt that the Duke had only rarely been at Bagshot before Currey's landscaping of the property, which included 'wood walks, fine large trees' and a 'variety of ground that is striking for so small a park'. She could see opportunities for thinning here and planting there, she wrote. Gardening, an activity in which Mary had taken little interest till now, was to become her passion, under the tutelage of the personable Mr Currey and with an excellent gardener, Mr Toward. She intended to make a flower garden, once the Duke and her brother the Prince had settled on which side of the house additions should be made, she told Miss Henrietta Finch in October.

For the Regent had sent Mr John Nash, the celebrated architect, to survey the house and grounds with the plan of making additions. 'He passed two hours with us yesterday, and will put his ideas on paper for you to approve or disapprove,' she wrote to her brother. She had told Mr Nash again and again that he should add only what was necessary 'from comfort', having no wish to 'drive any unnecessary expenses upon any of the [government] Offices'. Nevertheless, Mary had found on arrival at Bagshot that what the Duke thought necessary for a lady's comfort was very far from her own. 'You know how many things are required in a lady's apartment,' she wrote to Miss Finch on 4 October 1816, 'and that never can come into the head of any man, still less one who never was used to live with ladies before he married me.'

Even before he married, the Duke had been badly off at Bagshot for lodging rooms for his staff and even for servants' rooms. All was now to be rationalized and adapted by Mr Nash for the new couple's convenience. According to Princess Mary, the house had only two good rooms, her own and the Duke's. The apartment – and dressing room – that her sister-in-law Princess Sophia Matilda of Gloucester had occupied when she stayed had recently been greatly 'injured' by rain, and, as for the Duke's gentlemen, they had to sleep in a garret. Only their long attachment to the Duke made them put up with being lodged among the servants. The basics for the 'common convenience of a family' were not to be found in the house, and she continued to beg the Regent to urge Lord Liverpool to give his consent for their supply.

The Duke, when not out in his newly stocked woods with his gun, or travelling England in pursuit of game elsewhere, had found his comfort till now not at home, but in his sister Princess Sophia Matilda's house in London, or in male society at the numerous London clubs that he belonged to. With a marked liking for institutional life, he felt most strongly about the African Institution, of all the many bodies whose dinners he attended and whose meetings he chaired. Promoting the rights of African slaves, he thus found himself in company with Mr William Roscoe of Liverpool, lawyer Mr Henry Brougham and other Radical MPs. Gloucester was here, as in other charitable enterprises, always a generous donor. But it was whispered that he did not always fully follow the arguments that raged around him at Cambridge, at the African Institution or in other committee rooms.

The new Duchess, taking a hand at philanthropy herself, was building a small schoolroom for Bagshot parish which was 'much wanted'. In case these activities palled, the new Duchess was going to have 'a master for landscapes, which', she said, 'I think will amuse me very much'.

She and the Duke received morning visits from her mother and sisters, the Regent called from Royal Lodge at Windsor, and Charlotte and Leopold came to stay. But their most frequent guests were Princess Sophia Matilda, with her companion, formerly her governess, Miss Dee, and the guests who came on shooting parties during the autumn. When the Duke was away shooting – often for ten days or more at a time – his bride generally visited her mother and sisters at Windsor. Thus she made good her promise that she would continue to play as full a part as possible in Castle life.

Poor health dominated the lives of the Queen and of Mary's sisters at Windsor, where every ailment became a hideous encumbrance. Sophia was now never long free from spasms, although there were days when she could sit up and play at cards. And, mysteriously, there were days when the invalid went out for a hearty ride with her sister Augusta. Mary, visiting from Bagshot, was drawn into this world of indisposition and was laid up for several days in November with a very bad chilblain on her foot, reminding her, she wrote to her brother, of another chilblain 'in the very spot that caused me so much suffering two years ago'.

The Queen's poor health – her bilious complaints and her sinking spirits – was apparent to all her daughters. On certain anniversaries, like the day on which the King fell ill, 25 October, grief overcame her. When she received the news of the death of her brother Grand Duke Charles, Elizabeth wrote, 'She was struck so cold ... that I was privately anxious.' Years earlier Royal had written of her mother's difficulty in giving vent to the strong emotions that disturbed her, and the years had not altered that failing. 'After all that has passed, one cannot wonder at its being a most painful thing to her to feel that, in acting the part of a truly great and excellent Queen, she was obliged to take a step which for the sake of the country was so extremely painful to herself ... if she had not done what she did, the morals of the country were gone.' But the Queen gained some pleasure from visiting her granddaughter Charlotte and Prince Leopold at Claremont. Their plans to attend the Lord Mayor's Banquet and to take part in public life met with the Queen's firm approval, and though she tried to dissuade her own daughters from attending Charlotte and Leopold, frailty made her less obdurate in general. Only in one matter was she unbending. She would not quit Windsor, though the King did not register her presence when she made her impassive visits to his northern apartments, for the 'cure' her doctors implored her to take.

For Princess Mary, marriage was a brave new world. Among other difficulties to contend with, she had to reconcile her loyalty to her brother the Regent with her new duty to her husband. Her dreams, expressed before marriage, of acting as hostess – which she could never do in her spinster state – to her brother at Brighton were with difficulty realized. Although the Gloucesters spent the New Year of 1817 there with the Regent, who was, according to Charlotte, 'as well with them as can be', the Duke's feelings for his cousin remained ones of anger and envy. And the Regent did not forget that, throughout his battles with their mutual cousin his wife, the Gloucester family had played an ambiguous part and had never ceased to visit the Princess of Wales till she left England.

When an assassin made an attempt on the life of the Prince Regent early in 1817, the Duchess of Gloucester seized the opportunity to rush to the Castle, where her brother was recovering. Royal wrote from Württemberg warmly, if not knowledgeably, of 'the spirit of anarchy' abroad in Britain, and praised her brother for cancelling the drawing room – for fear of riots – at which their mother had been due to preside. 'It would be terrible to have her exposed to any hurry', she wrote of the Queen, 'at this time of life.' She said of her mother further that 'at her time of life, she ought to give up having long drawing rooms ... Augusta and Eliza might with great propriety do the honours of them at Carlton House or ... like our late aunt Princess Amelia they might once a month have their own drawing room, which would help to keep up trade.' Royal was referring to the silk merchants, dressmakers and milliners who benefited from orders for the new outfits that were de rigueur for drawing rooms.

Royal herself had no wish to return to England and host any such drawing room, although she was now free to do so. Momentous news had come from Stuttgart in November. Royal's husband, Frederick, King of Württemberg – that great survivor who had twisted and turned his way through the Napoleonic Wars – had died on 30 October 1816. And the Duke of Kent, who had by chance been with his sister when the King expired, would do justice to their mutual attachment to the last, wrote Royal. Her sisters and brothers were less convinced about that attachment, and considered that the Queen was too proud to admit that she was the victim of domestic violence. Over the years, reports of the King's mishandling his wife had filtered back to England, but, given Württemberg's status as a French vassal state, it had seemed impolitic to raise the issue. Now the matter must be allowed to rest, with the King in his grave.

Royal's stepson Wilhelm and his new wife Catherine had also stayed with her to the last – although Catherine was 'taken in labour as she was sitting in the next room to the late King when he was dying'. (Bewitched by the Grand Duchess of Oldenburg in London the Hereditary Prince had divorced his wife and married the Russian Princess, who was now expecting their first child.) With great firmness of mind, hours after the King's death and twelve hours after the delivery of her own child, this new Queen of Württemberg wrote to Queen Charlotte 'to ease her mind' about Royal, Elizabeth told Lady Harcourt.

As Dowager Queen of Württemberg, Royal wrote six months later to Lady Harcourt that, although supported wonderfully by the Almighty throughout 'the severe trial it has pleased him to afflict me with', her heart was 'too deeply wounded' not to mourn constantly her 'dearest friend' – the dead King. She thought of her husband constantly, led the same sort of life he had been partial to, and employed herself in those things that had given him satisfaction. And this, she found, was 'in a degree prolonging his existence beyond the grave'. In Stuttgart and Ludwigsburg she had a respected position and could live, on her generous English jointure, an extremely grand and luxurious life. Each year she kept up a sort of summer court at Teinach, the watering place in the Black Forest where she had first gone years before, after the stillbirth of her daughter. This year she wrote of the waters, 'But although I submit to their prescription, I have little faith in it as nothing can ease a broken heart.' Why would Royal wish to exchange this respectable life of mourning for the daughter's lot in England that would be hers, queen and widow though she might be?

The day after her husband died, Royal wrote to Sir John Coxe Hippisley, one of the trustees who had been appointed on her marriage to invest her dowry: 'I believe that from the day of the King's death, I am entitled to the whole interest of my fortune' – £80,000 in 1797. For dowager residences she chose apartments in the new Palace at Stuttgart, a set of rooms in the great complex at Ludwigsburg, and the pretty villa, Mon Repos, outside the latter town. It was from Ludwigsburg in August 1817 that she wrote to wish her brother the Regent a happy birthday: 'I look forward with delight to the moment which will make you a happy grandfather.'

Princess Charlotte was expecting a baby in November 1817. Even before she was pregnant she had surprised visitors who remembered her rakish teenage habits by the taste she exhibited for domestic life at Claremont. She and Leopold sang, sharing a piano stool. As the pregnancy advanced, they went hand in hand for slow walks in the grounds. Charlotte sat to Mr Thomas Lawrence the fashionable painter, and in the portrait, her happiness outshines even the lavish gold embroidery on her Russian blue dress. People began to say that she would make – in due course – an excellent queen. Charlotte's old foibles – her impulsiveness, her arbitrary favouritisms and dislikes – were forgotten. And she moved happily about her new home, entertaining family and friends with pleasure. 'It is not à façon de parler to say that this is Liberty Hall, and that we are only too happy to dispense with form and ceremony,' she said contentedly one evening. But that was going too far for one visitor who found the circle they sat in impossibly formal and German, and the conversation deadly.

The weather cleared in September, and the Duchess of Gloucester – and her sister Augusta, who visited – quite lived out of doors at Bagshot and Windsor. On receiving a letter from Lady Harcourt, Augusta wrote that it was a real pleasure to reply to her – 'but so many people would expect me to correspond with them because my sisters are fond of writing that I give out I cannot bear writing which really is not the case, but the fact is, I love my few friends so very much that I cannot make a hospital of my heart – a phrase I have often made use of to dear Miss Gouldsworthy, who entered perfectly on my feelings upon the subject...'

They heard that the Princess of Wales – having learnt that she was to be a grandmother in November – was coming to England, and that Miss Frances Garth, her former lady, was to meet her at Dover. But Mary placed hope in a forged bond that the Princess had given her brother the Duke of Brunswick before his death, and which she hoped would help to expose and bring down her sister-in-law.

Mary forgot about the Princess of Wales on a bridal visit with her husband to Weymouth, originally a Gloucester 'fiefdom', where they were besieged by a host of friendly inhabitants. When they visited the Ilchesters at Nutting, a house 'full of fine old chinoise and japan and some good pictures', the Duchess noticed, among a sea of Frampton and Seymour relations, 'a most agreeable old Lady with a wonderful memory' who told her stories of fifty years back 'with a degree of cheerfulness that is delightful'. Was Mary thinking of her mother, now aged seventy-three, who was neither cheerful nor delightful, but ill and old and cross? Weymouth seems to have awakened in Mary no painful recollections of her last visit there with Amelia, and triumphantly she proceeded to Brighton, to batten on her brother from the comfort of one of his houses – ostensibly to see if a course of sea bathing would keep off 'the Saint', or erysipelas, that coming winter.

Princess Elizabeth, meanwhile, was spending her time painting glass for a window in her new 'castle in the air' – the dairy she dreamt of building at her Old Windsor cottage. 'I have no such thing,' she told Augusta Baynes, who had traced her a design for her project, 'but I love living on hope. She is at times a sad girl, but still one cannot live without her.' Elizabeth now planned to japan a large screen with 'bold patterns of birds, plants and figures', and asked Augusta to trace her some. She would ask Mr Festrage, the great japanner, to send her some tracing paper of quality that did not stick.

After her hopes of marriage with the Duke of Orleans had been dashed eight years earlier, Elizabeth had increasingly inhabited the role of eccentric in her cottage at Old Windsor. Adhering to her rustic character, she wrote of putting the pieces of wedding cake her friends sent her under her pillow and lying in wait for bridegrooms. But of course this was daft nonsense; bridegrooms could not 'come along' for Princess Elizabeth as they might for a Miss Compton or even a Miss Perceval. If she were to come by a husband, it would be by treaty with a foreign state. Meanwhile, outside were the cattle and Chinese pigs that she bred. Inside, the house was chock-a-block with the 'old china' and teapots that she collected, her library of books, and her portfolios of prints and drawings. There were also to be found the raw materials of myriad artistic endeavours – scissors and black paper for the silhouette scenes of mothers and babies which she cut out with such dexterity, screens and inks and paints for her japanning projects, the large albums which she illuminated with texts and then grangerized, or filled with appropriate prints and engravings in the margins, and even a decorative garland or two from the countless fêtes and parties that she delighted in arranging for her friends and family.

Her artistic plans were put on hold in November 1817 when she was appointed companion to her mother on a journey to Bath. The Queen had at last consented to try the waters there. The physicians' dire warnings about the consequences of her remaining without remedy had at last overcome her aversion to leaving the King at Windsor. With the experienced and faintly ominous remark, after a visit to Claremont, that Charlotte was very large indeed, although some way off full term, and with anxious imprecations to Princess Augusta, left in charge at Windsor, about the care of the King, the Queen departed.

At Bath, Princess Elizabeth and Queen Charlotte settled into a routine of going to the Pump Room in the morning and dining early with their ladies at the capacious house in New Sydney Place which they had rented. But only days after they had arrived, on the morning of 6 November, before they left for the Pump Room, they received the unhappy news that Charlotte had gone into labour a month early the previous evening, and that her baby – a large and handsome boy – had been stillborn. The Princess's labour had been unexpected. She had come in from a walk and was laying aside her bonnet and cloak when the pains began. It was ago-nizing and protracted, they heard, and Sir Richard Croft, her accoucheur, and the midwives had done their best, but to no avail. When she was told the news, they learnt, Princess Charlotte had been stoic and, before set-tling to rest, had comforted her afflicted husband by speaking of many chil-dren to come.

Queen Charlotte in Bath, who had 'long been uneasy about Charlotte', did not at all like the account of her granddaughter's condition after the delivery, and all day worried and waited for a further express to bring more news. The Duke of Clarence, who had taken a house at the other end of the terrace, supported his mother before leaving to dress for a banquet that the City and Corporation of Bath were giving him at the Guildhall. The Queen and Elizabeth meanwhile – after some hesitation, and in all their diamonds – received the Lord Mayor and Deputation in advance of the dinner, as had been arranged. Worse news, the worst of news then arrived, and Princess Elizabeth wrote that night of the 'tremendous blow' they were dealt, when that second fateful express arrived while they were at dinner in New Sydney Place.

'General Taylor was asked out; our hearts misgave us. He sent out for Lady Ilchester, which gave us a moment for to be sure that something dreadful had happened.' The moment General Taylor came back into the dining room, Queen Charlotte said, 'I am sure it is over.' The express did indeed bring the news for which the Queen seemed to have been prepar-ing herself. Princess Charlotte, not yet twenty-two years old, a beaming bride a year before, a proud wife and mother-to-be days earlier, had died in the night from complications following the stillbirth of her premature son.

'Horror, sorrow and misery', wrote Elizabeth to Lady Harcourt, 'struck the heart, and no word could fall after such a dreadful shock.' And dole-fully she wrote to one of her brother's confidential attendants, 'In our lives have we never been so completely shocked.' At the Bath Guildhall, where the King's messenger had stopped to give the news to the dead Princess's uncle, the Duke of Clarence, the banquet was abandoned. In Bath, as throughout the country, as the news spread, the reaction was shock – and universal and genuine mourning. The lawyer Henry Brougham wrote, 'It really was as if every household throughout Great Britain had lost a favour-ite child.' The Prince Regent was prostrate with grief and 'deep affliction'.

At Windsor Princess Augusta, who had so recently written happily to Lady Harcourt, now told her, 'I even dared to expect the poor child could have lived, after all the sufferings, to the third day – You may suppose that

I am exactly in that situation of the man who stands till he falls. It is so sad a calamity that I am still quite stunned.' After Sir Brent Spencer had broken the news to her, it had been her 'very cruel' task to 'tell the fatal conclusion' to Sophy, and she dreaded the effect it would have on her. 'I sent for Battiscombe [the apothecary] to be with us and, thank God, the last accounts had been so bad that she expected a sad close as much as I did.' As she wrote, they were waiting for the Queen and Elizabeth, and then 'All our meetings and seeing Baillie will be over.' But, thinking of the funeral ahead, she added, 'till the necessary distressing scenes are past, we shall be constantly tracing open the wound afresh'.

The Queen, who returned with Elizabeth to Windsor on 7 November, continued to be the chief object of concern for Princess Augusta. She had dinner ready half an hour after the Queen arrived, having travelled ninety miles from Bath overnight. She had Dr Baillie tell 'the grievous tale' to her mother 'at least two hours before she went to bed', and tried in every way to 'lessen all the horror she had to meet with.' And she hoped that the Queen would adhere to Sir Henry's advice, to return to Bath to complete the cure – 'what little of the waters she had taken had acted like a charm upon her stomach' – after the funeral. But still, she admitted, not being able to go about their usual avocations, they all brooded too much upon their 'severe affliction'.

The details of the 'grievous tale' were enough to keep anyone awake, whether told at midday or late at night. Hours after the commotion surrounding the stillbirth, when the house was quiet, Charlotte had begun to moan and cry aloud in her room at Claremont. She called for Leopold, but he had ingested an opiate to help him sleep, and they did not at first wish to wake him. It took a while to shake him into consciousness, and by the time he arrived it was too late. His loving wife, despite her promise of more children only hours earlier, was a corpse, and guarding it were Mrs Louis, Charlotte's old nurse, and Croft, the wretched accoucheur, who had watched aghast as Princess Charlotte, before their eyes, suffered a fatal haemorrhage and died.

Augusta wrote again on the day of Charlotte's funeral, 'This most melancholy sad day … it is true that we see nothing of the last sad ceremony, but I shall be glad when it is all over.' They spoke to Prince Leopold, who talked to them of Charlotte's character as it had unfolded to him in the last happy year of her life: 'Her disposition expanding from prejudice into justice, and a self examination of the nervousness of her former ideas.' He said she had told him how 'long before she married … her mind had been impressed with a very unjust character of the Queen and her aunts. That she had been repeatedly told that she was brought to Windsor to be meddled and interfered with, and dictated to by them; that she found out, at last, it was false.' This comforted Augusta.

And the Queen, who had so short a time before chosen her granddaughter's bridal dress and trousseau and had now returned to Windsor to bury her, wrote of Charlotte, 'Claremont was indeed her earthly Paradise.' When the Queen returned from Bath, where she had gone in obedience to her doctors to complete her cure after Charlotte's funeral was over, she still looked 'ill in the face', and was nervous and easily overcome. The force of her grief for Charlotte shocked the Queen's dressers the Beckedorffs, mother and daughter.

Prince Leopold, whom the Queen and her daughters visited towards the end of November at Claremont, was also desolate, though calm. He had not yet returned to live in his former married quarters, he said, although he 'made it a rule to walk into these rooms every day'. The bonnet and cloak that 'she' had taken off before she was confined still lay where 'she' had placed them. He could not bear to move them yet, he said, and he meant to keep all – he gestured to the house and grounds where he and Charlotte had walked and planned their life to come – as 'she' had liked it.

Prince Leopold, as the widower rather than as the husband of the heir presumptive to the throne of England, all of a sudden faced a very different future, and his new income of £50,000 a year – the sum allotted him in the event of Charlotte's death – was as yet little consolation. Not so slowly, other reverberations of the heir presumptive's death were felt among Charlotte's uncles and aunts. The Prince Regent pursued with new vengeance his old project to divorce Charlotte's mother, now that 'much delicacy' had been set aside by his daughter's death. Caroline wrote from Italy, 'England, that grand country, has lost everything in losing my ever beloved daughter,' and doubted she would return there. Rumours redoubled that the Duchess of Cumberland was expecting a baby. And Charlotte's uncles Clarence and Kent began to look about them for wives, while the Duke of Cambridge, who had fallen in love with a young Hesse-Cassel princess at Hanover, pressed for his brother's consent to his marriage, and a Parliamentary grant to reflect that status.

Princess Sophia, who had loved Charlotte's spirit, was overcome with grief, and a 'melancholy meeting' with her sister Mary, who came to the Castle on her return from Brighton, only increased it. The Duchess of Gloucester herself, whose feelings were shallow by comparison with those of most of her family, was shocked to see the Duchess of York, who came on a visit from Oatlands and who had loved Charlotte, 'so altered'. Even so, the Duchess of Gloucester twined strands of Amelia's and Charlotte's hair together in 'two eternities' as a gift for her brother, the Regent, and told him that 'The two hearts open with a little hasp.' But in the midst of this mourning, when the Duke of Gloucester went to Norfolk in the New Year of 1818 to shoot, Mary found Princess Elizabeth in unaccountably high spirits, declaring that the waters at Bath had set her up: 'I am twenty years younger and walk and do as I usually do.'

Their mother was the reverse of well. The Queen's breathing had grown short and laboured, and the doctors were so nervous about her condition that Sir Henry warned the princesses that 'any sudden surprise, be it pain or pleasure, might cause sudden death'. A sudden surprise, and pain unmixed with pleasure, came barely a week later when Princess Elizabeth read a letter to her mother. Frederick, the Hereditary Prince of Hesse-Homburg – who had once offered for Augusta, and who had hung about Charlotte a year or so earlier – had offered for Elizabeth's hand in marriage. Elizabeth said it was a surprise to her. It was certainly a surprise, not only to the Queen but to all Elizabeth's sisters, Princess Mary wrote to the Prince Regent. And she enclosed, at Elizabeth's urging, the letter that had confounded their mother – but had, by good fortune, not caused her sudden death. She was too angry with her daughter for that.

The Duchess of Gloucester was calm itself. There was no reason for any consternation, she wrote. 'Eliza having never concealed her wish and desire to marry,' she argued, 'she is only acting up to what she has always said.' Naturally Elizabeth wanted the Prince Regent's approbation, Mary continued, but she was old enough, in her younger sister's opinion, to judge for herself. She would be a dreadful loss to the Queen, Mary feared. And yet, if the match did not take place, she warned her brother, 'she will make the Queen more unhappy in the long run than the act of leaving her'.

The Hereditary Prince of Hesse-Homburg's reasons for seeking Princess Elizabeth as his bride at this point were obscure. At the age of forty-eight, his bride could hardly be considered a strong candidate in the royal race to provide an heir to the British throne, or even for Homburg itself. But the Prince had seven brothers to do battle for the latter cause. Still, members of both their families – Royal, the Duke of Kent, the Duchess of York and her brother Prince William of Prussia, who had married the Hereditary Prince's sister Marianne – had acted in concert to advance the scheme, of which the bridegroom had written as early as February 1817. And it had advantages for both parties. Elizabeth would gain a property to administer, a husband, freedom from her mother. And her dowry would have a huge effect in the tiny domain of Hesse-Homburg. The state debts were growing, as the Hereditary Prince's father grew old, and the buildings and lands had been neglected for years. In short, a capable wife with means seemed the answer to the Prince – a professional soldier who 'shone' at fortifications – as he contemplated the duty that would soon be his to superintend his Hessian homeland.

And as for his choice of Elizabeth? A report from Frankfurt in 1818 names her as the only princess of England available as a wife for those wishing to ally themselves with that prosperous country. Two princesses – Royal and Mary – were married, ran the note; one – Sophia – was a permanent invalid, and one was privately married. The rumours, if not the truth, about Augusta and Sir Brent had spread wide.

To Sophia the Queen talked fully and, her daughter thought, very reasonably one evening on 'Eliza's subject'. She admitted that her daughter, at nearly fifty, was of an age to decide for herself. However, the Queen was 'vexed and flurried at the quickness with which she had taken her resolution'. Sophia attempted to soothe her mother and palliate her distress – although the Queen still cried bitterly at times – by reminding her repeatedly that 'she knew this was always Eliza's object'.

While the Regent declared that he entered deeply into the feelings of *all* parties – which he would endeavour to conciliate – the Hereditary Prince came to London, where, despite his preference for Elizabeth, he had to have his bride pointed out to him from among her sisters. He was 'much hurt at the Queen's manner'. The Queen tried to prevent him on various pretexts from seeing Elizabeth as she had earlier tried to prevent Mary and William of Gloucester having interviews before marriage. But the Hereditary Prince could arrange nothing until he saw his bride, he told the Duchess of Gloucester. He hated writing, and would far rather talk over his proposals in person with Princess Elizabeth. The sooner Elizabeth and the Queen were parted, the better for both their sakes, wrote Princess Mary on 3 February. All comfort was at an end between them, and Mary blamed Elizabeth's 'injudicious friends'. Her departure would be a sad blow to the Queen, she predicted – 'heaven grant she may not sink under it'. With Sophia a tactical invalid and Mary busy with duties at Bagshot, it was surely Augusta who would now 'sink under' the attendance on her mother.

Two days later Sir Henry Halford was called in to assess the Queen's health. He found that her 'suppressed anger made it difficult for him to judge correctly of her pulse or of her breathing', and he came out astonished at the 'perturbation and distress of feelings which she manifested'.

Even the Regent was powerless to assuage her mood. Elizabeth, meanwhile, was 'broken-hearted' after the series of 'severe speeches' that her mother made her. The Queen refused to believe that her daughter had as yet made her 'final irrevocable decision' and stuck to her refusal to bless the match, given that the King had never answered the earlier proposal from Hesse-Homburg for one of his daughters. It was not a match he would have liked, she said. By degrees, however, the Queen was brought round, and within a couple of weeks was counselling the Regent that Elizabeth's wedding should take place 'as soon as you can manage it should'. And the sooner the bridal couple left England after that, she instructed Sophia to tell her brother, the better it would be.

Elizabeth now began to receive notes of blessing and congratulations on her forthcoming marriage to 'Bluff' (her name for Frederick; like her brother-in-law the King of Württemberg, however, the Hereditary Prince was usually called Fritz), and to Miss Gomm, the former nursery governess, she wrote, 'I have great reason to bless God.' No man 'ever stood higher in the world', she wrote of her Fritz, and his manner and conduct towards her were perfect. Others thought that he stank to high heaven of stale tobacco from the meerschaum pipes he smoked addictively. On one occasion he made a bow at Court and the seat of his breeches ripped loudly. His ruddy face obscured by coarse whiskers and moustachioes gained few admirers. Princess Elizabeth did not know of a letter written by Leopold's mother to his sister Victoria, Princess of Leiningen, in which the match was called 'stupid'. And Napoleon, far away on St Helena, was contemptuous. 'The English royal family', he said in February 1818, 'va incanagliarsi [mean to lower themselves] with little petty princes, to whom I would not have given a brevet of sous lieutenant.' But she would have condemned Leopold – the likely source of his sister's comment – and Napoleon too, had she heard of their remarks. For Elizabeth and her reeking warrior prince were, quite by chance, to have a very happy marriage.

The Regent and Council approving the match, Elizabeth in virginal white married the Hereditary Prince in the drawing room of the Queen's House on 7 April. The maids of honour who had been at Royal's wedding were summoned, and all the Queen's 'family' was present, as were the great officers of state. With the promise that he would bring her back to England within a year, Fritz gathered up his bride and the many belongings she insisted on taking, and made for the Channel, after a honeymoon during which he would be so considerate as to smoke fewer pipes than usual. Among other possessions Elizabeth took with her to Bad Homburg were exercise books in which she had written down advice from Sir Joseph Banks on rose-growing and comments by Lord Harcourt on feeding orange trees. She took commonplace books and sketchbooks and artists' paraphernalia – and her dear old china. At the last, Elizabeth's resolve quivered. She and her sisters were aware that their mother was far from well. But she set her face for the Continent and looked forward to what lay across the Channel after the honeymoon she and the Prince were taking along the Sussex coast.

Bluff, for his part, sent an urgent letter to Bad Homburg to his chamberlain, ordering all the poultry to be removed from beneath the windows of his bride's proposed apartments and the stables near by to be cleaned. The family, used to their own company and able to put on a show for meals or entertain at Frankfurt when distinguished or royal visitors passed through, were not over-scrupulous in their living habits or in overseeing those of their servants.

In the following few weeks in London the Regent, astonishingly, gave his consent for three of his brothers – Clarence, Kent, and Cambridge – to marry. During the battle to secure royal married allowances for all these bridegrooms, Mr Thomas Creevey, the waggish Whig MP, commented that the royal dukes were 'the damndest millstone about the necks of any Government that can be imagined'. One of them had to get rid of what others might have considered a millstone round his own neck. The Duke of Kent, who had been living for over fifteen years first in North America and now at Brussels with Mme de St Laurent, simply handed her the newspaper to reveal to her his engagement to Victoria, Princess Leiningen, Prince Leopold's widowed sister.

While Elizabeth was still at Brighton on honeymoon, her mother's health worsened. On a journey in June 1818 from the Queen's House to Windsor, she had to stop at Kew when she developed breathing problems. Sir Henry Halford was summoned, and advised that it would be dangerous to move his royal patient.

'What my feelings must be at this time being away from my mother that I have always adored since I had sense of reason,' Elizabeth wrote, distraught, from Brighton. 'My trial has been severe and only proves how little happiness there is in this world for had I not had these tremendous blows, I might have been much too happy, as I assure you every hour increases my affection, esteem and admiration of my husband, who expresses himself so lucky that I only wish that I really was all he thinks me.' She and Bluff had had a very quiet time, were going to Worthing for a few days, and then embarked at Dover.

My spirits at times are not what they used to be, but I try to hide it from him, for though my family must be dearer than life to me, the kinder he is the more I ought to bear up. My dear sisters are angels, and I think Augusta particularly deserves every reward that this world can give by her uncommon firm steady friendship and affection for me, and exerting herself as she does for my mother dearest. They say her conduct is angelic – I have sacrificed my comfort in going away when I did, but that is of little consequence if I have done right, which I firmly believe I have, and that must make me content, but feeling that I might have shared with them the attendance on my mother, often occasions me a pang.

And with that, Elizabeth crossed to the German coast and made her way down the Rhine to her new life.

At Kew the Queen fretted that she was away from the King, but her doctor was adamant that she should remain where she was. And at least Princess Sophia, still not well, remained at Windsor. Princess Augusta, however, and the Duchess of Gloucester joined their mother at Kew, while the Duke, as Augusta told Lord Arran, tactfully went abroad. 'If he stayed at home,' Augusta explained, 'and Mary was at Kew the illustrious world would certainly say they had had a quarrel.'

Royal wrote from Ludwigsburg to Lady Harcourt:

Entre nous, when I first heard of the Duke of Gloucester's intending to make a tour without Mary, I was quite vexed, as all the English appeared to think there was some secret cause of his taking this step. Indeed, reports that reached me made me tremble for my dear Mary's happiness, and this worked me so much, that nothing but my thinking it wrong to offer advice unasked prevented my entreating Mary to reflect seriously on the consequences of so long a separation; as too frequently when married people have been parted for months, they take up tricks which are calculated to destroy their domestic happiness, and often that confidence which must reign between husband and wife is destroyed by their having accustomed themselves to confide in others.

Although the Duke had longed to marry his cousin Mary, as her husband he grew to delight in inflicting domestic privation on her. And his adoring sister, Princess Sophia Matilda, became for Mary a 'meddling, fussy' sister-in-law, who made the Duke's domestic tyranny still harder to bear. In one turbulent incident Mary was summoned by Sophia Matilda from a family crisis at Windsor to tend the Duke who was ill. The Duke then said he did not want her there, made his sister write to Windsor to say his wife was returning, and refused to send for Mary's dresser when she stayed. Mary wrote: 'to have one's feelings so little considered is to add an unnecessary distress; and want of concern since, nearly drove me wild last night'. Now Royal was quite happy to hear the Duke had been so kind as to let Mary attend the King, 'and assist poor dear Augusta, who I should fear would have been too wretched, had she been quite alone at Kew'. She herself was of course not able to come. 'My complaints are of a nature not to allow of my being two hours in a carriage,' she wrote ominously.

While the Queen was confined to her bedroom at Kew, her nurses Augusta and Mary were passing judgement on their new sisters-in-law, Kent, Cambridge and Clarence. Victoria, Duchess of Kent was the 'livelier', they considered, although not handsome. The Duchess of Cambridge – Princess Augusta of Hesse-Cassel – was 'proud'. And the young Duchess of Clarence – Princess Adelaide of Saxe-Meiningen – was, although pious, sadly without looks or fortune. But the Queen's daughters had little enough time to spare for their brothers and their new wives. For they lived in a permanent state of alarm about their mother's health.

Elizabeth wrote from Homburg in August 1818 to Lady Harcourt:

Alas, all my letters are daggers to my heart when I read of the state of my mother. That really kills me, for to know her so very suffering and not to be near her is almost death, though you will do me the justice to say that, of such an illness, I never dreamt. My agonies have been dreadful, but I can say with truth to you who will not show my letter, that my dread of losing her was always such that I did wish to settle, and my feelings regarding the sentiments I have ever held forth, and the opinion I have given regarding improper society, when once she was out of the way, has been fully justified by those asked to the last party at Carlton House where I hear many were offended at the Dss of A appearing there.

The princesses, in September, thinking their mother's end near, begged Lord Liverpool, the Prime Minister, to send the Archbishop of Canterbury to Kew. They hoped that that prelate might prevail on their mother to receive the Last Rites, which she was reluctant to have administered. Liverpool, in his turn, wrote of the Queen, 'For a person whose conduct through life has been so free from reproach she has a strange unaccountable fear of death.' The Queen was reluctant even to make a will and took a dislike to General Taylor when he raised the subject. She prayed ceaselessly, with her eyes and hands lifted up – alarming her assistant dresser, Miss Mary Rice. And she tried various remedies for her condition, including an invalid's chair to pull her upright. Her swollen legs were not the least of her problems. But the Queen herself feared mostly for her heart, which she was convinced must stop soon, so difficult was it for her to breathe.

From Württemberg and from Bad Homburg came the sighs of daughters not present. The Dowager Queen of Württemberg was conscious of the Regent's goodness to their mother. Elizabeth agreed with her sisters at Kew that 'it is almost unkind to wish that precious life prolonged'. Vanished was any hint of the tensions that had existed between and among the sisters and their mother. Augusta and Mary waited at Kew for the end, walked daily in the gardens of Kew and Richmond, and indeed made some 'improvements' there, planting coverts for their brothers' shooting. But their daily work lay inside the Dutch House that stood between the gardens at Kew and the River Thames. Here their brothers, the Prince and the Duke of York, and their father before them, had been educated, here their father had stayed during his illness in 1804, and here now their mother lay dying. Her sufferings on her chest made it uncomfortable for her to lie in bed, and so she sat day and night in a chair propped up with pillows and with a pillow on a table in front of her on which she often rested her head.

General Taylor informed the Regent in August that the Queen had still not made a will. And Princess Augusta, he added, believed that Frogmore would be hers under the terms of the Crown grant for that property, she being the senior unmarried daughter. Was this indeed explicit, Taylor asked, in the document that she had cited to him? Nearly a month later he returned to the subject, but the Queen herself at last solved the problem of her intestacy when she roused herself at the end of October to confront death. With her old directness she requested an assessment of her condition from the doctors, and Princess Augusta read out their latest bulletin. The Queen heard her daughter out in silence, 'but under visible emotion'. She asked if the opinion implied there was 'danger', and Augusta replied that the doctors had not applied that word to 'any other state than that of spasm, which certainly occasioned considerable uneasiness to them'. Hump-backed now and crooked with pain, the Queen spoke of her sufferings to Augusta, and of their distressing effect on her mind. She 'lamented most feelingly their effect upon her temper' to her daughter, and 'expressed her anxiety to control that effect'. She said 'her time was chiefly spent in prayer, and often so when she was thought to be asleep'.

The Queen then interrogated Millman and Halford about her illness. Halford said afterwards that she had 'not mistaken the opinion [they] conveyed'. And though she still spoke of 'soon going to Frogmore', the Queen secretly employed her dressers, the Beckedorffs, to send for General Taylor to settle her will. 'The Queen received me in her bedroom,' Taylor wrote in a later memorandum, 'and I observed a packet of papers lying upon the table which at once explained to me the object of her Majesty's summons.'

She told him to look through the draft of her will, and see if anything else needed doing 'to provide more especially for her unmarried daughters' and to consider more generally the others. He asked if he might break the seal. 'She answered, "Oh yes, Sir, do so", and she laid her head forward on the pillow seemingly much oppressed by her feelings, in which position her Majesty remained a considerable time.' He suggested assigning Lower Lodge to Sophia. 'Yes, sir, I think that would be very right. You will put it in so.'

On 11 November Taylor returned and read the Queen her will, and she approved it: 'Quite right.' But she ordered him to leave it for her to read over before she signed it. Five days later Mrs Beckedorff found her mistress 'in a state which alarmed her, seemingly struggling for breath, under violent perspiration and hardly capable of answering a question, apparently quite exhausted'. Halford and Millman went in and, coming back, told Taylor her life was in danger, there was no time to lose, if the act of signing the will was of importance. Taylor said he 'considered the completion as of the utmost importance to the Queen's character and to the credit of her name'. The physicians went up ahead to tell the Queen 'she was in immediate danger'. Taylor followed and 'found her sitting at the table, her head reclined, and Sir Henry Halford on his knees by the left side, holding her hand and feeling her pulse with a most anxious expression of countenance'. The Queen, looking up and seeing Taylor, 'gave me her hand with a most affectionate look and a painful smile'. Pressing his hand, she continued to hold it in hers, but soon 'reclined her head. The perspiration was running down her face, her eyes were moist. She breathed quick and appeared under great suffering.' He asked whether she would sign the will. She 'did not hear me (being very deaf on the right side),' he wrote, 'and asked Sir Henry Halford, what I said.' While Sir Francis Millman held her right hand to feel the pulse, Taylor 'got the will which was in a sealed packet which Mrs Beckedorff took out of a press'. While the Queen was signing it, and the doctors witnessing it, Halford – in Latin – urged Taylor to send for the Prince Regent. 'I then apprised the Princesses,' wrote Taylor, 'who had remained ignorant of the Queen's state, and Sir Henry Halford wrote to the Princess Sophia at Windsor.'

Princess Augusta could not afterwards forget 'the seeing her sinking so fast ... never complaining more to Mary and myself than that she was very ill – and in great pain – but she exerted herself so much when we were with her that it was often too much for her'. Sometimes she weakened. 'I wish to God I could see your brothers,' she told Augusta at one point, crying terribly, 'tell them I love them ... I wish I was near the dear King.'

On Friday the 13th – 'the last day we were with her to speak to her ... she sent for us rather late,' wrote Augusta. 'And after speaking most kindly to us both, but evidently under great oppression and pain, she said, "I am so miserably oppressed, so utterly, I don't know what to do".' Augusta 'moved her pillow for her on the table, and said, "Shall I call anybody?" [The Queen] said, "No, the doctors will come soon." Mary said, "Had we better not leave you to be quite quiet?" She looked up and smiled, and with tears in her eyes ... gave her hand to each of us, nodded her head, but could not speak. And I said to Mary, when we quitted the room, "Believe me, she will not be equal to see us again!" And I was but too correct in my judgement.'

On the morning of Wednesday, 18 November 1818, Queen Charlotte died, sitting up in her chair and holding her son the Regent's hand. 'We were, thank God, in the room when she expired,' wrote Princess Augusta of herself and Mary. With them also was the Duke of York. 'The countenance was so placid and her poor features which, for many months, we had never seen free from expression of pain, were quite become natural, and she looked so very free from all care, that the last impression was one I would not forget for worlds.'

Elizabeth, from Homburg, agreed with what Lord Sidmouth had said of the Queen, 'That the whole nation would for ever mourn the loss of a person who had ... performed every duty by it, as well as by her own family – and that morals, conduct and decency would be at an end.' Speaking of which, she added indignantly, she herself had recently had to see her cousin the Duchess of Cumberland, whom her mother had refused to receive. It was 'the bitterest pill I had ever swallowed', she wrote. It had been her duty, as she saw it, to submit to her husband, who had requested it, but she had told Bluff, 'Civil I would be, intimate never, and ... if her husband [the Duchess's husband, Elizabeth's brother Ernest] ever names my mother disrespectfully ... whether in my own room or one of the public dinners, I should say nothing but walk out of the room.'

16

Princesses at Large

~

PRINCESS AUGUSTA AND her sister Mary moved out of the Dutch House and into their brother Adolphus's house at Kew, Cambridge Cottage, so as not to be present for the laying out of their mother's corpse and its removal to Windsor. And they walked a last time in late November 1818 round the grounds of Kew that they had tramped daily since the summer – 'to take leave of everything we love here, at least forever in the style we have hitherto lived here'. They remembered, Augusta better than her younger sister, the gay young mother Queen Charlotte had been at Kew, superintending the education of her children, taking tea in her thatched cottage, enjoying the music of Bach and Cramer and Fischer in her drawing room at Kew House. Frogmore had darker associations, for it had been for the Queen a retreat from the world – a world of anxiety and dread – that she inhabited following the King's first illness.

'Very little oversets Augusta,' Mary wrote, but they were 'fumbling' into their old ways. With awe they observed the preparations being made to inter in the royal vault the woman whose will and authority had so dominated and crushed theirs. The blind, deluded King, once Queen Charlotte's loving husband, knew nothing of his wife's death or funeral when she was laid beside the coffins of her granddaughter Princess Charlotte and of that Princess's stillborn son, whose deaths a year earlier had instigated the race for the succession.

Sophia inherited Lower Lodge, where she had spent so much time as a child, under the terms of her mother's will so painfully made only days before her death. But it seemed clear that, in her invalid state, Sophia should remain instead in the Castle at Windsor, where she was well cared for by the doctors and, above all, by Sir Henry – who attended her father. She was very conscious of his presence in the apartments that lay across the quadrangle and through Engine Court.

While her mother was at Kew, Sophia had received a daily report on her father's health from the physicians, 'to be transmitted to the Queen in her absence from Windsor – This was by her own special order – Now alas!

The mouth that gave the order is shut for ever!' Sophia wrote that it would give her great pain to be 'without the daily comfort' of an authentic report of her father's state. The trembling invalid's request was duly granted, and a copy of the report continued to be furnished to her every day.

In the following months, the effect of Queen Charlotte's death on Augusta and Sophia at the Castle went deep. At Windsor was everything to remind them of the Queen, and when on 4 January 1819 they bid good-bye to Lady Harcourt, who had sustained them these six months at Kew, Augusta was again overcome. 'My heart was so full,' she wrote, 'when I saw you there this morning, not only with the thoughts of parting with your kind self but with the thoughts of going to the Cathedral, that I hardly knew what I was about. The only chance I had of behaving tolerably was not speaking at all, and I fear that my silence might appear lacking in grat-itude or want of affection, both of which I deeply feel for you and more particularly so since the sorrows have been so equally shared between us which we have gone through the last seven months ...' Augusta and Mary had made a pact to go that morning to St George's Chapel, in whose vault the remains of their sister Amelia and their mother now lay. She wrote, 'Our visit to the cathedral was very affecting indeed, particularly as ... it is eight years and two months since I put my foot into it.' She and Mary passed to the right of 'the two great chairs where my excellent parents always sat, and which will never be filled by either of them. I am glad I have been there ... now we will go there every Sunday. It is right and what I am sure the dear King would approve and that is all I wish.' And so Augusta condemned herself to more suffering, in the cause her mother had taught her, of doing 'what the dear King would approve'.

She wrote in February: 'With all the letters I have to write abroad I have not a minute to myself. I have all Eliza's business to do besides my own – and to write, or at least try to write, very clearly to her upon various sub-jects. Beckedorff is here, and every day she has something to say or to show to consult me about. And I must account to the trustees for everything that is done for Eliza ... My time does not hang heavy on my hands, for they are always full from morning to night, but the subject is always painful. I get my walks daily, and go some days to Frogmore.' But she did not go often into her mother's room there 'whilst all her effects are still laying about ... It is so very melancholy that I avoid seeing them as much as pos-sible. I fear it will take full another week before it is all cleared away, and then I trust I can go with pleasure.'

The Queen had left her house but not its contents to Augusta. Almost all her possessions, including her library, were to be sold, with the proceeds going to her daughters. Before her books went on sale, however, at Mr Christie's auction rooms in London, the princesses chose to keep some of those in which their mother had written or which she had annotated. Some others the Regent retained for the royal library, with the portfolios of drawings and etchings that Royal and Augusta and Elizabeth had done under the eye of their drawing masters fifty years earlier. Kept back also were the great illustrated albums the Queen and princesses had filled in their hours at Frogmore – the 'Extracts of the History of England' that Princess Mary had copied from Hume and that her mother had illustrated, the badges of the 'Dukes of York' with their armorial bearings which Princess Elizabeth had painted so beautifully.

Bacon's bust of the King the princesses donated to the royal library, after having casts made for themselves. They gave to the Prince Regent the red and white tents that Tippoo Sultan had once owned and that the Queen had used for garden fêtes. The Beckedorffs, mother and daughter, cleared from the Queen's presses and bureaux her dresses, 'made and unmade', and all her lace and trinkets, their reward for long service. As for the Queen's magnificent jewels, those that had been hers were for her four younger daughters to keep or sell. Difficulties arose when the Regent declared that the Queen's jewels were really Crown jewels, and not hers to dispose of. But her daughters were adamant that they were not, that they had been bought by George III for his wife at their marriage, on the births of their children and after his periods of illness.

And now the executors obeyed one of the Queen's last instructions: 'Of the papers all that were material have been destroyed,' they announced, 'including, with their Royal Highnesses' permission, the letters from the Princesses.' Only those from Elizabeth were not burnt, and were 'reserved for her pleasure' when she should next visit England. It was a pyre of paper in which the most inflammable topics touched on included the King's illnesses, Princess Sophia's own illness and its outcome at Weymouth in 1800, and Princess Amelia's passion for General Fitzroy.

By the terms of her mother's will – and by the terms of the original grant – although Princess Augusta had inherited Frogmore, she did not move in immediately. As General Sir Brent Spencer lived close to Frogmore, the situation would seem to have been ideal, but while her father lived she refused to abandon her apartment in the Castle, for all that she never saw him. And Sophia, who equally refused to move, could not be left alone at Windsor. So, much though Augusta might have wished to take up residence at Frogmore – which had always provided balm for her spirits – and although she and Sophia were among the least compatible of the sisters, the elder Princess remained in residence at the Castle. She had anyway to refurnish Frogmore after the depredations of the auctioneers.

'The Executors must take it upon themselves to act as they think best,' Augusta wrote, as the Queen's possessions were parcelled up for sale. 'We cannot do better than to leave everything to them. I have made up my service of plate,' she announced, and she kept back looking glasses, chandeliers and linen besides. She agreed that the further reduction on the King's establishment being meditated in Parliament – the grant for his establishment including that of his daughters at Windsor, following the Queen's death, was to be cut to £50,000 – was 'a poor way of proving the love and respect of so great a nation for a King who has protected them and defended them and saved them by his religion, his integrity, his firmness and his morality – but all these qualities are registered "where neither mirth nor wit doth corrupt" – I own this subject makes me low.'

Royal, in Stuttgart, was 'most deeply affected by the sad debates in Parliament' concerning the Windsor establishment. 'It makes me shudder to see all ready to give up the rights of my beloved father ... It is not only the King's dignity, but the honour of the country which suffers from his being deprived of the small remnant he had hitherto kept of Royalty.' When she thought of all these dreadful changes at Windsor, Royal remembered the day in the Great Room at Kew during her father's first illness, when he had said he was better off than King Lear in his madness, for he had no Regan or Goneril, but three Cordelias to look after him: 'Poor dear angel, how good of him to say this, which is frequently a comfort to me when I am much out of spirits.'

While Augusta and Sophia led a twilit existence at Windsor, mourning their mother and honouring their father, that November the Duke of York visited their father, who looked now very like King Lear. 'He was amusing himself with playing upon the harpsichord,' recorded York, 'and singing with as strong and firm a voice as ever I heard him ... but we must not conceal from ourselves that His Majesty is greatly emaciated within the last twelve months ... the frame is so much weaker that we can no longer look forward ... to his being preserved to us for any length of time.'

In Württemberg her sisters' situation continued to grieve Royal, and she was sorry they had remained at the Castle. 'Nothing should have induced me to continue in a situation which appears to me lowering their dignity, and in which they are exposed to many disagreeables. Never could I have borne the thought of applying to others to invite the company I wished to have; or not have it in my power to give direction about what I thought necessary to be done in the house.' And 'not from pride but from propriety', she insisted, 'I would never have submitted to accept as a favour the dining at the table of the Custos [or Governor of the Castle], when I had a sufficient income to keep my own.' She would have dined in her own apartment with her ladies, and now and then have invited some of the gentlemen to join her party.

Royal continued to brood on the disgrace done her father and sisters. She remembered Pitt defending the King's dignity in both his first and his third illness, and lamented to Lady Harcourt Pitt's and Fox's passing: 'They certainly had, as you rightly say, another manner of seeing and feeling from their great connections, which accustoms people from their youth to have a noble way of thinking.' But Royal was low in spirits. The unexpected death of Catherine, Queen of Württemberg, had been another blow. She wanted her sister Elizabeth to come to her, so that they could combine in grief for their mother, but it proved difficult. Elizabeth appeared 'too much taken up' to be able to fix 'that happy moment' when they would meet. 'I cannot press her as I feel what a melancholy companion I am.'

The entrance into the world of new sprigs of royalty brought a sentimental reaction from the Dowager Queen of Württemberg. Very much the older sister, she rejoiced with the Duke of Cambridge on the birth of his son, Prince George, in March 1819 in Hanover. 'Only think of me remembering your birth as if it was yesterday,' she wrote to him. Enquiring if the Duchess suckled the child, she approved there being an Englishwoman at the head of the nursery. 'By that means the baby will learn at once English and German.' There were soon more royal pregnancies to interest her. Sadly the Duchess of Clarence gave birth to a stillborn child in April 1819, but endured with strength of mind and goodness the christening of the Cambridge Prince in Hanover. Princess Augusta tried to cheer her brother Clarence with news that the May weather at Windsor was delightful, and she rode and walked and went out in the open carriage. 'The thorns – trees in blossom – and the verdure is quite wonderful.' But Clarence's ill luck in childbearing with Adelaide gave Kent – next in line to his brother – every ground for hope for the future of his own coming child.

Kent was soliciting funds for his return to England with his pregnant Duchess, on the ground that a birth of such possible importance should not occur out of the country. But the Duke of Clarence stood nearer the throne, his sister Augusta replied, refusing the request on the Regent's behalf, and that Duke's return for the birth of his child had not been thought necessary. She reminded him also that the princesses were anxious to do justice to the Prince's feelings – 'which are most delicate upon the occasion'. The implication was that the death of Princess Charlotte in childbirth was still much in the Regent's mind. But he was also forging ahead with his plans to divorce Caroline, and had prevailed on his Cabinet to appoint a team of lawyers and other agents to go out to Italy and sift such evidence against her as they might find there.

Kent and his pregnant Duchess set out anyway, though his brother Sussex warned that his rooms at Kensington Palace were not yet ready. These rooms where the Kents were to take up residence had belonged to the Princess of Wales. 'So fearful have they been that she should return', Augustus added, 'that they have been rendered totally unusable by all the features having been removed.' At Frankfurt Princess Elizabeth saw the Duchess of Kent en route – by cheap and easy stages – to the unsatisfactory apartments at Kensington. 'She is very big [with child] and, not being tall, shows it much,' wrote Elizabeth.

When the Duchess of Kent gave birth at Kensington to a daughter, Princess Victoria, on 24 May 1819, the Duke was ecstatic. In August he instructed the gardener at Kew to produce three bunches of flowers on the Duchess's birthday by 6.00 a.m. – 'a very large posy for myself to give her, and 2 smaller ones'. One was for his stepdaughter Feodora to give her mother. The other was 'to be put into the hands of our little baby, which, of course, must be so composed as to have nothing to prick her hands'.

It was not paternity alone that caused the Duke to be so tender. If the Duchess of Clarence continued to miscarry, Princess Victoria, by dint of Kent's own position in the royal family, must one day be queen of England – unless, should the Regent remarry, a younger sibling supplanted her. Prince George of Cambridge, though born earlier, and though male, ranked after Victoria in the succession, being the child of Kent's younger brother Adolphus – as indeed did Prince George of Cumberland, the child whom Frederica, Duchess of Cumberland produced in Berlin days after her sister-in-law in England produced 'Vicky'.

Mme d'Arblay (née Fanny Burney) visited Princess Augusta in the summer of 1819 at Frogmore during one of the Princess's first tentative occupations of the estate. She found there the 'Queen presumptive', as she named the baby Princess Victoria, with her proud father the Duke of Kent. Burney's propensity for sentiment where royal females were concerned remained boundless. She proposed to Princess Augusta, now enjoying her 'maternal bequest' at Frogmore, that one day an urn recording 'she who made it' would look well in the grounds.

Augusta, with Mary, lived quietly, but kept up the connections with their expanding family, dining at Oatlands with the Duchess of York, whom they found 'in high spirits', and joining the Kents at Kensington on the Duchess's birthday – after she had earlier received her abundance of posies at Kew. The sober doings of the turtledove Kents entertained the Duke's brothers and sisters time and again. At Windsor in September the Duke and Duchess and entourage, including baby, all retired together at nine o'clock for the night 'and actually went to bed, to the very great amusement of the whole society of Windsor', Mary reported.

Princess Sophia began to show signs of improving in health, and of improving in affection towards her sisters. Augusta invited Lady Harcourt to join her and Sophy at Frogmore in July 1819: 'It is cool there and you shall have tea, cold meat or white soup at your command. I can from my heart say I would kill any fatted calf, if I had one, upon the joyful occasion.' Sophy would meet her, and Augusta would see her after her sister went to dinner. It was so hot, the new mistress of the estate said, that she had for once not ridden, but had sat enjoying the shade under her trees.

Mary took Sophia to see the Regent's 'Cottage' or Royal Lodge in the Great Park, which her sister had never seen. 'It was a great exertion to Sophy walking about the house and garden, and certainly fatigued her, but the ice being broke,' the energetic elder sister reported, 'I hope it is the beginning of getting on and of more improvements in strength.' Indeed, the invalid Princess showed some signs of interest when the Regent sent three bracelets as presents to his sisters. Augusta chose the one 'in squares', Sophia reported. As to the others 'the debate was a long one between Mary and me', her invalid sister wrote. Mary decided at last on the 'turquoise, ruby and gold', leaving the one with 'ruby and brilliants' for Sophia. What clinched it was that Mary objected to 'any bracelet on the upper part of the arm', while her younger sister said mysteriously that she was 'compelled from necessity to wear such an ornament'.

But Mary was nowhere nearer breaking the ice between her brother the Regent and her husband. A request to her brother for the Duke to be allowed to shoot occasionally in the Great Park brought a resounding refusal from General Taylor. 'I felt awkward in making the request,' Mary acknowledged to her brother, 'but sometimes one can not help being under the necessity of doing what in one's heart one had rather not.'

She was still torn between her husband and her brother, with her brother generally the easy winner. She wrote a long letter to the Regent outlining in distress the various obstacles which she believed would make the Duke, when asked, reluctant to go to Brighton for Christmas. She ended quaintly, 'for man is man and does not like to be put out of his way – and still less by a wife than anybody else'. The Duchess was happiest with the Duke when they were visiting friends of his who were at best formerly acquaintances to her and could now form part of the expanding circle of society she craved. At Hatfield, she was breathless with excitement over a 'very uncomfortable business concerning Lord and Lady Westmeath'. Although the Marquess and Marchioness of Salisbury, her hosts, and their son Lord Cranborne were doing all they could to keep it out of a 'public court', Lady Westmeath, the Salisburys' daughter, was accusing her husband of adultery with five women, all of whom she wished to name.

Her sisters' company at Windsor was very tame for Mary after this taste of high life and country-house visits. The prospect of a visit from the Regent, however, was enough to keep her sitting on till five with them, at the Castle, 'hoping every time the door opened it might be you'. And to Brighton that Christmas she went without her husband – to be the hostess she had dreamt of being to her brother. The Conynghams, the Warwicks, Colonel Whately were all at dinner with her, as she had supposed would be the glorious case. But to her consternation the Regent was called away by inconsiderate ministers.

'I felt so dull and stupid', wrote Mary, 'when your carriage drove off that I thought I could not make myself agreeable.' His servants and household were 'all attention and kindness', she assured him, 'but still the master was missing.' She went shopping and met an old friend, Lady Elizabeth Berkeley – 'so altered I did not know her, and I suppose time has altered me likewise, as she did not me'. Mary was now aged forty-three. (Her dark hair, pink cheeks and blue eyes in Lawrence portraits of this time recall her earlier self, although her complexion has grown florid; her figure is still handsome, though stouter.) The two ladies then took a long walk to celebrate finding each other out. 'I have begged for the band,' Mary told her brother, 'as I feel I shall be a bad substitute in your absence to keep up the ball.' And she wished his ministers at the bottom of the sea for calling him away. 'Nobody can tell how dull Brighton is without you.' She bathed and walked with Lady Charlotte Belasyse, and dined, and hoped she would eat her Christmas dinner with her brother. Once Mary was back at Bagshot in the New Year, however, her Brighton days glowed in her memory. 'I follow you about from room to room like a tame dog fawning,' she wrote to the Regent. 'I see you at dinner offering the punch and brown bess all round the table. I see your calling for all the favoured music.'

But there were alarms in the New Year to discompose even the Duchess of Gloucester. Word came towards the end of January 1820 – the Kents' governess wrote to Sophia – that the Duke of Kent was seriously ill with a fever at Sidmouth, where he and the Duchess and the children had gone before Christmas in search of sea air. Prince Leopold meant to go down to his sister, if the Duke's condition worsened. And Mary wrote to her brother the Regent asking for a further bulletin. Edward had his faults, she wrote, but he had ever been a most affectionate brother to her. 'I own I feel his distance from us sadly.'

In the meantime, Dr Robert Willis had returned to Windsor after Christmas to find the King 'very much weaker and thinner'. At first he called it 'a very gradual decay with no appearance of immediate danger'. But days later he spoke of a 'great change in the King's whole appearance'. The Duke of York, heavy with grief, stood inside his father's apartment to witness 'the prodigious alteration in the poor King's face and countenance'.

Shocking news came on 24 January. The Duke of Kent, whom his brothers and sisters had considered so hale and hearty that he would out-live them all, had died at Sidmouth. He left his widow, her children and their baby daughter, Princess Victoria, virtually penniless. The weather was cold and damp at Windsor, where his sisters gathered to mourn their brother as best as they could. Mary wrote of 'many circumstances that go to my heart', and Sophia was 'much shocked' by her brother's death. But of all the royal siblings, dark, clever Edward had always been the least like-able – awkward, exacting and quick to give and take offence. Only Elizabeth had felt a bond with him, and Mary warned that care should be taken to break the news gently at Homburg. 'It is an event that will go very hard with her.' Sure enough, Elizabeth wrote, 'Upon the Continent he will be much regretted as he was very thoroughly esteemed by all those who lived with him.' She added, 'Poor fellow, he has been taken off in a moment when he was enjoying much domestic comfort, and that broke up is a very sad, sad thing.' All Edward's disappointments had been forgotten, not only in his contentment with the Duchess of Kent, but in his pride at produc-ing the heir presumptive to the throne.

Above all else that made the month of January 1820 'gloomy and melan-choly' was the prospect, as Mary wrote, that this misfortune of Edward's death would soon be followed by another. The King had had a mammoth paroxysm at Christmas, when he neither slept nor stopped talking for fifty-eight hours. 'Thank God he does not suffer,' Mary said of him. 'Our beloved father,' wrote Augusta, 'I find from the physicians, is daily declin-ing and growing weaker. And what makes the thing of worse import, per-haps, I do not make out that he has any disease.' Two days later in those apartments on the north terrace at Windsor where he had idled away the years since Amelia died, abusing his keepers, plucking at the bedclothes and ordering worlds of 'ideal' inhabitants conjured up from the past, King

George III himself died, just after half-past eight in the evening of 29 January – the eve of the anniversary of the execution of Charles I, whose martyrdom he revered. He had borne his own sufferings with grace.

Augusta wrote a letter to Lady Harcourt at a dark hour. The Prince Regent, now, at the age of fifty-seven, King George IV, had sent Frederick to Sophy. 'He spent the evening alone with us two,' and the Duke of Gloucester had sent Mary to them.

> This letter has been written over strange intervals … and I hope you can understand it but really my heart is so full and so much that is necessary but disagreeable I must attend to this morning I hope you will pardon my not looking over it again. I am very glad we shall be some days quite alone and Sophy wants quiet, and we are the best company for each other when we can meet. I am fully employed in writing all I can pick up to my two sisters – I dread their hearing of the fatal conclusion before they receive my letter of yesterday.

Augusta told of her 'poor stricken heart' and of the 'very very great sorrow' they had gone through in ten days. 'The blow is struck but now the first recovery opens our eyes to our affliction. I have cried a great deal today, and feel relieved by it,' she wrote on 4 February. Mary and Augusta and Sophia sat and worked in the evenings as they waited for the interment, first of their brother Edward and then of their father.

When the Duchess of Gloucester visited Windsor four days later she found that Princess Augusta and Princess Sophia were 'making great exertions to get their things all packed up to leave the Castle'. Mary herself thanked the new King for the gift of the furniture 'in the room I used to live in in the Castle', which would embellish Bagshot, and also for the gift of one of her father's carriages. Mary was always a materialist, and these acquisitions helped dull the pain of the two January deaths and the loss of Windsor.

Princess Augusta and Princess Sophia departed the Castle the day after their father's funeral, an event at which their brother Frederick was chief mourner in place of the King. While his father lay dying, George IV had fallen suddenly and gravely ill and, still weak, feared the night air. His feelings were as ever overset by death, this time to the point of contracting a pleurisy that had made some of his doctors think a third royal funeral might be in the offing. But it was not to be.

'The seeing this dear old place at this moment', Mary wrote from Windsor, 'is very melancholy.' She believed that Sophia's 'strength of mind' would help her to survive the move. It was a 'great object to get her to town' and into the care of Sir Henry Halford. She was to occupy apartments first in her brother Adolphus's home, Cambridge House in Mayfair, and then at Kensington Palace.

Augusta, on the other hand, was bound for Frogmore, where she meant to live most of the time, keeping apartments at the Queen's House for forays to town. She had sent for Lady Harcourt, who had been with them after the Queen's death, to join her there. And although she 'began to flag sadly' while making her final arrangements in early February at Windsor, within the month she was beginning to have things as she wanted, even promising her brother, General (newly Sir) Herbert Taylor, Sir Benjamin Bloomfield and others of the new King's inner circle a 'famous good dinner' at her new home.

From now on the princesses and, indeed, their brothers would be welcome only as the King's guests at Windsor. And although he was too preoccupied with putting together further damning evidence against his wife to feel any urge as yet to take possession of the Castle, Augusta and Sophia had a home, as well as a parent, to mourn.

With George III's death came an outpouring of reverent prose in the public press and a flood of images for sale extolling his virtues in life – balm to his daughters' eyes and ears when they had so minded his treatment the year before. The sentiments they expressed in the days after George III's death – 'clouded as his precious life has been for many years, it has pleased the Almighty to spare him many a pang which would have severely tried him' – were to be repeated and printed in newspapers and sermons and broadsheets. This image of a pious, benevolent father of the people might have come as a surprise to earlier subjects of George III, whose caricaturists and pamphleteers had not been so kind. But now, with the prospect of George IV as monarch, there was no stopping the pious flow.

'May you when your hour comes be as much loved, respected and regretted as he must be,' Elizabeth intoned, writing to her brother, the new King, on 6 February after hearing the news. That seemed unlikely, however, although Mary had recently told her brother that she could 'only lament you are not known all over the world as you are in your own house and at Brighton, for you are not done justice to by anybody'. For some, like his sister, George IV's charm was undimmed from when he was a boy, and he enlivened and brightened every occasion at which he was present, for all his auburn wig and florid, womanish face, his great girth and gouty legs. But this was not the case with most. In particular, his estranged wife Caroline endorsed Leigh Hunt's 1812 judgement that her husband was 'a violator of his word, a libertine over head and ears in debt and disgrace, a despiser of domestic ties'. When she heard that he had, almost as the first act of his reign, ordered that her name be omitted from the prayers for the royal family in church, the new Queen of England made plans immediately to return to England.

The oddities of the situation that the regency of ten years had created at Windsor were identified by Sophia when she wrote of her father's death to the new King: 'While I am mourning the loss of one who must and ever will live in my recollection, I am addressing one who has acted as such [that is, as fatherly protector and ruler] for some years.'

Princess Elizabeth had a hard time adjusting to the idea that her father was dead and that her brother was king in his stead. She even found it difficult to address her brother by his new title: 'I am a strange mortal and cannot help being easy with what I love. Therefore he must forgive me if I am not proper enough.' Then she heard in Homburg of the new King's dreadful pleurisy. According to Princess Mary, when a second express arrived, announcing his recovery, Elizabeth 'completely lost her head and for some time would not attend to reason'. So her English maid, Sarah Brawn, wrote home to the housekeeper at Kew, and she said she never saw her poor mistress 'in such a state of nerves in her life'. Perhaps Elizabeth had not forgotten that dark day in Bath when they learnt of Princess Charlotte's stillbirth – and then came that fateful second express, bearing the news of the young mother's own death.

Elizabeth refused – 'at great personal sacrifice to her own private feeling' – her brother's invitation to come over in the spring of 1820 for his Coronation, an invitation which her brothers Ernest in Berlin and Adolphus in Hanover had already accepted. Bluff, her husband, had only just become sovereign in his father's place, she explained, and not only did they have to look after his widowed mother, but they had found everything 'at 6's and 7's', with terrible debts to pay. Elizabeth would not wish to appear, should she make the journey, 'otherwise than as your sister ought to appear', but she could not think of making the necessary outlay at this time of hardship in Homburg. 'I make my excuse with running-over eyes,' she concluded, 'but my duty and affection for Bluff make me feel I am acting right.'

Royal, far away in Ludwigsburg, also refused her brother's invitation to attend the Coronation he was planning in London. Gratified as she was, she wrote, the health to which she was a martyr, and her 'grandchildren' – Prince Paul's daughters, whose care was her delight, as well as King Wilhelm's children on whom she doted – were twin duties forbidding her to take her place in Westminster Abbey. She only regretted that the peeresses were to walk at the Coronation – 'much as I shall ever rejoice at every-thing that can encourage trade'. She feared this would bring forward 'fresh fuel for those who are resolved to begin many unpleasant discussions con-cerning an illustrious lady [Queen Caroline], who I understand will force herself on the public, and is determined to run any risk for the sake of mis-chief'.

But it seemed that, while Royal and Elizabeth would not see their brother crowned, his sister Sophia might be well enough to be present. Her move to London had given her a new lease of life, and she wrote to her brother, 'I am very well satisfied with my abode ...' She added, 'the hopes of being able to see so much more of you and to be near at hand' to Carlton House had been a prime reason, an 'essential inducement', for fixing upon Cambridge House as a permanent home.

Emerging at last from long years immured in twilit sickrooms, Sophia wrote of 'trying to look at all around one in a favourable light'. She was, she reckoned – and in this she mistook the matter sorely – 'not very diffi-cult to please'. And she said she wished only for a 'quiet snug home' – which was what she now had. With an energy that was new to her, she walked in the gardens of the empty Queen's House, drove out to Hyde Park and Regent's Park with her sister Mary, and had one or two ladies in for the evening. She sat in a red dress to the painter Thomas Lawrence. She even mimicked her mother talking to one of Amelia's doctors: 'Really, had I shut my eyes,' Mary said of their dead mother, 'I should have thought she was in the room.' And finally one morning in April Sophia excelled her-self. 'Judge of my joy,' wrote Mary, 'when the door opened, and who should walk into the room but dear Sophy. The first visit she had made – and she actually came up to the top of the house, and really did not appear the worse for it, went all over it, and sat with me nearly an hour.' Mary told their brother, 'All nervous people must be a little humoured in regard to their health.' She did not, therefore, like to let Sophia know how well she thought her. But, she concluded, 'being her own mistress ... has been of great use to her general health'. She showed insight into Sophia's tur-bulent mind that dictated her varying poses from invalid to intrepid horse-woman when she concluded that it was 'by doing it her own way' that her sister would flourish.

And then reports came of an impediment to a peaceful Coronation. Queen Caroline, the wife whom the King refused adamantly to have crowned or to allow to be present at his own ceremony – was about to set out for England. Mary was quick in her outrage at the prospect of what she called 'the Illustrious Traveller' coming to England. She had heard that before the Liturgy was changed someone had said it ought to read 'Praise our gracious Queen Caroline.' 'Good Lord defend us ...' she exclaimed.

The rest of the year was dedicated to 'the Queen's affair'. It had been a rare year since 1795, when George and Caroline's misconceived marriage took place, that the Treasury and ministers – not to mention the royal family – were not dealing with fresh and unreasonable demands from one or the other. Not for nothing did one of the myriad cartoons published in this momentous year feature Queen Caroline as a kettle calling George IV – a coalscuttle – black. It had been a relationship which had caused untold damage to their daughter Charlotte before her marriage. But in this year of 1820 the couple's private and public disagreements lit the fuse of seething political discontent in the country. Now the rancorous arguments of King and Queen fed the nation, as the Radicals took up the Queen's cause. All the Parliamentary time that might have been devoted to debating reform of rotten boroughs was given to searching out the details of this rotten marriage. In the process, 'Silly Billy', as the Duke of Gloucester was aptly named, did untold damage to his own marriage when he rose in Parliament to support his cousin Caroline and denounce his brother-in-law the King.

Before the breach the Duchess of Gloucester had heard with pleasure Lord Hutchinson, one of the many who had been drawn into the 'Queen's affair', speak 'affectionately' of the King 'to please my feelings'. 'Both your ears ought to have burnt,' she told him. But Hutchinson failed in his brief – to offer Caroline in France the enormous sum of £50,000 a year to stay away and renounce the title of queen. An ambitious alderman, Matthew Wood, got to Caroline first, and persuaded her to continue her journey to England.

A former lord mayor, Wood, with other City Radicals – merchants and bankers among them, who wished to end the monopoly of aristocratic political power – took up Caroline's cause with gusto from February when the *Republican* newspaper proclaimed her virtues as an 'injured princess'. Princess Augusta, horrified with all her family by Caroline's dependence on a 'Cit', heard later that Wood had laid a massive bet that the Queen would come to England. And he had made his trip to France, she declared, simply to ensure that she did cross the Channel so that he could obtain his winnings.

Mary told the King on 12 June, 'I am not surprised at the arrival as I never doubted she would come.' And in a gesture of support for their brother – who stayed at Windsor – Augusta came up from Frogmore and Mary from Bagshot, to be present in London on 19 August. On this day, the Bill of Pains and Penalties, a punitive measure to deprive Caroline of her rights as queen and to condemn her for adultery with her Italian 'low man', began its second reading in the House of Lords. Notwithstanding the Duchess of York's grave illness – she died later that day – her husband, the Duke of York, was there in the House, with his brothers Clarence and Sussex, to support the honour of their brother.

A small dumpy figure in a black wig and with heavily arched eyebrows and rouged cheeks, Caroline was unrecognizable even in private life to those who had known her earlier in England. But none of the princesses met their strange sister-in-law during her residence now in London. In a letter later in the year to her brother Ernest, Augusta made her views clear, writing of 'the wicked who have made this horrid woman their tool. Bad as she is I am sure' – and here she differed from Mary – 'she never would have come to England', Augusta believed, 'if it had not been for Wood'.

The evidence brought against the Queen in the House of Lords and given by a couple of naval captains and by nearly ninety Italian witnesses – boatmen, ostlers, grooms and maidservants of varying degrees of respectability – failed, overall, in its effect. And when Henry Brougham, Caroline's lawyer, browbeat the Lords in November into abandoning the bill – he prophesied revolution should they continue with it – George IV's 'language and manner were those of a Bedlamite', Charles Arbuthnot recorded. Fulminating against those who had brought the catastrophe about, the King blamed particularly his cousin Gloucester for supporting a woman whom he knew to be a virtual criminal.

Mary suffered greatly from the double strain of her husband's support for Caroline – a woman she had long detested – and her brother's anger against her husband. It was impossible for her to see the King or even correspond normally with him, as it would be rank disloyalty to her husband. But how she longed to! The Queen's affair drove a wedge not so much between King and Duke as between Duke and Duchess. For Mary concluded that the Duke's support for Caroline was born of his jealousy of the King, though it was probably just muddle-headed chivalry. When the trial was over, the Duke took up his gun and resumed his annual slaughter of game, but the damage was done between him and Mary. The King moreover did not forgive him or show him one mark of favour till 1827, when he made him governor of Portsmouth.

The other princesses raised the King's spirits with reports that the Queen's popularity was waning in the New Year. 'Loyal addresses are coming in every day,' Augusta wrote to Ernest, now a supporter of the King, in Hanover. Their brother Frederick, staunch Tory and also loyal to the King, had been given the Freedom of the City of Norwich and had been very well received there, though it was 'all but a Radical town'. She concluded, 'Things getting better by degrees are more sure to hold.' In Ludwigsburg, where Elizabeth was at last visiting her sister Royal – they met after more than twenty years – welcome news arrived that a thanksgiving service for Queen Caroline in St Paul's, following the abandonment of the bill, had been a paltry affair and ill attended. The Queen's conduct had disgusted everyone, Elizabeth wrote to Bluff in Homburg, and her pious hope was that, at the end, even the most blind would have their eyes opened.

At home in England, the King felt popular enough to warrant holding a drawing room at the Queen's House, with a ball to follow in the evening at Carlton House. Augusta, her brother's hostess, informed Ernest in Hanover that the attendance had been splendid. 'Every person of proper feelings made it a point to come up to London on purpose to be present at it.' By midnight the Princess was 'pretty well fagged', having already received Society for four and a half hours before dinner at six. Having optimistically ordered her carriage for three in the morning, she was delighted to accept the offer of her brother's a good hour and a half earlier. The drawing room and ball had been especially splendid, in the King's view, as his wife had failed to appear at either. Caroline was not yet a spent force, but her power had waned dramatically with the grab at £50,000 a year she had made when it was offered her for a second time (after her earlier refusal) as an inducement to leave the country. This behaviour contradicted all that she had supposedly stood for, and made her supporters look fools. The game was not yet over, however.

At the Coronation of George IV on 12 July – or rather, hours before – Caroline of Brunswick, Queen Consort of England, made her last attempt to breach her husband's defences and demanded entrance at first one door and then another of Westminster Abbey. Denied at each of them, to a chorus of cheers that turned to jeers from the crowd waiting for the ceremony, she at last turned away – with a cry as if mortally afraid. Hours later, the King – effulgent in gold brocade and velvet bloomers, feathers nodding from his cap – stepped along the royal blue carpet that led from Westminster Hall to the welcoming Abbey doors. When the crown was placed upon his head and the peers and peeresses rustled obeisance, his expression was one of deep satisfaction. It had been a long time coming.

When George had first dreamt of kingship – in 1788, when his father had seemed mortally ill – the Irish Parliament had offered him the unrestricted regency of Ireland. Now king of that country, he determined to pay his subjects there, who had been so generous in the past, a visit. As he departed, Queen Caroline, uncrowned and ill, lay at Brandenburg House, her home at Hammersmith. Before the King's yacht had reached Holyhead, news came: she was dead, of an obstruction on the liver. The King had been on board shockingly drunk, or, as the Tory scribe John Croker put it, 'gayer than it might be proper to tell'. But after he heard of the Queen's death the royal widower did not appear on deck and Croker heard that he was, if not 'afflicted', at least 'affected at the first accounts of this event'.

But Caroline's hour was not yet over. Honouring her wish to be buried at Brunswick, her executors negotiated with the government for her coffin to be carried to Harwich to be embarked for Stade. But tempers ran high, and, when the authorities tried to turn the procession aside from a route leading to the City, where the Queen's support had been greatest, two protesters were killed in the fray that developed in Hyde Park. Princess Mary condemned from Bagshot 'all the disgraceful and disgusting scenes that have taken place within this last week, first at Brandenburg House and then as the Procession went on'. She regretted, particularly, the part of Caroline's executors, her lawyers Stephen Lushington and Thomas Denman. 'How thankful I feel', she told her brother, 'that you was not in town, for whatever blame may be attached to any of those who made the arrangements you ... have had little or nothing to do with it.' Citing 'infamous, designing invidious people' and those in Brandenburg House and Radicals besides who had 'espoused her cause from the beginning', Mary ended, 'hand and head ought to join hand and heart to spurn them out of society'.

Augusta had been spared the 'disgraceful and disgusting scenes' of her sister-in-law's funeral procession, having set out at the end of July for Germany to visit both her sisters. The newly crowned George IV, too, felt the need to travel abroad, and, leaving the United Kingdom for the first time in his life, he spent a happy month in the restored Electorate, newly a kingdom, of Hanover, where he was fêted whenever his gout allowed him to appear.

It was all that he could have wished, as there was no Caroline to disturb his Coronation, no Radicals to taunt him, not even the threat of Napoleon – dead this year on St Helena – to alarm him. He wept when presented with an address from the University of Göttingen where his younger brothers long before had harassed their tutors. Perhaps what meant most to the King, however, was his visit to the battlefield of Waterloo en route to Hanover. None other than the Duke of Wellington was his guide as he visited the different battle positions adopted on that fateful day. It poured with rain but George persevered – to inspect the spot where his friend Lord Anglesey's leg lay buried. Given time, he was to declare that he had been present at Waterloo not just on this visit, but on the day of the battle itself, six years earlier in June 1815. And with the dawning of another era, when memories dimmed of what had occurred and what had not in a previous age, he came to believe his own story.

BOOK FIVE
PIANO PIANO
1822–1857

17

Royal – Queenly Dowager

~

Following the débâcle of the 'Queen Caroline affair' in 1820, there was a welcome diversion for the Dowager Queen of Württemberg in Ludwigsburg. Elizabeth at last came from Homburg to stay with her sister for several weeks over Christmas 1820 and New Year 1821, while Fritz – newly Landgrave Friedrich VI of Hesse-Homburg – attended the Austrian Emperor to Munich. The sisters had not seen each other since the elder left England in 1797, when Royal the bride had been aged thirty and Elizabeth twenty-seven. Now fifty years old, the new Landgravine was shocked by her sister's size, which made her appear older than her age, and by her immobility. The Dowager Queen did not walk, but was carried in an armchair everywhere in the palace by attendants.

Once she had recovered from her surprise at her sister's condition, Elizabeth wrote daily to her husband of the state and opulence by which she was surrounded. 'Even you, dear angel, who is the grand mogul in your presents,' Elizabeth told Bluff on Christmas Eve 1820, after partaking in her sister's Christmas Eve rituals, 'would have been enchanted to see the magnificence.' The Dowager Queen had arranged 'thirteen tables filled with all sorts of things, silverware, jewellery, clothes, toys, bonbons …' Charlotte and Pauline, her stepson Prince Paul's daughters, for whom the majority of the gifts were destined, were overcome.

The Dowager Queen had been delighted earlier this year when her good-for-nothing stepson in Paris had given her custody of these princesses, his daughters. She had been determined to make this, their first Christmas together, special. But Baroness Veronica de Stein, Elizabeth's lady, was also 'aux anges' when she received from the Queen Dowager, among other treasures, an amethyst cross and a silk dress. Elizabeth herself was given her sister's portrait and was pleased to see that Royal got a handsome porcelain vase – doubtless from the Ludwigsburg factory – from her 'son' the King.

The contrast between the sisters' living standards could not have been more marked. On his father's death in January that year, Fritz had found the small state or landgraviate of Hesse-Homburg still deeper in debt to the bankers of Frankfurt and further afield than he had suspected. And he and Elizabeth had only her English income with which to service the debts that his father had incurred over many years. Stoically the new Landgravine declared herself very glad to be going home, and in general very glad not to be a rich widowed queen with a doting family and a busy life. She was stifled by the heat of the apartments at Ludwigsburg, she said, and exhausted by the number of steps leading from one apartment to another.

While the Dowager Queen still had her sister Elizabeth at Ludwigsburg, good news came from England. Following several miscarriages, Adelaide, William, Duke of Clarence's ugly but agreeable wife, had given birth to a daughter in early December. 'She was born nearly without assistance,' Elizabeth heard, and sent further details to her husband on 28 December 1820 of this interesting royal baby. The accoucheur had been in the country, and the wet-nurse had not yet been brought to bed, the baby being two months premature. 'Good old Halford ran for Sir William Knighton. A lady en couche [in labour] gave up her accoucheur, and they found a wet-nurse in three hours.' The reason for the early delivery, Elizabeth believed, was that six days before she gave birth, Adelaide 'went to church with Eliza Fitzclarence when she was marrying [the Earl of Erroll], and after that she was never well.'

Princess Sophia, in England, paid a visit of three hours to St James's Palace to see her new niece, and told her sisters in Germany that she had come away enchanted. 'She will be a worthy Queen if she does not have a brother,' wrote Elizabeth to her husband from Ludwigsburg. Born at seven months, the child, although small, thrived 'beyond anything that was ever known', and was given the name of Elizabeth, to the pleasure of her Homburg aunt. It was 'a name very dear to the English and in these cruel times I think they have done very well to choose what will please,' the Landgravine told her husband.

The princesses took malicious pleasure in the knowledge that the Clarences had produced an heir who would now knock eighteen-month-old Princess Victoria of Kent – who had been, from birth, heir presumptive – on to a lower rung in the succession to the throne. The princesses mistrusted their Coburg sister-in-law, the Duchess of Kent, and her brother Prince Leopold – still living on his £50,000 a year at Claremont. They wondered, however, that the Clarences, 'as they both are so fond of the country', did not spend more time at Bushey Park, the Duke's house on the Thames, now made 'very neat all fresh papered and yet furnished into thorough comfortable plain gentleman's rooms', as Augusta wrote to her brother Ernest on 8 May 1821. The couple's apartments at St James's were 'so dreadfully small that none but such contented creatures as they are could endure it'. But Bushey was where William had earlier raised his Fitzclarence family with Mrs Jordan. Perhaps, even for an insensitive man like William, the ghost of his children's mother whom he had cast off – and who had died two years before in France – was still strong.

Sophia, meanwhile, had moved from her brother Adolphus's house in Mayfair into a new house in Connaught Place north of the Park, near Kensington Palace. And the Duchess of Kent and her household comptroller Sir John Conroy – the Duke's former attaché – visited her there regularly. The house was 'quite clean, he [the landlord] furnished it only three years ago', Augusta recorded on 17 December 1820, and Sophia would have only two rooms to paper or paint, 'on account of his having had some large pictures against the wall'. The situation was very good, she added. 'It faces the south and looks over all the best part of Hyde Park and is particularly dry and clear of smoke.' Augusta told her correspondent, their brother Ernest, a few months later in May 1821 that it was quite like being in the country, with all the advantages of London – the Park 'making a constant gay scene, particularly a string of carriages daily which full still continues notwithstanding the heat and dust'.

There were no more mentions of spasms in connection with Sophia. She paid visits to Kensington Palace in her carriage where her bibliophile brother Sussex occupied rooms stacked with 50,000 volumes. She rode with the Duchess of Kent and Princess Feodora of Leiningen, the Duchess's daughter by her earlier marriage, in Mr Fozard's riding establishment behind the Queen's House. The Duchess of Kent had papered and furnished her apartments, formerly Queen Caroline's, at Kensington in rich, warm tones according to German taste. Princess Victoria's cradle was preserved as an object of sentimental regard, her cot was in the room next to her mother's, her father's portrait was prominent.

Nothing could have been more intimate – nor, some objected, more stifling. But Sophia was a regular visitor to Kensington, and at least part of the attraction there was the charismatic Sir John Conroy. The Duchess hung on the comptroller's every word, and included Lady Conroy and their several children – one of them a girl named Victoire of her daughter's age – in her affection. Sir John was assiduous, and Sophia soon matched her sister-in-law in her attachment to him and his family. Conroy's son Edward later wrote, 'We were one family.'

Sophia's sisters had another reason to dislike the Duchess of Kent. She was linked too closely for their liking not only to the Conroys, but also to her brother Prince Leopold, who had become distinctly unpopular with the princesses following Charlotte's death. A remark by Royal in Württemberg on 26 November 1824 shows the animus she felt towards him: 'Will you believe it that Prince Leopold is gone to Paris without having sent me the prints of my two elder brothers which Augusta had given him to have forwarded to me?' The Duchess of Kent often took her daughters down to Claremont to see Leopold, which hardly helped – and then made difficulties about the royal family visiting Victoria. But Sophia, the Duchess's Kensington neighbour, was allowed into the charmed circle.

Augusta was more objective about their brother Edward's child than was her sister Sophia. She wrote to their brother Ernest, who had settled with his family for reasons of economy in Berlin, on 8 May 1821, 'Our little Victoria is a handful and a very engaging child. She is tall and speaks very plain and is a capital mimic ... but her Mama is trying to break her of it ... she is too young to understand it is wrong.' But Augusta of all the princesses was the least involved with her nieces and nephew – except for the Fitzclarences, for whom she had a protective kindness. Her affections she reserved for her siblings, and they reciprocated.

When Augusta voyaged to the Continent to visit her sisters in July 1821 Elizabeth could not do enough for her at Homburg. She introduced her to her brother- and sister-in-law, Gustav and Louise, who had married the same year as she and Fritz, and who lived in the castle with a baby daughter. She drove her around the 'dear little town' of Homburg that surrounded the castle and that Elizabeth described in a letter to Mme d'Arblay as 'not larger than a village'. And they drove around the fertile plain below Homburg, and beyond to what Elizabeth called 'the finest mountains you can conceive, some covered with wood, others barren and chiefly rock, which makes the scenery picturesque'. Despite the state's debts, Elizabeth and Fritz were everywhere contemplating 'improvements'.

At Ludwigsburg, however, to which Augusta proceeded after two harmonious weeks with the Landgravine at Homburg, she had a great shock. Affection for her sister led the Dowager Queen of Württemberg to drive to a frontier post to greet Augusta. But the younger sister found that the elder had changed dramatically. 'She says', Mary wrote to Mrs Adams on 6 October 1821, 'she never should have known Royal again barring her eyes.' In her white cap and apron and with her huge girth, her jaw line and neck a solid slab, Royal was enormous, to the point that she found it more comfortable to do without any corsetry. Moreover, she was swollen in every part of her limbs and even in her face from dropsy, and lopsided from where her left breast had grown unaccountably large one year.

Royal, on the other hand, Mary told Mrs Adams, thought Augusta 'fatter and older, but she should have known her in any part of the world'. The sisters' days together were sour–sweet – Augusta still the determined British patriot, Royal after years of exposure to Continental warfare more fluid in her opinions. But they were united in lamenting the death of little Princess Elizabeth of Clarence at only four months. Until William and Adelaide produced another child, Princess Victoria of Kent would once more succeed her uncles George, York and Clarence on the throne. Should she and any issue fail, the throne would go to the Duke of Cumberland, a result many in England were loath to see occur.

Augusta returned to her apartments in the Queen's House in London, and to Frogmore, via the kingdom of Hanover where Adolphus, vice-regent since 1813, and his Augusta and their son George were living in domestic contentment. After this journey to the Continent, Augusta had sated to some degree the desire to travel abroad that she had long felt, and first expressed when – nearly twenty years before – she had envied her brother Augustus his sightseeing in Italy.

But Augusta was not to be allowed to rest yet. Her brother the King had made up his mind to pull down Carlton House and make the Queen's House – where Augusta had apartments – a showpiece for the monarchy. When it was proposed that it would be cheaper to build afresh, he said that youthful memories made the choice of his parents' home sacred to him. And swiftly installing a throne room, larger state rooms and modern fittings, as well as rooms for all the functions for which George III and Queen Charlotte had looked to St James's, this pious son rendered his parents' old home unrecognizable, and rechristened it Buckingham Palace.

The King also toyed with the idea of demolishing St James's Palace, but ended by leaving it. And here Augusta was shown by her brother's clerk of works a very desirable small house, Stable House, as a substitute for her apartments in the Queen's House. The King, in a very good mood, after a thunderous welcome in Edinburgh, promised that the house, an annexe to St James's Palace, across the courtyard from William and Adelaide's apaartments, could be made comfortable with a door leading from the garden into Green Park, so that his sister need not walk in the streets to visit her family. Augusta did not take the same pleasure in walking the streets that Mary and Sophia did.

But just when she was preparing to take the house, she was persuaded to set off again for Germany. The house at St James's would not be ready for some months. The King warmly seconded the proposal made by their brother Adolphus, who was in England, that Augusta join him and his family at Hanover for the winter. Meanwhile, in the waltz of siblings that grew a little more ponderous every year, Adolphus and Mary were off to Brighton for a few days, from where Mary would then proceed to stay with the Clarences at Bushey.

When Augusta returned to England early the following year, her brother Adolphus sent her from Hanover a clock as a housewarming present for her new home in Stable Yard, and she placed it, she told him happily, in her drawing room. Whether it was a wrench to leave the Queen's House, a home she had known for fifty years, she did not disclose. At times she and her sisters had been more miserable there with their mother than anywhere else. Her views on her brother's proposed changes for Windsor Castle she also kept to herself, describing on 26 March 1824 a dinner there as 'very cheerful and pleasant'. She invited Lady Harcourt to a housewarming in her new abode in London on 29 March, begging her not to dress up, and thanking her for so ably managing a committee for the foundation of an orphanage, to which Augusta planned to donate a library of good works. And several times she invited Mme d'Arblay to join her and Mary, who was with her a great deal, being ill and 'under the care of Sir Henry Halford and ... other medical attendants' for much of the year.

Royal, from Ludwigsburg, praised Augusta for inviting Mary to stay with her. She herself had been two months at Teinach with her own Court, bathing and attempting to cure pains in her hands that tortured her. At this Black Forest spa, set among velvety woods and precipitous ravines where she had first gone for a 'cure' after the stillbirth of her daughter nearly thirty years before, Royal was always happy. Now Miss Cornelia Knight, Charlotte's former lady, who had been visiting Elizabeth, was staying with her in Ludwigsburg. 'All my young people much amused,' Royal noted with satisfaction on 26 November 1824 after a little ball she gave for a Württemberg nephew who had settled in the town to study for the military. The affair lasted from six to eleven-thirty – 's'entend, both ball and supper, which is just a good length of time without allowing any dawdling between the dances', wrote the hostess.

The young consumed Royal's attention as she prepared to enter her sixties. Prince George of Cambridge's fifth birthday in Hanover – the age at which he came, according to German tradition, under the care of male governors – had occasioned a generous present from her of a topaz seal (to bear in due course his crest, orders and arms), and a silver fork, knife and spoon. Following German tradition again in making these presents, Royal promised to add pieces each year till he had two dozen of each, and then match that set with another two dozen. 'I wish I could do more,' she had concluded her letter to Adolphus on 24 March 1824. 'I can only go on piano piano.'

Princess Sophia in England had an opportunity of enjoying daily the company of her brother Edward's child, Victoria, when she left Connaught Place for apartments in Kensington Palace abutting those of the Duchess of Kent. Not only did she see Victoria by day, but she spent nearly every evening with the Duchess, with her daughter by her first marriage, Princess Feodora of Leiningen, and with the Conroys. When the Kent and Conroy group left town for a spell at the seaside, Victoria, aged five, wrote – with the aid either of her mother or of her newly appointed governess, Miss Louise (later Baroness) Lehzen – to her 'dear Aunt'. Sophia wrote back, on 3 September 1824, 'You will be sorry to hear that Aunt is quite deaf and cannot hear a word with her left ear. It is very distressing and very uncomfortable. I hope it will be well before I see you again, as you will find it a little troublesome to make me understand you.'

All the princesses, as we have seen, took a close interest in their nieces and nephews, and much appreciated news of them – be they legitimate or their brother William's Fitzclarence family. And their brothers were no less interested in the coming generation. On 29 March 1825 the Duke of Cumberland from Berlin gave his old tutor a laconic description of his six-year-old nephew, Prince George of Cambridge, and of the boy's sister Augusta. 'The little boy is two months older than George [of Cumberland, his own son] but mine is fatter, the little girl is delightful and much more lively than the boy.' Consumed with pride in his own son, Ernest contin-ued, 'George [of Cumberland] is very like the picture of [Benjamin] West's where I am with my two younger brothers and the big black Newfoundland dog.' He did not mention that his son's eyesight was a source of anxiety.

The Cambridges, meanwhile, visited England from Hanover in the summer of 1825 and stayed in the very house on Kew Green where William and Edward had grown up. It was renamed Cambridge Cottage, and, once all were settled in, the Duchess of Cambridge begged her sister-in-law Victoria of Kent to bring her daughter to play for the day. But the Duchess was short in her responses. It would appear that she preferred Victoria to play with comptroller Conroy's children rather than with her cousins.

In February 1826 Lady Harcourt, that remarkable correspondent to whom all the princesses had written their most intimate confidences, that friend who had known all their secrets, died. But the princesses kept up other long-standing, if less intimate, relationships. When Princess Sophia invited Mme d'Arblay to spend one Good Friday evening with her, the reply was effusive:

> Madam, Oh yes! Sweet princess, yes! Good Friday evening I shall feel – I dare not say more good, but more devout I will venture to assert, for spending it with so unchanged, unchangeable and kindly invariable, though so august a personage as the dear and fair Princess, who, from her childhood upwards, has so graciously deigned to receive and to encourage the warm attachment of her Royal Highness's most obliged, most faithful, most grateful and most respectfully devoted F d'Arblay.

The cold winds of the spring in 1826 were succeeded by a ferocious summer heat. The Duchess of Gloucester longed to sit beneath the shade of her trees at Bagshot, but she was staying in London to see her brother Frederick, who was seriously ill with dropsy. The Duke, aged sixty-two, suffered from this dropsical tendency which some of Queen Charlotte's children had inherited from her. In addition, he – like the King his brother – had the tendency to gout which George III had suffered, and made no pretence at diminishing his consumption of food or drink, or at increasing the exercise he took to counter his ill health.

This time he had been lucky, and Mary set off for Bagshot on 23 July where she found that a planned 'party on the water' which the King had devised for Virginia Water had to be postponed because of the weather, now turned from heat to torrential rain. 'From the vast quantity of wet that has fallen,' the King wrote that same day from Royal Lodge, his house in the Great Park at Windsor, 'the tents will be so wet, and what is sure, will continue damp in consequence for some days to come, that it would be downright madness to think of dining there tomorrow. This, my dearest Mary, is abominably provoking, but I hope by the end of the week we shall be able to make our party on the water good.'

Augusta still liked new experiences, if they were pleasant, and was gratified to have been present – with the rest of the royal family – to observe Lord Liverpool, that good conservative, lay the first stone of a new bridge in Kingston-on-Thames. 'It was a very pretty town, quite a new one to me,' Augusta observed, and she was delighted with her invitation from the Corporation and with the 'deservedly handsome reception' they gave the Prime Minister. On another occasion she was to stand patron to an 'Extraordinary Exhibition' of 'industrious fleas' in Regent Street in London, but whether curiosity drew her to see her protégés perform is not known.

She visited Petworth, Lord Egremont's seat in Sussex, motivated by a reasonable curiosity to see her host's famous 'fine statues' and even the grounds modelled by Capability Brown. The Boulle tables, she noted, 'would be much the better for Bramble's polishing'. But there was something of a family connection to explore as well. Her brother William's eldest son by Mrs Jordan, Captain George Fitzclarence, had married Lord Egremont's 'natural' daughter Mary Wyndham in 1819. With his wife and his father-in-law, George now received his aunt Augusta at Petworth. 'I wished Lord Egremont to feel that I loved William's son's wife, which I really do,' wrote Augusta to her friends the Arrans, and she kissed Mrs Fitzclarence. 'I hope you think I was right.'

King George IV was not stopping at making the Queen's House into a palace or embellishing a lodge in Windsor Great Park as sumptuous Royal Lodge. At Windsor he had decided to 'Gothicize' the whole Castle with the aid of architect Jeffry Wyatt. Wyatt, enraptured with the grandeur of the scheme, asked permission to change his name to Wyatville. 'Veal or mutton. Call yourself what you like,' came the King's grumpy answer. A visit to the altered Castle, which was now emerging from under Wyatville's scaffolding, put the King's sister Augusta in an equally grumpy mood. 'The main garden and Bastion terrace is frightful to the greatest degree. Wyatville', she said with scorn on 13 September 1826, 'says it's Classical. I never saw such an unmilitary appearance in my life.'

To soothe such upsets, Augusta and her lady, Lady Mary Taylor, played on the piano and harp for two hours together most evenings at Frogmore – 'and I have got some new songs which I hope you will command here or at St James's Palace in the spring', she told the Arrans later that month. She had had a harp made for Lady Mary by Egan in Dublin. It was 'in the highest order' and 'a great addition to the piano. We play little trifles of our own arranging which, as we play so much together, go very well indeed.'

Augusta's skill in arranging 'medleys' for her instruments of choice – including the Irish songs of Tom Moore, to that poet's pleasure – had been noted by Fanny Burney not long before. The Princess had begun this hobby of setting words to well-known tunes with the collaboration of Lady Harcourt at the outset of the French wars, when it was the fashion to stir up patriotic feeling by distributing song sheets with suitable sentiments around the theatres. And Tom Moore himself, whom Augusta greatly admired, had recently listened to her perform the 'new airs' that she had composed for two of his songs – 'The Wreath You Wove' and 'The Legacy'. Moore in return sang to her his rebel song, 'Oh, Where's the Slave!' and wrote, 'it was no small triumph to be chorused in it by the favourite sister of his Majesty George IV'.

Augusta also played for Tom Moore a march that she said she had composed for her brother Frederick's regiment. But the news about Frederick was bad again in September. His limbs were badly swollen. And Sophy wrote a melancholy account from London. Frederick, who thought it was a secret he was dropsical, talked of going to Brighton for a week, but his nerves were irritable – he liked a change 'even of rooms'. With the New Year it became clear that, racked by spasms and no longer able to swallow food, he had not long to live. Sophia was there when Frederick died on 5 January 1827 at the Duke of Rutland's house in London. She wrote afterwards to her brother the King: 'I am still a piece of marble, and can catch myself for ever inclined to call out, "So is it all true?" when the worst I know but too well.'

Frederick had been, according to Adolphus, 'the chief object' of Sophia's life, and her grief was 'poignant'. She wrote proudly to Lady John Thynne on 18 January, 'I occupied his last thoughts. Alas! All his property, you know too well what must become of it.' (It was to be auctioned to pay his creditors.) But the Duke had written, 'If there is anything over I name my beloved sister Sophia as residuary legatee.' She continued, 'Of course there is nothing to inherit, but the naming me in such a manner has made me feel I am Heir of his affection which is the most precious gift I could receive.' Sophia could be quite nonsensical, but she busied herself distributing mementoes of their brother to the rest of the family. Mary, who helped her, received a print of the Duke. To the King Sophia sent the last opera glass that Frederick had used, for, in showing it to her, she told him, he had said the King much approved it 'as suiting his eye'.

Sophia tried to be optimistic and chose some new cloth for habits with a view to recommencing her riding. But a series of spasms weakened her, and it was not till April that she felt able to drive out with Augusta, as the latter told Ernest on the 20th of that month, to 'one of the fine gardens on the King's Road to see the spring plants in their greatest beauty, that is to say, in the greenhouses'.

The death of Frederick, the father's favourite who had ever been devoted to his brother's service, went deep also with George IV. Harking back to former days, he commissioned Augusta to beg a visit from their sister Royal at Ludwigsburg.

The Queen Dowager was thrown into an almighty palaver about this enterprise. She consulted her 'son' the King about the journey – and her physician about bringing forward, or omitting, her usual summer trip to Teinach to take the waters. It was 'not a water drinking place one can go to in general in the spring', she explained, 'as the snow remains there often till June'. She wondered if there was a 'metzo terminé' (*mezzo termine*, or middle course) she could take, but she was so flattered by 'our dear brother's wishing to see me once more in this world' that she resolved to make the journey. Requesting the use of Mary's apartment at Frogmore, the Queen Dowager worried to her sister Augusta on 25 March 1827 that she would be able to do so little. 'I am troublesome from not being able either to go in a shut carriage or walk. My breath being now so short that I must be carried downstairs as well as upstairs.' Royal, cataloguing these frailties, finished, 'Though the shell is altered, the heart ever remains most affectionate.' And she was 'quite wild' with the idea of Augusta meeting her at Greenwich Stairs, as she had once driven herself to Bessig in Germany, 'to wait for your arrival and first catch the sight of your horses driving over the little bridge'. To her brother the King she wrote the same day, 'I am only afraid that you will be rather hurt ... at my appearance as I am very old of my age and infirm, owing to the gout in my hands and feet and a constant shortness of breath.' She implored him, 'Look on me as an old woman ...' She was sixty years old.

When the *Royal Sovereign*, the King of England's yacht, sailed up the Thames in early June to land the Queen Dowager at Greenwich Stairs, Augusta was duly waiting for her. Together the two sisters entered the City of London, a much larger place than when the elder had left it thirty years before. But it was at Windsor that Royal most marvelled at the changes. The Queen's Lodge had been pulled down, and following her brother's Gothic 'improvements', the Round Tower had gained a foot for each of the years she had been away. She went all over the Castle 'without any fatigue – being carried about in her armchair and by her own servants', Augusta told Ernest, and was 'pleased and astonished' with what she saw.

In early July the Dowager Queen sat out in the Priory Woods at Frogmore and told Augusta she was 'quite delighted to find that the outline of the walks had not been materially altered'. 'Indeed, Mr Price laid them with so much discretion and taste', the younger sister fought back gently, as she told their brother Ernest, 'that they could scarcely be improved, but ... taking down some trees and opening places in the shrubbery has given an appearance of depth to the garden which is hardly credible.'

The Duchess of Gloucester made a third late in July at Frogmore, so 'the house is literally what the common people call "chock full"', Augusta wrote cheerfully to the Arrans on 25 July. 'Our sitting room every morning after breakfast is the Colonnade, which is lovely. Mary and I have each our table opposite each other and a good large couch in the middle of which we sit, making a second and third table of each end of it, for all our superfluous articles of baskets, dictionaries, trays for the wafers and wax, etc.' Every morning at midday the Dowager Queen, who breakfasted in her room, summoned her younger sisters, and they then arranged the rest of the day. 'Royal', Augusta told Ernest on 26 July, 'has enchanted the Eton boys by begging a week's holidays for them … She delights everybody by her learning and she knows as much and as correctly about all the families in England as if she had never been out of it.'

Royal was happiest when with the King her brother, whom she had feared to disappoint with her appearance. Lady Louisa Stuart wrote kindly, after seeing her old friend, that she was 'rather shapeless than fat, not having worn stays of any kind these twenty years. And her dress is nothing extraordinary, what anybody's would be who went with their own few grey hairs instead of wearing a wig.' But then the King who greeted his sister the Queen Dowager now resembled more a pantomime dame – with rouged cheeks and a slipping wig – than anything else. The Dowager Queen was entranced anyway – and in ecstasy to see her brother Edward's child Victoria at last, who had been invited with her mama to stay with the King and meet her great-aunt from Germany.

Till now, Royal had had to content herself with sending presents – an amethyst cross and earrings on one occasion – and accompanying notes to Princess Victoria. The eight-year-old Princess was not at all shy. In fact, she was 'quite at home with the King and Queen, very merry and jumping about and never was so happy in her life'. With an eye to the future, Mary wrote that if her brother saw their niece Victoria long enough for her to be at her ease with him, 'he must be enchanted with her'.

Royal complained to her sisters of ill health, but when the King begged her to 'send him word at any moments when she felt herself equal to joining an early dinner party by the lake in the Great Park', she recovered miraculously. 'The very thoughts of it gave her new life,' wrote Augusta. Under an August moon, Royal and Augusta joined their brother at the lakeside dinner party that he hosted at Virginia Water. And after dinner, 'six strong pullers' rowed the ladies over to an island where they took coffee with the gentlemen of the party in a Chinese pavilion, papered inside 'with the grey ground and bamboo panels, the same as at the Pavilion at Brighton'. Augusta ended her account, 'we took a delightful row on the lake till after nine o'clock by moonlight'.

Royal's time in England drew slowly to a close. She and Augusta went up to the Castle to inspect the 'magnificent' designs for wallpapers – and even floor papers – that Mr Robson, the King's paperhanger, had produced. 'He is a very clever man,' wrote Augusta to Ernest at the end of September 1827. 'He has produced a floor paper with gold, and by a process with oil the floor loses its roughness and looks like a velvet ground.' Her brother the King spoke of inhabiting the Castle after Easter, she added, but she doubted it would be ready. 'The gilding of the library has left such a very strong smell of oil paint, that it needs fire and air and sun to get it out of the rooms, before it can be pleasant to sleep in them.'

Royal did not forget her family at home in Württemberg, and told Lady Louisa Stuart, showing her some ornaments she had bought from the jewellers Rundell and Bridge, that they were for her 'granddaughter' Pauline. But the Queen Dowager was 'very low' when she had to leave England. Her brother the King escaped the last farewells, telling Augusta to make his excuses and say 'he had a little gout'. Augusta, on whom the burden of Royal's slow and cumbersome tour of scenes past and present had rested, wrote crisply, 'I rather think it was nonsense not to see her again.'

Shortly before Royal departed, Sophia wrote to her niece Victoria excusing her lack of letters. 'Since my sisters have been in town, my mornings have been so occupied and so many interruptions occurring.' After her sister had left, Sophia conceded to a friend, 'She certainly tried all she could to show how rejoiced she was to see us again, and naturally kindness begets a return.' But if Sophia and Royal had not warmed to each other, the Queen Dowager returned to the Continent glad to have rekindled with others relationships of which she had cherished the memory all these years.

Augusta was ordered to Brighton for a 'cure' in the winter months following her sister's departure, but before she went, William and Adelaide, now in a new-built house at St James's, Clarence House, came to dine with her at Stable House. 'We had some of my favourite Irish melodies,' Augusta told her friends the Arrans, 'simple ballads which we like better than anything else, and then I played to amuse William every Paddy tune I could think of – O'Carrol – O'Rafferty – O'Casey, all his delights.'

That December it grew dark in St James's Palace by half-past three. 'Dear William has just been with me,' Augusta wrote again, 'and pulled down my blinds and had the candles lighted, for he said it was too melancholy.' At Brighton she lived comfortably in the White House, a house belonging to the King on the Steyne, and, having promised Sir Henry Halford that she would walk, she attempted a quarter of a mile along the sea front with a stick. Days later, she proclaimed triumphantly, 'I am grown bold, and stomp away with my stick in a most happy independent manner.' When indoors, she again abided by Sir Henry's instructions, the physician having charged her 'on no account to sit in hot rooms'. Accordingly, she sat in the evening in the light of very few candles.

Augusta remained nearly three months in the Brighton house, determined to persevere and walk sturdily once more. The spectre of Royal, who had effectively lost the use of her lower limbs, may have frightened her into this determined action. Occasionally, melancholy thoughts occurred to the Princess. She regretted Frederick's death – she had visited him here at Brighton shortly before it – and the loss of another link in the family chain. But she bound up her knee, and in January 1828 she announced she could walk on flat ground as firmly and as fast as ever. 'When in the streets or on the chain pier', she added, however, 'I take my stick for safety.'

Later that year Princess Sophia was at Kensington Palace reading a letter from her sister Royal that had just arrived, when a message was brought to her that her correspondent had died on 6 October. The Dowager Queen's sufferings had been dreadful, Augusta told Ernest, but short. She had spent her Saturday as usual, was indisposed on the Sunday and on the following day: 'The water rose so much to her chest and occasioned such palpitations at the heart' that, 'had her existence been prolonged, it would have been but for her to suffer torture and misery'.

In Ludwigsburg, so Elizabeth heard, the Dowager Queen's death had aroused strong emotion. Her 'son' King Wilhelm had earlier irritated Elizabeth by selling off the china that Royal had painted for his father, but now he redeemed himself by his constant watch, with his family, at his stepmother's deathbed. And his niece Pauline could not be detached from the side of the Dowager Queen's dead body for some hours.

Royal herself had written of her hopes to be reunited after death with the daughter whose stillbirth she had never forgotten. Now those two sets of baby clothes that she had brought with her from England, and which had so long lingered among her effects, were sold off with a dress of cloth of gold and other costly possessions dating from more recent times. In England Augusta was consoled by the thought that Royal had been so happy in England the previous year. Sophia agreed, and admitted to Lady Louisa Murray, 'Her visit last year revived feelings which I do not conceal from you were dormant after an absence of thirty years …'

Augusta was vexed by the behaviour of her brother-in-law the Duke of Gloucester. He had 'taken it as a heinous offence' when Robinson, a page of many years' service, expressed a desire to become a messenger, and had sacked him. Augusta asked Sir William Fremantle, who appointed her brother the King's household, if Robinson might try out as a King's page. Mary, she said, had begged her to help.

The Duchess of Gloucester was often very unhappy with her husband's behaviour, but she had found a spiritual refuge at Bagshot in the flower garden and arboretum she had made with the help of her husband's agent Mr Edmund Currey and of Mr Toward, her gardener. She would always love Mr Currey, she wrote later, 'for all the amusement and pleasure he afforded me in first giving me taste and pleasure in my garden and for the country'. The agent had had only one object when he originally undertook the management of Bagshot Park – 'to make the Duke like it and give him a taste for that place, and prevent him leaving it, as he used to do for shooting before he had game enough at Bagshot Park'. But with Mary's enthusiastic support the flower garden and arboretum flourished too.

At Frogmore Augusta was apparently fully engaged in charitable works, gardening, farming and playing duets with Lady Mary Taylor. Whether General Spencer still formed part of her life is not known, just as it is not known whether they ever succeeded in marrying. When he died in December 1828 at his estate at Great Missenden in Buckinghamshire, his obituarist wrote: 'Since the peace [of 1815] Sir Brent Spencer has passed his time in perfect retirement, enjoying the pleasures of a rural life, and the society of a few chosen friends ...' Augusta herself, whether one of Spencer's 'few chosen friends' or not, made no reference to his death.

Meanwhile, others were very concerned about the behaviour of Tommy Garth, now a captain on half-pay aged twenty-eight. Following a year in Paris after Harrow, learning French – and visiting the gaming tables – he had made little of the career in the army offered to him. Despite every kind of assistance, his progress had foundered on his own lack of enthusiasm. By the early 1820s, on the other hand, he was a familiar sight on the Leicestershire hunting fields, and had become a member of the 'wild Meltonians' set who hunted round Melton Mowbray in Leicestershire. His first crime was to fall in love with a fellow Meltonian's wife, Lady Astley. The second was to elope with her in 1826, carrying her off from the London house where she left behind her not only Sir Jacob Astley, her husband, but two tiny children.

Tommy Garth's elopement with Georgiana Astley, earlier a Miss Dashwood of West Wycombe, was the talk of the town, and his relationship with Princess Sophia was hinted at in caricatures of the night-time escape. Sir Jacob, betrayed, sued his fellow Meltonian for 'crim con' damages. ('Criminal conversation' was the term then used for adultery in legal proceedings.) But Astley was allotted a shilling after Garth brought counterclaims that Astley was no stranger to prostitutes and girls of the town in London and Leicestershire. Astley's petition for divorce failed, too, as the supplicant needed 'clean hands', and the evidence brought by Garth's lawyers in the civil suit had proved they were filthy. So Garth and Georgiana, with great effrontery, lived a sort of twilight existence together in a series of inns and lodgings. Georgiana's husband asked her to return to him, but she refused. Tommy and she were apparently oddly happy.

So was Princess Sophia in the late summer of 1828 when she wrote tranquilly to her niece Victoria: 'Has Polly learnt any new words?' Princess Victoria's parrot had gone with her to Tunbridge Wells and Ramsgate. Sophia apologized for not writing earlier, and thanked her eight-year-old niece for her well-written letter. 'I have walked very often all around the gravel walks under your windows,' wrote Aunt Sophia on 29 September at the palace in Kensington Gardens. 'In looking up at your windows how I missed that little voice which always makes me cheerful, as it gives me the delight of feeling that my dear Vicky is near me.'

Then Tommy's past, or rather his birth, caught up with him, indeed with everyone concerned. General Garth, thinking himself in 1828 on the point of death, summoned his 'protégé' and showed him an iron box containing letters and documents relating to his birth, which Tommy took away with him to study. The General recovered, but his son did not give the documents back. On the point of going to prison for debt the following spring, he was 'compelled to address the illustrious lady', he recorded later, by whom he meant Princess Sophia, for assistance. Sir Herbert Taylor, private secretary to King George IV as he had been to George III, and the Duke of York before him, was then entrusted with the delicate business of engaging young Garth to deposit at a bank the box of documents he had received from the General. In return he would receive an annuity of £3,000, and the payment of his debts. But all parties played unfair, and Sir Herbert took the box from the bank, while young Garth publicized his wrongs in an affidavit declaring robbery.

Meanwhile, the Duke of Cumberland came over to England as a guest of his brother the King this spring – and one determined to oppose the Duke of Wellington's cowardly volte-face, as he saw it, in sponsoring a bill for Catholic Emancipation shortly after becoming Prime Minister. Among allegations levelled against the Duke by those who favoured the bill were the old – false but potent – claims of his incestuous relationship with his sister Princess Sophia. These intensified with newspaper hints at Captain Garth's doubly royal parentage. It all made for a harrowing year for Sophia. And when General Garth – Captain Garth's real father – died in November 1829, and left the bulk of his estate to his nephew Captain Thomas Garth RN, in the belief that Tommy Garth was provided for, it was the harbinger

When Princess Charlotte married Prince Leopold of Saxe-Coburg, *above*, her aunt Princess Mary married their cousin the Duke of Gloucester, *right*, whom Charlotte had spurned

Princess Elizabeth,
at her desk at
Frogmore, *left*,
continued to paint
and publish when
she married
Frederick of Hesse-
Homburg, *below
left*. Seen *below
right*, as a widow,
again at her desk

The Princess Royal, *above*, as Queen of Württemberg, and Princess Augusta, *right*. The two eldest princesses met again after many years, once the Napoleonic Wars were over

General Sir Herbert Taylor,
left, deflected the demands
of Captain Tommy Garth,
below, for money and
access to his mother,
Princess Sophia

Cartoon showing Tommy Garth's elopement with Georgiana, Lady Astley, and hinting publicly at his parentage with the letter marked 'To Sophia' poking out of his pocket

Showman King, George IV, *above*, was beloved by his sisters the princesses. The Duke of Clarence, on succeeding as William IV, was a comfortable host to his sisters at Windsor with his kind-hearted wife, Queen Adelaide, *below*

For Queen Victoria, seen in a self-portrait *above*, her aunts the princesses were
authorities on royal etiquette. Blind and deaf latterly, Princess Sophia, *below*, is seen here
winding wool

Princess Mary, Duchess of
Gloucester, the last surviving
princess, *left*, and *below*, with
Queen Victoria, the future
King Edward VII and his sister
Princess Alice

of a further trail of misfortunes. But for the moment Tommy Garth played the part of chief mourner for his protector – and continued to stave off attacks from Sir Jacob Astley, who still, despite all, wanted his Georgiana back.

While Sir Herbert Taylor defended Princess Sophia's tarnished name against all comers, Sophia herself made no public or known private response to the allegations and rumours about the birth of Tommy Garth, but continued her correspondence with her niece in the next-door apartments at Kensington Palace. Ten-year-old Victoria announced that August from her uncle Leopold's Surrey home, 'Claremont is in high beauty now. I have been this morning sitting in the flower-garden.' Later in the summer she wrote from Broadstairs, enquiring after her aunt's dog. 'How is poor little Cosmo? I hope that he does not whine any more.' The younger Princess spoke proudly of her own dog: 'Fanny comes every morning to the breakfast table to get some biscuits; and Shrewsbury [the Duchess of Kent's new horse] comes close to the door in the morning to be fed with carrots.'

Victoria thanked her aunt for offering to make a dress for her – 'I shall like the pattern very much,' she told her – and announced that Sir John Conroy's daughter Victoire was tormented by a boil. Aunt Sophia responded with thanks for Victoria's letters: 'I know my dear little friend is not *very* fond of letter writing, therefore I am doubly pleased with your so kindly devoting so much time to me.' And she asked for news of Victoria's drawing and singing with Mama. 'Cosmo I must speak for,' she reported in October 1829; 'he is very well now' – he had fallen from a window ledge – 'and fancies himself fond of me, but I think him a little of a rogue ... he makes up to his mistress, as within the last few days we have had fires, and he enjoys lying on the rug before the fire, and follows me for that purpose.'

Earlier in the year George IV, lying in bed and increasingly gout-ridden at Royal Lodge, his mansion in Windsor Great Park, had been incensed that his sister Sophia should have such trouble brought upon her by these public airings of her past. At one point, he wanted to sack both Garths – the elderly General and his half-pay Captain son – from the army. Most of the time, however, he plotted peaceably with Jeffry Wyatville to 'Gothicize' still further the medieval fastness of Windsor Castle. But this brother, who meant more than anyone to the princesses, and whose appearance in their lives had always represented light and hope, was dying. George IV was so puffed up with dropsy, wrote the Duchess of Gloucester in dismay, that he resembled a feather counterpane. He rallied, but he was mortally ill. Days before he died, the King was 'as clear, as communicative, as agreeable, nay as facetious as he ever had been', his physician and man of business Sir William Knighton wrote. Wellington visited the King, and was 'astonished at his strength, both of body and mind'. On 26 June 1830 George IV summoned Knighton at three in the morning, after calling out, 'Sir Henry, Sir Henry! Fetch him – this is death!' After Halford – and Knighton – duly appeared, the King's 'lips grew livid, and he dropped his head on the page's shoulder'. At 3.15 a.m., confirming his prophecy, came death.

The Times asserted on 16 July, 'There never was an individual less regretted by his fellow-creatures than this deceased King.' But the newspaper forgot the sisters of George IV. One and all they were stricken by the death of a brother who had ever been kind to them, and especially kind when they were in deep distress. He had raised their spirits with letters and presents and jewellery, with his effulgent regard, with his confident promises. Now the glow of George IV's personality was extinguished, and with his death the princesses had virtually lost a third parent. Bluff, friendly William was a very different sort of brother, and would be a very different kind of king.

18

Elizabeth – The Largesse of a Landgravine

~

GEORGE IV'S DEATH in June 1830 was hard for Princess Elizabeth in Homburg. She had been much affected by her sister Royal's death twenty months before, especially because, after their initial reunion at Ludwigsburg at Christmas in 1820, the two had visited each other several times. Then Elizabeth's husband, the Landgrave, died in April 1829 after complications, following a bout of influenza, when an old leg wound broke out. 'No woman was ever more happy than I was for eleven years,' she wrote, 'and they will often be lived over again in the memory of the heart.' But the train of Elizabeth's life as a widow did not alter greatly, given that Bluff's younger bachelor brother Louis, the new Landgrave, was so congenial, so eager to enter into all her ideas for embellishing Homburg – with her income.

Now the death of George IV had removed a brother who had, in the widowed Landgravine's eyes, been 'all heart, and had he been left to his own judgement, would ever have been kind and just. But people got hold of him, and flattery did more harm in that quarter than anything'. Comparing her brother and father, she observed, 'My brother was always in a dazzle. My father was always seeing things composedly, sensibly, and seeing much further into the danger of what such and such things would produce.'

Elizabeth had been at Hanover and, around the time of her sixtieth birthday, on the point of setting out for England with the Cambridges in May 1830 to spend a year there, 'making the dear King my first object', as she told Sir William Knighton, when she heard that George IV was ill. She had written cheerfully to him a month earlier, 'Only promise when I am with you, that you look upon me as a quiet old dog to whom you can say, "Now leave me, go for a month to Mary" – and so on, without an idea of offending. In the way I shall not be, for once in my own room and not with you, I have employment enough never to annoy anyone.' Now, surmising correctly that she would not see the King again, she begged Knighton from Hanover, 'Put by a glass or a cup, or any trifle, ever so small, that he has used, even a pocket handkerchief which he has used, for me.'

Elizabeth proceeded, despite her brother's death, to England with the Cambridge family, who were going to leave eleven-year-old Prince George to be educated there. It would never, she told Knighton, in a letter she wrote from Brighton later that year, have been an easy journey, as she had 'nearly lost the use of her legs' since the 'shock of the Landgrave's death'. Now it was a journey made in sorrow. Not only was King George IV dead, but every corner of London and Windsor recalled him to his sister's mind. Windsor Castle, in particular, called forth painful thoughts. It was 'a very severe trial' to Elizabeth to find herself in 'that magnificent castle, and the being I most valued and loved gone; everything which I saw showing his taste, and every spot calculated to please and delight – his own formation.' She told Knighton, 'I give you my word, I went about half dead … you may believe the wound is far from healed, though I am able to show myself and appear cheerful in society.'

To reflect the changes that had occurred in Homburg since Fritz's death, Elizabeth had recently remade her will, leaving to the new Landgrave Louis all her 'funded property' – £36,000 – in England, and her 'library, prints, drawings', many of which she had brought on marriage from England. The rest of her bequests were mementoes, snuffboxes, bracelets, which she parcelled out in her will between her family in England and her in-laws in Homburg. Now in London she herself received mementoes. George IV had left her two snuffboxes filled with his own mixture. Elizabeth, who had once said she hated the stuff her mother and eldest brother took with such enjoyment, was overjoyed, and declared, 'The snuff will never be taken out, so dear is it to me.'

But barely a month after she had arrived in England, Elizabeth spoke of leaving, her nerves frayed by the double exertion of mourning her brother and of adapting to the new reign. Her brother King William's behaviour was lamented by many. First, he created his eldest son George Fitzclarence, Earl of Munster, and gave all his illegitimate children the titles of the younger sons and daughters of a marquess. Then he went into mourning upon the death of the husband of his illegitimate daughter Augusta Fitzclarence, the Hon. John Kennedy-Erskine, which scandalized many. After a military review, the new King put on plain clothes and went rambling up Pall Mall. To cap it all, his wife Adelaide's complexion was muddy.

There was nothing of majesty here, and people began to remember George IV with kindness. However, Elizabeth took a liking to the comfortable company of William and Adelaide, and busily 'sided' with her brother when he condemned the Duchess of Kent's upbringing of their niece Victoria, his heir. In September, after spraining her knee and becoming completely 'fixed' to her chair, she tried the 'warm bath' at Brighton, and did not return to Homburg till the following summer.

King William IV had much to undergo in the first years of his reign. Not only was he beset by members of his family, and by members of the current and previous administrations, with exhortations and advice about Parliamentary reform. But his eldest son, George Fitzclarence, now Earl of Munster, chose this moment to denounce his father to the Duchess of Gloucester – for failing to provide him with the funds and estate necessary to the dignity of a peer. He quoted a previous letter of his father in which he had refused him money, saying, 'Dear George, I cannot admit primogeniture, and must give 10,000 to each of your brothers and sisters before I can think of any other money for you.' Munster pointed out to his aunt 'the utter contradiction ... the virtual acknowledgement of primogeniture in raising me to the hereditary peerage.' When Duke of Clarence, and in comparative financial difficulty, his father had made 'every use' of him. Now he was king, he was trying to get rid of him 'at the cheapest rate possible'. Munster gained nothing by his appeal to his aunt Gloucester but kind words. However, he and the 'Fitzclarence set' that he headed continued to hang about their father and about Queen Adelaide, who accepted their existence with pious resignation.

Meanwhile, the Duke of Gloucester left the Whigs over the issue of reform, and remonstrated with the King on the danger it presented, warning that the measures proposed would deprive him of the crown. 'Very well, very well,' said William equably. 'But sir,' the Duke pressed, inspired for a moment by wit, 'your Majesty's head may be in it.' Nevertheless the second Reform Bill was approved in the summer of 1832, following a letter from William to Tory peers warning them not to vote against it again, or else he would be constrained to create enough new Whig peers to pass it. So just as Mary's husband, when a Whig, had fallen out with her brother George IV over one Parliamentary bill in 1820 – the Pains and Penalties against Queen Caroline – so, now that he was a Tory, he fell out with her brother the new King. And once again she was in a quandary – whether to visit her brother in Brighton, where her husband would not go, or remain on uneasy terms with her husband at Bagshot.

Before his death George IV had discreetly arranged that his sister Elizabeth should no longer make repayment of Homburg state debts to Mayer Amschel Rothschild, the banker in Frankfurt, without her English trustees' approval. Early on in her marriage she had impulsively sent her jewels to the banker without her husband's knowledge, naively wishing to secure a sum to ease Fritz's worries over the debt he had inherited with his principality when his father died. Rothschild then informed an aghast Fritz that he could not produce the sum Elizabeth had requested for over three months, but instead 'he would buy the jewels for his wife, who would like to have them'. Elizabeth had remarked to her brother the King in England, 'if you had seen Fritz's face of horror ...'. Fritz said he would sell his woods rather than do as the banker suggested.

As a widow, Elizabeth continued to pay £6,000 of her 'appanage' from England to settle other state debts in Homburg. And with the £5,000 she kept for herself, she carried on supporting the variety of projects she had already begun while Bluff was alive. She built a new coach house and stables at the castle, and she planted an English garden, and erected buildings and follies in the Little Wood immediately below the castle. Just as Elizabeth had arranged her collection of china in her cottage at Windsor, now she installed her 'china closet' in a house she had built for it in the Little Wood, and 'peu à peu' she hoped to make the house pretty, which was now ready to receive furniture. In the Great Forest that lay beyond, she worked with a pliant Louis on a great Gothic house roofed with copper to serve as a location for woodland picnics.

In the town, she supported, among other charities, a sewing and knitting school for poor children, and arranged for the distribution of layettes for expectant mothers in need. The quality of life for inhabitants of castle and town had improved dramatically, thanks to the energy of this busy Princess. Things had, in fact, been transformed since Bluff had written home urgently from St James's in 1818, bidding his steward to cleanse the Augean stables of the castle, and paint afresh the hallmark white tower. She was optimistic that she and her brother-in-law Louis could continue the work she had laboured at with Fritz, simultaneously to enhance the country and clear it of debt.

Elizabeth still occupied the married quarters in the castle at Bad Homburg which she and Fritz had restored with the Hesse Darmstadt architect Georg Moller, and which had become known as the 'English wing'. When the writer Fanny Trollope visited Homburg, Elizabeth walked her, as she recorded, through 'a suite of rooms ... from the windows of which a beautiful view was enjoyed. The library contained a large and excellent collection of books. The Princess said, "I brought these volumes with me from England", adding, with a smile, "I am very proud of my library." Speaking of the beauty of the scenery, she said, "I can never forget Windsor and Richmond, but Germany is a glorious country."' Mrs

Trollope stopped before a portrait of George III. 'You know that portrait,' said the Princess. 'It is my father. It is quite perfect.'

But life as a dowager was not quite as agreeable as the Landgravine had hoped it would be. Optimism, Elizabeth's chief characteristic, waxed and waned now. The children of her brother- and sister-in-law Gustav and Louise, thirteen-year-old Caroline, nine-year-old Elizabeth and their two-year-old brother Friedrich, had the scarlet fever in December. And although the children recovered, the whole family was in quarantine over Christmas. Young Elizabeth sent word to Aunt Elizabeth to say that her dolls all had the scarlet fever and she had put their clothes in the fire. 'The poor dear children are peeling and they have forbid Gustav and Louise to come near me,' wrote Elizabeth, 'for the infection is much stronger at that time.' So the Christmas tables heaped with presents that she had bought in Frankfurt for the children were not wanted this year.

Elizabeth's letters were always full of coded allusions to the shortcomings and oddities of her in-laws at Homburg. Gustav and Louise's habit of keeping themselves to themselves meant she saw little of their children, which upset her. But she tried to avoid 'clashing with those whom I love ... How strange it is! But one must smile often upon what would at times make me cry, for I always wish to be kind.' She wrote again, 'I never ask questions or meddle with anybody else's concerns. If they tell me, I hear, if not, I do not take it ill. It is the only way to go on when one has such various people in one house ...'

The numerous charities Elizabeth had established or to which she contributed at Homburg occupied much of her time. 'I am wanted for rich and poor, halt, maimed, etc., and it is one's duty to do what one can, and I don't like to appear to run away, as if I would not assist,' she told a new English acquaintance, Miss Louisa Swinburne, who had settled with her family at nearby Wiesbaden. Nevertheless, she left her cares at Homburg behind her in the first half of 1833 on a visit to her brother Adolphus in Hanover, where she lived in a whirl at his vice-regal Court. Appointed godmother to her brother's latest child, Princess Mary Adelaide of Cambridge, she was amused at the christening by the enormous weight of the infant's dress and the cushions which formed part of the ensemble she had to lift to the font. Elizabeth's sister Mary in England, another godmother, wrote to her elder Cambridge niece, eight-year-old Augusta, as the ceremony approached: 'You have no idea how a kind and good elder sister assists a younger one.' Augusta could save Mary Adelaide from getting into many scrapes, she suggested, and help her in her education. 'I speak from experience,' the Duchess of Gloucester wrote, 'as I once had three elder sisters, and your Aunt Eliza who was always most particularly good natured to me when a child always came forward to give me good advice.'

Elizabeth obliged her brother by holding a drawing room in Hanover, and an assembly afterwards. But as a widow, she explained, she never took off her black, except for a birthday. 'Then I wear white as my grand dress, and grey for the smaller days when colours are expected.' Abhorring idleness, she hosted a party of thirty to hear a Swede, whom her sister-in-law the Duchess of Cambridge supported, lecture on French literature. Back at Homburg she no longer sighed for London. 'All that is going on so affects my feelings that I might unintentionally sport sentiments which would be very highly improper,' she wrote, referring to the meetings of the first reformed Parliament. 'I am no politician, I hate the whole trade.' She preferred to 'watch my poor, my gardens, my cows'.

With widowhood and with the passing of years, Elizabeth made friends with the Cumberlands – her brother Ernest and his wife Frederica – who now lived in a house newly christened Royal Lodge across the way from Cambridge Cottage on Kew Green, but who still made visits to the Continent. Even so, she kept her distance, and when the Cumberlands paid her a visit in Homburg in the autumn of 1833, she hung back. 'I wish to be friendly and kind, but not to push, so I don't worry them of a morning which is better for all parties.' No such injunction governed meetings with her nephew Prince George of Cumberland, who had been born nearly blind in one eye, and had recently lost all the sight of his good eye in a most unfortunate accident. Playing with a curtain cord at a window at Royal Lodge, he had swung it and the brass weight hit him square in the eye. The thirteen-year-old was at first thought able to see 'much as usual', as Prince George's preceptor Dr Jelf told Dr Thomas Hughes, once tutor to the boy's father. But this proved to be far from the case. 'To see that lovely creature led about is not to be told – his good humour, his sweet way of expressing himself …' grieved Elizabeth. And she feared that the operation planned to restore his sight would not answer. 'The only thing is to make him forget himself,' she declared, and consoled herself with the apparent pleasure the blind young Prince took in talking and laughing with her.

Shortly after her brother George IV's death Sophia's eyes too had begun to cause her trouble. She had worn spectacles for years – and had long lost the self-consciousness that years before had made her hesitate to wear them to the theatre. But now no spectacles seemed to help, and her sisters Mary and Augusta grew concerned. Nevertheless, despite her anxiety, Sophia maintained her cheerful letters to her niece. 'Today all looks very la la,' she wrote to Victoria early in the New Year of 1832. 'Damp and dull, and does not tempt me much to go out, but I shall try, for if once in this season one is shut up, there is no end to it.' She was glad Victoria was coming home to Kensington. 'All is gay when the house is full, and I hear the sound of carriages.' When the Kents were in town, she still went, according to her niece's diary, almost every evening after dinner to their apartments, and sometimes played the piano with the Duchess.

And then the blow fell. Resigned as Sophy was to an existence impaired by nerves and spasms, and lately by deafness, the misfortune that befell her now required reserves of iron. 'The affliction with which the Almighty has thought fit to try me with ... is the total loss of my right eye,' she informed her brother Adolphus in January 1832. She woke up blind in that eye on a Monday morning, and sent for Mr Alexander, the eye surgeon, after she had continued some time in the same way. 'Pray treat me like a rational being,' she said firmly when he arrived, 'and tell me the real truth, for I assure you I am prepared for the worst.' Alexander duly informed her that it was a decided cataract come in abruptly, but he did not advise the operation of couching, or removing it, while her left eye still functioned,

Sophia was remarkably spirited in the face of this setback, and continued to ride and to play music as though nothing had happened. She even decided to learn German, recalling, for her niece Victoria's benefit, that the measles had stopped her education in that language years before. She was playing the piano a great deal, and trying some new waltzes and quadrilles – but she had to admit that what she called her 'poor blind eyes' were a 'sad drawback'.

Dolls, dogs, Mr Fozard's riding school – where Princess Sophia, the Duchess of Kent, Victoria and her governess, Baroness Lehzen, were all keen pupils – and summer holidays continued the subjects of the easy correspondence with Victoria which Sophia kept up, as the Duchess of Kent led her daughter off to ever fresh resorts and watering places. From the Isle of Wight Victoria wrote in September 1833 of her dog: 'Dash has distinguished himself several times by swimming.' And she was pleased to hear her aunt had ridden some other horses at Mr Fozard's. Avril was 'a nice quiet creature', she agreed. 'Still, you must have been very tired of riding her always.' And a further letter contained the information: 'I don't think you will know Dash when you see him, his ears are grown so long and curly.'

Princess Elizabeth in Homburg was sad not to know her niece Victoria better, or to see more of Gustav and Louise's children, but she sought out others. A young niece of Miss Swinburne, her Wiesbaden friend, was invited to visit her aunt when she was staying with the Dowager Landgravine. 'Someone knocked at the door,' she recalled later, 'which, being opened, the Landgravine, a very fat old lady dressed in black, appeared with her apron full of toys and presents for us.' Later in the day the party drove 'all through the grounds, crossing a good many little streams with rustic bridges'. They all met at a summerhouse on an island where the Princess gave them tea. 'She poured her own tea into the saucer to drink it, and, as we children laughed at this, she laughed too and said she was like an old English washerwoman.'

Elizabeth had been all this time hatching a charitable scheme, to benefit the poor of Hanover, where she now spent her winters. A young lady of the town, Miss Minna Witte, had written some German sonnets to accompany Elizabeth's 1806 series of prints, *The Power and Progress of Genius*. These plates had now been 'improved' by the Hanoverian artist Ramberg, and Princess Elizabeth herself had supplied prefatory remarks in English to each of them.

In June 1833 Elizabeth wrote in great anxiety about this production to Edward Harding, once her mother's librarian at Frogmore, who was to produce the book. There was so much to do, and she asked him to settle with Ackermann the printseller in London how many he would take. Elizabeth had an immense list of people she must send copies to, diminishing the profits – 'out of my two hundred I give fifty to the young woman who made the poetry ... she [Minna Witte] has behaved with such modesty, that I cannot say too much of her.'

'It has turned out very well,' the Landgravine was able to tell Miss Swinburne at last in the spring of 1834. And her dedication to Adolphus in the finished book read, 'It will give me the greatest pleasure if this work should turn out of use to a town I so much love, and where you and all have shown me such proofs of kindness, and, without compliment, your own manner of acting has served me as an example to throw in my widow's mite into the general Poor Box.' The publication was a success, and the school or crèche that Elizabeth envisaged was soon founded from the proceeds. Within months there were sixteen, then thirty-two pupils. It would not be renowned for its 'learning', she admitted, but would be 'of much use, for the infant children of poor women who go out to work all day; it prevents their being killed'. She referred to incidents of these unsupervised children playing in the streets and being run down by passing carriage-horses.

Mary became, quite unexpectedly, a widow in the winter of 1834. Her husband the Duke of Gloucester had been as usual keen for the shooting season to begin, and had set off the month before to meet 'a large shooting party at Sir George Stanley's in Buckinghamshire', Augusta told Ernest, while the Duchess tended her autumn garden. But he was taken ill with a fever, returned home, and – fifteen days later – died on 30 November at the age of fifty-eight. The 'family complaint' was, as usual, blamed for this latest royal death, the politician John Wilson Croker claiming that 'the immediate cause of death was the internal bursting of a scrofulous swelling in the head'. At the end, the Duke had been quiet and grave. On the morning he died, being told that Princess Victoria and her mother had asked after him, he said, as the Princess wrote in her diary on 2 December, 'Tell them that I say, God bless them, and that I love them.' According to her sister Elizabeth, the Duchess wrote that 'So fine a death was rarely witnessed ... she should feel the better for it as long as she lived.'

But it had been all so sudden, a strange end to a curious life and a difficult marriage. The Duchess of Gloucester's maid Mrs Gold said much later, 'Their marriage had not been a happy one, and she was not attached to the Duke, but she had been a most humble and obedient wife, though he plagued her much and could not bear her being of higher rank than him.' Indeed, reported her sister Elizabeth, Mary spoke of her feelings being fully alive to 'his [the Duke's] poor broken hearted sister who, she is aware, has lost her all in him'. The implication was that, while Princess Sophia Matilda of Gloucester was a broken reed, she herself was not.

Mary had her own ideas from the beginning about how to live as a widow – in London, and without the stricken Princess Sophia Matilda's companionship. Shortly after the Duke's body had been placed, where his father and mother already lay, in St George's Chapel at Windsor, she moved into his late apartments on the ground floor of Gloucester House. This was, Aunt Sophia told Princess Victoria on Christmas Day 1834, 'a good plan for herself and her friends as the high staircase is so steep [to her former top-storey apartments], but I sometimes think she may regret the gaiety of the scene from the windows above'. The Duchess showed no signs of regretting the view she had been obliged to enjoy after her husband had banished her to the top of the house – on the ground that she kept the downstairs drawing room untidy. Now, within a month of his death, she took over his quarters.

Princess Victoria paid an afternoon visit to her aunt Mary a few weeks later, on 1 February 1835, and wrote in her journal, 'She looks uncommonly well. She is in the deepest mourning and shows no hair at all from under her widow's cap.' And Sophia wrote to Victoria that summer from Bagshot, 'She does everything like her neighbours, and except keeping to her earlier dinner hour, I see no difference in health ... and strength.' Anxiety about her recovery from the Duke's death was no longer necessary, Sophia wrote drily. Comptroller Currey – newly Sir Edmund – and his wife Louise were besides on hand to comfort her.

But Elizabeth, who came to England again to cheer her widowed sister in January 1835, was gloomy. 'We are like a pack of cards,' she wrote, 'and run so near together that we all are sensible we are going down hill.' Princess Augusta had always enjoyed taking exercise, boasting once ten years before that she was 'in fine walking order' and managed three miles every day for a fortnight at Bushey – except on two days, when it rained hard. But then she was laid up for months with a stiff knee. Although she wrote to her brother Ernest robustly when she was some way to recovery, 'I have walked several times about my two rooms with my crutch and the assistance of [her dresser] Wright's arm,' from now on Augusta's exercise was limited to airings in a carriage, and, if she wanted to promenade about the Frogmore estate, she had to resort to a garden chair. The Duke of Sussex was now blind too – at least, until he got his cataracts couched, and he would not undergo the operation until after the annual meeting of the Royal Society, of which he was president. Ernest had had a throat operation in Hanover. And Sophia's health did not bear thinking about; as she approached sixty, her eyesight was now failing at great speed, although she continued, undeterred, her correspondence with her niece Victoria.

Princess Victoria's responses to Sophia from Ramsgate in the autumn of 1835 gave no hint of Sir John Conroy's attempts there while she was ill with a fever to make her promise that he should be her private secretary when she ascended the throne. But the incident turned Victoria, now aged sixteen, not only against Conroy but against her mother and against her aunt Sophia, his supporters.

Some years later, Victoria spoke of her aunt Sophia being 'quite in the power and à la merci of Sir J.C.'. Sir John Conroy's power over Sophia probably stemmed from his ability to turn away the bullying demands of Tommy Garth, as we have seen. But Sophia also found in Sir John a confidant of the kind she had always favoured, like Miss Garth and Sir Henry Halford, with whom she could weave conspiratorial melodrama without resolution. Victoria later recalled that 'Princess Sophia used to court him [Sir John] more than anyone.' The affairs of the different households at Kensington Palace and of royalty elsewhere were grist to Sophia's mill, and Conroy was an appreciative correspondent. 'Tell her how well she writes and always to write with the blackest stuff,' he instructed his son Edward. Sophia, appreciative in her turn, paid a large part of the purchase price of a Welsh estate for Sir John, and bought for him besides a family house in Vicarage Gate, off Church Lane in Kensington.

Sophia might court Sir John with the purchase of residences, but she was getting old and accident-prone, now that she saw with only one eye. Victoria wrote solemnly in her diary on 26 February 1836, 'Poor Aunt Sophia could not come to dinner as she met with a sad accident in the morning; she set her cap, handkerchief and dress on fire and came to her servants all in a blaze; most fortunately they instantly put it out and she is not much burnt; only a little on her neck and behind her ear.' But the Princess recovered and that summer, ever intellectually curious, took up Italian lessons and read *Le Favole* with a Signor Guazzi. Later she acquired a new dog, and wrote to Victoria for Dash's diet. It was very simple, her niece replied: 'A compound of potatoes broken up and with gravy mixed up, a very few little slices of meat being put at the top of all.'

Elizabeth had cheered up over the course of her long stay in England, especially when her brother-in-law, Landgrave Louis, joined her towards its end in June 1836 and was warmly welcomed by William and Adelaide. He was the King and Queen's companion in their coach, driving through 'the beautiful park of Windsor' and 'to Busche [Bushey], a country estate of the King, where he lived before, when he was Duke of Clarence', as the Landgrave's chamberlain Christian Jacobi informed his wife in Homburg. Elizabeth meanwhile had been staying with Augusta during a series of unseasonable 'cold and rainy' days, 'covered with mist and fog'. She admired her sister Augusta's management of Frogmore, where she herself had played such a part before her marriage. 'All the plants which I saw planted, and planted so many with my own hands, we are now walking under their shade,' she had written the previous summer. 'I must say that Augusta keeps it in admirable order, she has taken the farm into her own hands and it is quite lovely, and the drive round her fields is very pretty and interesting to me. She is the best of mistresses, and is adored by all around her, and with reason, for being so benevolent, so kind, so good as she is I cannot tell you – she ought to have a mine. That she certainly wants, for she impoverishes herself from all going on in good deeds.'

With regret, in July 1836 Elizabeth left her elder sister – and Sophia as well – to travel back to Homburg with Louis. But as compensation her widowed sister Mary went out to Homburg on her very first visit to the Continent. From there she wrote to the Duchess of Kent 'in high spirits'. Being out of England, Victoria's two aunts missed the occasion later that summer when King William turned on his sister-in-law the Duchess of Kent in front of a hundred guests. The normally affable King, aged seventy-one, spoke wildly against his younger brother's widow, who was sitting at his right hand. Princess Victoria burst into tears, and the Duchess abruptly ordered her carriage.

The source of the King's irritation was ostensibly that the Duchess had commandeered a suite of rooms at Kensington contrary to his express orders. But he was perhaps maddened into this unbecoming show of wrath against his sister-in-law by a very recent miscarriage that his queen, Adelaide, had suffered, defeating his hopes that a child of his own could supplant Victoria as his heir. 'The regularity of drives and of walks on alternate days, very excellent spirits and looking particularly well' – all these signs had led Augusta, correctly, to conclude that Adelaide was pregnant again in 1835. But this Clarence child did not transpire. With Victoria's approach to adulthood, it was at last allowed among those of the royal family – Augusta among them – who frowned on the pretensions of the Duchess of Kent and her brother Leopold – that, like it or not, Victoria would almost certainly succeed her uncle William.

'My aunt Gloucester was taken very ill last week with a violent nervous fever,' Princess Victoria wrote in her diary on 10 January 1837, following Mary's return to England and journey to Brighton at the New Year, 'and continues still very ill. She is quite delirious.' William and Adelaide remained at Brighton with the Duchess of Gloucester, and her sanity was feared for. However, she recovered enough to order chicken broth for nourishment in the last week of January, and indeed organize payment of her servants' wages. Shortly before her niece Victoria's eighteenth birthday, in May 1837, the Duchess was enough recovered to host a large dinner party at Gloucester House. She was 'very well dressed', her niece noted, 'and looked remarkably well, better than last year … Two men called Ganz played, one on the violin and the other on the violoncello, very well but not very amusingly.' The Princess's majority, when she turned eighteen a month later, was warmly celebrated by her relations, and Aunt Augusta 'made the honneurs' at the ball that night, as the King was unwell. Whenever she succeeded her uncle William, there would now be no call for her mother, the Duchess of Kent – whom King William detested – to play the part of regent, with her brother Leopold hovering.

Victoria's accession came unexpectedly soon. In early June 1837, William IV became seriously ill and for many days the devoted Adelaide did not stir from his bedside even so long as to change her clothes. But her nursing and the efforts of Sir Henry Halford and the King's other doctors were in vain. William Henry, Duke of Clarence, King William IV, died on 20 June. Victoria was famously called down from the bedroom she shared with her mother to hear that she was queen, and her aunt Sophia wrote to her: 'My dear Victoria, The awful day is arrived which calls you to fill the most exalted and important station in this country.'

Despite the loss of William, all the princesses – even the Landgravine in Homburg – regarded Victoria as a sacred charge, the child of their brother Edward, and their sovereign. She in turn invited all her aunts to sup and to dine with her at Buckingham Palace, which became her new home, but Sophia had to turn down the invitations. 'I really find my sight so rapidly diminishing that I am sensible of being a trouble.' Looking ahead to an operation, to remove cataracts, she wrote on 16 August, 'I therefore must look forward a few months hence to be enabled, if still wished for, to appear before you more like others.' The natural gaiety with which Sophia had written to her Kensington neighbour was much curtailed now that she was queen.

Victoria took trouble with all her aunts, although she was absorbed by public business with her accession, and thanked the Landgravine for an album she sent to her. Elizabeth was realistic – 'we are all so much older, that we cannot expect the sort of attachment we have been spoilt with', she wrote, referring to the attentions of King George and King William to their sisters. But the departure of her brother Adolphus and his family from Hanover for England in the wake of their brother Ernest's accession as king of Hanover was a cruel blow to her. Following Salic law no woman could reign in Hanover – once an electorate, since 1813 a kingdom – and the kingdoms of Great Britain and of Hanover now had to divide. While Queen Victoria moved into Buckingham Palace, King Ernest entered with pomp into the city of Hanover, and took up residence in the palace of Herrenhausen.

After Ernest had left for Hanover, Augusta visited Royal Lodge, the home he had left at Kew, and, she reported to him, 'your pretty little bitch terrier puppy rushed up to me in the most cordial manner'. Her remarks about the new Queen of England, however, were for a time not especially cordial. This was to be expected, perhaps, as she spent a good deal of the winter following her brother William's death with his widow Adelaide. Mary too mourned William – 'his most hospitable home was open at all times to us'. The changes were hard to bear, she wrote to Lady Currey in July 1837, and mentioned 'the anxiety that so youthful a Queen must occasion to all those of her relations'. Victoria had no knowledge of the world, 'poor child' – and she was unavoidably, 'poor soul, completely in the hands of the Ministers'. But soon the youthful Queen's diary records the eagerness with which the Duchess of Gloucester forged ties with her. At Windsor, the Queen made much of her aunt Gloucester, and sat on a sofa between her and her uncle the Duke of Cambridge for an entire evening. 'It is impossible to be with her (I must say),' wrote the aunt to Queen Louise – whose husband Prince Leopold had become king of the Belgians – 'though she is my niece, and not feel a particular interest about her – and she gains much on acquaintance.'

The arrival of the Cambridge family back from Hanover to live in Cambridge Cottage at Kew in the autumn of 1837 irked Victoria as much as it delighted her aunts. 'It is a great pity Augusta is so high-shouldered,' she noted of her fifteen-year-old cousin. The Duchess, meanwhile, told Queen Louise that Gussy – Princess Augusta of Cambridge – was 'an affectionate creature', and that 'the little one' – Princess Mary Adelaide – was 'quite a darling and a great pet with all of us'. Victoria agreed about 'the little one', declaring that same month after a family afternoon at Buckingham Palace that 'Minny [Mary Adelaide] was beyond everything merry and funny.'

Just as the Duchess had fêted her niece Victoria's eighteenth birthday in May, now she gave 'a sort of juvenile fête' at Gloucester House to mark her niece Mary Adelaide's fourth in November, with 'dancing dolls, jugglers, etc' to amuse the children. 'I went down and saw the children and supper, and then came away,' wrote a very adult Victoria. As her aunt Gloucester had earlier said to Queen Louise, 'Poor dear, she is very young to be brought forth into so responsible a situation.'

On 22 December Augusta poured out all her grievances, which amounted to grief, in a passionate letter to Sir William Fremantle, who had been treasurer of the royal household since 1826. 'I indeed lament the changes in the Great Park's beauty,' she told him, 'usefulness and what is more melancholy, many individuals will greatly suffer from them. But what could be expected from a poor, young creature who is completely a puppet in the hands of others, kind and amiable as I believe her really to be. She is totally ignorant, even of her own position, and she can but trust to those who are about her. She has no taste for the country – and only likes it now because she is fond of riding – consequently an additional ride made under her own eye will very naturally have charm for her.'

Augusta became more reasonable, and considered her niece's decision to spend six weeks a year at the Pavilion in Brighton, although Victoria did not like it, very proper. Her niece's attentions to Queen Adelaide had been great, she conceded, and her eagerness to have members of her family about her – whom she had seen little of before she came to the throne – evidently proceeded from a good heart. But Victoria was, in turn, not always complimentary about her aunts. Three months before her Coronation, she spoke to Lord Melbourne of 'the fuss the Princesses were in about their robes', and told him in some amusement that the Duchess of Gloucester had offered to hold the tip of her train when she was crowned, as the Duchess of Brunswick had done for Queen Charlotte.

In time for the Queen's Coronation on 28 June 1838 the 'old royal family' played out a game of 'budge'. At St James's, the Dowager Queen Adelaide left Clarence House, and Princess Augusta moved into it. Meanwhile at Kensington, Sophia had to find a new home, as the dilapidated part of the Palace where she and the Kents had resided was to be pulled down. It was shortly after she moved into her new residence, York House in Vicarage Place, close to the Conroys, that Sophia found that the sight in her good − left − eye was diminishing.

To the grief of her sisters Augusta and Mary, Sophia's sight failed completely in December 1837. The operation of which she had written with such hope to the new Queen had done no good. And by the following year she could see no light at all, except when she was out of doors. Victoria visited Sophia in February 1838 with Lady Durham. 'She tells me that day and night', the Queen wrote in her diary, 'she sees nothing but snow, and that only when she is brought very close to the light, she can distinguish shades. She bears it very patiently, but seems at times very much disheartened.' In her helpless state, Sophia found, not surprisingly, a visit to her sister at Bagshot Park later that year perilous. 'It is wonderful to me that she can be so cheerful,' wrote the Duchess of Gloucester on 30 August. 'She walks out a great deal and drives out with me ...'

Queen Victoria did not much like her aunt Augusta's answers to her private secretary Sir Benjamin Stephenson in April and July 1838 on the subject of Queen Charlotte's jewels, which Ernest now claimed for the crown of Hanover. On the eve of their wedding in 1761, her mother had often told her, her father had handed his bride 'into the room where her bridal attire was placed, and he showed her the jewels in question'. They were hers, and hers to dispose of, he told her then. And Augusta had often seen her mother look at the jewels and say they were to go to Hanover, 'in failure of a King in this country'. Princess Augusta herself wanted to know the size of Victoria's wrist, as she was ordering a bracelet for her − a gold band or gold chains just as she liked − on which was to be mounted the Duke of Kent's picture. This pleased her niece, but Victoria was startled when her composed aunt nearly caught fire − as her sister Sophie had before her − by standing too near to a candle when she was giving the Queen and the Prime Minister dinner.

The tireless Duchess of Gloucester gave a ball for Victoria on 5 July 1838 which the young Queen enjoyed – with reservations. 'The rooms are of course extremely small in comparison to those here. All the windows were taken out which made it very cool, too cool almost at last,' Victoria noted. But she did not depart till half-past three in the morning, and danced eight times, five before supper and three after. A while later the Queen recorded her displeasure with the Cambridge family, who gave her another fête: 'The house is ill adapted for a ball, and the whole was not half as well arranged or half so gay as at Gloucester House. The heat was awful, and what was dreadful, all the candles melted and covered everybody, as well as the floor, with wax. They should at least have taken the windows out.' The next day Victoria was still musing on her wrongs: the Duchess of Cambridge had not received her at the door, and was 'only coming down the staircase' when she arrived. Her aunt Gloucester, on the other hand, had very properly received her at the door, and shown her 'every possible civility'.

The Duchess of Gloucester travelled on serenely. 'I really pity the Queen,' she wrote on 13 July to Ernest, 'for she has no soul about her to tell her what she ought to do, as I really think that she is disposed to do what is right if put in the right way.' Princess Mary was sure she knew the cause of the problem: 'Unfortunately never having been brought up to live with any of us (though always kind when we meet) yet there is no intimacy ... I hope by and by when her mind is more quiet and got more used to her situation and she finds we do not push ourselves, that she may find out how sincerely and truly we are her friends.'

Elizabeth gave up wintering at Hanover now that her brother Dolly had left the city where he had been vice-regent so long, and had taken a 'pied-à-terre', as she named it, in a house on the main street in Frankfurt. She had 'neither heart, power or strength to go to Hanover', she admitted, 'my legs have been so very painful and weak, so care I must take of them'. This pied-à-terre would enable her to have her whist party 'most evenings'. And, should she want more company, the castle at Bad Homburg was often as 'full as an egg' with a great crew of relations, including Prince Wilhelm and Princess Marianne of Prussia, 'nephews and ladies'. But the company there was no longer all to her taste, as earlier it had been.

Elizabeth's relations with Gustav and Louise were no easier. 'I hope this week to accomplish seeing some of the natives,' she wrote, but she saw little of them and their children. 'One must in this world make up one's mind to contretemps,' she added staunchly. When their elder daughter Caroline married Prince Reuss, however, she roused herself to decorate the corridors and state apartments with 'Gothick screens' and evergreen branches.

The wish of her imbecile brother-in-law Prince Philip of Hesse-Homburg, who lived at Greiz in Thuringia, to marry a lowborn Frau had vexed Elizabeth, but the marriage won Landgrave Louis's acquiescence, providing it was a morganatic affair. Then Philip and his Frau came to live at the castle. It was impossible for Elizabeth to be comfortable there under such circumstances, but she promised, 'I will do all in my power to make [the new Princess] happy, for Philip's sake ... I have made all visit her – and I went the other evening to please the natives, upon the Salle being opened for the first time near the well, which is a great event, and I made her sit next to me to let them see how very well I was with her.'

The 'well' to which she referred was a project of Louis's, a spa at Bad Homburg, which Elizabeth had encouraged and helped to finance. 'All that is doing at the Source – beautiful, all done with good taste,' she wrote, 'so is all the Landgrave does.' She had prevailed on Louis not only to develop the spring or Source at Bad Homburg, but also to lay out gardens and esplanades around it, and now a Salle for refreshments. The success of the Source Elizabeth was a great pleasure to its namesake. Her portrait was hung above the entrance to the spa, and was held by everyone, she said, to be 'like, but not flattered, *tant mieux pour moi*'.

The disagreeable atmosphere in the castle receded as Elizabeth spent more and more of her time down on the promenades at the Source. 'All those that are here appear pleased with the place and the waters,' she reported with satisfaction. Elizabeth became with an effort resigned to much that might have annoyed her in her domestic circumstances. 'I say to you with truth', she insisted, 'that no one enjoys their old age more than me, and am convinced that I have been a much happier being since the spring and summer of my life are over.'

The Landgravine, no longer lachrymose, wrote from Frankfurt to Augusta Hicks, Lady Charlotte Finch's granddaughter, in the winter of 1838: 'Princes, Princesses &c [have] been worrying me with questions I cannot answer – none more than the question who will the Queen of England marry. How in the world can I tell? Who most probably will be the last to know ...' Elizabeth protested, as ever, that she had no wish to 'meddle'. But in fact, whether her aunt in Homburg knew it or not, in England Queen Victoria was weighing up the merits as a bridegroom of a certain Prince Albert of Saxe-Coburg, her first cousin.

The death of Landgrave Louis early in 1839 did much to undo Elizabeth's fragile happiness and sour her mood. Now that they had together turned Homburg into a watering place of distinction, it was for Philip and his Frau to inherit their work – and undo it, Elizabeth feared. She remarked that already the castle had begun to resemble more the unkempt building it had been on her arrival in Germany, rather than the smart home with modern comforts within medieval walls that she had made it.

Elizabeth had once before spoken of her sister Mary being much in the world. This June she thanked Sir Samuel Higgins, the Duchess's steward, for letting her know when Mary was ill. But when the Duchess was well, she added rancorously, she was 'so taken up with the world and its amusements' that she did not keep in touch anyway. The Dowager Landgravine shared with Sir Samuel, in lieu of her gadabout sister, some unusually hostile thoughts about her once beloved Homburg: 'You would be half crazy was you to see any stables but mine, so dirty so hot – so unwholesome and the carriages never brushed or cleaned. I make a great fuss to keep mine in order, but the neatness of England you never will find here – privately, there is a natural love of dirt amongst the Germans that makes me wild.' Her peevish remarks and disenchantment with German manners were born of her continuing dissatisfaction with the upstart Princess Philip's jurisdiction in the castle on which she, Elizabeth, had lavished time and money for twenty years. With every day, she told Sir Samuel in June 1839, she regretted the death of 'my excellent Louis' more.

The arrival of Queen Victoria's portrait in Homburg caused the Dowager Landgravine's stock to rise a few points in the castle. 'I sent it up to my sister[-in-law] Louise to look at,' Elizabeth wrote to her niece in thanks on 26 June, 'as she could not come down to me ... I never trouble you with letters,' she added, 'feeling you must be rejoiced not to be plagued with them from places you know nothing about.' In a letter she sent to Augusta on New Year's Eve, Elizabeth was more outspoken. It ended, 'now I am useless'.

Word came to England on 15 January 1840 that the Queen's aunt, Princess Elizabeth, the Dowager Landgravine, had died on the 10th of that month 'without any suffering' at the age of sixty-nine, in what she had recently termed her 'miserable pied-à-terre' at Frankfurt. Only her lady, Stein, and Brawn, her maid, had been with her. True to character, the members of the Hesse-Homburg family whose very residences she had embellished and part-financed for years came to visit, but, on reflecting that there was little they could do, went away again.

Drawn by black-plumed horses, an immense catafalque covered in black velvet and bearing on its top the coronet to which she was entitled as a princess of England carried her coffin from Frankfurt through a country-side lined with mourners. To the castle of Bad Homburg to which Elizabeth had come with such high expectations twenty-two years before, the procession ascended, and in the chapel there, Philip and Gustav were the chief mourners. The Anglican burial service was read at the deceased's request, before her body was committed to the Hesse-Homburg family vault.

Landgravine Elizabeth had at the last left the capital of her estate, pre-viously willed to Louis, back to England, with numerous keepsakes to her family there. The Duchess of Gloucester in England regretted that the Landgravine had not done more for Baroness de Stein, the German lady who had been with her for more than two decades, than leave her 500 flo-rins and some coral jewellery, 'instead of shawls'. But she put no faith in Elizabeth's in-laws to make amends. Landgrave Philip was in a 'deplorable' state, Mary told her brother Ernest, and Gustav and Louise, in her opin-ion, were 'interested selfish dirty minded people and have shown very little feeling either'. But to Elizabeth, her relations with her husband's family had been a sacred duty, and her jewels she duly bequeathed to her 'sister' Louise – whatever her faults – in Homburg.

19

Augusta – A Princess for All Seasons

~

IN ENGLAND, PRINCESS Augusta was 'a good deal affected' by the news of the death in Germany of her younger sister Elizabeth in January 1840. Augusta wrote to a friend, Mrs Dering, that she had known that a pain in her side had been troubling Elizabeth all the previous year. Indeed, the Landgravine had written to Augusta that she was 'like the late Earl of Huntingdon, whose knees were so bent outward that he appeared as if he was making a minuet curtsy'. But no one, Augusta wrote sorrowfully, had thought it 'a disease likely to terminate her precious life'.

Mary and Sophia could not feel as their elder sister did. From childhood and right up until Elizabeth's marriage, Augusta and this third Princess had been intimate. Royal, although an indispensable part of the elder trio of princesses, had always set herself apart a little, with her lofty temperament and her position as eldest daughter of the King. Moreover, when not together in Homburg or in England, Augusta and Elizabeth had written to each other twice a week, ever since Elizabeth first married Bluff and left for Germany in 1818.

For all her grief, Augusta was her usual rational self and, when Queen Victoria spoke of attending the State Opening of Parliament in February 1840 despite the Landgravine's death, approved her plan. 'Of course you must go, my dear,' she said, 'it is right you should do so and your duty to do so.' She added that, if Queen Victoria liked, she might say that she, Augusta, had told her she should go. Augusta was further benign in her dictum that the Queen might wear mourning for only two months, and then black gloves for six weeks. The Landgravine's brothers and sisters would, however, wear full mourning for three months. The approaching wedding of Queen Victoria and Prince Albert would of course be an exception.

Mary, with her sister Augusta, had once been eager to see their niece Charlotte 'settled'. Now they were eager to see Victoria in what they regarded as that happy state. 'In her situation it is a great object that she should be married,' Aunt Mary had written on 17 September 1839 to Queen Louise. Fortunately Queen Louise's husband (and Charlotte's former husband) Uncle Leopold had the business well in hand. And his choice had never strayed from his nephew and Victoria's cousin, Prince Albert of Saxe-Coburg-Gotha.

Victoria had pleaded three years earlier, on meeting this paragon, that she and Albert were too young to marry. Not for Victoria's eyes, but for those of her own brother Ernest, Augusta had written on 21 February 1839, regretting the influence of Prince Leopold. Victoria, she expostulated, was 'totally inexperienced and without a friend'. The match that Leopold promoted — for his nephew and niece Albert and Victoria — was born of political ambition, and she prophesied would never succeed. But when Uncle Leopold convinced Victoria otherwise in the late summer of 1839, and when Albert came over to England that October, Augusta welcomed the Coburg Prince. It was common knowledge, even before Albert and his brother arrived, that a match had been made. And Princess Mary had written in September that she was pleased that her niece had already had 'the great advantage of having had an opportunity of seeing more of him than, in general, falls to the lot of Princesses, and still less of Queens'.

Queen Victoria summoned Albert to the Blue Closet at Windsor on 15 October and proposed to him. It was an infinitely 'nervous thing' to do, she told the Duchess of Gloucester. But, as the bride was Queen of England, the formal proposal had to come from her. Moreover, the Queen told Aunt Gloucester, Albert would never have presumed to take the liberty.

The Duchess of Gloucester apparently made a favourable impression on Albert, and she was much consulted by Victoria — while Albert travelled to Coburg and Gotha in turn — in the approach to the royal wedding that was to take place in February 1840. No favours had been given at her parents' wedding, she reliably informed her niece — eighty years after an event at which she had not been present. Lord Melbourne was inclined to think she was right, for the daughters of George III brought an august, if sometimes spurious, authority to their pronouncements.

Queen Victoria was not slow to invent her own rules of etiquette. Accepting an invitation for herself and Albert — who returned to England in January — and a retinue of six to dine at Aunt Gloucester's days before their wedding, Queen Victoria declared that she was 'happy to meet anybody you choose at your table'. But the Duchess had mentioned to Albert that she intended inviting all the royal family. 'Allow me to say that, if that is to be the case,' Victoria wrote, 'I must beg that, if Albert does not lead me into dinner (which he always does here but which I conclude you would do as you did last year) he should take in the next person in rank immediately after me.' Victoria added that she felt anxious upon this point, 'and I feel certain that my uncles and aunts will make no difficulty …'. If they did, she warned, it would be almost impossible for her to meet her uncles except in her house and at her Court.

That old warhorse Ernest, King of Hanover was immediately up in arms at the idea of being cut out by Albert from his place as senior male member of the royal family. 'All letters speak of the marked incivility … as to the conduct of Her Majesty and her Court to the members of the old Royal Family,' he wrote from Hanover. 'Mark my prophecy of three years ago,' he continued, the Coburgs would insult them.

The Duchess of Gloucester had her own troubles in the months following Albert's arrival – and following her sister the Landgravine's death in Homburg. She was unwell and unable to attend Victoria's wedding on 10 February, and Princess Augusta alone of the daughters of George III was present. When Queen Victoria and Prince Albert visited Aunt Mary in April at Gloucester House, Sir Henry Halford received them at the top of the stairs and whisked them into another room to give them a report on her health. The Duchess was 'very low and excessively nervous', he said, 'having all sorts of fancies preying upon her mind, like at the beginning of her illness at Brighton'.

As a result, Albert stayed in the carriage outside while Victoria went in to see her aunt, She 'kept holding my hand and looking up into my face very sadly,' wrote Victoria. 'In her other hand she held a paper,' which she began telling Victoria about. It was all about some conversation, wrote a puzzled Victoria, between George IV and his daughter, Princess Charlotte, 'which she maintains she had been forced to write'. The Duchess of Gloucester was thinking back to those short December days in 1814 when she had extracted her niece Charlotte's troubled confidences about her mother and Captain Hesse. Victoria, knowing nothing of Princess Mary's qualms of conscience in that affair, lost interest when Halford, who knew better, reassured her that 'it was all imagination'.

Princess Mary recovered, and was fit to receive her brother the Duke of Cambridge when he visited her as usual on her birthday later that month. But Augusta stated of her sister dispassionately this year, when she herself was not well, 'She is unfortunately nervous about her health, in which she is totally unlike the rest of her family.'

Augusta was by now finally reconciled to the changes that the new reign had brought, and she was fond of Victoria in a straightforward way. When she had told her niece the previous year that her health prevented her from appearing at the Birthday Court, she said she would gladly come to the dressing room where the Queen retired after the drawing room – 'that I may make you my loyal courtesy as your subject, and maybe you will let me kiss your dear face en passant'. And she gave her niece words of encouragement, complimenting Victoria on going to Adelaide, the Queen Dowager, directly the widow returned from a voyage abroad. She was indignant when her niece was attacked in the newspapers, and wrote with delight from Frogmore on 15 July 1839 that *John Bull*, the journal, had reformed its ways: 'My poor child [Queen Victoria] has been cruelly calumniated, but yesterday she was spoken of as she ought to be.'

As she grew older, Augusta, like her brother Ernest, found change more and more repugnant. 'The railroads are doing incalculable mischief to the great roads,' she wrote, 'the innkeepers are in great distress and are obliged to sell their horses and part with their boys which is melancholy – so many turned out of employment.' Instances she had in plenty, and she named a blacksmith in Egham, 'so very expert a man that he was in constant employ; and by calculation he will now lose the shoeing of 160 horses, which will be the ruin of the poor man'. Furthermore the two 'capital' inns at Bagshot were to be given up.

'It is all detestable, I think,' Augusta had written to Ernest on 3 October 1838. Now confined to her chair, she had once been a fervent rider who knew those roads and those inns from her long courses with her father and his equerries. Turning away from what could never please her, she sent a 'very pretty book called "Chit Chat" with agreeable stories' and a magic album to little Mary Adelaide at Cambridge Cottage for her birthday. Augusta had found the bright and boisterous children of her brother Adolphus a great entertainment since the family had returned from Hanover in 1837 and, with Prince George of Cambridge, settled at Cambridge Cottage in Kew. Augusta especially liked seven-year-old Princess Mary Adelaide, whom she entranced with story-telling skills developed long ago as a child at Kew. (Princess Mary Adelaide called Augusta a 'capital Aunt' when she resumed a story that she had stopped when her niece was naughty.) The print at the top of her letter, Aunt Augusta mentioned, showed the Amphitheatre at Brighton decorated for Queen Victoria's visit to the Pavilion there. 'You may cut it off and paste it into a book,' she directed her niece.

Augusta gave her older niece Queen Victoria for her birthday in this year of her marriage 'a turquoise heart with a bit of my old grey locks,' and a blessing incorporating some words of advice for her future:

My hand shakes so I can hardly write – but as long as I can hold it, it will trace the truth from my heart of my affection for you, my beloved Victoria – May you as you increase in years, increase in domestic happiness, and comfort. Your solid and real happiness must be your home. Thank God you have a happy home. The life of a sovereign cannot be one of peace, it must be more or less chequered. But my dear father always said, 'I could not have met with such locals and disagreeables, if I had not felt that when my public duty was done – and that, I always thank God, I thought first of, what was my duty to my country and for its good, before I thought of my own feelings – I say, I then thanked God that I had a peaceable happy quiet … home to return to.' As years roll on, dearest dear Victoria, you must expect to meet with trials – for kings cannot do what they will, but what they can. And when, my dearest child, these troubles come upon you, you will have the blessing of the affection, confidence and devotion of dear Albert, which will be like balm to your soul. May God bless you, my dearest children, both together for many and many years, love your affectionate friend and aunt, Augusta.

Augusta became unwell herself at Clarence House in the summer of 1840, following Victoria's wedding. A year earlier Brighton had been thought of as a cure for her deteriorating health, and she had written from there to her niece Victoria in February 1839 that she went out – never later than a quarter to three, and always in the best chaise – 'with cloaks and an ermine tippet and a vile muff besides Welsh whittles [or blankets] round my feet and legs which is reckoned warmer than anything in the world'. But even so she was eleven days in bed with influenza, and she detailed her bizarre appearance, with 'leeches all round my throat – a brown necklace with a tailed fringe – very disgusting'. She had concluded then, 'My beautiful writing will betray me, so I may as well tell you that I am still in bed.'

Wright, Princess Augusta's dresser of long service, was with her mistress now at Clarence House. Sir Henry Halford told Lord Melbourne in June that the Princess's condition was not hopeless, but the Duchess of Gloucester was so distressed after seeing her invalid sister that she could not attend a concert. And the members of Princess Augusta's household at Frogmore received a lithograph of their mistress that she sent to them from London, but waited for her in vain, as her condition worsened in town. On 2 July 1840 the Windsor paper carried a report of 'the serious and alarming illness of the Princess Augusta'. It concluded, 'the inhabitants of this town (amongst whom Her Royal Highness has so long resided, and where her charity has been as unostentatious as her benevolence has been unbounded) … fear the worst'.

At Windsor and in its neighbourhood, Princess Augusta had been a familiar figure for years, exercising her 'unostentatious' charity and her 'unbounded' benevolence even while living at the Castle with her parents.

But when she had taken possession of the Frogmore estate, following the deaths of both parents, this Princess whose personality was always less 'marked' than that of her sisters had flourished. She relished changes that she made to the garden and the walks there. Her mother's estate, although extremely pretty with the ample white house facing the lake, with groves of trees bisected by Uvedale Price's walks, had had, as her daughter saw it, its flaws. Augusta had greatly disliked looking in winter from her favourite room in the house, past a lime tree, at 'a plain piece of grass, too large to be left unplanted and too small to be called a lawn', in her flower garden, 'just the other side of the lime tree opposite my own window'. In place of the turf, she wrote early on in her occupation of the estate, she had now made 'a beautiful new basket' so that 'when the leaves drop from the tree, I shall have a small handsome clump to look at'.

Augusta continued delighted with the 'basket' outside her window, and indeed was to sniff at one the King installed at Windsor as not nearly so nice as her own. She had planted carefully, she told a correspondent, so that there was a 'profusion of flowers' throughout the year. And the contented mistress of Frogmore laid down her pen in favour of communing with the spirits of the place. 'I am now going to take my walk.'

Several visitors to Frogmore commented that the water in front of the house was an eyesore, and a touring German prince, Hermann von Pückler-Muskau, wrote that it was 'now only a swamp for frogs, though surrounded by hedges of rose and yew'. John Claudius Loudon, the influential editor of a new publication, the *Gardener's Magazine*, gave his opinion of Augusta's beloved Frogmore as 'a remarkably dull place'. He did admit that the walled kitchen gardens, where strawberries and melons were successfully grown, were fruitful, and he approved her gardener Mr Thomas Ingram's wiring of walls and grafting of geraniums and passion flowers. But, recalling the landscaping of the garden when originally planted in the 1790s and 'rendered interesting by a very long, winding piece of water' and by 'extensive planting', Loudon was disapproving of Augusta's stewardship of the garden. 'The trees and shrubs seem now to occupy the greater part of the surface, and the water being very extensive, stagnant, and not very free from aquatic plants, the situation appears to us as unhealthy a one as could well be chosen for a residence,' he wrote. 'The shrubbery is too old to have the freshness of youth, the shrubs in general too common to have the beauty of variety.' In other words, Frogmore — for all Augusta's 'baskets', it had not changed substantially since first laid out by Queen Charlotte and Major William Price in the 1790s — was old fashioned and even overgrown, just what Loudon did not like, and just what Augusta did. 'It is not tidy from the falling of leaves and that discomposes me sadly,' she acknowledged one autumn to Miss Garth. But, as she said, her gardener would shortly dig in the leaves and it would look better.

With their own hands she and her sisters had planted some of the original seedlings which were now large and vigorous bushes, 'Memory is a blessed delight,' she wrote, although she admitted that 'at times it tortures the feelings sadly'. Frogmore in every season, whatever Prince Pückler-Muskau's or Mr Loudon's strictures, was enchanting to Augusta. She loved it, whether the 'early trees' were losing leaves, and the garden bore 'a wintry appearance' or when, 'from the beauty of the verdure', it was uncommonly summer-looking.

Mary at Bagshot got off more lightly when that stern horticultural critic Mr Loudon visited the Bagshot Park grounds on behalf of the readers of the *Gardener's Magazine*. Through a rustic gate, he told them, close to the Duke and Duchess's house, an arbour trellis gave on to a rosary or rose garden, a showy herbaceous garden and an 'American garden on turf' that the Duchess had laid out and planted. Loudon approved what he saw at Bagshot, and he returned there several times, although he regretted that the Duchess's gardener Mr Toward was not better housed. He kindly included on his first visit a diagram for his readers showing all the features of Mary's flower garden, and on his second particularly admired the American garden, 'in which the tufted masses of peat-earth shrubs, magnolias, rhododendrons, andromedas, azaleas, kalmias, ericas, etc., looked admirably'.

With Edmund Currey and Mr Toward, Mary had undoubtedly created something quite special at Bagshot. Visitors began to come, asking to see the pleasure ground, and on one occasion a dropsical Mary deputed her sister Augusta to escort them where the little garden chair in which she tooled around the paths could not reach. Augusta appears to have borne her sister no malice for her better 'review' from Mr Loudon, but she seems also to have been undaunted by criticism in her love of her 'swamp' at Frogmore.

As a hostess at Frogmore as well as in London, Augusta was always generous with her invitations. One year she implored her friends, the Arrans, to visit her come spring. 'I can promise you that the house is as warm as toast. Your rooms shall be to the south and you shall do everything you please from morning till night,' sang the siren. But she was content to be alone, whatever the weather. In the wake of a downpour, she toured Windsor in an open carriage, watched the Eton boys play cricket on the playing fields, and observed the Thames crowded with pleasure boats, before she walked in the garden at Frogmore. 'Everything looks clean and refreshed by the rain,' she remarked, 'and the Thames has recovered its beauty, for it was quite dull and low ... The Castle is looking magnificent just now from my own little sanctum.'

Mary stayed with Augusta a good deal, especially when invalid. Miss Garth often stayed with her before Christmas on her way to her brother and his family in Surrey. Her uncle General Thomas Garth kept up ties of friendship with Augusta till his death, sending her once a 'magnificent present of game' for which she begged Miss Garth to thank her uncle. If he would 'now and then be so good as to use his gun for me', Augusta wrote, she would be very much obliged to him.

Miss Peggy Planta, Augusta's old English teacher, stayed at Frogmore with her former pupil, and passed her mornings at Windsor, seeing her old acquaintances there – of which there were many, following her long years in harness to the royal family. Old acquaintances, old stories and old jokes going back thirty years and more provided a comfortable diet for Augusta at Frogmore. Mary 'laughed ready to choke herself' on one occasion, Augusta reported, when the Duchess and Miss Garth were both staying with her. Augusta had remarked on the death of an old Windsor acquaintance, Mrs Coleman, whom General Gouldsworthy had used to call 'cross-patch' and 'grumpibus' when they were young, and Miss Garth in answer had declared herself surprised that the death had been announced 'in one paper' only. Did they think, Mary asked, that it should have been announced to the public 'by the common crier, or ... proclaimed like a general peace by the heralds with Sir Bland Burges at their head?'

Such innocent diversions at Frogmore were at an end now. Three days after the Windsor paper had reported its alarm at Princess Augusta's illness in London in the summer of 1840, Queen Victoria ordered the park keepers to keep the gates of Green Park closed day and night, so that the traffic would not disturb Princess Augusta. Her death was now expected, but, as Halford wrote on 21 July to Lord Melbourne, the elderly Princess's strong constitution made it impossible to forecast its date. When Leopold, King of the Belgians, and his wife Louise visited England in August, the Princess was still in this world. Halford spoke at the end of the month to Lord Melbourne again of the Princess's 'natural powers of constitution'. And Queen Victoria, down at Windsor, on the same day despatched a messenger 'by the railroad' to London to establish the latest information.

Prince Albert had declined to remain at the Mansion House for the great dinner being given to celebrate his receiving the Freedom of the City that day. Queen Victoria held that he could not appear 'when our poor aunt is dying'. The Duke of Cambridge, however, did attend the dinner and said robustly that if he, as the Princess's brother, felt able to celebrate Prince Albert's Freedom, there was no reason why the Prince himself should hang back. Unfortunately, it became clear that the banqueters, deprived of the spectacle of the Coburg bridegroom, were in a sullen mood, and one or two even turned over their plates in reproach to their hosts. Whereupon the Duke of Cambridge rose, and made a woolly-headed attempt to placate the angry tables with references to Prince Albert's recent marriage and to the charms of Queen Victoria at Windsor. This speech did nothing to endear him to his niece, who was outraged – at six months pregnant – to be the subject of such immodest talk. And still Augusta bore up and manifested 'a consciousness of what is passing when she is awake', wrote Halford in September.

Leopold and Louise departed England early that month, and still Augusta struggled on. 'Fixed mischief in the tract of the intestine' threatened daily to end her life, but manfully she took 'liquid nourishment', digested it and lived, as Halford told Melbourne on 16 September. Her niece Victoria wrote, with a hint of irritation: 'Under the circumstances I can't well walk in public this afternoon.'

But now Augusta was in dreadful pain. Moore, the royal apothecary, was at Clarence House all day – and he stayed the night, too, so as to administer the opiates and other drugs he had brought. Prince Albert went up by train to see the Princess, and she was unconscious. The Duke of Sussex, looking ahead now, said that when his sister died word must be sent immediately to the King of Hanover. Ernest would take it ill if he did not hear 'directly', and Queen Victoria passed the comment to Melbourne on 21 September.

The Queen told her uncle Leopold, 'Almost the last thing she said, when she was still conscious, the day before she died, was to Mr Moore (the apothecary), who wrote me every morning a report: "Have you written to my darling?" Is this not touching?' Victoria was overcome, when she received that report, and told Lord Melbourne on 22 September, 'It is wonderful that she even struggles so long.' But she had heard from Sir Henry that afternoon that her aunt could not live more than a few hours, 'and that probably before the evening closed in, all would be over'. Victoria wrote in her diary that she talked over that evening after dinner with 'Lord M' her aunt's 'dying condition, her having no will, and uncle Sussex likely to mix himself up in everything'.

At Clarence House in London, meanwhile, and oblivious of such worldly considerations, Princess Augusta Sophia of England had died at twenty past nine that evening. Her sister-in-law and friend Queen Adelaide held her hands while her sisters Mary and Sophia and her brother Adolphus looked on. And then the Queen Dowager closed the dead Princess's eyes.

Augusta, as a child and later, had greatly valued her family and had delighted in her hours with them at the Queen's House, at Kew and at Windsor. But at Frogmore and in her London homes after her parents' deaths she had also been able to enjoy the hours alone without which, as she had said as a young girl, she was not fit for company. Her faith, her duties and works in the parish, and her attentions to the brothers and sisters she 'doted on' kept her busy. For recreation she had gardening, walking in the grounds she laid out, and in the evening playing duets with Lady Mary Taylor while the shadows thickened over the lake. In many ways Princess Augusta's life recalls that of the medieval English gentlewoman, her private passions — for General Spencer and perhaps others — occluded from view. But her lively wit and sense of the ridiculous moor her firmly in the Georgian age, where for some, this reserved Princess was, as King Leopold wrote from Wiesbaden on 1 October 1840, 'certainly the best of the whole family'. Joining those members of her family whom she had most loved, her father, her mother, her brothers George IV and William IV, and her sister Princess Amelia, she was buried in the vault under St George's Chapel at Windsor.

20

Sophia – The Little Gypsy

~

NOT LONG AFTER the accession of her niece Victoria, Princess Sophia lost the sight in her good eye, and became blind, as we have seen. Augusta wrote sadly, shortly before her death in September 1840, that her sister's mind was now made up 'never to be any better'. She found it painful to 'witness the poor dear, who used to be so often and so well employed, reduced now only to open [that is, cut the pages of] books and tear up paper for couch-pillows'. (Sophia had apparently heard that hospital patients found pillows stuffed with paper comforting.) When Princess Sophia attended her sister's deathbed, she could see neither her sister nor the other mourners.

A metal mesh firescreen that Sophia had once embroidered stood before the fireplace in her house in Vicarage Place, Kensington and bore a large S within a wreath of pink roses and purple and yellow pansies. The days at Windsor when Sophia had taken pleasure in this 'work', the days at Kensington Palace when she had embroidered dresses for her neighbour and niece Victoria, were over. Now she tore her paper or wound silk, while a series of readers came to read to her at Kensington for an hour each in English, French, German or Italian, The Princess would not allow them to read longer – 'the fatigue would … be too great for them'. And, easily irritated, she refused to have a lady-in-waiting live with her, but relied on her dresser, Mrs Cochrane, for help. 'Not being able to see,' she confided to Amelia Murray, 'she should always fancy the lady sitting opposite her, looking wearied.'

Sophia had a life that would have made anyone 'sink', as she did occasionally. 'In addition to her blindness she was in some degree deaf,' wrote Amelia Murray, 'and could not move from her seat without being carried; yet still she was as patient and uncomplaining as ever.' The artist Sir William Ross drew Princess Sophia at the task of carding wool, and she looks the picture of composure, with braided loops of hair, under a ribboned cap, and with sleeves massy with lace. The older woman yet has, about her smile and cast-down blind eyes, something of the elusive 'gypsy'

380

quality that Lord Melbourne had detected in Princess Sophia when he and she were young.

However, Sophia did not withdraw from family life, despite her infirmities. On either side of her chair at York House hung two chequered beadwork bags, bordered and tasselled, of maroon and lemon, that she had once ornamented. The one held family letters recently received, the other those ready for despatch. (Those that arrived were read to her, but enough virtually indecipherable letters from these years survive to show that Sophia continued to write at least some of her correspondence herself.) Though she could not see, she could feel the trinkets and bibelots that all her family exchanged and amassed through legacy on tables all around her and within her reach.

Sophia's intimacy with her niece Victoria had ended for good and all when the Queen moved out of Kensington Palace and into Buckingham Palace. Moreover, Queen Victoria gave birth months after her aunt Augusta's death to her first child — another Victoria and a princess royal to succeed her aunt Württemberg. 'I am very proud of her eyes, they are so large, and so dark blue; her hair is light brown; and her complexion too with pink cheeks is very pretty,' wrote the Queen to Uncle Leopold on 22 December 1840. From now on, the Queen would be absorbed in her own family, and less curious about and considerate of the earlier generation — except for dear Aunt Mary, who took such a keen interest in Victoria and Albert and in their domestic circumstances. But the Queen still corresponded with her aunt Sophia and, as her family grew, brought them on visits to York House, Sophia's home in Vicarage Place that had previously been the residence of the clerk of the works at Kensington Palace.

The Duchess of Gloucester, with her enormous social appetite, was Sophia's saviour in some ways. Brooking no argument, she carried off the crumpled heap that was her sister on carriage drives around Hyde Park. Augusta's death had left Mary bereft of a sister with whom she had for twenty years exchanged visits down at Bagshot and Frogmore, a companion at the yearly round of Court events, a friend with whom she could exchange frank remarks on the subject of their vast and vexing array of relations. The Duchess of Gloucester now visited Sophia in her seclusion all the more devotedly for the want of their elder sister.

The Duke of Cambridge was an affectionate brother too in whose company Sophia rejoiced, and his children had been trained to love Aunt Sophia, although Prince George of Cambridge later recalled her as a 'shrivelled old lady'. In addition, the Duke of Cambridge, like his sister Mary Adelaide, was extremely charitable, and no church, hospital or Bible society asked in vain for his presence on a committee. Philanthropy was life's blood to his wife, the Duchess of Cambridge, and to the other ladies of the 'old Royal Family', too. It was said that, as Queen Dowager, William IV's widow Adelaide spent £20,000 a year on charities benefiting children. And for the Duchess of Kent, religion and education were her watchwords, as patron of the Servants' Society and of the Kent Dispensary, named after her deceased husband. When she moved into Frogmore, following Princess Augusta's death, she took over many of her sister-in-law's pet charities at Windsor.

In town Sophia, Mary and their sisters-in-law were all successfully courted by Charles Blomfield, the energetic Bishop of London, with sermons of his own printed for the royal ladies' delectation and with offers of visits and acceptances of dinners with his wife at their homes. They happily subscribed to his programme of building churches in outlying parts of the metropolis, and supported his work in colonial bishoprics. Indeed, with his encouragement Queen Adelaide gave large sums for the establishment of an Anglican church in Malta.

Just as her interest in Queen Victoria as a child had helped Sophia to shrug off despond in the 1820s, so the Cambridge children now – George, Augusta and Mary Adelaide – were important diversions for her. In many ways the healthy appetites and boisterous spirits of the three children recreated those of their father and his siblings in youth at Kew and Windsor, and Dolly and Mary themselves – though not Sophia – continued in their seventies to display those characteristics. 'There is such heartiness and seemingly endless good temper about all the Royal family, to judge from manner and look,' wrote Lady Lyttelton when a fellow guest with the Duke of Cambridge at Bagshot. Prince George of Cambridge and his sisters inherited from their father, besides, principles of benevolence which were to lead the youngest, Princess Mary Adelaide, into a positive addiction to charitable work. No bazaar was to be free of her. Others might question Adolphus's intellect, as when he joined in unexpectedly and disastrously with professional singers at a musical evening and then applauded himself. Victoria found fault with her uncle's extreme deafness, and others with his yellow wig. But Princess Sophia felt only warmth for the family who came so regularly and uncomplainingly to see her at York House.

The rest of her family visited her, too – the Duke of Sussex and Lady Cecilia Buggin, the widow whom he had married on Lady Augusta Murray's death in 1830 and whom Queen Victoria, on coming to the throne, had created Duchess of Inverness. Uncle Sussex took Victoria's part against his brother Ernest in a matter of royal precedence, and this elevation of his wife – the second whom he had married without reference to the Royal Marriages Act – was by way of a reward. Characteristically, there was an exact value placed on the Duchess of Inverness's honours. She was never to be seated at the royal table for dinner, and was to approach it only after the most junior of other duchesses had advanced. But at the words, 'His Grace the Duke of Sussex and Her Grace the Duchess of Inverness', the couple could enter shambling and smiling into a reception or ball. And together the elderly Graces visited Sophia.

In April 1843, only three years after his Cecilia was made a duchess, the Duke of Sussex died, from that old-established family complaint, erysipelas. Most unusually he was buried in a granite sarcophagus in the new public cemetery of Kensal Green, north of Paddington. Incompetent arrangements for his brother William's interment in St George's Chapel at Windsor in 1837 had upset the Duke, it was said. But that had not stopped their sister Princess Augusta being buried in that chapel very decorously, three years later. The more romantic truth was that he wished Lady Cecilia to be laid at his side when she died, and so he arranged for the huge grey tomb in the public plot at Kensal Green to be his resting place.

News of other family matters was brought to Sophia in her Kensington home. There was the birth of another great-niece – Victoria and Albert's second daughter Alice – in April 1843, four days after her brother Sussex's death. And in July of that year her niece Gussy – Princess Augusta of Cambridge – departed to make a home in Germany following her marriage to Friedrich, Hereditary Prince of Mecklenburg-Strelitz. At Gussy's wedding at Buckingham Palace, Ernest, King of Hanover, as the male head of the English royal family, rather than her father, gave the bride away. Over seventy now, bent and 'grown very old and excessively thin', he was still combative, and tried to stop Prince Albert taking precedence over him when it came to signing the marriage register. But the Queen defeated her uncle, who was poised to take the pen from her fingers after she had signed. She 'nipped round the table like lightning, had the register passed across to her, signed and gave the pen to the Prince before the King of Hanover knew what was happening'.

A year later, the expected death of Prince Albert's father, Duke Ernest of Coburg, led Princess Mary to ruminate: 'This Court mourning coming just as one season begins and when all our shops are full of their new fashions does not please the trades people.' The death of her sister-in-law Princess Sophia Matilda struck deeper, reviving memories of Mary's childhood as much as of her marriage to the deceased Princess's brother. From the age of twelve, she wrote, Sophia Matilda had been 'a warm and kind friend', and ever 'the same towards me'. It was a blank that would not easily be filled up, she wrote, and the loss would be greatly felt at Blackheath, where, like a medieval saint, Princess Sophia Matilda has done 'much good to the poor and passed her retired life in acts of charity'. Mary had forgotten those days when Sophia Matilda, as her sister-in-law, had been that 'meddling fussy sister'. Unfortunately, Sophia Matilda's 'anxiety to save pain', the Duchess wrote, had made her order those about her to give no alarm when she fell ill. As a result, there was no family with her when she died, and the news came upon all of them 'like a thunderbolt'.

The Duchess of Gloucester was always content when with Victoria and Albert and their children. She watched 'Puss' – Princess Vicky – play as a toddler in the Grand Corridor at Windsor when she stayed there one November, and was delighted when her great-niece and her great-nephew Bertie were brought down to luncheon. Bertie, Prince of Wales, received a letter from his great-aunt four years later, thanking him for the pretty drawing he had made for her birthday. She told the five-year-old she had just seen his grandmama, the Duchess of Kent. 'I fear in this cold weather you will not have found your garden much advanced as to flowers,' she said, 'and that the east wind will make it very cold by the seaside.' The Queen had taken her growing family to holiday on the Isle of Wight, which had remained a favourite spot from her childhood – even though her first acquaintance with it had come through her bête noire, Sir John Conroy.

Meanwhile the Duchess summered at her new country retreat, White Lodge in Richmond Park. Having previously demurred at moving from Bagshot, she took up residence in this new home after Lord Sidmouth, the old premier and its previous inhabitant, died in 1843. Her sister Sophia's increasingly weak condition made Mary reluctant to be out of easy reach of her at Bagshot. White Lodge was a charming solution. The Duchess established all her furniture and pictures there, and soon the Lodge was redolent of comfortable chairs and feminine charm.

Queen Victoria took her five-year-old daughter Vicky with her on a visit to her aunt Sophia one January day after luncheon in 1846. They found 'a sad sufferer and a complete cripple, unable to move, and quite blind', as the Queen recorded afterwards in her diary. 'In spite of it all,' she marvelled, 'she is quite cheerful. She was much pleased at my bringing Vicky who was very civil and good.' Six months later, however, after another visit the Queen was less sanguine. Sophia was 'in a very sad state', she wrote in her diary, and she felt 'the greatest pity for her ... her existence is dreadful and she bears it so admirably, without ever complaining.'

Eighteen months later in January 1848 there came a change. At seventy years old Sophia was suddenly, as the Duke of Cambridge reported to Queen Victoria, 'in a very precarious state and, I fear, sinking ... she seems herself not to wish to live on'. Queen Victoria drove to see her aunt on Valentine's Day, and found her 'much altered. She is nearly bent double, and very much wasted, and her voice is very feeble.'

In the midst of anxiety about Aunt Sophia, Victoria and Albert had cause for concern about the Queen's other aunt, the Duchess of Gloucester. Aunt Mary was 'again in one of her nervous states', wrote her niece Victoria to Uncle Leopold in May 1848, 'and gave us a dreadful fright at the christening [of Victoria and Prince Albert's latest daughter, Princess Louise] by quite forgetting where she was and ... kneeling at my feet in the middle of the service. Imagine our horror.' Leopold's reply was swift: 'You must have been terrified by the poor Duchess of Gloucester.' And he added quite untruly, 'There is a little madness in her case.' But Victoria believed everything that Leopold said about the 'old Royal Family', of which he had so briefly been part – and with whom he had fought over Charlotte's memory.

In fact, the elderly Duchess had been much affected by having to give her opinion, as her sister Augusta had years earlier, in a case that rumbled on. Should Victoria or Ernest in Hanover inherit Queen Charlotte's jewels? Plumping, like Augusta before her, for Ernest, Mary still felt all the weight of her niece's disapproval at her answer, and it had preyed on her mind. Soon she was to be further disturbed in her old age, for, one after- noon in May 1848, the Duchess's remaining sister Princess Sophia died quite dramatically for one so weak.

'It was terribly sudden and melancholy in the midst of such rejoicing,' Queen Victoria wrote in her journal. She and Albert had held a very suc- cessful drawing room that day at St James's – Mary was not there, 'Aunt Sophia not being so well'. When it was over, Prince Albert decided to ride down to Kensington and enquire at York House after the invalid's health. Meanwhile, Queen Victoria took a drive around the Park to get some air with her younger children, Princess Alice and Prince 'Affie' or Alfred. She had just returned and was in the garden of Buckingham Palace when Albert's equerry, Captain Gardiner, came running in. Victoria was terrified that some harm had come to Albert. But the Captain explained – to her 'utter astonishment', as the Queen wrote in her journal – that Albert had sent him from Kensington with word that 'poor Aunt Sophia had just expired'. The Prince himself had gone at once to Aunt Gloucester.

At Gloucester House the Duchess, who was calm and composed, revealed that, after seeing her sister at Kensington that afternoon, she had told the rest of the family who were gathered there of Sophia's mortal danger, but she had begged them not to send word to Victoria, as the drawing room should not be put off. The Duchess had then gone home, and, by the time she returned to York House at about six, Princess Sophia had 'passed away almost imperceptibly' – with her hand in that of her sister-in-law, the Duchess of Cambridge. Mary reported that Sophia looked in death at last 'most placid'.

Sophia's had not been a life to remember with pleasure, or one that anyone could have wished prolonged. 'She was blind, helpless and suffered martyrdom; a very clever, well-informed woman but [one] who never lived in the world,' was the diarist Charles Greville's cold assessment. But she had been much loved by the few to whom she had allowed a degree of friendship. The Duchess of Kent, who went to her daughter Queen Victoria after dinner that evening, was 'much shocked' by the news, 'having been very intimate', Victoria wrote, 'with poor Aunt Sophia, for, when we lived at Kensington, we saw her almost daily and she was always very kind and amiable'. There was immense curiosity in the family about Sophia's financial affairs and about her directions for burial. The Duchesses of Gloucester and Cambridge searched at Sophia's house in Kensington, as Queen Victoria noted in her journal, for 'any will or papers, directing what was to be done'. Finding nothing, and knowing that Sir John Conroy 'had done everything' for the Princess, reluctantly they thought it best to send for him. He reported, as Queen Victoria put it, that everything was in 'the greatest order', but confirmed that there was no will, 'though he had several times expressed the wish [for her] to make one'. (Princess Augusta too had died intestate, but her sister Sophia should have had more to leave. With every death of the royal sisters who lived in England, the Parliamentary sum that the remaining princesses received – and that had been allotted them for division as far back as 1812 – grew larger.) Princess Sophia had always answered that 'she knew her brother and sister Dolly and Minny would do all that was right'. To the surprise – and disappointment – of the royal family, it emerged that Sophia had left practically nothing. She had expended all that she had had, at different times, on Sir John Conroy, on the purchase of his residences and on the maintenance of his family in a superior style, and on her charities.

Members of the royal family, following Sophia's death, visited her corpse at Vicarage Place, where it had been laid out by her dresser Mrs Cochrane. Although the Princess had left no will, she had, as it turned out, left clear instructions about where that corpse should be buried. Two days after her death her banker Mr Drummond brought to Queen Victoria a letter dated 11 March of that year, in which Sophia expressed the wish to be buried 'on the south side of the cemetery of Kensal Green', close to where her brother Augustus was buried, and her funeral 'to be as private as possible'.

Where her brother Augustus had been buried earlier and where his widow the Duchess of Inverness was to be laid in due course, Princess Sophia's coffin was put to rest on 6 June 1848 — for the moment, within the cemetery vault. (Prince Albert's artistic adviser, Professor Ludwig Grüner of Dresden, had been given the task of designing a casket tomb to stand on the plot opposite that of the Duke of Sussex, long Sophia's fellow inmate at Kensington Palace.) The Duke of Cambridge was much affected, and all Sophia's ladies attended the interment, but, as Sophia had wished, and as Queen Victoria recorded in her journal, 'There were only mourning coaches, no royal ones.'

A year later, the Princess's tomb was ready, and Princess Sophia's remains were duly transferred to 'grave plot number 8028', and to Grüner's wreathed and swagged quattrocento sarcophagus. Carved of Carrara marble by the eminent Signor Bardi, with lions' paws for legs and bearing the name Sophia, this elegant casket perched atop a high stone podium made by Edward Pearce. On one panel of the podium ran the fitting legend, 'Come unto me all ye that labour and are heavy laden and I will give you rest.' Sophia's royal relations, while following her instructions for a private funeral, had ensured that her burial place would always attract attention. For while, across the way, her brother Augustus's sarcophagus was, if massive, plain, Sophia's ornate casket tomb was, in the public cemetery, highly noticeable, being surmounted by a large coronet.

As for the last remaining daughter of George III, the Duchess of Gloucester's dresser Mrs Gold said she 'never thought of being, or wished to be, buried anywhere but at Windsor and ... was much shocked at her brother, the Duke of Sussex, and her sister being buried at Kensal Green, remarking at the time, "They shall not carry me there."' Accordingly the Duchess of Gloucester set down immediately after Princess Sophia's death the directions for her own interment at Windsor, whenever it should occur.

There were those who thought that Sophia chose Kensal Green as a burial place where her son Tommy Garth might one day also lie, but she left no such instructions. It seems likely that the idea would have been repugnant in the extreme to Sophia, but Tommy Garth himself may have believed that this wish directed her choice of burial ground. He certainly expected to inherit a fortune on her death, as he later told George, Duke of Cambridge – and he swore it was George's own father, Adolphus, who had told him so immediately after Sophia's death. But of course there was nothing.

Shortly after his passage of arms with Sir Herbert Taylor in 1829, Tommy Garth, failing to fend off creditors any longer, had taken up residence in the King's Bench debtors' prison in south London. He remained there five years – years during which his lover Georgiana Astley stayed close by and gave birth to his daughter, Georgiana Rosamund Garth. Adding further melodrama to a story already overladen with it, Lady Astley died in childbirth. And her daughter, whom we must assume to have been Sophia's granddaughter, although she was baptized confusingly after her mother's death as the daughter of Sir Jacob and Lady Astley, was reared in the neighbourhood of the King's Bench, while her father Tommy Garth lingered inside. Appeals to Sir Herbert from prison eventually brought Garth in 1834 a lump sum of £10,000 to effect his release and establishment, and when he emerged from jail he took his young daughter to live with him.

Princess Sophia's death in 1848 and the disappointment of his hopes that he was the heir to a fortune came at a moment when Tommy Garth's lump sum of £10,000 from Sir Herbert had dwindled to nothing. Repeated appeals to the royal purse secured, as the scandal faded, a less generous settlement, a pension of £300 a year. When, following her father's death in 1875, Georgiana Garth made claims of her own to the royal family for assistance, she failed entirely in her attempts. If Tommy Garth's life had been blighted from birth by the mystery of his parentage, Georgiana Rosamund was doubly cursed. She never married, apparently feeling that the scandal of her birth and its circumstances made such an enterprise impossible. In this she echoed her grandmother Sophia's own sentiments from years before.

21

Mary – Last of the Line

~

FOLLOWING SOPHIA'S DEATH in May 1848, Victoria and Albert were tender in their care of the Duchess of Gloucester. Seaside air, they decided, would help to ease her suffering. That July she was invited to Osborne, their new house on the Isle of Wight, to 'walk around by the sea' and to play with her great-nephews and nieces. Uncle Cambridge, as a great concession, was invited too, and the brother and sister planted trees at their niece's request, then sat under their shade. 'Aunt Gloucester is a most kind, amiable old lady and very sensible,' was Victoria's judgement.

With Princess Sophia's death the Duchess of Gloucester and her brother the Duke of Cambridge were released from their dutiful daily attendance at York House in Kensington, just as their sister was released from her circumscribed life. But the loss for the Duchess was frightful, and her sister's death no blessing. Sophia had been to her a cherished companion, the sister nearest in age, the last of the sisterhood whose memories were long and active. A year later, back at Osborne, Mary 'talked with grief of Aunt Sophia and many things which had distressed her'. The Queen took her aunt for a drive after lunch to distract her, and a beach expedition the next day with the Prince of Wales, the Princess Royal, Princess Alice and Affie was still more successful. They floated about on two barges until eight in the evening.

That same year, 1849, the Duchess went with her brother Cambridge and his family to the Isle of Anglesey, when he was ordered there for his health, and they mourned together the death of their pious sister-in-law Adelaide, the Queen Dowager. But neither the Duchess nor the Cambridge household at Kew suspected that they were soon to be dealt a far worse blow. In July 1850 'dear Dolly' was taken fatally ill at his London home, Cambridge House in South Audley Street, and an express was sent to Mecklenburg-Strelitz to urge his daughter Gussy to leave for England at once if she wished to see him alive.

The Hereditary Princess, accompanied by her young son, named Adolphus after her father, arrived in London hours too late. Earlier that evening at Cambridge House her aunt Mary had been sitting with the Duchess of Cambridge when a servant entered to summon the latter 'instantly' to the dying Duke's side, and that Duchess entered the room where her husband lay, 'only to hear the last gasp'. The Duchess of Gloucester, Mary Adelaide and Prince George, now Duke of Cambridge, and all the Cambridges' servants besides, then joined the newly widowed Duchess and knelt to pray with her round the bed.

'His dear face looks just as if he was in a happy sleep,' wrote the Duchess of Gloucester to her 'sister', the Duchess of Kent, after viewing her brother Adolphus's corpse the following day. He deserved his rest, she added, 'after a life spent in charities and good deeds'. The Duke, Queen Victoria echoed her aunt, had been 'charitable and popular, and even his peculiarities' – like his bright yellow wig – were well liked. Aunt Gloucester was calm, Victoria recorded, though, while the Duke of Cambridge had been alive, 'not a day [had] passed without his writing to her, or, if he was in London or at Kew, going to see her'. Now, of all the brothers and sisters on whom, throughout a long life, Princess Mary had lavished affection, only Ernest, the widowed old King of Hanover, still resisting change and even revolution in northern Germany, remained. But he never visited England now, for, when not absorbed in Hanoverian matters of state, he was reluctant to leave his young grandson Ernst – blind Crown Prince George's son – on whom he doted.

Mary of Gloucester spent the morning of Dolly's funeral at home in London with her niece Queen Victoria, who had volunteered to keep her company, while the Cambridge ladies attended the Duke's funeral at the church on Kew Green. The Duke of Wellington disapproved of their being at the funeral – it was against all royal etiquette – and thought they would have been better off at Gloucester House.

There, the Duchess of Gloucester, her niece the Queen and all the servants huddled into the dining room where Mr Nepean, the chaplain, 'read prayers and parts of the burial service', and gave an address. Afterwards Mary and Queen Victoria sat upstairs, and the Duchess gave her niece a beautiful diamond bracelet that Queen Adelaide had only the year before left her in her will. In sombre mood the Duchess said she would prefer to give, 'rather than bequeath', it to Victoria.

Now that her brothers and sisters – all but Ernest – were dead, the Duchess of Gloucester confided to Victoria stories of the Courts of George III and of George IV which she said she had never till now revealed to anyone. 'She talked much of former times,' Queen Victoria recorded later that year, 'and the very painful quarrel between the Duke of

Gloucester and George IV about the late Queen Caroline, whom the Duke defended. My aunt could in consequence not go to Court for a long time, as she naturally did not wish to go alone, and could not do so with her husband, exposed to see him insulted.'

The Duchess of Gloucester was encouraged to reminisce further over the next years. And she happily criticized with her niece Victoria the 'strange, rather over-lively and undistinguished manners' of Augusta d'Este, the daughter of her brother Sussex by Lady Augusta Murray who was now Lady Truro, wife of the Lord Chancellor, and very handsome. With Princess Mary Adelaide of Cambridge, now in her twenties, the Duchess shared a memory from sixty years before of her first bathe in the sea at Weymouth. Her bathing dress was a 'regular one' made for the occasion, she recalled, which 'no floating about deranged'. The Duchess wrote, 'If the world had been looking on, they would have seen me as well dressed as at a drawing room.'

Energetic — and lonely — in her old age, the Duchess of Gloucester thanked Mary Adelaide for her share, on a visit she made to the Cambridge ladies at Plas Newydd, on the Isle of Anglesey, the summer after the Duke died, 'in making me laugh of an evening. I am sure for years I had not laughed as I did the evening you brought up the Address from Bangor ...' She said she was 'almost ashamed' — at her age — 'to have been so amused with ... such wonderful nonsense'. Back at home she drove about the grounds of Frogmore — now the Duchess of Kent's retreat — in a garden chair belonging to her hostess, only to regret it next day. She wrote to Princess Mary Adelaide that it had shaken her 'nearly into a jelly, and I am aching all over'.

Mary looked forward greatly to the opening, set for May Day 1851, of the Great Exhibition in Paxton's 'Glass Palace' in Hyde Park. And she was firmly of the opinion that Prince George, the new Duke of Cambridge, should return from military duties in Dublin for the event. She told his mother, the Duchess, in April: 'My own feeling is that as there are so few of us left of the royal family to attend her [Victoria] ... he ought to come.' Aunt Mary did not count among the royal family the actress Louisa Fairbrother, who had been going under the name of Mrs Fitzgeorge since she and George — ignoring the Royal Marriages Act — had married, and with whom, when in London, together with their three small sons, the Duke lived contentedly in a house in Queen Street. George's marriage was a matter that was rarely discussed within the royal family, his aunt Mary limiting herself to counselling him, after his father's death, to honour Adolphus's wishes and 'disembarrass himself of what would trouble him more every year'. George did not take her advice.

Ten days after the opening of the Exhibition, Mary wrote of her 'admiration' for it to her niece Victoria – 'it far surpassed anything I ever saw before and requires days and days to see everything. Then I was nearly blinded with looking and seeing such magnificent and such a fine collection of things from all parts of the world – and my chair went about very comfortably.' She went a further three times that month. 'Every day I find more to admire,' she exclaimed, singling out the Russian exhibits for special commendation, in a letter to her niece Mary Adelaide, who was on a visit to her mother's Hesse relations at Rumpenheim in Germany. 'I wish I had wings to fly to make you a visit,' the Duchess of Gloucester told her, 'and wake you up of a morning by pecking at the window to be let in and oblige you to get out of bed.'

It is 'well worth your making the exertion to go there', the Duchess told her sister-in-law, the Duchess of Cambridge, a year or two later when she visited the Crystal Palace, which had housed the Great Exhibition, in its new home in Sydenham in south London. 'There are plenty of chairs to be drawn about in, and plenty of room for everybody to walk about and sit down ... and more than you can possibly eat and drink for 2 shillings a head and all well conducted, no noise and the building – as clean and sweet as possible ... come and meet me there some day ... no soul will disturb you as the conductors are all attention and do all they can to oblige everybody.'

The Duchess was as much fascinated by the visitors to the Exhibition in Hyde Park as by the construction itself. She went there in September 1851, she wrote to Mary Adelaide, on 'one of the shilling days ... to see the lower classes milling about in the greatest order looking so happy and pleased amused me ... the seeing them sitting down in groups to eat their dinner and displaying the contents of their baskets [was] almost as curious a sight as the Exhibition'. Enthralled by the Exhibition and its exotic wares, she wrote after a State Ball at Buckingham Palace that one of the guests, the Duchess of Norfolk, had been so hung about with jewels that she looked 'as if she had put on all the Indian things ... in the Exhibition'.

News arrived of the death at Herrenhausen of Ernest, King of Hanover in November 1851. And the Duke of Wellington, who had been Ernest's political opponent, was not unmoved when he commented, 'He had the disorder in his lungs which they all have!' Queen Victoria wrote in November 1851, 'Poor Aunt G feels it very much, though there never could have been great love for him on her part, but she has always been kind to all her brothers and sisters, and it is a sad feeling to be the last left of so large a family.' As for the Queen herself, Ernest had been 'an uncle whom I could not love ... I never saw anyone like him, who liked to hurt in everything he said. He was of an extraordinary unflinching courage, for which one must admire him, but there were many dark stories connected with his name which I will not touch upon, but which make me shudder.'

'My nephews and nieces ... are now my chief object of care and interest,' the Duchess of Gloucester wrote solemnly to Victoria after learning of her brother's death. And, with every intention of keeping up ties of affection with her blind nephew George, the new King of Hanover, she prayed that Victoria might be guided in friendship with him. 'I consider Hanover an old family estate that it is impossible not to wish to keep in the family,' she explained. 'Compared with the great country' – the United Kingdom – she conceded that Hanover was 'a drop in the sea', but she counselled her niece that, 'well managed and a good understanding kept up', the former Electorate was a useful channel for obtaining information of affairs on the Continent. Regrettably, King George began almost immediately, as Queen Victoria informed her aunt, on 'a track of reaction, so unfortunately the course pursued by almost all the German princes'. The 'good understanding' for which Mary had hoped perished before it was born. Indeed, the new King of Hanover and his wife soon incurred the old Duchess's wrath by not acknowledging her 'four letters . Christmas presents and New Year letter'. Her only solace, she told the Duchess of Cambridge, was King George's resolve to 'keep up all his father's charities at Kew in regard to the school and church ... He says he never can forget his happy childish days there.'

Marking the anniversary of the Cambridges' wedding in May 1852, Mary surrendered to gloom. 'Without you,' she told the widowed Duchess of Cambridge, 'I should be all alone in the world ... sometimes I think I must be a dead weight upon you. I feel I grow so stupid, so dull and so old ... all and everything', she concluded drearily, 'is changed as to our family and the world in general.' But she kept up her rituals, and as usual marked the Fourth of June, her father's Birthday, with a party. Gout did not cramp her style. 'I managed by going to one chair and then another (like a child beginning to walk),' she reported. But it was the first time that there were no brothers or sisters with whom to mark the day.

'Here I am all alone by myself today to drink the health', she wrote to Mary Adelaide, 'of the only one of my once large family left of us brothers and sisters – It made me low when I first awoke this morning.' She comforted herself with the reflection that 'such dear ones as yourself, George and Gussy are left to us to love and care about'. And she seized the moment to keep up other old ties: 'Now I am going to drive down to Brompton Square to see the King of Hanover's foster sister, old Miss Cheveley'. (Miss Cheveley's mother Louisa had been Ernest's wet-nurse.)

Occasionally lachrymose, the Duchess of Gloucester generally enjoyed a sociable old age. She offered on one occasion 'a quiet evening with a stupid dull old lady' at Gloucester House to an old friend, Sarah, Lady Abinger. But the tall house on the corner of Park Lane and Piccadilly often hosted greater numbers. And candidates for the crowded children's balls she gave in the upper room there – she brought in 'little wonders', musical prodigies six years old, and ventriloquists to amuse her junior guests – were not hard to find. An elderly Duke of Argyll much later recalled attending children's balls there with his cousins annually. 'The Duchess of Gloucester, with grey curls on each side of her head and a small cap above her good natured face, was most kind and attentive to us all.'

All beauty fled, all bosom and benevolence, with a comfortable shawl pulled around her and with a large lace cap drawn over her smooth and braided hair and tied under her fleshy chin, the Duchess was now the picture of a complacent Victorian lady – which, indeed, is what she was. She travelled between White Lodge and Windsor, Gloucester House and Brighton – and even Osborne. And she bore with resignation the deaths of public and private characters which the years brought, while rejoicing in the burgeoning royal family at Windsor. The Queen gave birth to an eighth child – Prince Leopold – on 7 April 1853 and used 'that blessed chloroform' for the first time.

But hanging over all else was the threat of war with Turkey and Russia. And when hostilities broke out in 1854, in the thick of it was the Duchess of Gloucester's nephew George, Duke of Cambridge, who had been promoted lieutenant-general and sent out to the Crimea that February in command of a division of Guards and Highlanders. At the battle of Alma in September his men came forward, when the Light Division had fallen back before the Russian counter-attack, and won the engagement. 'When all was over,' he recorded, 'I could not help crying like a child.' Disaster then followed success, when he had his horse shot from under him at the battle of Inkerman, and lost half his brigade of Guards.

Shocks and losses, and the suffering of others, to say nothing of the primitive conditions out in Turkey – fever, salt pork, and no vegetables, tobacco or soap – preyed on George's nerves, and he described himself as 'dreadfully knocked up and quite worn out'. Encamped on the heights within view but just out of sight of Sebastopol, he wrote gloomily to his mother and aunt Mary in early October 1854 that cholera had broken out again very badly among the troops. And he felt there was no likelihood that Sebastopol would fall.

News was sparse in England. Word of battles and of the killed or wounded came slowly, and Aunt Gloucester's sleep was disturbed by the anxiety she felt on her nephew's behalf. A month later, following news from George of Russian counter-attacks, she told the Duchess of Cambridge, 'I am still in a shake with thinking what danger he was in.' But, responding to the news that her nephew meditated coming home, Mary added: 'I feel sure, without it is necessary, George never could think of doing so at such a moment.' But George, exhausted, left the scene of war following the battle of Inkerman on 5 November and rested in a hospital ship, the *Retribution*, off Balaclava. Even there he was not left undisturbed, and had to retreat, after a thunderbolt hit the ship, to Constantinople to convalesce.

'I should be miserable if his health obliged him to come home,' Queen Victoria told her aunt Mary, as the latter informed George's mother the Duchess of Cambridge in December. The Queen expressed the hope that her cousin had gone back to his post, and, as if to deny the possibility of his return to England, reported to Aunt Gloucester that she was at work making the Duke a comforter, to send out to him. But the Duke was homeward bound, regardless of his female relations' views. 'You can not be more annoyed or more miserable [than I] at George having asked to come home on sick leave,' lamented Aunt Mary to Queen Victoria as the new year of 1855 dawned. Thinking of 'all the disagreeable things that ... will be said', she wrote, 'it is a sad pity his nerves have been so shaken'.

Before George returned to England in late January, his examination by a medical board at Constantinople had confirmed — to the invalid's relief — his opinion that he should not rejoin the army for the moment. Still, his martial aunt did not give up hope, and she wrote to the Duke's mother on 23 March, 'I consider George's return [to the Crimea] ... only put off for the time and, as a proof of this, all his horses are left there.' Meanwhile Mary took up her paintbrush to produce sixteen paintings for the Patriotic Fund exhibition in aid of Crimean War victims.

When not fretting over her nephew's nerves, the Duchess of Gloucester had passed the festive season arranging her glass cabinets and bringing out the treasures she had accumulated and inherited over many years. Among them was a satin pochette containing a prayer she had written when she was twelve and frightened during her father's strange illness at Kew. And she had, should she wish to sigh over it, wrapped up in tissue paper the hair of many of her sisters — a great auburn coil from Amelia's head — and even some iron-grey wisps identified as her mother's during her last years. There were as well items of her sisters' 'work' to turn over — including the maroon and lemon chequered workbags in which her sister Sophia had hung her correspondence on her chair arms.

But there were more cheerful mementoes of the past – her family's 'pictures', ranging from miniatures of her parents and Reynolds's painting of her sister-in-law Sophia Matilda as a child to recent photographs of the Cambridges and of Victoria's family. There was even one prized photograph taken by the fashionable photographer Claudet. It showed not only Queen Victoria, her son Bertie, Prince of Wales and his younger sister Alice, but also their great-aunt Mary, tiny and hunched but smiling, in a highly decorated dress. Her equerry the Hon. Augustus Liddell took another photograph of the Duchess of Gloucester – alone this time, but again in a very striking outfit adorned with a shawl. Other treasures at Gloucester House included books, Bibles and almanacs that had once belonged to her brothers and sisters. And the Duchess owned besides a magpie collection of jewellery and less substantial trinkets now all hers as sole survivor of a large family who had religiously exchanged gifts all their lives on high days and holidays.

While staying in Brighton in the autumn of 1855, the Duchess of Gloucester was gratified to hear – in confidence – from Queen Victoria of another royal marriage to come. Vicky, Princess Royal, was engaged to Prince Friedrich Wilhelm, future King of Prussia, and the couple met the Duchess's criteria for happiness – 'the young people have been allowed (fortunately) opportunities of becoming well acquainted with each other'. Mary welcomed 'an alliance that is so desirable in every way and one I always considered as the most natural to be thought of'. But she then turned tearful. 'It is not likely I should live to see this event take place.'

'It appears like a dream to me', she told Victoria, 'that you should have a daughter old enough to begin to think of settling down for life – when I remember your birth as if it happened only yesterday.' In fact, Vicky would not marry her Prince of Prussia for another two years, and, in visiting this long engagement on their daughter, Victoria and Albert were breaking the Duchess's tenet that long love affairs were 'very disagreeable'. But they were at least providing for their daughter the dynastic match that Mary's own father, King George III, had so singularly failed to produce for her.

The guns that sounded the end of war in the Crimea in March 1856 led the Duchess to speak of 'the blessings of peace'. She had lived through three terrible carnages – the American War of Independence, the Napoleonic Wars and now this. 'Pray God it may be a lasting one,' she wrote to Queen Victoria on 30 March. Honour was restored in July when,

as one of the blessings of peace, George, Duke of Cambridge became commander-in-chief. But Bertie, the Prince of Wales, rather than his cousin
George, was now the old Duchess's pride and joy. As the future sovereign,
he naturally attracted her attention, and she was delighted when, with his
tutor Mr Gibbs, he paid her a visit at White Lodge in Richmond Park
when she was recovering from a serious illness. 'She had become so thin,'
her dresser Mrs Gold later recalled, that 'her bones had nearly come
through the skin'. But Mary received visitors, sitting up in bed supported
by cushions, and looked 'very cheerful and … so nice and venerable' –
according to Queen Victoria – 'in her white night-cap and everything so
neatly and prettily arranged'.

When the fourteen-year-old Prince of Wales visited his great-aunt
during her convalescence, he brought her five game birds he had shot himself. 'I hear', wrote the Duchess to the boy's mother, 'the keeper says he
will be an admirable shot as he sets about it so steadily.' A few years before
she had encouraged Bertie's earliest sporting attempts: 'I can well believe
how delighted you must have been at being allowed to go out shooting for
the first time, and the being so fortunate as to have killed two rabbits gives
every hope that you will be a good sportsman by and by.'

After receiving her great-nephew in bed, the Duchess roused herself to
entertain him downstairs. 'He made himself very agreeable, full of wishing to have the particulars of every picture that hangs up in the room and
the history of every picture in the house, making very sensible remarks …
in short, I was delighted with him,' she told Queen Victoria, 'and I hear
he gained all hearts below stairs.' Already a ladies' man, the future King
Edward VII said, before he left to catch his train, that 'he was so glad he
had seen Aunt Gloucester up and dressed, as she looked so much prettier
up than in bed'.

The only one of the family who now worried Aunt Gloucester was
Princess Mary Adelaide of Cambridge. At twenty-three she had spurned
one suitor, the Prince of Sardinia – which she now regretted – and she was
growing disquietingly large. But the Duchess of Gloucester endorsed the
tour of Germany on which the Duchess of Cambridge led her younger
daughter, and, while wishing marriage for Princess Mary Adelaide, did not
for a moment neglect her other great-nieces and -nephews. The ninth
birthday of Princess Louise in March 1857 produced a packet of books and
a letter from her great-aunt Gloucester, and in addition, twenty pounds
despatched separately to her mother 'for any trinket you may fancy for her'.
Mary, who had had little money herself when young, liked to give generous sums to children, once sending a 'little bit of paper' for three sisters to

divide, with the message, 'As there are balls, it may assist in making you all a little smart.'

Queen Victoria and Prince Albert were not neglectful of Aunt Gloucester in their turn. When he heard that Mary had been taken ill in April 1857, Prince Albert sent over to Gloucester House 'a very handsome useful piece of furniture' – a sofa that could be raised 'an inch at a time' and was a 'perfect convenience'. The Duchess had had it brought upstairs and would probably try it in the course of the day, her equerry Liddell wrote in thanks. The Duchess was 'very weak and much oppressed' that day, as her niece Mary Adelaide noted, but she nevertheless wrote to Albert herself: 'It is impossible to express, my dear Albert, how deeply I feel your kindness in sending me so beautiful and useful a chair, and one that I feel sure will be such a comfort for me when once I get used to use it, and how much I am impressed with your kindness. Thank God that dear Victoria is going on well, my affte love to her, Yours, Mary, April the 15th, GH.' This was to be the last letter she ever wrote.

Next morning an account came to Cambridge Cottage of the Duchess of Gloucester having had 'an attack of spasms at the heart in the night'. That afternoon George – who was out of London – and Gussy – in Mecklenburg-Strelitz – were telegraphed for, and the rest of the family, forbidden for the moment to see the Duchess, waited downstairs in the small front drawing room at Gloucester House. It was 'wretched work', wrote Princess Mary Adelaide after some hours of sitting there, talking and reading with her mother. And the next two days were much the same. But on the 18th, after the Duchess of Cambridge and Mary Adelaide returned from seeing the Queen's new baby, Princess Beatrice, at Buckingham Palace, back at Gloucester House the ailing Duchess awoke from a doze and kissed her hand to her niece Mary Adelaide, when she visited her. But this small sign of life meant little, and Hawkins the Duchess's surgeon* said ominously on 18 April that 'he felt much alarmed as a torpor was stealing over the brain'.

Visitors continued to come to Gloucester House – Prince Albert, the Prince of Wales and Vicky, the Princess Royal, the Duchess of Inverness, Aunt Kent, even Princess Feodora and her husband, Prince Ernest of Hohenlohe-Langenburg. Queen Victoria visited with her daughter Alice.

---

* This was Mr Caesar Henry Hawkins, grandson of Sir Caesar and one of Queen Victoria's surgeons. He was a great-nephew of Mr Pennell Hawkins, who inoculated Princess Mary against smallpox in 1779 and a nephew of Mr Charles Hawkins, who treated her arm in 1788.

George, Duke of Cambridge arrived, and then on the 21st Gussy, from Mecklenburg-Strelitz with her son Dolphy. Mary Adelaide peeped at her aunt from behind a screen as the Duchess was given beef tea, and wondered at her marvellous tenacity. But the days hung heavy for those assembled at the house.

The Prince of Wales sneaked up the back way to look in on his aunt. On the 25th, her eighty-first birthday, Mary gave signs of life, and pressed Mary Adelaide's hand twice when her niece kissed hers. Two days later she was confused, and did not know her visitors. She asked if the Duchess of Cambridge was coming. They replied that she was in the house. Would Aunt Mary like her to come? 'By all means, let her come,' was their great-aunt's reply. But when the Duchess of Cambridge came, the patient did not speak.

The Duchess stopped eating the next day, on 28 April, and there was a 'marked change' in the night that followed. After seeing her aunt on the 29th, Mary Adelaide of Cambridge cried in the room of Mary's dresser Mrs Gold, and after dinner Hawkins directed the family that they should remain for the night. At three-thirty the following morning the family knelt around the Duchess's bed. Mr Nepean, the chaplain, read the prayers for the dying. 'The pulse was beating feebler and feebler and death had set its stamp upon her much loved features,' recorded Mary Adelaide. The old Princess's heavy breathing was loud in the room, and she hovered 'between life and eternity'. At five-fifteen in the morning of 30 April 1857, 'with another stretch and a momentary convulsive contraction of the face', Princess Mary, Duchess of Gloucester died.

'With her is gone the last link, which connected us with a bygone generation,' Victoria wrote, on receiving the news of her aunt's death in a note from George, written at half-past five that morning. 'She was an authority on everything, a bright example of loyalty, devotion and duty, the kindest and best of mistresses, and friends. She had become like a grandmother to us all, from her age, and from her being the last of the family.' Meanwhile the mourners at Gloucester House wandered sadly from room to room, watching the servants unbar the shutters and draw the blinds as day dawned. Then they drove away, leaving Mrs Gold to wash and dress and lay out the corpse of the mistress whom she had served so long. The story of the six daughters of George III, which had begun with the Princess Royal's birth in the Queen's House ninety-one years before on Michaelmas Day 1766, was concluded.

Notes

FAMILY ABBREVIATIONS

George III, Queen Charlotte and their children are shown in bold

Adolphus: Prince Adolphus, seventh son of George III, later Duke of Cambridge

Amelia: Princess Amelia, sixth daughter of George III

Augusta: Princess Augusta, second daughter of George III

Augustus: Prince Augustus, sixth son of George III, later Duke of Sussex, husband of Lady Augusta Murray and of Lady Cecilia Buggin, Duchess of Inverness

Bertie: Edward, Prince of Wales, later King Edward VII, eldest son of Queen Victoria and Prince Albert

Dowager Princess of Leiningen: Victoria of Saxe-Coburg-Gotha, widow of Prince Charles of Leiningen, later wife of Edward, Duke of Kent and mother of Queen Victoria

Dowager Princess of Wales: Augusta of Saxe-Gotha, Dowager Princess of Wales, widow of Frederick, Prince of Wales and mother of George III

Duchess of Brunswick: Augusta, formerly Hereditary Princess, wife of Charles, Duke of Brunswick, sister of George III and mother of Caroline, Princess of Wales

Duchess of Cambridge: Princess Augusta of Hesse, wife of Adolphus, Duke of Cambridge

Duchess of Kent: Victoria of Saxe-Coburg, widow of Prince Charles of Leiningen, wife of Edward, Duke of Kent and mother of Queen Victoria

Duke Charles: Prince/Duke Charles, later Grand Duke Charles of Mecklenburg-Strelitz, Queen Charlotte's brother

Duke Frederick: Frederick, Duke, formerly Hereditary Prince, later Elector and King of Württemberg, and husband of Royal

Duke of Gloucester: William Henry, first Duke of Gloucester and brother of George III, father of William Frederick, second Duke, and of Sophia Matilda

Edward: Prince Edward, fourth son of George III, later Duke of Kent, father of Queen Victoria

Elizabeth: Princess Elizabeth, third daughter of George III, later Hereditary Princess and Landgravine of Hesse-Homburg, wife of Fritz

Ernest: Prince Ernest, fifth son of George III, later Duke of Cumberland, and first King of Hanover

Frederick: Prince Frederick, Duke of York and Albany, second son of George III

Fritz: Friedrich/Friedrich VI, Hereditary Prince, later Landgrave of Hesse-Homburg, husband of Elizabeth

GIII: King George III, Elector of Hanover, husband of Queen Charlotte

GIV: King George IV, eldest son of George III, formerly George, Prince of Wales and Prince Regent

George: Prince George, later second Duke of Cambridge, only son of Adolphus, Duke of Cambridge

GP: George, Prince of Wales, eldest son of George III, later Prince Regent and George IV

Grand Duchess of Mecklenburg-Strelitz: see Gussy

Grand Duke Charles: Grand Duke, formerly Duke Charles of Mecklenburg-Strelitz, Queen Charlotte's brother

Gussy: Princess Augusta of Cambridge, Hereditary Princess, later Grand Duchess of Mecklenburg-Strelitz, elder daughter of Adolphus, Duke of Cambridge and wife of Friedrich Wilhelm, Hereditary Prince, later Grand Duke of Mecklenburg-Strelitz

Hereditary Prince: Frederick, Hereditary Prince, later Duke, Elector and King of Württemberg, husband of Royal

Hereditary Princess: Augusta, later Duchess of Brunswick, wife of Charles, Hereditary Prince of Brunswick, sister of George III and mother of Caroline, Princess of Wales

King Frederick: Frederick, King, formerly Hereditary Prince, Duke and Elector of Württemberg, husband of Royal

Leopold: Prince Leopold of Saxe-Coburg-Gotha, later King Leopold I of the Belgians, husband of Princess Charlotte, uncle of Queen Victoria

Mary: Princess Mary, fourth daughter of George III, later Duchess of Gloucester, wife of William Frederick

Mary Adelaide: Princess Mary Adelaide, younger daughter of Adolphus, Duke of Cambridge, later Duchess of Teck and mother of Queen Mary

PR: Prince Regent, eldest son of George III, formerly George, Prince of Wales and later King George IV, father of Princess Charlotte

Prince Albert: Prince Albert of Saxe-Coburg-Gotha, nephew of Leopold and Prince Consort of Queen Victoria

Princess Charlotte: Princess Charlotte of Wales, only child of George IV and Queen Caroline, when Prince and Princess of Wales, and first wife of Leopold

Princess of Wales: Caroline of Brunswick, Princess of Wales, wife of George, Prince of Wales and later Queen Caroline, mother of Princess Charlotte

Queen Charlotte: Charlotte of Mecklenburg-Strelitz, Queen Consort of King George III

Queen Mary: Mary of Teck, daughter of Mary Adelaide and of the Duke of Teck, wife of King George V

Queen Victoria: Queen Victoria, formerly Princess Victoria of Kent, daughter of Edward, Duke of Kent and wife of Prince Albert

Royal: Princess Charlotte Augusta Matilda, Princess Royal, eldest daughter of George III, and later, as second wife of Frederick, first King of Württemberg, Hereditary Princess, Duchess, Electress and Queen of Württemberg

Sophia: Princess Sophia, fifth daughter of George III

Sophia Matilda: Princess Sophia Matilda of Gloucester, daughter of William Henry, first Duke of Gloucester, sister-in-law of Mary

Victoria: Princess Victoria, only child of Edward, Duke of Kent, later Queen Victoria

WIV: William IV, third son of George III, formerly Prince William and Duke of Clarence

William: Prince William, third son of George III, later Duke of Clarence, then William IV, husband of Adelaide

William Frederick: Prince William Frederick of Gloucester, son of William Henry, first Duke of Gloucester, later second Duke of Gloucester, husband of Mary

OTHER ABBREVIATIONS

Add	Additional
BL	British Library
Col	Collection
Corr	Correspondence
Eg	Egerton
(Fr)	translated from French
GEO	Georgian Papers
(Ger)	translated from German
HMC	Historical Manuscripts Commission
LB	Letter Book
LC	Lord Chamberlain's Papers
LRO	Leicestershire Record Office
LWL	Lewis Walpole Library
(M)	Microfilm
Ms(s)	Manuscript(s)
NYPL	New York Public Library
PML	Pierpont Morgan Library
PRO	Public Record Office
QVJ	Queen Victoria's Journal
RA	Royal Archives
RC	Royal Collection
RCP	Royal College of Physicians

RL   Royal Library
RPC   Royal Photographic Collection
VIC   Victorian Papers
YCBA   Yale Center for British Art, New Haven

CHAPTER 1: EARLY DAYS

'princess'. Home, *Lady Mary Coke*, 1, 59
'understanding'. Greig, *Diaries of a Duchess*, 63
'sons'. Home, *Lady Mary Coke*, 1, 59
'House'. LRO/DG7, Lady Charlotte Finch's Journal, 29 September 1766
'goose'. Cf Dobson, *d'Arblay Diary*, 4, 107
'figure'. LRO/DG7/Box 4953, Bundle 31, Henrietta Finch to Charlotte Finch,
    11 August 1766
'petticoats'. LRO/DG7/Box 4953, Bundle 31, Lady Charlotte Finch to Lord
    Winchilsea, 26 September 1765
'sometimes'. Finch, *Burley-on-the-Hill*, 1, 294
'reflections'. Huish, *George III*, 1, 13
'comical', 'her?'. Home, *Lady Mary Coke*, 1, 30–1
'jewels'. Lybbe Powys, *Passages*, 116–17
'evening'. LRO/DG7/ Box 4953, Bundle 31, Sophia Finch to Lord Winchilsea,
    19 September 1766
'away'. Greig, *Diaries of a Duchess*, 63
'worse'. Home, *Lady Mary Coke*, 1, 35
'lodgings'. Ibid, 1, 67
'lesson'. LRO/DG7, Lady Charlotte Finch's Journal, 24 November 1766
'covers'. PRO, LC 9/293
'sea'. RA GEO/Add 21/101, Royal to Lady Charlotte Finch, 14 March 1805
'noise'. Buckingham and Normanby, *Works*, 2, 223
'coat'. LRO/DG7, Lady Charlotte Finch's Journal, 19 January 1767
'bed'. Ibid, 1766–7 passim; LRO/DG7, Box 4953, Bundle 50, Henrietta to
    Frances Finch, 5 June [1766]
'abandoned'. Lewis, *Walpole Correspondence*, 38, 434
'disconcerted'. Ibid, 116–17
'Ranelagh ...'. Ibid, 127–8
'parrots'. RA GEO(M)/Add 21/91/1 (Fr), Queen Charlotte to Duke Charles, 9
    January 1778
'timidity'. Harcourt, *Papers*, 4, 80
'dead'. Finch, *Burley-on-the-Hill*, 286
'Princes'. BL Add Ms 35839, f250, 'Character of the Queen', 1761
'to her'. Ibid
'see this'. Harcourt, *Papers*, 4, 79
'nothing'. Greig, *Diaries of a Duchess*, 51

'Guido'. Millar, *Later Georgian*, 22

'Tuscan'. Lewis, *Walpole Correspondence*, 37, 69

'daughter'. LRO/DG7, Lady Charlotte Finch's Diary, 1766–7 passim

'pretty'. Home, *Lady Mary Coke*, 2, 44

'to her'. Ibid, 401

'family'. RA VIC/Y 67/8, Leopold to Queen Victoria, 1 October 1840

'served up'. Huish, *George III*, 1, 326

'health'. Home, *Lady Mary Coke*, 2, 434

'please them'. Ibid, 247

'accent'. RA GEO/50177, Royal to Martha, Lady Elgin, 31 January 1799

'return'. Home, *Lady Mary Coke*, 2, 326

'forget them …'. RA GEO/50173, Royal to Martha, Lady Elgin, 20 February 1798

superintendents. RA GEO/50171–2, RA GEO/50181, Royal to Martha, Lady
    Elgin, 23 December 1797–20 February 1798, 9 November 1799

'character'. RA GEO/15884–5, 'Description of an entertainment … September
    1769'

'head'. Greig, *Diaries of a Duchess*, 93–5

'thing'. RA GEO/50177, Royal to Martha, Lady Elgin, 31 January 1799

'sylph'. Greig, *Diaries of a Duchess*, 93–5

'herself'. RA GEO/50181, Royal to Martha, Lady Elgin, 9 November 1799

'plain'. Home, *Lady Mary Coke*, 2, 429

'boughs'. Ibid, 387

'unattended'. Ibid, 3, 114

'access'. Watkins, *Her Majesty*, 591

'prospect'. Lewis, *Walpole Correspondence*, 23, 66

courtyard. Doran, *Lives of the Queens*, 2, 67

'tired'. Home, *Lady Mary Coke*, 3, 153

'wall', try her. Greig, *Diaries of a Duchess*, 145

'unreasonably', 'ever was'. Home, *Lady Mary Coke* 3, 258

'yours'. RA GEO/Add 15/8152, Queen Charlotte to Lady Charlotte Finch, 6
    November 1771

'people'. RA GEO/Add 15/8154, Queen Charlotte to Lady Charlotte Finch,
    [before 31 October] 1774

twins. HMC, *Dartmouth*, 443, GIII to Lord Dartmouth, 14 May 1804

'Brunswick family'. RA GEO/50286, Royal to Martha, Lady Elgin, 14 May 1801

CHAPTER 2: GROWING UP

'infant'. Home, *Lady Mary Coke*, 3, 439

'hitherto'. RA GEO/36346, Queen Charlotte to GP, 12 August 1770

'yourself'. LRO/DG7, Box 4953, Bundle 31, Lord Winchilsea to Lady Charlotte
    Finch, July 1771

'on them'. LRO/DG7, Box 4953, Bundle 31, Lady Juliana Penn to Lady Charlotte Finch, 5 August 1771

'showy'. Dobson, *d'Arblay Diary*, 2, 409

'men', 'turn'. RA VIC/Y 171/81, Mary Campbell to Rebecca Fraser, Philadelphia, 1774

'hour'. RA GEO/50195–6, Royal to Martha, Lady Elgin, 16 March 1802

'employment'. Home, *Lady Mary Coke*, 4, 424

'my sister'. RA GEO/Planta/6 (Fr), Miss Elizabeth Planta to Lady Strathmore 14 July 1771

Christian. RA VIC/Y 171/81, Mary Campbell to Rebecca Fraser, Philadelphia, 1774

'about them'. RA GEO/Add 15/8154, Queen Charlotte to Lady Charlotte Finch, [before 31 October] 1774

'price'. Greig, *Diaries of a Duchess*, 28–9

'pounds'. Lewis, *Walpole Correspondence*, 22, 540

'crust'. Fitzgerald, *Queen Charlotte*, 97

'followed them'. Dyce, *Rogers' Table Talk*, 116

'whip'. Murray, *Recollections*, 69

'children'. RA GEO/50181, Royal to Martha, Lady Elgin, 9 November 1799

'better'. RA GEO/50178, Royal to Martha, Lady Elgin, 4 February 1799

'alone'. RA GEO/50181, Royal to Martha, Lady Elgin, 9 November 1799

'idle'. RA GEO/50196, Royal to Martha, Lady Elgin, 16 March 1802

'separation'. RA GEO(M)/Add 21/91/1 (Fr), Queen Charlotte to Duke Charles, 3 September 1771

'likewise'. *Annual Register* (1765), 25

'fool'. Lady Louisa Stuart's *Memoir* in Home, *Lady Mary Coke*, 1, lxxxvi

'help her'. Lewis, *Walpole Correspondence*, 21, 530

'untruth'. RA GEO/15948, GIII's Memorandum, after 1 December 1771

'family'. RA GEO/15934, GIII to Dowager Princess of Wales, 3 November 1771

'example'. RA GEO/15938, GIII to Duke of Gloucester, draft 9 November 1771

'thought'. RA GEO/15939–40, GIII to Duke of Gloucester, 9 November 1771

'hopes ... door'. Home, *Lady Mary Coke*, 4, 15ff

'pardon him'. RA GEO/54250, Dowager Princess of Wales to GIII (Fr), [?November 1771]

'to see'. RA GEO/15942, GIII to Duke of Gloucester, 19 November 1771

'viscera'. Hedley, *Queen Charlotte*, 111

'groan'. Lewis, *Walpole Correspondence*, 23, 379

'bitterly'. RA VIC/Y 171/81, Mary Campbell to Rebecca Fraser, Philadelphia, 1774

'revolution'. Lewis, *Walpole Correspondence*, 23, 375

'character'. RA GEO/15975, GIII to Hereditary Princess, 8 May 1772

'shades'. Home, *Lady Mary Coke*, 4, 22

'prettiest'. Ibid, 119

'nieceling'. Lewis, *Walpole Correspondence*, 32, 118

'red'. Home, *Lady Mary Coke*, 4, 178

'abroad'. Ibid, 283

'than ever'. RA GEO(M)/Add 21/91/1 (Fr), Queen Charlotte to Duke Charles, 20 March 1772

house. RA GEO/Add 16/69, List of inhabitants at Kew, 1779

'sorry to go'. Home, *Lady Mary Coke*, 4, 180–1

'repining'. RA GEO/Add 15/8154, Queen Charlotte to Lady Charlotte Finch, [before 31 October] 1774

'nursery'. RA GEO/Add 15/8155, Lady Charlotte Finch to Queen Charlotte, 31 October 1774

'figure'. RA VIC/Y 171/81, Mary Campbell to Rebecca Fraser, Philadelphia, 1774

'fitted for it'. RA GEO Add 15/8155, Lady Charlotte Finch to Queen Charlotte, 31 October 1774

'anything'. LRO/DG7, Box 4953, Bundle 32, Henrietta Finch to Sophia Feilding, née Finch, 2 September 1774

'three years ago …'. RA VIC/Y 171/81, Mary Campbell to Rebecca Fraser, Philadelphia, 1774

'memory'. Ibid

'learnt'. RA GEO/50186, Royal to Martha, Lady Elgin, 14 May 1801

'Roberts'. BL Add Ms 17870, Queen Charlotte's Treasurer's Accounts [1771–6] ff 92, 108

'writing'. Anson Mss, A1, Writing exercises

'geography teacher'. Shefrin, *Affectionate Care*, 7

'French'. RA, Royal Household Index

'geography'. RA VIC/Y 171/81, Mary Campbell to Rebecca Fraser, Philadelphia, 1774

'children'. Ibid

'with me'. Ibid

'naughty child'. Ibid

'find'. NYPL, Berg Col, Elizabeth to Fanny Burney, 21 April 1819

'habit'. Home, *Lady Mary Coke*, 4, 418

'nothing'. BL, Eg Ms 3491 (Leeds Papers, 168), f135, Frederick to Lord Holderness, 26 November 1774

'bed'. Home, *Lady Mary Coke*, 4, 119

'fearful'. RA GEO/Add 15/8156, Queen Charlotte to Lady Charlotte Finch, 17 April 1775

'o clock'. Ibid

'entirely'. RA GEO(M)/Add 21/91/1 (Fr), Queen Charlotte to Grand Duke Charles, 15 July 1776

'particularly well'. Stuart, *Daughters*, 73

'boys' play'. RA GEO/50186, Royal to Martha, Lady Elgin, 14 May 1801

'inhabited'. van Thal, *Ernest Augustus*, 301, 2 August 1845

CHAPTER 3: THE YOUNGER ONES

Dacres. RA GEO/Add 12/2/1, Bounty Warrant, 8 December 1777

'mummies'. Harcourt, *Papers*, 6, 294

'women'. Anson, *Hamilton*, 84

'truth'. Hibbert, *Prince of Wales*, 11

'good'. RA GEO/Add 15/946, Augusta to Mary Compton, 26 November 1777

'take place'. RA GEO(M)/Add 21/91/2 (Fr), Queen Charlotte to Duke Charles, 6 October 1779

'autre face'. RA GEO(M)/Add 21/91/1 (Fr), Queen Charlotte to Duke Charles, 9 July 1776

'£4000'. RA GEO(M)/Add 21/91/1 (Fr), Queen Charlotte to Duke Charles, 17 January 1777

'*campagnarde*'. RA GEO(M)/Add 21/91/1 (Fr), Queen Charlotte to Duke Charles, 18 June 1776

'week'. RA GEO(M)/Add 21/91/1 (Fr), Queen Charlotte to Duke Charles, 3 May 1782

'flowers'. Anson, *Hamilton*, 55

'tender years'. Ibid, 58

'clergy'. Ibid, 56

'weak side'. Ibid, 59–60

'have …'. Anson Mss, A1, Augusta to Mary Hamilton, 1777

'to me'. Anson Mss, A1, Augusta to Mary Hamilton, nd [1777]

'minutes'. RA GEO(M)/Add 21/91/1 (Fr), Queen Charlotte to Duke Charles, 19 December 1777

'heard it'. Anson Mss, A1, Misc, Augusta to Mary Compton, 20 October 1777

'Dacres'. Anson Mss, A1, Misc, Augusta to Martha Gouldsworthy, 20 October 1777 (copy)

'for you'. RA GEO/Add 15/930, Augusta to Mary Compton, nd

'from her'. RA GEO/Add 15/943, Augusta to Mary Compton, [1777]

'good'. RA GEO/Add 15/946, Augusta to Mary Compton, 26 November 1777

'London'. RA GEO/Add 10/1, Augusta to Queen Charlotte, 26 December 1777

'undone'. RA GEO/Add 15/929, Royal to Mary Compton, 4 November 1777

soon. RA GEO/Add 15/941, Royal to Mary Compton, 22 November 1777

'do you'. Ibid

'think so'. RA GEO/Add 15/940, Royal to Mary Compton, 25 November 1777

'o clock'. RA GEO/Add 15/935, Royal to Mary Compton, December 1777

'window'. RA GEO/Add 15/939, Royal to Mary Compton, 23 November 1777

'tomorrow'. RA GEO/Add 15/944, Royal to Mary Compton, 26 November 1777

'mama'. RA GEO/Add 15/952, Royal to Mary Compton, 5 December 1777

'ground'. RA GEO/Add 15/953, Royal to Mary Compton, 7 December 1777

Windsor. RA GEO/Add 2/81, Royal to Queen Charlotte, 27 December 1777

'often'. RA GEO/Add 15/924, Elizabeth to Mary Compton, nd

'establishment', 'Court'. Anson, *Hamilton*, 127, 50

'show'. Anson Mss, A1, Writing exercises, Augusta, 17 July 1788

'Sophia'. Anson Mss, A1, Augusta to Mary Hamilton, Kew House, 1778

'sleepy'. Anson Mss, A1, Augusta to Mrs Hamilton, 28 November [1777]

'night'. Anson Mss, A1, Royal to Mary Hamilton, 20 December 1777

'Matilda'. Anson Mss, A1, Royal to Mary Hamilton, 13 January 1778

'mama'. Anson Mss, A1, Royal to Mary Hamilton, 14 January 1778

'with me'. Anson Mss, A1, Royal to Mary Hamilton, 17 January 1778

'esteem you'. Anson Mss, A1, Royal to Mary Hamilton, nd

'character'. Anson Mss, A1, Royal to Mary Hamilton, nd

'heureuse'. Anson Mss, A1, Royal to Mary Hamilton, 28 Janvier 1778

'continue it'. Anson Mss, A1, Royal to Mary Hamilton, 28 January 1778

'friend'. Anson Mss, A1, Royal to Mary Hamilton, 30 January 1778

'Matilda'. Anson Mss, A1, Royal to Mary Hamilton, 1 February 1778

'loved them'. Anson Mss, A1, Royal to Mary Hamilton 3 February 1778

'tomorrow'. Anson Mss, A1, Royal to Mary Hamilton, 6 February 1778

'rhubarb'. Anson Mss, A1, Augusta to Mary Hamilton, 8 August 1778

Palace. Anson Mss, A15, Lady Charlotte Finch to Mary Hamilton, nd [February 1778]

'breakfast'. Anson Mss, A1, Royal to Mary Hamilton, 6 June 1780

library. Roberts, *Royal Artists*, 69ff

'malgré moi'. RA GEO(M)/Add 21/91/1 (Fr), Queen Charlotte to Duke Charles, ?January 1778

'look for you'. RA GEO/36352–4, Queen Charlotte to GIII, 26 April 1778

'ground'. Anson, *Hamilton*, 66

'the place'. Llanover, *Mrs Delany*, 2, 379

'living at it'. RA GEO/Add 21/1/3, Queen Charlotte to William, [9 July 1779]

'everybody'. Llanover, *Mrs Delany*, 2, 370–82

'good sense'. Dobson, *d'Arblay Diary*, 3, 49

'advantage'. Anson Mss, A9, Louisa Cheveley to Mary Hamilton, 25 July 1778

'weighed'. Anson Mss, A9, Louisa Cheveley to Mary Hamilton, 15 November 1779

'*ear*'. Llanover, *Mrs Delany*, 2, 379–80

'style'. LWL, Clement Col, Laura Keppel to Jane Clement, 8 August 1776

'Windsor'. Ibid

'autumn'. RA GEO/Add 21/1/3, Queen Charlotte to William, 9 July 1779

attendants. RA GEO/Add 16/69, List of inhabitants at Kew, 1779

departed. Anson Mss, A2, Mary Hamilton to GP, June 1779

'friend?'. Llanover, *Mrs Delany*, 2, 473–4

'suffice'. Anson Mss, A17, Martha Gouldsworthy to Mary Hamilton, 4 July 1779

'dinner'. Anson Mss, A1, Elizabeth to Mary Hamilton, 26 September 1779

'mischief'. Anson Mss, A1, Queen Charlotte to Mary Hamilton, 30 August 1780

'confidence in'. RA GEO/Add 15/8157, Queen Charlotte to Lady Charlotte Finch, ?9 October 1775 'table'. Anson Mss, A17, Martha Gouldsworthy to Mary Hamilton, 2 May 1779

'wide world'. Anson Mss, A2, GP to Mary Hamilton, 14 November 1779

'virtuous'. Anson, *Hamilton*, 90

'object'. Anson Mss, A2, Mary Hamilton to GP, 7 December 1779

'possible'. Anson Mss, A17, Martha Gouldsworthy to Mary Hamilton, 20 June 1780

CHAPTER 4: ADOLESCENCE

'egg'. RA GEO(M)/Add 21/91/1 (Fr), Queen Charlotte to Duke Charles, 29 October 1775

'there'. RA GEO(M)/Add 21/91/2 (Fr), Queen Charlotte to Duke Charles, 15 June 1783

'world'. Ibid

'teachers'. Anson, *Hamilton*, 95

'revenge'. Anson Mss, A1, Writing exercises, Elizabeth, nd

'violence'. Anson Mss, A1, Writing exercises, Elizabeth, 1 January 1779

'lessons'. Anson, *Hamilton*, 95

'to you'. Ibid, 96

'happy'. RA GEO(M)/Add 21/91/1 (Fr), Queen Charlotte to Duke Charles, 6 September 1780

'them all'. RA GEO/Add 15/8159, Queen Charlotte to Lady Charlotte Finch, 8 July 1780

'right'. RA GEO/Add 15/8158, Queen Charlotte to Lady Charlotte Finch, 20 June 1780

'delicacy'. Anson Mss, A1, Queen Charlotte to Mary Hamilton, 23 June 1780

'so well'. Anson Mss, A1, Queen Charlotte to Lady Charlotte Finch, July 1780

'Friday'. Anson Mss, A1, Royal to Mary Hamilton, 18 June 1780

'to her'. Anson Mss, A1, Royal to Mary Hamilton, 13 July 1780

'bed'. Anson Mss, A17, Martha Gouldsworthy to Mary Hamilton, 20 June 1780

'Windsor'. Anson Mss, A17, Martha Gouldsworthy to Mary Hamilton, 27 July 1780

'to her'. Anson Mss, A9, Margaret Planta to Mary Hamilton, 24 July 1780

Gouldsworthy. Anson Mss, A17, Martha Gouldsworthy to Mary Hamilton, 16 September 1780

'presents ...'. Anson Mss, A1, Augusta to Mary Hamilton, 8 November 1779

'titles'. Anson Mss, A1, Augusta to Mary Hamilton, 17 July 1780

'inhabitants'. Lewis, *Walpole Correspondence*, 33, 225–6 and notes

'colours'. Ibid

'King'. Anson Mss, A1, Augusta to Mary Hamilton, recd 15 September 1780

'Elizabeth'. RA GEO/Add 11/1, Elizabeth to GIII, 23 September 1780

'nurse'. RA GEO/Add 15/442, Queen Charlotte to Lady Charlotte Finch, 27 February 1781

September, 'after you'. Anson Mss, A15, Mary Hamilton to Lady Charlotte Finch, 2 September 1781

'done'. Anson Mss, A1, Misc, Lady Charlotte Finch to Elizabeth, 4 August 1781

'Spectators'. Anson Mss, A1, Elizabeth to Mary Hamilton, 10 June 1781

'for you'. Anson Mss, A1, Queen Charlotte to Mary Hamilton, 30 August 1780

'indeed'. Anson Mss, A1, Queen Charlotte to Mary Hamilton, 16 July 1780

'said …', 'person'. Anson Mss, A1, Queen Charlotte to Mary Hamilton, 25 June 1781

'very fine'. Anson Mss, A15, Mary Hamilton to Lady Charlotte Finch, 2 September 1781

'Genii'. Anson Mss, A15, Mary Hamilton to Lady Charlotte Finch, 2–4 September 1781

'very well'. Lewis, *Walpole Correspondence*, 33, 291, n18

'cathedral'. Anson Mss, A15, Mary Hamilton to Lady Charlotte Finch, 2–4 September 1781

'collection'. Anson Mss, A15, Lady Charlotte Finch to Augusta, 24 July 1781

'themselves'. Anson Mss, A1, Writing exercises, Augusta, 5 February 1781

'see you'. Anson Mss, A1, Augusta to Mary Hamilton, 13 March 1781

'again'. Anson Mss, A1, Augusta to Mary Hamilton, nd

'bid me'. Anson Mss, A1, Augusta to Mary Hamilton, nd

'Hamilton'. Anson Mss, A1, Augusta to Mary Hamilton, docketed by same, 14 August 1781

'stir'. RA GEO/Add 21/1/16, Frederick to William, 29 June 1781

'dress'. RA GEO/Add 21/1/20, Royal to William, 30 March 1782

'my good'. Anson Mss, A1, Augusta to Mary Hamilton, 27 May 1782

occur. RA GEO/Add 15/8160, Queen Charlotte to Lady Charlotte Finch, 8 June 1782

'terrace'. Anson Mss, A1, Augusta to Mary Hamilton, 17 July 1780

'Augusta'. RA GEO/Add 15/8160, Queen Charlotte to Lady Charlotte Finch, 8 June 1782

'pleasure'. Anson Mss, A1, Augusta to Mary Hamilton, 20 September 1782

weak. Anson Mss, A9, Louisa Cheveley to Mary Hamilton, August 1782

'doctor'. RA GEO/Add 15/8161, Queen Charlotte to Lady Charlotte Finch, 19 July 1782

'anything'. RA GEO(M)/Add 21/91/1 (Fr), Queen Charlotte to Duke Charles, 1776

'King also'. RA GEO/Add 15/8183, Lady Charlotte Finch to Sophia Feilding, 31 August 1782

'mean to do'. Anson Mss, A1, Augusta to Mary Hamilton, 20 November 1782

'angel'. Anson Mss, A9, Miss Margaret Planta to Mary Hamilton, 5 May 1783

'point'. Anson Mss, A9, Louisa Cheveley to Mary Hamilton, 5 May 1783

continue. Fulcher, *Gainsborough*, 111

'remembrance'. Millar, *Later Georgian*, 38

'talk to'. BL Add Ms 33131 (Chichester Papers), ff54–6, Queen Charlotte to Mary, Lady Holderness, January 1783 'object'. HMC, *Dartmouth*, 442

'wishes'. RA GEO/Add 21/1/39, Royal to William, 15 September 1783

CHAPTER 5: BROTHERS AND SISTERS

'there'. RA GEO(M)/Add 21/91/2 (Fr), Queen Charlotte to Duke Charles, 1 July 1783

'established'. RA GEO/52107, Duchess of Brunswick to GIII, 7 November 1782

'pin'. RA GEO/Add 4/22, Augusta to William, 6 November 1783

'letters'. RA GEO/Add 21/1/48, 13 February 1784

'brothers'. RA GEO/Add 21/1/47, Queen Charlotte to William, 29 December 1783

'emulation'. RA GEO/Add 15/476 (Fr), Jacob Budé to GIII, c January 1784

'way'. RA GEO/Add 21/1/50, Royal to William, 28 March 1784

'soon'. RA GEO/Add 21/1/51, Augusta to William, 28 March 1784

'dancing'. RA GEO/Add 21/1/50, Royal to William, 28 March 1784

'pencils and paper'. Llanover, *Mrs Delany*, 3, 308

Saracens. Roberts, *Royal Artists*, 73–6

'feathers'. Llanover, *Mrs Delany*, 3, 148

'low'. Ibid, 2, 496

'pearls'. Ibid, 3, 150

'scarlet'. Ibid, 2, 473

'actress'. RA GEO/Add 21/1/51, Augusta to William, 28 March 1784

'sum'. RA GEO(M)/Add 21/91/2 (Fr), Queen Charlotte to Duke Charles, winter 1783?

'grew up'. HMC, *Ailesbury*, 269–70

'Royalty', 'attentive'. Campbell, *Mrs Siddons*, 128ff, 136ff

'preceptress'. Boaden, *Kemble*, 1, 118–19

'enunciate'. Delves Broughton, *Mrs Papendiek*, 1, 205

'emolument'. Campbell, *Mrs Siddons*, 136n

'comedy'. Delves Broughton, *Mrs Papendiek*, 1, 204

'face'. Dobson, *d'Arblay Diary*, 3, 254

'engagements'. Aspinall, *Later Correspondence*, 1, 168–70

'alliance'. RA GEO/52351, GIII to Lord Carmarthen, ?November 1785

'think of it'. Aspinall, *Later Correspondence*, 1, 209

'fool!'. Dobson, *d'Arblay Diary*, 3, 223–6

'monks'. RA GEO/Add 15/8054, Ernest to Thomas Hughes, 4 April 1788

'known'. Harcourt Mss, Augusta's narrative, September 1785

'needle'. Dobson, *d'Arblay Diary*, 2, 424

'together'. RA GEO/Add 13/3 (Fr), Sophia to GIII, nd

'amused'. RA GEO/Add 12/11 (Fr), Mary to GIII, nd

'Sophie'. RA GEO/Add 13/1 (Fr), Sophia to GIII, nd

'ourselves'. RA GEO/Add 13/4 (Fr), Sophia to GIII, after 8 August 1783 'very obligingly'. Adams, *Works*, 8, 266

'Copley'. Millar, *Later Georgian*, 20

'better'. RA GEO/Add 12/10 (Fr), Mary to GIII, nd [supposed 1785]

'lungs'. Llanover, *Mrs Delany*, 3, 315

'spasms'. Ibid, 326

'side'. Delves Broughton, *Mrs Papendiek*, 1, 265

'embroidery'. Lewis, *Walpole Correspondence*, 33, 498–500

'attacks'. RA GEO(M)/Add 21/91/2 (Fr), Queen Charlotte to Duke Charles, 20
    January 1786

'distresses'. Stuart, *Daughters*, 144

'more'. RA GEO/Add 9/16, Elizabeth to Augustus, c 6 September 1786

'yours'. RA GEO/Add 9/7, Augusta to Augustus, July [1786]

'House'. RA GEO/Add 9/10, Royal to Augustus, 26 July [1786]

'stabbed'. Dobson, *d'Arblay Diary*, 2, 414

'her so'. Harcourt, *Papers*, 11, 262

'fathers'. RA GEO/Add 9/11, Royal to Augustus, August 1786

'misfortune'. RA GEO/Add 9/13, Augusta to Augustus, ?8 August 1786

'having'. RA GEO/Add 9/59, Elizabeth to Augustus, ?November 1786

'long'. RA GEO/Add 9/25, Elizabeth to Augustus, c March 1787

'Matilda'. RA GEO/Add 9/20, Royal to Augustus, 20 January 1787

'fortune'. RA GEO/Add 9/21, Royal to Augustus, early 1787

'characters'. RA GEO/Add 9/25, Elizabeth to Augustus, 30 March 1787

'no more'. RA GEO/Add 9/27, Augusta to Augustus, spring 1787

'knew him'. RA GEO/Add 9/34, Augusta to Augustus, 1–2 August 1787

'liquors'. Ibid

'bed'. RA GEO/Add 9/36, Elizabeth to Augustus, ?19 August 1787

'again'. RA GEO/Add 9/34a, Augusta to Augustus, after 19 August 1787

'in it'. RA GEO/Add 9/34, Augusta to Augustus, 1–2 August 1787

'very much'. RA GEO/Add 9/34a, Augusta to Augustus, after 19 August 1787

'improve'. RA GEO/Add 9/40, Royal to Augustus, 28 November 1787

'desire'. RA GEO/Add 21/212, Augusta to William, spring 1788

'daughter'. Dobson, *d'Arblay Diary*, 2, 401

'manner'. Ibid, 3, 103

'respect'. Ibid, 2, 386

'world'. Ibid, 427

'young'. Ibid, 411

'age'. Ibid, 410–11

'sustaining it'. Ibid, 403

'them'. Ibid, 411

'over'. Ibid, 411–12

'way'. Mountstuart Mss, BU/114/5, Queen Charlotte to Lord Bute, 19 March 1788

'honour'. Roberts, *Royal Artists*, 65

'doing it'. Hedley, *Queen Charlotte*, 138

'assist'. Mountstuart Mss, BU/114/5, Queen Charlotte to Lord Bute, 19 March
	1788
'being'. Delves Broughton, *Mrs Papendiek*, 1, 228
'sweetness'. Philobiblon, 'Mrs Harcourt's Diary', *Miscellanies*, 13, 35–6
'darling'. Buchan, *Lady Louisa Stuart*, 195
'to them'. RA GEO/Add 9/47, Royal to Augustus, 3 July 1788
'aspect'. Aspinall, *Later Correspondence*, 1, 378, n2
'wanting'. Ibid, 380–1

CHAPTER 6: FEAR

'defend him …'. Aspinall, *Later Correspondence*, 1, 390
draught. Dobson, *d'Arblay Diary*, 4, 68
bed. Ibid, 76
'head', 'face'. Dobson, *d'Arblay Diary*, 4, 4–5
'purgative'. Aspinall, *Later Correspondence*, 1, 383
'beaucoup'. RA GEO/Add 13/5, Sophia to GIII, 22 July 1788
'today'. RA GEO/Add 12/14, Mary to GIII, 22 July 1788
'Amelia'. RA GEO/Add 14/2, Amelia to GIII, 22 July 1788
'happy'. RA GEO/Add 13/6, Sophia to GIII, 5 August 1788
'gypsy'. Esher, *Girlhood of Queen Victoria*, 1, 309
'done', 'pleased', 'exceedingly'. RA GEO/Add 12/16, Mary to GIII, 7 August
	1788
'spirits'. RA GEO/Add 9/51, Augusta to Augustus, 26 September 1788
'Cheltenham'. RA GEO/Add 9/55, Royal to Augustus, 26 September 1788
'of them'. RA GEO/Add 9/56, Elizabeth to Augustus, c 26 September 1788
'geese'. Dobson, *d'Arblay Diary*, 4, 107
'use to him'. HMC, *Ailesbury*, 293
'ones'. RA GEO/Add 9/57, Royal to Augustus, 17 October [1788]
'cords'. Harcourt, *Papers*, 4, 10
Richmond. Minto, *Life*, 1, 228–9
'attack'. Macalpine and Hunter, *Mad-business*, 14
'lame'. Ibid
'delirium'. Ibid, 17
'rest'. Buckingham and Chandos, *George III*, 1, 429
'own'. Macalpine and Hunter, *Mad-business*, 17
'skin'. Aspinall, *Later Correspondence*, 1, 397
'stiffness'. Macalpine and Hunter, *Mad-business*, 18
'moment'. Buckingham and Chandos, *George III*, 1, 431
'inexpressibly'. Dobson, *d'Arblay Diary*, 4, 120
calmer. Harcourt, *Papers*, 4, 16
'mind'. Ibid, 14

waist. HMC, *Ailesbury*, 297

'Princesses'. Harcourt, *Papers*, 4, 20–1

know. Dobson, *d'Arblay Diary*, 4, 128

'remove'. Aspinall, *Correspondence*, 1, 360

'irresolution'. Dobson, *d'Arblay Diary*, 4, 125

'alarmed'. Ibid, 126

twice. Ibid, 127

'desultory'. Macalpine and Hunter, *Mad-business*, 24

mouth. Harcourt, *Papers*, 4, 21–2

'water'. Ibid, 22

'mind'. Macalpine and Hunter, *Mad-business*, 25

'unconfiding'. Dobson, *d'Arblay Diary*, 4, 129

'ill too'. Harcourt, *Papers*, 4, 24

'nervous'. Dobson, *d'Arblay Diary*, 4, 136

'restored'. Harcourt, *Papers*, 4, 28

'of me!', 'apprehensions'. Dobson, *d'Arblay Diary*, 4, 140

'grief'. Ibid, 141

'death'. Aspinall, *Correspondence*, 1, 366–7

'whatever'. Ibid, 369

effect. Moore, *Sheridan*, 2, 23

curtsey. Dobson, *d'Arblay Diary*, 4, 150

'dog'. Moore, *Sheridan*, 2, 24

'dropsical'. *Gentleman's Magazine*, October 1788

'now'. BL Add Ms 41579, Lady Elizabeth Foster's Journal, copy, f4, 20 November 1788

'skin'. Bessborough, *Georgiana*, 138

'throughout'. Bladon, *Robert Fulke Greville*, 81

'retirement'. Dobson, *d'Arblay Diary*, 4, 152

'rowing'. Bladon, *Robert Fulke Greville*, 81

hours. Ibid, 82–3

'churches'. Dobson, *d'Arblay Diary*, 4, 159

'must not'. BL Add Ms 41579, copy, f4, 20 November 1788

'flourishes'. Eden, *Auckland Correspondence*, 2, 244

'Buckingham'. Ibid

'house'. Harcourt, *Papers*, 4, 59–60

wake, LRO, DG7, Box 4953, Bundle 32, Lady Charlotte Finch to Lord Winchilsea, November 1788

'cure'. RA, King's Physicians' Reports, 23, 27 November 1788

'strait waistcoat'. BL Add Ms 41579, Lady Elizabeth Foster's Journal, copy, f6, 2 December 1788

'destroy them'. Dobson, *d'Arblay Diary*, 4, 199

'person'. Hunter and Macalpine, *Three Hundred Years of Psychiatry*, 511–13

'house'. Iremonger, *Love and the Princesses*, 103

'frightened'. BL Add Ms 41579, Lady Elizabeth Foster's Journal, copy, ff13 and 15, 14 and 19 December 1788

'days'. RA, King's Physicians' Reports, 17 December 1788

'talking about'. RA, King's Physicians' Reports, 18 December 1788

'stage'. Hayward, *Lady of Quality*, 122

'doing so'. Hutton, *Bland Burges*, 114

'as ever'. RA, King's Physicians' Reports, 24 December 1788

'hitherto'. RA, King's Physicians' Reports, 28 December 1788

'Majesty'. RA, King's Physicians' Reports, Francis Willis to GP, 1 January 1789

'wild'. Macalpine and Hunter, *Mad-business*, 77

'Cordelias'. Harcourt Mss, Royal to Elizabeth, Lady Harcourt, 22 February 1819

'properly'. Harcourt, *Papers*, 4, 221

'illness'. Macalpine, *Mad-business*, 86

'recovery'. RA, King's Physicians' Reports, Sir George Baker, Sir Lucas Pepys and Francis Willis to GP, 27 February 1789

CHAPTER 7: HOPE

'appearance'. Wraxall, *Historical and Posthumous Memoirs*, 3, 369–70

'this'. Dobson, *d'Arblay Diary*, 4, 269–70

'horseback'. Ibid, 271

'time'. Anson Mss, A1, Misc, Leonard Smelt to Mary Dickenson, née Hamilton, 14 March 1789

'bedposts'. Philobiblon, 'Mrs Harcourt's Diary', *Miscellanies*, 13, 37

'anything'. Jesse, *George III*, 3, 116

'Hanover'. RA GEO/Add 9/67, GIII to Augustus, 24 March 1789

'Englishwoman'. RA GEO/Add 9/68, Elizabeth to Augustus, 16 April 1789

'dressed', 'great'. Doran, *Lives of Queens*, 2, 147

'Jubilate'. Hedley, *Queen Charlotte*, 347

'walking'. Minto, *Life*, 1, 304–5

'millions'. Dobson, *d'Arblay Diary*, 4, 285

'opinion'. RA GEO(M)/Add 21/91/1 (Fr), Queen Charlotte to Duke Charles, 9 May 1789

'dejection', 'papers'. Macalpine and Hunter, *Mad-business*, 96

'Lennox's'. Minto, *Life*, 1, 313–22, and cf Hutton, *Bland Burges*, 121–5

lover. RA GEO/Add 11/214, [Ashe, Thomas], *The Claustral Palace*, Ms 'Programma'

'sea'. Aspinall, *Later Correspondence*, 1, 400, n4

'relaxation'. Macalpine and Hunter, *Mad-business*, 96

'year'. Harcourt, *Papers*, 8, 281

'faces'. Hemlow, *Burney Journals*, 1, 21

'crowns'. Harcourt, *Papers*, 8, 280

'King'. Dobson, *d'Arblay Diary*, 4, 298

'other [day]'. Aspinall, *Later Correspondence*, 1, 433

'men'. Ibid

'greatcoats!'. RA GEO/Add 9/75, Royal to Augustus, 10 August 1789

'fat'. Harcourt, *Papers*, 8, 312

'room'. RA GEO/Add 9/73, Augusta to Augustus, c 20 July 1789

'scene'. RA GEO(M)/21/91/2 (Fr), Queen Charlotte to Duke Charles, 1789

'woman'. Hemlow, *Burney Journals*, 1, 27

'battery', 'keep it', 'wood'. Harcourt, *Papers*, 8, 282–7

round her. Philobiblon, 'Mrs Harcourt's Diary', *Miscellanies*, 13, 11

'employment'. Delves Broughton, *Mrs Papendiek*, 2, 141–2

'equalized'. *Royal Children exhibition*, Queen's Gallery, 1963, 17

'man'. RA GEO(M)/Add 21/91/2 (Fr), Queen Charlotte to Duke Charles, 23 December 1789

'France'. Aspinall, *Later Correspondence*, 1, 440

'people'. RA GEO(M)/Add 21/91/2 (Fr), Queen Charlotte to Duke Charles, 23 December 1789

'way'. Aspinall, *Later Correspondence*, 1, 443

'cheap'. RA GEO/Add 9/78, Augusta to Augustus, 15 September 1789

'ever saw'. RA GEO/Add 2/48, Lady Mary Howe to Louisa, Lady Altamont, 2 January 1790

'painting'. RA GEO(M)/Add 21/91/2 (Fr), Queen Charlotte to Duke Charles, 23 February 1789

'consequence'. RA GEO/Add 9/84, Augusta to Augustus, end February 1790

'wish most to see'. Ibid

'most wish to see'. RA GEO/Add 9/91, Elizabeth to Augustus, 30 May and 14 June 1790

'close'. RA GEO/Add 9/88, Royal to Augustus, May 1790

'just got'. RA GEO/Add 9/85, Augusta to Augustus, 1 March 1790

'again'. RA GEO/Add 9/91, Elizabeth to Augustus, 30 May and 14 June 1790

'about'. Clement Col, LWL, Charlotte Keppel to Anne Clement, June 1790

'particular'. RA GEO/Add 9/92, Augusta to Augustus, 18 June 1790

'forward'. Aspinall, *Later Correspondence*, 1, 488

'service'. RA GEO/Add 10/2, Augusta to Ernest, 20 July 1790

'while'. RA GEO/Add 9/100, Augusta to Augustus, 2 September 1790

'women'. RA GEO/Add 9/103, Royal to Augustus, 24 September 1790

'hair'. RA GEO/Add 9/107, Sophia to Augustus, 23 November 1790

'nothing'. RA GEO/Add 9/75, Royal to Augustus, 10 August 1789

'breakfasted there'. RA GEO/Add 9/99, Royal to Augustus, 17 August 1790

'vastly well'. Harcourt Mss, Elizabeth, Lady Harcourt to Lord Harcourt, August 1790

'old'. RA GEO/Add 9/110, Queen Charlotte to Augustus, 22 December 1790

Court. Montbrison, *d'Oberkirch Memoirs*, 3, 63

'months'. RA GEO/Add 9/111, Augusta to Augustus, 23–25 December 1790

'desired of'. Harcourt Mss (Fr), Prince Ferdinand of Württemberg to Elizabeth, Lady Harcourt, 3 January 1791

'number'. RA GEO/Add 11/2, Elizabeth to Augustus, finished 1 January 1791

'behold'. Delves Broughton, *Mrs Papendiek*, 2, 208

'forward'. Ibid

'night'. RA GEO/Add 9/119, Augusta to Prince Augustus, 22 [finished 29] January 1791

'to their Majesties'. Harcourt Mss (Fr), Prince Ferdinand of Württemberg to Elizabeth, Lady Harcourt, 19 January 1791

'Augusta'. Ibid, docket by Elizabeth, Lady Harcourt, 29 January 1791

'of their majesties'. Harcourt Mss (Fr), Prince Ferdinand of Württemberg to Elizabeth, Lady Harcourt, 20 January 1791

'elder'. Delves Broughton, *Mrs Papendiek*, 2, 208

'everything'. RA GEO/Add 9/119, Augusta to Augustus, 22 [finished 29] January 1791

'taken'. RA GEO/Add 9/135, Augusta to Augustus, 30 April 1791

'my life'. RA GEO/Add 9/119, Augusta to Augustus, 22 [finished 29] January 1791

'done up for'. RA GEO/Add 9/135, Augusta to Augustus, 30 April 1791

'morning'. Delves Broughton, *Mrs Papendiek*, 2, 216–17

'screamed'. RA GEO/Add 11/5, Elizabeth to Augustus, finished 27 May 1791

'liable'. RA GEO/Add 9/132, Augusta to Augustus, 8–10 April 1791

'ladies'. RA GEO/Add 9/135, Augusta to Augustus, 30 April 1791

'Mary'. RA GEO/Add 9/131, Frederick to Augustus, 29 March 1791

'pretty'. RA GEO/Add 9/122, Mary to Augustus, c 7 February 1791

'thing'. RA GEO/Add 9/121, Sophia to Augustus, 1 February 1791

'royalty'. RA GEO/Add 9/137 Augusta to Augusta, 10 June 1791

'infant', 'postponed'. Aspinall, *Correspondence*, 2, 162

'assist'. Ibid, 163

'response'. Ibid, 170

'severity', 'woman'. Delves Broughton, *Mrs Papendiek*, 2, 217

'botanized'. RA GEO/Add 11/9, Elizabeth to Augustus, 30 July–1 August 1791

'paradise', 'success'. RA GEO/Add 9/124, Queen Charlotte to Augustus, 11 February 1791

'it did', 'first', 'about it'. RA GEO/Add 9/123, Elizabeth to Augustus, c 8 February 1791

'day'. RA GEO/Add 9/140, Elizabeth to Augustus, 28 August 1791

'for it', 'each other', 'apple'. Harcourt, *Papers*, 4, 295–8

'faith', 'Terrace', 'wax'. RA GEO/Add 9/144, Augusta to Augustus, 4 September 1791

'charming'. RA GEO/Add 9/153, Royal to Augustus, end November 1791

'to you'. RA GEO/Add 9/151, Royal to Augustus, c 4 November 1791
'broke'. RA GEO/Add 9/153, Royal to Augustus, end November 1791
'to you'. RA GEO/Add 9/158, Queen Charlotte to Augustus, 13 January 1792

CHAPTER 8: DESPOND

'whiles'. RA GEO/Add 9/160, Augusta to Augustus, 3 February 1792
'other', 'laughable'. RA GEO/Add 9/162, Sophia to Augustus, 19 February
     1792
'Amelia.' Hemlow, *Burney Journals*, 1, 110
'cards'. RA GEO/Add 9/162, Sophia to Augustus, 19 February 1792
'secret'. RA GEO/Add 15/8092, Augustus to Thomas Hughes, 10 January 1792
'one', 'Frogmore'. Hemlow, *Burney Journals*, 1, 149
'amusement'. Harcourt Mss, Elizabeth to Elizabeth, Lady Harcourt, 1792
'for them'. Hemlow, *Burney Journals*, 1, 220
'degree'. Harcourt Mss, Sophia to Elizabeth, Lady Harcourt, c 14 October 1792
'each other'. Hemlow, *Burney Journals*, 1, 109
'particular'. Ibid, 149
'given up'. RA/VIC/Add A 8/330, Mary to Mary Adelaide, 6 August [1850]
'dressing'. Harcourt Mss, Elizabeth to Elizabeth, Lady Harcourt, 3 October
     1792
'very good'. Harcourt Mss, Sophia to Elizabeth, Lady Harcourt, 14 November
     1792
'campaign'. RA GEO/48401, Adolphus to GIII, 1 February 1793
'1793'. Harcourt Mss, Verses vol
'ever since'. RL, Miss Lucy Kennedy's Diary, Oct 1793
'swallow'. RA GEO(M)/Add 21/91/2 (Fr), Queen Charlotte to Duke Charles, 28
     May 1793
'attends her'. RL, Miss Lucy Kennedy's Diary, October 1793
'own room'. Harcourt Mss, Elizabeth to Elizabeth, Lady Harcourt, 8 July 1793
'illness'. RA GEO/Add 13/9, Sophia to GIII, 19 August [1793]
'to you'. Aspinall, *Correspondence*, 2, 388
'life'. RL, Miss Lucy Kennedy's Diary, October 1793
'mention that'. RA GEO/Add 13/11, Sophia to GIII, 15 October 1793
'well'. RA GEO(M)/Add 21/91/2 (Fr), Queen Charlotte to Duke Charles, 2
     August 1793
'very much'. Harcourt, *Papers*, 5, 365–6
'angel'. Harcourt Mss, Elizabeth to Elizabeth, Lady Harcourt, 17 September 1793
'ever saw'. Aspinall, *Correspondence*, 2, 467
'roses'. RA GEO/Add 15/982, Queen Charlotte to Henry H. Compton, 6
     October 1793
'a coming'. Harcourt Mss, Elizabeth to Elizabeth, Lady Harcourt, 17 September 1793

'is in'. Gillen, *Royal Duke*, 75

'immediately'. RL, Miss Lucy Kennedy's Diary, 14 November 1793

'England'. Harcourt, *Papers*, 5, 403–4, 414

'themselves'. RL, Miss Lucy Kennedy's Diary, January 1794

'till one'. RA GEO/Add 43/3, Queen Charlotte's Journal, 25, 29 January 1794

'Murray'. Gillen, *Royal Duke*, 85

'Frederick'. Ibid, 86

'proudest'. RA GEO/Add 15/8166, Elizabeth to Lady Charlotte Finch, 26 June 1794

'glory'. Hemlow, *Burney Journals*, 3, 182

'conversation'. Harcourt Mss, Elizabeth to Elizabeth, Lady Harcourt, 25 July 1794

'possible'. Harcourt Mss, Sophia to Elizabeth, Lady Harcourt, 24 July 1794

'bread'. Hutton, *Bland Burges*, 284

'weak and sick', 'as she is'. Harcourt, *Papers*, 5, 562–4

'face'. Aspinall, *Correspondence*, 3, 32

'House'. Ibid, 33

'weapons'. Harcourt Mss, Royal to Lord Harcourt, 13 May 1795

'condescension'. Hemlow, *Burney Journals*, 6, 53

'heat'. RA GEO/Add 43/3, Queen Charlotte's Diary, 24 August 1794

'rose'. Aspinall, *Correspondence*, 3, 85

'to you'. Aspinall, *Correspondence*, 3, 119

'express'. RA GEO/Add 15/8168, Elizabeth to Lady Charlotte Finch, 6 November 1795

'noise'. Harcourt Mss, Augusta to Elizabeth, Lady Harcourt, 7 November 1795

'on him'. HMC, *Fortescue*, 3, 147

'united with hers'. RA GEO/51398–9 (Fr), Hereditary Prince to GIII, 12 December 1795

'little girl'. RA GEO/Add 15/8169, Mary to Lady Charlotte Finch, 9 January 1796

'and soul'. Aspinall, *Correspondence*, 3, 132ff

'follow'. RA GEO/Add 11/54, Elizabeth to GP, [6 June 1796]

'accomplishment'. Harcourt Mss, Memo re Counts Zeppelin and Worontzow, 5 May 1796

'negotiations'. RA GEO/51400 (Fr), Hereditary Prince to Sir John Coxe Hippisley, 4 June 1796

'take place'. RA GEO/51401 (Fr), GIII to Hereditary Prince, 15 July 1796

'amused'. Aspinall, *Correspondence*, 3, 267

'country'. RA GEO/51404 (Fr), Hereditary Prince to GIII, 6 October 1796

'marriage'. HMC, *Fortescue*, 3, 265

'from it'. Harcourt Mss, Augusta to Elizabeth, Lady Harcourt, 4 December 1796

'lamb'. Harcourt Mss, Augusta to Elizabeth, Lady Harcourt, 6 January 1797 'with him'. RA GEO/Add 15/8171, Elizabeth to Lady Charlotte Finch, April 1797

'bursting'. Childe-Pemberton, *Princess Amelia*, 25

'lover'. Buckingham and Chandos, *George III*, 2, 377

'answers'. Hemlow, *Burney Journals*, 3, 314

'spoken of'. Harcourt, *Papers*, 6, 73, 148

three. Disbrowe, *Old Days*, 179

'life'. Hemlow, *Burney Journals*, 4, 7

'herself', gold. Ibid, 14

'heralds'. Hutton, *Bland Burges*, 301

'procession'. George, *Political and Personal Caricature*, 7, 350

'show'. Harcourt, *Papers*, 6, 146

'attention'. Ibid, 147

'follow', late. RA GEO/Add 37/5, Anne Hayman to Eleanor Hayman, 2 June 1797

'regretted'. RA GEO(M)/Add 21/91/2 (Fr), Queen Charlotte to Duke Charles, 11 October 1802

'possessing it'. Hemlow, *Burney Journals*, 4, 8

'very much'. Aspinall, *Correspondence*, 3, 347

'daughter'. Aspinall, *Later Correspondence*, 2, 590

'happy'. RA GEO(M)/Add 21/91/2 (Fr), Queen Charlotte to Grand Duke Charles, 12 June 1797

'overcome'. Aspinall, *Later Correspondence*, 2, 595

CHAPTER 9: IN SPIRITS

'away'. Aspinall, *Later Correspondence*, 2, 609–10

'sister'. RA GEO/Add 37/7, Anne Hayman to Eleanor Hayman, 5 June 1797

'room'. Harcourt Mss, Elizabeth to Elizabeth, Lady Harcourt, 1 August 1797

Tomkins. Tomkins, *Birth and Triumph*

'*Love*'. Bland Burges, *Birth and Triumph of Love*; Egerton, *Birth and Triumph of Love* [plates]

'HRH'. Hutton, *Bland Burges*, 276–7, 295–6

'poem'. Ibid, 296–7

'verse'. Ibid, 298

'poets'. Ibid

'very much'. Harcourt Mss, Elizabeth to Lord Harcourt, ?1795

'Doll'. Tomkins, *Birthday Gift*

'dog'. Harcourt Mss, Elizabeth to Elizabeth, Lady Harcourt, 6 March 1796

Elizabeth. Harcourt Mss, 'Verses' vol

'Love'. Hemlow, *Burney Journals*, 3, 187

'first'. Ibid, 191

'gold'. Ibid, 195

'forward'. Harcourt Mss, Elizabeth to Lord Harcourt, 7 June 1795

'redecoration'. Hemlow, *Burney Journals* 3, 181

gardens. Dobson, *d'Arblay Diary*, 5, 216

'effects'. Hemlow, *Burney Journals*, 3, 185

'lines'. Harcourt Mss, Elizabeth to Lord and Lady Harcourt, ?4 December 1796

'else'. RA GEO/Add 21/8/36, Elizabeth to Frances Garth, 7 July 1797

'performers'. Hemlow, *Burney Journals*, 4, 10–11

'please'. Ibid, 11–12

'greatly'. RA GEO/Add 21/8/21, Sophia to Frances Garth, nd

'head'. RA GEO/Add 21/8/22, Sophia to Frances Garth, c 12 June 1796

'long'. RA GEO/Add 21/8/25, Sophia to Frances Garth, nd

'devil'. Strachey and Fulford, *Greville Memoirs* 1, 271

'même'. Aspinall, *Correspondence*, 3, 465

'presence'. Strachey and Fulford, *Greville Memoirs*, 1, 271

'enquiries'. RA GEO/Add 21/8/29, Sophia to Frances Garth, c April 1797

'repaired'. Aspinall, *Later Correspondence*, 2, 611–12

'with child'. Ibid, 618

'grandchildren'. Ibid, 633

'dreadful'. Ibid, 641

nine. Stuttgart State Archives, G245/B15, Royal to Hereditary Prince, 22 November 1797

that day. Stuttgart State Archives, G245/B15, Royal to Hereditary Prince, 23 November 1797

'heroes'. Harcourt Mss, Elizabeth to Elizabeth, Lady Harcourt, 12 November 1797

'Court'. Aspinall, *Later Correspondence*, 2, 611–12

'closet'. Ibid, 3, 24–5

'to us'. Ibid, 36

'to me'. Ibid, 30–1

'Schrader'. Ibid, 43

'in life'. Ibid, 35

'submit'. Ibid, 43

'safety'. RA GEO/51472, Charles Arbuthnot to GP, 2 May 1798

'preparing her'. Harcourt, *Papers*, 6, 148 (Fr)

'recovery'. Ibid

'my child'. Aspinall, *Later Correspondence*, 3, 57–8

'cure me'. Ibid, 58

'blow there'. Ibid, 209

'sight'. Ibid, 111

snow, 'stomach'. Brownlow, *Eve of Victorianism*, 3–4

'pain'. RA GEO/50179, Royal to Martha, Lady Elgin, 4 May 1799

rocking horse. Aspinall, *Correspondence*, 3, 415

'which it is'. RA GEO/Add 37/5, Anne Hayman to Eleanor Hayman, 2 June 1797

'left hand'. Aspinall, *Correspondence*, 3, 457

'King's'. RA GEO/Add 21/8/60, Sophia to Frances Garth, summer 1798

'lips', 'captivating'. Hemlow, *Burney Journals*, 4, 95

'attend to'. Delves Broughton, *Mrs Papendiek*, 2, 216

lessons. Ibid

sands. Aspinall, *Later Correspondence*, 3, 107

'better'. Ibid 103

thanks. Aspinall, *Correspondence*, 3, 448 n2

'motion'. Aspinall, *Later Correspondence*, 3, 109

'amendment'. Ibid, 122

'stronger'. RA VIC/Add A/8/2202, Amelia to Jane Gomm, 23 September 1798

'minute'. Aspinall, *Correspondence*, 3, 482

'lapels'. Hemlow, *Burney Journals*, 4, 232

'Keate'. Ibid, 225

'seized me'. RA VIC/Add A 8/2202 enc, Amelia to Jane Gomm, 23 September 1798

'hurts'. Aspinall, *Later Correspondence*, 3, 157

'canter'. RA VIC/Y 19/54, Amelia to Anne Parker, 20 December 1798

'what is right', 'to do right'. Aspinall, *Later Correspondence*, 3, 103

'know'. Ibid, 3, 122

'originated'. Bickley, *Glenbervie*, 2, 94

'letters'. RA GEO/Add 14/1/1 and passim, Amelia to Charles Fitzroy

'to me'. Aspinall, *Correspondence*, 4, 102

bride. Moremen, *Steadfast Son*, 92-3

'problem'. Stuart, *Daughters*, 102

'whims'. Aspinall, *Correspondence*, 2, 367

'again'. Ibid, 4, 67

'happy'. Ibid, 3, 501

'calm'. Aspinall, *Later Correspondence*, 3, 198

'death'. Minto, *Life*, 3, 177-8

'bêtise'. RA GEO(M)/Add 21/91/2 (Fr), Queen Charlotte to Duke Charles, 16 June 1800

'joy', 'custody'. RA GEO(M)/Add 21/91/2 (Fr), Queen Charlotte to Duke Charles, 16 June 1800

'hot rooms', Weymouth. RA GEO/Add 21/8/55, Sophia to Frances Garth, 25 May 1800

'sociable'. *Gentleman's Magazine*, August 1800

'shortly'. Aspinall, *Correspondence*, 4, 150

'excursions'. *Gentleman's Magazine*, September 1800

beef. Strachey and Fulford, *Greville Memoirs*, 1, 271

'paper house'. Aspinall, *Later Correspondence*, 3, 447

'prisoner'. Ibid

'Review', 'success'. Ibid, 452–3
armistice. Aspinall, *Later Correspondence*, 3, 464, 468
peace. Ibid, 470

CHAPTER 10: AGITATION

'testify'. BL Add Ms 41692, Willis Journal, f109, 17 March 1801
'unjustly'. Harcourt Mss, Sophia to Elizabeth, Lady Harcourt, 30 December 1800
'nurse'. RA GEO/Add 13/100, Sophia to Theresa Villiers, 10 January 1805
intimate. BL Add Ms 52483, f4, Sophia to 'My very dear, dear General', nd
'father'. Bickley, *Glenbervie*, 1, 363–4
'daughters'. Ibid
'Wales'. RA GEO/Add 21/179/5, Elizabeth to Thomas Willis, 6 June 1801
'person'. Wardroper, *Wicked Ernest*, 136–7
'once more'. BL Add Ms 52483, f4, Sophia to 'My very dear, dear General', nd
slept. Jesse, *George III*, 3, 245
'chilled'. Malmesbury, *Diaries*, 4, 27
nothing more. BL Add Ms 41692, Willis Journal, f5, 16 February 1801
quiet. Colchester, *Diary*, 1, 243
'ill'. BL Add Ms 41692, Willis Journal, ff9–10, 21 February 1801
'arranging'. Buckingham and Chandos, *George III*, 3, 144
'letter'. Aspinall, *Correspondence*, 4, 203
'anything', 'angry'. BL Add Ms 41692, Willis Journal, ff27–85, 2–14 March 1801
'spirits', 'sent for'. Harcourt Mss, Augusta to Lord Harcourt, 16 March 1801
'more'. Harcourt Mss, Augusta to Elizabeth, Lady Harcourt, 17 November 1801
'fondness'. HMC, *Carlisle*, 733–4
'live'. Macalpine and Hunter, *Mad-business*, 126–7
'family'. RA GEO/Add 21/179/5, Elizabeth to Thomas Willis, 6 June 1801
'fatigued'. Ibid
'minute'. Doran, *Lives of the Queens*, 2, 180
'for her'. Bickley, *Glenbervie*, 1, 224–5
'sisters'. RA GEO/Add 21/8/72, Sophia to Frances Garth, summer 1801
'home'. Aspinall, *Later Correspondence*, 3, 540
'girl'. RA GEO/50188, Royal to Martha, Lady Elgin, 24 May 1801
'timidity'. RA GEO/50189, Royal to Martha, Lady Elgin, 25 June 1801
'Adolphus's'. Aspinall, *Later Correspondence*, 3, 603
'trouble'. Ibid, 552
'in it'. Ibid, 578
'amusement'. Ibid, 591
'long'. Ibid, 584
'England'. Ibid, 606
'headaches'. Ibid, 630

'apply [myself]', 'determined'. Ibid

'followed'. Ibid, 625

'war'. Ibid, 633

'father'. Harcourt Mss, Sophia to Elizabeth, Lady Harcourt, 25 July 1801

'partout'. Harcourt Mss, Augusta to Elizabeth, Lady Harcourt, 17 November 1801

'ball'. Aspinall, *Later Correspondence*, 4, 3

'work'. Ibid, 30

'landscapes'. Ibid, 62

'wholly'. RA GEO(M)/Add 21/91/2 (Fr), Queen Charlotte to Duke Charles, 11 October 1802

'afraid'. Aspinall, *Later Correspondence*, 4, 65–6

'day'. Aspinall, *Correspondence*, 4, 303

'usual'. Ibid, 304

'understanding'. Harcourt Mss, Elizabeth to Elizabeth, Lady Harcourt, 23 July 1802

'it had'. RA GEO/Add 15/8174, Mary to Lady Charlotte Finch, 2 January 1803

'world'. RA GEO/Add 21/90/40, Princess of Wales to Elizabeth, Lady Townshend, 7 September 1807

'charming'. RA GEO/Add 15/8174, Mary to Lady Charlotte Finch, 2 January 1803

'expected'. Harcourt Mss, Elizabeth to Elizabeth, Lady Harcourt, 26 December 1803

'fine trees'. RA GEO(M)/Add 21/91/2 (Fr), Queen Charlotte to Duke Charles, 8 October 1803

'service'. RA GEO/52412 (Fr), Friedrich V, Landgrave of Hesse-Homburg to GIII, 12 January 1804

'well'. RA GEO(M)/Add 21/91/2 (Fr), Queen Charlotte to Duke Charles, 19 July 1803

'way …'. Harcourt Mss, Elizabeth to Elizabeth, Lady Harcourt, 31 July 1803

'mire'. Harcourt Mss, Augusta to Elizabeth, Lady Harcourt, 17 September 1803

'I have'. Childe-Pemberton, *Princess Amelia*, 79

'she was'. Harcourt Mss, Elizabeth to Elizabeth, Lady Harcourt, 26 December 1803

'do well'. Harcourt Mss, Amelia to Elizabeth, Lady Harcourt, 1 January 1804

'together'. Aspinall, *Correspondence*, 4, 437–8

'through'. Ibid, 496

'sensation'. HMC, *Fortescue*, 7, 215

'necessary'. Colchester, *Diary*, 1, 481

'passés'. Harcourt Mss, Elizabeth to Elizabeth, Lady Harcourt, 3 March 1804

'at 50'. RA GEO(M)/Add 21/91/2 (Fr), Queen Charlotte to Duke Charles, 20 April 1804

'miracle'. Harcourt Mss, Elizabeth to Elizabeth, Lady Harcourt, 7 May 1804

'Amelia'. Childe-Pemberton, *Princess Amelia*, 85–7

'occasion'. Ibid, 87-9

'extraordinary', 'martyrdom'. Harcourt Mss, Augusta to Elizabeth, Lady Harcourt, 3 July 1804

'Princess'. Aspinall, *Correspondence*, 5, 59

'mercy'. Ibid, 70

'ill'. Ibid, 86

'sisters'. Ibid

'vexatious'. RA GEO/Add 13/86, Sophia to Theresa Villiers, 20 August 1804

'sano'. HMC, *Fortescue*, 7, 232-3

'coach'. Ibid, 223

'duty'. Aspinall, *Correspondence*, 5, 114

'else', 'right'. Eden, *Auckland Correspondence*, 4, 213-14

'childish'. HMC, *Fortescue*, 7, 232

'illness'. RA GEO/Add 14/54, Amelia to Edward, 12 November 1804

'happiness'. RA GEO/Box 11/32c, GIII to Princess of Wales, 13 November 1804

'odious!'. RA GEO/Add 13/88, Sophia to Theresa Villiers, December 1804

'feels'. RA GEO/Add 13/91, Sophia to Theresa Villiers, 9 December 1804

'spirits'. RA GEO/Add 13/90, Sophia to Theresa Villiers, December 1804

'forgive'. RA GEO/Add 13/92, Sophia to Theresa Villiers, 24 December 1804

'whole'. Ibid

'Frogmore'. Ibid

'quiet'. Ibid

'unfavourable'. HMC, *Fortescue*, 7, 247

'eyes'. RA GEO/Add 13/95, Sophia to Theresa Villiers, 30 December 1804

'my life'. Harcourt Mss, Elizabeth to Elizabeth, Lady Harcourt, 26 December 1804

'consequence'. RA GEO/Add 13/103, Sophia to Theresa Villiers, ?19 January 1805

'lament it'. RA GEO/Add 13/106, Sophia to Theresa Villiers, ?22 January 1805

'from it'. RA GEO/Add 13/109, Sophia to Theresa Villiers, 17 February 1805

'stone'. RA GEO/Add 13/108, Sophia to Theresa Villiers, 18 February 1805

'mother'. RA GEO/Add 15/8129, William Cookson to Thomas Hughes, 19 January 1805

'attended to'. Twiss, *Lord Eldon*, 1, 481-2

'possible'. RA GEO/Add 37/32, Anne Hayman to Eleanor Hayman, 30 January [1805?]

'blame them'. RA GEO(M)/Add 21/91/2 (Fr), Queen Charlotte to GIII, ?9 April 1805

'Germany'. RA GEO(M)/Add 21/91/2 (Fr), GIII to Queen Charlotte, 9 April 1805

'separation'. Ibid

'invalids'. RA GEO(M)/Add 21/91/2 (Fr), Queen Charlotte to Duke Charles, 11 April 1805

'hands'. Hare, *Bunsen*, 1, 70-1

'evil'. PRO 30/70/6/400, Hoare Pitt Papers, Queen Charlotte to Mary Elizabeth, Lady Chatham, 3 August 1805

'here'. RA GEO/Add 13/122, Sophia to Theresa Villiers, 16 July 1805

'alive', 'over'. RA GEO/Add 13/126, Sophia to Theresa Villiers, [1805]

'things'. Ibid

'himself'. Ibid

'kangaroo'. Ibid

'exalted'. RA GEO/Add 15/8176, Elizabeth to Lady Charlotte Finch, 6 November 1805

'march'. RA GEO/Add 21/101/8, Royal to Lady Charlotte Finch, 6 November 1805

'happy'. RA GEO(M)/Add 21/91/2 (Fr), Queen Charlotte to Duke Charles, 27 May 1805

'tyrant'. RA GEO(M)/Add 21/91/2 (Fr), Queen Charlotte to Duke Charles, 12 December 1805

'esteem'. Aspinall, *Correspondence*, 5, 305–6

'situation'. RA GEO/Add 21/101/9, Royal to Lady Charlotte Finch, 2 January 1806

'names'. Aspinall, *Correspondence*, 5, 305–6

'received'. Stuart, *Daughters*, 48

'great'. Aspinall, *Correspondence*, 5, 305–6

'marriage'. O'Meara, *Napoleon*, 372–3

CHAPTER 11: OUTCRY

'blow'. Childe-Pemberton, *Princess Amelia*, 108

'Wales'. Fairburn, *The Book*, 1–4

'morning'. RA GEO/Add 21/90/6, Princess of Wales to Elizabeth, Lady Townshend, 31 May–1 June 1806

lawyers. RA GEO/Add 21/90/1, Princess of Wales to GIII, 8 June 1806

'receive her', 'good humoured'. RA GEO/Add 14/1/5, Amelia to Charles Fitzroy, 'Thursday night, I have so much to say to you ...'

'story ...'. RA GEO/Add 13/100, Sophia to Theresa Villiers, 10 January 1805

'perfect rag'. RA GEO/Add 13/103, Sophia to Theresa Villiers, ?19 January 1805

'too often'. RA GEO/Add 13/107, Sophia to Theresa Villiers, 23 January 1805

'world'. RA GEO/Add 21/8/185, Thomas Garth to Frances Garth, 17 July 1806

'tears'. RA GEO/Box 8/15, Duchess of Brunswick to GIII, 25 August 1806

'release'. Harcourt Mss, Elizabeth to Elizabeth, Lady Harcourt, 1 December 1806

'alone'. RA/GEO/Add 21/90/59, Spencer Perceval to Elizabeth, Lady Townshend, 10 December 1806

'concern'. Aspinall, *Correspondence*, 6, 127

'powder'. Fairburn, *The Book*, Appendix, 63–4

'reprimand'. RA GEO/Add 37/43, Princess of Wales to Anne Hayman, 2 February 1807

'succession'. RA GEO/Box 8/3, GP to GIII, 1 February 1807

'Eagle'. Granville, *Private Correspondence*, 2, 251

'sufferings'. Aspinall, *Later Correspondence*, 4, 521

'England'. Aspinall, *Correspondence*, 6, 325−6

'shook'. RA GEO/Add 37/55, Princess of Wales to Anne Hayman, 29 November 1807

'taste'. RA GEO/52252, Duchess of Brunswick to GIII, 3 September 1807

'cats'. RA GEO/Add 37/54, Princess of Wales to Anne Hayman, after 3 September 1807

'ago'. RA GEO/Add 37/48, Princess of Wales to Anne Hayman, 14 July 1807

'loss'. Harcourt Mss, Augusta to Elizabeth, Lady Harcourt, 7 September 1807

'escaped'. Ibid

'better'. *United Service Journal* (1829), 2, 83−8

'choice'. Harcourt Mss, Augusta to Elizabeth, Lady Harcourt, 28 June 1808

'endeavour'. Harcourt Mss, Augusta to Elizabeth, Lady Harcourt, 17 August 1808

'myself'. RA GEO/Add 15/991, Elizabeth to Augusta Compton, 13 February 1808

'lonely'. Aspinall, *Correspondence*, 6, 265

'toe'. Ibid, 298

'father'. Ibid, 308−10

'country'. RA GEO/Add 12/2/36, Mary to Anna Maria Adams, 11 July 1808

'with her'. Ibid

'ruined'. Childe-Pemberton, *Princess Amelia*, 136

'outrageous'. Ibid, 137

'this year'. RA GEO/Add 12/2/36, Mary to Anna Maria Adams, 11 July 1808

'pay for'. RA VIC/Y 19/34, Amelia to Charlotte Williams, 25 January 1808

'rogue'. Aspinall, *Correspondence*, 6, 356 n1

'give up'. Harcourt Mss, Elizabeth to Elizabeth, Lady Harcourt, 17 September 1807

'unwholesome'. Aspinall, *Correspondence*, 6, 308−9

'desk'. Ibid

'tail', 'kindness'. Ibid

'nameless'. Ibid, 316

'upon it'. Ibid, 317

'of it', 'theirs'. Ibid

'again'. Ibid

'lot'. Ibid, 323

'wife'. Ibid

'set'. Ibid, 324

'way'. RA GV/CC/35/10, Grand Duchess of Mecklenburg-Strelitz to Queen Mary, 9 March 1910 'for me'. Aspinall, *Correspondence*, 6, 324

'law'. Ibid, 338–9

'children'. RA GEO/Add 13/30, Sophia to GP, 5 October 1808

'by it'. Bickley, *Glenbervie*, 1, 383–4

'properly'. RA GEO/Add 15/993, Elizabeth to Augusta Compton, 30 November 1808

'sadly'. Ibid

'taken'. Aspinall, *Correspondence*, 6, 373

'adviser'. Ibid

'wish'. Ibid, 364

'immaterial'. RA VIC/Add W 3/6, Elizabeth to Dorothea, Lady Banks, nd

'flaws'. Harcourt Mss, Elizabeth to Elizabeth, Lady Harcourt, 1 December 1808

CHAPTER 12: PASSION

'way'. RA GEO/Add 14/1/11, Amelia to Charles Fitzroy, nd [before 1808], begins: 'AFR, I trust I may say your opinion'

'servants'. RA GEO/Add 14/1/83, Amelia to Charles Fitzroy, nd, begins: 'dear Lord E, how I love him'

'devils'. RA GEO/Add 13/147, Sophia to Theresa Villiers, 6 February 1809

'flippant'. Harcourt Mss, Augusta to Elizabeth, Lady Harcourt, 10 March 1809

'swim for them'. RA GEO/Add 13/147, Sophia to Theresa Villiers, 6 February 1809

'dressing'. RA GEO/Add 14/1/11, Amelia to Charles Fitzroy, nd, begins: 'AFR, I trust I may say your opinion'

'rights'. Childe-Pemberton, *Princess Amelia*, 180–1

'inseparable'. Ibid, 173

'breath …'. RA GEO/Add 14/1/60, Amelia to Charles Fitzroy, nd, begins: 'Oh God I am almost mad for you'

'unpleasant'. RA GEO/Add 14/1/51, Amelia to Charles Fitzroy, begins: 'Wed night, I must begin by blessing you'

'womb'. RA GEO/Add 14/1/14, Amelia to Charles Fitzroy, nd, begins: 'Tell me, my own dear precious darling, Have I done anything you don't like'

'name'. RA GEO/Add 14/1/60, Amelia to Charles Fitzroy, begins: 'Oh God, I am almost mad for you'

'leads to'. RA GEO/Add 14/1/8, Amelia to Charles Fitzroy, nd, begins: 'As I have the pamphlets to send you'

'longed for'. RA GEO/Add 14/1/11, Amelia to Charles Fitzroy, nd, begins: 'AFR, I trust I may say your opinion'

'anything'. RA GEO/Add 14/1/8 Amelia to Charles Fitzroy, begins: 'As I have the pamphlets to send you'

'give me'. RA GEO/Add 14/1/10, Amelia to Charles Fitzroy, begins: 'My own dear angel, I must begin by telling you my worry …'

'should be'. Add 14/1/8, Amelia to Charles Fitzroy, nd, begins: 'As I have the pamphlets to send you'

'providence'. RA GEO/Add 13/155, Sophia to Theresa Villiers, [1809]

'assistance'. RA GEO/Add 46/14, Sophia to Sir William Parsons, 14 May 1809

'skeleton', 'illness'. RA GEO/Add 13/149, Sophia to Theresa Villiers, 8 April 1809

'recover'. Aspinall, *Correspondence*, 6, 412

'either'. Ibid

'pain'. Childe-Pemberton, *Princess Amelia*, 237

'meeting'. Bickley, *Glenbervie*, 2, 23−4

'her side'. Aspinall, *Correspondence*, 6, 412−13

'cure'. Ibid, 414

'air'. RA GEO/Add 12/2/43, Mary to Anna Maria Adams, 17 August 1809

'remaining'. Aspinall, *Later Correspondence*, 5, 319

'life'. Childe-Pemberton, *Princess Amelia*, 200

'speak'. Aspinall, *Correspondence*, 6, 423

'better'. Ibid

'health'. Childe-Pemberton, *Princess Amelia*, 78

'water'. Aspinall, *Later Correspondence*, 5, 370

'hide it'. RA VIC/Y 19/37, Amelia to Charlotte Williams, 23 August 1809

'satisfied'. Aspinall, *Later Correspondence*, 5, 333

'side'. Ibid, 354

'through'. Ibid, 370

'roof'. Ibid, 333

'entirely'. Ibid, 352

'witness'. Ibid, 370

'distressing'. Ibid, 356

'issues'. Ibid, 389

'caustic'. Aspinall, *Correspondence*, 6, 455

'nothing'. Ibid, 471

'recommended'. Aspinall, *Later Correspondence*, 5, 436

'eastward'. Ibid, 411

'mind'. Aspinall, *Correspondence*, 6, 478

'quarter'. Ibid, 479

'quiet'. RL, Miss Lucy Kennedy's Diary, October 1810

'death'. Ibid

'Münster [the Hanoverian Minister]'. Aspinall, *Correspondence*, 6, 516

'cross words'. Bickley, *Glenbervie*, 2, 24

'room', 'Weymouth'. Aspinall, *Correspondence*, 6, 518

'unfavourable', 'case'. Ibid, 517

'reasonable'. Aspinall, *Later Correspondence*, 5, 476

'grapes'. RA GEO/Add 14/180−90, Matthew Baillie to GIII, letters of May 1810

'exhaustion'. Aspinall, *Later Correspondence*, 5, 590

'suffering'. Aspinall, *Correspondence*, 7, 33

'abhor'. RA GEO/Add 14/176, Amelia to Charlotte Williams, 11 May 1810

'him'. RA GEO/Add 14/256, plate inventory, 1810

'locked'. RA GEO/Add 14/168, jewellery invoice, 1809

'gratitude', 'world'. Childe-Pemberton, *Princess Amelia*, 214–15

'unparalleled'. LRO/DG24/822/3, Halford Papers, Sir Henry Halford to Mary, with encl (copy) [autumn 1810]

'regret'. LRO/DG24/822/4, Halford Papers, Amelia to Sir Henry Halford, 9 September 1810 (copy)

'like'. Aspinall, *Correspondence*, 7, 48–9

'account'. LRO/DG24/822/4, Halford Papers, Amelia to Sir Henry Halford, 9 September 1810 (copy)

'indescribable'. Harcourt Mss, Augusta to Elizabeth, Lady Harcourt, 26 September 1810

'as I do'. Ibid

'minute'. Harcourt Mss, Amelia to Elizabeth, Lady Harcourt, [1810]

'kindness'. Childe-Pemberton, *Princess Amelia*, 222–3

'released'. RA GEO/Add 21/101/50, Elizabeth to Henrietta Finch, 19 October 1810

'transparent'. Knight, *Autobiography*, 1, 174

'to it'. Ibid

'life'. Harcourt Mss, Augusta to Elizabeth, Lady Harcourt, 26 October 1810

'sleep'. RA GEO/Add 14/228, Sir Henry Halford to GP, 28 October 1810

'countenance'. Knight, *Autobiography*, 1, 174

'of her'. RL, Miss Lucy Kennedy's Diary, October 1810

'mornings'. Ibid

'coffin with him'. Ibid

'to ask'. RA GEO/Add 14/289, J. D. Bridges, Memorandum, [1810]

'sounds'. Harcourt Mss, Augusta to Elizabeth, Lady Harcourt, 6 November 1810

'Queen'. RL, Miss Lucy Kennedy's Diary, 2 November 1810

'wishes'. Childe-Pemberton, *Princess Amelia*, 227

'tear'. Harcourt Mss, Augusta to Elizabeth, Lady Harcourt, 6 November 1810

'hear'. Aspinall, *Correspondence*, 7, 67, n1

'time'. Ibid, 65–6, n1

'illness'. RA GEO/Add 15/1027, Elizabeth to Augusta Compton, c 2 November 1810

'under them'. Buckingham, *George III*, 4, 462–3

'rank'. Macalpine and Hunter, *Mad-business*, 145–6

'Amelia'. Aspinall, *Correspondence*, 7, 67, n1

'insanity'. Munk, *Halford*, 143

'purpose'. Aspinall, *Correspondence*, 7, 73

'to me'. Aspinall, *Later Correspondence*, 5, 607

'blindness'. HMC, *Fortescue*, 10, 60

'her'. Harcourt Mss, Augusta to Elizabeth, Lady Harcourt, 6 November 1810

'right'. RA GEO/Add 10/121, Augusta to Anna Maria Adams, [1810]

'grief'. Harcourt Mss, Augusta to Elizabeth, Lady Harcourt, 6 November 1810

'believe it'. Harcourt Mss, Elizabeth to Elizabeth, Lady Harcourt, 9 November 1810

'taken off'. Macalpine and Hunter, *Mad-business*, 146

'Prince'. RL, Miss Lucy Kennedy's Diary, November 1810

'tears'. RA GEO/Add 15/1030, Elizabeth to Augusta Compton, 5 January 1811

CHAPTER 13: BREAKING UP

'of dress'. RA GEO/Add 14/270, Inventory taken ... 1 December 1810

'apartments'. RA GEO/Add 14/278, Theresa Villiers to Charles Bicknell, 10 December 1810

'poor'. RL, Miss Lucy Kennedy's Diary, November 1810

'confidence'. Colchester, *Diary*, 2, 293

'shock'. Aspinall, *Correspondence*, 7, 67–8 n1

'despair'. RA GEO/Add 12/2/75, Elizabeth to Anna Maria Adams, 15 December 1810

'mind'. RA GEO/Add 12/2/78, Elizabeth to Anna Maria Adams, 20 December 1810

'might', 'like'. RA GEO/Add 12/2/68, Mary to Anna Maria Adams, 26 November 1810

'nerves is'. RA GEO/Add 12/2/74, Elizabeth to Anna Maria Adams, 14 December 1810

'alive'. Colchester, *Diary*, 2, 308

'manner'. Macalpine and Hunter, *Mad-business*, 152

'dexterity', 'not so good'. Harcourt, *George Rose*, 2, 474–5

'life'. Macalpine and Hunter, *Mad-business*, 155

'calmness'. RA GEO/Add 12/2/107, Mary to Anna Maria Adams, c 5 February 1811

'recovering'. RL, Miss Lucy Kennedy's Diary, 6 February 1811

'formerly'. RL, Miss Lucy Kennedy's Diary, 20 May 1811, and Phipps, *Plumer Ward*, 1, 344

'door'. RA, Princess Mary's Reports to PR, 21 May 1811

'help trade'. RA, Princess Mary's Reports to PR, May 1811

'sick room'. RA GEO/Add 12/2/94, Mary to Anna Maria Adams, May 1811

'boxes, etc'. RA GEO/50262–4, General Herbert Taylor's Memorandum, 23 December 1811

'key'. Ibid

'daughter'. Buckingham and Chandos, *Regency*, 1, 102

'situation'. RA GEO/Add 12/2/94, Mary to Anna Maria Adams, May 1811 meditated. RA GEO/Add 15/882, Mary to Sir Henry Halford, 4 June 1811

'worse'. RA, Princess Mary's Reports to PR, 1812

'time'. RA, GEO/Add 12/116, Mary to Anna Maria Adams, June 1811

'voice'. Ibid

'dull'. Aspinall, *Princess Charlotte*, 1

'reason'. RA GEO/Add 12/2/95, Mary to Anna Maria Adams, 19 July 1811

'hour'. RA GEO/Add 12/2/109, Mary to Anna Maria Adams, 8 August 1811

'know me'. RA GEO/Add 10/46, Augusta to Charlotte Williams, 15 August 1811

'stillness'. Knight, *Volume of Varieties*, 78

'mind'. RA GEO/Add 15/874, Sir Henry Halford's Diary, 6 December 1811

'evening'. RA, Princess Mary's Reports to PR, 1812

'upon it'. RA GEO/Add 15/874, Sir Henry Halford's Diary, 17 October 1811

'disagreed'. RA GEO/Add 12/2/101, Mary to Anna Maria Adams, 9 November 1811

'Saturday'. Harcourt Mss, Mary to Elizabeth, Lady Harcourt, 20 October 1811

'Quadrangle'. Harcourt Mss, Augusta to Elizabeth, Lady Harcourt, 10 October 1811

'reduced'. Ibid

'ears'. Harcourt Mss, Elizabeth to Elizabeth, Lady Harcourt, 23 October 1811

'castle'. Aspinall, *Princess Charlotte*, 12

'otherwise'. Harcourt Mss, Elizabeth to Elizabeth, Lady Harcourt, 23 October 1811

'heart'. RA GEO(M)/Add 21/91/1 (Fr), Queen Charlotte to Duke Charles, 19 November 1811

'world'. RA GEO/Add 15/874, Sir Henry Halford's Diary, 2 December 1811

'state'. RA, Princess Mary's Reports to PR, 20 January 1812

'Yes'. RA GEO/Add 15/874, Sir Henry Halford's Diary, 4 January 1812, Proposed questions …

'together'. RA GEO/Add 13/51, Sophia to PR, 12 December 1811

'of us'. RA, Princess Mary's Reports to PR, 2 January 1812

'gratified'. RA GEO/Add 21/88/86, William Fremantle's draft speech, 22 March 1812

'account'. RA GEO/Add 13/52, Sophia to PR, March 1812

'myself'. RA GEO/Add 10/50, Augusta to PR, 23 January 1812

'heart'. RA GEO/Add 15/1037, Elizabeth to Augusta Compton, 29 February 1812

'conduct'. Harcourt Mss, Elizabeth to Elizabeth, Lady Harcourt, 9 January 1812

'bilious'. Harcourt Mss, Elizabeth to Elizabeth, Lady Harcourt, 12 February 1812

'to us'. RA GEO/Add 15/1037, Elizabeth to Augusta Compton, 29 February 1812

'thought of'. Harcourt Mss, Elizabeth to Elizabeth, Lady Harcourt, 23 January 1812

'happiness'. RA GEO/Add 10/56, Augusta to PR, 5 March 1812

'for us'. RA GEO/Add 10/51, Augusta to PR, 2 April 1812

'criticized'. RA GEO/Add 10/52, Queen Charlotte to Princesses, 2 April 1812

'footing'. RA GEO/Add 10/51, Augusta to PR, 2 April 1812

'looks'. RA GEO/Add 12/2/123, Mary to Anna Maria Adams, 9 June 1812

'large'. Ibid

'yourself …'. RA GEO/Add 10/55, Augusta to PR, 12 June 1812

'character'. RA GEO/Add 10/56, Augusta to PR, 5 March 1812

'married'. Walker, *Miniatures: Eighteenth and Early Nineteenth Centuries*, 167–8

'right'. RA GEO/Add 12/2/123, Mary to Anna Maria Adams, 9 June 1812

'life'. RL, Miss Lucy Kennedy's Diary, 30 April 1811 [12]

'subdued', 'fever'. RA GEO/Add 12/2/118, Mary to Anna Maria Adams, 3 January 1812

'sick'. Ibid

'saw him'. Colvin, *Maria Edgeworth*, 127

'nervous'. LRO/DG24/844, Sophia's correspondence with Sir Henry Halford

'overcome'. RA GEO/Add 12/2/122, Mary to Anna Maria Adams, 15 May 1812

'monster'. Ibid

'overset'. RA GEO/Add 15/1038, Elizabeth to Augusta Compton, 26 May 1812

'children'. RA GEO/Add 12/2/122, Mary to Anna Maria Adams, 15 May 1812

'hand and pen'. RA GEO/Add 15/1037, Elizabeth to Augusta Compton, 29 February 1812

'idea'. RA GEO/Add 15/1038, Elizabeth to Augusta Compton, 26 May 1812

'bedrooms'. RA GEO/Add 15/1039, Elizabeth to Augusta Compton, 13 June 1812

'visit her'. RA GEO/Add 12/2/124, Mary to Anna Maria Adams, 28 June 1812

'uncertainties'. Aspinall, *Princess Charlotte*, 30

'fled'. Ibid, 27

'games'. Ibid, 19

'everybody'. Ibid, 28

'heart'. RA GEO/Add 12/2/64, Mary to Anna Maria Adams, 12 July 1812

'repeater'. Aspinall, *Princess Charlotte*, 33

'loves'. Ibid, 32

'round'. RA GEO/Add 12/2/126, Mary to Anna Maria Adams, 24 August 1812

'older'. Ibid

'cold'. RA, Princess Mary's Reports to GP, 1813

'without end'. RA GEO/Add 12/2/116, Mary to Anna Maria Adams, June 1811

'upon'. RA GEO/Add 15/49694–5, Mary to PR, 21 December [1812]

'there'. Stuart, *Daughters*, 223

'yet'. Aspinall, *Princess Charlotte*, 38

'place'. Ibid, 37

'best'. RA GEO/Add 12/2/117, Mary to Anna Maria Adams, 27 November 1812

'scene'. RA GEO/Add 10/57, Augusta to PR, 2 December 1812

'please'. RA GEO/36622–3, Queen Charlotte to PR, 2 December 1812

'met with'. RA GEO/Add 10/57, Augusta to PR, 2 December 1812 'mind'. Ibid

'mind it'. RA GEO/Add 12/191, Mary to PR, 7 December 1812

'most deeply'. RA GEO/Add 10/57, Augusta to PR, 2 December 1812

'humour'. RA GEO/Add 12/190, Mary to PR, 6 December 1812

'at all'. RA GEO/Add 12/193, Mary to PR, 9 December 1812

'towards us'. RA GEO/Add 10/59, Augusta and sisters to PR, c 12 December 1812

'famous for'. RA GEO/Add 12/2/138, Mary to Anna Maria Adams, 29 December [?1812]

'Christmas day'. RA GEO/Add 21/101/41, Mary to Henrietta Finch, 10 December [1812]

'low'. RA GEO/Add 12/2/141, Mary to Anna Maria Adams, [1812]

CHAPTER 14: EMANCIPATION

'arrangements'. RA GEO/Add 12/2/147, Mary to Anna Maria Adams, January 1813

'directly'. RA GEO/49725–6, Elizabeth to PR, 11 January 1813

'Charlotte'. RA GEO/49749–50, Mary to PR, 19 January 1813

'trifles'. Aspinall, *Princess Charlotte*, 51

'everything'. Ibid, 52

'before'. Ibid

'doings'. RA GEO/Add 23/8, Unknown to William Frederick, 6 January 1813

'amorous', 'foolish'. RA VIC/QVJ, 1 August 1838

'death'. RA GEO/Add 12/196, Mary to PR, 25 January [1813]

'stand'. Ibid

'influence'. Aspinall, *Princess Charlotte*, 71

'England'. Harcourt Mss, Royal to Elizabeth, Lady Harcourt, 21 May 1814

'thank God'. RA GEO/Add 10/63, Augusta to Sir Henry Halford, 2 May 1813

'adoration'. RA GEO/Add 12/197, Mary to PR, 18 February 1813

'together'. Ibid

'*faut*'. RA GEO(M)/Add 21/91/2 (Fr), Queen Charlotte to Duke Charles, 2 April 1813

'was'. RA GEO/Add 12/2/160, Mary to Anna Maria Adams, 1 November 1813

'shyness'. RA GEO/Add 12/2/154, Elizabeth to Anna Maria Adams, 16 May 1813

'intended'. RA GEO/Add 12/2/155, Mary to Anna Maria Adams, 18 May 1813

'folly'. RA GEO/Add 12/2/154, Elizabeth to Anna Maria Adams, 16 May 1813

'by and by'. RA GEO/Add 15/1046, Elizabeth to Augusta Compton, 19 May 1813

'HRHs'. RA GEO/Add 15/1048, Elizabeth to Augusta Compton, 11 June 1813

'that's all'. RA GEO/Add 15/1051, Elizabeth to Augusta Compton, 8 August [1813]

'meddle'. Aspinall, *Princess Charlotte*, 67

'violent'. Ibid, 55

'front'. Ibid, 72

'else'. Aspinall, *Princess Charlotte*, 65

'over'. Ibid, 78

'glorious'. Ibid, 80

'true'. Ibid, 92, 95

'married'. Ibid, 97

'advice'. Ibid

'faces'. Ibid

'used'. Ibid, 102

'strength'. Ibid, 99

'me'. Ibid 105–6

'cough'. Harcourt Mss, Royal to Elizabeth, Lady Harcourt, 21 May 1814

'ferociously'. RA GEO/Add 15/8180, Elizabeth to Sophia Feilding, 11 June 1814

'conduct'. RA GEO/51774–5, Royal to PR, 30 June 1814

'end'. Aspinall, *Princess Charlotte*, 118

'interfere'. RA GEO/Add 21/122/12, Lord Liverpool to Princess of Wales, 28 July 1814

'low'. Aspinall, *Princess Charlotte*, 135

'pleasure'. RA GEO/Add 12/207, Mary to PR, 27 July 1814

'lovely'. Aspinall, *Princess Charlotte*, 131

'impossible'. Ibid, 144

'inaccessible'. Ibid

'subjected'. Ibid

'settled'. Harcourt Mss, Royal to Elizabeth, Lady Harcourt, 16 March 1814

'agreed'. Aspinall, *Princess Charlotte*, 145

'cat's paw'. Ibid

'sulks'. Ibid, 147

'again'. Ibid, 146

'certainly'. Ibid, 149

'else'. Ibid, 153

'of him'. Ibid, 151

'that kind'. Ibid, 152, 154–5

'the way'. Ibid, 161

'overstrained'. Ibid, 165

'of him'. Ibid, 180

'quiet'. Ibid, 191

'quarantine'. RA GEO/Add 22/92, Sophia to Princess Charlotte, late 1815

'firm'. Aspinall, *Princess Charlotte*, 191–2

'miserable'. Ibid, 193

'Dutch man'. Ibid

'year'. Aspinall, *Letters*, 2, 45

'difficulties'. RA GEO/Add 12/214, Mary to PR, 18 September [1815]

'letter'. Harcourt Mss, Elizabeth to Elizabeth, Lady Harcourt, 4 September [1815] 'world'. RA GEO/Add 12/238, Mary to PR, 3 September [1815]

'err'. RA GEO/Add 9/188, Elizabeth to Augustus, 3 September 1815

'concur'. RA GEO/Add 10/70, Augusta to PR, 28 August 1815

'myself'. Aspinall, *Princess Charlotte*, 209–10

'mine'. Aspinall, *Letters*, 1, 515–23

'bosom'. RA GEO/49888-9, Princess Charlotte to Mary, 26 December 1814

'*qui vive*'. Aspinall, *Princess Charlotte*, 210–11

'happy'. Ibid, 212

'I believe'. Ibid, 207

'Austin'. Ibid, 217

'perfect'. RA GEO/Add 12/261, Mary to PR, 6 February 1816

'starved'. RA GEO/Add 21/101/34, Augusta to Henrietta Finch, 29 December 1815

'down'. Aspinall, *Princess Charlotte*, 224

'fine lace'. Ibid, 221

'people'. Ibid, 224

'married'. Ibid, 235

'about her'. Ibid, 237

'awkwardness', 'animals'. Ibid 242–3

'nearly'. Ibid, 243

'fainted'. Childe-Pemberton, *Princess Amelia*, 296–7

'cheeks'. Twiss, *Lord Eldon*, 2, 284

'Smelt'. RA, Princess Mary's Reports to GP, 1813

'distress'. RA GEO/Add 21/64, Mary to Helena Trench, née Perceval, 21 June 1816

'happiness'. RA GEO/Add 21/65, Augusta to Helena Trench, 23 June 1816

'situation'. RA GEO/Add 12/274, Mary to PR, 14 July 1816

'can now'. RA GEO/Add 12/276, Mary to PR, 20 July 1816

'occasions'. Aspinall, *Princess Charlotte*, 243

'tiresome'. Ibid, 245

'with him'. Ibid

CHAPTER 15: DAUGHTERS IN DISTRESS

'state'. RA GEO/Add 12/282, Mary to PR, 29 September 1816

'heart'. RA GEO/Add 12/278, Mary to PR, 26 July 1816

'supper'. RA GEO/Add 15/1064, Elizabeth to Augusta Baynes, née Compton, 26 September 1816

'park'. RA GEO/Add 12/278, Mary to PR, 26 July 1816

'Offices'. RA GEO/Add 12/283, Mary to PR, 8 October 1816

'married me'. RA GEO/Add 21/101/18, Mary to Henrietta Finch, 4 October 1816

'family'. RA GEO/Add 12/305, Mary to PR, 3 December [1817]

'very much'. RA GEO/Add 21/101/18, Mary to Henrietta Finch, 4 October 1816

'ago'. RA GEO/Add 12/286, Mary to PR, 2 November 1816

'gone'. Harcourt Mss, Elizabeth to Elizabeth, Lady Harcourt, 29 November 1816

'can be'. Aspinall, *Princess Charlotte*, 246

'life'. RA GEO/51808, Royal to PR, 12 February 1817

'trade'. Harcourt Mss, Royal to Elizabeth, Lady Harcourt, 23 May 1817

'dying'. Harcourt Mss, Elizabeth to Elizabeth, Lady Harcourt, 29 November 1816

'mind'. Ibid

'grave'. Harcourt Mss, Royal to Elizabeth, Lady Harcourt, 23 May 1817

'heart'. Ibid

'fortune'. Aspinall, *Letters*, 2, 171

'grandfather'. RA GEO/51809, Royal to PR, 12 August 1817

'ceremony'. Bury, *Diary*, 2, 272

'subject'. Harcourt Mss, Augusta to Elizabeth, Lady Harcourt, 19 September 1817

'delightful'. RA GEO/Add 12/297, Mary to PR, 26 October 1817

'figures'. RA GEO/Add 15/1066, Elizabeth to Augusta Baynes, 24 August 1817

'Charlotte'. RA GEO/50048–9, Elizabeth to [?Sir Benjamin Bloomfield], 6 November 1817

'blow'. Ibid

'dreadful shock'. Harcourt, *Papers*, 6, 265

'completely shocked'. RA GEO/50048–9, Elizabeth to [?Sir Benjamin Bloomfield], 6 November 1817

'child'. Brougham, *Memoirs*, 2, 332

'deep affliction'. Aspinall, *Letters*, 2, 213

'afresh'. Harcourt Mss, Augusta to Elizabeth, Lady Harcourt, 8 November 1817

'severe affliction'. Harcourt Mss, Augusta to Elizabeth, Lady Harcourt, 13 November 1817

'over'. Harcourt Mss, Augusta to Elizabeth, Lady Harcourt, 19 November 1817

'false'. Ibid

'Paradise'. Harcourt Mss, Queen Charlotte to Elizabeth, Lady Harcourt, 11 November 1817

'face'. RA GEO/Add 12/309, Mary to PR, 23 December [1817]

'day'. Holme, *Prinny's Daughter*, 241

'delicacy'. RA GEO/Add 21/179/159, PR to Lord Eldon, 1 January 1817

'daughter'. RCP, Hunter-Baillie Mss, 8, Princess of Wales to Matthew Baillie, 2 December 1817 (copy)

'meeting'. RA GEO/Add 46/48, Sophia Beckedorff to Lady Parsons, 12 November 1817

'altered'. RA GEO/Add 12/307, Mary to PR, 11 December 1817

'hasp'. RA GEO/Add 12/311, Mary to PR, 18 January 1818

'usually do'. RA GEO/Add 15/1075, Elizabeth to Augusta Baynes, 7 January 1818

'death'. RA GEO/Add 12/312, Mary to PR, 23 January 1818

'leaving her'. RA GEO/Add 12/314, Mary to PR, 29 January 1818

'shone'. Harcourt Mss, Elizabeth to Elizabeth, Lady Harcourt, 16 November 1825
'object'. RA GEO/Add 13/63, Sophia to PR, 30 January 1818
'manner'. RA GEO/Add 12/316, Mary to PR, February 1818
'under it'. RA GEO/Add 12/317, Mary to PR, 3 February 1818
'manifested'. RA GEO/Add 13/60, Sophia to PR, 5 February 1818
'decision'. Ibid
'should'. RA GEO/Add 13/62, Sophia to PR, 16 February 1818
'world'. RA VIC/A 8/2204, Elizabeth to Jane Gomm, 20 February 1818
'stupid'. RA VIC/M 45/26 (Ger), Augusta, Dowager Duchess of Saxe-Coburg to
     Dowager Princess of Leiningen, 13 February 1818
'sous–lieutenant'. O'Meara, *Napoleon*, 372–3
cleaned. Hesse-Homburg papers, Fritz to Christian Jacobi, February 1818
'imagined'. Maxwell, *Creevey Papers*, 1, 276–7
'pang'. Harcourt Mss, Elizabeth to Elizabeth, Lady Harcourt, 12 June 1818
'quarrel'. RA GEO/Add 10/94, Augusta to Lord Arran, 7 July 1818
'others'. Harcourt Mss, Royal to Elizabeth, Lady Harcourt, 2 September 1818
'night'. PML, Rulers of England, Box 13b, Mary to Lady Charlotte Belasyse, 16
     February 1820
'carriage'. Harcourt Mss, Royal to Elizabeth, Lady Harcourt, 2 September 1818
'appearing there'. Harcourt Mss, Elizabeth to Elizabeth, Lady Harcourt, 4 August
     1818
'death'. Hedley, *Queen Charlotte*, 294
'prolonged'. NYPL, Berg Col, Elizabeth to Fanny Burney, 8 November 1818
'improvements'. NYPL, Berg Col, Mary to Fanny Burney, 11 December 1818
'danger', 'to them'. RA GEO/50343–4, Sir Herbert Taylor to PR, 31 October 1818
'effect', 'asleep'. Ibid
'signed it'. RA GEO/50353–65, Sir Herbert Taylor's Memorandum, 17 November
     1818
'Windsor'. Ibid
'for her'. RA GEO/Add 7/1332, Augusta to Edward, 23 November 1818
'King'. RA GEO/Add 10/75, Augusta to PR, 31 October 1818
'judgement'. RA GEO/Add 7/1332, Augusta to Edward, 23 November 1818
'worlds'. Ibid
'room'. Harcourt Mss, Elizabeth to Elizabeth, Lady Harcourt, 4 August 1818

CHAPTER 16: PRINCESSES AT LARGE

'here'. RA GEO/Add 7/1334–5, Augusta to Edward, 30 November 1818
'fumbling'. RA GEO/Add 12/324, Mary to PR, 7 December 1818
'comfort'. RA GEO/Add 13/65, Sophia to PR, 18 November 1818
'wish'. Harcourt Mss, Augusta to Elizabeth, Lady Harcourt, 4 January 1819
'with pleasure'. Harcourt Mss, Augusta to Elizabeth, Lady Harcourt, 4 February 1819

'her pleasure'. RA GEO/50375–6, Sir Herbert Taylor's Instructions to Mr Nichol

'plate'. Harcourt Mss, Augusta to Elizabeth, Lady Harcourt, 4 February 1819

'low'. Ibid

'spirits'. Harcourt Mss, Royal to Elizabeth, Lady Harcourt, 22 February 1819

'time'. Aspinall, *Letters*, 2, 298–9

'my own'. Harcourt Mss, Royal to Elizabeth, Lady Harcourt, 22 March 1819

'I am'. Ibid

'German'. RA GEO/51812–3, Royal to Adolphus, 29 March 1819

'wonderful'. RA GEO/Add 21/1/70, Augusta to William, 17 May 1819

'occasion'. RA GEO/Add 7/1334–5, Augusta to Edward, 30 November, 17
     December 1818

'removed'. RA GEO/Add 21/15/2, Augustus to Ernest, 5 April 1819

'much'. RA GEO/Add 15/1079, Elizabeth to Augusta Baynes, 30 March 1819

'hands'. RA VIC/Y 19/22, Edward to William Townsend Aiton, 11 August 1819

'made it'. NYPL, Berg Col, Fanny Burney to Augusta, 12 August 1819

'high spirits'. RA GEO/Add 12/329, Mary to PR, 19 August 1819

'Windsor'. RA GEO/Add 12/333, Mary to PR, 10 September 1819

'occasion'. Harcourt Mss, Augusta to Elizabeth, Lady Harcourt, 30 July 1819

'strength'. RA GEO/Add 12/328, Mary to PR, 12 August 1819

'ornament'. RA GEO/Add 13/64, Sophia to PR, 10 November 1819

'rather not'. RA GEO/Add 12/332, Mary to PR, 3 September 1819

'else'. RA GEO/Add 12/339, Mary to PR, 10 November 1819

'court'. RA GEO/Add 12/335, Mary to PR, 26 September 1819

'be you'. RA GEO/Add 12/337, Mary to PR, 3 October 1819

'ball'. RA GEO/Add 12/343, Mary to PR, 3 December 1819

'without you'. RA GEO/Add 12/345, Mary to PR, 6 December 1819

'music'. RA GEO/Add 12/353, Mary to PR, 16 January 1820

'sadly'. RA GEO/Add 12/356, Mary to PR, 23 January 1820

'appearance'. RA GEO/Add 12/355, Mary to PR, 20 January 1820

'countenance'. Ibid

'heart'. RA GEO/Add 12/358, Mary to PR, 27 January 1820

'shocked'. Ibid

'with her'. RA GEO/Add 12/357, Mary to PR, 24 January 1820

'sad thing'. RA GEO/Add 11/324, Elizabeth to PR [GIV], 30 January 1820

'melancholy'. RA GEO/Add 12/358, Mary to PR, 27 January 1820

'suffer'. RA GEO/Add 12/361, Mary to PR, 28 January 1820

'disease'. RA GEO/Add 9/192, Augusta to Augustus, [27 January 1820]

'yesterday'. Harcourt Mss, Augusta to Elizabeth, Lady Harcourt, 25–26 January 1820

'by it'. Harcourt Mss, Augusta to Elizabeth, Lady Harcourt, 4 February 1820

'carriages'. RA GEO/Add 12/368, Mary to PR, now GIV, 13 February 1820

'town'. RA GEO/Add 12/355, Mary to PR, 20 January 1820

'dinner'. RA GEO/Add 12/364, Mary to PR, now GIV, February 1820

'him'. RA GEO/Add 11/325, Elizabeth to GIV, 6 February 1820

'must be'. Ibid
'anybody'. RA GEO/Add 12/351, Mary to PR, 6 January 1820
'ties'. *The Examiner*, 19 March 1812
'years'. RA GEO/Add 13/67, Sophia to PR, now GIV, 2 February 1820
'enough'. RA GEO/Add 12/374, Mary to GIV, 7 March 1820
'life'. Ibid
'right'. RA GEO/Add 12/378, Mary to GIV, 17 March 1820
'mischief'. Harcourt Mss, Royal to Elizabeth, Lady Harcourt, 20 April 1820
'inducement'. RA GEO/Add 13/68, Sophia to GIV, 12 March 1820
'home'. Ibid
'room'. RA GEO/Add 12/376, Mary to GIV, 12 March 1820
'her own way'. RA GEO/Add 12/386, Mary to GIV, 11 April 1820
'defend us'. RA GEO/Add 12/379, Mary to GIV, 20 March 1820
'Silly Billy'. Brownlow, *Eve of Victorianism*, 195
'burnt'. RA GEO/Add 12/382, Mary to GIV, 28 March 1820
'come'. RA GEO/Add 12/389, Mary to GIV, 12 June 1820
'Wood'. RA GEO/Add 21/15/9, Augusta to Ernest, 17 December 1820
'Bedlamite'. Bamford and Wellington, *Mrs Arbuthnot*, 1, 53
'hold'. RA GEO/Add 21/15/9, Augusta to Ernest, 17 December 1820
'fagged'. RA GEO/Add 21/15/10, Augusta to Ernest, 8 May 1821
'event'. Jennings, *Croker Papers*, 1, 201
'with it'. RA GEO/Add 12/393, Mary to GIV, 18 August 1821
'society'. Ibid

CHAPTER 17: ROYAL – QUEENLY DOWAGER

the King. RA GEO/52484–5 (Fr), Elizabeth to Fritz, 24 December 1820
'never well'. RA GEO/52488–9 (Fr), Elizabeth to Fritz, 28 December 1820
'brother'. RA GEO/52484–5 (Fr), Elizabeth to Fritz, 24 December 1820
'please'. RA GEO/52480–1 (Fr), Elizabeth to Fritz, 21 December 1820
'endure it'. RA GEO/Add 21/15/10, Augusta to Ernest, 8 May 1821
'smoke'. RA GEO/Add 21/15/9, Augusta to Ernest, 17 December 1820
'dust'. RA GEO/Add 21/15/10, Augusta to Ernest, 8 May 1821
'one family'. Hudson, *Royal Conflict*, 72
'to me?'. RA GEO/Add 12/410, Royal to Mary, 26 November 1824
'wrong'. RA GEO/Add 21/15/10, Augusta to Ernest, 8 May 1821
'picturesque'. NYPL, Berg Col, Elizabeth to Fanny Burney, 21 April 1819
'eyes'. RA GEO/Add 12/2/131, Mary to Anna Maria Adams, 6 October 1821
'world'. Ibid
'pleasant'. RA GEO/Add 10/87, Augusta to Adolphus, 26 March 1824
'attendants'. RA GEO/Add 12/410, Royal to Mary, 26 November 1824
'dances'. Ibid

'piano'. RA GEO/51820, Royal to Adolphus, 24 March 1824

'you'. RA VIC/Z 480/149, Sophia to Victoria, 3 September 1824

'dog'. RA GEO/Add 15/8062, Ernest to Thomas Hughes, 29 March 1825

'd'Arblay'. Hemlow, *Burney Journals*, 11, 510

'good'. RA GEO/Add 12/422, GIV to Mary, 23 July 1826

'reception'. RA GEO/Add 21/8/118, Augusta to Frances Garth, [1825]

known. YCBA, Ephemera Col (T395.5 G74E87 1833+), *Extraordinary Exhibition! Under the Patronage of HRH the Princess Augusta … the Industrious Fleas etc* [?1833]

'right'. RA GEO/Add 10/97, Augusta to Lord and Lady Arran, 1 September 1826

'my life'. RA GEO/Add 10/99, Augusta to Lord and Lady Arran, 13 September 1826

'indeed'. RA GEO/Add 10/100, Augusta to Lord and Lady Arran, 28 September 1826

before. Hemlow, *Burney Journals*, 11, 111n

theatres. Harcourt Mss, Verses, 'A Word to the Wise', by Elizabeth, Lady Harcourt, December 1792

'Legacy'. Russell, *Thomas Moore*, 8, 203

'George IV'. Ibid, 4, 193

'rooms'. RA GEO/Add 10/99, Augusta to Lord and Lady Arran, 13 September 1826

'too well'. RA GEO/Add 13/71, Sophia to GIV, 18 January 1827

'receive'. RA GEO/Add 13/72, Sophia to Lady John Thynne, 18 January [1827]

'greenhouses'. RA GEO/Add 21/15/11, Augusta to Ernest, 20 April 1827

'wild', 'bridge'. RA GEO/51825–6, Royal to Augusta, 25 March 1827

'woman'. RA GEO/51827–8, Royal to GIV, 25 March 1827

'servants', 'astonished'. RA GEO/Add 21/15/12, Augusta to Ernest, 5 July 1827

'credible'. Ibid

'wax, etc'. RA GEO/Add 10/103, Augusta to Lord and Lady Arran, 25 July 1827

'out of it'. RA GEO/Add 21/15/12, Augusta to Ernest, 26 July 1827

wig. Home, *Lady Louisa Stuart*, 75

'with her'. RA VIC/Add U 72/4, Mary to Charlotte, Duchess of Northumberland, 18 August [1827]

'new life'. RA GEO/Add 10/104, Augusta to Lord and Lady Arran, 3 August 1827

'Brighton', 'moonlight'. RA GEO/Add 10/104, Augusta to Lord and Lady Arran, 3 August 1827

'in them'. RA GEO/Add 21/15/13, Augusta to Ernest, [between 20 and 27 September 1827]

Pauline. Home, *Lady Louisa Stuart*, 131

'again'. RA GEO/Add 21/15/13, Augusta to Ernest, [between 20 and 27 September 1827]

'occurring'. RA VIC/Z 480/155, Sophia to Victoria, 29 September 1827

'return'. RA GEO/Add 13/80, Sophia to Lady Louisa Murray, 28 October [1827?]

'delights'. RA GEO/Add 10/106, Augusta to Lord and Lady Arran, 12 December 1827

'melancholy'. Ibid

'manner'. RA GEO/Add 10/107, Augusta to Lord and Lady Arran, 27 December 1827

'hot rooms'. RA GEO/Add 21/15/14, Augusta to Ernest, 7 January 1828

'safety'. Ibid

'torture and misery'. RA GEO/Add 21/15/15, Augusta to Ernest, 16 October 1828

some hours. Home, *Lady Louisa Stuart*, 131

times. Disbrowe, *Old Days*, 179

'years …'. RA GEO/Add 13/80, Sophia to Lady Louisa Murray, 28 October [1828]

'offence'. RA GEO/Add 21/88/152, Augusta to Sir William Fremantle, 24 December 1828

'country'. RA GEO/Add 23/52, Mary to Louise, Lady Currey, end 1836

'Park'. Ibid

'friends …'. *United Service Journal*, (1829) 2, 83–8

happy. Wardroper, *Wicked Ernest*, 130–45

'words?'. RA VIC/Z 480/155, Sophia to Victoria, 29 September [1828]

'near me'. Ibid

'lady'. RA VIC/PP 1/80/3, Captain Thomas Garth to George, 25 November 1862

Georgiana back. Wardroper, *Wicked Ernest*, 130–45

'flower-garden'. RA VIC/LB 1/30, Victoria to Sophia, 3 August 1829

'much'. RA VIC/LB 1/36, Victoria to Sophia, 1829

boil. RA VIC/LB 1/39, Victoria to Sophia, 6 September 1829

'time to me'. RA VIC/Z 480/157, Victoria to Sophia, 4 November 1829

'purpose'. RA VIC/Z 480/156, Sophia to Victoria, 5 October 1829

death. Parissien, *George IV*, 7

'King'. *The Times*, 16 July 1830

CHAPTER 18: ELIZABETH – THE LARGESSE OF A LANDGRAVINE

'heart'. RA GEO/Add 11/346, Elizabeth to Sir William Knighton, 23 August 1829

'produce'. Stuart, *Daughters*, 193

'anyone'. RA GEO/Add 11/349a, Elizabeth to GIV, 25 April 1830

'for me'. RA GEO/Add 11/351, Elizabeth to Sir William Knighton, 1 June 1830

'death'. Yorke, *Princess Elizabeth*, 130–1

'society'. Ibid

'to me'. Ibid

'fixed'. Ibid

'possible'. RA GEO/Add 39/575, Lord Munster to Mary, 24 November 1832, draft

'in it'. Jennings, *Croker Papers*, 2, 113

'horror …'. RA GEO/Add 11/333, Elizabeth to GIV, 22 December 1821

'peu à peu'. Yorke, *Princess Elizabeth*, 190

'perfect'. Trollope, *Frances Trollope*, 191–2

'time'. Yorke, *Princess Elizabeth*, 162

'kind'. Ibid

'house …'. Ibid, 151

'assist'. Ibid, 155

'advice'. RA VIC/Add A 8/503a, Mary to Gussy, 1833

'expected'. Yorke, *Princess Elizabeth*, 179

'improper', 'cows'. Ibid, 178

'parties'. Ibid, 195

'usual'. RA GEO/Add 15/8081, Richard Jelf to Thomas Hughes, 10 October 1832

'himself'. Yorke, *Princess Elizabeth*, 196–7

'carriages'. RA VIC/Z 480/159, Sophia to Victoria, 14 January 1832

'eye'. RA GEO/Add 13/75, Sophia to Adolphus, 27 January 1832

'worst'. Ibid

'drawback'. RA VIC/Z 480/164, Sophia to Victoria, 12 September 1832

'swimming'. RA VIC/LB 4/1, Victoria to Sophia, 1833

'always'. RA VIC/LB 3/36, Victoria to Sophia, 1833

'curly'. RA VIC/LB 4/10, Victoria to Sophia, 1833

'washerwoman'. Yorke, *Princess Elizabeth*, 192, n1

'of her'. RA GEO/Add 21/196, Elizabeth to Edward Harding, 15 June 1833

'well', 'Box'. Yorke, *Princess Elizabeth*, 228–9

'killed'. Ibid, 255–6

'Buckinghamshire'. RA GEO/Add 21/15/17, Augusta to Ernest, 14 October 1834

'head'. Jennings, *Croker Papers*, 2, 250

'love them'. RA VIC/QVJ, 2 December 1834

'lived'. RA GEO/Add 23/38, Elizabeth to Louise, Lady Currey, 13 December 1834

'than him'. RA VIC/QVJ, 4 May 1857

'in him'. RA GEO/Add 23/35, Elizabeth to Louise, Lady Currey, 2 December 1834

'above'. RA VIC/Z 480/174, Sophia to Victoria, 25 December 1834

'cap'. RA VIC/QVJ, 1 February 1835

'strength'. RA VIC/Z 480/176, Sophia to Victoria, 26 August [1835]

'down hill'. Yorke, *Princess Elizabeth*, 273

'order'. RA GEO/Add 21/8/118, Augusta to Frances Garth, [1825]

'arm'. RA GEO/Add 21/15/16, Augusta to Ernest, 2 October 1833

'Sir J.C.'. RA VIC/QVJ, 15 March 1838

'anyone'. RA VIC/QVJ, 21 January 1839

'stuff'. Hudson, *Royal Conflict*, 83

'ear'. RA VIC/QVJ, 26 February 1836

'of all'. RA VIC/LB 32/15, Victoria to Sophia, 6 November 1836

'Clarence'. Hesse-Homburg Papers, Christian Jacobi to Frau Jacobi, 29 June 1836

'fog'. Ibid

'deeds'. Yorke, *Princess Elizabeth*, 278

'spirits'. RA VIC/LB 29/8, Victoria to Sophia, 1 September 1836

'well'. RA GEO/Add 21/15/17, Augusta to Ernest, 3 February 1835 'delirious'. RA VIC/QVJ, 10 January 1837

'amusingly'. RA VIC/QVJ, 24 April 1837

'country'. RA VIC/Z 480/191, Sophia to Queen Victoria, 26 June 1837

'others'. RA VIC/Z 480/198, Sophia to Queen Victoria, 16 August [1837]

'spoilt with'. Yorke, *Princess Elizabeth*, 321

'manner'. RA GEO/Add 21/15/22, Augusta to Ernest, 26 June 1837

'Ministers'. RA GEO/Add 23/54, Mary to Louise, Lady Currey, July 1837

evening. RA VIC/QVJ, 24 September 1837

'acquaintance'. RA VIC/Y 19/95, Mary to Queen Louise, 5 January 1838

'high-shouldered'. RA VIC/QVJ, 6 November 1837

'of us'. RA VIC/Y 19/95, Mary to Queen Louise, 5 January 1838

'funny' RA VIC/QVJ, 19 January 1838

'away'. RA VIC/QVJ, 27 November 1837

'situation'. RA VIC/Y 19/90, Mary to Queen Louise, 3 July 1837

'for her'. RA GEO/Add 21/88/181, Augusta to Sir William Fremantle, 22 December 1837

'robes'. RA VIC/QVJ, 12 February 1838

'disheartened'. Ibid

'with me …'. RA GEO/Add 21/15/27, Mary to Ernest, 30 August [1838]

'country'. RA VIC/C 58/7 and 7a, Augusta to Sir Benjamin Stephenson, 27 April 1838, 7 July 1838

dinner. RA VIC/QVJ, 2 May 1838

'at last'. RA VIC/QVJ, 5 July 1838

'windows out'. RA VIC/QVJ, 13 July 1838

'civility'. RA VIC/QVJ, 14 July 1838

'way', 'friends'. RA GEO/Add 21/15/27, Mary to Ernest, 13 and 24 July [1838]

'pied-à-terre'. Stuart, *Daughters*, 195

'ladies'. Yorke, *Princess Elizabeth*, 323

'natives', 'contretemps'. Ibid, 330

'Gothick screens'. Stuart, *Daughters*, 197

'well … with her'. Ibid, 196

'does'. Yorke, *Princess Elizabeth*, 328

'*moi*'. Ibid, 332

'waters'. Ibid, 336

'over'. Ibid, 353

'concerns'. RA GEO/Add 15/454, Elizabeth to Augusta Hicks, 15 December 1838

'amusements'. RA VIC/Add W 5/13, Elizabeth to Sir Samuel Higgins, 15 June 1839

'wild'. Ibid

'Louis'. Ibid

'about'. RA VIC/Z 480/74, Elizabeth to Queen Victoria, 26 June 1839

'useless'. Stuart, *Daughters*, 199

'suffering'. RA VIC/QVJ, 15 January 1840

'shawls'. RA GEO/Add 11/352, Elizabeth's will, 12 February 1830
'either'. RA GEO/Add 21/15/31, Mary to Ernest, 3 March 1840

CHAPTER 19: AUGUSTA – A PRINCESS FOR ALL SEASONS

'affected'. RA VIC/QVJ, 15 January 1840
'curtsy'. Stuart, *Daughters*, 199
'life'. Ibid
'do so'. RA VIC/QVJ, 15 January 1840
'married'. RA VIC/Y 19/96, Mary to Queen Louise, 17 September 1839
'friend'. RA GEO/Add 21/15/24, Augusta to Ernest, 21 February 1839
'Queens'. RA VIC/Y 19/96, Mary to Queen Louise, 17 September 1839
'thing'. Strachey and Fulford, *Greville Diary*, 2, 115
liberty. Longford, *Victoria RI*, 134
'difficulty ...'. RA VIC/LB 101/1, Queen Victoria to Mary, 2 February 1840
'ago'. RA VIC/A 31/750, Ernest to Sir Frederick Watson, 20 February 1840
'Brighton', 'write'. RA VIC/QVJ, 27 April 1840
'imagination'. Ibid
'family'. RA VIC/Z 480/51, Augusta to Queen Victoria, [1840]
'en passant'. RA VIC/Z 480/56, Augusta to Queen Victoria, 22 May 1839
'ought to be'. RA VIC/Add C 12/17, Augusta to Sir Henry Whately, 15 July 1839
'think'. RA GEO/Add 21/15/23, Augusta to Ernest, 3 October 1838
'book'. RA VIC/Add A 8/2B, Augusta to Mary Adelaide, 17 November 1838
'Augusta'. RA VIC/Z 480/66, Augusta to Queen Victoria, 22 May 1840
'bed'. RA VIC/Z 480/53, Augusta to Queen Victoria, 3 February 1839
'worst'. RA GEO/Add 10/120, *Morning Herald*, 2 July 1840
'look at'. RA GEO/Add 21/8/112, Augusta to Frances Garth, 4 October 1823
'walk'. Ibid
'yew'. Pückler-Muskau, *Tour*, 4, 153
'variety'. *Gardener's Magazine*, 4 (1828), 176–7
better. RA GEO/Add 21/8/118, Augusta to Frances Garth, [autumn 1825]
'feelings sadly'. RA GEO/Add 10/111, Augusta to Lord and Lady Arran, 11 November 1829
'verdure'. RA GEO/Add 10/110, Augusta to Lord and Lady Arran, 1 October 1829
'turf'. *Gardener's Magazine*, 4 (1828), 433–7
'admirably'. Ibid, 5 (1829), 570–1
'night'. RA GEO/Add 10/98, Augusta to Lord and Lady Arran, 9 September 1826
'sanctum'. Ibid
'for me'. RA GEO/Add 21/8/112, Augusta to Frances Garth, 4 October 1823
'head?'. RA GEO/Add 21/8/114, Augusta to Frances Garth, 4 December 1823

'constitution'. RA VIC/MP, 122/95, Sir Henry Halford to Lord Melbourne, 27 August 1840

information. RA VIC/C 3/60, Queen Victoria to Lord Melbourne, 27 August 1840

Windsor. Strachey and Fulford, *Greville Memoirs*, 4, 289

'awake'. RA VIC/MP 122/99, Sir Henry Halford to Lord Melbourne, September 1840

'nourishment'. RA VIC/MP 122/104, Sir Henry Halford to Lord Melbourne, 16 September 1840

'afternoon'. RA VIC/C 3/61, Queen Victoria to Lord Melbourne, ?30 August 1840

'directly'. RA VIC/C 3/64, Queen Victoria to Lord Melbourne, 21 September 1840

'touching'. RA VIC/Y 90/2, Queen Victoria to Leopold, 26 September 1840

'so long'. RA VIC/C 3/65, Queen Victoria to Lord Melbourne, 22 September 1840

'everything'. RA VIC/QVJ, 22 September 1840

'family'. RA VIC/Y 67/8, Leopold to Queen Victoria, 1 October 1840

CHAPTER 20: SOPHIA – THE LITTLE GYPSY

'couch-pillows'. Stuart, *Daughters*, 314

'wearied'. Murray, *Recollections*, 70

'as ever'. Ibid, 71

'gypsy'. Esher, *Girlhood of Queen Victoria*, 1, 309

'pretty'. RA VIC/LB 125/10, Queen Victoria to Leopold, 22 December 1840

'old lady'. RA PP/VIC/1/80/28, Sir Arthur Bigge's Memorandum, 1 November 1896

Malta. Beinecke Library, Osborn Col, Osborn Files, Folder 81, Queen Adelaide to Charles Blomfield, 22 November 1824

'look'. Wyndham, *Lady Lyttelton*, 279

'thin'. Hibbert, *Queen Victoria Letters*, 95

'happening'. Longford, *Victoria RI*, 171

'trades people'. RA VIC/Add A 8/324, Mary to Gussy, 11 February [1844]

'thunderbolt'. RA VIC/Y 19/94, Mary to Queen Louise, 8 December 1844

luncheon. RA VIC/QVJ, 5 November 1843

'seaside'. RA VIC/T 1/9, Mary to Bertie, 10 May [1846]

'good'. RA VIC/QVJ, 29 January 1846

'complaining'. RA VIC/QVJ, 24 July 1846

'live on'. RA VIC/QVJ, 7 January 1848

'feeble'. RA VIC/QVJ, 14 February 1848

'horror'. RA VIC/Y 93/32, Queen Victoria to Leopold, 16 May 1848

'case'. RA VIC/Y 74/54, Leopold to Queen Victoria, 19 May 1848

'expired'. RA VIC/QVJ, 27 May 1848

'placid'. Ibid

'world'. Strachey and Fulford, *Greville Memoirs*, 6, 69
'amiable', 'done'. RA VIC/QVJ, 27 May 1848
'right'. RA VIC/QVJ, 29 May 1848
'Green', 'possible'. Ibid
'ones'. RA VIC/QVJ, 6 June 1848
'number 8028'. Curl, *Kensal Green*, 122–3
'me there'. RA VIC/QVJ, 4 May 1857
live with him. Wardroper, *Wicked Ernest*, 241–2
attempts. RA PP/VIC/1/80/20–9; Miss Georgiana Garth's Claims, 1875

CHAPTER 21: MARY – LAST OF THE LINE

'sea'. RA VIC/QVJ, 27 July 1848
'sensible'. RA VIC/QVJ, 29 July 1848
'distressed her'. RA VIC/QVJ, 15 July 1849
'gasp'. RA VIC/QVJ, 8 July 1850
'deeds'. RA VIC/Add A 8/927, Mary to Duchess of Cambridge, 9 July 1850
well liked. RA VIC/QVJ, 8 July 1850
'see her'. Ibid, 9 July 1850
'bequeath'. RA VIC/QVJ, 16 July 1850
'insulted'. RA VIC/QVJ, 12 November 1850
'manners'. RA VIC/QVJ, 13 November 1850
'drawing room'. RA VIC/Add A 8/330, Mary to Mary Adelaide, 6 August [1850]
'nonsense'. RA VIC/Add A 8/331, Mary to Mary Adelaide, 14 September [1850]
'over'. RA VIC/Add A 8/330, Mary to Mary Adelaide, 6 August [1850]
'come'. RA GEO/Add 12/407, Mary to Duchess of Cambridge, 26 April 1851
'year'. RA VIC/Add A 8/329, Mary to Duchess of Cambridge, 3 July [1850]
'comfortably'. RA VIC/Z 480/116, Mary to Queen Victoria, 11 May 1851
'bed'. RA VIC/Add A 8/332, Mary to Mary Adelaide, 23 May [1851]
'everybody'. RA VIC/Add A 7/208, Mary to Duchess of Cambridge, 22 August
      [?1854]
'as the Exhibition'. RA VIC/Add A 8/340, Mary to Mary Adelaide, 10 September
      [1851]
'in the Exhibition'. RA VIC/Add A 8/338, Mary to Gussy, ?15 June 1851
'have!'. Burghclere, *Great Man's Friendship*, 143
'family'. RA VIC/QVJ, 12 November 1851
'shudder'. RA VIC/QVJ, 20 November 1851
'kept up'. RA VIC/Z 480/117, Mary to Queen Victoria, 21 November 1851
'princes'. RA VIC/Z 480/119, Queen Victoria to Mary, 29 November 1851
'days'. RA VIC/Add A 8/349, Mary to Duchess of Cambridge, 11 January [1852]
'general'. RA VIC/Add A 8/353, Mary to Duchess of Cambridge, 8 May 1852
'Cheveley'. RA VIC/Add A 8/335, Mary to Mary Adelaide, 5 June 1851

'old lady'. RA VIC/Add C 2/1, Mary to Sarah, Lady Abinger, 4 May [1850s]

'wonders'. Argyll, *Passages from the Past*, 1, 200

'us all'. Ibid

'chloroform'. Longford, *Victoria RI*, 234

'child'. St Aubyn, *Royal George*, 91

troops. RA VIC/Add A 8/199–200, George to Mary and to Duchess of Cambridge, 3 October 1854

'moment'. RA VIC/Add A 8/357, Mary to Duchess of Cambridge, 3 November [1854]

out to him. RA VIC/Add A 8/358, Mary to Duchess of Cambridge, 11 December 1854

'shaken'. RA VIC/Z 480/133, Mary to Queen Victoria, 1 January 1855

'there'. RA VIC/Add A 8/365, Mary to Duchess of Cambridge, 23 March 1855

victims. Roberts, *Royal Artists*, 71

dress. RPC, RCIN 54306, Queen Victoria, with Edward, Prince of Wales, Princess Alice and Mary, Duchess of Gloucester, by Antoine Claudet

shawl. RPC, RPC.01/0170/18b, Princess Mary, Duchess of Gloucester, by Augustus Liddell

'place'. RA VIC/Z 61/19, Mary to Queen Victoria, 3 October [1855]

'yesterday'. Ibid

'disagreeable'. RA VIC/Add U 142/26, Mary to Frances Paget, 23 February [no year]

'one'. RA VIC/Z 480/137, Mary to Queen Victoria, 30 March 1856

'skin'. RA VIC/QVJ, 4 May 1857

'arranged'. RA VIC/QVJ, 27 August 1856

'steadily'. RA VIC/Z 480/144, Mary to Queen Victoria, 7 September 1856

'by and by'. RA VIC/T 1/10, Mary to Bertie, 11 November [?1850]

'stairs'. RA VIC/Z 480/144, Mary to Queen Victoria, 7 September 1856

'bed'. Ibid

'for her'. RA VIC/Z 480/148, Mary to Queen Victoria, 18 March 1857, marked: 'the last letter to me. She was taken ill on the night after 15 April and died April 30, 1857'

'smart'. RA VIC/Add U 142/28, Mary to Frances Paget, nd

'convenience'. RA PP/VIC/Add 751, Augustus Liddell to Sir Thomas Biddulph, 15 April 1857

'April the 15th, GH'. RA VIC/M 54/22, Mary to Prince Albert, 15 April 1857

'night'. RA VIC/Add A 8/3441/222, Mary Adelaide's Diary, 16 April 1857

'work'. RA VIC/Add A 8/3441/222–3, Mary Adelaide's Diary, 16 April 1857

'brain'. RA VIC/Add A 8/3441/224, Mary Adelaide's Diary, 18 April 1857

'come'. RA VIC/Add A 8/3441/233, Mary Adelaide's Diary, 27 April 1857

'face', 'sadly'. RA VIC/Add A 8/3441/237–8, Mary Adelaide's Diary, 28–30 April 1857

'family'. RA VIC/QVJ, 30 April 1857

Select Bibliography

DOCUMENTARY

Additional and Egerton Mss, British Library, London
Anson Mss, private collection
Henry W. and Albert A. Berg Collection, New York Public Library, New York
Clement Collection, Lewis Walpole Library, Yale University, Farmington, Connecticut
Ephemera Collection, Yale Center for British Art, New Haven
Finch Mss, DG7, Leicestershire Record Office, Wigston Magna
Georgian and Additional Georgian, Victorian and Additional Victorian, and George V Papers, Royal Archives, Windsor Castle
Halford Mss, DG24, Leicestershire Record Office, Wigston Magna
Harcourt Mss, private collection
Hesse-Homburg Papers, Gothic House, Bad Homburg
Hoare Pitt Papers, Public Record Office, Kew
Miss Lucy (known as Mrs) Kennedy's Diary, Royal Library, Windsor Castle
Lord Chamberlain's Papers, Public Record Office, Kew
Lower Saxony State Archives, Hanover
Mountstuart Mss, Isle of Bute, Scotland
James Marshall and Marie-Louise Osborn Collection, Beinecke Library, Yale University, New Haven
Rulers of England Papers, Pierpont Morgan Library, New York
Stuttgart State Archives, Stuttgart

PRINTED

Place of publication is London unless otherwise stated.

Adams, Charles Francis, ed, *Works of John Adams, with a Life* ... 10 vols (Boston, 1850–6)
Annual Register, 1st series, 104 vols (1758–1862)
Anson, Elizabeth and Florence, eds, *Mary Hamilton, afterwards Mrs John Dickenson, at Court and at Home: From Letters and Diaries, 1756–1816* (1925)

Argyll, John, Duke of, *Passages from the Past*, 2 vols (1907)

Aspinall, Arthur, ed, *The Letters of King George IV, 1812–1830*, 3 vols (Cambridge, 1938)

Aspinall, Arthur, ed, *Letters of the Princess Charlotte, 1811–1817* (1949)

Aspinall, Arthur, ed, *The Later Correspondence of George III*, 5 vols (Cambridge, 1962–70)

Aspinall, Arthur, ed, *The Correspondence of George, Prince of Wales, 1770–1812*, 8 vols (1963–71)

Bamford, Francis, and the Duke of Wellington, eds, *The Journal of Mrs Arbuthnot, 1820–32*, 2 vols (1950)

Beattie, William, *Journal and residence in Germany, 1822, 1825 and 1826*, 2 vols (1831)

Bessborough, Earl of, ed, *Georgiana: Extracts from the Correspondence of Georgiana, Duchess of Devonshire* (1955)

Bickley, Francis, ed, *Diaries of Sylvester Douglas, Lord Glenbervie*, 2 vols (1928)

Bladon, F. McKno, ed, *Diaries of Colonel the Hon. Robert Fulke Greville* (1930)

Bland Burges, Sir James, *Birth and Triumph of Love: a poem* (1796)

Boaden, James, *Memoirs of the Life of John Philip Kemble*, 2 vols (1825)

Boaden, James, *Memoirs of the Life of Mrs Siddons*, 2 vols (1827)

Boddy, Maureen, and Jack West, eds, *Weymouh: An Illustrated History* (Wimborne, 1983)

Brougham, Henry, *Memoirs of Henry Brougham by himself*, 3 vols (1871)

Brownlow, Emma, Countess of, *The Eve of Victorianism: Reminiscences of the Years 1802 to 1834* (1940)

Buchan, Susan, *Lady Louisa Stuart: Her Memories and Portraits* (1932)

Buckingham and Chandos, Richard Grenville, 2nd Duke of, *Memoirs of the Court and Cabinets of George the Third*, 4 vols (1853, 1855)

Buckingham and Chandos, Richard Grenville, 2nd Duke of, *Memoirs of the Court of England, during the Regency, 1811–1820*, 2 vols (1856)

Buckingham and Normanby, John Sheffield, Duke of, *Works*, 4th edn, 2 vols (1753)

Burghclere, Winifred, Lady, ed, *A Great Man's Friendship: Letters of the Duke of Wellington to Mary, Marchioness of Salisbury, 1850–1852* (1927)

Bury, Lady Charlotte, *The Court of England under George IV, founded on a diary …*, 2 vols (1896)

Bury, Shirley, *History of Jewellery, 1789–1910*, 2 vols, vol 1: *The International Era, 1789–1861* (1991)

Bute, John, Earl of, *Botanical Tables*, 9 vols (1785)

Campbell, Thomas, *Life of Mrs Siddons* (1839)

Campbell Orr, Clarissa, 'Queen Charlotte as Patron', *Society for Court Studies*, 6 (2001)

Childe-Pemberton, William S., *The Romance of Princess Amelia* (1910)

Climenson, E. J., ed, *Passages from the Diaries of Mrs Philip Lybbe Powys* (1899)

Cloake, John, *Palaces and Parks of Richmond and Kew*, 2 vols, vol 2: *Richmond Lodge and the Kew Palaces* (Chichester, 1996)

Cokayne, G. E., *The Complete Peerage ... revised by Vicary Gibbs et al.*, 13 vols (1910–59)

Colchester, Charles, 2nd Baron, ed, *The Diary and Correspondence of Charles Abbot, Lord Colchester*, 3 vols (1861)

Colvin, Christina, ed, *Maria Edgeworth: Letters from England, 1813–44* (1971)

Cooke, Sir Charles Kinloch, *Memoir of HRH Princess Mary Adelaide, Duchess of Teck*, 2 vols (1900)

Curl, James Stevens, ed, *Kensal Green Cemetery: The Origins and Development of the General Cemetery of All Souls, Kensal Green, London, 1824–2001* (2001)

Delves Broughton, Mrs Vernon, ed, *Court and Private Life in the Time of Queen Charlotte, being the journals of Mrs Papendiek, Assistant Keeper of the Wardrobe and Reader to her Majesty*, 2 vols (1887)

Desmond, Ray, *Kew: The History of the Royal Botanic Gardens* (1995)

Disbrowe, Charlotte Anne Albinia, *Old Days in Diplomacy: Recollections of a Closed Century* (1903)

Dobson, Austin, ed, *Diary and Letters of Madame d'Arblay, 1778–1840, edited by Charlotte Barrett*, 6 vols (1904–5)

Donald, Diana, *The Age of Caricature: Satirical Prints in the Reign of George III* (1996)

Doran, Dr John, *Lives of the Queens of England of the House of Hanover*, 2 vols (1855)

Dyce, A., ed, *Recollections of the Table Talk of Samuel Rogers* (1856)

Eden, R. J., ed, *The Journal and Correspondence of William, Viscount Auckland*, 4 vols (1861)

Egerton, T., *The Birth and Triumph of Love* [plates] (1796)

Esher, Reginald, Viscount, *The Girlhood of Queen Victoria: A Selection from Her Majesty's Diaries between the Years 1832 and 1840*, 2 vols (1912)

Fairburn, John, *The Book ... An Inquiry, or Delicate Investigation, into the Conduct of Her Royal Highness, the Princess of Wales*, 4th edn (1820)

Finch, Pearl, *History of Burley-on-the-Hill, Rutland*, 2 vols (1901)

Fitzgerald, Percy, *Good Queen Charlotte* (1899)

Fraser, Flora, *The Unruly Queen: The Life of Queen Caroline* (1996)

Fulcher, George W., *Life of Thomas Gainsborough ...* (1856)

Gardener's Magazine, ed. J. C. Loudon, 9 vols (1826–43): vols 4 (1828) and 5 (1829)

Garlick, Kenneth, and Angus Macintyre, *The Diary of Joseph Farington*, 17 vols (1978–98)

George, D. M., ed, *Catalogue of Political and Personal Caricature in the British Museum*, 12 vols (1870–1958): vols 5–12 (1935–58)

Gentleman's Magazine, 303 vols (1731–1907)

Gillen, Mollie, *Royal Duke. Augustus Frederick, Duke of Sussex, 1773–1843* (1977)

Granville, Castalia, Countess, ed, *Lord Granville Leveson Gower, 1st Earl Granville: Private Correspondence, 1781–1821*, 2 vols (1917)

Greig, James, ed, *The Diaries of a Duchess: Extracts from the Diaries of the first Duchess of Northumberland, 1716–1776* (1926)

Guiffardière, Charles de, *Cours élémentaire d'histoire ancienne, à l'usage des LL. AA. Royales, Mesdames les Princesses d'Angleterre*, 2 vols (Windsor, 1798)

Harcourt, Edward William, ed, *Harcourt Papers*, 14 vols (Oxford, 1880–1905)

Harcourt, L. V., ed, *Diaries and Correspondence of the Rt Hon George Rose*, 2 vols (1860)

Hare, Augustus, ed, *Life and Letters of Frances, Baroness Bunsen*, 2 vols (1879)

Harris, John, Martin Snodin et al, eds, *Sir William Chambers: Architect to George III* [exhibition catalogue] (1996)

Hayward, Abraham, ed, *Diaries of a Lady of Quality* [Miss Frances Williams Wynn] *from 1797 to 1844* (1864)

Hedley, Olwen, *Queen Charlotte* (1975)

Hemlow, Joyce, et al, eds, *The Journals and Letters of Fanny Burney (Madame d'Arblay)*, 12 vols (Oxford, 1972–84)

Hibbert, Christopher, *George IV, Prince of Wales, 1762–1811* (1972)

Hibbert, Christopher, *George IV, Regent and King, 1811–1830* (1973)

Hibbert, Christopher, ed, *Queen Victoria in her Letters and Journals: A Selection, 1819–1901* (1985)

HMC, *Manuscripts of ... the Marquis of Ailesbury ...* (1897), Fifteenth Report, Appendix 7

HMC, *Manuscripts of the Earl of Carlisle ... at Castle Howard* (1897), Fifteenth Report, Appendix 6

HMC, *Manuscripts of the Earl of Dartmouth* (1887), Eleventh Report, Appendix 5

HMC, *Manuscripts of J. B. Fortescue, Esq., preserved at Dropmore*, Thirteenth Report, Parts 3 (1899), 7 (1910), 10 (1927)

Holme, Thea, *Prinny's Daughter: A Life of Princess Charlotte of Wales* (1976)

Home, Hon James A., ed, *The Letters and Journals of Lady Mary Coke*, 4 vols (Edinburgh, 1889–96)

Home, Hon James A., ed, *Letters of Lady Louisa Stuart to Miss Louisa Clinton*, 2nd series (Edinburgh, 1903)

Hudson, Katherine, *A Royal Conflict: Sir John Conroy and the Young Victoria* (1994)

Huish, Robert, *The Public and Private Life of George III*, 2 vols (1821)

Hunter, Richard, and Ida Macalpine, *Three Hundred Years of Psychiatry, 1535–1860* (1963)

Hutton, James, ed, *Selections from the Letters and Correspondence of Sir James Bland Burges, Bart.* (1885)

Iremonger, Lucille, *Love and the Princesses* (New York, 1958)

Jennings, Louis J., ed, *The Croker Papers: The Correspondence and Diaries of the Late Rt. Hon. J. W. Croker*, 3 vols (1884)

Jesse, John Heneage, *Memoirs of the Life and Reign of George III*, 3 vols (1867)

Knight, Charles, *Passages of a Working Life during Half a Century*, 3 vols (1861)

Knight, Charles, *A Volume of Varieties* (1844)

Knight, Ellis Cornelia, *Autobiography of Miss Cornelia Knight*, 2 vols (1861)

Knighton, Dorothea, Lady, *Memoirs of Sir William Knighton, Bart.*, 2 vols (1838)

Lewis, W. S., ed, *The Yale Edition of Horace Walpole's Correspondence*, 48 vols (Oxford, 1937–65)

Llanover, Lady, ed, *Autobiography and Correspondence of Mary Granville, Mrs Delany*, 2nd series, 3 vols (1862)

Lloyd, Christopher, *Masterpieces in Little: Portrait Miniatures from the Collection of Her Majesty Queen Elizabeth II* (1996)

Longford, Elizabeth, *Victoria RI* (1964, paperback 1966)

Longford, Elizabeth, *Wellington: Pillar of State* (1969)

Loudon, J. C., *In Search of English Gardens* (1829)

Macalpine, Ida, and Richard, Hunter, *George III and the Mad-business* (1969, 1991)

Malmesbury, 3rd Earl, ed, *Diaries and Correspondence of James Harris, 1st Earl of Malmesbury*, 2nd ed, 4 vols (1844)

Martineau, Harriet, *Biographical Sketches, 1852–1868* (1869)

Maxwell, Sir Herbert, ed, *The Creevey Papers: A Selection from the Correspondence and Diaries of the Late Thomas Creevey, MP*, 2 vols (1903)

Millar, Oliver, *Later Georgian Pictures in the Royal Collection* [text and plates] (1969)

Minto, Emma, Countess of, ed, *Life and Letters of Sir Gilbert Elliot, 1st Earl of Minto, 1751–1806*, 3 vols (1874)

Montbrison, Count de, ed, *Memoirs of Baroness d'Oberkirch, written by herself*, 3 vols (1852)

Moore, Thomas, *Memoirs of the Life of the Rt Hon R. B. Sheridan*, 2 vols (1825)

Moremen, Grace E., *Adolphus Frederick, Duke of Cambridge – Steadfast Son of King George III, 1774–1850* (New York, 2002)

Munk, William, *The Life of Sir Henry Halford* (1895)

Murray, Hon Amelia, *Recollections from 1803–1837, with a conclusion in 1868* (1868)

O'Meara, Barry Edward, *Napoleon in Exile: or A Voice from St Helena: The Opinions and Reflections of Napoleon ...* (1822)

Parissien, Steven, *George IV: The Grand Entertainment* (2001)

Parliamentary Debates from the year 1803 to the present time, ed. T. C. Hansard, 41 vols (1812–20)

Parliamentary History of England from the earliest period to the year 1803, ed. William Cobbett, 36 vols, vol 17 (1806–20)

Philobiblon Society, 'Mrs Harcourt's Diary of the Court of George III' *Miscellanies of the Philobiblon Society*, 13 (1871–2)

Phipps, Hon Edmund, ed, *Memoirs of the Political and Literary Life of Robert Plumer Ward*, 2 vols (1850)

Pointon, Marcia, *Hanging the Head: Portraiture and Social Function in Eighteenth Century England* (1993)

Pointon, Marcia, *Strategies for Showing: Women, Possession, and Representation in English Visual Culture, 1665–1800* (Oxford, 1997)

Pope Hennessy, James, *Queen Mary* (1959)

Prochaska, Frank, *Royal Bounty: The Making of a Welfare Monarchy* (1995)

Pückler-Muskau, Prince Hermann von, *Tour of Germany, Holland and England in 1826, 1827 and 1828 in a series of letters by a German prince*, 4 vols (1832)

Ribeiro, Aileen, *The Art of Dress: Fashion in England and France, 1750 to 1820* (1995)

Roberts, Jane, *Royal Artists, from Mary Queen of Scots to the Present Day* (1987)

Roberts, Jane, *Royal Landscape: The Gardens and Parks of Windsor* (1997)

Robertson, Emily, ed, *Letters and Papers of Andrew Robertson* (1895)

Rohl, John, *Purple Secret: Genes, 'Madness' and the Royal Houses of Europe* (1998)

Royal Children [Queen's Gallery exhibition catalogue] (1963)

Russell, Lord John, ed, *Journal and Correspondence of Thomas Moore*, 8 vols (1853–6)

St Aubyn, Giles, *The Royal George: The Life of HRH Prince George, Duke of Cambridge* (1963)

Scrase, David, *Flower Drawings* (Cambridge, 1997)

Shefrin, Jill, *Such Constant Affectionate Care: Lady Charlotte Finch – Royal Governess and the Children of George III* (Los Angeles, 2003)

Sheppard, Edgar, *Memorials of St James's Palace*, 2 vols (1894)

Sloan, Kim, *'A Noble Art': Amateur Artists and Drawing Masters, c. 1600–1800* (2000)

Smythies, Raymond, *Historical Records of the 40th (2nd Somersetshire) Regiment ...* (Devonport, 1894)

Strachey, Lytton, and Roger Fulford, *The Greville Memoirs*, 8 vols (1938)

Stuart, D. M., *Daughters of George III* (1939)

Taylor, Ernest, ed, *The Taylor Papers, Being a Record of ... the Life of Lieut. General Sir Herbert Taylor* (1913)

Thackeray, William, *The Four Georges* (1861)

Tomkins, Peltro, *The Birth and Triumph of Cupid, from papers cut by Lady Dashwood* [24 plates] (1795)

Tomkins, Peltro, *The Birthday Gift or The New Doll, from papers cut by a lady* (1796)

Trollope, Frances E., *Memoir of Frances Trollope* (1895)

Twiss, Horace, ed, *Public and Private Life of Lord Chancellor Eldon*, 3 vols (1844)

United Service Journal (1829–72)

Vallone, Lynne, *Becoming Victoria* (2001)

van Thal, Herbert, *Ernest Augustus, Duke of Cumberland and King of Hanover* (1936)

Walker, Richard, *Miniatures in the Collection of Her Majesty the Queen: The Eighteenth and Early Nineteenth Centuries* (Cambridge, 1992)

Walsh, Gerta, et al, eds, *'Ich schreibe, lese und male ohne Unterlass': Elizabeth, englische Prinzessin und Landgräfin von Hessen-Homburg (1770–1840) als Künstlerin und Sammlerin* (Bad Homburg, 1995)

Wardroper, John, *Wicked Ernest* (2002)

Watkin, David, *Royal Interiors of Regency England* (1984)

Watkins, John, *Memoirs of Her Majesty Sophia Charlotte, Queen of Great Britain,* (1819)

Withers, Philip, *History of the Royal Malady, with a variety of entertaining anecdotes* (1789)

Wraxall, Sir Nathaniel, *The Historical and Posthumous Memoirs of his Own Time, 1772–1784*, 5 vols (1884)

Wyndham, Hon Mrs Hugh, ed, *Correspondence of Sarah Spencer, Lady Lyttelton, 1787–1870* (1912)

Yorke, Philip, ed, *Letters of Princess Elizabeth of England, Landgravine of Hesse-Homburg* (1898)

Index

Abbott, Charles, 244
Abbott, Alice, 20
Abinger, Sarah, Lady, 394
Abington, Frances, 82
Ackermann, Rudolph, Junior, 358
Act of Succession (1689), 84
Adams, Anna Maria, 48–9, 223, 236, 239,
    245, 251, 266, 268, 270, 272
Adams, John, 88
Addington, Dr Anthony, 193
Addington, Henry *see* Sidmouth, Viscount
Adelaide of Saxe-Meiningen, Queen of
    William IV (*earlier* Duchess of Clarence):
    qualities, 309; gives birth to stillborn
    child, 317; birth and death of daughter,
    334, 336; appearance, 352; and Earl of
    Munster's complaints, 353; welcomes
    Landgrave Louis to England, 361; and
    husband's death, 362; miscarriage, 362;
    leaves Clarence House, 365; with dying
    Augusta, 379; philanthropy, 382; death,
    389
Adolphus, Prince, Duke of Cambridge
    ('Dolly'): birth, 34; childhood, 41; and
    Mary Hamilton, 48; dancing, 56;
    inoculated, 58; character, 85; visits
    Nuneham Courtenay, 85–7; serves in
    Hanoverian army, 142, 146, 152; wounded
    in battle and returns to England, 148;
    returns to war on continent, 150; meets
    Princess Royal after her marriage, 162;
    love with Frederica of Prussia frustrated,
    175, 182–3; visits England (1801), 194–5;
    dukedom, 199; visits Princess Royal, 199;
    Caroline abuses, 218; as Amelia's executor,
    240, 249; attends Amelia's funeral, 246; on
    father's selection of music for concert,
    254; attends to sick father, 267; asks
    permission to marry, 303; granted consent
    to marry, 307; birth of son, 317; accepts
    invitation to George IV's Coronation, 324;
    Augusta visits in Hanover, 337–8; as vice-
    regent of Hanover, 337–8, 355; visits
    England (1825), 339; Elizabeth visits, 355;

leaves Hanover for England, 363, 366;
    gives fête for Victoria, 366; visits Mary,
    372; attends dinner for Albert's Freedom of
    City of London, 378; at Augusta's
    deathbed, 379; companionship with
    Sophia in infirmity, 381–2; charitable
    works, 382; attends Sophia's funeral, 387;
    freedom after Sophia's death, 389; illness
    and death, 389–90
Adolphus, Prince of Mecklenburg-Strelitz,
    399
African Institution, 295
Ailesbury, Thomas Brudenell-Bruce, 1st Earl
    of, 105–6
Aiton, William, 98, 138
Albert Edward, Prince of Wales
    (Victoria/Albert's son; 'Bertie'), 384,
    396–9
Albert of Saxe-Coburg-Gotha, Consort of
    Queen Victoria: as potential husband for
    Victoria, 367; wedding, 370–2; and dying
    Augusta, 377; given Freedom of City of
    London, 377–8; and Sophia's death, 385;
    and Mary in old age, 398
Alexander I, Tsar, 219, 279, 281
Alexander, Henry, 357
Alfred, Prince (George III/Charlotte's son):
    birth, 61, 66; inoculated, 71; death,
    72–4, 89–90
Alfred, Prince (Victoria/Albert's son; 'Affie'),
    385
Alice, Princess (Victoria/Albert's daughter),
    383, 385, 398
Altamont, John, 3rd Earl of, 94
Alvensleben, Baron (Hanoverian Minister in
    London), 79
Amelia, Princess (George II's daughter), 6,
    12, 34, 297
Amelia, Princess (George III/Charlotte's
    daughter): birth, 74–5; character, 74, 98,
    131; expenses to mother, 82; Sarah
    Siddons sees as child, 83; education, 87,
    144; at Kew, 88; in Copley painting, 89;
    writes to parents in Cheltenham, 102–3;

fifth birthday, 104; and father's illness,
112, 118; and father's recovery, 121, 206;
Lawrence portrays, 128; inoculation, 131;
caricatured, 140; needlework, 145;
reading, 145; and Princess Royal's
pregnancy, 176; appearance, 179–80; in
Worthing for treatment to knee, 180–2;
attachment to sister Mary, 181; religious
faith, 182; supposedly infected by Keate's
nephew, 182; visits Weymouth, 182, 186,
199, 235–7; affection for niece Charlotte,
199, 221; dress, 199–200, 224; romance
with General Charles Fitzroy, 200, 202–4,
224, 231–5, 238–9, 241, 253, 274, 315; ill
health and attempted cures, 202, 234–42;
makes wills, 202, 231, 236, 240, 249;
friendship with Mrs Villiers, 203; fall from
horse, 205; fears for father, 214; and
charges against Caroline, 215; measles,
223–4; economies and debts, 224; twenty-
fifth birthday, 224; fears of infection, 233;
writes to Lady Harcourt, 241;
reconciliation with mother, 242, death,
243, 264, 274; funeral, 245–6
America: unrest in, 19, 27, 41–2, 70;
Declaration of Independence (1776), 42;
peace negotiations with, 73–4
Amiens, Peace of (1801), 189, 197, 202,
221n
Anglesey, Henry William Paget, 1st Marquess
of, 330
Anne, Princess of Orange (George II's
daughter), 4
Arblay, Madame d' *see* Burney, Fanny
Arbuthnot, Charles, 177, 327
Argyll, Elizabeth, Duchess of, 40
Astley, Georgiana, Lady (*née* Dashwood),
347–9, 388
Astley, Sir Jacob, 347–9
Auckland, William Eden, 1st Baron, 205,
245
Auersperg, Prince, 211
Auerstädt, battle of (1806), 217–18
Augusta, Dowager Princess of Wales (George
III's mother), 10, 29–30, 32–3
Augusta, Duchess of Brunswick (Caroline's
mother): unhappy marriage, 8, 31–20;
seeks marriage for son to Princess Royal,
79; death and burial, 156, 274–5; on
Delicate Investigation into Caroline's
behaviour, 217; widowhood and move to
England, 218–20; relations with Mary in
old age, 393
Augusta of Hesse-Cassel, Duchess of
Cambridge: marriage, 309; birth of son,
317; in Hanover, 337–8; visits England
(1825), 339; gives fête for Victoria, 366;

philanthropy, 382; with dying Sophia,
386; and Sophia's financial and funeral
arrangements, 386; and Adolphus's death,
390; visits Great Exhibition, 392; visits
dying Mary, 399
Augusta, Princess of Bavaria, 213
Augusta, Princess of Brunswick, Hereditary
Princess of Württemberg, 156–7
Augusta, Princess of Cambridge, Hereditary
Princess of Mecklenburg-Strelitz, 282,
364, 383, 389, 399
Augusta Sophia, Princess: birth, 15;
character and appearance, 15, 18, 22, 35,
38–40, 44, 48, 83, 85, 171, 379; infancy,
17–18; fondness for Mary Dacres, 20;
visits great-aunt Amelia at Gunnersbury,
34; education, 37, 39–40, 51, 69; portraits,
39; wilful behaviour, 39, 69–70; political
views, 41; sports as child, 42; writes to
Mary Hamilton's mother, 48; on
departure of Mary Dacres, 49; writes to
mother, 50; meets uncle Duke of
Cumberland, 60; at Lower Lodge,
Windsor, 67, 96; letter to Lady Charlotte
Finch in Portugal, 69; writes to Mary
Hamilton, 69–70; debut at King's
Birthday, 70–1; acquires first lady-in-
waiting, 73; letters to brothers, 79, 91,
93–7, 104, 129–32, 135, 140–1; dress, 82,
122, 133; proposed as bride for Prince
Royal of Denmark, 85; relations with
younger brothers, 85; visit to Nuneham
Courtenay, 85–7, 93; musical studies and
playing, 96, 128, 140, 341–2, 345, 379;
friendliness to attendants, 97; and father's
illnesses, 107–8, 113, 120, 193–4, 255;
twentieth birthday, 113; attends theatre
after father's recovery, 122; dances with
Charles Lennox, 123–4; in Weymouth,
124–6, 140, 186; on French Revolution,
128; on father's recovery, 129; on brother
William's naval service, 131; attachment to
Ferdinand of Württemberg, 132–4, 156;
reading, 134; friendships, 135–6, 340–1;
sea-bathing, 140; relations with Duchess
of York, 142; pride in Ernest's wound,
152; and Prince of Wales's marriage, 154;
allowance, 155; and mob attack on father,
156; writes to Lady Harcourt, 156, 159,
198, 202, 204, 221–2, 241, 243, 245, 299,
301, 322; and Princess Royal's marriage,
159, 161; marriage prospects and suitors,
183, 201, 231; relations with General Sir
Brent Spencer, 183, 215, 222, 260–1, 305,
379; sympathy towards Queen, 207; and
niece Charlotte, 221; on success in Baltic,
221–2; on Amelia in sickness, 236, 239,

Augusta Sophia, Princess (*cont.*)
241, 243; gives bird to Amelia, 242–3,
245; and Amelia's death, 243, 245;
discussion with General Taylor, 256;
Prince Regent makes financial provisions
for, 259; horses, 260; mother's relations
with, 260–2, 269–70; writes to Prince
Regent requesting permission to marry
Spencer, 260–3; visits Lord Liverpool,
268; hopes for independent life in London,
271; on Davenport's nervous collapse, 275;
on Mary's marriage, 292; visits Mary, 299;
on Princess Charlotte's death, 301–2;
attends sick mother at Kew, 308–12; at
mother's deathbed, 312; moves to
Cambridge Cottage, Kew, 313; effect of
mother's death on, 314; inheritance from
mother, 314–16; drawings, 315; stays at
Windsor after mother's death, 315–16; at
Frogmore with Mary, 318–19, 376; on
father's death, 322; lives at Frogmore,
322–3, 347, 375, 379; at George IV's
Coronation, 326; supports brother George
against Caroline, 326; hosts ball for
brother George, 328; visits sisters and
brother in Germany, 329, 336–8; on
Sophia's Connaught Place house, 335;
writes to Ernest, 335, 343–5, 359–60, 373;
in Stable House, 337–8, 345; invites
Mme d'Arblay to stay, 338, 340; visits
Kingston-on-Thames, 340; dislikes
George IV's changes to Windsor Castle,
341; entertains Princess Royal on visit to
England (1827), 343–5; in Brighton for
health, 345–6; on Princess Royal's death,
346; reduces exercise, 360; manages
Frogmore estate, 361; and Victoria's claim
to throne, 362; spends time with Adelaide
after William's death, 363; on Victoria's
accession, 364; claims mother's jewels
meant for Hanover, 365; moves into
Clarence House, 365; near-accident with
fire, 365; on Elizabeth's death, 370; and
Victoria's marriage, 370–1; attends
Victoria's wedding, 372; attitude to
Victoria as Queen, 372–3; reads to niece
Mary Adelaide, 373; resistance to change,
373; charitable works at Windsor, 374;
health deteriorates, 374, 377–8; garden
design, 375–6; Mary stays with, 377;
death and burial, 378–9, 383
Augusta Lodge, Windsor, 238
Augusta Frederick, Prince of Prussia, 182,
280, 285, 290
Augustus, Prince, Duke of Sussex and
Inverness: birth, 32, 34; infancy, 35; and
Mary Hamilton, 48; supports Keppel, 65;

Augusta writes to, 73, 91, 93–7, 104,
129–30, 132, 135, 140; asthma, 85, 95,
104, 131; naval ambitions, 85, 91, 130;
visits Harcourts at Nuneham Courtenay,
85–6; in Germany, 91–4, 96, 105, 122;
letters from Princess Royal and mother,
99–100, 104–5, 122, 128–9, 138, 140–1;
letter from father on illness, 107; travels,
129, 138, 141, 142, 150; considers
academic career, 143; marriage and
children with Lady Augusta Murray,
149–51, 184, 232; return visits to England,
149, 204; lives at Kensington Palace, 184;
dukedom, 199; attends to sick father, 267;
in dispute between George and Caroline,
274, 327; and Princess Charlotte's marriage
prospects, 279, 281; bibliophile, 335; in
Kensington Palace, 335; temporary
blindness, 360; and dying Augusta, 378;
second marriage to Duchess of Inverness,
382; visits Sophia in infirmity, 382; death
and burial at Kensal Green, 383, 387
Austerlitz, battle of (1805), 211
Austin, William, 201, 214, 285, 289
Austria: war with France, 142, 145; peace
with France (1800–1), 187–8, 193;
defeated at Ulm (1805), 211

Bach, John Christian, 128
Bad Homburg: spa water, 367–8
Bagshot Park, Surrey, 291–2, 294–5, 340,
347, 376
Baillie, Dr Matthew, 239, 242, 249, 253, 256,
264, 276, 279, 302
Baker, Sir George: attends royal family, 90,
99, 101–2; and George III's illness,
106–12, 115, 118–19
Banks, Dorothea, Lady, 229
Banks, Sir Joseph, 26, 39, 98, 121, 162, 229,
260, 307
Bannister, Charles, 122
Bardi, Pietro, 387
Bastille: stormed (1789), 126
Bath, 61, 300
Baynes, Augusta (*née* Compton), 223, 228,
236, 265, 294, 299; marriage, 276–7
Baynes, Captain Thomas, 276
Beatrice, Princess (Victoria/Albert's
daughter), 398
Beckedorff, Charlotte, 275, 303, 310–11,
314–5
Beckedorff, Sophia, 303, 310, 315
Bedford, Francis Russell, 5th Duke of, 138
Belasyse, Lady Charlotte, 182, 320
Bellingham, John, 264
Berkeley, Lady Elizabeth, 320
Bertie, Lady Charlotte, 94

Bessborough, Henrietta Frances, Countess of, 212

Blackheath, 172, 179, 195, 220

Blomberg, Frederick William ('Master'), 17–18

Blomfield, Charles, Bishop of London, 382

Bloomfield, Sir Benjamin, 274, 323

Blücher, General Gebhard Eberecht von, 279

Bolton, Sir George, 54, 224

Bolton, David, 224–5

Boston, Mass., 19, 27

Bott, Joseph, 252

Brande, Augustus, 71, 210

Brawn, Sarah, 324, 368

Brighton: Prince of Wales in, 90; Augusta visits, 345–6; Victoria visits, 364

Brougham, Henry (later Baron), 282, 288, 295, 301, 327

Bruce, Lady Charlotte, 147, 153

Bruce, Lady Frances, 94

Brunswick: incorporated in Confederation of the Rhine, 218

Buckingham, George Nugent-Temple, 1st Marquess of, 116, 205, 207

Buckingham Palace: George IV rebuilds Queen's House and renames, 3n 337, 341; Victoria makes home in, 363

Buckley, Lady Georgiana, 232

Budé, Major General Jacob, 23, 57, 80

Bulley, John, 37

Bulstrode, 81

Burges, Sir James Bland, 161, 168–70, 208

Burney, Dr Charles, 145

Burney, Fanny (Mme d'Arblay): on princesses as children, 97–8; consults apothecary, 101; on George III's illness, 107–10, 120; and Queen's depression, 111–12; hears prayers for George III, 114; at Kew, 117; writes lines for Amelia to recite to father, 121; on visit to Weymouth, 124; on Queen's appearance, 127; on Amelia, 142, 181; visits Frogmore, 143–4; reads to Mary, 144; and Augusta's pride in Ernest's wound, 152; and Princess Royal's marriage, 160, 162; visits Windsor, 169–70; on Sophia, 171; praises Amelia, 180; visits Augusta at Frogmore, 318; Elizabeth writes to from Homburg, 336; Augusta invites to Stable House, 338, 340; Camilla, 169–70

Bushey Park, 334–5, 360

Bute, John Stuart, 3rd Earl of, 10, 12, 98

Cambridge Cottage, Kew Green, 313, 339, 356

Cambridge, Duke of see 1. Adolphus, Prince, 1st Duke; 2. George, Prince, 2nd Duke

Cambridge House, London, 323, 366, 389

Camperdown, battle of (1797), 173, 175

Canning, George, 250

Cape St Vincent, battle of (1794), 175

Cardigan, Elizabeth, Countess of see Waldegrave, Lady Elizabeth

Cardigan, James Brudenell, 6th Earl of, 106, 135

Carlton House, London: Prince of Wales hopes to move to, 59; paintings at, 83; Mrs Fitzherbert entertains at, 89–90; renovated and decorated, 90; life at, 171, 272–3; Prince Regent gives ball for daughter Charlotte at, 272; George IV intends to demolish, 337

Carmarthen, Francis Osborne, Marquess of, 105

Caroline of Brunswick, Princess of Wales, Queen of George IV: marriage, 153–5; pregnancy and birth of daughter, 156–7; poor marriage relations, 157–8, 200, 219, 266; Elizabeth supports, 171; forces resignation of Lady Jersey, 171; in Blackheath, 172, 179, 195; separation, 175; on paternity of Sophia's child, 191; George III's schemes for, 195; and rights over daughter, 195; and George III's plans for Princess Charlotte's care, 204, 206; George III visits in Blackheath, 206; visits daughter Charlotte at Windsor, 208; adopts children, 214, 285; charges against ('Delicate Investigation'), 214, 217–19, 274; abuses brothers-in-law, 218; illness on father's death, 218; lovers and affairs, 218; received by George III, 218–19; public support for, 219, 274; maintains contact with daughter, 266; rejected at Windsor, 266; daughter reads Parliamentary Report on, 274–5; 2nd Duke of Gloucester supports, 274, 326–7, 391; protests at being denied access to daughter, 274; daughter's anxieties over, 279, 288–9, 372; refuses to harbour daughter in flight from Prince Regent, 282; travels abroad, 282–3, 285; relations with courier (Pergami), 289; travels to England, 299; and daughter's death, 303; Prince Regent plans to divorce, 303, 318, 323; plans return to England on husband's accession, 324–5; public arguments with husband ('the Queen's affair'), 326–7; refused entry to Abbey at George IV's Coronation, 328; death, funeral and burial, 329

Caroline Matilda, Queen of Denmark, 4, 8, 31, 85

Caroline, Princess of Hesse-Homburg (*later* Princess Reuss), 355, 366
Castlereagh, Robert Stewart, Viscount, 285
Cathcart, Elizabeth, Lady, 147–8
Catherine II (the Great), Empress of Russia, 132, 157
Catherine, Grand Duchess, of Oldenburg and Queen of Württemberg, 279, 281–2, 297–8; death, 317
Catherine, Princess of Württemberg ('Trinette'), 176, 185, 187, 196; marriage to Jérôme Bonaparte, 213, 219, 275
Catholic emancipation, 41, 193, 208, 348
Chambers, Sir William, 26, 44
Chapman, Elizabeth, 9
Charles, Duke of Brunswick (*later* Grand Duke of Mecklenburg-Strelitz, Queen Charlotte's brother): Queen Charlotte writes to, 8, 11, 27, 33, 44, 61–2, 72, 79, 82, 129, 153, 163; proposes son as husband for one of princesses, 209; Queen Charlotte's love for, 287; death, 296
Charles, George, Hereditary Prince of Brunswick, 79
Charles William Ferdinand, Duke of Brunswick (Caroline's father), 145, 218
Charlotte Augusta Matilda, Princess Royal, Queen of Württemberg ('Royal'): birth, 4–5; infancy, 7, 9, 14; appearance, 14, 16, 18, 22, 38, 83, 178, 199; education, 16–17, 37–8, 54; inoculated against smallpox, 16; and childhood performances, 18–19; fondness for Mary Dacres, 20–1; stammer, 21, 38, 163; on children's upbringing, 27; memory, 37; portraits, 38, 178; at Windsor, 46; on Mary Dacres's departure to marry, 50; letters to Mary Hamilton, 52–3, 64; drawing and painting, 54, 73, 81, 96–7, 128–9, 131, 141, 197, 315; dancing, 56, 63; and brother William's departure for navy, 57; meets uncle Duke of Cumberland, 60; restricted social life, 61; rudeness to Miss Gouldsworthy, 63–4; debut at King's Birthday (1781), 66–7; opens brother George's nineteenth birthday ball, 68; acquires first lady-in-waiting, 73; on birth of sister Amelia, 75; Duchess of Brunswick seeks as bride for son, 79; writes to brother William in Hanover, 80; dress, 82, 160–1; visits Nuneham Courtenay, 87; advises Augustus on preventing tinnitus, 91–2; writes to Augustus in Germany, 91, 93–4, 104–5, 122, 129; female friends, 92; insensitivity to music, 96, 105, 140; welcomes Frederick's return from Germany, 96; character and manner, 97, 99; and Fanny Burney, 97; copies botanical specimens, 98; gives secretarial aid to mother, 98–9; affection for father, 99; marriage prospects, 99, 105–6, 137–8, 140; uneasy relations with mother, 99, 155, 161; in Cheltenham, 101; celebrates twenty-second birthday, 105–6; and father's illness, 108, 116, 120, 122; hosts gala celebration for father's recovery, 123; in Weymouth, 124–5, 131; describes Twelfth Night Ball, 133; isolation, 135, 155; twenty-sixth birthday, 145; Sophia suspects, 147; allowance, 155; courtship and marriage, 155–6, 158–64, 290; and Prince of Wales's marriage, 159–60; jaundice, 159–60; writes to Lady Harcourt, 160, 280, 283, 308, 317; leaves England for Württemberg, 162–3; life in Württemberg, 167, 172–4, 176, 184, 199; pregnancy, 173–5; and husband's accession, 175; child stillborn, 177–8; and younger sisters' education, 180; learns engraving, 184; evacuates to Erlangen, 185, 187; and Austrian surrender to France (1801), 186–7; gardening and farming, 196–7; returns to Württemberg, 196; on winter in Württemberg, 198; writes to father from Württemberg, 198–9; flees from Austrian advance (1805), 211; Napoleon visits, 212–13; and husband's alliance with France, 219; marriage relations, 219, 297; finds note from Amelia to Fitzroy, 235; and sisters' hopes for independent life, 270; financial difficulties, 275; resumes correspondence with family in England, 275; hopes for sisters' marriages, 280; disavows Prince Paul's behaviour in England, 281; and Princess Charlotte's relations with William of Orange, 285–6; widowhood in Württemberg, 297–8; writes on hearing of assassination attempt on Prince Regent, 297; on Mary's marriage relations, 309; and mother's health decline, 310; on situation of father and sisters after mother's death, 316–17; refuses invitation to George IV's Coronation, 324; Elizabeth visits in Ludwigsburg, 328, 333–4; life-style as Queen Dowager, 333–4; obesity and immobility, 333, 336, 346; Augusta visits in Germany, 336–7; hostility to Leopold, 336; takes waters at Teinach, 338, 342; visit to England (1827), 342–4; death, 346
Charlotte Augusta, Princess (daughter of George IV and Caroline): birth, 157; childhood, 179, 182, 199; mother's rights

to, 195; given ball at Frogmore, 200;
upbringing, 200; George III's plans for,
204, 206; settles in Windsor, 208, 220;
character and temperament, 220–1, 255,
267, 270; dines with grandmother
Brunswick in Blackheath, 220; visits
princesses at Windsor, 255, 257, 266;
Elizabeth criticizes, 257, 266; Whiggism,
258, 268; and parents' difficult marriage
relations, 266; amuses grandmother
Charlotte, 267; accompanied to London
by Elizabeth and Mary, 268–9, 272; hopes
for independence, 268; Prince Regent
arranges to spend time at Warwick House,
268; Queen's attitude to, 269; flirtations,
272; life in London, 272–3; reads
Parliamentary Report on mother, 274;
prospective marriage to Hereditary Prince
of Orange, 277–80, 285–6; confirmation,
278; suitors, 280–2, 288; ends engagement
with Prince of Orange, 281; father
banishes to Cranbourne Lodge, Windsor,
282–3; relations with father, 283–4; visits
Weymouth, 283–4; decides to marry
Prince Leopold, 285, 288–9; concern for
mother, 288–9, 372; marriage to Leopold,
289–91, 294; on Mary's marriage, 292–4;
visits Mary at Bagshot, 296; domestic life,
298; portrait, 298; pregnancy and birth of
stillborn child, 298, 300–1; death, 301–3
Charlotte, Princess (daughter of Paul) of
Württemberg, 333
Charlotte, Princess of Mecklenburg-Strelitz
(Queen Charlotte's niece, 'Lolo'), 80, 175
Charlotte, Queen of George III: birth of
children, 3–4, 6, 13, 15, 21, 32, 49, 55, 61,
65, 74; fondness for son George, 5; and
children's upbringing and education, 7,
13, 21, 22, 24, 37, 45, 50, 54, 81, 88;
informal home life, 11–12, 18–19; love of
music, 11, 82; character and appearance,
12–13, 126–7; marriage, 12–13; and
dismissal of Mrs Abbott, 20; portraits, 25,
38, 127–8; and brother Charles's departure,
27; differences with Lady Charlotte Finch,
34–5; and American War of Independence,
41–2, 55; social activities, 45, 61; at
Windsor, 46–8, 55–8, 205–6; and
children's visit to Eastbourne, 62–3; good
relations with princesses' attendants, 67;
and Augusta's debut, 70–1; and death of
son Alfred, 72; refuses marriage of
Princess Royal to Prince of Brunswick,
79; letter to William in Hanover, 80; dress,
81; financial problems, 82; summons
actors to perform, 82–3, 88; greets John
Adams, 88; on Elizabeth's ill-health, 90;

botanical interests and gardening, 98–9,
138–9, 144, 276; relations with Princess
Royal, 98–9, 155, 161; and George III's
illnesses, 106, 108–12, 114, 120, 203,
256–7; falls ill, 110; and prospective
regency, 111–12; at Kew with sick George
III, 117, 194; and George III's recovery,
122; visits Weymouth and West Country,
124–7, 146, 187, 210; on French
Revolution, 126, 128; effect of King's
illness on personality, 127–8, 149; interest
in art, 129; occupies and improves
Frogmore house, 131, 138–9, 143, 146,
170; and daughters' marriage prospects,
135; fan painting, 141; reading, 143; and
Sophia's Court debut, 144; dismay at
Prince of Wales's marriage to Caroline,
153; supports Prince of Wales against wife,
158; and Princess Royal's marriage, 160–1,
163; attitude to Frederick of Württemberg,
167; and attempted assassination of George
III, 186; on Princess Royal's obesity, 199;
life at Frogmore, 201, 276; bans husband
from bedchamber, 205, 210; Sophia
blames for father's unhappiness, 207; and
nephew as prospective husband for one of
princesses, 209; criticizes granddaughter
Charlotte, 221; Miss Gomm blames for
Amelia's continuing affair with Fitzroy,
224; puts on weight, 225; opposes
Elizabeth's romance with Louis Philippe,
226–7; depression, 228; Amelia turns
against, 234, 238; Amelia's reconciliation
with, 242; Council advises on King's care,
251; coolness towards princesses, 254, 261;
regard for Prince of Wales, 254; refuses to
leave Windsor, 256; jealousy of Prince
Regent's provisions for princesses, 258–9;
gives annual present to Miss Planta, 259;
and Augusta's wish to marry Spencer,
260–3; advice to newly independent
princesses under regency, 261–2; amused
by granddaughter Princess Charlotte, 267;
opposes daughters accompanying Princess
Charlotte to Warwick House, 268–9;
worsening relations with daughters,
268–70; Prince Regent effects
reconciliation with princesses, 270; and
Princess Charlotte's companions in
London, 272; encourages Augusta
Compton's marriage, 276; health decline,
276, 287, 296, 304, 307–10; erysipelas,
286; and Princess Charlotte's marriage
prospects, 286; refuses to meet Frederica,
Duchess of Cumberland, 287; approves of
Princess Charlotte's marriage to Leopold,
289–90; visits Charlotte and Leopold at

Charlotte, Queen of George III (*cont.*)
  Claremont, 296; takes waters at Bath,
  300; and Princess Charlotte's death,
  301–3; opposes Frederick of Hesse-
  Homburg's proposal to Elizabeth, 305–6;
  will and disposal of belongings, 310–11,
  313–16; death, 312; funeral, 313; family
  claims on jewels, 365, 385
Chatham, William Pitt, 1st Earl of, 13
Cheltenham, 100–5
Cheveley, Miss (Louisa's daughter), 393
Cheveley, Louisa ('Che Che'), 56, 61, 66,
  71–3, 88, 147–8, 182, 393
Choiseul, Etienne François, Duc de, 12
Christian VII, King of Denmark, 8, 31, 85
Christian, Prince Royal of Denmark (*later*
  King Christian VIII), 85, 134
Claremont, Surrey, 290–1, 294, 349
Clarence, Duke of *see* William IV, King
Clarence House, London, 345, 365
Clarke, Mary Anne, 229
Claudet, Antoine, 396
Clayton, Lady Louisa, 105
Clement, Dorothy, 8
Clifford, Sophia, Lady de: as governess to
  Princess Charlotte, 208, 220, 257; resigns,
  272
Clive, Robert, Baron, 25
Cochrane, Mrs (Sophia's dresser), 380, 386
Coke, Lady Mary: observations on royal
  children, 3, 6, 14, 16, 18–22, 32, 34, 40,
  56; on Mrs Cotesworth's drinking, 23; and
  death of Edward, Duke of York, 28; and
  1st Duke of Gloucester's illness, 29; on
  Queen Caroline of Denmark's behaviour,
  31; and 1st Duke of Gloucester's marriage,
  32–3
Coleman, Mrs (of Windsor), 377
Compton, Augusta *see* Baynes, Augusta
Compton, Henry, 49–50, 265
Compton, Mary (*née* Dacres), 21, 39, 43,
  49–51, 72, 223, 259
Confederation of the Rhine, 201n, 218
Connaught Place, Bayswater, 282, 335
Conroy, Edward, 335, 360
Conroy, Elizabeth, Lady, 3356
Conroy, Sir John, 335, 339, 360–1, 384, 386
Conroy, Victoire, 335, 349
Continental System, 221n
Cook, Captain James, 26, 39
Copenhagen: battle of (1801), 194; falls to
  British, 221
Copley, John Singleton, 88–9
Corn Laws, 286
Cornwallis, Charles, 1st Marquess, 70, 197
Cotes, Francis, 14, 38
Cotesworth, Henrietta, 3, 14, 20, 23, 34

Coventry, George William Coventry, 6th Earl
  of, 102
Cranbourne Lodge, Windsor Great Park,
  282–3
Crawfurd, James ('Fish'), 114
Creevey, Thomas, 307
Crimean War (1854–5), 394–6
Croft, Sir Richard, 301–2
Croker, John Wilson, 329, 359
Crystal Palace, Sydenham, 392
Cumberland, Lady Albinia, 291
Cumberland, Duke of *see* 1. Ernest, Duke of
  Cumberland, King of Hanover; 2. Henry
  Frederick, Duke of Cumberland; 3.
  William, Duke of Cumberland
Cumberland, Captain William, 181, 182
Currey, Sir Edmund, 294, 347, 360, 376
Currey, Louise, Lady, 360, 363

Dacres, Mary *see* Compton, Mary
d'Arcy, Lady Amelia, 16
Dartmouth, William Legge, 2nd Earl of, 74
Davenport, Miss, 275
Dee, Leonara (Sophia Matilda's governess),
  130, 296
Delany, Mary, 55–7, 81–2, 87, 89, 97
Deluc, Jean André, 99, 127, 136
Denman, Thomas, 329
Denoyer, Philip, 38
Dering, Mrs (Augusta's friend), 370
d'Este, Augusta *see* Truro, Lady Augusta Emma
d'Este, Augustus Frederick (son of Prince
  Augustus and Lady Augusta Murray),
  150–1, 279, 281
Devonshire, Georgiana, Duchess of, 83–4
Devonshire, William Spencer Cavendish, 6th
  Duke of, 258, 278
Dickenson, Mary *see* Hamilton, Mary
Digby, Colonel Stephen, 117
Digby, Rear Admiral Robert, 57
Dillen, Count Karl, 174
Disbrowe, Colonel Edward, 238
Dundas, Sir David, 106, 242, 249, 253, 256
Dunkirk, 148

Eastbourne, 61–3
Edgeworth, Maria, 264
Edridge, Henry, 276
Edward, Duke of York (Caroline Matilda's
  brother), 8, 28
Edward, Prince, Duke of Kent: house at
  Kew, 23, 26; appearance, 35; childhood,
  40; differences with brother William, 57;
  health visit to Eastbourne, 61–2; sister
  Elizabeth's fondness for, 65–6; in Hanover,
  84, 91, 94; studies in Geneva, 97; believes
  father unlikely to travel to Hanover, 130;

in Canada, 142, 152, 186; relations with
Mme de St Laurent, 142, 307; dukedom,
186; informs Caroline of investigation,
214; encourages Louis Philippe's interest in
Elizabeth, 226; behaviour, 228; attends to
sick father, 267; supports Caroline against
Prince Regent, 274; and Princess
Charlotte's marriage prospects, 281; and
death of Frederick of Württemberg, 297;
seeks wife, 303; engagement and marriage
to Victoria of Leiningen, 307; return to
England, 317–18; and succession, 317–18;
birth of daughter Victoria, 318; home life,
319; illness and death, 320–1; funeral, 322
Effingham, Catherine, Countess of, 19–20
Egremont, George Wyndham, 3rd Earl of,
340–1
Eldon, John Scott, 1st Earl of, 251, 256, 291
Elgin, Martha, Countess of: as Princess
Charlotte Augusta's governess, 158, 204;
and Burges, 168; Princess Royal writes to
from Württemberg, 179
Elizabeth, Princess (daughter of William and
Adelaide): birth, 334; death, 337
Elizabeth, Princess, Landgravine of Hesse-
Homburg: birth, 20; acquires own
establishment at Kew, 22; infancy, 22;
appearance and character, 32, 39–40, 83,
225, 234, 266; visits great-aunt Amelia at
Gunnersbury, 34; education, 37, 39–40,
62; attachment to Mary Compton, 51;
complains of Lady Weymouth, 58; visit to
Eastbourne, 61–2; artistic
accomplishments, 62, 81, 91, 128–9, 135,
138–9, 141, 149, 168–70, 225, 265,
299–300, 315, 358; fondness for brother
Edward, 65–6, 321; at Lower Lodge,
Windsor, 67; dress, 82, 122, 133, 209;
illness and recovery, 89–90, 93, 169;
rumours of children by Ramus, 90–1;
spends time in Kew, 90–1; writes to
Augustus in Germany, 93, 105; at
celebrations for Edward's return from
Germany, 95; musical studies, 96, 128;
and father's illness, 106, 108, 120; and
father's recovery, 122; in Weymouth,
124–5, 146, 152, 186, 200; at father's
Birthday ball, 130; at Frogmore, 139, 143,
170; reading, 141; relations with Duchess
of York, 142; writes to Lady Harcourt,
143, 146, 152, 200, 202, 225, 229, 259,
298, 301, 309; on Sophia's illness, 147; and
Augustus's becoming father, 150; praises
Howe's 1794 victory, 152; and Prince of
Wales's marriage, 154; and attack on
father's coach, 156; on Prince of Wales's
marriage relations, 158; on Princess

Royal's marriage prospects, 160; on
Frederick of Württemberg's broken arm,
168; debts, 170; life-style, 170–1; and
rumours of Sophia's illegitimate child,
189; and King's plans for Caroline, 195;
longing for marriage, 200, 229, 231, 300;
on French invasion threat, 201; on
Amelia's ill health, 202, 235, 241; relations
with Sophia, 207; on Napoleon's victories,
218; on public support for Caroline, 219;
acquires cottage at Old Windsor, 221, 225,
235; farming and gardening interests, 221,
225, 228, 307; friendship with Augusta
Compton, 223, 236; and Miss Gomm's
resignation, 223–4; dissatisfactions, 225–6;
portrait, 225; hopes of marriage to Louis
Philippe, 226–30, 300; desire for children,
228; Amelia turns against, 234; and Select
Committee enquiry into George III's
condition, 250; father discusses Amelia's
death with, 252; relations with niece
Charlotte, 257, 266; and reorganization
under regency, 259–60; suffers face
ailment, 262; financial independence
under regency, 265; invites Augusta
Compton to Windsor as companion, 265;
organizes fêtes at Frogmore, 268; Prince
Regent arranges to accompany Princess
Charlotte to London, 268–9; quarrel with
mother, 269; reads to mother, 270; hopes
for independent life in London, 271;
Princess Charlotte believes influences
Prince Regent, 273; and Augusta
Compton's marriage, 276–7; visiting
royalty call at Windsor, 280–1; on
mother's unbending nature, 287, 296;
gives marriage feast for Mary, 294; builds
dairy at Old Windsor, 299; life at Windsor,
299–300; accompanies mother to Bath,
300; on Princess Charlotte's death, 301–2;
Frederick of Hesse-Homburg sues for
hand, 304–6; recovers spirits in Bath, 304;
and Homburg finances, 305, 334, 336,
352–4; marriage to Frederick and move to
Homburg, 306–8; on mother's health
decline, 309–10; on mother's death, 312;
letters to mother preserved, 315; unable to
visit Princess Royal, 317; sees brother
Kent and wife en route to England, 318;
on brother Edward's death, 321; and
brother George's accession, 323–4; refuses
invitation to George IV's Coronation, 324;
visits Princess Royal in Ludwigsburg, 328,
333–4; life in Homburg, 334, 367;
Augusta visits in Germany, 336; and death
of George IV, 351–2; husband's death,
351; visits England on George IV's death,

Elizabeth, Princess, Landgravine of Hesse-
  Homburg (*cont.*)
  352; will, 352, 369; charitable works, 354,
  358; improves Homburg property, 354; life
  in widowhood, 354–8; visits Adolphus in
  Hanover, 355–6; visits sisters in England
  (1836), 360–1; and Adolphus's departure
  from Hanover, 363; and Victoria's
  accession, 363; relations with Hesse-
  Homburg family, 366–7, 369; takes
  apartments in Frankfurt, 366; criticizes
  Mary for worldliness, 368; death and
  funeral, 368–70; *The Birth and Triumph of
  Cupid* (designs; later *The Birth and Triumph
  of Love*), 168–70; *Cupid Turned Volunteer*,
  225; *The Power and Progress of Genius*, 225,
  358
Elliot, Sir Gilbert *see* Minto, Baron
Elliot, Lady Harriot, 92, 94
Elliot, Hugh, 84–5
Elphinstone, Mercer, 268, 277, 279, 281–2,
  288–9
Erfurt, 219–20
Erlangen, 185, 187
Ernest, Duke of Coburg (Albert's father),
  383
Ernest, Prince, Duke of Cumberland, King
  of Hanover: birth, 22; education, 23;
  father's devotion to, 25; excursion to
  Gunnersbury, 34; childhood at Kew, 42,
  57; and Mary Hamilton, 48; Mrs
  Cheveley on, 56; character and behaviour,
  85, 150, 191, 228; on life at Kew, 85; visits
  Harcourts at Nuneham Courtenay, 85–6;
  letter from Augusta, 131; serves in
  Hanoverian army, 142, 146, 150; wounded
  and return to England, 152; dukedom,
  186; in Weymouth, 186–7; supposed
  incest with sister Sophia, 191, 348; with
  Caroline in Blackheath, 195; Augusta
  writes to, 271, 335, 343–5, 359–60, 373;
  visits Continent after Napoleon's defeat,
  286–7; marriage to Frederica, 287;
  Elizabeth on, 312; accepts invitation to
  George IV's Coronation, 324; and
  Augusta's hostility to Caroline, 327–8; in
  line for throne, 337; describes nephew and
  niece, 339; and Princess Royal's death,
  346; opposes Wellington on Catholic
  Emancipation, 348; friendship with sister
  Elizabeth, 356; accession as King of
  Hanover, 363; claims mother's jewels for
  crown of Hanover, 365, 385; Mary writes
  to, 366; in dispute over precedence, 372,
  383; resistance to change, 373; and death
  of sister Augusta, 378; gives away Princess
  Augusta of Cambridge in marriage, 383;

survives brothers, 390; death, 392
Ernest, Prince of Hohenlohe-Langenburg,
  398
Ernest, Duke of Mecklenburg-Strelitz
  (Queen Charlotte's brother), 19, 27, 31,
  42
Ernst August, Prince of Hanover, 390
Euston, George Henry Fitzroy, Earl of, 231

Fairbrother, Louisa (Mrs Fitzgeorge), 391
Fauconberg, Henry, 3rd Earl of, 101, 114
Feilding, Sophia (*née* Finch), 7, 48
Feodora, Princess of Leiningen (*later* Princess
  of Hohenlohe-Langenburg), 318, 335,
  339, 398
Ferdinand IV of Naples and Sicily, 229
Ferdinand, Prince of Württemberg: courts
  Augusta, 132–4, 156
Ferdinand, Princess of Württemberg
  (Albertine Wilhelmina), 184
Festrage (japanner), 300
Finch, Lady Charlotte: as royal governess,
  3–4, 7, 9, 11, 16, 20, 22, 24–5, 37, 40, 51,
  61, 144; on George III's devotion to
  children, 5; mourns husband's death, 10;
  worldliness, 13; domestic and family
  difficulties, 14, 18; at Kew, 17, 19, 43, 48;
  informal dress, 19; and dismissal of Mrs
  Abbott, 20; Lady Mary Coke visits, 22;
  on 1st Duke of Gloucester's illness, 29; on
  1st Duke of Gloucester's marriage, 32;
  requests reduction in hours as governess,
  34–6; introduces Princess Royal to adult
  world, 50; organizes children's displays,
  56; in Eastbourne with royal children,
  61–3; in Lisbon to nurse son, 66; letter
  from Augusta, 69; and Augusta's debut,
  70; nurses dying Alfred, 72; Elizabeth
  copies portrait of, 81; botanical interests,
  98; Prince of Wales drives recklessly at
  Windsor, 117; leads prayers for George
  III's recovery, 118; resigns, 144; letter
  from Elizabeth, 152; princesses assemble at
  apartments of, 209; letters from Princess
  Royal, 211–12; and Trafalgar victory, 211;
  sends snuffbox on Amelia's 25th birthday,
  224
Finch, Charlotte (Lady Charlotte's eldest
  daughter), 14
Finch, Frances (Lady Charlotte's daughter):
  death, 14
Finch, Henrietta (Lady Charlotte's daughter),
  5, 36, 295
Finch, Sophia (Lady Charlotte's daughter) *see*
  Feilding, Sophia
Finch, William (Lady Charlotte's husband),
  10, 12, 14

Fisher, John, Bishop of Exeter, then of Salisbury, 62, 220, 268

Fite, Elizabeth de la, 127

Fitzclarence, Eliza, 334

Fitzclarence, George *see* Munster, Earl of

Fitzclarence, Mary (*née* Wyndham), 341

Fitzclarence, Sophia, 278

Fitzherbert, Maria: Prince of Wales introduced to, 83–4; wears Prince of Wales's ring, 84; Prince of Wales marries clandestinely, 89; in Brighton, 142; in Prince of Wales's will, 155; Prince of Wales returns to, 179, 183–4, 235

Fitzroy, General Charles: romance with Amelia, 200, 202–4, 210, 215, 224, 231–6, 239–40, 241, 253, 274, 315; and dying Amelia, 238; Queen Charlotte reproaches, 238; told of Amelia's death, 243; Amelia leaves possessions to, 249

Floyer, Mr: Queen buys Frogmore Farm from, 131

Foulon, Joseph-François, 126

Fox, Charles James, 83, 111, 113, 115–16, 317

France: intervenes in American war, 49; breaks off relations with Britain (1778), 54; war with Prussia and Austria, 142; mob behaviour, 145; republic declared (1792), 145; declares war on Britain and United Netherlands (1793), 146; captures Holland, 154; threatens Württemberg, 184–5; peace with Austria (1801), 187, 193; invasion threat to Britain, 201; defeat at Trafalgar, 211; land victories (1805–6), 211, 217; economic war on Britain, 221n; in Peninsular War, 222 & n; Bourbon restoration (1814), 279

Frederica of Prussia, Duchess of York and Albany: marriage, 137, 139–40, 142; arrival in England, 140; breach with Frederick, 151, 158; lends house for Princess Charlotte's honeymoon, 290; Augusta and Mary visit at Oatlands, 318; death, 327

Frederica, Princess Louis of Prussia, Duchess of Cumberland (Queen Charlotte's niece): marriage to Prince Louis of Prussia, 140; Adolphus's infatuation with, 174, 182–3; marriage to and divorce from Prince of Solms, 182, 287; marriage to Ernest, Duke of Cumberland, 287; supposed pregnancy, 303; Elizabeth sees, 312; birth of son, 318; friendship with Elizabeth, 356

Frederick, Duke of Württemberg (*earlier* Hereditary Prince, *later* King): courtship and marriage to Princess Royal, 156, 158–60, 163; breaks arm in fall from horse, 167; George III's attitude to, 167; succeeds to Duchy, 175; and stillbirth of daughter, 177; obesity, 178; and French threat to Württemberg, 185; makes peace with France (1801), 188; welcomes Princess Royal's return to Württemberg, 196; territorial claims after Lunéville Treaty, 197; signs private treaty with Napoleon, 199, 219–20; as Elector of Holy Roman Empire, 201; proclaimed King, 201n, 212; Napoleon on, 213; realigns with Austria and Russia, 275; death, 297; supposed mistreatment of wife, 297

Frederick, Hereditary Prince of Hesse-Homburg *see* Friedrich VI, Landgrave of Hesse-Homburg

Frederick of Hesse, Prince, 154

Frederick, Prince, Duke of York and Albany: birth and upbringing, 3; inspects Princess Royal, 4; father adores as child, 5, 91; childhood activities, 18; installed as Knight of Garter, 23; education, 26; influenced by brother George, 58; supports Keppel, 65; in Hanover for military training, 66, 70, 80, 84; dukedom, 84; returns to England (1787), 95–6; visits father in Cheltenham, 102; Windsor ball for, 104; and father's illness, 109, 112–13; mimics father's mania, 117; duel with Lennox, 123; misbehaves at Thanksgiving service for father's recovery, 123; marriage, 137, 139, 142; and Princess Royal's marriage prospects, 137–8; visits Berlin, 137; as commander-in-chief of British forces against French, 146–9, 183; marriage breakdown, 151, 158; recalled from command, 151; returns to Flanders, 152; and mob hostility, 156; borrows from Bolton, 225; removed as C.-in C. after investigation, 229; on Amelia's illness, 239; at mother's deathbed, 312; at father's death and funeral, 322; supports brother George against Caroline, 327; given Freedom of City of Norwich, 328; dropsy, 340, 342; death, 342, 346

Frederick, Prince of Orange, 154, 210

Frederick, Prince of Wales: death (1751), 8, 10

Frederick William II, King of Prussia, 142, 158

Frederick William III, King of Prussia (*earlier* Crown Prince): as prospective husband for Princess Royal, 137–8, 140; with Adolphus at Pyrmont, 174; occupies Hanover, 194; defeated by Napoleon, 217; visits Elizabeth at Windsor, 281

Frederick William, Duke of Brunswick (known as William; Caroline's brother), 176–7, 273, 275, 283, 299

Fremantle, Sir William, 258–9, 346, 364

French Revolution (1789), 126, 128

Friedrich VI, Landgrave (*earlier* Hereditary Prince) of Hesse-Homburg ('Bluff'; 'Fritz'): character, 288–9; as suitor for Charlotte, 288; courtship and marriage to Elizabeth, 304–8; and finances, 305, 334, 354; succeeds father, 324, 333; attends Austrian Emperor to Munich, 333; death, 351–2

Friedrich, Hereditary Prince of Mecklenburg-Strelitz, 209–10, 383, 387

Friedrich, Prince of Hesse-Homburg, 355

Friedrich Wilhelm, Crown Prince of Prussia, 396

Frogmore House: Sir Edward Walpole lives at, 8; Queen buys and maintains, 143, 170, 313; gardens, 139, 375–6; life at, 143–4, 146, 201; ball for Princess Charlotte, 290; Augusta inherits, 314–15; Augusta lives at, 323, 347, 375, 379; Duchess of Kent occupies, 391; Mary visits, 391

Frogmore Farm (Amelia Lodge): Queen buys and embellishes, 131, 138–9, 143, 146

Gainsborough, Thomas, 73, 83, 127, 163

Gardiner, Captain (Albert's equerry), 385

Garrick, David, 50, 83

Garth, Frances: friendship with Sophia, 171–2, 179, 186; in Weymouth with royal family, 187; gout, 192; and Sophia's suspicions of Caroline's behaviour, 195; and uncle's commitment to son, 217; meets Caroline at Dover, 299; and Augusta's Frogmore garden, 376; stays with Augusta, 377

Garth, Georgiana Rosamund, 388

Garth, General Thomas: and Sophia, 171, 179, 210; as putative father of Sophia's child, 190–2, 217; in Weymouth with Tommy, 210, 215–17; Sophia ends relations with, 215–16; supposed marriage to Sophia, 264; in Weymouth with Princess Charlotte, 283–4; death and will, 348; gives documents to Tommy, 348; friendship with Augusta, 377

Garth, Thomas (*earlier* Ward; Princess Sophia's illegitimate child): birth and paternity, 190–2, 284; in Weymouth with General Garth, 210, 215–17; father presses on Princess Charlotte, 284; career, 347; elopes with Lady Astley, 347–8; demands settlement on receiving documents from father, 348, 360; inherits from General

Garth, 348–9; and Sophia's death, 387–8; birth of daughter, 388; imprisoned for debt, 388

Gaskoin, Mary, 224, 237, 239, 241, 249

Genlis, Stéphanie de St Aubin, Comtesse de, 88

George II, King, 11–12

George III, King: children, 3, 15, 20; relations with children, 5, 13–14, 21, 25, 57, 74; informal home life, 11–12, 19, 57; accession, 12; marriage, 12–13; and unrest in America, 19, 27, 41–2, 55, 70; portraits, 25; conflicts with brother Duke of Cumberland, 28; introduces Royal Marriages Act (1772), 30, 32; and sister Caroline's adultery, 31; Horace Walpole's hostility to, 33; undertakes own official correspondence, 37; opposes Catholic emancipation, 41, 208; at Windsor, 44–5, 48, 55–7, 205–7; hunting, 44–5, 130; relations with Prince of Wales, 44, 59, 84, 194; and death of sons Alfred and Octavius, 72–4; and American peace negotiations, 73–4; refuses Princess Royal as bride for Prince of Brunswick, 79, 135; love of music, 82; summons actors to perform, 82–3; and younger sons' education, 85; informality with Mrs Delany, 87; greets John Adams, 88; assassination attempts on, 92–3, 186; and Edward's return from Germany, 95–6; suffers violent attacks, 100; in Cheltenham for health, 101–5; illness and mental disturbance (1788), 106–20; leaves Windsor for Kew, 117–18; placed in straitjacket, 119, 122, 194–5, 203; recovers, 120–1, 129; Thanksgiving service for recovery, 122–3; visits to Weymouth and West Country, 124–7, 139, 146, 152, 187, 198, 204–5, 210; refuses Ferdinand of Württemberg's suit for Augusta, 133–5; opposes son Augustus's marriage to Lady Augusta Murray, 150; illness returns (1794), 152; approves Prince of Wales's marriage to Caroline, 153; mob abuses, 156; supports Caroline, 158; and Princess Royal's marriage, 159, 162; refuses separation for Prince of Wales, 175; illness returns (1801), 192–4; interest in gardening and farming, 196–7; signs agreement for Peace of Amiens, 198; and restoration of Windsor Castle, 199; return of illness and recovery (1804), 202–4; arranges care of Princess Charlotte, 204, 206, 208; Prince of Wales refuses to meet, 204–5; deteriorating marriage relations, 205; improper behaviour towards daughters, 205–6; weakening eyesight, 207, 210, 234; resists marriage for daughters, 208–9; suffers headaches, 210; and charges against Caroline, 214–15; agrees to receive Caroline, 218–19; Amelia's fondness for, 234; and Amelia's health trip to Weymouth, 235–8; and dying Amelia, 242; further illness (1810–11), 242, 244, 249–52, 255–8, 267; and Amelia's death, 244–5, 246, 252; describes decline into illness, 244; regency during mental collapse, 246, 250–1; and Amelia's estate, 249; daughters visit during illness, 251, 253; selects music for concert, 254; fantasies and hallucinations, 255–7; life at Windsor during late illness, 268; irrational behaviour, 291; unaware of wife's death and funeral, 313; allowance reduced after wife's death, 316; succession question, 318; decline and death, 321–2; obituary tributes, 323

George IV, King (*earlier* Prince of Wales and Prince Regent): precocity, 3, 6; inspects sister Charlotte, 4; father's attitude to, 5; birth, 13; resents Master Blomberg, 17–18; childhood and upbringing, 18, 40; and Spitalfields silk-weavers, 19; acquires establishment at Kew, 22; education, 22, 26, 37, 44; installed as Knight of Garter, 23; relations with father, 44, 58–9, 84, 194; fifteenth birthday celebrations, 46–7; behaviour as young man, 58–9, 71, 96; infatuation with Mary Hamilton, 58–9; supports Keppel, 65; nineteenth birthday ball, 68; shooting, 68; London apartments, 69; commissions Gainsborough to portray princesses, 83; meets Mrs Fitzherbert, 83–4; debts, 84, 111, 153; marries Mrs Fitzherbert clandestinely, 89; and father's illness, 109, 111–13, 115–16; prospective regency, 111; takes over management of royal house, 114; politicking and scheming during father's illness, 116–17; wild driving, 117; misbehaves at Thanksgiving service for father's recovery, 123; at Sophia Matilda's debut, 130; invites Ferdinand of Württemberg to Hampshire estate, 133; praises sister Mary's appearance, 136; plans marriage for Princess Royal, 137; in Brighton with Mrs Fitzherbert, 142; marriage to Caroline, 153–5; public hostility to, 156, 219; marriage relations, 157–8, 200, 219, 266; attachment to Mrs Fitzherbert, 158; makes will, 158; separation, 175; returns to Mrs Fitzherbert, 179, 183–4, 235; and Amelia's

illness in Worthing, 180–1; spreads reports of Sophia's illegitimate child, 189; fails to meet father to discuss Princess Charlotte, 204; hopes for regency during father's illness, 204; and charges against Caroline ('Delicate Investigation'), 215, 218–19; supports Elizabeth's romance with Louis Philippe, 226–7; mother's attachment to, 228; Amelia confides in, 235; as Amelia's executor, 240, 249; attends Amelia's funeral, 245–6; as Prince Regent, 251; holds fête at Carlton House, 252; cost of regency court, 254; unreserved regency powers, 257–8; financial provisions for sisters, 258–9; Augusta requests permission to marry Spencer, 261–3; visits Windsor for father's birthday (1812), 262; arranges Warwick House stay for daughter Charlotte, 268; attempts to heal breach between mother and princesses, 269–70; and daughter Charlotte's life in London, 272–3; life at Carlton House, 272–3; and daughter Charlotte's marriage prospects, 278, 281; entertains victorious Allies in England (1814), 279–80; banishes Charlotte to Cranbourne Lodge, 282; relations with daughter Charlotte, 283–4; and Corn Bill riots, 286; recognizes Frederica as brother Ernest's wife, 287; interest in Princess Charlotte's relations with Caroline, 288; agrees to Leopold as suitor for Princess Charlotte, 289; Mary's devotion to, 292, 297, 319–20, 324; visits Mary at Bagshot, 296; assassination attempt on, 297; and death of Princess Charlotte, 301; plans to divorce Caroline, 303, 318, 323; and Elizabeth's proposal from Frederick of Hesse-Homburg, 304–5; gives consent for brothers to marry, 307; and mother's decline, 310; at mother's deathbed, 312; retains some of mother's books, 315; coolness to Mary's husband, 319; gives bracelets to sisters, 319; illness after father's funeral, 322, 324; succeeds on father's death, 322–3; appearance in early life, 323, 344; Coronation, 324–5, 328; public arguments with Caroline, 326; disfavours 2nd Duke of Gloucester, 327; holds ball at Queen's House, 328; offered regency of Ireland, 328; reaction to Caroline's death, 329; visits Hanover, 329; visits Waterloo battlefield, 329–30; rebuilding and improvements, 337, 341; rebuilds Queen's House as Buckingham Palace, 337; and Frederick's death, 342; receives brother Frederick's opera glass, 342; Princess Royal visits in England

George IV, King (*earlier* Prince of Wales and Prince Regent) (*cont.*) (1827), 343–4; decline and death, 349–51; and Garth affair, 349; helps Elizabeth with debts, 353

George Augustus Frederick, Prince of Wales *see* George IV, King

George, King of Hanover (*earlier* Prince George of Cumberland; Ernest's son), 318, 356, 390, 393

George, Prince (*later* 2nd Duke of Cambridge; Adolphus's son): birth, 317–18; childhood in Hanover, 337–9; education in England, 352; Sophia's interest in, 382; and Tommy Garth's hopes of fortune, 388; at father's death, 390; military career, 391; serves in Crimean War, 394–5; appointed Commander-in-Chief, 397; and Mary's illness and death, 399

George, of Cumberland, Prince *see* George, King of Hanover

Gibbs, Frederick, 397

Gillray, James: *The Bridal Night* (cartoon), 161

Glenbervie, Sylvester Douglas, Baron: and Amelia's stay in Worthing, 182; and Sophia's illegitimate child, 189–90, 215; on George III's visits to Caroline in Blackheath, 195; on Queen Charlotte's depression, 228

Glenton (tailor), 5

Gloucester, Duchess of (*earlier* Lady Waldegrave) *see* Maria, Duchess of Gloucester

Gloucester, Duke of *see* 1. William Frederick, 2nd Duke of Gloucester; 2. William Henry, 1st Duke of Gloucester

Gloucester House, London, 292

Gloucester Lodge, Weymouth, 90, 125, 153

Gold, Sarah (*née* Byerley), 359, 387, 397, 399

Gomm, Jane: as princesses' sub-governess, 87, 112; disagreements with Margaret Planta, 144; Amelia writes to, 181; and Amelia's affair with Fitzroy, 200, 224; resigns, 223–4; and Elizabeth's prospective marriage to Frederick of Hesse-Homburg, 306

Gordon, Lord George: riots (1780), 60

Göttingen, University of: younger princes attend, 91, 97

Gouldsworthy, Martha ('Gouly'): as princesses' sub-governess, 36, 48–9, 51, 53, 61, 103, 112, 144; at Windsor, 58, 112; and princesses' inoculation, 58; Princess Royal's misbehaviour towards, 63–4; ill health, 66, 144; attends Elizabeth at Kew, 90; attends Queen in sickness, 110; acompanies sick Sophia to Kew, 147; accompanies Amelia to Worthing, 180, 182; retires, 223–4; and Augusta's friendships, 299

Gouldsworthy, General Philip, 103, 115, 179, 181–2, 186, 190, 377

Great Exhibition (1851), 391–2

Grenville, William Wyndham, Baron, 107, 156–7, 159–60, 205

Gresse, John Alexander, 54, 81, 97, 138, 155

Greville, Charles, 386

Greville, Robert Fulke, 114, 122

Grey, Charles Grey, 2nd Earl, 258, 278, 281

Grovestein, Mesdames de, 29, 32

Grüner, Ludwig, 387

Guazzi, Signor, 361

Guiffardière, Charles de, 51, 53–4, 65, 85, 127, 134, 141

Guilford, Francis North, 1st Earl of, 82

Gunnersbury, 34

Gustav, Prince of Hesse-Homburg (*later* Landgrave), 336, 355, 366, 369

Hadfield, James, 186

Hagedorn, Johanna-Louisa, 9

Hagget (Lord Harcourt's chaplain), 93

Halford, Sir Henry: and Amelia's illness and death, 239, 243, 245; and Amelia's wish to marry Fitzroy, 240; attends George III, 242, 244–5, 250–1, 253, 256; questioned by Privy Council on King's condition, 249; letters from Sophia, 264; and Villiers' blackmail attempts with Amelia's letters, 273–4; and Queen Charlotte's illness and death, 302, 304–5, 307, 310–11; attends Sophia, 313, 323, 360; attends Mary, 338; attends Augusta, 345; and George IV's death, 350; reports on Mary's health to Victoria and Albert, 372; on Augusta's health, 374

Hamilton, Mary (*later* Dickenson): as assistant governess to princesses, 45–8, 51–2, 62; letters from princesses, 52–3, 64–5, 69–70; on departure of Prince William for navy, 57; Prince of Wales's infatuation with, 58–9; in Eastbourne, 62–3; leave of absence, 66; Queen Charlotte's relations with, 67–8; on Prince of Wales's shooting, 68; ill health, 69; leaves royal service, 72; botanical interests, 98; marriage, 105; told of George III's recovery, 121

Hanover: Prince Frederick, Duke of York in, 66, 70, 84; Prince William in, 75, 79–80; Prince Edward sent to, 84; Court at, 122; in war with France, 146, 148; Prussians occupy (1801), 194, 202; restored to England, 276; George IV visits, 329; Adolphus's vice-regency in, 337–8, 355; Ernest accedes as King, 363; George succeeds to throne, 393

Harcourt, Edward Venables Vernon, Archbishop of York, 251

Harcourt, Elizabeth, Countess (earlier Lady Nuneham): letter from Duchess of Gloucester, 43; royals visit at Nuneham Courtenay, 85, 139; on attempted assassination of George III, 92; and George III's illness, 106, 108–9, 193–4; Mrs Siddons reports on Queen to, 126; on Frogmore Farm, 131; Ferdinand of Württemberg writes to, 132–3; Elizabeth writes to, 143, 146, 152, 200, 202, 225, 229, 259, 298, 301, 309; on Duke of York's command, 147; Sophia writes to from Weymouth, 153, 198; and attack on George IV's coach, 156; and princesses' marriage prospects, 156; Augusta writes to, 159, 198, 202, 204, 221–2, 241, 243, 245, 299, 301, 322; letters from Princess Royal, 160, 280, 283, 308, 317; and Princess Royal's marriage, 161; keeps princesses informed, 169; Sophia confides to of illegitimate child, 189; leaves Nuneham, 236; maintains correspondence with princesses, 236; Amelia writes to, 241; Mary writes to, 256; sustains Augusta and Sophia at Kew, 314; visits princesses at Frogmore, 319; joins Augusta at Frogmore, 323; Augusta invites to Stable House, 338; death, 339; musical settings, 341; Philip, A Tale, 169

Harcourt, George Simon Harcourt, 2nd Earl: royals visit at Nuneham Courtenay, 85, 139; recommends backless stools for princesses, 102; Elizabeth sends engravings to, 169; Elizabeth writes to, 170; comforts Augusta, 194; death, 236; on feeding orange trees, 307

Harcourt, Mrs William, 92, 116, 139–40, 148, 150, 154

Harcourt, General William, 148, 154

Harding, Edward, 358

Hawkins, Sir Caesar, 7, 71, 398n

Hawkins, Caesar Henry, 398

Hawkins, Charles, 102–3, 398n

Hawkins, Pennell, 7, 57, 71, 398n

Hayman, Anne, 161, 168, 208

Heberden, Dr William, 108, 113, 238

Heberden, Dr William, Jr, 242, 249, 252–3, 256

Henley, Morton Eden, 1st Baron, 205

Henry Frederick, Duke of Cumberland: conflicts with brother George III, 28–30; marriage, 28, 31–2, 151; lives abroad after marriage, 33; relations with Prince of Wales, 59

Herschel, William, 211

Hertford, Isabella, Marchioness of, 289

Hesse, Captain Charles, 272, 279, 288, 372

Hesse-Homburga: debts, 305, 334, 336, 352–4

Hicks, Augusta (née Feilding) 48, 367

Higgins, Sir Samuel, 368

Hippisley, Sir John Coxe, 159, 177, 298

Hobart, Robert, Baron (later 4th Earl of Buckinghamshire), 205

Holderness, Mary, Countess of, 13, 16, 26, 58, 73

Holderness, Robert d'Arcy, 4th Earl of: as princes' governor, 13, 23–4, 26, 35, 40; royals poach French governess from, 16; goes abroad for health, 40; resigns, 44

Holland: French capture (1795), 154

Holy Roman Empire: ends (1801), 187, 201n

Horn, Charles, 96, 128

Horton, Lady Anne, Duchess of Cumberland, 28

Hoskyns, Lady, 24

Howe, Lady Louisa, 92, 94, 128

Howe, Lady Mary, 92, 94, 129, 136, 140

Howe, Admiral Richard, Earl: Glorious First of June victory (1794), 152, 175

Howe, General Sir William (later 5th Viscount), 41

Hughes, Dr Thomas, 143, 356

Hunt, Leigh, 323

Hunter, Dr William, 3, 7, 15

Hurd, Richard, Bishop of Worcester, 102–3

Hutchinson, John Hely-Hutchinson, 1st Baron (later 2nd Earl of Donoughmore), 326

Ilchester, Maria, Countess of, 283–4, 299, 301

Inverness, Cecilia, Duchess of (Duke of Sussex's second wife; earlier Lady Cecilia Buggin), 382–3, 387, 398

Jacobi, Christian, 361

Jebb, Sir Richard, 95

Jelf, Dr Richard, 356

Jena, battle of (1806), 217

Jérôme (Bonaparte), King of Westphalia, 213, 219

Jersey, Frances, Countess of, 156, 172

John Bull (journal), 373

Johnson, Mrs (midwife), 49, 74

Jordan, Dorothea, 142, 335

Joseph (Bonaparte), King of Spain, 223

Josephine, Empress of Napoleon I, 212
Juliana, Dowager Queen of Denmark, 31

Keate, Dr Robert, 182
Keate, Dr Thomas, 180–2
Keith, Sir Robert Murray, 30–1
Kennedy, Lucy, 147, 149, 242, 249, 252, 263
Kennedy-Erskine, John, 352
Kensal Green cemetery, 383, 387
Kent, Duchess of (Queen Victoria's mother)
  see Victoria, Princess of Leiningen
Kent, Duke of see Edward, Prince
Kent, Edwardine, 285
Keppel, Admiral Augustus, 1st Viscount, 65
Keppel, Laura, 57
Kew (or White) House, Kew: 4, 33–4; Prince
  of Wales's House at, 22, 33; botanic
  gardens, 26; royal children at, 26, 33,
  42–3, 47–8, 57, 85, 88; George III and
  Charlotte move to, 33; conditions, 64;
  Princess Elizabeth recovers at, 90–1; sick
  George III moved to, 117; Augusta and
  Mary move into Cambridge Cottage, 313;
  Royal Lodge, Kew Green, 356, 363
Knight, Ellis Cornelia, 241–2, 272, 282, 338;
  Marcus Flaminius, 143
Knighton, Sir William, 334, 350, 351–2
Krohme, Anne Dorothée, 16, 49, 54
Krohme, Julie, 17, 23

Lawrence, Thomas, 128, 276, 298, 320, 325
Leeds, Charlotte, Duchess of, 272
Lehzen, Louise (later Baroness), 339, 357
Lennox, Captain Charles, 123–4
Lennox, Sir George, 47
Leopold II, Emperor of Austria, 142
Leopold, Prince of Saxe-Coburg-Gotha (later
  King of the Belgians): Princess Charlotte's
  interest in, 280, 282, 284–5, 288–9;
  marriage to Princess Charlotte, 289–90,
  298; fears divorce of Waleses, 290; made
  field marshal, 292; visits Bagshot Park,
  296; and Charlotte's death, 302–3; and
  Elizabeth's prospective marriage to
  Frederick, 306; hopes to visit sister in
  Sidmouth, 321; allowance, 334;
  mistrusted by princesses, 334, 336; as King
  of the Belgians, 364; organizes marriage
  of Victoria and Albert, 371; leaves
  England (1840), 378; praises Augusta,
  379; Victoria writes to, 381, 385
Leopold, Prince (Victoria/Albert's son), 394
Liddell, Augustus, 396, 398
Liverpool, Robert Banks Jenkinson, 2nd Earl
  of, 268, 290, 309, 340
Livesay, Richard, 128
Loudon, John Claudius, 375–6

Louis XVI, King of France, 126, 136, 146
Louis, Landgrave of Hesse-Homburg, 351–2,
  354, 361, 367; death, 367–8
Louis, Louisa, 302
Louis Philippe, Duke of Orleans (later King
  of the French), 200, 226–7, 239, 300
Louis, Prince, of Prussia, 140, 175
Louise, Princess of Hesse-Homburg (later
  Landgravine), 336, 355, 366, 368–9
Louise, Princess (Victoria/Albert's daughter),
  385, 397
Louise, Queen of the Belgians, 364, 370, 378
Louise, Queen of Frederick William III of
  Prussia (Queen Charlotte's niece), 140,
  280–1
Lower Lodge, Windsor, 57, 67, 238, 313
Ludwigsburg, 163, 173, 176, 178, 196–7,
  211–12, 336
Lunardi, Vincenzo, 80
Lunéville, Treaty of (1801), 187, 197, 221n
Lushington, Stephen, 329
Luttrell, Lady Elizabeth, 28
Lyttelton, Sarah, Lady, 382

Mack, Karl, Freiherr von, 211
Majendie, Dr Henry, 57
Manby, Captain Thomas, 285
Mann, Sir Horace, 30
Mansfield, William Murray, 1st Earl of, 60
Maria, Duchess of Gloucester (earlier
  Countess of Waldegrave): marriage and
  children, 8–9, 29, 32–3, 43; on royal
  informality, 56–7; King and Queen's
  coolness to, 130
Marianne of Hesse-Homburg, Princess of
  Prussia, 304, 366
Maria Amalia of Bourbon (later Queen of the
  French), 229
Marie Antoinette, Queen of France, 126,
  136, 149
Mary, Princess of Orange (Charles I's
  daughter): styled Princess Royal, 4
Mary, Princess, Duchess of Gloucester: birth,
  42; appearance, 47, 56, 136, 209, 264, 284,
  320; at Windsor, 48, 57; affection for
  father, 55; dancing, 56; inoculated, 58,
  362; on Juliana Penn, 66; attends opera and
  theatre, 80, 142; education, 80, 87–8;
  allowance, 82; expenses to mother, 82;
  singing voice, 87; in Copley painting,
  88–9; Fanny Burney meets, 97–8;
  operation for tumour in arm, 102–3;
  writes to parents in Cheltenham, 102, 104;
  and father's illnesses, 112, 118, 120, 202,
  251, 256–7, 267; debut, 136; dress, 136,
  199, 264; marriage prospects, 137, 227,
  284; Fanny Burney reads to, 144; love of

children, 144; in Weymouth, 145, 179, 299; and Sophia's illness, 147–8; Adolphus praises, 149; welcomes birth of niece Charlotte, 157; on Thomas Garth, 172; Amelia's attachment to, 181; helps dress Amelia, 199; Amelia keeps romance with Fitzroy secret from, 203; romantic attachments, 207, 210; on Peninsular campaign, 223; gout, 228, 393; accompanies Amelia on health trip to Weymouth, 235–7; helps nurse sick Amelia, 239; and Amelia's request to marry Fitzroy, 240; and dying Amelia's gift of ring to father, 242–3; collapse after Amelia's death, 250; on niece Charlotte's behaviour, 255, 267–8; writes to Lady Harcourt, 256; close relations with niece Charlotte, 257; Prince Regent's financial provisions for, 258; mother's relations with, 262–3, 270; nurses Sophia, 263; disapproves of Elizabeth's relations with Augusta Compton, 265; niece Charlotte criticizes, 266; on niece Charlotte's neglected upbringing, 266; Prince Regent arranges to accompany Princess Charlotte, 268–9; visits Lord Liverpool, 268; and mother's attitude to Princess Charlotte, 269; hopes for independent life in London, 271; life in London, 272–3; cousin William, Duke of Gloucester proposes to, 273, 278; George Villiers attempts to blackmail, 274; portraits, 276, 320; Princess Charlotte's wariness of, 284; relates Princess Charlotte's experiences with Caroline, 288; marries William, Duke of Gloucester, 291–4; devotion to Prince Regent, 292, 297, 319–20, 324; gardening, 294–5, 347, 376; on Princess Charlotte's marriage, 294; life at Bagshot, 295–6, 347, 376; married life, 297, 299, 308, 319–20, 346–7, 353, 359; hostility to Caroline, 299, 325–6; and Princess Charlotte's death, 303–4; on Elizabeth's marriage prospects, 304–5; attends sick mother at Kew, 308–10, 312; at mother's deathbed, 312; moves to Cambridge Cottage, Kew, 313; visits mother's vault, 314; copies from Hume, 315; lives with Augusta, 318; on brother Edward's death, 321; and father's death, 322; and Sophia's improved health, 325; supports brother George in case against Caroline, 326–7; conflict over husband's support for Caroline, 327; condemns behaviour over Caroline's funeral procession, 329; with Augusta at Stable House, 338; in Brighton and Bushey, 338, 362; ill health, 338, 372; and

brother Frederick's death, 342; at Frogmore with visiting sister Charlotte, 343; on George IV's dropsy, 349; and Cambridge children, 355; husband's death, 358–9; life in widowhood, 359–60; visits Homburg, 361; mourns brother William's death, 363; on Sophia's fortitude in blindness, 365; and Victoria's Coronation, 365; gives ball for Victoria, 366; writes to Ernest, 366; Elizabeth criticizes for worldliness, 368; on Elizabeth's will, 369; and Elizabeth's death, 370; and Victoria's marriage, 370–1; unable to attend Victoria's wedding, 372; distress at Augusta's ill health, 374; stays with Augusta, 377; at Augusta's deathbed, 379; charitable works, 381; supports Sophia in infirmity, 381; Victoria's relations with, 381; on death of Sophia Matilda, 383–4; at White Lodge, Richmond Park, 384; with Victoria's children, 384; and disposal of mother's jewels, 385; health decline, 385; and sister Sophia's death, 385–6, 389; directions for burial at Windsor, 387; Victoria and Albert care for in old age, 389; and Adolphus's death, 390; reminisces over family stories with Victoria, 390–1; visits Great Exhibition and Crystal Palace, 391–2; activities in old age, 393–6; on King George of Hanover, 393; on George, 2nd Duke of Cambridge's, service in Crimean War, 394–6; paints for Patriotic Fund, 395; portrait photographs, 396; Albert Edward, Prince of Wales, visits, 397; final illness and death, 398–9

Mary Adelaide, Princess of Cambridge (later Duchess of Teck) 355, 364, 373, 382, 390–3, 397–9

Mecklenburg-Strelitz, Hereditary Prince of see Friedrich, Hereditary Prince of Mecklenburg-Strelitz

Meen, Margaret, 96

Melbourne, William Lamb, 2nd Viscount, 103, 365, 371, 374, 381

Millman, Sir Francis, 187, 236, 238–9, 276, 310–11

Mills, Sir Charles, 124

Minicks, Mrs (née Planta), 38

Minto, Gilbert Elliot, Baron (later 1st Earl of), 115, 178, 185, 197

Moller, Georg, 354

Monro, Dr John, 93, 186, 256

Monson, Elizabeth, Lady, 289

Montague, George Brudenell, 1st Duke of, 44

Montmollin, Charlotte-Salomé de, 87–8, 112, 135

Montmollin, Julie de, 135, 145
Moore, Edward Duke, 378
Moore, General Sir John, 222–3
Moore, John, Archbishop of Canterbury, 75, 114, 122, 150
Moore, Tom, 341–2
More, Hannah, 37; *Hints Towards Forming the Character of a Young Princess*, 268
Moreau, General Jean Victor, 184, 187
Mortimer, John Hamilton, 81
Moser, Mary, 129
Moula, Suzanne, 54
Mount Edgcumbe, Emma, Countess of, 127
Mount Edgcumbe, George Edgcumbe, 1st Earl of, 127
Müller, Friedrich, 184
Münster, Count Ernst von, 238
Munster, George Fitzclarence, Earl of, 272, 341, 352–3
Murray, Amelia, 380
Murray, Lady Augusta: marriage and children with Augustus, 149–51, 184, 232; death, 382
Murray, Lady George, 236, 246
Murray, Lady Louisa, 346
Muttlebury, Mrs (wet-nurse), 7, 9, 14

Napoleon I (Bonaparte), Emperor of the French: private treaty with Duke of Württemberg, 199; threatens invasion of Britain, 201; crowned emperor, 202; visits Württembergs at Ludwigsburg, 212–13; defeats Frederick William III at Jena and Auerstädt, 217; and Duke of Brunswick, 218; meets Tsar Alexander I, 219; introduces Continental System against Britain, 221n; imprisoned on Elba, 279; escape from Elba, defeat and exile to St Helena, 286; disparages Elizabeth's marriage to Frederick of Hesse-Homburg, 306; death, 329
Nash, John, 295
Nelson, Admiral Horatio, 1st Viscount, 180, 194
Nepean, Revd Evan, 390, 399
New Forest (Hampshire), 124
Ney, Marshal Michel, 211
Nicolson, Margaret, 92, 186
Nile, battle of the (1798), 180
Norfolk, Charlotte Sophia, Duchess of, 392
North, Frederick, Lord, 27, 32
Northumberland, Elizabeth, Duchess of (*née* Seymour), 13, 25
Nuneham Courtenay, near Oxford, 85–6, 93, 139, 221, 225
Nuneham, Lady *see* Harcourt, Elizabeth, Countess

Oatlands (house), near Weybridge, 102, 140, 290, 318
Octavius, Prince: birth, 7, 65; in Eastbourne, 61; father's fondness for, 72; death, 73–4, 90; Princess Royal's etching of, 81
Omai (Tahitian), 39
Osborne, Isle of Wight, 389

Pains and Penalties Bill (1820), 327
Papendiek, Charlotte, 83, 89, 133, 138, 180
Parsons, Sir William, 234
Paul, Emperor of Russia, 157
Paul, Prince, of Württemberg, 163, 185, 187, 196, 279, 281; daughters, 324
Pauline, Princess (daughter of Paul) of Württemberg, 324, 333, 345–6
Payne, John ('Jack') Willett, 113–14
Pearce, Edward, 387
Pembroke, Elizabeth, Countess of, 117, 120, 126–7
Penn, Lady Juliana, 23, 66
Pepys, Sir Lucas, 119, 147, 159, 180–1
Perceval, Spencer: on Caroline's illness, 218; premiership, 223; and George III's illness, 245, 251; introduces 1810 Regency Bill, 250–1; Prince Regent retains as Prime Minister, 257; and Prince Regent's provisions for princesses, 259; assassinated, 264
Peter Frederick, Duke of Oldenburg, 156
Peter, Prince, Duke of Oldenburg (son of Peter Frederick), 279
Petworth, 340–1
Philip, Prince of Hesse-Homburg, 367–9
Philippe Egalité (Duke of Orleans), 228
Phipps, Jonathan Wathen, 207, 234
Pitt, William, the Younger: George III meets, 107; Prince of Wales's hostility to, 111; and George III's illnesses, 112, 119, 317; George III works with, 123; discusses French Revolution with George III in Weymouth, 126; and recall of Duke of York from army command, 151; resigns over Catholic emancipation, 193; resumes premiership (1803), 203; death, 214; and Regency Bill, 250
Planta, Andreas, 24
Planta, Elizabeth, 24
Planta, Frederica: as princesses' assistant governess, 23–4, 30, 35–40; death, 54; on Augusta, 69
Planta, Joseph, 24, 54
Planta, Margaret (Peggy): teaches princesses, 54, 63; at Kew, 64; in Cheltenham, 101; and George III's illness, 110; disagreements with Miss Gomm, 144; resigns, 259–60; stays at Frogmore, 377

Pope, Dr Robert, 234–9
porphyria, 114n
Portland, Margaret Cavendish, Duchess of (née Harley), 56
Portland, William Henry Cavendish Bentinck, 3rd Duke of: and George III's illness, 115; and Princess Royal's prospective marriage, 159; hostility to Prince Regent, 258
Portugal: France declares war on (1807), 222n; in Peninsular War, 254
Powney, Peniston Portlock, 65
Pressburg, Treaty of (1805), 212
Price, Major William, 375
Princess Royal see 1. Charlotte Augusta Matilda, Princess Royal, Queen of Württemberg ('Royal'); 2. Victoria, Princess Royal ('Vicky')
Prussia: war with France, 142
Pückler-Muskau, Prince Hermann von, 375–6

Queen's House, London, 3n, 6, 25, 328, 337; also see Buckingham Palace
Queen's (or Upper) Lodge, Windsor, 44–6, 55, 57, 205–6

Ramberg, Johann Heinrich, 358
Ramsay, Allan, 25
Ramus, William ('Billy'), 65, 90–1
Rebecca, Biagio, 121
Reform Bill, Second (1832), 353
Regency Bill: (1789), 121, 203, 250; (1810–11), 250–1, 257–8
Reid, Lady, 103
Reuss, Heinrich XX, Prince, 366
Reynolds, Dr Henry Revell, 111–12, 119, 244
Reynolds, Sir Joshua, 54, 396
Rice, Mary, 309
Richmond Lodge, 4, 7, 25, 34
Rieger, Baron de, 159
Roberts, Peter (writing master), 37, 54
Robinson (Gloucesters' page), 346
Robinson, Mary ('Perdita'), 59
Robinson (Sophia's emissary), 172
Robson, Horatio, 344
Roscoe, William, 295
Ross, Sir William, 380
Rothschild, Mayer Amschel, 353–4
Royal Lodge, Windsor Great Park, 319, 341, 349, 363
Royal Marriages Act (1772), 30, 32, 149, 231–2
Russia: supports France in Peninsular War, 222n; in Crimean War, 394

St Helens, Alleyne Fitzherbert, Baron, 229
St James's Palace: court life at, 6

St Laurent, Julie de: relations with Prince Edward, 142, 307
Saunders, Dr William, 238–9
Schrader, Heinrich, 38, 54, 176
Schwellenberg, Juliana-Elizabeth, 9, 97, 136, 144
scrofula (king's evil), 10, 90
Secker, Thomas, Archbishop of Canterbury, 8
Shah Alam, Mogul Emperor, 25
Shakespeare, William: King Lear, 119–20
Sharland, Samuel and Charlotte, 190, 192
Sheffield, John Baker Holroyd, 1st Baron (later 1st Earl of), 115
Sheridan, Richard Brinsley, 115, 186
Siddons, Sarah, 82–3, 88, 105, 113, 125–7
Sidmouth, Henry Addington, Viscount, 193, 203, 312; death, 384
Simmons, Dr Samuel, 202–4, 244, 256–7
Sion Hill, Middlesex, 26
Smelt, Leonard, 35, 44, 91, 121, 169
Smith, Sir Sidney, 285
Sophia, Princess: birth, 49, 55; allowance, 55, 82; in Eastbourne, 61–2; attends opera and theatre, 80, 142; education, 80, 87; expenses to mother, 82; singing voice, 87; writes to father in French, 87–8; in Copley painting, 88–9; reading, 88, 145; and Fanny Burney, 97; writes to parents in Cheltenham, 102–3; character and manner, 103–4, 171; eleventh birthday, 106; and father's illness, 112, 120; has locket made containing family hair, 131; debut at Court, 144; needlework, 145; at Frogmore, 146; fears for brother Frederick in war, 147; ill health, 147–8, 179, 186–7, 210, 216–17, 262–4, 267, 279, 296, 305, 308, 313, 315, 322–3; and Augustus's becoming father, 150; in Weymouth, 152, 179, 186–7, 198, 205–6, 210; appearance, 171; relations with Colonel Garth, 171–2; on attempted shooting of father, 186; illegitimate child, 189–92, 216–17, 315, 348–9; supposed incest with brother Ernest, 191, 348–9; suspects Caroline of impropriety, 195; as father's confidante and supporter, 206, 210; on George III's visit to Blackheath, 206; blames mother for father's unhappiness, 207, 210; nervous spasms, 207, 210, 296, 342; father's treatment of, 208; ends relations with Garth, 215–16; confesses to love for unknown man, 216; and niece Charlotte, 221, 266–7; invests through Mr Bolton, 224; and Elizabeth's frustrated courtship with Louis Philippe, 228; on Amelia's romance with Fitzroy, 232; on Amelia's ill health, 234, 237; thanks Prince Regent for

Sophia, Princess (*cont.*)
making provisions for future, 258–9;
horses and riding, 260, 357; on Victoria's
accession, 262–3; and assassination of
Spencer Perceval, 264–5; visits Lord
Liverpool, 268; hopes for independent life
in London, 270–1; supports niece
Charlotte, 283; and Princess Charlotte's
death, 303; at Windsor, 308, 315–16;
inherits Lower Lodge in mother's will,
311, 313; effect of mother's death on, 314;
told daily of father's state, 314; health
improvement, 319, 325; and brother
Edward's death, 321; and father's death,
322; leaves Windsor Castle, 322; on
brother's regency, 324; and George IV's
Coronation, 325; portraits of, 325, 380;
visits Adelaide and daughter, 334; moves
to Connaught Place, 335; relations with
Victoria, Duchess of Kent, 336; sees
Princess Victoria as child, 339; grief at
Frederick's death, 342; on Princess Royal's
visit to England (1827), 345; and Princess
Royal's death, 346; correspondence with
Princess Victoria, 348–9, 357, 359–60,
363; Tommy Garth appeals to for help,
348; eyesight deteriorates, 356–7, 360–1,
363, 365; piano playing, 357; on Mary's
widowhood, 359–60; confides in and
helps Conroy, 360–1; sets clothes on fire,
361; takes Italian lessons, 361; moves into
York House, 365; and Elizabeth's death,
370; at Augusta's deathbed, 379; blindness
and infirmity, 380–1, 384; Mary's devotion
to in infirmity, 381; death and burial,
385–8
Sophia Matilda of Gloucester, Princess: birth,
33, 43, 55; allowance, 55; debut, 130;
present at King's Birthday, 136;
accompanies brother Duke of Gloucester,
273; denied title of Royal Highness, 273;
apartments at Bagshot Park, 295; visits
Mary at Bagshot, 296; meddles in Mary's
domestic arrangements, 308; and brother's
death, 359; death, 383–4; portrait, 396
Spain: Peninsular campaign in, 222–3
Spencer, General Sir Brent: effect on
Augusta, 183; rides with Augusta, 215; in
Baltic and Peninsular campaigns, 222, 254;
Queen reports on, 238; Augusta hopes to
marry, 260–2, 379; reports Princess
Charlotte's death to Augusta, 302;
relations with Augusta, 305, 315, 347;
death, 347
Spiegel, Mme de, 163, 167, 173, 174
Spinluffe, Elizabeth, 20, 39
Spitalfields: silk-weavers riot, 19

Stable House, St James's, 337, 345
Stanhope, Lady Anna Maria, 142
Stanley, Lady Betty, 40
Stanley, Sir George, 359
Stein, Baroness Veronica de, 333, 368–9
Stephenson, Sir Benjamin, 365
Strawberry Hill, 170
Struensee, Count Johann, 31
Stuart, Sir John, 172
Stuart, Lady Louisa, 345
Stuttgart, 176, 197
Sussex, Duke of *see* Augustus, Prince
Sutton, Charles Manners, Archbishop of
Canterbury, 309
Swinburne, Louisa, 355, 357–8

Taylor, General Sir Herbert: as George III's
secretary, 207, 234; Princess Mary's
attachment to, 207, 210; rides with
Amelia, 215; resigns as secretary, 253;
relations with George III, 256; and
princesses' allowances, 259; and Villiers'
attempted blackmail, 274; reports death of
Princess Charlotte, 301; suggests Queen
Charlotte make will, 309–11; refuses Duke
of Gloucester permission to shoot at
Windsor Great Park, 319; and Augusta at
Frogmore, 323; as George IV's secretary,
348; and settlement with Tommy Garth,
348–9, 388
Taylor, Lady Mary, 341, 347, 379
Thurn and Taxis, Thérèse, Princess of
(Queen Charlotte's niece), 199
Thynne, Lady Isabella, 264
Tilsit, Treaty of (1807), 220
Tippoo Sultan, 315
Tomkins, Peltro, 168–9
Tories: and George's regency, 251
Toward, Andrew, 294, 347, 376
Trafalgar, battle of (1805), 211
Trimmer, Sarah: *The Story of the Robins*, 88
Trollope, Frances, 354–5
Truro, Lady Augusta Emma (*earlier* d'Este,
daughter of Prince Augustus and Lady
Augusta Murray), 184, 391
Tuck, I. and L. (jewellers), 239
Turkey: and Crimean War, 394
Turton, Dr John, 192
Tyrwhitt, Sir Thomas, 280

Ulm, battle of (1805), 211
Upper Lodge *see* Queen's (or Upper) Lodge,
Windsor

Valmy, battle of (1792), 145
Vesey, Elizabeth, 58
Victoria, Queen (*earlier* Princess): birth, 318;

as heir presumptive, 334, 337, 362;
babyhood, 335; Augusta's view of, 336,
372–4; Sophia sees as child, 339; Princess
Royal sees on visit to England, 343;
Sophia corresponds with, 348–9, 357,
359–60, 363; William IV criticizes
upbringing, 353; riding, 357; and Duke
of Gloucester's death, 359; visits aunt
Mary, 359; hostility to Conroy, 360;
accession on death of William IV, 362–3;
and George IV's attack on mother, 362;
reaches majority (age 18), 362; princesses'
attitude to on accession, 363–4; and claim
to Queen Charlotte's jewels, 365, 385;
Coronation, 365; visits Sophia after loss of
sight, 365; considers marriage to Albert,
367; wedding, 370–2; and Augusta's
impending death, 377–8; birth of
children, 381, 383, 385, 394; relations with
aunts, 381; writes to Leopold, 381, 385;
on uncle Adolphus, 382, 390; in Isle of
Wight, 384; visits Sophia, 384; and
Sophia's death and funeral, 385–7; takes
care of Mary in old age, 388, 389; attends
Adolphus, Duke of Cambridge's, funeral,
390; Mary confides in, 390–1; on uncle
Ernest, 392–3; and George, Duke of
Cambridge's, service in Crimean War,
395; and daughter Vicky's engagement,
396; portrait photograph, 396; visits dying
Mary, 398; on Mary's death, 399
Victoria, Princess of Leiningen, Duchess of
Kent: marriage, 306–7; character, 309;
pregnancy and birth of daughter, 317–18;
home life in England, 319, 335; and
husband's illness and death, 320–1;
mistrusted by princesses, 334–6; visits
Augusta at Connaught Place, 335; Sophia
visits, 339; William IV criticizes for
upbringing of daughter, 353; riding, 357;
William IV attacks, 361; loses claim to
regency, 362; visits Brighton, 364;
relations with princesses, 365–6;
philanthropy, 382; told of Adolphus's
death, 390; visits dying Mary, 398
Victoria, Princess Royal (Victoria/Albert's
daughter; 'Vicky'), 381, 383–4, 396, 398
Vienna, Congress of (1815), 279–80
Villiers, George, 203, 234; attempts to
blackmail Mary, 273–4
Villiers, Theresa, 203, 206–7, 216, 231, 234,
274

Waddington, Frances, 209
Waldegrave, Lady Caroline, 86, 106, 136
Waldegrave, Lady Elizabeth (later Countess of
Cardigan): as lady-in-waiting to Princess

Royal and Augusta, 73; comforts Queen
during George III's illness, 109;
seasickness, 126; marriage to Cardigan,
135
Walpole, Sir Edward, 8
Walpole, Horace, 11, 14, 19, 30, 33, 61, 90,
170
Walpole, Sir Robert, 27
Wangenheim, General George von, 97
Warburton, Dr Thomas, 193
Wardle, Gwyllym, 229
Warren, Sir Richard, 111–12, 115, 119
Warwick House, London, 220, 268
Washington, George, 41, 42
Waterloo, battle of (1815), 286, 329–30
Weimar, Dr de, 174
Wellesley, Richard Colley, Marquess, 244
Wellington, Arthur Wellesley, 1st Duke of:
Peninsular campaign, 222–3; and
Hereditary Prince of Orange, 277;
accompanies George IV to Waterloo
battlefield, 329; supports Catholic
emancipation, 348; visits dying George IV,
350; on Duke of Cambridge's funeral,
390; on death of Ernest, King of Hanover,
392
West, Benjamin, 38–9, 74, 81, 89, 127
Westmeath, Anne Bennet Elizabeth,
Countess (later Marchioness) of, 320
Weymouth (Dorset), 124–5, 131, 139–40,
145–6, 152–3, 156, 159, 179, 182, 186,
195, 198–200, 204–6, 210, 235–7, 283–4,
299
Weymouth, Elizabeth, Viscountess, 58
Whigs: propose economy on royal court, 65;
attack Queen, 127; and George's regency,
251; support Caroline, 274
White House, Kew see Kew: Kew (or White)
House
White Lodge, Richmond Park, 384
Wilhelm, King (earlier Prince) of
Württemberg, 163, 185, 297–8, 324, 346,
366
Wilhelm, Prince of Solms, 287
Wilhelmina of Prussia, Princess of Orange,
139, 154
Wilkes, John, 19
William IV, King (earlier Duke of Clarence):
birth and upbringing, 3–5; inoculated
against smallpox, 16; punished by nurse,
20; education, 23, 57; house at Kew, 23,
34; and grandmother's death, 30;
childhood, 40; twelfth birthday, 48;
begins naval service, 57, 66; character and
behaviour, 57, 228; on leave, 67; serves in
American war, 70; in Hanover, 75,
79–80; letters from sisters, 79–80; mother

William IV, King (*earlier* Duke of Clarence) (*cont.*)
writes to, 80; debts, 84; sails for West Indies, 84; writes from West Indies, 95; dukedom, 125; rejoins navy in war against Spain, 131; drinking, 136; partners sister Mary, 136; relations with Mrs Jordan, 142; favours Duke of Devonshire as bride for daughter Sophia, 278; and Princess Charlotte's death, 301; seeks wife, 303; granted consent to marry, 307; supports brother George against Caroline, 327; London apartments, 334–5; visits Augusta at Stable House, 345; accession on death of George IV, 350; behaviour as King, 352; son George (Earl of Munster) complains to, 353; supports Second Reform Bill, 353; attacks Duchess of Kent, 361; welcomes Landgrave Louis to England, 361; death, 362–3; interment, 383

William, Duke of Brunswick (Caroline's brother) *see* Frederick William, Duke of Brunswick

William, Duke of Cumberland, 28–9, 32

William Frederick, 2nd Duke of Gloucester: birth, 43; allowance, 55; present at King's Birthday, 136; military service in Flanders, 152; Caroline abuses, 218; succeeds to dukedom, 218; on Prince Regent's life at Carlton House, 273; proposes to Mary, 273, 278; supports Caroline against Prince Regent, 274, 326–7, 391; Princess Charlotte rejects, 277–8; rejected by Lady Monson, 289; marriage to Mary, 291–4, 297; shooting and hunting, 294–5, 304; involvement in African Institution, 295; marriage relations, 308, 346–7, 359; travels abroad, 308; Prince Regent's coolness to, 319; and George III's death, 322; behaviour, 346–7; leaves Whigs over reform, 353; death, 358–9

William Henry, 1st Duke of Gloucester: at Caroline Matilda's wedding, 8; marriage status, 8, 29–30, 32; relations with brother George III, 28–9; illness abroad, 29–30; birth of daughter, 33; lives abroad after marriage, 33; returns to court, 59–60; meets royal family on visit to Weymouth, 124–5; King and Queen's coolness to, 130; George III buys Weymouth Lodge from, 195; death, 218

William, Hereditary Prince of Orange (*later* King William II), 277–82, 285–6

William, Prince, of Hesse Philippsthal, 227

William, Prince, of Prussia, 304

Williams, Charlotte, 235–6, 238–9, 255

Willis, Dr Francis: treats George III, 118–20, 123, 193; sees illuminations in London, 121; advises George III against moving to Hanover, 124

Willis, Dr John, 118, 193–6, 203, 256–8

Willis, Dr Robert, 195–6, 203, 245, 249, 252–3, 256–8, 275, 291, 321

Willis, Revd Thomas, 118, 152, 189, 193–6

Wimpfen, Baron de (Württemberg Minister in London), 156, 177

Winchilsea, George Finch, 9th Earl of (Lady Charlotte Finch's son), 18, 22, 66, 251

Windsor: George III and Charlotte occupy, 44–6, 48, 55–7, 205–7; hunting at, 44; Prince of Wales's fifteenth-birthday celebrations at, 46–7; life at, 57–8, 64–5; entertainments at, 104–5; Home Park, 144; Fanny Burney visits, 169–70; George III plans restoration of, 199, 205; Princess Charlotte settles in, 208, 220–1, 285; Elizabeth acquires cottage at, 221, 225; Amelia returns to from health trip to Weymouth, 238; during George III's final illness, 255; Princess Charlotte visits, 255, 257; Augusta and Sophia stay in after mother's death, 315–16; George IV alters, 338, 341, 343, 345, 349; Princess Royal visits (1827), 343; Augusta's charitable works in, 374

Witte, Minna, 358

Wood, Alderman Matthew, 326–7

Worcester, 102–3

Woronzow, Count Simeon Romanovich, 159

Worthing, 179, 182

Wright, Elizabeth, 374

Württemberg, 173–4, 184, 196, 198

Wyatville, Sir Jeffry, 146, 341, 349

Yarmouth, Francis Charles Seymour-Conway, Earl of (*later* 3rd Marquess of Hertford), 277

York, Duke of *see* 1. Edward, Duke of York; 2. Frederick, Prince, Duke of York and Albany

York House, Vicarage Place, 365, 380–1

Yorktown, battle of (1781), 70

Zastrow, Baron, 138

Zeppelin, Count Johann Karl, 158–9, 173–4

Zoffany, Johann, 25, 88